(Continued from the front flap)

lyric, narrative, and dramatic verse are
represented, and the range of verse forms
and meters is unlimited. American poetry
(as distinct from British) is more fully covered than in any other general anthology.
Contemporaries down to the mid-twen-
tieth century are given a proportionate
place with the poets of the past.

In addition to its outstanding contents,
the reliability of its text, its excellent editorial features, and its attractiveness of
format make this volume the ideal gift
book for any occasion, or for one's own
basic collection.

THE VIKING BOOK OF
Poetry
OF THE ENGLISH-SPEAKING WORLD

'Tis with our judgments as our watches, none
Go just alike, yet each believes his own.
In poets as true genius is but rare,
True taste as seldom is the critic's share.

ALEXANDER POPE

THE VIKING BOOK OF

Poetry

OF THE
ENGLISH-SPEAKING
WORLD

Edited by Richard Aldington

New York · The Viking Press

The Viking Book of Poetry of the English-Speaking World
Revised, Mid-Century Edition

TWO-VOLUME EDITION PUBLISHED IN 1958
ONE-VOLUME EDITION PUBLISHED IN 1962
BY THE VIKING PRESS, INC.
625 MADISON AVENUE, NEW YORK 22, N.Y.

ORIGINAL ONE-VOLUME EDITION PUBLISHED IN 1941
FOURTH PRINTING 1946

Note to the Revised, Mid-Century Edition

The additions and revisions in this edition were most kindly
undertaken for me by the editorial staff of The Viking Press,
assisted by Malcolm Cowley, since pressure of work made it
impossible for me to give the time for an adequate revision.
Since no two persons ever think alike or choose alike in
anthology-making, I leave to them all the responsibility and
praise for the alterations and additions from page 1122 on.

RICHARD ALDINGTON

LIBRARY OF CONGRESS CATALOG CARD NUMBER: 58-8134

PRINTED IN THE UNITED STATES OF AMERICA
BY THE COLONIAL PRESS INC.

INTRODUCTION

THIS anthology is "general" rather than "personal." By "general" I mean such works as *The Oxford Book of English Verse* and *The Oxford Anthology of English Poetry*. By "personal" I mean anthologies where the compiler puts in only what appeals to his own special taste and ignores popular poems. Aldous Huxley's *Texts and Pretexts* and *The Spirit of Man* by the late Dr. Bridges will at once occur to everybody as examples of the "personal" anthology. The difference between these two types of anthologist is that the "personal" anthologist is on the lookout for unusual or neglected poetry, whereas the "general" anthologist tries to give the best of a period—which in the present case is poetry in the English language. But then the most personal of anthologists, even Mr. Huxley, cannot avoid quoting some poems which other people have heard of; and the most conventional of general anthologists does display a personal taste, even if that taste turns out to be merely timid, academic, and correct.

This book is not a re-shuffling of anthology pieces, but is based on a re-reading of the complete works of the poets quoted and of a good many which were not quoted. Of course, collections have been used, such as *The Oxford Book of Ballads*, Sidgwick and Chambers's useful little selection of medieval lyrics, and Bullen's *Lyrics from the Elizabethan Song-Books*. Other anthologies were used only as a check, and the number of poems added as a result has been surprisingly small.

In a very few cases, a poem is given solely on the authority of an anthologist. There is, for example, Mr. Gilfillan, a mid-Victorian gentleman who, among other activities, published three volumes of *Lesser-Known British Poets*. There I found the anonymous eighteenth-century poem supposed to have been written with a diamond on the window of a London lodginghouse. Mr. Gilfillan doesn't say where he found it, and I have never found anyone who could tell me.

Every "general" anthology must be built round a self-selecting nucleus of universally admired poems. Even if he wanted to do anything so absurd, the "general" anthologist could not omit Spenser's "Epithalamion," Shakespeare's songs and sonnets, "Lycidas," the "Ode to a Nightingale," and scores of other poems which must be included in such a book. Around that nucleus I have collected the less obvious poems, in choosing which there is room for the play of personal taste. This has been done on liberal lines, reaching far back into the past and coming down to include numerous living writers. "English" poetry has been interpreted as "poetry written in the English language" and not poetry written by Englishmen.

Among the advantages resulting from a re-survey of poetry is that even in standard poets the reader may find work that is new to him. Two examples from many—the "Epithalamium" of Richard Crashaw was first printed from MS. in 1924, and the last four lines which now complete Clough's well-known satirical poem "The Latest Decalogue" were not made public until 1936.

This book contains over 1200 poems by about 300 known poets and a considerable number of anonymous writers. But no matter how voluminous an anthology is, it cannot possibly claim to be complete in the sense of being beyond the elementary criticism which is invariably applied to all anthologies: "If A is included, why is B omitted?" All that criticism means is that an anthology is a selection, that selection is a matter of taste, and that people differ in their tastes. The most the anthologist may hope for is that readers will not find too many of their pet aversions included or too many of their favourite pieces omitted.

There is a difference of some importance between an anthology which is academic and historical and one, such as this, which is popular and aesthetic—in the sense that the poems are chosen in the hope of giving pleasure to all people who enjoy poetry for its own sake. The popular anthologist must take into account certain human limitations which his more austere confrere of the academic world very properly disregards. The most important is the fact that for the modern reader without some little specialist training real pleasure in English poetry begins about the early Tudor period, for the simple reason that the poets then began writing an English which is still substantially ours—at any rate, it can be modernized fairly easily, with no particular damage to sense and rhythm.

That takes us back four centuries or more, which is a long

time. And yet such is the antiquity of English poetry that when Skelton was writing in the days of Henry VIII and Cardinal Wolsey there was then nearly a thousand years of it behind him. Among the literatures which succeeded classical Latin none has greater antiquity than the English. Unfortunately, in the course of thirteen or fourteen centuries a language is apt to change, and Old English poetry (or Anglo-Saxon poetry) was written at a stage of the language so remote from our own that to all intents and purposes it is a foreign tongue. If you found somebody who had never read anything but modern English and put before him a page of *Beowulf* or of Caedmon, he would probably strenuously deny that it is the same language.

Here, for example, are three lines which are said to be "perhaps among the oldest our language has to show":

> *Hal wes thu, folde, fira modor,*
> *beo thu growende on guiles faethine;*
> *fodre gefylled firum to nytte.*

They are a pre-Christian invocation to the Earth goddess, and are translated by Stopford Brooke:

> *Hale be thou, Earth, Mother of men!*
> *Fruitful be thou in the arms of the god.*
> *Be filled with thy fruit for the fare-need of man!*

But when we come to the Early Transitional English of the period following the Conquest, the similarity to our own tongue is at once apparent. These lines from the "Luve Run" (Love Runc) of Thomas de Hales were written before 1240:

> *Hwer is Paris and Heleyne*
> *That weren so bryht and feyre of bleo:*
> *Amadas, Tristram, and Dideyne,*
> *Yseude and alle theo;*
> *Ector with scharpe meyne*
> *And Cesar riche of worldes feo?*
> *Heo beoth iglyden ut of the reyne,*
> *So the schef is of the cleo.*

I have substituted the modern "th" for the obsolete letter, but even our imaginary person who had never read anything except modern English would have to admit there were some words he recognized. And if we jump on about a century and a half to the Middle English of *Piers the Plowman,* the identity is obvious:

> *Pore peple, thi prisoneres, Lord, in the put of myschief,*
> *Comforte tho creatures that moche care suffren,*
> *Thorw derth, thorw drouth, alle her dayes here,*
> *Wo in wynter tymes for wanting of clothes,*
> *And in somer tyme selde soupen to the fulle;*
> *Comforte thi careful, Cryst, in thy ryche!*

If it is explained that "put" means "pit," "moche" "much," "thorw" "through," "her" "their," "selde" "seldom," and "ryche" "kingdom," anyone can understand that passage.

If this early poetry were to be properly illustrated in an anthology, we should have at least to quote from *Beowulf,* "Widsith," "The Wanderer," "The Seafarer," "Deor," and the Christian Saxon poets, Caedmon and Cynewulf. From the post-Conquest epochs of Transitional and Middle English we should have to put in something from Layamon's *Brut,* "The Owl and the Nightingale," "Ormulum," the metrical romances such as *Sir Gawayne and the Grene Knight, Havelok,* and *Guy of Warwick,* the anonymous poem "The Pearl," Robert Mannyng of Brunne, Langland, Lydgate, Occleve, Gower, and of course Chaucer. And we should have to quote from the poets of medieval Scotland, who were quite as gifted as their rivals south of the border but wrote an even more crabbed "Ynglis."

Now, an academic and historical anthology would very properly include specimens of all these and more. But it would be absurd to burden a popular anthology with pages of Old English which most of its readers wouldn't want, or with translations. So I have contented myself with quoting the opening lines of *Beowulf* in the modern version by C. K. Scott-Moncrieff. This "token" extract is given merely as a reminder that there was a flourishing English poetry between the sixth century and the Norman Conquest.

For the Middle English period preceding Chaucer a similar token representation has been adopted. The English school is shown by three exquisite and very well-known anonymous lyrics, and the Scottish school by the equally famous lines on freedom from John Barbour's lengthy poem, *The Bruce.*

There is one Middle English poet who is too important
from his humanity, his humour, his mastery of the art, to be
passed over with a merely token representation; and he of
course is Chaucer. Even though his lines must be accom-
panied by a glossary I think most readers would not have
wished him left out. Yet if there is one negative truth about
Chaucer which hardly admits of dispute, it is that we do not
value him chiefly or even very highly as a purely lyric poet.
He is a great narrative poet, a teller of stories and a brilliant
recorder of human character, who gives the first real indica-
tion of coming triumphs in the drama and the novel, and one
of the most attractive personalities of the Middle Ages. Of
course, Chaucer cannot be equalled to Dante in depth, passion, power of intellect, and beauty of expression, but then
he had a something the virulent Italian lacked. I think it will
be obvious why I have specially emphasized the character
sketches in the Prologue to *The Canterbury Tales*,

For the period between Chaucer and Skelton I have gone
back to token representation with a handful of lyrics by
anonymous authors—a couple of carols, a love song, a mock
aubade, and two drinking songs. After Skelton, Dunbar, and
Hawes, I give my selection from the ballads and a small
group of carols.

There has been controversy about both the date and the
possible authorship of the ballads, but it seems to me that
they ought to come before the great and expanding achievement of Tudor-Stuart poetry. Obviously many of the texts as
we have them come from that and even later periods, but
practically no genuine ballads were composed after the end
of the fifteenth century. Why not, therefore, quote them at
about the time of their fullest expansion, even if the texts are
not exactly of that time and in spite of the fact that later and
spurious work may be mixed in?

I have never been able to go along with those who think
that ballads were written by "the people." Just how do "the
people" set about writing a poem? Such a collective enterprise either in a village or in a town seems highly improbable.
But I do think the ballads were popular, in the sense that they
were composed *for* the people by forgotten poets who most
probably were *of* the people. I would also agree that the
people made alterations to them, but quite unintentionally,

as they passed by oral tradition from generation to generation. But I doubt whether this collaboration was always an
improvement. For instance, in the early version of "Chevy
Chase" (given here) we find this quatrain:

> For Witherington my heart was woe
> That ever he slain should be:
> For when both his legs were hewn in two
> Yet he kneeled and fought on his knee.

which in the later version becomes:

> For Witherington needs must I wail
> As one in doleful dumps,
> For when his legs were smitten off
> He fought upon the stumps.

I should have liked to give more specimens of the early
Scottish poets. There are passages in their work which I feel
would be greatly appreciated by those who believe that poetry is spoiled by being made too clear. It would be gratifying to be able to include something to please everybody and
I fear that most of this book errs on the side of clarity. But
how about this by William Dunbar?

> Bot fowll, jow-jowrdane-hedit jevellis,
> Cowkin-kenseis, and culroun kewellis;
> Stuffettis, strekouris, and stafische strummellis;
> Wyld haschbaldis, dysouris, dyvouris, drewellis;
> Misgydit memberis of the dewellis . . .

It would be unfair to Gavin Douglas to say that his translation of Vergil is written in the same style, but it is near
enough to make one see why Douglas has been taken up as
the "only translator" of Vergil—I can't say in English, but
in the British Isles.

From the time of Henry VIII onwards the language difficulty disappears, and the anthology becomes comparatively
full. Of course, if you read yourself into any period or into
one of the major poets, it is possible to go on almost indefi-
nitely adding more and more examples. A halt has to be called
somewhere if any proportion is to be kept. But naturally
every anthologist tends to emphasize his own tastes, and I
find that in my case the Tudor-Stuart period comes first.

During the Middle Ages a good deal of English poetry was written by ecclesiastics; some, if not written by the people, came out of the people; and there was a certain amount of Court poetry. The great enemy of all culture is prolonged war and its miseries. At the time of Edward III and Chaucer, English poetry stood high and seemed to have a brilliant future. But when, after the Hundred Years War and the Wars of the Roses, Henry VII found leisure to look around for a poet laureate, he had to pick a Frenchman, as there were apparently no Englishmen available. This gives some idea of the destruction that took place, and the situation was not improved by Henry VIII's suppression of the monasteries.

When English poetry really revived again, in the reign of Elizabeth, it had much to assimilate—the New Learning, the poetry of Renaissance Italy, the French Pléiade, and the Spaniards. As was natural, the assimilation occurred first with Court poets —fine gentlemen who were rich enough to travel and to buy expensive books. Henry VIII's laureate, Skelton, was no doubt a more vigorous poet than either Wyatt or Surrey, yet he seems uncouth and old-fashioned in comparison with them. A generation or so later they were followed by other Court poets—Dyer, Raleigh, Sidney, Brooke.

The greatest, though perhaps not the most read, of these poets is Spenser. His pastorals suffer from a theory of rusticity which makes them sometimes clumsy, and he went archaizing in *The Faery Queen* when he should have done just the opposite. If that enormous suite of tapestry designs in words has grown faded and perhaps a little tedious, few poems have had such lasting and happy effects on later poets. It is surely an achievement to have inspired *The Castle of Indolence* and *Childe Harold's Pilgrimage*. And, although Spenser's sonnets are too closely modelled after French and Italian originals, he made a unique contribution with his two odes, the "Prothalamion" and the "Epithalamion." Everybody drank of that Pierian source, from Shakespeare and Milton to Dryden, to Coleridge, Wordsworth, and Keats, to Arnold and Swinburne.

If Elizabethan poetry had gone no farther than these poets —and we may throw in with them such happy lyrics as Lyly and Lodge, Greene and Peele—the achievement would have been gratifying but not remarkable. After all, much of what they did had already been done on the Continent. Boiardo, Ariosto, and Tasso showed the way for *The Faery Queen*; and one can never be quite sure of any sonnet and lyric of the period that it will not turn out to have an Italian or French original. Spenser translated du Bellay, and Ronsard and his Pléiade were very popular. There is a lyric of Greene's, for instance, which has a French refrain, very much in the manner of the Pléiade:

> *N'oserez-vous, mon bel, mon bel,*
> *N'oserez-vous, mon bel ami?*

There was a learned movement in England—Ascham, Gabriel Harvey, the Countess of Pembroke's efforts to uplift British drama on the lines of Robert Garnier's synthetic Roman tragedies—but luckily it didn't amount to much. The most learned of the Stuart poets, Milton, Donne, and Ben Jonson, managed to hammer their learning into poetry.

The emancipation of Elizabethan poetry came through the stage, as we all know. Here the poet was given that most precious of opportunities, a general and not a specialist audience. When Voltaire came to England he was amazed to see a peer take off his coat and fight ten rounds with a Covent Garden porter to settle a point in dispute. And Voltaire's sixteenth-century predecessor would have been equally amazed to see young nobles from the Court in the same theatre with citizens, prentices, and punks. It was also an advantage for the actors that they were rogues and vagabonds before they were noblemen's servants, so they were spared the upper-class amateur. And though they had to pray for the queen at every performance, that mattered very little, since their poets seldom had to write for her.

All these valuable advantages would have been wasted if there had been nobody to make use of them. Lyly and Peele and Greene and the earlier, forgotten dramatists were all very well, but the man who changed everything and in turn gave Shakespeare his stimulus was Christopher Marlowe. This lewd, atheistic, overweening, bombastic genius worked on the grand scale. He endowed the English stage with his "drumming decasillabons" and showed it how to treat great themes in terms of great poetry.

All Marlowe's greatest writing is in his plays, and it seems absurd to represent him only by the pretty pastoral, "Come live with me and be my love." Marlowe's plays are quotable because they contain passages of splendid rhetoric and lyrical quality. The same is true of other Tudor-Stuart dramatists, and while I don't pretend to have given a complete set of extracts, something like a cross-section will be found. The one exception is Shakespeare. On the one hand, his songs and sonnets are sufficient to show his commanding position in English literature; and, on the other, I found that to quote the plays adequately I should need an impossibly large number of pages. *Venus and Adonis* and *The Rape of Lucrece* are passed over for similar reasons.

Among the glories of Tudor-Stuart poetry are its songs. Many of these were written to be sung on the stage; a few may be found in the novels of the time; but a large number, including some of the finest, come from the song books. After Shakespeare, the most successful of the song-writing dramatists is John Fletcher; and among the purely lyrical writers Campion and Herrick are deservedly very popular. But there are so many great poets in this epoch! Rather apart from the rest is Donne. He is the inventor of what Johnson attacked as the "metaphysical school," and from time to time he is taken up as an exclusive fad by the cliques. Yet Ben Jonson had more insight than Sam Johnson when he said Donne was the first poet in the world for some things.

After the death of Shakespeare and the slow decline of the great poets of the theatre, the Tudor-Stuart period ends as it began with a covey of Court poets. Herrick is that and something more, but it applies to the Carews and Lovelaces and Sucklings and the rest of them. But what grace and elegance and command of subtle rhythm these careless fashionables possessed! In search of these virtues I have gone through George Saintsbury's valuable collection of minor Caroline poets.

On the other side from the king's poets we have the great figure of Milton, the lesser figure of Marvell, and the still lesser figure of Wither. Milton, the Milton of "Arcades" and *Comus* and "Lycidas" and "L'Allegro" and "Il Penseroso," is one of those supreme artists who close an epoch by giving the last polish of consummate style to themes and methods inherited from their predecessors. It is quite true that Milton

is filled with reminiscences, but without him we should have
lost some of the most beautiful poetry in English. The fact
that he also possessed and used all the scholarship of the late
Renaissance should not be held against him. It was, I think,
Mark Pattison who pointed out that a real appreciation of
Milton is one of the rewards of a liberal education.

It is not possible to fix any hard and fast date for the end
of this epoch any more than for its beginning. The names of
Crashaw, Cowley, Marvell, Herbert, Vaughan, and even Cotton still suggest links with the age of Shakespeare. But Dryden, Swift, Gay, Pope, Thomson, Gray, Collins at once suggest
a totally different epoch with quite different views of poetry.

Samuel Johnson was a great man and in his day a great
critic, but from our point of view his taste in poetry seems
wrong. I know of course that he did not select the poets in
the collected edition for which he wrote his critical *Lives*—
that was the work of the booksellers. But Johnson did arrange
for four poets to be added to the list, and if anything they
seem more perverse than the original choice. I have gone
through the *Lives* again, and find some curious statistics. If
Dr. Johnson and his bookseller friends had compiled this anthology, they would have omitted everything before Milton
and Cowley—a little more than the first third of the book.
There would have been thirty-two poets whose work I have
omitted, and only nineteen in common.

It is interesting to consider Johnson's list, which I give
here, printing in italics those names which are found in this
anthology: *Cowley, Denham, Milton, Butler, Rochester,* Ros-
common, *Dryden, Waller,* Pomfret, Dorset, Stepney, J. Philips,
Walsh, Otway, Smith, Duke, King, Sprat, Halifax, Parnell,
Garth, Rowe, Addison, Hughes, Buckingham, *Prior, Con-
greve,* Blackmore, Fenton, *Gay,* Granville, Yalden, Tickell,
Somervile, Savage, *Swift,* Broome, *Pope,* Pitt, *Thomson,*
Watts, A. Philips, West, *Collins,* Dyer, *Shenstone, Young,*
Mallet, Akenside, *Gray,* Lyttleton.

Period specialists can of course say that all this only goes
to show that I don't properly appreciate Augustan poetry. To
which I should reply that the majority of poetry readers to-
day are less interested in Augustan poetry than in the poetry
which preceded and followed it. The dominant poets of the
epoch are Dryden and of course Pope, and their taste on the

whole was that of the French in the age of Louis XIV, with Dryden inclining more to Corneille and Pope to Boileau. But even in France, where it produced great work, this taste was essentially narrow and arrogant, concentrating on a few selected models and rejecting much that now seems to us more valuable than those very models.

Each country had its critical clichés which were thought to dispose of whole generations of poets without more ado. *"Enfin Malherbe vint."* But to a modern reader of French poetry the coming of Malherbe seems no great happiness, since he succeeded merely in quenching for a long period a lyric beauty which had existed in France for centuries. (Amusingly enough, his most admired and quoted fragment has been proved to owe its charm to a printer's error.) The equivalent in England is: "Waller was smooth." But who now cares about Waller's smoothness, and who would dream of ranking him with the Tudor-Stuart poets he was supposed to have superseded for ever?

One of the greatest glories of England is that its poetry counts twice in the history of world literature: that after producing the age of Spenser, Shakespeare, and Milton there were still enough energy and imagination to produce the secondary but still splendid epoch of Blake, Wordsworth, and Shelley. It is due to the Romantic poets that we now rate the poetry of the eighteenth century below its own complacent estimate of itself, and it is also due to them that we value so highly the Tudor-Stuart poets, whom the Augustans wanted to throw on the scrap-heap as obsolescent. An epoch of great poetry will always sympathize with the others, but an age of little poets will have little critics. *"Cosa bella mortal passa, ma non d'arte,"* said Leonardo da Vinci. It is the little criticism which passes, and not the great poetry.

There is an often-quoted line from Elizabethan drama:

Cover her face; mine eyes dazzle; she died young.

It seems the appropriate epitaph for English Romantic poetry partly because two of its two brightest Occidental stars, Shelley and Keats, died young, and partly because the period itself was brief. We cannot put it much before the publication of the Kilmarnock Burns in 1786, and it died at Missolonghi with Byron in 1824. Romantic poetry is the poetry of young men, who either died into immortality or survived like hoary Tithonuses incapable of the Muse's bed.

The poets of England and America who succeeded the Romantics and tried to carry on their tradition succeeded in giving the impression of fabulous respectability. I will not go so far as to say that poetry and respectability are incompatible, but it is hard to think of respectable poets in any other epoch. Even Vergil wrote on dubious themes, and neither Sophocles nor Racine was a member of the Anglican Church or even a Quaker. Of course the Victorians were not so respectable as people thought they were. Tennyson used to get drunk on port, but it was all hushed up, and neither the queen nor the British public ever heard of it. And the same is true of that little scandal of Wordsworth's youth in France, the discovery of which triumphantly restored Wordsworth to the human race. If I am told that Wordsworth ranks among the Romantics, I shall point out that while he was enthusiastically cooperating with the French Revolution he certainly was a great Romantic poet, but by the time he had qualified to be the good and great queen's poet laureate and a piece of indispensable furniture in every home, he was reduced to the mental indigence of writing "Ecclesiastical Sonnets."

These views have naturally influenced the building up of this anthology. I have not given as much attention to the Augustans and their successors as would be expected from a contemporary of Boswell or from a modern critic who tries to persuade us that "The Hind and the Panther" is greater poetry than "Prometheus Unbound." Yet it will be found that I have allowed both Dryden and Pope to have their say, and have included some of those whom Dodsley the publisher used to call "eminent hands." But at the same time I have used the eighteenth century also to bring out those occasional foretastes of the coming Romantics which show what the more sensitive poets were vaguely and perhaps unconsciously trying to express. Kit Smart (so renowned for trying to make Dr. Johnson say his prayers in Fleet Street) may have been mad when he wrote his "Song to David" and sane when he wrote his frightful odes, but for us his madness was more fruitful than his sanity. I have ventured to give more of this interesting poem than is included in many anthologies because it is the gradual working up which brings out the full effect of the grand finale.

The feebleness of English poetry in the latter part of the eighteenth century is well described by an early poem, "To the Muses," by a then totally unknown poet, William Blake, who now ranks very high indeed:

> How have you left the ancient love
> That bards of old enjoy'd in you!
> The languid strings do scarcely move!
> The sound is forc'd, the notes are few!

The last two lines could very appropriately be used to describe the poetical labours of Blake's unsatisfactory patron, William Hayley, who enjoyed a greater reputation than Blake ever did in his lifetime, and who (I blush to say) was actually praised by Gibbon. Among the more preposterous creations of eighteenth-century poetry I would recommend to the curious in such things the incredible "epic" of "Leonidas" by Richard Glover, and Grainger's didactic poem on the sugar cane. There is even one on hop gardens, which contains a superb passage on manure.

I have now accounted for most of the main groups of poets, however superficially. There remain the American poets, the Victorians proper, the poets of the nineties, and the moderns. I don't think the Victorians are under-represented, although I admit they do not stir me as the Romantics do, except perhaps Browning and Swinburne. Browning seems to me the most important of the post-Romantic poets of England. Indeed, I am inclined to think he was the last really major poet England produced. I think it indisputable that there is a decline in the second half of the nineteenth century, in spite of such interesting figures as Hardy, Blunt, Hopkins, Bridges, and Henley.

While standard American poetry gave me anxious moments and I realized that my taste might not always be acceptable, all that was nothing compared with the difficulties of the modern section, American, British, and Dominions.

It is impossible to include everybody who might be held to deserve the attention of posterity, so the partisans of somebody—and probably of many poetical somebodies and nobodies—are going to be offended. On the other hand, by including even a little new and experimental work which has not yet acquired a trace of patina or prestige, the anthologist exposes himself to the charge of gross incompetence by including trash in a volume which contains Shakespeare and Milton. Moreover, by allotting only one or two poems to as many poets as possible, the effect may be given that they are all of equal importance or unimportance. Thus, the treatment of the moderns is a return to the "token" system used at the beginning of this book, though the difficulty here is the mass of material. This is especially true of Dominions poetry, of which I have been able to give only a very few "token" examples.

There remain two or three points which I should like to make clear to avoid any misapprehensions about the scope and limits of this book. I have given examples of light verse from "I Have a Gentil Cok" in the fifteenth century to G. K. Chesterton in the twentieth, but I hope I have succeeded in keeping out the facetious and the whimsy-whamsy. I have tried to limit translations to such universally admired works as Fitzgerald's Omar and William Cory's "Heraclitus," which are poems in their own right, and I have tried to track down and to eliminate the unacknowledged translation or paraphrase. Thus Drummond of Hawthornden's "Sweet Spring, Thou Turn'st" and "Alexis, Here She Stay'd" and "The Beauty and the Life" were all rejected because they are translated respectively from Petrarch, Ronsard, and Guarini.

A standard anthology of the English-speaking world should limit itself to poems in standard English, and therefore I have rejected dialect poets, even the pleasant Dorset poet Barnes. Scots is not a dialect but that branch of Middle "Ynglis" which has been spoken and written for centuries in the ancient Kingdom of Scotland. Anybody who doubts this statement is requested to take up the matter with the first Scotsman he meets. I felt some doubt about two of the Kipling poems, but on discovering that not a word needs to be glossed I thought they might scrape by as standard English. The same prohibition applies to poems in thieves' jargon and in jabberwocky, neither of which can be called standard English. Parody and nonsense verses were also barred as being outside the book's logical scheme and because if you admit one you must admit a host. If you admit the Lewis Carroll parodies which delighted our childhood (when we didn't know they were parodies) then you must admit *Rejected Addresses* and "Quoth the Raven: Nelly Moore,"

and "Butter and Eggs and a Pound of Cheese" and the
brilliant parodies by Chesterton and Sir John Squire and
Swinburne's parody of himself and A. E. Housman's parody
of a Greek tragedy and more and more. Though usually light-
hearted, parody can be cruel. For instance, Byron's two
parodies of Cowper's "Stanzas to Mary" rather mercilessly
killed the original.

In the case of all standard and early writers I have tried to
use a good text, by which I mean a text edited by a reputable
scholar or published by a university press or by one of the
large publishing houses which specialize in producing accu-
rate texts of standard authors. In the case of some rare poets I
have had to be content with the editions of Grosart, who, I
discover, is not very highly esteemed by more recent and
exact scholars.

The spelling of modern poets has of course been left un-
changed—English spelling for the British, American for the
Americans. But I must point out that some American poets
seem to prefer English spelling or a style closer to it than to
modern American standards. I have tried to respect these
individual preferences. For Middle English and Scots I have
made a glossary at the foot of each page. For that long period
in England when spelling differed from modern usage, I
have modernized. There are objections to this, I know, in
the cases of Spenser and Milton and even of Dryden, but
I justify these liberties (which some readers will certainly
dislike) on the ground that the object is to make as much
poetry as possible accessible to as many readers as possible.

There was evidently a period when a past participle such
as "looked" could be pronounced either "lookéd" or "look'd."
Poets continued to write "look'd" and similar words long after
the necessity for the usage had gone. Where I thought it
desirable an improvement, I have ventured to write "looked"
instead of "look'd," and where in reading I found a "lookéd"
word unmarked and it held me up in scanning the line I have
also ventured to accent the "e." But I have *not* tried to make
this a uniform "style." I have simply trusted my eye and ear
in the individual poem or line, so that there may be variations
on the same page. My reason for this liberty is once again the
convenience of the modern reader.

As far as I could, I have freed the poems in this book of

the fancy titles imposed on untitled poems by editors or anthologists. These are often confusing and a positive hindrance in search, because different people give different titles to the same poem. The obvious method of identifying an untitled poem is by part or the whole of the first line. If any invented titles are used here, the reason is that some editor has misled me.

A worse deception on the reader than this is to print an extract from a poem as if it were actually a whole short poem, or to drop one or more stanzas from a poem without warning the reader. This objectionable practice is very common. In this book whenever there is an extract from a longer poem, or if any line or stanzas has been omitted from a short poem, the reader is always warned that what he is about to read is not a complete work by the fact that the title is preceded by "FROM." Thus under Milton the description of Athens in *Paradise Regained* is not printed as if it were a separate complete poem under some invented title; it is marked "FROM *Paradise Regained*." And so throughout the book.

Since many songs and lyrics originally appeared as part of a longer work such as a play or novel, I thought it might be worth noting the fact at the foot of the poem by giving the title of the play or novel from which it is quoted. This does not mean that the song or lyric is incomplete; it is complete in itself but taken from a play or novel and not from a collection of lyrics. I have also given the names of Elizabethan and Jacobean song books and collections, such as *England's Helicon*, followed by their dates. The dates of plays are of the first performance, whenever that is known; in other cases, the dates are of the earliest known publication.

RICHARD ALDINGTON

1956

CONTENTS

CAROLS
"Joseph Was an Old Man"   58
"As Joseph Was A-Walking"   59
"As I Sat under a Sycamore Tree"   60
"God Rest You Merry, Gentlemen"   61
"The First Nowell . . ."   62
ANONYMOUS (15TH–16TH CENTURY)
FROM "The Maidens Came"
"THE MAIDENS CAME"   64
"Back and Side Go Bare . . ."   64
ANONYMOUS (16TH CENTURY)
"Western Wind, When Wilt Thou Blow"   66
KING HENRY VIII (1491–1547)
"As the Holly Groweth Green"   66
ANONYMOUS (16TH CENTURY)
Harpalus' Complaint   67
A Praise of His Lady   70
Against Women either Good or Bad   72
As You Came from the Holy Land   73
"Fain Would I Have a Pretty Thing"   74
SIR THOMAS WYATT (1503–1542)
The Lover Sheweth How He Is Forsaken . . .   76
The Lover Beseecheth His Mistress . . .   77
The Lover Complaineth the Unkindness of His Love   77
HENRY HOWARD, EARL OF SURREY (1516–1547)
A Vow to Love Faithfully . . .   79
The Means to Attain Happy Life   79
FROM The Fourth Book of Virgil's Aeneid
"THEN MERCURY 'GAN BEND HIM TO OBEY"   80
GEORGE GASCOIGNE (1525?–1577)
The Praise of Philip Sparrow   81
NICHOLAS BRETON (1542–1626)
A Sweet Lullaby   82
FROM The Passionate Shepherd
"WHO CAN LIVE IN HEART SO GLAD"   84
Phillida and Coridon   85
FROM An Invective against the Wicked of the World
"LET BUT A FELLOW IN A FOX-FURRED GOWN"   85
THOMAS DELONEY (1543?–1607?)
Song   87

Sonnets

THE VIKING BOOK OF
Poetry
OF THE ENGLISH-SPEAKING WORLD

ANONYMOUS

(A.D. 600–800)

FROM *Beowulf*

What! We of Spear-Danes in spent days,
Of the Folk-Kings' force have heard,
How the Athelings excelled in fight.
Oft Shield of the Sheaf from scathing hordes,
From many meinies their mead-stools tore.
Affrighted them the Earl, since erst he was
Found, unwealthy; then friendship he awaited,
Waxed under the welkin, in worship throve,
Until each one of those out-dwelling
Over the whale-road, must hearken to him,
Gold must give him. That was a good King.
His offspring was afterwards known,
Young in the yards, whom God sent
The folk to befriend, the fierce dearth He knew
They had ere then endured, lacking elders
A long while. To him the Life-Lord
Glory's Wielder, world-honour gave.
Noble was Beowulf (bloomed wide his name)
Shielde's son in the Scede-lands.
So shall a young groom work his own good,
By full fees given to friends of his father,
That with him in his age they may ever abide,
Willing comrades, whenas war cometh,
To serve the people; by praised deeds shall
One man thrive among all man-kind.
Turned aside then Shield in the time shaped for him,
Full-ripe, to fare in Frea's keeping.
Him then out they bare to the brink of ocean,
His sweet companions, so himself had bidden,
While his words had weight, welcome friend of Shieldings;
A beloved land-chief, long had he reigned.
There in the roads ring-stemmed she stood,
Icy, out-faring, an atheling's craft:
Laid they down then the lovely Prince,
Bestower of bracelets, in the breast of the ship,
Their man by the mast. There was a mass of wealth,
Fretted gold ferried from far away.

1

Nor heard I of a keel more comely-wise garnished
With brave weapons and battle-weeds,
With bills and byrnies; on his breast lay
Many treasures that must with him
In the flood's keeping fare afar.
Nothing less of gifts they allowed him,
Of their possessions than had those
Who at his first faring forth had sent him
Alone over ocean, an infant indeed.
Still more, they stood up for him a golden standard
High over head; they let the holm bear him,
Sent him to the Spear-Man; sad was their soul,
Mournful their mood. For men knew not
How soothly to say, men seely in council,
Of their hero under heaven who that lading received.

Translated from Old English by C. K. SCOTT-MONCRIEFF

ANONYMOUS

(13TH CENTURY)

"Sing Cuccu..."

Sing cuccu nu! Sing cuccu!
Sing cuccu! Sing cuccu nu!

Sumer is icumen in,
    Lhudë sing cuccu;
Groweth sed and bloweth med
    And springeth the wdë nu.
        Sing cuccu!
Awë bleteth after lomb,
    Lhouth after calvë cu;
Bulluc sterteth, buckë verteth;
    Murie sing cuccu.
        Cuccu, cuccu,
    Well singës thu, cuccu,
    Ne swik thu naver nu.

Nu, now. Lhudë, loud. Sed, med, seed, mead. Wdë, wood. Awë, ewe.
Lhouth, loweth. Cu, cow. Verteth, hides in the green wood. Murie,
merry. Swik, cease.

ANONYMOUS

(14TH CENTURY)

"Bytuenë Mersh and Averil"

Bytuenë Mersh and Averil,
   When spray biginneth to springe,
The lutel foul hath hire wyl
   On hyre lud to synge.
Ich libbe in love-longinge
For semlokest of allë thinge;
He may me blissë bringe;
Icham in hire baundoun.
     An hendy hap ichabbe yhent;
     Ichot from hevene it is me sent;
     From allö wymmen mil love is lent
   Ant lyht on Alysoun.

On heu hire her is fayr ynoh,
   Hire browë broune, hire eyë blake;
With lossum chere he on me loh,
   With middel smal ant wel ymake.
Bote he me wollë to hire take,
Fortë buen hire owen make,
Longe to lyven ichulle forsake,
Ant feye fallen adoun.

Nihtës when I wende ant wake,
   Forthi myn wongës waxeth won.
Levedi, al for thinë sake
   Longinge is ylent me on.
In world nis non so wytermon,
That al hire bountë tellë con.
Hire swyre is whittore then the swon
Ant feyrest may in toune.

Lutel foul, *little bird*. Hire, *her*. Lud, *voice*. Ich libbe, *I live*. Sem-lokest, *seemliest*. He, *she*. Icham, *I am*. Baundoun, *lordship*. Hendy, *fair*. Hap, *fortune*. Ichabbe, *I have*. Yhent, *gained*. Ichot, *I wot*. Lyht, *lights*. Heu, *hue*. Hire her, *her hair*. Lossum, *lovesome*. He, *she*. Loh, *laughed*. Bote, *unless*. Fortë buen, *for to be*. Make, *mate*. Ichulle, *I shall*. Feye, *lifeless*. Wende, *turn*. Forthi, *therefore*. Wongës, *cheeks*. Won, *wan*. Levedi, *lady*. Nis, *is not*. Wytermon, *wise man*. Swyre, *neck*. May, *maid*.

Icham for wowing al forwake,
  Wery so water in wore.
Lest eny revë me my make,
  Ichabbe y-yernéd yore.
Betere is tholien whylë sore,
  Then mournen evermore.
Geynest under gore,
Herknë to my roun.
    An hendy hap ichabbe yhent;
    Ichot from hevene it is me sent;
    From allë wymmen mi love is lent
  Ant lyht on Alysoun.

ANONYMOUS

(14TH CENTURY)

"Lenten Is Come..."

Lenten is come with love to toune,
With blosmen and with briddës roune,
  That al this blissë bringeth,
Dayës-eyës in this dales,
Notës suete of nytëgales;
  Uch foul song singeth.
The threstelcoc him threteth oo;
Away is huere wynter woo,
  When wodërovë springeth.
This foulës singeth ferly fele
And wlyteth on huere wynter wele,
  That al the wodë ryngeth.

The rosë rayleth hire rode;
The levës on the lyhtëwode
  Wexen all with wille.

Wowing, wooing. Wore, weir. Revë, rob. Yore, long. Tholien, to endure.
Geynest, most graceful. Gore, skirt. Roun, song.

Lenten, Lent. Briddës, birds. Roune, song. Uch, each. Foul, bird.
Threstelcoc, blackbird. Threteth oo, ever chides. Huere, their. Woo, woe.
Wodërovë, wood-ruff. Ferly fele, wondrous many. Wlyteth, whistle. Wele,
joy. Rayleth, sends forth. Rode, red. Wille, desire.

The monë mandeth hire bleo;
The lilie is lossom to seo,
 The fenyl ant the fille.
Wowës thisë wildë drakes;
Milës murgeth huere makes,
 Asc strcm that striketh stille.
Mody meneth, so doth mo.
Ichot ycham on of tho
 For love that likës ille.

The monë mandeth hire lyht;
So doth semly sonnë bryht,
 When briddës singeth breme.
Deawës donketh the dounes,
Deores with huere dernë rounes,
 Domes forte domo.
Wormës woweth under cloude;
Wymmen waxeth wounder proude,
 So wel hit wol hem seme.
Yef me shal wontë wille of on,
This wunnë weole I wole forgon,
 Ant wyht in wode be fleme.

JOHN BARBOUR

(1320?–1395)

FROM *The Bruce*

A! fredome is a noble thing!
Fredome mayss man to haiff liking;
Fredome all solace to man giffis:
He levys at ess that frely levys!

Mandeth hire bleo, *sends out her light.* Lossom to seo, *lovesome to see.*
Fenyl, *fennel.* Fille, *thyme.* Wowës, *woos.* Milës murgeth huere makes,
Wild things make merry (with) their mates. Ase, *as.* Striketh, *flows.* Mody
meneth, so doth mo, *The passionate man complains, and so do others.*
Ichot ycham, *I wot I am.* On of tho, *one of those.* Breme, *valiantly.*
Deawës, *dews.* Donketh, *moisten.* Dounes, *downs.* Deores, *animals.* Dernë,
secret. Domës fortë deme, *whereby they converse.* Wormës woweth under
cloude, *Worms woo under clod.* Hit, *it.* Yef, *if.* Wontë, *want.* Wunnë
weole, *wealth of delight.* Fleme, *fugitive.*

Mayss, *makes.* Haiff, *have.* Liking, *happiness.* Giffis, *gives.* Levys, *lives.*

A noble hart may haiff nane ess
Na elles nocht that may him pless,
Gyff fredome failhe; for fre liking
Is yharnyt our all othir thing.
Na he, that aye hass levyt fre
May nocht knaw weill the propyrte,
The angyr, na the wrechyt dome,
That is cowplyt to foule thyrldome;
Bot gyff he had assayit it
Than all perquer he suld it wyt,
And suld think fredome mar to pryss
Than all the gold in warld that is.

GEOFFREY CHAUCER

(1340?–1400)

FROM *The Prologue to the Canterbury Tales*

1.

Whan that Aprille with his shoures soote
The droghte of March hath perced to the roote,
And bathed every veyne in swich licour
Of which vertu engendered is the flour;
Whan Zephyrus eek with his sweete breeth
Inspired hath in every holt and heeth
The tendre croppes, and the yonge sonne
Hath in the Ram his halve cours yronne,
And smale fowles maken melodye,
That slepen al the nyght with open ye
(So priketh hem nature in hir corages);
Thanne longen folk to goon on pilgrimages,
And palmeres for to seken straunge strondes,
To ferne halwes, kowthe in sondry londes;

Ess, *ease.* Nane, *no.* Na elles nocht, *nor aught else.* Pless, *please.* Gyff, *if.*
Failhe, *fail.* Yharnyt, *desired.* Our, *above.* Na, *nor.* Nocht knaw, *not know.*
Dome, *fate.* Cowplyt, *coupled.* Thyrldome, *thralldom.* Bot, *but.* Assayit,
experienced. Perquer, *thoroughly.* Suld, *should.* Mar, *more.* Pryss, *prize.*

Whan, *when.* Shoures, *showers.* Soote, *sweet.* Droghte, *drought.* Veyne,
sap-vessel. Swich, *such.* Licour, *moisture.* Flour, *flower.* Inspired, *breathed.*
Holt, *cultivated land.* Heeth, *heath, wild land.* Yonge, *young.* His haive
cours yronne, *has run half his course.* Fowles, *birds.* Ye, *eye.* Priketh, *stirs.*
Hem, *them.* Corages, *desires.* Thanne, *then.* Strondes, *strands.* Ferne
halwes, *distant saints.* Kowthe, *known.* Londes, *lands.*

And specially from every shires ende
Of Engelonde to Caunterbury they wende,
The hooly blisful martir for to seke,
That hem hath holpen whan that they were seeke.

2.

There was also a Nonne, a Prioresse,
That of hir smylyng was full symple and coy;
Hire gretteste ooth was but by Seinte Loy;
And she was cleped madame Eglentyne.
Ful weel she soong the service dyvyne,
Entuned in hir nose ful semely,
And Frenssh she spak ful faire and fetisly,
After the scole of Stratford atte Bowe,
For Frenssh of Paris was to hire unknowe.
At mete wol ytaught was she with alle:
She leet no morsel from her lippes falle,
Ne wette hir fyngres in hir sauce depe;
Wel koude she carie a morsel and wel kepe
That no drope ne fille upon hire brest.
In curteisie was set ful muchel hir lest.
Hir over-lippe wyped she so clene
That in her coppe there was no ferthyng sene
Of grece, whan she dronken hadde hir draughte.
Ful semely after hir mete she raughte.
And sikerly she was of greet desport,
And ful plesaunt, and amyable of port,
And peyned hire to countrefete cheere
Of court, and to been estatlich of manere,
And to ben holden digne of reverence.
But, for to speken of hire conscience,
She was so charitable and so pitous
She wolde wepe, if that she saugh a mous
Kaught in a trappe, if it were deed or bledde.
Of smale houndes hadde she that she fedde

Seeke, *sick.*

Nonne, *nun.* Hir, hire, *her.* Ooth, *oath.* Seinte Loy, *Saint Eligius.* Cleped,
named. Semely, *pleasantly.* Fetisly, *gracefully.* Mete, *meat.* Ne, *nor.*
Koude, *could.* Fille, *fell.* Lest, *desire.* Ferthyng, *farthing, bit.* Grece, *grease.*
Raughte, *reached.* Sikerly, *certainly.* Desport, *mirth.* Port, *behaviour.*
Peyned, *took pains.* Estatlich, *dignified.* Digne, *worthy.* Pitous, *full of pity.*

With rosted flessh, or milk and wastel-breed.
But soore wepte she if oon of hem were deed,
Or if men smoot it with a yerde smerte;
And al was conscience and tendre herte.
Ful semyly hir wympul pynched was;
Hir nose tretys, hir eyen greye as glas,
Hir mouth ful smal, and thereto softe and reed;
But sikerly she hadde a fair forheed;
It was almoost a spanne brood, I trowe;
For, hardily, she was nat undergrowe.
Ful fetys was hir cloke, as I was war.
Of smal coral aboute hire arm she bar
A peire of bedes, gauded al with grene,
And theron heng a brooch of gold ful sheene,
On which ther was first write a crowned A,
And after *Amor vincit omnia.*

3.

A Marchant was ther with a forked berd,
In mottelee, and hye on horse he sat;
Upon his heed a Flaundryssh bever hat,
His bootes clasped faire and fetisly.
His resons he spak ful solempnely,
Sownynge alwey th' encrees of his wynnyng.
He wolde the see were kept for any thyng
Betwixe Middelburgh and Orewelle.
Wel koude he in eschaunge sheeldes selle.
This worthy man ful wel his wit bisette:
Ther wiste no wight that he was in dette,
So estatly was he of his governaunce
With his bargaynes and with his chevyssaunce.
For sothe he was a worthy man with alle,
But, sooth to seyn, I noot how men hym calle.

Wastel-breed, *fine white bread.* Yerde, *stick.* Tretys, *well-shaped.* Hardily,
certainly. Fetys, *graceful.* War, *aware.* Peire, *pair.* Gauded, *trimmed.*
Sheene, *bright.*

Berd, *beard.* Mottelee, *parti-coloured cloth.* Flaundryssh, *Flanders.* Resons,
opinions. Sownynge, *proclaiming.* Encrees, *increase.* Wynnyng, *gains.* He
wolde the see were kept, *he wanted the sea held.* Middelburgh, *Mid-
delburg, Holland.* Orewelle, *the river Orwell, England.* Sheeldes, *French
money.* His wit bisette, *applied his mind.* Wiste, *knew.* Wight, *person.*
Estatly, *dignified.* Governaunce, *demeanour.* Chevyssaunce, *dealing in
money.* Noot, *know not.*

4.

A Clerk ther was of Oxenford also,
That unto logyk hadde longe ygo.
As leene was his hors as is a rake,
And he nas nat right fat, I undertake,
But looked holwe, and therto sobrely.
Ful thredbare was his overeste courtpey;
For he hadde geten hym yet no benefice,
Ne was so worldly for to have office.
For hym was levere have at his beddes heed
Twenty bookes, clad in blak or reed,
Of Aristotle and his philosophie,
Than robes riche, or fithele, or gay sautrie.
But al be that he was a philosophre,
Yet hadde he but litel golde in coffre;
But al that he myghte of his freendes hente,
On bookes and on lernynge he it spente,
And bisily gan for the soules preye
On hem that yaf hym wherwith to scoleye.
Of studie took he moost cure and moost heede.
Noght o word spak he moore than was neede,
And that was seyd in forme and reverence,
And short and quyk and ful of hy sentence;
Sownynge in moral vertu was his speche,
And gladly wolde he lerne and gladly teche.

5.

A Frankeleyn was in his compaignye.
Whit was his berd as is the dayesye;
Of his complexioun he was sangwyn.
Wel loved he by the morwe a sop in wyn;
To lyven in delit was evere his wone,
For he was Epicurus owene sone,
That heeld opinioun that pleyn delit

Hadde longe ygo, *had long been studying.* Nas nat, *was not.* Holwe, *hollow.* Overeste courtpey, *short overcoat.* Geten, *gotten.* Office, *secular employment.* Hym was levere, *he would rather.* Fithele, *fiddle.* Sautrie, *psaltery.* Hente, *obtain.* Preye, *pray.* Yaf, *gave.* Scoleye, *study.* Cure, *care.* Noght o, *not one.* Sentence, *significance.* Sownynge in, *making for.*

Frankeleyn, *a franklin, a wealthy land-owner.* Dayesye, *daisy.* Morwe, *morning.* Sop in wyn, *bread dipped in wine.* Wone, *custom.* Pleyn, *complete.*

Was verraily felicitee parfit.
An householdere, and that a greet, was he;
Seint Julian he was in his contree.
His breed, his ale, was always after oon;
A bettre envyned man was nowher noon.
Withoute bake mete was nevere his hous
Of fissh and flessh, and that so plentevous,
It snewed in his hous of mete and drynke,
Of all deyntees that men koude thynke.
After the sondry sesons of the yeer,
So chaunged he his mete and his soper.
Ful many a fat partrich hadde he in muwe,
And many a breem and many a luce in stuwe.
Wo was his cook but if his sauce were
Poynaunt and sharp, and redy al his geere.
His table dormant in his halle alway
Stood redy covered al the longe day.
At sessiouns ther was he lord and sire;
Ful ofte tyme he was knyght of the shire.
An anlaas and a gipser all of silk
Heeng at his girdel, whit as morne milk.
A shirreve hadde he been, and a countour.
Was nowher such a worthy vavasour.

6.

A good Wif was ther of biside Bathe,
But she was somdele deef, and that was scathe.
Of clooth-makyng she had swich an haunt,
She passed hem of Ypres and of Gaunt.
In al the parisshe wif ne was ther noon
That to the offrynge bifore hire sholde goon;
And if ther dide, certayn so wrooth was she,

Seint Julian, *saint of hospitality.* Breed, bread. After oon, *uniformly good.* Envyned, *stocked with wine.* Noon, none. Snewed, snowed. Deyntees, *dainties.* Koude, could. Soper, supper. Muwe, coop. Breem, bream. Luce, *pike.* Stuwe, *stew.* Geere, utensils. Table dormant, *a permanently fixed table.* Anlaas, anlace, *a dagger.* Gipser, purse. Heeng, hung. Morne, morning. Shirreve, sheriff. Countour, accountant or non-professional pleader *in the law courts.* Vavasour, *a minor feudal land-holder.*

Somdele, somewhat. Deef, deaf. Scathe, a pity. Swich an haunt, *so much skill.* Ne was ther noon, *there was none.* Offrynge, offering in church. Wrooth, angry.

That she was out of alle charitee.
Hir coverchiefs ful fyne weren of ground;
I dorste swere they weyeden ten pound
That on a Sonday weren upon hir heed.
Hir hosen weren of fyn scarlet reed,
Ful streite yteyd, and shoes ful moyste and newe.
Boold was hir face, and fair, and reed of hewe.
She was a worthy womman al hir lyve:
Housbondes at chirche dore she hadde fyve,
Withouten oother compaignye in youthe,
But thereof nedeth nat to speke as nowthe.
And thries hadde she been at Jerusalem;
She hadde passed many a straunge strem;
At Rome she hadde been, and at Boloigne,
In Galice at Seint Jame, and at Coloigne.
Sho koude muchel of wandrynge by the weye.
Gat-tothed was she, soothly for to seye.
Upon an amblere esily she sat,
Ywympled wel, and on hir heed an hat
As brood as is a bokeler or a targe;
A foot-mantel about her hipes large,
And on hir feet a paire of spores sharpe.
In felaweshipe wel koude she laughe and carpe.
Of remedies of love she knew per chaunce,
For she koude of that art the olde daunce.

7.

The Millere was a stout carl for the nones;
Ful byg he was of brawn, and eek of bones.
That proved wel, for over al ther he cam,
At wrastlynge he wolde have alwey the ram.

Coverchiefs, head-dress. Ground, texture. Dorste, durst. Weyeden, weighed.
Hosen, stockings. Reed, red. Streite yteyd, tightly tied. Moyste, soft. Hewe,
hue. As nowthe, now. Thries, thrice. Boloigne, Boulogne sur Mer. Galice
at Seint Jame, Sant' Iago de Compostela in Galicia. Coloigne, Cologne.
Koude, knew. Gat-tothed, teeth set wide apart. Amblere, an ambling horse.
Ywympled, wrapped in a wimple. Bokeler, buckler. Targe, shield. Foot-
mantel, a cloth covering worn over the skirt in riding. Hipes, hips. Spores,
spurs. Felaweshipe, fellowship. Koude, could. Carpe, talk. Koude, knew.

Carl, fellow. For the nones, indeed, exceedingly. Over al ther he cam,
above all others in the place from which he came. The ram, the prize.

He was short-sholdred, brood, a thikke knarre;
Ther was no dore that he nolde heve of harre,
Or breke it at a rennyng with his heed.
His berd as any sowe or fox was reed,
And thereto brood, as though it were a spade.
Upon the cop right of his nose he hade
A werte, and theron stood a toft of herys,
Reed as the brustles of a sowes erys;
His nosethirles blake were and wyde.
A swerd and bokeler bar he by his syde.
His mouth as greet was as a greet forneys.
He was a janglere and a goliardeys,
And that was moost of synne and harlotries.
Wel koude he stelen corn and tollen thries;
And yet he hadde a thombe of gold, pardee.
A whit cote and blew hood wered he.
A baggepipe wel koude he blowe and sowne,
And therwithal he broghte us out of towne.

FROM *The Reeve's Tale*

At Trumpyngtoun nat fer from Cantebrigge,
Ther gooth a brook, and over that a brigge,
Upon the whiche brook ther stant a melle;
And this is verray sooth that I yow telle:
A millere was ther dwellynge many a day.
As any pecok he was proud and gay.
Pipen he koude and fisshe, and nettes beete,
And turne coppes, and wel wrastle and sheete;
Ay by his belt he baar a long panade,
And of a swerd ful trenchant was the blade.

Brood, broad. Thikke knarre, *thickset heavy man.* Nolde heve of harre, *could not lift off its hinge.* Rennyng, *running.* Heed, *head.* Berd, beard. Reed, red. Cop, *tip.* Werte, wart. Toft of herys, *tuft of hairs.* Brustles, *bristles.* Erys, ears. Nosethirles, *nostrils.* Bokeler, *buckler.* Bar, *carried.* Greet, great. Forneys, *furnace.* Janglere, *chatterer.* Goliardeys, *coarse buffoon.* Tollen thries, *charge people three times over.* A thombe of gold, *a thumb of gold; i.e., honest for a miller.* Pardee, *truly.* Koude, could.

Cantebrigge, *Cambridge.* Brigge, *bridge.* Melle, *mill.* Koude, *could.* Nettes beete, *weave nets.* Turne coppes, *make wooden cups.* Sheete, *shoot.* Baar, *carried.* Panade, *cutlass.*

A joly poppere baar he in his pouche;
Ther was no man, for peril, dorste hym touche.
A Sheffeld thwitel baar he in his hose.
Round was his face, and camus was his nose;
As piled as an ape was his skulle.
IIe was a market-betere atte fulle.
Ther dorste no wight hand upon hym legge,
That he ne swoor he sholde anon abegge.
A theefe he was for sothe of corn and mele,
And that a sly, and usant for to stele.
His name was hoote deynous Symkyn.

A wyf he hadde, ycomen of noble kyn;
The person of the toun hir fader was.
With hire he yaf ful many a panne of bras,
For that Symkyn sholde in his blood allye.
She was yfostred in a nonnerye.
And she was proud, and peert as is a pye.
A ful fair sight was it upon hem two;
On halydayes biforn hire wolde he go
With his typet bounden aboute his heed,
And she cam after in a gyte of reed;
And Symkyn hadde hosen of the same.
Ther dorste no wight clepen hire but "dame";
Was noon so hardy that wente by the weye
That with hire dorste rage or ones pleye,
But if he wolde be slayn of Symkyn
With panade, or with knyf, or boidekyn.
For jalous folk ben perilous everemo;
Algate they wolde hire wyves wenden so.
And eek, for she was somdel smoterlich,

Joly poppere, neat dagger. For peril, because of the risk. Dorste, durst.
Sheffeld thwitel, large Sheffield knife. Camus, snub-nosed. Piled, usually
"bald," but here probably "hairy." Market-betere, swaggerer at market
places. Wight, person. Swoor, swore. Abegge, pay dearly for it. For sothe,
forsooth. Usant, accustomed. Stele, steal. Hoote, called. Deynous, scornful.
Ycomen, come. Person, parson. Hire, her. Yaf, gave. Panne, pan. Bras,
brass. Allye, ally. Yfostred, reared. Nonnerye, nunnery. Peert, saucy. Pye,
magpie. Halydayes, holidays. Biforn, before. Typet, tippet. Heed, head.
Gyte of reed, red garment. Clepen, call. Noon, none. Hardy, bold. Rage,
flirt. Ones, once. Pleye, make jokes. But if he wolde, unless he wanted to
be. Boidekyn, bodkin. Perilous, dangerous. Everemo, evermore. Algate,
nevertheless. Hire, their. Wenden so, go in this way. Somdel smoterlich,
somewhat besmirched (i.e., as illegitimate daughter of a priest).

She was as digne as water in a dich,
And ful of hoker and of bisemare.
Hir thoughte that a lady sholde hire spare,
What for her kynrede and hir nortelrie
That she had lerned in the nonnerie.

FROM *The Wife of Bath's Tale*

In th'olde dayes of the Kyng Arthour,
Of which the Britons speken greet honour,
Al was this land fulfild of fayerye.
The elf-queene, with hir joly compaignye,
Daunced ful ofte in many a grene mede.
This was the olde opinion, as I rede;
I speke of manye hundred yeres ago.
But now kan no man se none elves mo,
For now the greet charitee and prayeres
Of lymytours and othere hooly freres,
That serchen every lond and every streem,
As thikke as motes in the sonne-beem,
Blessynge halles, chambres, kichenes, boures,
Citees, burghes, castels, hye toures,
Thropes, bernes, shipnes, dayeryes—
This maketh that ther been no fayeryes.
For ther as wont to walken was an elf,
Ther walketh now the lymytour hymself
In undermeles and in morwenynges,
And seyth his matyns and his hooly thynges
As he gooth in his lymytacioun.
Wommen may go now saufly up and doun
In every bussh or under every tree;
Ther is noon oother incubus but he,
And he ne wol doon hem but dishonour.

Digne, *haughty.* Dich, *ditch.* Hoker, *disdain.* Bisemare, *scorn.* Spare, *be
reserved.* Kynrede, *kindred.* Nortelrie, *education.*

Greet, *great.* Fulfild, *full.* Fayerye, *fairy-folk.* Joly, *merry.* Grene mede,
green meadow. Rede, *think.* None elves mo, *no more elves.* Lymytours, *begging friars.* Hooly freres, *holy friars.* Serchen, *visit.* Lond, *land.* Thikke,
thick. Sonne-beem, *sunbeam.* Boures, *women's rooms.* Hye, *high.* Thropes,
villages. Bernes, *barns.* Shipnes, *stables.* Dayeryes, *dairies.* Undermeles,
afternoons. Morwenynges, *mornings.* Matyns, *matins.* Lymytacioun, *friar's
limit.* Saufly, *safely.* Noon, *none.*

FROM *The Parliament of Fowls*

The lyf so short, the craft so long to lerne,
Th'assay so hard, so sharp the conquerynge,
The dredful joye, alwey that slit so yerne:
Al this mene I by Love, that my felynge
Astonyeth with his wonderful werkynge
So sore iwis, that whan I on hym thynke,
Nat wot I wel wher that I flete or synke.

Of usage—what for lust and what for lore—
On bokes rede I ofte, as I yow tolde.
But wherfore that I speke al this? Not yoore
Agon, it happede me for to beholde
Upon a bok, was write with lettres olde,
And therupon, a certeyn thing to lerne,
The longe day ful faste I redde and yerne.

For out of olde feldes, as men seyth,
Cometh all this newe corn from yer to yere,
And out of olde bokes, in good feyth,
Cometh al this newe science that men lere.
But now to purpos as of this matere
To rede forth hit gan me so delite,
That al that day me thoughte but a lyte.

FROM *Troilus and Criseyde*

Go, litel bok, go, litel myn tragedye,
Ther God thi makere yet, er that he dye,
So sende myght to make in some comedye!

Assay, trial. Dredful, timid. Slit so yerne, passes so quickly. Astonyeth, confounds. Iwis, assuredly. Whan, when. Nat wot I, I know not. Wher,
whether. Flete, float. Lust, pleasure. Lore, learning. Yow, you. Yoore, long.
Ful faste, eagerly. Redde, read. Yerne, desired. Feldes, fields. Seyth, say.
Yer, yere, year. Feyth, faith. Lere, learn. Gan, did. A lyte, a little, i.e., short.

Bok, book. Ther God &c., and so may God grant that thy poet may write
comedy before he dies. Makere, poet. Make, write poetry.

But litel book, no makyng thow n'envie,
But subgit be to alle poesye;
And kis the steppes, where as thow seest pace
Virgil, Ovide, Omer, Lucan, and Stace.

And for ther is so gret diversitie
In Englissh and in writyng of oure tonge,
So prey I God that non myswrite the,
Ne the mysmetre for defaute of tonge.
And red wherso thow be, or elles songe,
That thow be understonde, God I beseche!
But yet to purpos of my rather speche.

O yonge, fresshe folkes, he or she,
In which that love up groweth with youre age,
Repeyreth hom fro worldly vanyte,
And of youre herte up casteth the visage
To thilke God that after his ymage
Yow made, and thynketh al nys but a faire
This world, that passeth soon as floures faire.

And loveth hym, the which that right for love
Upon a crois, oure soules for to beye,
First starf, and roos, and sit in hevene above;
For he nyl falsen no wight, dar I seye,
That wol his herte al holly on hym leye.
And syn he best to love is, and most meke,
What nedeth feyned loves for to seke?

Lo here, of payens corsed olde rites,
Lo here, what alle hire goddes may availle;
Lo here, this wrecched worldes appetites;
Lo here, the fyn and guerdoun for travaille

No makyng thow n'envie, *do thou envy no other writing.* Subgit, *subject.*
Omer, *Homer.* Stace, *Statius.* Tonge, *tongue.* Non, *none.* The, *thee.* Mysmetre, *falsify the metre.* Red, *read.* Elles songe, *or else sung.* Repeyreth
hom, *return home.* Fro, *from.* Thilke, *that.* Al nys, *all is*—negative. Floures,
flowers. Loveth, *love*—imperative. The which, *who.* Crois, *cross.* Beye,
redeem. Starf, *died.* Roos, *rose.* Sit, *sits.* Nyl falsen, *will not betray.* Wight,
person. Holly, *wholly.* Leye, *recline.* Syn, *since.* Meke, *meek.* Feyned, *pretended.* Seke, *seek.* Payens, *pagans.* Corsed, *accursed.* Hire, *their.* Fyn, *end.*
Guerdoun, *reward.*

Of Jove, Appollo, of Mars, of swich rascaille!
Lo here, the forme of olde clerkis speche
In poetrie, if ye hire bokes seche.

O moral Gower, this book I directe
To the and to the, philosophical Strode,
To vouchen safe, ther nede is, to correcte,
Of your benignities and zeles goode.
And to that sothefast Crist, that starf on rode,
With al myn herte of mercy evere I preye,
And to the Lord right thus I speke and seye:

Thow oon, and two, and thre, eterne on lyve,
That regnest ay in thre, and two, and oon,
Uncircumscript, and al maist circumscrive,
Us from visible and invisible foon
Defende, and to thy mercy, everichon,
So make us, Jesus, for thi mercy digne,
For love of mayde and moder thyn benigne.
        Amen.

FROM *The Legend of Good Women*

And as for me, though that my wit be lite,
On bokes for to rede I me delyte,
And in myn herte have hem in reverence,
And to hem yeve swich lust and swich credence
That there is wel unethe game non
That fro my bokes make me to gon,
But be it other upon the halyday,
Or ellis in the joly tyme of May,
What that I here the smale foules synge,

Swich rascaille, *such a mob*. Seche, *seek*. Gower, *English poet*. The, **thee.**
Strode, *probably Ralph Strode, the scholar*. Ther, *where*. Benignities, *gra-
ciousness*. Sothefast, *true*. Rode, *rood*. Oon, *one*. Eterne on lyve, *eternally
living*. Maist, *mayest*. Foon, *foes*. Everichon, *every one*. Digne, *worthy*.
Benigne, *gracious*.

Lite, *slight*. Rede, *read*. Hem, *them*. Yeve, *give*. Swich lust, *such pleasure*.
Wel unethe game non, *scarcely any amusement*. Fro, *from*. Gon, *go*. Halyday, *holiday*. Ellis, *else*. Here, *hear*. Foules, *birds*.

And that the floures gynne for to sprynge.
Farwel my stodye, as lastynge that sesoun!
Now have I therto this condicioun,
That of alle the floures in the mede,
Thanne love I most these floures white and rede,
Swyche as men calle dayesyes in oure toun.
To hem have I so gret affeccioun,
As I seyde erst, whan comen is the May,
That in my bed there daweth me no day
That I n'am up and walkynge in the mede
To sen these floures agen the sonne sprede,
The longe day thus walkynge in the grene.

Balade de Bon Conseil

Flee fro the prees, and dwelle with sothfastnesse,
Suffyce unto thy good, though it be smal;
For hord hath hate, and climbing tikelnesse,
Prees hath envye, and wele blent overal;
Savour no more than thee bihove shal;
Reule wel thyself, that other folk canst rede;
And trouth thee shal delivere, it is no drede.

Tempest thee noght al croked to redresse,
In trust of hir that turneth as a bal:
Gret reste stant in litel besinesse;
Be war also to sporne ayeyns an al;
Stryve not, as doth the crokke with the wal.
Daunte thyself, that dauntest otheres dede;
And trouthe thee shal delivere, it is no drede.

Floures, flowers. Gynne, begin. Stodye, study. As lastynge, during. Condicioun, state of mind. Mede, meadow. Thanne, then. Rede, red. Dayesyes, daisies. Erst, at first. Whan, when. Daweth, dawneth. N'am, am not. Agen, towards.

Fro, from. Prees, throng. Sothfastnesse, truth. Hord, avarice. Tikelnesse, instability. Wele blent, success blinds. Bihove, behove. Rede, advise. Drede, doubt. Tempest, distress. Noght, not. Al croked, all crooked things. Hir, here, i.e., Fortune. Reste, repose. Be war, beware. Sporne, kick. Ayeyns, against. Al, awl. Crokke, crock. Daunte, control.

That thee is sent, receyve in buxumnesse,
The wrastling for this world axeth a fal.
Her is non hoom, her nis but wildernesse:
Forth, pilgrim, forth! Forth, beste, out of thy stal!
Know thy contree, look up, thank God of al;
Hold the heye way, and lat thy gost thee lede;
And trouthe thee shal delivere, it is no drede.

ENVOY

Therfore, thou Vache, leve thyn old wrecchednesse
Unto the world; leve now to be thral;
Crye him mercy, that of his hy goodnesse
Made thee of noght, and in especial
Draw unto him, and pray in general
For thee, and eek for other, hevenlich mede;
And trouthe thee shal delivere, it is no drede.

The Complaint of Chaucer to His Purse

To yow, my purse, and to noon other wight
Complayne I, for ye be my lady dere!
I am so sory, now that ye been lyght;
For certes, but ye make me hevy chere,
Me were as leef be layd upon my bere;
For which unto your mercy thus I crye:
Beth hevy ageyn, or elles mot I dye!

Now voucheth sauf this day, or yt be nyght,
That I of yow this blissful soun may here,
Or see your colour lyk the sonne bryght,
That of yelownesse hadde never pere.
Ye be my lyf, ye be myn hertes stere,
Quene of comfort and of good companye:
Beth hevy ageyn, or elles moote I dye!

Buxumnesse, *submission.* Axeth, *asketh.* Her is non hoom, *here is no home.*
Contree, *country.* Gost, *spirit.* Lede, *lead.* Vache, *cow.* Hevenlich mede,
heavenly reward.

Stere, *pilot.*

Now purse, that ben to me my lyves lyght
And saveour, as doun in this world here,
Out of this toune help me thurgh your myght,
Syn that ye wole nat ben my tresorere;
For I am shave as nye as any frere.
But yet I pray unto your curtesye:
Beth hevy agen, or elles moote I dye!

LENVOY DE CHAUCER

O conqueror of Brutes Albyon,
Which that by lyne and free eleccion
Been verray king, this song to yow I send;
And ye, that mowen alle oure harmes amende,
Have mind upon my supplicacion!

ANONYMOUS

(15TH CENTURY)

"I Sing of a Maiden"

I sing of a maiden
    That is makëles,
King of all kinges
    To her sone sche ches.

He cam also stille
    There his moder was,
As dew in Aprille
    That falleth on the grass.

He cam also stille
    To his moderës bour,
As dew in Aprille
    That falleth on the flour.

Nye, *close.* Frere, *friar.* Lyne, *descent.* Mowen, *have power to.* Harmes, *misfortunes.*

Makëles, *mateless.* Sche, *she.* Ches, *chose.* Moder, *mother.* Bour, *bower.*

He came also stille
　　There his moder lay,
As dew in Aprille
　　That falleth on the spray.

Moder and maiden
　　Was never non but sche;
Well may swich a lady
　　Godës moder be.

ANONYMOUS

(15TH CENTURY)

"Can I Not Sing..."

Can I not sing but "Hoy,"
Whan the joly shepard made so much joy?

The shepard upon a hill he satt;
He had on him his tabard and his hat,
His tarbox, his pipe, and his flagat;
His name was called Joly Joly Wat,
　　For he was a gud herdës boy.
　　　　Ut hoy!
　　For in his pipe he made so much joy.

The shepard upon a hill was laid;
His dog to his girdell was taid;
He had not slept but a litill braid,
But "Gloria in excelsis" was to him said.
　　　　Ut hoy!
　　For in his pipe he made so much joy.

The shepard on a hill he stode;
Round about him his shepe they yode;
He put his hond under his hode,
He saw a star as rede as blode.
　　　　Ut hoy!
　　For in his pipe he made so much joy.

Swich, such.

Tabard, short coat. Flagat, flagon. Taid, tied. Braid, time. Yode, went.
Hond, hand. Hode, hood. Blode, blood

The shepard said anon right,
"I will go see yon farly sight,
Where as the angel singeth on hight,
And the star that shineth so bright."
                    Ut hoy!
        For in his pipe he made so much joy.

"Now farewell, Mall, and also Will!
For my love go ye all still,
Unto I cum again you till,
And evermore, Will, ring well thy bell."
                    Ut hoy!
        For in his pipe he made so much joy.

"Now must I go there Crist was born;
Farewell! I cum again to morn.
Dog, keep well my shepe from ye corn,
And warn well 'Warroke' when I blow my horn!"
                    Ut hoy!
        For in his pipe he made so much joy.

Whan Wat to Bedlem cum was,
He swet, he had gone faster than a pace;
He found Jesu in a simpell place,
Between an ox and an ass.
                    Ut hoy!
        For in his pipe he made so much joy.

"Jesu, I offer to thee here my pipe,
My skirt, my tar-box, and my scripe;
Home to my felowes now will I skipe,
And also look unto my shepe."
                    Ut hoy!
        For in his pipe he made so much joy.

"Now farewell, mine owne herdes man Wat!"
"Yea, for God, lady, even so I hat;
Lull well Jesu in thy lape,
And farewell, Joseph, with thy round cape!"
                    Ut hoy!
        For in his pipe he made so much joy.

Farly, *marvellous.* Scripe, *scrip.* Hat, *am called.*

"Now may I well both hope and sing,
For I have bene at Cristes bering;
Home to my felowes now will I fling.
Crist of heven to his bliss us bring!"
Ut hoy!
For in his pipe he made so much joy.

ANONYMOUS

(15TH CENTURY)

"I Am as Light as Any Roe"

I am as light as any roe
To preise womene where that I go.

To onpreise womene it were a shame,
For a woman was thy dame.
Our blessèd lady bereth the name
Of all womene where that they go.

A woman is a worthy thing;
They do the washe and do the wringe;
"Lullay, lullay!" she dothe thee singe;
And yet she hath but care and wo.

A woman is a worthy wight;
She serveth a man both day and night;
Thereto she putteth alle her might;
And yet she hath but care and wo.

ANONYMOUS

(15TH CENTURY)

"I Have a Gentil Cok"

I have a gentil cok
Croweth me day;
He doth me risen erly
My matines for to say.

Bering, *birth.*

I have a gentil cok;
  Comen he is of grete;
His comb is of red corel,
  His tail is of get.

I have a gentil cok;
  Comen he is of kinde;
His comb is of red corel,
  His tail is of inde.

His leggës ben of asour,
  So gentil and so smale;
His sporës arn of silver white
  Into the wortëwale.

His eyen arn of cristal,
  Loken all in aumber;
And every night he percheth him
  In mine ladyes chaumber.

ANONYMOUS

(15TH CENTURY)

"Bring Us in Good Ale..."

Bring us in good ale, and bring us in good ale;
For our blessëd Lady sake bring us in good ale!

Bring us in no browne bred, for that is made of brane,
Nor bring us in no white bred, for therein is no gane.
  But bring us in good ale!

Bring us in no befe, for there is many bones,
But bring us in good ale, for that goth downe at ones,
  And bring us in good ale!

Bring us in no bacon, for that is passing fate,
But bring us in good ale, and gife us enough of that;
  And bring us in good ale!

Get, *jet.* Inde, *indigo.* Asour, *azure.* Sporës, *spurs.* Wortëwale, *the skin of the claws.* Loken, *set.*

Bring us in no mutton, for that is often lene,
Nor bring us in no tripes, for they be seldom clene,
   But bring us in good ale!

Bring us in no eggs, for there are many schelles,
But bring us in good ale, and gife us nothing elles;
   And bring us in good ale!

Bring us in no butter, for therein are many heres,
Nor bring us in no pigges flesch, for that will make us bores,
   But bring us in good ale!

Bring us in no podinges, for therein is all Godes good,
Nor bring us in no venesen, for that is not for our blod;
   But bring us in good ale!

Bring us in no capons flesch, for that is ofté dere,
Nor bring us in no dokes flesch, for they slober in the mere,
   But bring us in good ale!

ANONYMOUS
(15TH CENTURY)

"How, Butler, How!"

  How, butler, how!
   Bevis a tout!
  O fill the boll, jentill butler,
   And let the cup rout!

  Jentill butler, bellamy,
  Fill the boll by the eye,
  That we may drink by and by,
   With "How, butler, how!"
    Bevis a tout!
   Fill the boll, butler,
    And let the cup rout!

Brane, bran. Heres, hairs. Bores, boars. Podinges, puddings. Dokes, ducks.
Slober, slobber.

Bevis a tout, drink to all (Fr.). Rout, move. Bellamy, fair friend (Fr.).
Boll, bowl.

Here is metë for us all,
Both for grete and for small,
I trow we must the butler call,
  With "How, butler, how!"

I am so dry I cannot speke;
I am nigh chokëd with my mete;
I trow the butler be aslepe.
  With "How, butler, how!"

Butler, butler, fill the boll,
Or elles I beshrewe thy noll.
I trow we must the bell toll,
  With, "How, butler, how!"

If the butler's name be Water,
I would he were a galow claper;
But if he bring us drink, the rather
  With "How, butler, how!"

JOHN SKELTON

(1460?–1529)

FROM *Philip Sparrow*

How shall I report
All the goodly sort
Of her features clear,
That hath none earthly peer?
The favour of her face
Ennewed all with grace,
Comfort, pleasure and solace.
Mine heart doth so embrace,
And so hath ravished me
Her to behold and see,
That in wordës plain
I cannot me refrain
To look on her again:

Noll, *noddle.* Galow claper, *Gallows clapper.* But if, *unless.*

Alas, what should I feign?
It were a pleasant pain
With her aye to remain.

Her eyen gray and steep
Causeth mine heart to leap;
With her brows bent
She may well represent
Fair Lucrece, as I ween,
Or else fair Polexene,
Or else Calliope,
Or else Penelope;
For this most goodly flower,
This blossom of fresh colour,
So Jupiter me succour,
She flourisheth new and new
In beauty and virtue.

The Indy sapphire blue
Her veins doth ennew;
The orient pearl so clear,
The whiteness of her lere;
Her lusty ruby ruddies
Resemble the rose buddës;
Her lips soft and merry
Enbloomèd like the cherry:
It were an heavenly bliss
Her sugar'd mouth to kiss.

FROM *Elinor Rumming*

And this comely dame,
I understand, her name
Is Elinor Rumming,
At home in her wonning;
And as men say

Lere, *complexion.*

Wonning, *dwelling.*

She dwelt in Surrey,
In a certain stead
Beside Leatherhead.
She is a tonnish gib,
The devil and she be sib.

But to make up my tale,
She breweth nappy ale,
And maketh thereof pot-sale
To travellers, to tinkers,
To sweaters, to swinkers,
And all good ale-drinkers,
That will nothing spare
But drink till they stare
And bring themselves bare,
With *"Now away the mare!*
And let us slay care."
As wise as an hare!

Come who so will
To Elinor on the hill
With "Fill the cup, fill!"
And sit there by still,
Early and late.
Thither cometh Kate,
Cisly, and Sare,
With their legs bare,
And also their feet
Hardely full unsweet;
With their heelës daggéd,
Their kirtles all to-jaggéd,
Their smockës all to-raggéd,
With titters and tatters,
Bring dishes and platters,
With all their might running
To Elinor Rumming
To have of her tunning:
She lendeth them on the same,
And thus beginneth the game.

Tonnish gib, *stylish cat.* Sib, *kin.* Swinkers, *labourers.* Hardely, *hardly.*
Daggéd, *bemired.*

FROM *Against Garnesche*

What, have ye kithéd you a knight, Sir Douglas the Doughty,
  So currishly to beknave me in the king's palace?
Ye sturdy strong stallion, so stern and stouty,
  Ye bear ye bold as Barrabas, or Sir Terry of Thrace;
  Ye grin grimly with your gummës and with your grisly face!
But say me yet, Sir Satrapas, what authority ye have
In your challenge, Sir Chesten, to call me a knave?

Your wind-shaken shanks, your long loathly legs,
  Crooked as a camock, and as a cow calfless,
Brings you out of favour with all female tegs:
  That Mistress Punt put you off, it was not all causeless;
  At Orwell her haven your anger was lawless.
But say me yet, Sir Satrapas, what authority ye have
In your challenge, Sir Chesten, to call me a knave?

I say, ye solemn Saracen, all black is your ble;
  As a glede glowing, your eyen glister as glass,
Rolling in your hollow head, ugly to see;
  Your teeth tainted with tawny; your snively snout doth pass
  Hookéd as an hawkës beak, like Sir Thopas.
Boldly bend you to battle, and busk yourself to save:
Challenge yourself for a fool, call me no more knave!

FROM *Speak, Parrot*

So many moral matters, and so little used;
  So much new making, and so mad time spent;
So much translation into English confused;
  So much noble preaching, and so little amendment;
  So much consultation, almost to none intent;
So much provision, and so little wit at need—
Since Deucalion's flood there can no clerkës read.

Camock, *hockey stick*. Tegs, *sheep*. Ble, *visage*. Glede, *ember*.

So little discretion, and so much reasoning;
    So much hardy dardy, and so little manliness;
So prodigal expence, and so shameful reckoning;
    So gorgeous garments, and so much wretchedness;
    So much portly pride, with purses penniless;
So much spent before, and so much unpaid behind—
Since Deucalion's flood there can no clerkës find.

So much forecasting, and so far an after deal;
    So much politic prating, and so little standeth in stead;
So little secretness, and so much great council;
    So many bold barons, their hearts as dull as lead;
    So many noble bodies under a daw's head;
So royal a king as reigneth upon us all—
Since Deucalion's flood was never seen nor shall.

To Mistress Margery Wentworth

With margerain gentle,
    The flower of goodlihead,
Embroidered the mantle
    Is of your maidenhead.
Plainly I cannot glose;
    Ye be, as I divine,
The pretty primrose,
    The goodly columbine.
With margerain gentle,
    The flower of goodlihead,
Embroidered the mantle
    Is of your maidenhead.
Benign, courteous, and meek,
    With wordës well devised;
In you, who list to seek,
    Be virtues well comprised.
With margerain gentle,
    The flower of goodlihead,
Embroidered the mantle
    Is of your maidenhead.

To Mistress Isabel Pennell

By Saint Mary, my lady,
Your mammy and your daddy,
Brought forth a goodly baby!

My maiden Isabel,
Reflaring rosabel,
The fragrant camomel;
The ruddy rosary,
The sovereign rosemary,
The pretty strawberry;
The columbine, the nept,
The gillyflower well set,
The proper violet:
Ennewéd your colour
Is like the daisy flower
After the April shower;
Star of the morrow gray,
The blossom on the spray,
The freshest flower of May;
Maidenly demure,
Of womanhood the lure;
Wherefore I make you sure
It were an heavenly health,
It were an endless wealth,
A life for God himself,
To hear this nightingale
Among the birdës smale
Warbling in the vale,
Dug, dug,
Jug, jug,
Good year and good luck,
With chuck, chuck, chuck, chuck!

To Mistress Margaret Hussey

Merry Margaret,
As midsummer flower,
Gentle as falcon
Or hawk of the tower:

With solace and gladness,
Much mirth and no madness,
All good and no badness;
 So joyously,
 So maidenly,
 So womanly
 Her demeaning
 In every thing,
 Far, far passing
 That I can indite,
 Or suffice to write
 Of Merry Margaret
  As midsummer flower
 Gentle as falcon
 Or hawk of the tower.
  As patient and still
 And as full of good will
 As fair Isaphill,
 Coliander,
 Sweet pomander,
 Good Cassander,
 Steadfast of thought,
 Well made, well wrought,
 Far may be sought
 Ere that he can find
 So courteous, so kind
 As Merry Margaret,
  This midsummer flower,
 Gentle as falcon
 Or hawk of the tower.

WILLIAM DUNBAR

(1460–1520?)

FROM *The Lament for the Makaris*

I that in heill was and gladness
Am trublit now with great sickness
And feblit with infirmitie;
 Timor Mortis conturbat me.

Makaris, *poets.* Heill, *health.* Trublit, *troubled.* Feblit, *enfeebled.* Timor
Mortis conturbat me, *fear of death troubles me.*

Our plesance here is all vain glory,
This fals world is but transitory,
The flesh is bruckle, the Feynd is slee;
    Timor Mortis conturbat me.

The state of man does change and vary,
Now sound, now sick, now blyth, now sary,
Now dansand mirry, now like to die;
    Timor Mortis conturbat me.

No state in Erd here standis sicker,
As with the wynd wavis the wicker,
So wannis this world's vanitie;
    Timor Mortis conturbat me.

Unto the ded gois all Estatis,
Princes, Prelatis, and Potestatis,
Baith rich and poor of all degree;
    Timor Mortis conturbat me.

He takis the knichtis in to the field
Enarmit under helm and scheild,
Victor he is at all mellie;
    Timor Mortis conturbat me.

That strong unmerciful tyrand
Takis, on the motheris breast sowkand,
The babe full of benignitie;
    Timor Mortis conturbat me.

He takis the campion in the stour,
The captain closit in the tour,
The lady in bour full of bewtie;
    Timor Mortis conturbat me.

He spairis no lord for his piscence,
Na clerk for his intelligence,
His awful straik may no man flee;
    Timor Mortis conturbat me.

Bruckle, *brittle.* Feynd, *fiend.* Slee, *sly.* Sary, *sorry.* Mirry, *merry.* Erd, *earth.*
Sicker, *sure.* Wicker, *willow.* Wannis, *wanes.* Mellie, *battle.* Sowkand,
sucking. Campion, *champion.* Stour, *battle.* Tour, *tower.* Piscence, *puis-*
sance. Straik, *stroke.*

Art-magicianis and astrologgis,
Rethoris, logicianis, and theologgis,
Them helpis no conclusionis slee;
   Timor Mortis conturbat me.

In medicine the most practicianis,
Leechis, surrigianis, and physicianis,
Themself fra ded may not supplee;
   Timor Mortis conturbat me.

I see that makaris amang the lave
Playis here their padyanis, syne gois to grave,
Sparit is nocht their facultie;
   Timor Mortis conturbat me.

Sen he has all my brethren tane,
He will naught let me live alane,
Of force I man his next prey be;
   Timor Mortis conturbat me.

Since for the Death remeid is none,
Best is that we for Death dispone,
After our death that live may we;
   Timor Mortis conturbat me.

STEPHEN HAWES

(1475?–1523?)

FROM *The Passetyme*

O mortal folk, you may behold and see
 How I lie here, sometime a mighty knight;
The end of joy and all prosperity
 Is death at last, thorough his course and might:
 After the day there cometh the dark night,
  For though the day be never so long,
  At last the bells ringeth to evensong.

Fra, *from.* Supplee, *save.* Makaris, *poets.* The lave, *the rest.* Padyanis,
pageants. Syne, *soon.* Sparit, *spared.* Sen, *since.* Tane, *taken.* Alane, *alone.*
Man. *must.* Remeid, *remedy.* Dispone, *make ready.*

ANONYMOUS

(PERIODS UNCERTAIN)

Sir Patrick Spens

The king sits in Dumferling toune,
　　Drinking the blude-reid wine:
O quhar will I get guid sailór,
　　To sail this schip of mine?

Up and spak an eldern knicht,
　　Sat at the king's richt knee:
Sir Patrick Spens is the best sailór,
　　That sails upon the sea.

The king has written a braid letter,
　　And signed it wi' his hand;
And sent it to Sir Patrick Spens,
　　Was walking on the sand.

The first line that Sir Patrick red,
　　A loud lauch lauched he:
The next line that Sir Patrick red,
　　The teir blinded his ee.

O quhar is this has don this deid,
　　This ill deid don to me;
To send me out this time o' the zeir,
　　To sail upon the sea?

Mak haste, mak haste, my mirry men all,
　　Our good schip sails the morn.
O say na sae, my master deir,
　　For I feir a deadlie storme.

3 5

Late late yestreen I saw the new moone
    Wi' the auld moone in hir arme;
And I feir, I feir, my deir mastér,
    That we will come to harme.

O our Scots nobles wer richt laith
    To weet their cork-heild schoone;
But lang owre a' the play were played,
    Their hats they swam aboone.

O lang, lang, may the ladies stand
    Wi' their fans into their hand,
Or e'er they see Sir Patrick Spens
    Come sailing to the land.

O lang, lang, may the ladies stand
    Wi' thair gold kems in their hair,
Waiting for their ain deir lords,
    For they'll see them na mair.

Have owre, have owre to Aberdour,
    It's fifty fadom deip:
And thair lies guid Sir Patrick Spens,
    Wi' the Scots lords at his feit.

The Falcon

Lully, lulley! lully, lulley!
The faucon hath borne my make away!

He bare him up, he bare him down,
He bare him into an orchard brown.

In that orchard there was an halle,
That was hangéd with purple and pall.

And in that hall there was a bed,
It was hangéd with gold sa red.

And in that bed there li'th a knight,
His woundés bleeding day and night.

At that bed's foot there li'th a hound,
Licking the blood as it runs down.

By that bed-side kneeleth a may,
And she weepeth both night and day.

And at that bed's head standeth a stone,
Corpus Christi written thereon.

Lully, lulley! lully, lulley!
The faucon hath borne my make away.

FROM *The Birth of Robin Hood*

And mony ane sings o' grass, o' grass,
  And mony ane sings o' corn,
And mony ane sings o' Robin Hood
  Kens little whare he was born.

It wasna in the ha', the ha',
  Nor in the painted bower;
But it was in the gude green-wood,
  Amang the lily-flower.

FROM *Robin Hood and the Monk*

In somer, when the shawes be sheyne,
  And leves be large and long,
Hit is full mery in feyre foreste
  To here the foulys song:

To se the dere draw to the dale,
  And leve the hillés hee,
And shadow hem in the levés grene,
  Under the grene-wode tre.

Hit befel on Whitsontide,
  Erly in a May mornyng,
The Son up feyre can shyne,
  And the briddis mery can syng.

"This is a mery mornyng," said Litull John,
  "Be Hym that dyed on tre;
A more mery man then I am one
  Lyves not in Christianté.

"Pluck up thi hert, my dere mayster,"
  Litull John can sey,
"And think hit is a full fayre tyme
  In a mornyng of May."

FROM *The Death of Robin Hood*

"I never hurt maid in all my time,
  Nor at mine end shall it be;
But give me my bent bow in my hand,
  And a broad arrow I'll let flee;
And where this arrow is taken up
  There shall my grave digged be.

"But lay me a green sod under my head,
  And another at my feet;
And lay my bent bow at my side,
  Which was my music sweet;
And make my grave of gravel and green,
  Which is most right and meet.

"Let me have length and breadth enough,
  And under my head a sod;
That they may say when I am dead,
  Here lies bold Robin Hood."

The Three Ravens

There were three ravens sat on a tree,
They were as black as they might be.

The one of them said to his make,
"Where shall we our breakfast take?"

"Down in yonder greené field
There lies a knight slain under his shield;

"His hounds they lie down at his feet,
So well they their master keep;

"His hawks they flie so eagerly,
There's no fowl dare him come nigh."

Down there comes a fallow doe
As great with young as she might go.

She lift up his bloudy head
And kist his wounds that were so red.

She got him up upon her back
And carried him to earthen lake.

She buried him before the prime,
She was dead herself ere evensong time.

God send every gentleman
Such hounds, such hawks, and such a leman.

The Unquiet Grave

"The wind doth blow to-day, my love,
    And a few small drops of rain;
I never had but one true-love;
    In cold grave she was lain.

"I'll do as much for my true-love
   As any young man may;
I'll sit and mourn all at her grave
   For a twelvemonth and a day."

The twelvemonth and a day being up,
   The dead began to speak:
"Oh who sits weeping on my grave,
   And will not let me sleep?"

" 'Tis I, my love, sits on your grave,
   And will not let you sleep;
For I crave one kiss of your clay-cold lips,
   And that is all I seek."

"You crave one kiss of my clay-cold lips;
   But my breath smells earthy strong;
If you have one kiss of my clay-cold lips,
   Your time will not be long.

" 'Tis down in yonder garden green,
   Love, where we used to walk,
The finest flower that e'er was seen
   Is withered to a stalk.

"The stalk is withered dry, my love,
   So will our hearts decay;
So make yourself content, my love,
   Till God calls you away."

Thomas the Rhymer

True Thomas lay on Huntlie bank;
   A ferlie he spied wi' his e'e;
And there he saw a ladye bright
   Come riding down by Eildon Tree.

Ferlie, wonder.

Her skirt was o' the grass-green silk,
  Her mantle o' the velvet fyne;
At ilka tett o' her horse's mane
  Hung fifty siller bells and nine.

True Thomas he pu'd aff his cap,
  And louted low down on his knee:
"Hail to thee, Mary, Queen of Heaven!
  For thy peer on earth could never be."

"O no, O no, Thomas," she said,
  "That name does not belang to me;
I'm but the Queen o' fair Elfland,
  That am hither come to visit thee.

"Harp and carp, Thomas," she said;
  "Harp and carp along wi' me;
And if ye dare to kiss my lips,
  Sure of your bodie I will be."

"Betide me weal, betide me woe,
  That weird shall never daunten me."
Syne he has kissed her rosy lips,
  All underneath the Eildon Tree.

"Now ye maun go wi' me," she said,
  "True Thomas, ye maun go wi' me;
And ye maun serve me seven years,
  Thro' weal or woe as may chance to be."

She's mounted on her milk-white steed,
  She's ta'en true Thomas up behind;
And aye, whene'er her bridle rang,
  The steed gaed swifter than the wind.

O they rade on, and farther on,
  The steed gaed swifter than the wind;
Until they reached a desert wide,
  And living land was left behind.

Tett, *tuft.* Siller, *silver.* Harp and carp, *play and recite.*

"Light down, light down now, true Thomas,
 And lean your head upon my knee;
Abide ye there a little space,
 And I will show you ferlies three.

"O see ye not yon narrow road,
 So thick beset wi' thorns and briars?
That is the Path of Righteousness,
 Though after it but few inquires.

"And see ye not yon braid, braid road,
 That lies across the lily leven?
That is the Path of Wickedness,
 Though some call it the Road to Heaven.

"And see ye not yon bonny road
 That winds about the fernie brae?
That is the Road to fair Elfland,
 Where thou and I this night maun gae.

"But, Thomas, ye sall haud your tongue,
 Whatever ye may hear or see;
For speak ye word in Elfyn-land,
 Ye'll ne'er win back to your ain countrie."

O they rade on, and farther on,
 And they waded rivers abune the knee;
And they saw neither sun nor moon,
 But they heard the roaring of the sea.

It was mirk, mirk night, there was nae starlight,
 They waded thro' red blude to the knee;
For a' the blude that's shed on the earth
 Rins through the springs o' that countrie.

Syne they came to a garden green,
 And she pu'd an apple frae a tree:
"Take this for thy wages, true Thomas;
 It will give thee the tongue that can never lee."

Weird, doom, fate. Braid, broad. Leven, ? level or lawn. Abune, above.

"My tongue is my ain," true Thomas he said;
    "A gudely gift ye wad gie to me!
I neither dought to buy or sell
    At fair or tryst where I might be.

"I dought neither speak to prince or peer,
    Nor ask of grace from fair ladye!"
"Now haud thy peace, Thomas," she said,
    "For as I say, so must it be."

He has gotten a coat of the even cloth,
    And a pair o' shoon of the velvet green;
And till seven years were gane and past,
    True Thomas on earth was never seen.

Chevy Chase

FYTTE I

The Percy out of Northumberland,
    An avow to God made he
That he would hunt in the mountains
    Of Cheviot within days three,
In the maugre of doughty Douglas,
    And all that e'er with him be.

The fattest harts in all Cheviot
    He would kill and carry away.
"By my faith," said the doughty Douglas again,
    "I will let that hunting if I may!"

Then the Percy out of Banborowe came,
    With him a mighty meinye,
With fifteen hundred archers bold
    Chosen out of shirés three.

This began on a Monday at morn,
    In Cheviot the hills so hye;
The child may rue that is unborn,
    It was the more pitye.

Dought, *could.*

Fytte, *canto.* In the maugre, *despite.* Let, *hinder.* Meinye, *train.*

The drivers through the woodés went
   All for to raise the deer,
Bowmen bicker'd upon the bent
   With their broad arrows clear.

Then the wild thoro' the woodés went
   On every sidé shear;
Greyhounds thoro' the grevés glent
   For to kill their deer.

This began on Cheviot the hills abune
   Early on a Monenday;
By that it drew to the hour of noon
   A hundred fat harts dead there lay.

They blew a mort upon the bent,
   They 'sembled on sidés shear;
To the quarry then the Percy went
   To the brittling of the deer.

He said, "It was the Douglas' promise
   This day to meet me here;
But I wist he would fail, verament!"
   A great oath the Percy sware.

At the last a squire of Northumberland
   Lookéd at his hand full nigh;
He was ware o' the doughty Douglas coming,
   With him a great meinye.

Both with speär, bill and brand,
   'Twas a mighty sight to see;
Hardier men both of heart nor hand
   Were not in Christianté.

They were twenty hundred spearmen good,
   Withouten any fail:
They were born along by the water o' Tweed
   I' the boun's o' Teviotdale.

Bicker'd, *skirmished.* Bent, *heath.* Shear, *sheer.* Grevés, *?.* Glent, *glitter or move swiftly.* Abune, *above.* Mort, *bugle call at the kill.* Brittling, *cutting up.* Wist, *thought.* Verament, *truly.* Bill, *halberd.*

"Leave off the brittling of deer," he said;
    "To your bows look ye take good heed,
For sith ye were on your mothers born
    Had ye never so mickle need."

The doughty Douglas on a steed
    Rode all his men beforn;
His armour glitter'd as did a gleed,
    Bolder bairn was never born.

"Tell me whose men ye are," he says,
    "Or whose men that ye be;
Who gave you leave in this Cheviot chase
    In the spite of mine and of me?"

The first man that him answer made
    It was the good Lord Percye:
"We will not tell whose men we are,
    Nor whose men that we be;
But we will hunt here in this chase
    In spite of thine and of thee.

"The fattest harts in all Cheviot
    We have killed to carry away."
"By my troth," said the doughty Douglas again,
    "The one of us dies this day.

"Yet to kill allé these guiltless men
    Alas, it were great pitye!
But, Percy, thou art a lord of land,
    I an earl in my countrye—
Let all our men on a party stand,
    And do battle of thee and me!"

"Christ's curse on his crown," said the lord Percye,
    "Whosoever thereto says nay!
By my troth, thou doughty Douglas," he says,
    "Thou shalt never see that day,

Gleed, ember.

Neither in England, Scotland nor France,
   Nor for no man of woman born,
But, that and fortune be my chance
   I dare meet him, one man for one."

Then bespake a squire of Northumberland,
   Richard Witherington was his name;
"It shall never be told in South England
   To King Harry the Fourth for shame.

"I wot you bin great lordés two,
   I am a poor squire of land;
Yet I'll ne'er see my captain fight on a field
   And stand myself and look on.
But while that I may my weapon wield
   I'll not fail, both heart and hand."

That day, that day, that dreadful day!
   The first fytte here I find:
An you'll hear any more o' the hunting of Cheviot,
   Yet there is more behind.

FYTTE II

The Englishmen had their bows y-bent,
   Their hearts were good enow;
The first of arrows that they shot off
   Seven score spearmen they slew.

Yet bides the Earl Douglas upon the bent,
   A captain good enoghe;
And that was seené verament,
   For he wrought them both woe and wouche.

The Douglas parted his host in three,
   Like a chief chieftain of pride;
With suré spears of mighty tree
   They came in on every side;

Verament, *truly*. Wouche, *? pain.*

Throughé our English archery
  Gave many a woond full wide;
Many a doughty they gar'd to dye,
  Which gainéd them no pride.

The Englishmen let their bowés be,
  And pull'd out brands that were bright;
It was a heavy sight to see
  Bright swords on basnets light.

Thoro' rich mail and manoplie
  Many stern they struck down straight;
Many a freyké that was full free
  There under foot did light.

At last the Douglas and the Percy met,
  Like to captains of might and of main;
They swapt together till they both swat
  With swordés of fine Milan.

These worthy freykés for to fight
  Thereto they were full fain,
Till the blood out of their basnets sprent
  As ever did hail or rain.

"Yield thee, Percy," said the Douglas,
  "And i' faith I shall thee bring
Where thou shalt have an Earl's wages
  Of Jamie our Scottish king.

"Thou shalté have thy ransom free,
  I hight thee here this thing;
For the manfullest man thou art that e'er
  I conquered in field fighting."

But "Nay," then said the lord Percye,
  "I told it thee beforn
That I would never yielded be
  To man of a woman born."

Basnets, *helmets.* Manoplie, *panoply.* Freyké, *brave man.* Swapt, *fought.*
Swat, *sweated.* Hight, *promise.*

With that an arrow came hastily
  Forth of a mighty wane;
And it hath stricken the Earl Douglas
  In at the breasté-bane.

Thoro' liver and lungés both
  The sharp arrów is gone,
That never after in his life-days
  He spake mo words but one:
'Twas, "Fight ye, my merry men, whilst ye may,
  For my life-days bin gone!"

The Percy leanéd on his brand
  And saw the Douglas dee;
He took the dead man by the hand,
  And said, "Woe is me for thee!

"To have saved thy life I'd have parted with
  My lands for yearés three,
For a better man of heart nor of hand
  Was not in the north countrye."

All this there saw a Scottish knight,
  Sir Hugh the Montgomerye:
When he saw the Douglas to the death was dight,
  Through a hundred archerye
He never stint nor he never blint
  Till he came to the lord Percye.

He set upon the lord Percý
  A dint that was full sore;
With a suré spear of a mighty tree
  Thro' the body him he bore,
O' the t'other side that a man might see
  A large cloth-yard and more.

An archer of Northumberland
  Saw slain was the lord Percye:
He bare a bent bow in his hand,
  Was made of a trusty tree.

Wane, ? bow. Stint, ceased. Blint, stopped. Dint, blow.

An arrow that was a cloth-yard long
   To the hard steel haléd he,
A dint that was both sad and sair
   He set on Montgomerye.

The dint it was both sad and sair
   That he on Montgomerye set;
The swan-feathers that his arrow bare
   With his heart-blood they were wet.

There was never a freyké one foot would flee,
   But still in stoure did stand;
Hewing on each other, while they might dree,
   With many a baleful brand.

This battle began in Cheviot
   An hour before the noon,
And when the even-song bell was rung
   The battle was not half done.

They took their stand on either hand
   By the lee light of the moon;
Many had no strength for to stand
   In Cheviot the hills abune.

Of fifteen hundred archers of England
   Went away but seventy-and-three;
Of twenty hundred spearmen of Scotland
   But even five-and-fifty.

There was slain with the bold Percye
   Sir John of Agerstoune,
Sir Roger, the hendé Hartley,
   Sir William, the bold Herone.

Sir George, the worthy Loumlye,
   A knight of great renown,
Sir Ralph, the riché Rabye,
   With dints were beaten down.

Stoure, battle Dree, endure. Lee, dim. Abune, above.

For Witherington my heart was woe
 That ever he slain should be:
For when both his legs were hewn in two
 Yet he kneeled and fought on his knee.

There was slain with the doughty Douglas
 Sir Hugh the Montgomerye,
Sir Davy Lambwell, that worthy was,
 His sister's son was he.

Sir Charles a Murray in that place,
 That never a foot would flee:
Sir Hew Maxwell, a lord he was,
 With the Douglas did he dee.

So on the morrow they made them biers
 Of birch and hazel so gray;
Many widows with weeping tears
 Came to fetch their makes away.

Teviotdale may carp of care,
 Northumberland may make moan,
For two such captains as slain were there
 On the March-parts shall never be none.

Word is come to Edinboro',
 To Jamie the Scottish King,
Earl Douglas, lieutenant of the Marches,
 Lay slain Cheviot within.

His hands the King did weal and wring,
 Said, "Alas! and woe is me!
Such another captain Scotland within
 I' faith shall never be!"

Word is come to lovely London
 To the fourth Harry, our King,
Lord Percy, lieutenant of the Marches,
 Lay slain Cheviot within.

Dee, *die.* Makes, *mates.* Carp, *tell.* Weal, *twist.*

"God have mercy on his soul," said King Harry,
    "Good Lord, if thy will it be!
I've a hundred captains in England," he said,
    "As good as ever was he:
But Percy, an I brook my life,
    Thy death well quit shall be."

And as our King made his avow
    Like a noble Prince of renown,
For Percy he did it well perform
    After, on Homble-down;

Where six-and-thirty Scottish knights
    On a day were beaten down;
Glendale glittered on their armour bright
    Over castle, tower and town

This was the hunting of the Cheviot;
    That e'er began this spurn!
Old men, that knowen the ground well,
    Call it of Otterburn.

There was never a time on the Marche-partés
    Since the Douglas and Percy met,
But 'tis marvel an the red blood run not
    As the reane does in the street.

Jesu Christ! our balés bete,
    And to the bliss us bring!
This was the Hunting of the Cheviot:
    God send us all good ending!

Waly, Waly

O waly waly up the bank,
    And waly waly down the brae,
And waly waly yon burn-side
    Where I and my love were wont to gae!

Brook, keep. Quit, revenged. Spurn, ? contest. Reane, rain. Balés bete,
deaths conquer, i.e., redeem us to life.

Waly, exclamation of sorrow. Brae, slope. Burn-side, brook-side.

I leant my back unto an aik,
    I thought it was a trusty tree;
But first it bowed, and syne it brak,
    Sae my true love did lichtly me.

O waly waly gin love be bonny
    A little time while it is new;
But when it's auld it waxeth cauld
    And fades awa' like morning dew.
O wherefore shuld I busk my heid?
    Or wherefore shuld I kame my hair?
For my true love has me forsook,
    And says he'll never loe me mair.

Now Arthur-Seat sall be my bed;
    The sheets shall ne'er be fyl'd by me:
Saint Anton's Well sall be my drink,
    Since my true love has forsaken me.
Marti'mas wind, when wilt thou blaw
    And shake the green leaves aff the tree?
O gentle Death, when wilt thou come?
    For of my life I am wearie.

'Tis not the frost, that freezes fell,
    Nor blawing snaw's inclemencie,
'Tis not sic cauld that makes me cry,
    But my love's heart grown cauld to me.
When we came in by Glasgow town,
    We were a comely sight to see;
My love was clad in the black velvét,
    And I myself in cramasie.

But had I wist, before I kist,
    That love had been sae ill to win;
I had lockt my heart in a case of gowd
    And pinned it with a siller pin.
And O! if my young babe were born,
    And set upon the nurse's knee,
And I myself were dead and gane,
    For a maid again I'se never be.

Aik, oak. Syne, later. Gin, if. Busk, dress. Heid. head. Kame, comb. Fyl'd, defiled. Cramasie, crimson cloth. Gowd, gold. Siller, silver.

Fair Helen

I wish I were where Helen lies;
Night and day on me she cries;
O that I were where Helen lies
      On fair Kirconnell lea!

Curst be the heart that thought the thought,
And curst the hand that fired the shot,
And in my arms burd Helen dropt,
      And died to succour me!

O think na ye my heart was sair
When my love dropt down and spak nae mair!
There did she swoon wi' meikle care
      On fair Kirconnell lea.

As I went down the water-side,
None but my foe to be my guide,
None but my foe to be my guide,
      On fair Kirconnell lea;

I lighted down my sword to draw,
I hackéd him in pieces sma',
I hackéd him in pieces sma',
      For her sake that died for me.

O Helen fair, beyond compare!
I'll make a garland of thy hair
Shall bind my heart for evermair
      Until the day I die.

O that I were where Helen lies!
Night and day on me she cries;
Out of my bed she bids me rise,
      Says, "Haste and come to me!"

O Helen fair! O Helen chaste!
If I were with thee, I were blest,
Wnere thou lies low and takes thy rest
      On fair Kirconnell lea.

I wish my grave were growing green,
A winding-sheet drawn ower my een,
And I in Helen's arms lying,
    On fair Kirconnell lea.

I wish I were where Helen lies;
Night and day on me she cries;
And I am weary of the skies,
    For her sake that died for me.

Bonny George Campbell

Hie upon Hielands,
    And laigh upon Tay,
Bonny George Campbell
    Rade out on a day:
Saddled and bridled,
    Sae gallant to see,
Hame cam' his gude horse,
    But never cam' he.

Down ran his auld mither,
    Greetin' fu' sair;
Out ran his bonny bride,
    Reaving her hair;
"My meadow lies green,
    And my corn is unshorn,
My barn is to bigg,
    And my babe is unborn."

Saddled and bridled
    And booted rade he;
A plume in his helmet,
    A sword at his knee;
But toom cam' his saddle
    A' bloody to see,
O hame cam' his gude horse,
    But never cam' he!

Laigh, *low.* Greetin', *weeping.* Bigg, *build.* Toom, *empty.*

Barbara Allen's Cruelty

In Scarlet town, where I was born,
  There was a fair maid dwellin',
Made every youth cry *Well-a-way!*
  Her name was Barbara Allen.

All in the merry month of May,
  When green buds they were swellin',
Young Jemmy Grove on his death-bed lay,
  For love of Barbara Allen.

He sent his man in to her then,
  To the town where she was dwellin';
"O haste and come to my master dear,
  If your name be Barbara Allen."

So slowly, slowly rase she up,
  And slowly she came nigh him,
And when she drew the curtain by,
  "Young man, I think you're dyin'."

"O it's I am sick and very very sick,
  And it's all for Barbara Allen."
"O the better for me ye'se never be,
  Tho' your heart's blood were a-spillin'!

"O dinna ye mind, young man," says she,
  "When the red wine ye were fillin',
That ye made the healths go round and round,
  And slighted Barbara Allen?"

He turned his face unto the wall,
  And death was with him dealin':
"Adieu, adieu, my dear friends all,
  And be kind to Barbara Allen!"

As she was walking o'er the fields,
  one heard the dead-bell knellin';
And every jow the dead-bell gave
  Cried "Woe to Barbara Allen."

"O mother, mother, make my bed,
　O make it saft and narrow:
My love has died for me to-day,
　I'll die for him to-morrow.

"Farewell," she said, "ye virgins all,
　And shun the fault I fell in:
Henceforth take warning by the fall
　Of cruel Barbara Allen."

Get Up and Bar the Door

It fell about the Martinmas time,
　And a gay time it was then,
When our goodwife got puddings to make,
　And she's boiled them in the pan.

The wind sae cauld blew south and north,
　And blew into the floor;
Quoth our goodman to our goodwife,
　"Gae out and bar the door."

"My hand is in my hussyfskap,
　Goodman, as ye may see;
An' it shou'dna be barred this hundred year,
　It's no be barred for me."

They made a paction 'tween them twa,
　They made it firm and sure,
That the first word whae'er should speak,
　Should rise and bar the door.

Then by there came two gentlemen,
　At twelve o'clock at night,
And they could neither see house nor hall,
　Nor coal nor candle-light.

Martinmas, *Feast of St. Martin, Nov.* 11. Hussyfskap, *housewifery.*

"Now whether is this a rich man's house,
　　Or whether is it a poor?"
But ne'er a word wad ane o' them speak,
　　For barring of the door.

And first they ate the white puddings,
　　And then they ate the black.
Tho' muckle thought the goodwife to hersel'
　　Yet ne'er a word she spake.

Then said the one unto the other,
　　"Here, man, tak ye my knife;
Do ye tak aff the auld man's beard,
　　And I'll kiss the goodwife."

"But there's nae water in the house,
　　And what shall we do than?"
"What ails ye at the pudding-broo,
　　That boils into the pan?"

O up and then started our goodman,
　　An angry man was he:
"Will ye kiss my wife before my een,
　　And sca'd me wi' pudding-bree?"

Then up and started our goodwife,
　　Gied three skips on the floor:
"Goodman, you've spoken the foremost word!
　　Get up and bar the door."

Muckle, *much.* Than, *then.* Broo, *broth.* Bree, *broth.*

ANONYMOUS

(PERIODS UNCERTAIN)

"Joseph Was an Old Man"

Joseph was an old man,
　And an old man was he,
When he wedded Mary
　In the land of Galilee.

Joseph and Mary walked
　Through an orchard good,
Where was cherries and berries
　So red as any blood.

Joseph and Mary walked
　Through an orchard green,
Where was berries and cherries
　As thick as might be seen.

O then bespoke Mary,
　So meek and so mild,
"Pluck me one cherry, Joseph,
　For I am with child."

O then bespoke Joseph
　With words so unkind,
"Let him pluck thee a cherry
　That brought thee with child."

O then bespoke the babe
　Within his mother's womb,
"Bow down then the tallest tree
　For my mother to have some."

Then bowed down the highest tree
    Unto his mother's hand:
Then she cried, "See, Joseph,
    I have cherries at command!"

O then bespake Joseph—
    "I have done Mary wrong;
But cheer up, my dearest,
    And be not cast down.

"O eat your cherries, Mary,
    O eat your cherries now;
O eat your cherries, Mary,
    That grow upon the bough."

Then Mary plucked a cherry
    As red as the blood;
Then Mary went home
    With her heavy load.

"As Joseph Was A-Walking"

As Joseph was a-walking,
    He heard an angel sing:
"This night shall be born
    Our heavenly King.

"He neither shall be born
    In housen nor in hall,
Nor in the place of Paradise,
    But in an ox's stall.

"He neither shall be clothéd
    In purple nor in pall,
But all in fair linen,
    As were babies all.

Pall, *fine cloth.*

"He neither shall be rocked
In silver nor in gold,
But in a wooden cradle
That rocks on the mould.

"He neither shall be christened
In white wine nor red,
But with fair spring water
With which we were christenéd."

"As I Sat under a Sycamore Tree"

As I sat under a sycamore tree,
A sycamore tree, a sycamore tree,
I looked me out upon the sea
On Christ's Sunday at morn.

I saw three ships a-sailing there,
A-sailing there, a-sailing there,
Jesu, Mary and Joseph they bare
On Christ's Sunday at morn.

Joseph did whistle and Mary did sing,
Mary did sing, Mary did sing,
And all the bells on earth did ring
For joy our Lord was born.

O they sailed into Bethlehem,
To Bethlehem, to Bethlehem;
St. Michael was the sterésman,
St. John sate in the horn.

And all the bells on earth did ring,
On earth did ring, on earth did ring:
"Welcome be thou Heaven's King,
On Christ's Sunday at morn!"

"God Rest You Merry, Gentlemen"

God rest you merry, gentlemen,
  Let nothing you dismay,
For Jesus Christ, our Saviour,
  Was born upon this day,
To save us all from Satan's power
  When we were gone astray.
    O tidings of comfort and joy!
    For Jesus Christ, our Saviour,
    Was born on Christmas Day.

In Bethlehem, in Jewry,
  This blessèd babe was born,
And laid within a manger,
  Upon this blessèd morn;
The which His mother, Mary,
  Nothing did take in scorn.

From God, our Heavenly Father,
  A blessèd angel came;
And unto certain shepherds
  Brought tidings of the same:
How that in Bethlehem was born
  The Son of God by name.

"Fear not," then said the angel,
  "Let nothing you affright,
This day is born a Saviour
  Of virtue, power and might,
So frequently to vanquish all
  The friends of Satan quite."

The shepherds at those tidings
  Rejoicèd much in mind,
And left their flocks a feeding
  In tempest, storm and wind,
And went to Bethlehem straightway,
  This blessèd babe to find.

But when to Bethlehem they came,
   Whereat this infant lay,
They found Him in a manger,
   Where oxen feed on hay,
His mother Mary kneeling
   Unto the Lord did pray.

Now to the Lord sing praises,
   All you within this place,
And with true love and brotherhood
   Each other now embrace;
This holy tide of Christmas
   All others doth deface.
      O tidings of comfort and joy!
      For Jesus Christ, our Saviour,
      Was born on Christmas Day.

"The First Nowell..."

The first Nowell the angels did say
Was to certain poor shepherds in fields as they lay,
In fields where they lay keeping their sheep,
On a cold winter's night that was so deep.
   Nowell, Nowell, Nowell, Nowell,
   Born is the King of Israel.

They lookéd up and saw a star
Shining in the East beyond them far,
And to the earth it gave great light,
And so it continued both day and night.
   Nowell &c.

And by the light of that same star
Three wise men came from country far;
To seek for a King was their intent,
And to follow the star wherever it went.
   Nowell &c.

The star drew nigh to the north-west,
O'er Bethlehem it took its rest,
And then it did both stop and stay
Right over the place where Jesus lay.
   Nowell &c.

Then entered in those wise men three,
Most reverently upon their knee,
And offered there in His presence
Their gold and myrrh and frankincense.
   Nowell &c.

Then let us all with one accord
Sing praises to our heavenly Lord,
That hath made heaven and earth of naught,
And with His blood mankind hath bought.
   Nowell, Nowell, Nowell, Nowell,
   Born is the King of Israel.

ANONYMOUS

(15TH–16TH CENTURY)

FROM *"The Maidens Came"*

The maidens came
When I was in my mother's bower;
I had all that I would.
   The bailey beareth the bell away;
   The lily, the rose, the rose I lay.
The silver is white, red is the gold;
The robes they lay in fold.
   The bailey beareth the bell away;
   The lily, the rose, the rose I lay.
And through the glass window shines the sun.
How should I love, and I so young?
   The bailey beareth the bell away;
   The lily, the lily, the rose I lay.

ANONYMOUS

(15TH–16TH CENTURY)

"Back and Side Go Bare..."

Back and side go bare, go bare,
   Both hand and foot go cold,
But belly, God sent thee good ale enough
   Whether it be new or old!

But if that I may have truly
   Good ale my belly full,
I shall look like one, by sweet Saint John,
   Were shorn against the wool.
Though I go bare, take ye no care,
   I am nothing cold,
I stuff my skin so full within
   Of jolly good ale and old.

I cannot eat but little meat,
   My stomach is not good;
But sure I think that I could drink
   With him that weareth an hood.

64

Drink is my life; although my wife
   Some time do chide and scold,
Yet spare I not to ply the pot
   Of jolly good ale and old.

I love no roast but a brown toast,
   Or a crab in the fire;
A little bread shall do me stead;
   Much bread I never desire.
Nor frost, nor snow, nor wind I trow,
   Can hurt me if it wold,
I am so wrapped within and lapped
   With jolly good ale and old.

I care right naught, I take no thought
   For clothes to keep me warm;
Have I good drink, I surely think
   Nothing can do me harm.
For truly than I fear no man,
   Be he never so bold,
When I am armed and thoroughly warmed
   With jolly good ale and old.

But now and than I curse and ban,
   They make their ale so small;
God give them care and evil to fare!
   They stry the malt and all.
Such peevish pew, I tell you true,
   Nor for a crown of gold
There cometh one sip within my lip,
   Whether it be new or old.

Good ale and strong maketh me among
   Full jocund and full light,
That oft i sleep and take no keep
   From morning until night.
Then start I up and flee to the cup;
   The right way on I hold;
My thirst to staunch, I fill my paunch
   With jolly good ale and old.

And Kit, my wife, that as her life
    Loveth well good ale to seek,
Full oft drinketh she, that ye may see
    The tears run down her check.
Then doth she troll to me the bowl,
    As a good malt-worm shold,
And say "Sweet-heart, I have take my part
    Of jolly good ale and old."

They that do drink till they nod and wink,
    Even as good fellows should do,
They shall not miss to have the bliss
    That good ale hath brought them to.
And all poor souls that scour black bowls,
    And them hath lustily trolled,
God save the lives of them and their wives,
    Whether they be young or old!

ANONYMOUS

(16TH CENTURY)

"Western Wind, When Wilt Thou Blow"

Western wind, when wilt thou blow,
    The small rain down can rain?
Christ, if my love were in my arms
    And I in my bed again!

KING HENRY VIII

(1491–1547)

"As the Holly Groweth Green"

As the holly groweth green,
    And never changeth hue,
So I am, ever hath been
    Unto my lady true;

As the holly groweth green
    With ivy all alone,
When flowerës can not be seen
    And green wood leaves be gone.

Now unto my lady
　　Promise to her I make,
From all other only
　　To her I me betake.

Adieu, mine own lady,
　　Adieu, my special,
Who hath my heart truly,
　　Be sure, and ever shall!

ANONYMOUS

Harpalus' Complaint

Phyllida was a fair maid,
　　As fresh as any flower;
Whom Harpalus the herdman prayed
　　To be his paramour.

Harpalus and eke Corin
　　Were herdmen both yfere;
And Phyllida would twist and spin
　　And thereto sing full clear.

But Phyllida was all too coy
　　For Harpalus to win,
For Corin was her only joy,
　　Who forced her not a pin.

How often would she flowers twine,
　　How often garlands make
Of cowslips and of columbine?
　　And all for Corin's sake.

But Corin, he had hawks to lure,
　　And forcéd more the field;
Of lovers' law he took no cure,
　　For once he was beguiled.

Yfere, in comradeship. Forcéd, cared for.

Harpalus prevailéd nought,
 His labour all was lost;
For he was farthest from her thought,
 And yet he loved her most.

Therefore waxed he both pale and lean,
 And dry as clod of clay;
His flesh it was consuméd clean,
 His colour gone away.

His beard it had not long be shave,
 His hair hung all unkempt;
A man most fit e'en for the grave,
 Whom spiteful love had shent.

His eyes were red and all forwatched,
 His face besprent with tears;
It seemed unhap had him long hatched,
 In midst of his despairs.

His clothes were black, and also bare;
 As one forlorn was he;
Upon his head always he ware
 A wreath of willow tree.

His beasts he kept upon the hill,
 And he sat in the dale;
And thus with sighs and sorrows shrill
 He gan to tell his tale.

Oh Harpalus! thus would he say,
 Unhappiest under sun,
The cause of thine unhappy day
 By love was first begun.

For thou went'st first by suit to seek
 A tiger to make tame,
That sets not by thy love a leek,
 But makes thy grief her game.

Shent, ruined. Unhap, misfortune.

As easy 'twere for to convert
   The frost into the flame,
As for to turn a froward heart
   Whom thou so fain wouldst frame.

Corin he liveth careless,
   He leaps among the leaves;
He eats the fruits of thy redress;
   Thou reap's^t, he takes the sheaves.

My beasts a while your food refrain
   And hark your herdman's sound,
Whom spiteful love alas! hath slain
   Through girt with many a wound.

O happy be ye, beastës wild,
   That here your pasture takes,
I see that ye be not beguiled
   Of these your faithful makes.

The hart he feedeth by the hind;
   The buck hard by the doe;
The turtle dove is not unkind
   To him that loves her so.

The ewe she hath by her the ram;
   The young cow hath the bull;
The calf with many a lusty lamb
   Do feed their hunger full.

But well-away! that nature wrought
   Thee, Phyllida, so fair,
For I may say that I have bought
   Thy beauty all too dear.

What reason is that cruelty
   With beauty should have part?
Or else that such great tyranny
   Should dwell in woman's heart?

I see therefore to shape my death
    She cruelly is pressed,
To th'end that I may want my breath;
    My days be at the best.

O Cupid, grant this my request,
    And do not stop thine ears;
That she may feel within her breast
    The pains of my despairs.

Of Corin that is carëless
    That she may crave her fee,
As I have done in great distress
    That loved her faithfully.

But since that I shall die her slave,
    Her slave and eke her thrall,
Write you, my friends, upon the grass
    This chance that is befall:

"Here lieth unhappy Harpalus
    By cruel love now slain;
Whom Phyllida unjustly thus
    Hath murdered with disdain."

Tottel's Miscellany, 1557

ANONYMOUS

(16TH CENTURY)

A Praise of His Lady

Give place, you ladies, and begone,
    Boast not yourselves at all;
For here at hand approacheth one
    Whose face will stain you all.

The virtue of her lively looks
    Excels the precious stone;
I wish to have none other books
    To read or look upon.

In each of her two crystal eyes
   Smileth a naked boy;
It would you all in heart suffice
   To see that lamp of joy.

I think nature hath lost the mould
   Where she her shape did take,
Or else I doubt if nature could
   So fair a creature make.

She may be well compared
   Unto the phoenix kind,
Whose like was never seen nor heard
   That any man can find.

In life she is Diana chaste,
   In truth Penelopey,
In word and eke in deed steadfast;
   What will you more we say?

If all the world were sought so far,
   Who could find such a wight?
Her beauty twinkleth like a star
   Within the frosty night.

Her rosial colour comes and goes
   With such a comely grace,
More ruddier too, than doth the rose,
   Within her lively face.

At Bacchus' feast none shall her meet
   Ne at no wanton play,
Nor gazing in an open street,
   Nor gadding as astray.

The modest mirth that she doth use
   Is mixed with shamefastness,
All vice she doth wholly refuse
   And hateth idleness.

O Lord! it is a world to see
　　How virtue can repair,
And deck in her such honesty,
　　Whom nature made so fair.

Truly, she doth as far exceed
　　Our women nowadays,
As doth the gillyflower a weed;
　　And more a thousand ways.

How might I do to get a graff
　　Of this unspotted tree?
For all the rest are plain but chaff
　　Which seem good corn to be.

This gift alone I shall her give
　　When death doth what he can,
Her honest fame shall ever live
　　Within the mouth of man.

Tottel's Miscellany, 1557

ANONYMOUS

(16TH CENTURY)

Against Women either Good or Bad

A man may live thrice Nestor's life,
　　Thrice wander out Ulysses' race,
Yet never find Ulysses' wife;
　　Such change hath chancéd in this case.

Less age will serve than Paris had
　　Small pain (if none be small enough)
To find good store of Helen's trade;
　　Such sap the root doth yield the bough.

For one good wife Ulysses slew
　　A worthy knot of gentle blood;

For one ill wife Greece overthrew
   The town of Troy. Sith bad and good
      Bring mischief, Lord, let be Thy will
      To keep me free from either ill.

Tottel's Miscellany, 1557

ANONYMOUS

(16TH CENTURY)

As You Came from the Holy Land

As you came from the holy land
   Of Walsinghame,
Met you not with my true love
   By the way as you came?

How shall I know your true love,
   That have met many a one,
As I went to the holy land,
   That have come, that have gone?

She is neither white nor brown,
   But as the heavens fair;
There is none hath a form so divine
   In the earth or the air.

Such a one did I meet, good sir,
   Such an angelic face,
Who like a queen, like a nymph, did appear,
   By her gait, by her grace.

She hath left me here all alone,
   All alone, as unknown,
Who sometime did me lead with herself,
   And me loved as her own.

What's the cause that she leaves you alone,
   And a new way doth take,
Who loved you once as her own,
   And her joy did you make?

I have loved her all my youth,
    But now old, as you see;
Love likes not the falling fruit
    From the withered tree.

Know that Love is a careless child,
    And forgets promise past;
He is blind, he is deaf when he list,
    And in faith never fast.

His desire is a dureless content,
    And a trustless joy;
He is won with a world of despair,
    And is lost with a toy.

Of womenkind such indeed is the love,
    Or the word love abuséd,
Under which many childish desires
    And conceits are excuséd.

But true love is a durable fire,
    In the mind ever burning,
Never sick, never old, never dead,
    From itself never turning.

ANONYMOUS

(16TH CENTURY)

"Fain Would I Have a Pretty Thing"

Fain would I have a pretty thing
    To give unto my Lady:
I name no thing, nor I mean no thing,
    But as pretty a thing as may be.

Twenty journeys would I make,
    And twenty ways would hie me,
To make adventure for her sake,
    To set some matter by me:
      But fain would I &c.

Some do long for pretty knacks,
    And some for strange devices:
God send me that my lady lacks,
    I care not what the price is.
        Thus fain, &c.

Some go here, and some go there,
    Where gazes be not geason;
And I go gaping everywhere,
    But still come out of season.
        Yet fain &c.

I walk the town and thread the street,
    In every corner seeking:
The pretty thing I cannot meet,
    That's for my lady's liking.
        Fain would &c.

The mercers pull me, going by,
    The silk-wives say, "What lack ye?"
"The thing you have not," then say I,
    "Ye foolish fools, go pack ye!"
        But fain &c.

It is not all the silk in Cheap,
    Nor all the golden treasure,
Nor twenty bushels on a heap
    Can do my lady pleasure.
        But fain &c.

The gravers of the golden shows
    With jewels do beset me;
The sempsters in the shop that sews,
    They do no thing but let me.
        But fain &c.

But were it in the wit of man
    By any means to make it,
I could for money buy it then,
    And say, "Fair Lady, take it."
        Thus fain &c.

O Lady what a lack is this,
   That my good willing misseth
To find what pretty thing it is
   That my good lady wisheth.
Thus fain would I have had this pretty thing
   To give unto my lady:
I said no harm, nor I meant no harm,
   But as pretty a thing as may be.

Clement Robinson's A Handful of Pleasant Delights, 1584

SIR THOMAS WYATT

(1503–1542)

The Lover Sheweth How He Is Forsaken of Such as He Sometime Enjoyed

They flee from me, that sometime did me seek,
   With naked foot stalking within my chamber:
Once have I seen them gentle, tame and meek,
   That now are wild, and do not once remember,
   That sometime they have put themselves in danger
To take bread at my hand; and now they range
Busily seeking in continual change.

Thankéd be Fortune, it hath been otherwise
   Twenty times better; but once especial,
In thin array, after a pleasant guise,
   When her loose gown did from her shoulders fall,
   And she me caught in her arms long and small,
And therewithal so sweetly did me kiss,
And softly said, "Dear heart, how like you this?"

It was no dream; for I lay broad awaking:
   But all is turn'd now, through my gentleness,
Into a bitter fashion of forsaking;
   And I have leave to go of her goodness;
   And she also to use new fangleness.
But since that I unkindly so am served:
How like you this, what hath she now deserved?

The Lover Beseecheth His Mistress Not to Forget
His Steadfast Faith and True Intent

Forget not yet the tried intent
Of such a truth as I have meant;
My great travail so gladly spent,
   Forget not yet!

Forget not yet when first began
The weary life ye know, since whan
The suit, the service, none tell can;
   Forget not yet!

Forget not yet the great assays,
The cruel wrong, the scornful ways,
The painful patience in delays,
   Forget not yet!

Forget not! oh! forget not this,
How long ago hath been, and is
The mind that never meant amiss,
   Forget not yet!

Forget not then thine own approv'd,
The which so long hath thee so lov'd,
Whose steadfast faith yet never mov'd:
   Forget not this!

The Lover Complaineth the Unkindness
of His Love

My lute, awake, perform the last
Labour that thou and I shall waste;
And end that now I have begun:
And when this song is sung and past,
My lute, be still, for I have done.

As to be heard where ear is none;
As lead to grave in marble stone;
My song may pierce her heart as soon.
Should we then sigh, or sing, or moan?
No, no, my lute, for I have done.

The rocks do not so cruelly
Repulse the waves continually,
As she my suit and affection:
So that I am past remedy;
Whereby my lute and I have done.

Proud of the spoil that thou hast got
Of simple hearts thorough Love's shot,
By whom unkind thou hast them won:
Think not he hath his bow forgot,
Although my lute and I have done.

Vengeance shall fall on thy disdain,
That makest but game on earnest pain;
Think not alone under the sun
Unquit to cause thy lover's plain;
Although my lute and I have done.

May chance thee lie withered and old
In winter nights, that are so cold,
Plaining in vain unto the moon;
Thy wishes then dare not be told:
Care then who list, for I have done.

And then may chance thee to repent
The time that thou hast lost and spent,
To cause thy lover's sigh and swoon:
Then shalt thou know beauty but lent,
And wish and want as I have done.

Now cease, my lute, this is the last
Labour that thou and I shall waste;
And ended is that we begun:
Now is this song both sung and past;
My lute, be still, for I have done.

HENRY HOWARD, EARL OF SURREY

(1516–1547)

A Vow to Love Faithfully, Howsoever He Be Rewarded

Set me whereas the sun doth parch the green
Or where his beams do not dissolve the ice;
In temperate heat, where he is felt and seen;
In presence prest of people, mad or wise;
Set me in high, or yet in low degree;
In longest night, or in the shortest day;
In clearest sky, or where clouds thickest be;
In lusty youth, or when my hairs are grey:
Set me in heaven, in earth, or else in hell,
In hill, or dale, or in the foaming flood;
Thrall, or at large, alive whereso I dwell,
Sick, or in health, in evil fame or good,
Hers will I be; and only with this thought
Content myself, although my chance be nought.

The Means to Attain Happy Life

Martial, the things that do attain
The happy life, be these, I find:
The riches left, not got with pain;
The fruitful ground, the quiet mind:

The equal friend, no grudge, no strife;
No charge of rule, nor governance;
Without disease, the healthful life;
The household of continuance:

The mean diet, no delicate fare;
True wisdom join'd with simpleness;
The night dischargéd of all care,
Where wine the wit may not oppress:

The faithful wife, without debate;
Such sleeps as may beguile the night;
Contented with thine own estate;
Ne wish for Death, ne fear his might.

FROM *The Fourth Book of Virgil's Aeneid*

Then Mercury 'gan bend him to obey
His father's mighty will; and to his heels
His golden wings he knits, which him transport
With a light wind above the earth and seas.
And then with him his wand he took, whereby
He calls from hell pale ghosts; and other some
Thither also he sendeth comfortless,
Whereby he forceth sleeps, and them bereaves,
And mortal eyes he closeth up in death.
By power whereof he drives the winds away
And passeth eke amid the troubled clouds,
Till in his flight he 'gan descry the top
And the steep flanks of rocky Atlas' hill,
That with his crown sustains the welkin up;
Whose head forgrown with pine, circled alway
With misty clouds, is beaten with wind and storm;
His shoulders spread with snow; and from his chin
The springs descend; his beard frozen with ice.
Here Mercury with equal shining wings
First touched; and with body headling bent
To the water then took he his descent;
Like to the fowl that endlong coasts and strands
Swarming with fish, flies sweeping by the sea;
Cutting betwixt the winds and Libyan lands,
From his grandfather by the mother's side,
Cyllene's child so came, and then alight
Upon the houses with his wingéd feet,
Tofore the towers where he Aeneas saw
Foundations cast, arearing lodges new;
Girt with a sword of jasper starry bright,
A shining 'parel, flamed with stately eye
Of Tyrian purple, hung his shoulders down,
The gift and work of wealthy Dido's hand,
Stripéd throughout with a thin thread of gold.

GEORGE GASCOIGNE

(1525?–1577)

The Praise of Philip Sparrow

Of all the birds that I do know
   Philip my Sparrow hath no peer;
For sit she high or lie she low,
   Be she far off, or be she near,
There is no bird so fair, so fine,
Nor yet so fresh as this of mine.

Come in a morning merrily
   When Philip hath been lately fed,
Or in an evening soberly
   When Philip list to go to bed;
It is a heaven to hear my Phip
How she can chirp with cherry lip.

She never wanders far abroad,
   But is at hand when I do call,
If I command she lays on lode
   With lips, with teeth, with tongue and all;
She chants, she chirps, she makes such cheer,
That I believe she hath no peer.

And yet beside all this good sport
   My Philip both can sing and dance,
With new found toys of sundry sort
   My Philip can both prick and prance;
And if you say but "fend cut Phip"
Lord! how the peat will turn and skip!

Her feathers are so fresh of hue
   And so well provéd every day,
So lacks no oil, I warrant you,
   To trim her tail both trick and gay;
And though her mouth be somewhat wide,
Her tongue is sweet and short beside.

And for the rest I dare compare
   She is both tender, sweet and soft;
She never lacketh dainty fare,
   But is well fed, and feedeth oft;
For if my Phip have best to eat,
I warrant you, Phip lacks no meat.

And then if that her meat be good
   And such as like do love alway,
She will lay lips thereon, by rood!
   And see that none be cast away;
For when she once hath felt a fit,
Philip will cry still, "Yet, yet, yet!"

And to tell truth, he were to blame
   Which had so fine a bird as she,
To make him all this goodly game
   Without suspect or jealousy;
He were a churl and knew no good
Would see her faint for lack of food.

Wherefore I sing, and ever shall,
   To praise as I have often proved,
There is no bird amongst them all
   So worthy for to be beloved.
Let others praise what bird they will,
Sweet Philip shall be my bird still.

NICHOLAS BRETON

(1542–1626)

A Sweet Lullaby

Come little babe, come silly soul,
Thy father's shame, thy mother's grief,
Born as I doubt to all our dole
And to thyself unhappy chief;
   Sing lullaby, and lap it warm,
   Poor soul that thinks no creature harm.

Thou little think'st and less dost know
The cause of this thy mother's moan,
Thou want'st the wit to wail her woe,
And I myself am all alone;
 Why dost thou weep? why dost thou wail?
 And knowest not yet what thou dost ail.

Come, little wretch, ah, silly heart!
Mine only joy, what can I more?
If there be any wrong thy smart,
That may the destinies implore;
 'Twas I, I say, against my will,
 I wail the time, but be thou still.

And dost thou smile, Oh! thy sweet face,
Would God Himself He might thee see,
No doubt thou wouldst soon purchase grace,
I know right well, for thee and me;
 But come to mother, babe, and play,
 For father false is fled away.

Sweet boy, if it by fortune chance
Thy father home again to send,
If death do strike me with his lance,
Yet may'st thou me to him commend;
 If any ask thy mother's name,
 Tell how by love she purchas'd blame.

Then will his gentle heart soon yield,
I know him of a noble mind,
Although a lion in the field,
A lamb in town thou shalt him find;
 Ask blessing, babe, be not afraid,
 His sugared words hath me betrayed.

Then may'st thou joy and be right glad,
Although in woe I seem to moan,
Thy father is no rascal, lad,
A noble youth of blood and bone;
 His glancing looks if he once smile
 Right honest women may beguile.

Come, little boy, and rock asleep,
Sing lullaby, and be thou still,
I that can do nought else but weep,
Will sit by thee, and wail my fill;
  God bless my babe, and lullaby,
  From this thy father's quality.

The Arbour of Amorous Devices, 1597

FROM *The Passionate Shepherd*

Who can live in heart so glad
As the merry country lad?
Who upon a fair green baulk
May at pleasure sit and walk;
And amidst the azure skies
See the morning sun arise,
While he hears in every spring
How the birds do chirp and sing;
Or, before the hounds in cry,
See the hare go stealing by;
Or along the shallow brook
Angling with a baited hook,
See the fishes leap and play
In a blessed sunny day;
Or to hear the partridge call
Till she have her covey all;
Or to see the subtle fox,
How the villain plays the box,
After feeding on his prey
How he closely sneaks away,
Through the hedge and down the furrow
Till he gets into his burrow;
Then the bee to gather honey,
And the little black-haired coney
On a bank for sunny place
With her fore-feet wash her face:
Are not these with thousands moe
Than the court of kings do know?

Phillida and Coridon

In the merry month of May,
In a morn by break of day,
Forth I walked by the wood side
Whenas May was in his pride.
There I spiéd all alone
Phillida and Coridon.
Much ado there was, Got wot,
He would love and she would not.
She said, never man was true;
He said, none was false to you.
He said, he had loved her long;
She said, Love should have no wrong.
Coridon would kiss her then.
She said, maids must kiss no men
Till they did for good and all.
Then she made the shepherd call
All the heavens to witness truth,
Never loved a truer youth.
Thus with many a pretty oath,
Yea and nay, and faith and troth,
Such as silly shepherds use
When they will not love abuse;
Love, which had been long deluded,
Was with kisses sweet concluded.
And Phillida, with garlands gay,
Was made the lady of the May.

England's Helicon, 1600

FROM An Invective against the Wicked of the World

Let but a fellow in a fox-furred gown,
A greasy night-cap and a drivelled beard,
Grow but a bailiff of a fisher-town,
And have a matter 'fore him to be heard,
Will not his frown make half a street afeared?
　　Yea, and the greatest Codshead gape for fear
　　He shall be swallowed by this ugly bear.

Look but on beggars going to the stocks,
How master constable can march before them,
And while the beadle maketh fast the locks,
How bravely he can knave them and be-whore them,
And not afford one word of pity for them,
　　When it may be poor honest silly people
　　Must make the church make curtsy to the steeple.

Note but the beadle of a beggars' Spittle,
How in his place he can himself advance,
And will not of his title lose a tittle,
If any matter come in variance,
To try the credit of his countenance;
　　For whatsoever the poor beggars say
　　His is the word must carry all away.

Find out a villain, born and bred a knave,
That never knew what honesty became,
A drunken rascal and a doggéd slave,
That all his wits to wickedness doth frame,
And only lives in infamy and shame;
　　Yet let him tink upon the golden pan,
　　His word may pass yet for an honest man.

Look on old Beatrice with her beetle brows,
Begot betwixt a tinker and his Tib,
And but of late a silly cobbler's spouse;
If she have played the thrifty prowling scrib
To purchase grass to grase the bullock's rib,
　　She shall be fed with fine and dainty fare,
　　And wooed and wedded ere she be aware.

But for a poor wench, be she ne'er so fair,
Gracious and virtuous, wise and nobly born,
And worthy well to sit in Honour's chair,
Yet, if her kirtle or her gown be torn,
All her good gifts shall but be held in scorn,
　　And she, poor soul, in sorrow and disgrace,
　　Be forced to give a filthy baggage place.

So that by all these consequents I see
It is the money makes or mars the man,
And yet where judges will indifferent be
The hobby-horse best fits Maid Marian,
While greedy dogs may lick the dripping pan;
  For though that money may do many things,
  Yet virtue makes the truest kings and queens.

THOMAS DELONEY

(1543?–1607?)

Song

The primrose in the green forest,
  The violets, they be gay;
The double daisies, and the rest
  That trimly decks the way,
Doth move the spirits with brave delights,
  Who Beauty's darlings be:
With hey tricksy, trim-go-tricksy,
  Under the greenwood tree.

FROM A Joyful New Ballad

O noble England,
  Fall down upon thy knee,
And praise thy God with thankful heart,
  Which still maintaineth thee.
The foreign forces
  That seek thy utter spoil,
Shall then through His especial grace
  Be brought to shameful foil,
With mighty power
  They come unto our coast;
To over-run our country quite,
  They make their brag and boast.
In strength of men
  They set their only stay;
But we upon the Lord our God
  Will put our trust alway.

Great is their number
  Of ships upon the sea,
And their provision wonderful;
  But, Lord, Thou art our stay.
Their armed soldiers
  Are many by account;
Their aiders eke in this attempt
  Do sundry ways surmount.
The Pope of Rome
  With many blessed grains,
To sanctify their bad pretence
  Bestowed both cost and pains.
But little land
  Is not dismayed at all;
The Lord, no doubt, is on our side,
  Which soon will work their fall.

Our pleasant country,
  So fruitful and so fair,
They do intend by deadly war
  To make both poor and bare.
Our towns and cities
  To rack and sack likewise,
To kill and murder man and wife,
  As malice doth arise.
And to deflower
  Our virgins in our sight,
And in the cradle cruelly
  The tender babe to smite.
God's holy truth
  They mean for to cast down,
And to deprive our noble Queen
  Both of her life and crown.

But God Almighty
  Be blessed evermore,
Who doth encourage Englishmen
  To beat them from the shore,
With roaring cannons,
  Their hasty steps to stay,
And with the force of thundering shot
  To make them fly away.

Who made account,
    Before this time or day,
Against the walls of fair London
    Their banners to display.
But their intent
    The Lord will bring to naught,
If faithfully we call and cry
    For succour as we ought.

And you, dear brethren,
    Which beareth arms this day,
For safeguard of your native soil,
    Mark well what I shall say.
Regard your duties,
    Think on your country's good,
And fear not in defence thereof
    To spend your dearest blood;
Desiring you,
    True English hearts to bear,
To God, to Her, and to the land
    Wherein you nursed were.

SIR EDWARD DYER

(1545?–1607)

My Mind to Me a Kingdom Is

My mind to me a kingdom is;
    Such present joys therein I find,
That it excels all other bliss
    That earth affords or grows by kind:
Though much I want which most would have
Yet still my mind forbids to crave.

No princely pomp, no wealthy store,
    No force to win the victory,
No wily wit to salve a sore,
    No shape to feed a loving eye;
To none of these I yield as thrall:
For why? My mind doth serve for all.

I see how plenty suffers oft,
   And hasty climbers down do fall;
I see that those which are aloft,
   Mishap doth threaten most of all;
They get with toil, they keep with fear:
Such cares my mind could never bear.

Content I live, this is my stay,
   I seek no more than may suffice;
I press to bear no haughty sway;
   Look what I lack my mind supplies:
Lo, thus I triumph like a king,
Content with that my mind doth bring.

Some have too much, yet still do crave;
   I little have, and seek no more.
They are but poor though much they have,
   And I am rich with little store;
They poor, I rich; they beg, I give;
They lack, I leave; they pine, I live.

I laugh not at another's loss,
   I grudge not at another's gain;
No worldly waves my mind can toss:
   My state at one doth still remain:
I fear no foe, I fawn no friend;
I loathe not life nor dread my end.

Some weigh their pleasure by their lust,
   Their wisdom by their rage of will;
Their treasure is their only trust,
   A cloakéd craft their store of skill.
But all the pleasure that I find
Is to maintain a quiet mind.

My wealth is health and perfect ease;
   My conscience clear my choice defence;
I neither seek by bribes to please
   Nor by deceit to breed offence;
Thus do I live, thus will I die;
Would all did so as well as I.

BARTHOLOMEW GRIFFIN

(15—?–1602)

"Venus, with Young Adonis..."

Venus, with young Adonis sitting by her
Under a myrtle shade, began to woo him:
She told the youngling how god Mars did try her,
And as he fell to her, so fell she to him.
"Even thus," quoth she, "the warlike god embraced me,"
And then she clipped Adonis in her arms;
"Even thus," quoth she, "the warlike god unlaced me,"
As if the boy should use like loving charms;
"Even thus," quoth she, "he seizéd on my lips,"
And with her lips on his did act the seizure;
And as she fetchéd breath, away he skips,
And would not take her meaning nor her pleasure.
Ah, that I had my lady at this bay,
To kiss and clip me till I run away!

The Passionate Pilgrim, 1599

FROM *Sonnets*

Fair is my love that feeds among the lilies,
The lilies growing in that pleasant garden,
Where Cupid's mount, that well-beloved hill is,
And where the little god himself is warden.

See where my love sits in the bed of spices,
Beset all round with camphor, myrrh and roses,
And interlaced with curious devices,
Which her from all the world apart incloses.

ANONYMOUS

(16TH CENTURY)

"Crabbed Age and Youth..."

Crabbed age and youth cannot live together:
Youth is full of pleasance, age is full of care;
Youth like summer morn, age like winter weather;

Youth like summer brave, age like winter bare.
Youth is full of sport, age's breath is short;
  Youth is nimble, age is lame;
Youth is hot and bold, age is weak and cold;
  Youth is wild, and age is tame.
Age, I do abhor thee; youth, I do adore thee;
  O, my love, my love is young!
Age, I do defy thee: O, sweet shepherd, hie thee,
  For methinks thou stay'st too long.

> [*Attributed to* WILLIAM SHAKESPEARE]
> *The Passionate Pilgrim,* 1599

SIR WALTER RALEIGH
[See also page 169]

(1552–1618)

The Shepherd's Description of Love

Meliboeus: Shepherd, what's love, I pray thee tell?

Faustus: It is that fountain and that well,
Where pleasure and repentance dwell;
It is perhaps that sauncing bell,
  That tolls all in to heaven or hell:
  And this is love as I heard tell.

Meliboeus: Yet what is love, I prithee say?

Faustus: It is a work on holiday,
It is December match'd with May,
When lusty bloods in fresh array
  Hear ten months after of the play:
  And this is love, as I hear say.

Meliboeus: Yet what is Love, good shepherd, sain?

Faustus: It is a sunshine mix'd with rain,
It is a tooth-ache, or like pain,
It is a game, where none doth gain;
  The lass saith no, and would full fain:
  And this is Love, as I hear sain.

Meliboeus: Yet, shepherd, what is Love, I pray?

Faustus: It is a yea, it is a nay,
                  A pretty kind of sporting fray,
                  It is a thing will soon away,
                      Then, nymphs, take vantage while ye may:
                      And this is Love, as I hear say.

Meliboeus: Yet what is love, good shepherd, show?

Faustus: A thing that creeps, it cannot go,
                  A prize that passeth to and fro,
                  A thing for one, a thing for moe,
                      And he that proves shall find it so:
                      And, shepherd, this is love, I trow.

                                          [Authorship uncertain]

The Faery Queen

Methought I saw the grave where Laura lay,
    Within that temple where the vestal flame
Was wont to burn; and passing by that way,
    To see that buried dust of living fame,
Whose tomb fair Love and fairer Virtue kept,
    All suddenly I saw the Faery Queen,
At whose approach the soul of Petrarch wept;
    And from thenceforth those graces were not seen,
For they this queen attended; in whose stead
    Oblivion laid him down on Laura's hearse.
Hereat the hardest stones were seen to bleed,
    And groans of buried ghosts the heavens did pierce:
Where Homer's sprite did tremble all for grief,
And cursed th' access of that celestial thief.

The Silent Lover

Passions are likened best to floods and streams:
    The shallow murmur, but the deep are dumb;
So, when affections yield discourse, it seems
    The bottom is but shallow whence they come.
They that are rich in words, in words discover
That they are poor in that which makes a lover.

Wrong not, sweet empress of my heart,
    The merit of true passion,
With thinking that he feels no smart,
    That sues for no compassion;

Since, if my plaints serve not to approve
    The conquest of thy beauty,
It comes not from defect of love,
    But from excess of duty.

For, knowing that I sue to serve
    A saint of such perfection,
As all desire, but none deserve,
    A place in her affection,

I rather choose to want relief
    Than venture the revealing;
Where glory recommends the grief,
    Despair distrusts the healing.

Thus those desires that aim too high
    For any mortal lover,
When reason cannot make them die,
    Discretion doth them cover.

Yet, when discretion doth bereave
    The plaints that they should utter,
Then thy discretion may perceive
    That silence is a suitor.

Silence in love bewrays more woe
    Than words, though ne'er so witty:
A beggar that is dumb, you know,
    May challenge double pity.

Then wrong not, dearest to my heart,
    My true, though secret, passion:
He smarteth most that hides his smart,
    And sues for no compassion.

The Lie

Go, Soul, the body's guest,
   Upon a thankless arrant;
Fear not to touch the best;
   The truth shall be thy warrant:
Go, since I needs must die,
And give the world the lie.

Say to the Court, it glows
   And shines like rotten wood;
Say to the Church, it shows
   What's good, and doth no good:
If Church and Court reply,
Then give them both the lie.

Tell potentates, they live
   Acting by others' action;
Not loved unless they give,
   Not strong but by a faction:
If potentates reply,
Give potentates the lie.

Tell men of high condition
   That manage the Estate,
Their purpose is ambition,
   Their practice only hate:
And if they once reply,
Then give them all the lie.

Tell them that brave it most,
   They beg for more by spending,
Who, in their greatest cost,
   Seek nothing but commending:
And if they make reply,
Then give them all the lie.

Tell zeal it wants devotion;
   Tell love it is but lust;
Tell time it is but motion;

Tell flesh it is but dust:
And wish them not reply,
For thou must give the lie.

Tell age it daily wasteth;
  Tell honour how it alters;
Tell beauty how she blasteth;
  Tell favour how it falters:
And as they shall reply,
Give every one the lie.

Tell wit how much it wrangles
  In tickle points of niceness;
Tell wisdom she entangles
  Herself in over-wiseness:
And when they do reply,
Straight give them both the lie.

Tell physic of her boldness;
  Tell skill it is pretention;
Tell charity of coldness;
  Tell law it is contention:
And as they do reply,
So give them still the lie.

Tell Fortune of her blindness;
  Tell Nature of decay;
Tell friendship of unkindness;
  Tell justice of delay;
And if they will reply,
Then give them all the lie.

Tell arts they have no soundness,
  But vary by esteeming;
Tell schools they want profoundness,
  And stand too much on seeming:
If arts and schools reply,
Give arts and schools the lie.

Tell faith it's fled the city;
  Tell how the country erreth;
Tell manhood shakes off pity;

Tell virtue least preferreth:
And if they do reply,
Spare not to give the lie.

So when thou hast, as I
    Commanded thee, done blabbing—
Although to give the lie
    Deserves no less than stabbing—
Stab at thee he that will,
No stab the soul can kill.

FROM *The Pilgrimage*

Give me my scallop-shell of quiet,
    My staff of faith to walk upon,
My scrip of joy, immortal diet,
    My bottle of salvation,
My gown of glory, hope's true gage;
And thus I'll take my pilgrimage.

Blood must be my body's balmer;
    No other balm will there be given;
Whilst my soul, like quiet palmer,
    Travelleth towards the land of heaven;
Over the silver mountains,
Where spring the nectar fountains:
        There will I kiss
        The bowl of bliss;
And drink mine everlasting fill
Upon every milken hill.
My soul will be a-dry before;
But after, it will thirst no more.

Verses Written in His Bible

Even such is Time, that takes in trust
Our youth, our joys, our all we have,
And pays us but with earth and dust;
Who in the dark and silent grave

When we have wandered all our ways,
Shuts up the story of our days;
But from this earth, this grave, this dust,
My God shall raise me up, I trust.

EDMUND SPENSER

(1552–1599)

FROM *The Shepherd's Calender, April*

See where she sits upon the grassy green,
    (O seemly sight!)
Yclad in scarlet, like a maiden Queen,
    And ermines white:
Upon her head a crimson coronet
With damask roses and daffadillies set,
        Bay leaves between,
        And primroses green,
Embellish the sweet violet.

Bring hither the pink and purple columbine,
    With gillyflowers;
Bring coronations and sops-in-wine
    Worn of paramours;
Strew me the ground with daffadowdillies
And cowslips and kingcups and lovéd lilies;
        The pretty pawnce
        And the chevisaunce
Shall match with the fair flower de lys.

FROM *Sonnets*

LXX

Fresh spring, the herald of Love's mighty king,
In whose coat-armour richly are displayed
All sorts of flowers, the which on earth do spring,
In goodly colours gloriously arrayed;
Go to my love, where she is careless laid,
Yet in her winter's bower will not awake;

Tell her the joyous time will not be stayed
Unless she do him by the forelock take;
Bid her therefore herself soon ready make
To wait on Love among his lovely crew;
Where every one that misseth then her make
Shall be by him amerced with penance due.
Make haste, therefore, sweet love, whilst it is prime,
For none can call again the passéd time.

LXXV

One day I wrote her name upon the strand;
But came the waves and washéd it away;
Again I wrote it with a second hand;
But came the tide, and made my pains his prey.
"Vain man," said she, "that dost in vain essay
A mortal thing so to immortalise,
For I myself shall like to this decay,
And eke my name be wipéd out likewise."
"Not so," quoth I, "let baser things devise
To die in dust, but you shall live by fame;
My verse your virtues rare shall eternise,
And in the heavens write your glorious name.
Where, whenas death shall all the world subdue,
Our love shall live, and later life renew."

LXXVIII

Lacking my love, I go from place to place,
Like a young fawn, that late hath lost the hind,
And seek each where, where last I saw her face,
Whose image yet I carry fresh in mind.
I seek the fields with her late footing signed,
I seek her bower with her late presence decked;
Yet nor in field nor bower I her can find,
Yet field and bower are full of her aspect.
But when mine eyes I thereunto direct
They idly back return to me again;
And when I hope to see their true objéct
I find myself but fed with fancies vain.
Cease then, mine eyes, to seek herself to see
And let my thoughts behold herself in me.

Prothalamion

Calm was the day, and through the trembling air
Sweet-breathing Zephyrus did softly play
A gentle spirit, that lightly did delay
Hot Titan's beams, which then did glister fair;
When I, (whom sullen care,
Through discontent of my long fruitless stay
In Prince's Court, and expectation vain
Of idle hopes, which still do fly away,
Like empty shadows, did afflict my brain,)
Walked forth to ease my pain
Along the shore of silver streaming Thames;
Whose rutty bank, the which his river hems,
Was painted all with variable flowers,
And all the meads adorned with dainty gems
Fit to deck maidens' bowers,
And crown their paramours
Against the bridal day, which is not long:
　　Sweet Thames! run softly, till I end my song.

There, in a meadow, by the river's side,
A flock of nymphs I chancéd to espy,
All lovely daughters of the flood thereby,
With goodly greenish locks, all loose untied,
As each had been a bride;
And each one had a little wicker basket,
Made of the twigs, entrailéd curiously,
In which they gathered flowers to fill their flasket,
And with fine fingers cropt full feateously
The tender stalks on high.
Of every sort, which in that meadow grew,
They gathered some; the violet, pallid blue,
The little daisy, that at evening closes,
The virgin lily, and the primrose true,
With store of vermeil roses,
To deck their bridegrooms' posies
Against the bridal day, which was not long:
　　Sweet Thames! run softly, till I end my song.

With that I saw two swans of goodly hue
Come softly swimming down along the lea;
Two fairer birds I yet did never see;
The snow, which doth the top of Pindus strew,
Did never whiter show;
Nor Jove himself, when he a swan would be
For love of Leda, whiter did appear;
Yet Leda was (they say) as white as he,
Yet not so white as these, nor nothing near;
So purely white they were,
That even the gentle stream, the which them bare,
Seemed foul to them, and bade his billows spare
To wet their silken feathers, lest they might
Soil their fair plumes with water not so fair,
And mar their beauties bright,
That shone as heaven's light,
Against their bridal day, which was not long:
   Sweet Thames! run softly, till I end my song.

Eftsoons the Nymphs, which now had flowers their fill,
Ran all in haste to see that silver brood,
As they came floating on the crystal flood;
Whom when they saw, they stood amazéd still,
Their wondering eyes to fill;
Them seemed they never saw a sight so fair,
Of fowls, so lovely, that they sure did deem
Them heavenly born, or to be that same pair
Which through the sky draw Venus' silver team;
For sure they did not seem
To be begot of any earthly seed,
But rather angels, or of angels' breed;
Yet were they bred of summer's heat, they say,
In sweetest season, when each flower and weed
The earth did fresh array;
So fresh they seemed as day,
Even as their bridal day, which was not long:
   Sweet Thames! run softly, till I end my song.

Then forth they all out of their baskets drew
Great store of flowers, the honour of the field,
That to the sense did fragrant odours yield,

All which upon those goodly birds they threw
And all the waves did strew,
That like old Peneus' waters they did seem,
When down along by pleasant Tempe's shore,
Scattered with flowers, through Thessaly they stream.
That they appear, through lilies' plenteous store,
Like a bride's chamber floor.
Two of those Nymphs, meanwhile, two garlands bound
Of freshest flowers which in that mead they found,
The which presenting all in trim array,
Their snowy foreheads therewithal they crowned,
Whilst one did sing this lay,
Prepared against that day,
Against their bridal day, which was not long:
   Sweet Thames! run softly, till I end my song.

"Ye gentle birds! the world's fair ornament,
And heaven's glory, whom this happy hour
Doth lead unto your lovers' blissful bower,
Joy may you have, and gentle heart's content
Of your love's couplement;
And let fair Venus, that is queen of love,
With her heart-quelling son upon you smile,
Whose smile, they say, hath virtue to remove
All Love's dislike, and friendship's faulty guile
For ever to assoil.
Let endless Peace your steadfast hearts accord,
And blesséd Plenty wait upon your board;
And let your bed with pleasures chaste abound,
That fruitful issue may to you afford,
Which may your foes confound,
And make your joys redound
Upon your bridal day, which is not long:
   Sweet Thames! run softly, till I end my song."

So ended she; and all the rest around
To her redoubled that her undersong,
Which said their bridal day should not be long:
And gentle Echo from the neighbour ground
Their accents did resound.
So forth those joyous birds did pass along,

Adown the lea, that to them murmured low,
As he would speak, but that he lacked a tongue,
Yet did by signs his glad affection show,
Making his stream run slow.
And all the fowl which in his flood did dwell
'Gan flock about these twain, that did excel
The rest, so far as Cynthia doth shend
The lesser stars. So they, enrangéd well,
Did on these two attend,
And their best service lend
Against their wedding day, which was not long:
    Sweet Thames! run softly, till I end my song.

At length they all to merry London came,
To merry London, my most kindly nurse,
That to me gave this life's first native source,
Though from another place I take my name,
A house of ancient fame:
There when they came, whereas those bricky towers
The which on Thames' broad agéd back do ride,
Where now the studious lawyers have their bowers,
There whilom wont the Templar knights to bide,
Till they decayed through pride:
Next whereunto there stands a stately place,
Where oft I gainéd gifts and goodly grace
Of that great Lord, which therein wont to dwell,
Whose want too well now feels my friendless case;
But ah! here fits not well
Old woes, but joys, to tell
Against the bridal day, which is not long:
    Sweet Thames! run softly, till I end my song.

Yet therein now doth lodge a noble peer,
Great England's glory, and the world's wide wonder,
Whose dreadful name late through all Spain did thunder,
And Hercules' two pillars standing near
Did make to quake and fear:
Fair branch of Honour, flower of Chivalry!
Thou fillest England with thy triumph's fame,
Joy have thou of thy noble victory,
And endless happiness of thine own name

That promiseth the same;
That through thy prowess, and victorious arms,
Thy country may be freed from foreign harms;
And great Eliza's glorious name may ring
Through all the world, filled with thy wide alarms,
Which some brave muse may sing
To ages following
Upon the bridal day, which is not long:
   Sweet Thames! run softly, till I end my song.

From those high towers this noble Lord issuing,
Like radiant Hesper, when his golden hair
In th' ocean billows he hath bathéd fair,
Descended to the river's open viewing,
With a great train ensuing.
Above the rest were goodly to be seen
Two gentle knights of lovely face and feature,
Beseeming well the bower of any queen,
With gifts of wit, and ornaments of nature,
Fit for so goodly stature,
That like the twins of Jove they seemed in sight,
Which deck the baldrick of the heavens bright;
They two, forth pacing to the river's side,
Received those two fair brides, their love's delight;
Which, at th' appointed tide,
Each one did make his bride
Against their bridal day, which is not long:
   Sweet Thames! run softly, till I end my song.

Epithalamion

Ye learned sisters, which have oftentimes
Been to me aiding others to adorn,
Whom ye thought worthy of your graceful rhymes
That even the greatest did not greatly scorn
To hear their names sung in your simple lays,
But joyéd in their praise;
And when ye list your own mishaps to mourn,
Which death or love or fortune's wreck did raise,
Your string could soon to sadder tenor turn

And teach the woods and waters to lament
Your doleful dreariment;
Now lay those sorrowful complaints aside
And, having all your heads with garlands crowned,
Help me my own love's praises to resound;
Nor let the same of any be envied;
So Orpheus did for his own bride,
So I unto myself alone will sing;
The woods shall to me answer, and my echo ring.

Early, before the world's light-giving lamp
His early beam upon the hills doth spread,
Having dispersed the night's uncheerful damp,
Do ye awake; and with fresh lustihead
Go to the bower of my beloved love,
My truest turtle dove.
Bid her awake, for Hymen is awake
And long since ready forth his masque to move,
With his bright tead that flames with many a flake,
And many a bachelor to wait on him
In their fresh garments trim.
Bid her awake therefore, and soon her dight,
For lo! the wishéd day is come at last
That shall, for all the pains and sorrows past,
Pay to her usury of long delight;
And, while she doth her dight,
Do ye to her of joy and solace sing
That all the woods may answer, and your echo ring.

Bring with you all the nymphs that you can hear
Both of the rivers and the forests green
And of the sea that neighbours to her near,
All with gay garlands goodly well beseen.
And let them also with them bring in hand
Another gay garland,
For my fair love, of lilies and of roses,
Bound true-love wise with a blue silk riband.
And let them make great store of bridal posies,
And let them eke bring store of other flowers

Tead, torch.

To deck the bridal bowers.
And let the ground whereas her foot shall tread,
For fear the stones her tender foot should wrong,
Be strewed with fragrant flowers all along
And diapered like the discoloured mead.
Which done, do at her chamber door await,
For she will waken straight;
The whiles do ye this song unto her sing,
The woods shall to you answer, and your echo ring.

Ye Nymphs of Mulla, which with careful heed
The silver scaly trouts do tend full well
And greedy pikes which use therein to feed;
(These trouts and pikes all others do excel;)
And ye likewise, which keep the rushy lake,
Where none do fishes take;
Bind up the locks the which hang scattered light,
And in the waters, which your mirror make,
Behold your faces as the crystal bright,
That when you come whereas my love doth lie,
No blemish she may spy.
And eke ye lightfoot maids, which keep the deer
That on the hoary mountain used to tower,
And the wild wolves which seek them to devour
With your steel darts do chase from coming near;
Be also present here
To help to deck her and to help to sing,
That all the woods may answer, and your echo ring.

Wake now, my love, awake! for it is time;
The rosy Morn long since left Tithon's bed,
All ready to her silver coach to climb;
And Phoebus 'gins to show his glorious head.
Hark! how the cheerful birds do chant their lays
And carol of Love's praise.
The merry lark her matins sings aloft,
The thrush replies, the mavis descant plays,
The ousel shrills, the ruddock warbles soft;
So goodly all agree, with sweet consent,
To this day's merriment.
Ah! my dear love, why do you sleep thus long

When meeter were that you should now awake,
T'await the coming of your joyous make
And hearken to the birds' love-learned song
The dewy leaves among!
Now they of joy and pleasance to you sing
That all the woods may answer, and their echo ring.

My love is now awake out of her dreams,
And her fair eyes, like stars that dimméd were
With darksome cloud, now show their goodly beams
More bright than Hesperus his head doth rear.
Come now, ye damsels, daughters of delight,
Help quickly her to dight.
But first come ye fair hours, which were begot
In Jove's sweet paradise of Day and Night,
Which do the seasons of the year allot,
And all that ever in this world is fair
Do make and still repair.
And ye three handmaids of the Cyprian Queen,
The which do still adorn her beauty's pride,
Help to adorn my beautifullest bride;
And, as ye her array, still throw between
Some graces to be seen;
And, as ye use to Venus, to her sing
The whiles the woods shall answer, and your echo ring.

Now is my love all ready forth to come.
Let all the virgins therefore well await;
And ye, fresh boys, that tend upon her groom,
Prepare yourselves; for he is coming straight.
Set all your things in seemly good array,
Fit for so joyful day,
The fairest day that ever sun did see.
Fair Sun! shew forth thy favourable ray,
And let thy lifefull heat not fervent be,
For fear of burning her sunshiny face,
Her beauty to disgrace.
O fairest Phoebus! father of the Muse!
If ever I did honour thee aright
Or sing the thing that mote thy mind delight,
Do not thy servant's simple boon refuse;

But let this day, let this one day be mine;
Let all the rest be thine.
Then I thy sovereign praises loud will sing
That all the woods shall answer, and their echo ring.

Hark how the minstrels 'gin to shrill aloud
Their merry music that resounds from far,
The pipe, the tabor, and the trembling croud,
That well agree withouten breach or jar.
But most of all the damsels do delight
When they their timbrels smite,
And thereunto do dance and carol sweet
That all the senses they do ravish quite;
The whiles the boys run up and down the street,
Crying aloud with strong confused noise,
As if it were one voice,
"Hymen, io Hymen, Hymen", they do shout;
That even to the heavens their shouting shrill
Doth reach, and all the firmament doth fill;
To which the people standing all about,
As in approvance, do thereto applaud,
And loud advance her laud;
And evermore they "Hymen, Hymen" sing
That all the woods them answer, and their echo ring.

Lo! where she comes along with portly pace,
Like Phoebe from her chamber of the East,
Arising forth to run her mighty race,
Clad all in white, that 'seems a virgin best.
So well it her beseems that ye would ween
Some angel she had been.
Her long loose yellow locks like golden wire,
Sprinkled with pearl and pearling flowers atween,
Do like a golden mantle her attire;
And, being crownéd with a garland green,
Seem like some maiden queen.
Her modest eyes, abashéd to behold
So many gazers as do at her stare,
Upon the lowly ground affixéd are;
Nor dare lift up her countenance too bold,
But blush to hear her praises sung so loud,

So far from being proud.
Nathless do ye still loud her praises sing
That all the woods may answer, and your echo ring.

Tell me, ye merchants' daughters, did ye see
So fair a creature in your town before,
So sweet, so lovely, and so mild as she,
Adorned with beauty's grace and virtue's store?
Her goodly eyes like sapphires shining bright,
Her forehead ivory white,
Her cheeks like apples which the sun hath rudded,
Her lips like cherries charming men to bite,
Her breast like to a bowl of cream uncrudded,
Her paps like lilies budded,
Her snowy neck like to a marble tower;
And all her body like a palace fair
Ascending up with many a stately stair
To honour's seat and chastity's sweet bower.
Why stand ye still, ye virgins, in amaze
Upon her so to gaze,
Whiles ye forget your former lay to sing,
To which the woods did answer, and your echo ring?

But if ye saw that which no eyes can see,
The inward beauty of her lively spright,
Garnished with heavenly gifts of high degree,
Much more then would ye wonder at that sight
And stand astonished like to those which read
Medusa's mazeful head.
There dwells sweet love and constant chastity,
Unspotted faith and comely womanhood,
Regard of honour and mild modesty.
There virtue reigns as queen in royal throne
And giveth laws alone,
The which the base affections do obey
And yield their services unto her will;
Nor thought of thing uncomely ever may
Thereto approach to tempt her mind to ill.
Had ye once seen these her celestial treasures
And unrevealéd pleasures,
Then would ye wonder and her praises sing
That all the woods should answer, and your echo ring.

Open the temple gates unto my love,
Open them wide that she may enter in,
And all the post adorn as doth behove,
And all the pillars deck with garlands trim,
For to receive this saint with honour due,
That cometh in to you.
With trembling steps and humble reverence
She cometh in before th'Almighty's view;
Of her, ye virgins, learn obedience,
When so ye come into those holy places,
To humble your proud faces.
Bring her up to th'high altar that she may
The sacred ceremonies there partake,
And let the roaring organs loudly play
The praises of the Lord in lively notes;
The whiles, with hollow throats,
The choristers the joyous anthem sing
That all the woods may answer, and their echo ring.

Behold, whiles she before the altar stands,
Hearing the holy priest that to her speaks,
And blesseth her with his two happy hands,
How the red roses flush up in her cheeks,
And the pure snow, with goodly vermeil stain
Like crimson dyed in grain;
That even th'angels, which continually
About the sacred altar do remain,
Forget their service and about her fly,
Oft peeping in her face, that seems more fair
The more they on it stare.
But her sad eyes, still fastened on the ground,
Are governéd with goodly modesty,
That suffers not one look to glance awry,
Which may let in a little thought unsound.
Why blush you, love, to give to me your hand,
The pledge of all our band!
Sing, ye sweet angels, alleluia sing,
That all the woods may answer, and your echo ring.

Now all is done. Bring home the bride again,
Bring home the triumph of our victory,

Bring home with you the glory of her gain,
With joyance bring her and with jollity.
Never had man more joyful day than this,
Whom heaven would heap with bliss,
Make feast therefore now all this live-long day;
This day for ever to me holy is.
Pour out the wine without restraint or stay,
Pour not by cups but by the bellyful,
Pour out to all that wull,
And sprinkle all the post and walls with wine
That they may sweat and drunken be withal.
Crown ye god Bacchus with a coronal,
And Hymen also crown with wreaths of vine;
And let the Graces dance unto the rest,
For they can do it best;
The whiles the maidens do their carol sing,
To which the woods shall answer, and their echo ring.

Ring ye the bells, ye young men of the town,
And leave your wonted labours for this day.
This day is holy; do ye write it down
That ye for ever it remember may.
This day the sun is in his chiefest height,
With Barnaby the bright,
From whence declining daily by degrees
He somewhat loseth of his heat and light,
When once the Crab behind his back he sees.
But for this time it ill ordainéd was
To choose the longest day in all the year
And shortest night, when longest fitter were;
Yet never day so long but late would pass.
Ring ye the bells to make it wear away
And bonfires make all day,
And dance about them and about them sing,
That all the woods may answer, and your echo ring.

Ah! when will this long weary day have end,
And lend me leave to come unto my love?
How slowly do the hours their numbers spend!
How slowly does sad Time his feathers move!
Haste thee, O fairest planet, to thy home

Within the western foam;
Thy tired steeds long since have need of rest.
Long though it be, at last I see it gloom
And the bright evening star with golden crest
Appear out of the East.
Fair child of beauty! glorious lamp of love!
That all the host of heaven in ranks dost lead
And guidest lovers through the night's sad dread,
How cheerfully thou lookest from above
And seem'st to laugh atween thy twinkling light,
As joining in the sight
Of these glad many, which for joy do sing
That all the woods them answer, and their echo ring!

Now cease, ye damsels, your delights fore-past,
Enough it is that all the day was yours;
Now day is done, and night is nighing fast,
Now bring the bride into the bridal bowers.
The night is come; now soon her disarray
And in her bed her lay;
Lay her in lilies and in violets,
And silken curtains over her display,
And odoured sheets and Arras coverlets.
Behold how goodly my fair love does lie
In proud humility!
Like unto Maia whenas Jove her took
In Tempe, lying on the flowery grass
'Twixt sleep and wake, after she weary was
With bathing in the Acidalian brook.
Now it is night, ye damsels may be gone
And leave my love alone,
And leave likewise your former lay to sing.
The woods no more shall answer, nor your echo ring.

Now welcome night! thou night so long expected,
That long days' labour dost at last defray,
And all my cares which cruel Love collected
Hast summed in one and cancelléd for aye.
Spread thy broad wing over my love and me
That no man may us see,
And in thy sable mantle us enwrap

From fear of peril and foul horror free.
Let no false treason seek us to entrap,
Nor any dread disquiet once annoy
The safety of our joy;
But let the night be calm and quietsome
Without tempestuous storms or sad affray;
Like as when Jove with fair Alcmena lay
When he begot the great Tirynthian groom;
Or like as when he with thyself did lie
And begot Majesty.
And let the maids and young men cease to sing;
Nor let the woods them answer, nor their echo ring.

Let no lamenting cries nor doleful tears
Be heard all night within, nor yet without;
Nor let false whispers breeding hidden fears
Break gentle sleep with misconceivéd doubt.
Let no deluding dreams nor dreadful sights
Make sudden sad affrights;
Nor let house fires nor lightnings' helpless harms,
Nor let the Puck nor other evil sprights,
Nor let mischievous witches with their charms,
Nor let hobgoblins, names whose sense we see not,
Fray us with things that be not;
Let not the screech owl nor the stork be heard,
Nor the night raven that still deadly yells,
Nor damnéd ghosts called up with mighty spells,
Nor grisly vultures, make us once afeared;
Nor let th'unpleasant choir of frogs still croaking
Make us to wish their choking.
Let none of these their dreary accents sing,
Nor let the woods them answer, nor their echo ring.

But let still Silence true night-watches keep
That sacred Peace may in assurance reign;
And timely Sleep, when it is time to sleep,
May pour his limbs forth on your pleasant plain;
The whiles an hundred little wingéd Loves,
Like divers-feathered doves,
Their pretty stealths shall work, and snares shall spread
To filch away sweet snatches of delight,

Concealed through covert night.
Ye sons of Venus, play your sports at will!
For greedy pleasure, careless of your toys,
Thinks more upon her paradise of joys
Than what ye do, albeit good or ill.
All night therefore attend your merry play,
For it will soon be day;
Now none doth hinder you that say or sing,
Nor will the woods now answer, nor their echo ring.

Who is the same which at my window peeps?
Or whose is that fair face that shines so bright?
Is it not Cynthia, she that never sleeps,
But walks about high heaven all the night?
O! fairest goddess, do thou not envy
My love with me to spy;
For thou likewise didst love, though now unthought,
And for a fleece of wool which privily
The Latmian shepherd once unto thee brought,
His pleasures with thee wrought.
Therefore to us be favourable now;
And sith of women's labours thou hast charge
And goodly generation dost enlarge,
Incline thy will t'effect our wishful vow,
And the chaste womb inform with timely seed
That may our comfort breed.
Till which we cease our hopeful hap to sing;
Nor let the woods us answer, nor our echo ring.

And thou, great Juno! which with awful might
The laws of wedlock still dost patronise,
And the religion of the faith first plight
With sacred rites hast taught to solemnise,
And eke for comfort often callèd art
Of women in their smart;
Eternally bind thou this lovely band,
And all thy blessings unto us impart.
And thou, glad Genius! in whose gentle hand
The bridal bower and genial bed remain
Without blemish or stain,
And the sweet pleasures of their love's delight

With secret aid dost succour and supply
Till they bring forth the fruitful progeny,
Send us the timely fruit of this same night.
And thou, fair Hebe! and thou, Hymen free!
Grant that it so may be.
Till which we cease your further praise to sing;
Nor any woods shall answer, nor your echo ring.

And ye high heavens, the temple of the gods,
In which a thousand torches flaming bright
Do burn, that to us wretched earthly clods
In dreadful darkness lend desired light;
And all ye powers that in the same remain,
More than we men can feign!
Pour out your blessing on us plenteously,
And happy influence upon us rain,
That we may raise a large posterity,
Which from the earth, which they may long possess
With lasting happiness,
Up to your haughty palaces may mount;
And for the guerdon of their glorious merit
May heavenly tabernacles there inherit,
Of blessed saints for to increase the count.
So let us rest, sweet love, in hope of this,
And cease till then our timely joys to sing;
    The woods no more us answer, nor our echo ring!

Song! made in lieu of many ornaments,
With which my love should duly have been decked,
Which cutting off through hasty accidents,
You would not stay your due time to expect,
But promised both to recompense;
Be unto her a goodly ornament,
And for short time an endless monument.

FROM *The Faery Queen*

1.

The noble heart that harbours virtuous thought
And is with child of glorious great intent,
Can never rest until it forth have brought
Th'eternal brood of glory excellent;
Such restless passion did all night torment
The flaming courage of that Faery knight,
Devising how that doughty tournament
With greatest honour he achieven might:
Still did he wake, and still did watch for dawning light.

At last, the golden oriental gate
Of greatest heaven 'gan to open fair,
And Phoebus, fresh as bridegroom to his mate,
Came dancing forth shaking his dewy hair
And hurled his glistering beams through gloomy air.
Which when the wakeful Elf perceived, straightway
He started up, and did himself prepare
In sun-bright arms and battailous array;
For with that pagan proud he combat will that day.

And forth he comes into the common hall,
Where early waits him many a gazing eye,
To weet what end to stranger knight may fall.
There many minstrels maken melody
To drive away the dull melancholy,
And many bards that to the trembling cord
Can tune their timely voices cunningly,
And many chroniclers that can record
Old loves and wars for ladies done by many a lord.

Soon after comes the cruel Sarazin
In woven mail all arméd warily,
And sternly looks at him who not a pin
Does care for look of living creature's eye.
They bring them wines of Greece and Araby
And dainty spices fetched from furthest Ind
To kindle heat of courage privily;
And in the wine a solemn oath they bind
T'observe the sacred laws of arms that are assigned.

At last forth comes that far renownéd Queen.
With royal pomp and princely majesty
She is ybrought unto a paléd green,
And placéd under stately canopy,
The warlike feats of both those knights to see.
On th'other side in all men's open view
Duessa placéd is, and on a tree
Sansfoy his shield is hanged with bloody hue;
Both those the laurel garlands to the victor due.

A shrilling trumpet sounded from on high
And unto battle bade themselves address;
Their shining shields about their wrists they tie,
And burning blades about their heads do bless,
The instruments of wrath and heaviness,
With greedy force each other doth assail
And strike so fiercely that they do impress
Deep dinted furrows in the battered mail;
The iron walls to ward their blows are weak and frail.

The Sarazin was stout and wondrous strong,
And heapéd blows like iron hammers great,
For after blood and vengeance he did long;
The knight was fierce and full of youthful heat,
And doubled strokes like dreaded thunder's threat;
For all for praise and honour he did fight.
Both stricken strike, and beaten both do beat,
That from their shields forth flyeth fiery light,
And hewen helmets deep shew marks of either's might.

So th'one for wrong, the other strives for right,
And each to deadly shame would drive his foe;
The cruel steel so greedily doth bite
In tender flesh that streams of blood down flow,
With which the arms that erst so bright did show
Into a pure vermilion now are dyed.
Great ruth in all the gazers' hearts did grow,
Seeing the goréd wounds to gape so wide,
That victory they dare not wish to either side.

Book 1, Canto 5

2.

Mammon emovéd was with inward wrath;
Yet, forcing it to feign, him forth thence led
Through grisly shadows by a beaten path,
Into a garden goodly garnishéd
With herbs and fruits, whose kinds mote not be read;
Not such as earth out of her fruitful womb
Throws forth to men, sweet and well savouréd,
But direful deadly black both leaf and bloom,
Fit to adorn the dead and deck the dreary tomb.

There mournful cypress grew in greatest store,
And trees of bitter gall and ebon sad,
Dead sleeping poppy and black hellebore,
Cold coloquintida and tetra mad,
Mortal samnitis and cicuta bad,
With which th'unjust Athenians made to die
Wise Socrates, who therof quaffing glad,
Poured out his life and last philosophy
To the fair Critias, his dearest belamy!

The Garden of Proserpina this hight;
And in the midst thereof a silver seat,
With a thick arbour goodly over-dight,
In which she often used from open heat
Herself to shroud, and pleasures to entreat;
Next thereunto did grow a goodly tree,
With branches broad dispread and body great,
Clothéd with leaves, that none the wood might see,
And loaden all with fruit as thick as it might be.

Their fruit were golden apples glistering bright,
That goodly was their glory to behold;
On earth like never grew, nor living wight
Like ever saw, but they from hence were sold;
For those which Hercules with conquest bold
Got from great Atlas' daughters hence began,
And planted there did bring forth fruit of gold;
And those with which th'Euboean young man wan
Swift Atalanta, when through craft he her outran.

Here also sprung that goodly golden fruit
With which Acontius got his lover true,
Whom he had long time sought with fruitless suit;
Here eke that famous golden apple grew,
The which amongst the gods false Até threw,
For which th'Idaean ladies disagreed
Till partial Paris deemed it virtue's due,
And had of her fair Helen for his meed,
That many noble Greeks and Trojans made to bleed.

Book 2, Canto 7

3.

Eftsoons they heard a most melodious sound,
Of all that mote delight a dainty ear,
Such as at once might not on living ground,
Save in this paradiso, be heard elsewhere;
Right hard it was for wight which did it hear
To read what manner music that mote be;
For all that pleasing is to living ear
Was there consorted in one harmony;
Birds, voices, instruments, winds, waters all agree.

The joyous birds shrouded in cheerful shade
Their notes unto the voice attempered sweet;
Th'angelical soft trembling voices made
To th'instruments divine respondence meet;
The silver sounding instruments did meet
With the bass murmur of the water's fall;
The water's fall with difference discreet
Now soft, now loud, unto the wind did call;
The gentle warbling wind low answeréd to all.

The whiles some one did chant this lovely lay:
Ah! see, whoso fair thing dost fain to see,
In springing flower the image of thy day.
Ah! see the virgin rose how sweetly she
Doth first peep forth with bashful modesty,
That fairer seems the less ye see her may.
Lo! see soon after how more bold and free
Her baréd bosom she doth broad display;
Lo! see soon after how she fades and falls away.

So passeth in the passing of a day
Of mortal life the leaf, the bud, the flower;
Nor more doth flourish after first decay
That erst was sought to deck both bed and bower
Of many a lady' and many a paramour.
Gather therefore the rose whilst yet is prime,
For soon comes age that will her pride deflower;
Gather the rose of love whilst yet is time,
Whilst loving thou mayst lovéd be with equal crime.

Book 2, Canto 12

ANTHONY MUNDAY

(1553–1633)

To Colin Clout

Beauty sat bathing by a spring,
    Where fairest shades did hide her,
The winds blew calm, the birds did sing,
    The cool streams ran beside her.
My wanton thoughts enticed mine eye
    To see what was forbidden,
But better memory said, fie,
    So vain desire was chidden.
        Hey nonny nonny O!
        Hey nonny nonny!

Into a slumber then I fell,
    When fond imagination
Seeméd to see, but could not tell
    Her feature or her fashion.
But even as babes in dreams do smile,
    And sometimes fall a-weeping,
So I awaked, as wise this while,
    As when I fell a-sleeping.

England's Helicon, 1600

JOHN LYLY?

(1553–1606)

"What Bird So Sings..."

What bird so sings, yet does so wail?
O 'tis the ravished nightingale.
"Jug, jug, jug, jug, tereu," she cries,
And still her woes at midnight rise.
Brave prick-song! who is't now we hear?
None but the lark so shrill and clear;
Now at heaven's gates she claps her wings,
The morn not waking till she sings.
Hark, hark, with what a pretty throat,
Poor robin redbreast tunes his note;
Hark how the jolly cuckoos sing,
Cuckoo to welcome in the spring!
Cuckoo to welcome in the spring!

Alexander and Campaspe, 1584

"Cupid and My Campaspe Played"

Cupid and my Campaspe played
At cards for kisses—Cupid paid;
He stakes his quiver, bow and arrows,
His mother's doves, and team of sparrows;
Loses them too; then down he throws
The coral of his lip, the rose
Growing on's cheek (but none knows how);
With these, the crystal of his brow,
And then the dimple of his chin:
All these did my Campaspe win.
At last he set her both his eyes,
She won, and Cupid blind did rise.
O Love! has she done this to thee?
What shall, alas! become of me?

Alexander and Campaspe, 1584

"Pan's Syrinx Was a Girl..."

Pan's Syrinx was a girl indeed,
Though now she's turned into a reed;
From that dear reed Pan's pipe does come,
A pipe that strikes Apollo dumb;
Nor flute, nor lute, nor gittern can
So chant it as the pipe of Pan:
Cross-gartered swains and dairy girls,
With faces smug and round as pearls,
When Pan's shrill pipe begins to play,
With dancing wear out night and day;
The bagpipe's drone his hum lays by,
When Pan sounds up his minstrelsy;
His minstrelsy! O base! this quill,
Which at my mouth with wind I fill,
Puts me in mind, though her I miss,
That still my Syrinx' lips I kiss.

Midas, 1592

FULKE GREVILLE, Lord Brooke
(1554–1628)

Song to His Cynthia

Away with these self-loving lads,
Whom Cupid's arrow never glads!
Away poor souls that sigh and weep
In love of them that lie and sleep!
  For Cupid is a meadow-god,
  And forceth none to kiss the rod.

God Cupid's shaft, like destiny,
Doth either good or ill decree;
Desert is borne out of his bow,
Reward upon his feet doth go.
  What fools are they that have not known
  That Love likes no laws but his own?

My songs they be of Cynthia's praise,
I wear her rings on holidays;
On every tree I write her name,
And every day I read the same.
　　Where Honour Cupid's rival is,
　　There miracles are seen of his.

If Cynthia crave her ring of me,
I blot her name out of the tree;
If doubt do darken things held dear,
Then welfare nothing once a year,
　　For many run, but one must win;
　　Fools only hedge the cuckoo in.

The worth that worthiness should move
Is love, which is the due of love;
And love as well the shepherd can
As can the mighty nobleman.
　　Sweet nymph, 'tis true you worthy be,
　　Yet without love naught worth to me.

To Myra

I, with whose colours Myra dressed her head,
I, that wear posies of her own hand-making,
I, that mine own name in the chimneys read
By Myra finely wrought ere I was waking;
　　Must I look on, in hope time coming may
　　With change bring back my turn again to play?

I, that on Sunday at the church-stile found
A garland sweet with true-love knots in flowers,
Which I to wear about mine arms was bound,
That each of us might know that all was ours;
　　Must I now lead an idle life in wishes,
　　And follow Cupid for his loaves and fishes?

I, that did wear the ring her mother left,
I, for whose love she gloried to be blamed,
I, with whose eyes her eyes committed theft,

I, who did make her blush when I was named;
   Must I lose ring, flowers, blush, theft, and go naked,
   Watching with sighs till dead love be awakéd?

I, that when drowsy Argus fell asleep,
Like jealousy o'erwatchéd with desire,
Was ever warnéd modesty to keep,
While her breath speaking kindled Nature's fire;
   Must I look on a-cold, while others warm them?
   Do Vulcan's brothers in such fine nets arm them?

Was it for this that I might Myra see
Washing the water with her beauties white?
Yet would she never write her love to me,
Thinks wit of change while thoughts are in delight?
   Mad girls must safely love, as they may leave;
   No man can print a kiss; lines may deceive.

Chorus

   O wearisome condition of humanity!
   Born under one law, to another bound;
   Vainly begot, and yet forbidden vanity,
   Created sick, commanded to be sound.
   What meaneth Nature by these diverse laws?
   Passion and reason self-division cause.
   Is it the mark or majesty of Power
   To make offences that it may forgive?
   Nature herself doth her own self deflower
   To hate those errors she herself doth give.
   For how should man think that he may not do
   If Nature did not fail and punish too?
   Tyrant to others, to herself unjust,
   Only commands things difficult and hard,
   Forbids us all things which it knows we lust,
   Makes easy pains, impossible reward.
   If Nature did not take delight in blood,
   She would have made more easy ways to good.
   We that are bound by vows and by promotion,
   With pomp of holy sacrifice and rites,

To preach belief in God and stir devotion,
To preach of Heaven's wonders and delights;
Yet when each of us in his own heart looks,
He finds the God there far unlike his books.

Mustapha, 1609

SIR PHILIP SIDNEY

(1554–1586)

"My True Love Hath My Heart..."

My true love hath my heart, and I have his,
By just exchange one for the other given.
I hold his dear, and mine he cannot miss;
There never was a better bargain driven.
His heart in me keeps me and him in one;
My heart in him his thoughts and senses guides;
He loves my heart, for once it was his own;
I cherish his, because in me it bides.
His heart his wound receivéd from my sight;
My heart was wounded with his wounded heart;
For as from me on him his hurt did light
So still methought in me his hurt did smart:
Both equal hurt, in this change sought our bliss;
My true love hath my heart, and I have his.

Arcadia

FROM Astrophel and Stella

1.   SONNET I

Loving in truth, and fain my love in verse to show,
That the dear she might take some pleasure of my pain:
Pleasure might cause her read, reading might make her know,
Knowledge might pity win, and pity grace obtain—
I sought fit words, to paint the blackest face of woe,
Studying inventions fine, her wits to entertain,
Oft turning others' leaves, to see if thence would flow
Some fresh and fruitful shower, upon my sun-burnt brain.
But words came halting out, wanting invention's stay,
Invention, nature's child, fled stepdame study's blows,

And others' feet still seemed but strangers in my way.
Thus great with child to speak, and helpless in my throes,
Biting my tongue and pen, beating myself for spite:
Fool! said my muse to me, look in thy heart and write.

2.   SONNET XXXI

With how sad steps, O moon, thou climb'st the skies!
How silently, and with how wan a face!
What! may it be that even in heavenly place
That busy archer his sharp arrows tries?
Sure, if that long-with-love-acquainted eyes
Can judge of love, thou feel'st a lover's case:
I read it in thy looks; thy languished grace
To me, that feel the like, thy state descries.
Then, even of fellowship, O Moon, tell me,
Is constant love deemed there but want of wit?
Are beauties there as proud as here they be?
Do they above love to be loved, and yet
Those lovers scorn whom that love doth possess?
Do they call virtue there ungratefulness?

3.   SONNET XXXIX

Come, Sleep; O Sleep! the certain knot of peace,
The baiting-place of wit, the balm of woe,
The poor man's wealth, the prisoner's release,
Th'indifferent judge between the high and low;
With shield of proof shield me from out the prease
Of those fierce darts Despair at me doth throw:
O make in me those civil wars to cease;
I will good tribute pay, if thou do so.
Take thou of me smooth pillows, sweetest bed,
A chamber deaf to noise and blind of light,
A rosy garland and a weary head;
And if these things, as being thine by right,
Move not thy heavy grace, thou shalt in me,
Livelier than elsewhere, Stella's image see.

4.   ELEVENTH SONG

"Who is it that, this dark night,
Underneath my window plaincth?"
"It is one, who from thy sight
Being, ah! exiled, disdaineth
Every other vulgar light."

"Why, alas! and are you he?
Be not yet those fancies changed?"
"Dear, when you find change in me,
Though from me you be estranged,
Let my change to ruin be."

"Woll, in absence this will die;
Leave to see, and leave to wonder."
"Absence sure will help, if I
Can learn how myself to sunder
From what in my heart doth lie."

"But time will these thoughts remove;
Time doth work what no man knoweth."
"Time doth as the subject prove,
With time still the affection groweth
In the faithful turtle dove."

"What if you new beauties see?
Will they not stir new affections?"
"I will think they pictures be,
Image-like of saint's perfection,
Poorly counterfeiting thee."

"But your reason's purest light
Bids you leave such minds to nourish."
"Dear, do reason no such spite,
Never doth thy beauty flourish
More than in my reason's sight."

"But the wrongs love bears will make
Love at length leave undertaking."
"No, the more fools it do shake
In a ground of so firm making,
Deeper still they drive the stake."

"Peace, I think that some give ear;
Come no more lest I get anger."
"Bliss, I will my bliss forbear,
Fearing, sweet, you to endanger,
But my soul shall harbour there."

"Well, begone, begone I say,
Lest that Argus' eyes perceive you."
"O unjust Fortune's sway!
Which can make me thus to leave you
And from louts to run away!"

FROM *Certain Sonnets*

1.   "RING OUT YOUR BELLS! ..."

Ring out your bells! Let mourning shows be spread,
For Love is dead:
All love is dead, infected
With plague of deep disdain;
Worth as nought worth rejected,
And faith fair scorn doth gain.
    From so ungrateful fancy,
    From such a female frenzy,
    From them that use men thus,
    Good Lord deliver us.

Weep, neighbours, weep, do you not hear it said
That Love is dead?
His death-bed, peacock's folly;
His winding sheet is shame;
His will false-seeming holy;
His sole executor blame.

Let dirge be sung, and trentals rightly read,
For Love is dead.
Sir Wrong his tomb ordaineth;
My mistress Marble-heart,
Which epitaph containeth,
His eyes were once his dart.

Alas, I lie! Rage hath this error bred,
Love is not dead.
Love is not dead, but sleepeth
In her unmatchéd mind,
Where she his counsel keepeth
Till due desert she find.
    Therefore from so vile fancy,
    To call such wit a frenzy,
    Who love can temper thus,
    Good Lord, deliver us.

2.   "THOU BLIND MAN'S MARK..."

Thou blind man's mark, thou fool's self-chosen snare,
Fond Fancy's scum and dregs of scattered thought,
Band of all evils, cradle of causeless care,
Thou web of will whose end is never wrought;
Desire! desire, I have too dearly bought
With price of mangled mind thy worthless ware;
Too long, too long asleep thou hast me brought,
Who should my mind to higher things prepare.
But yet in vain thou hast my ruin sought,
In vain thou mad'st me to vain things aspire,
In vain thou kindlest all thy smoky fire.
For virtue hath this better lesson taught,
Within myself to seek my only hire,
Desiring nought but how to kill desire.

3.   "LEAVE ME, O LOVE ..."

Leave me, O Love, which reachest but to dust;
And thou, my mind, aspire to higher things.
Grow rich in that which never taketh rust;
Whatever fades but fading pleasure brings.
Draw in thy beams, and humble all thy might,
To that sweet yoke where lasting freedom be,
Which breaks the clouds and opens forth the light,
That doth both shine and give us sight to see.
O take fast hold, let that light be thy guide
In this small course which birth draws out to death,
And think how evil becometh him to slide
Who seeketh heav'n, and comes of heav'nly breath.
Then, farewell world! thy uttermost I see;
Eternal Love, maintain thy life in me.

THOMAS LODGE

(1556?–1625)

Phoebe's Sonnet

"Down a down!"
   Thus Phyllis sung,
   By fancy once distress'd:
   "Whoso by foolish Love are stung
   Are worthily oppress'd.
And so sing I, with a down a down."

"When Love was first begot,
And by the mother's will,
Did fall to human lot,
His solace to fulfil,
Devoid of all deceit,
A chaste and holy fire,
Did quicken men's conceit,
And women's breasts inspire.
The gods that saw the good,
That mortals did approve,

With kind and holy mood
Began to talk of Love.
   Down a down!"
      Thus Phyllis sung
      By fancy once distress'd.

"But during this accord,
A wonder strange to hear,
Whilst Love in deed and word,
Most faithful did appear,
False semblance came in place,
By jealousy attended,
And with a double face
Both love and fancy blended;
Which made the gods forsake,
And men from fancy fly,
And maidens scorn a make;
Forsooth, and so will I.
   Down a down!"
      Thus Phyllis sung,
      By fancy once distress'd:
      "Whoso by foolish Love are stung
      Are worthily oppress'd.
And so sing I, with a down a down."

Rosalind's Madrigal

Love in my bosom like a bee
   Doth suck his sweet;
Now with his wings he plays with me,
   Now with his feet.
Within mine eyes he makes his nest,
His bed amidst my tender breast;
My kisses are his daily feast,
And yet he robs me of my rest.
   Ah wanton, will ye?

And if I sleep, then percheth he,
   With pretty flight,
And makes his pillow of my knee
   The livelong night.

Strike I my lute, he tunes the string;
He music plays if so I sing;
He lends me every lovely thing;
Yet cruel he my heart doth sting.
  Whist, wanton, still ye!

Else I with roses every day
  Will whip you hence,
And bind you, when you long to play,
  For your offence.
I'll shut mine eyes to keep you in,
I'll make you fast it for your sin,
I'll count your power not worth a pin,
Alas, what hereby shall I win,
  If he gainsay me?

What if I beat the wanton boy
  With many a rod?
He will repay me with annoy,
  Because a god.
Then sit thou safely on my knee,
Then let thy bower my bosom be;
Lurk in mine eyes, I like of thee.
O Cupid, so thou pity me,
  Spare not, but play me.

"The Earth, Late Choked..."

The earth, late choked with showers,
  Is now arrayed in green,
Her bosom springs with flowers,
  The air dissolves her teen;
    The heavens laugh at her glory,
    Yet bide I sad and sorry.

The woods are decked with leaves,
  And trees are clothéd gay,
And Flora crowned with sheaves,
  With oaken boughs doth play;
    Where I am clad in black,
    The token of my wrack.

The birds upon the trees
　　Do sing with pleasant voices,
And chant in their degrees
　　Their loves and lucky choices;
　　　　When I, whilst they are singing,
　　　　With sighs mine arms am wringing.

The thrushes seek the shade,
　　And I my fatal grave;
Their flight to heaven is made,
　　My walk on earth I have;
　　　　They free, I thrall; they jolly,
　　　　I sad and pensive wholly.

Scilla's Metamorphosis, 1589

To Phyllis, the Fair Shepherdess

My Phyllis hath the morning sun,
　　At first to look upon her;
And Phyllis hath morn-waking birds
　　Her risings for to honour.

My Phyllis hath prime-feathered flowers
　　That smile when she treads on them;
And Phyllis hath a gallant flock
　　That leaps since she doth own them.

But Phyllis hath so hard a heart,
　　Alas that she should have it,
As yields no mercy to desart,
　　Nor grace to those that crave it.

Sweet sun, when thou look'st on,
Pray her regard my moan;
Sweet birds, when you sing to her,
To yield some pity, woo her;
Sweet flowers whenas she treads on,
Tell her, her beauty deads one,
And if in life her love she nill agree me,
Pray her before I die she will come see me.

To Phyllis

Love guards the roses of thy lips
  And flies about them like a bee;
If I approach he forward skips,
  And if I kiss he stingeth me.

Love in thine eyes doth build his bower,
  And sleeps within their pretty shine;
And if I look the boy will lower,
  And from their orbs shoot shafts divine.

Love works thy heart within his fire,
  And in my tears doth firm the same;
And if I tempt it will retire,
  And of my plaints doth make a game.

Love, let me cull her choicest flowers,
  And pity me, and calm her eye,
Make soft her heart, dissolve her lowers,
  Then will I praise thy deity.

But if thou do not, Love, I'll truly serve her
In spite of thee, and by firm faith deserve her.

GEORGE PEELE

(1558?–1597)

"Fair and Fair..."

Oenone: Fair and fair, and twice so fair,
      As fair as any may be;
    The fairest shepherd on our green,
      A love for any lady.

Paris: Fair and fair, and twice so fair,
      As fair as any may be;
    Thy love is fair for thee alone,
      And for no other lady.

Oenone: My love is fair, my love is gay,
 As fresh as bin the flowers in May,
And of my love my roundelay,
 My merry, merry, merry roundelay,
Concludes with Cupid's curse—
 They that do change old love for new,
Pray gods they change for worse!

Both: They that do change &c.

Oenone: Fair and fair &c.

Paris: Fair and fair &c.

Oenone: My love can pipe, my love can sing,
My love can many a pretty thing,
And of his lovely praises ring
My merry, merry roundelays,
 Amen to Cupid's curse,
 They that do change old love for new,
Pray gods they change for worse!

Both: Fair and fair, and twice so fair,
 As fair as any may be;
The fairest shepherd on our green,
 A love for any lady.

The Arraignment of Paris, 1584

"His Golden Locks..."

His golden locks time hath to silver turned;
 O time too swift, O swiftness never ceasing!
His youth 'gainst time and age hath ever spurned,
 But spurned in vain; youth waneth by increasing:
Beauty, strength, youth, are flowers but fading seen;
Duty, faith, love, are roots, and ever green.

His helmet now shall make a hive for bees,
 And, lovers' sonnets turned to holy psalms,
A man-at-arms must now serve on his knees,

And feed on prayers, which are age his alms:
But though from court to cottage he depart,
His saint is sure of his unspotted heart.

And when he saddest sits in homely cell,
   He'll teach his swains this carol for a song—
"Blessed be the hearts that wish my sovereign well,
   Cursed be the souls that think her any wrong."
Goddess, allow this aged man his right,
To be your beadsman now that was your knight.

Polyhymnia, 1590

"Whenas the Rye..."

Whenas the rye reach to the chin,
And chopcherry, chopcherry ripe within,
Strawberries swimming in the cream,
And schoolboys playing in the stream;
Then, O then, O then, O, my true love said,
'Till that time come again
She could not live a maid.

The Old Wives' Tale, 1595

"Not Iris in Her Pride..."

Not Iris in her pride and bravery
Adorns her arch with such variety;
Nor doth the Milk-white Way in frosty night
Appear so fair and beautiful in sight,
As do these fields and groves and sweetest bowers
Bestrewed and decked with parti-coloured flowers.
Along the bubbling brooks and silver glide,
That at the bottom doth in silence slide,
The water-flowers and lilies on the banks
Like blazing comets burgeon all in ranks;
Under the hawthorn and the poplar tree,
Where sacred Phoebe may delight to be,
The primrose and the purple hyacinth,

The dainty violet and the wholesome minth,
The double daisy and the cowslip (Queen
Of summer flowers) do over-peer the green;
And round about the valley as ye pass,
Ye may not see, for peeping flowers, the grass.

The Arraignment of Paris, 1584

FROM *The Love of King David and Fair Bethsabe,*
1599
1.

Absalon: Now for the crown and throne of Israel,
To be confirmed with virtue of my sword,
And writ with David's blood upon the blade.
Now, Jove, let forth the golden firmament
And look on him with all thy fiery eyes,
Which thou hast made to give their glories light.
To show thou lovest the virtue of thy hand,
Let fall a wreath of stars upon my head,
Whose influence may govern Israel
With state exceeding all her other kings.
Fight, lords and captains, that your sovereign's face
May shine in honour brighter than the sun;
And with the virtue of my beauteous rays
Make this fair land as fruitful as the fields
That with sweet milk and honey overflowed.
God, in the whizzing of a pleasant wind,
Shall march upon the tops of mulberry-trees,
To cool all breasts that burn with any griefs;
As whilom he was good to Moses' men,
By day the Lord shall sit within a cloud,
To guide your footsteps to the fields of joy;
And in the night a pillar bright as fire
Shall go before you like a second sun,
Wherein the essence of his Godhead is;
That day and night you may be brought to peace,
And never swerve from that delightsome path
That leads your souls to perfect happiness.
This He shall do for joy when I am king.
Then fight, brave captains, that these joys may fly
Into your bosoms with sweet victory.

2.

Bethsabe: Come, gentle Zephyr, tricked with those perfumes
That erst in Eden sweetened Adam's love,
And stroke my bosom with thy silken fan.
This shade, sun-proof, is yet no proof for thee;
Thy body, smoother than this waveless spring,
And purer than the substance of the same,
Can creep through that his lances cannot pierce:
Thou and thy sister, soft and sacred Air,
Goddess of life and governess of health,
Keep every fountain fresh and arbour sweet;
No brazen gate her passage can repulse,
Nor bushy thicket bar thy subtle breath.
Then deck thee with thy loose delightsome robes,
And on thy wings bring delicate perfumes
To play the wanton with us through the leaves.

3.

David: Now comes my lover tripping like the roe,
And brings my longings tangled in her hair.
To joy her love I'll build a kingly bower,
Seated in hearing of a hundred streams,
That for their homage to her sovereign joys
Shall, as the serpents fold into their nests
In oblique turnings, wind their nimble waves
About the circles of her curious walks;
And with their murmur summon easeful sleep
To lay his golden sceptre on her brows.
Open the doors, and entertain my love;
Open, I say, and, as you open, sing:
Welcome fair Bethsabe, King David's darling.

CHIDIOCK TICHBOURNE
(1558?–1586)

Written the Night before His Execution

My prime of youth is but a frost of cares;
  My feast of joy is but a dish of pain;
My crop of corn is but a field of tares;

And all my good is but vain hope of gain;
My life is fled, and yet I saw no sun;
And now I live, and now my life is done.

The spring is past, and yet it hath not sprung;
    The fruit is dead, and yet the leaves be green;
My youth is gone, and yet I am but young;
    I saw the world, and yet I was not seen;
My thread is cut, and yet it is not spun;
And now I live, and now my life is done.

I sought my death, and found it in my womb,
    I looked for life, and saw it was a shade,
I trod the earth and knew it was my tomb,
    And now I die, and now I am but made:
The glass is full, and now my glass is run,
And now I live, and now my life is done.

ROBERT GREENE

(1560?–1592)

The Shepherd's Wife's Song

Ah, what is love? It is a pretty thing,
As sweet unto a shepherd as a king;
        And sweeter too,
For kings have cares that wait upon a crown,
And cares can make the sweetest love to frown;
        Ah then, ah then,
If country loves such sweet desires do gain,
What lady would not love a shepherd swain?

His flocks are folded, he comes home at night,
As merry as a king in his delight;
        And merrier too,
For kings bethink them what the state require,
When shepherds careless carol by the fire:

Ah then, ah then,
If country loves such sweet desires do gain,
What lady would not love a shepherd swain?

He kisseth first, then sits as blithe to eat
His cream and curds as doth the king his meat;
 And blither too,
For kings have often fears when they do sup,
Where shepherds dread no poison in their cup:
 Ah then, ah then,
If country loves such sweet desires do gain,
What lady would not love a shepherd swain?

To bed he goes, as wanton then, I ween,
As is a king in dalliance with a queen;
 More wanton too,
For kings have many griefs affects to move,
Where shepherds have no greater grief than love:
 Ah then, ah then,
If country loves such sweet desires do gain,
What lady would not love a shepherd swain?

Upon his couch of straw he sleeps as sound,
As doth the king upon his bed of down;
 More sounder too,
For cares cause kings full oft their sleep to spill,
Where weary shepherds lie and snort their fill:
 Ah then, ah then,
If country loves such sweet desires do gain,
What lady would not love a shepherd swain?

Thus with his wife he spends the year, as blithe
As doth the king at every tide or sithe;
 And blither too,
For kings have wars and broils to take in hand,
Where shepherds laugh and love upon the land:
 Ah then, ah then,
If country loves such sweet desires do gain,
What lady would not love a shepherd swain?

Sithe, *time.*

Samela

Like to Diana in her summer-weed,
Girt with a crimson robe of brightest dye,
         Goes fair Samela;

Whiter than be the flocks that straggling feed,
When washed by Arethusa's Fount they lie,
         Is fair Samela;

As fair Aurora in her morning-grey,
Decked with the ruddy glister of her love,
         Is fair Samela;

Like lovely Thetis on a calmèd day,
Whenas her brightness Neptune's fancy move,
         Shines fair Samela;

Her tresses gold, her eyes like glassy streams,
Her teeth are pearl, the breasts are ivory
         Of fair Samela;

Her cheeks like rose and lily, yield forth gleams,
Her brows bright arches framed of ebony:
         Thus fair Samela

Passeth fair Venus in her bravest hue,
And Juno in the show of majesty,
         For she's Samela;

Pallas in wit, all three, if you well view,
For beauty, wit and matchless dignity,
         Yield to Samela.

Weep Not, My Wanton

Weep not, my wanton, smile upon my knee;
When thou art old there's grief enough for thee.
  Mother's wag, pretty boy,
  Father's sorrow, father's joy;
  When thy father first did see

Such a boy by him and me,
He was glad, I was woe;
Fortune changéd made him so,
When he left his pretty boy,
Last his sorrow, first his joy.

Weep not, my wanton, smile upon my knee;
When thou art old there's grief enough for thee.
   Streaming tears that never stint,
   Like pearl-drops from a flint,
   Fell by course from his eyes,
   That one another's place supplies;
   Thus he grieved in every part,
   Tears of blood fell from his heart,
   When he left his pretty boy,
   Father's sorrow, father's joy.

Weep not, my wanton, smile upon my knee;
When thou art old there's grief enough for thee.
   The wanton smiled, father wept,
   Mother cried, baby lept;
   More he crowed, more we cried,
   Nature could not sorrow hide:
   He must go, he must kiss
   Child and mother, baby bliss,
   For he left his pretty boy,
   Father's sorrow, father's joy.
Weep not, my wanton, smile upon my knee;
When thou art old there's grief enough for thee.

A Mind Content

Sweet are the thoughts that savour of content;
   The quiet mind is richer than a crown;
Sweet are the nights in careless slumber spent;
   The poor estate scorns fortune's angry frown:
Such sweet content, such minds, such sleep, such bliss,
Beggars enjoy, when princes oft do miss.

The homely house that harbours quiet rest;
  The cottage that affords no pride nor care;
The mean that 'grees with country music best;
  The sweet consort of mirth and music's fare;
Obscuréd life sets down a type of bliss:
A mind content both crown and kingdom is.

"Ah, Were She Pitiful..."

Ah, were she pitiful as she is fair,
  Or but as mild as she is seeming so,
Then were my hopes greater than my despair,
  Then all the world were heaven, nothing woe.
Ah, were her heart relenting as her hand,
  That seems to melt even with the mildest touch,
Then knew I where to seat me in a land,
  Under wide heavens, but yet there is not such.
So as she shows, she seems the budding rose,
  Yet sweeter far than is an earthly flower,
Sovereign of beauty, like the spray she grows,
  Compassed she is with thorns and cankered bower,
Yet were she willing to be plucked and worn,
She would be gathered, though she grew on thorn.

Ah, when she sings, all music else be still,
  For none must be comparéd to her note;
Ne'er breathed such glee from Philomela's bill,
  Nor from the morning-singer's swelling throat.
Ah, when she riseth from her blissful bed,
  She comforts all the world, as doth the sun,
And at her sight the night's foul vapour's fled;
  When she is set, the gladsome day is done.
O glorious sun, imagine me the west,
Shine in my arms, and set thou on my breast!

Pandosto, the Triumph of Time, 1588?

FROM A Madrigal

The swans, whose pens as white as ivory,
Eclipsing fair Endymion's silver love,
Floating like snow down by the banks of Po,
Ne'er tuned their notes, like Leda once forlorn,
With more despairing sorts of madrigals,
Than I, when wanton Love hath with his gad
Pricked to the core of deep and restless thoughts.

"Sonnet"

Fair is my love, for April is her face,
    Her lovely breasts September claims his part,
And lordly July in her eyes takes place;
    But old December dwelleth in her heart.
Blest be the months that set my thoughts on fire,
Accursed that month that hind'reth my desire!

Like Phoebus' fire, so sparkle both her eyes;
    As air perfumed with amber is her breath;
Like swelling waves her lovely teats do rise;
    As earth her heart, cold, dateth me to death.
Ay me, poor man, that on the earth do live,
When unkind earth death and despair doth give!

In pomp sits Mercy seated in her face;
    Love 'twixt her breasts his trophies doth imprint;
Her eyes shine favour, courtesy and grace;
    But touch her heart, ah, that is framed of flint!
Therefore my harvest in the grass bears grain;
The rock will wear washed with a winter's rain.

GEORGE CHAPMAN

(1560–1634)

Song

O come, soft rest of cares! come, Night!
　Come, naked Virtue's only tire,
The reapéd harvest of the light
　Bound up in sheaves of sacred fire.
　　　Love calls to war;
　　　　Sighs his alarms,
　　　Lips his swords are,
　　　　The field his arms.

Come, Night, and lay thy velvet hand
　On glorious Day's outfacing face;
And all thy crownéd flames command
　For torches to our nuptial grace.
　　　Love calls to war;
　　　　Sighs his alarms,
　　　Lips his swords are,
　　　　The field his arms.

FROM *Bussy d'Ambois*, 1607

1.

Bussy　　As cedars beaten with continual storms,
d'Ambois:　So great men flourish; and do imitate
　　　Unskilful statuaries, who suppose
　　　In forming a Colossus, if they make him
　　　Straddle enough, strut, and look big, and gape,
　　　Their work is goodly: so men merely great
　　　In their affected gravity of voice,
　　　Sourness of countenance, manners' cruelty,
　　　Authority, wealth, and all the spawn of fortune,
　　　Think they bear all the kingdom's worth before
　　　　　them;
　　　Yet differ not from those colossic statues,
　　　Which, with heroic forms without o'erspread,
　　　Within are nought but mortar, flint and lead.

2.

Bussy   I long to know
d'Ambois: How my dear mistress fares, and be informed
          What hand she now doth hold on the troubled blood
          Of her incensèd lord. Methought the Spirit
          When he had uttered his perplexed presage,
          Threw his changed countenance headlong into clouds
          His forehead bent, as he would hide his face;
          He knocked his chin against his darkened breast,
          And struck a churlish silence through his powers.
          Terror of Darkness, O thou King of Flames,
          That with thy music-footed horse dost strike
          The clear light out of crystal, on dark earth;
          And hurl'st instructive fire about the world;
          Wake, wake the drowsy and enchanted night,
          That sleeps with dead eyes in this heavy riddle.
          Or thou, Great Prince of Shades, where never sun
          Sticks his far-darted beams; whose eyes are made
          To see in darkness and see ever best
          Where sense is blinded; open now the heart
          Of thy abashed oracle, that, for fear
          Of some ill it includes, would fain lie hid,
          And rise Thou with it in thy greater light.

FROM *Caesar and Pompey*, 1631

Cato: Poor slaves, how terrible this Death is to them!
          If men would sleep, they would be wroth with all
          That interrupt them; physic take, to take
          The golden rest it brings; both pay and pray
          For good and soundest naps; all friends consenting
          In those kind invocations; praying all
          "Good rest the Gods vouchsafe you." But when Death,
          Sleep's natural brother, comes, that's nothing worse
          But better (being more rich—and keeps the store—
          Sleep ever fickle, wayward still, and poor)
          O, how men grudge and shake and fear and fly
          His stern approaches! all their comforts, taken
          In faith and knowledge of the bliss and beauties

That watch their wakings in an endless life,
Drowned in the pains and horrors of their sense
Sustained but for an hour.

FROM *The Conspiracy of Charles,*
Duke of Byron, 1608

1.

Laffin: As when the moon hath comforted the night,
And set the world in silver of her light,
The planets, asterisms, and whole State of Heaven
In beams of gold descending; all the winds
Bound up in caves, charged not to drive abroad
Their cloudy heads; and universal peace
(Proclaimed in silence) of the quiet earth:
Soon as her hot and dry fumes are let loose,
Storms and clouds mixing suddenly put out
The eyes of all these glories; the creation
Turned into chaos; and we then desire
For all our joy of life the death of sleep.
So, when the glories of our lives (men's loves,
Clear consciences, our fames and loyalties)
That did us worthy comfort are eclipsed,
Grief and disgrace invade us; and for all
Our night of life besides, our misery craves
Dark earth would ope and hide us in our graves.

2.

Byron: Give me a spirit that on life's rough sea
Loves to have his sails filled with a lusty wind,
E'en till his sail-yards tremble, his masts crack,
And his rapt ship run on her side so low
That she drinks water and her keel ploughs air.
There is no danger to a man that knows
What life and death is; there's not any law
Exceeds his knowledge; neither is it lawful
That he should stoop to any other law.
He goes before them, and commands them all,
That to himself is a law rational.

FROM *The Sixth Book of Homer's Iliads*

She, with his sight made breathless haste to meet him; she,
    whose grace
Brought him withal so great a dower; she that of all the race
Of King Aetion only lived; Aetion whose house stood
Beneath the mountain Placius, environed with the wood
Of Theban Hypoplace, being court to the Cilician land.
She ran to Hector, and with her, tender of heart and hand
Her son, borne in his nurse's arms; when, like a heavenly sign
Compact of many golden stars, the princely child did shine,
Whom Hector called Scamandrius; but whom the town did
    name
Astyanax, because his sire did only prop the same.
Hector, though grief bereft his speech, yet smiled upon his joy.
Andromache cried out, mixed hands, and to the strength of
    Troy
Thus wept forth her affection: "O noblest in desire,
Thy mind, inflamed with others' good, will set thyself on fire;
Nor pitiest thou thy son, nor wife who must thy widow be,
If now thou issue; all the field will only run on thee.
Better my shoulders underwent the earth than thy decease;
For then would earth bear joys no more; then comes the black
    increase
Of griefs, like Greeks on Ilion. Alas, what one survives
To be my refuge? one black day bereft seven brothers' lives,
By stern Achilles; by his hand my father breathed his last,
His high-walled rich Cilician Thebes sacked by him and laid
    waste
The royal body yet he left unspoiled; religion charmed
That act of spoil; and all in fire he burned him complete
    armed;
Built over him a royal tomb; and to the monument
He left of him, th' Oreades (that are the high descent
Of aegis-bearing Jupiter) another of their own
Did add to it, and set it round with elms; by which is shown
In theirs the barrenness of death; yet might it serve beside
To shelter the sad monument from all the ruffinous pride
Of storms and tempests, used to hurt things of that noble kind.

The short life yet my mother lived he saved, and served his
    mind
With all the riches of the realm; which not enough esteemed
He kept her prisoner; whom small time but much more wealth
    redeemed;
And she in sylvan Hypoplace Cilicia ruled again,
But soon was overruled by death; Diana's chaste disdain
Gave her a lance, and took her life. Yet, all these gone from me
Thou amply render'st all; thy life makes still my father be,
My mother, brothers; and besides thou art my husband too,
Most loved, most worthy. Pity then, dear love, and do not go,
For, thou gone, all these go again; pity our common joy,
Lest, of a father's patronage, the bulwark of all Troy,
Thou leavest him a poor widow's charge; stay, stay then, in
    this tower,
And call up to the wild fig-tree all thy retired power;
For there the wall is easiest scaled, and fittest for surprise,
And there th' Ajaces, Idomen, th' Atrides, Diomed, thrice
Have both surveyed and made attempt; I know not if induced
By some wise augur, or the fact was naturally infused
Into their wits or courages." To this great Hector said:
"Be well assured, wife, all these things in my kind cares are
    weighed.
But what a shame and fear it is to think how Troy would
    scorn
(Both in her husbands and her wives, whom long-trained
    gowns adorn)
That I should cowardly fly off! The spirit I first did breathe
Did never teach me that; much less, since the contempt of
    death
Was settled in me, and my mind knew what a worthy was,
Whose office is to lead in fight, and give no danger pass
Without improvement. In this fire must Hector's trial shine;
Here must his country, father, friends, be in him made divine.
And such a stormy day shall come (in mind and soul I know)
When sacred Troy shall shed her towers, for tears of over-
    throw;
When Priam, all his birth and power, shall in those tears be
    drowned.
But neither Troy's posterity so much my soul doth wound,
Priam, nor Hecuba herself, nor all my brothers' woes

(Who though so many and so good must all be food for foes)
As thy sad state; when some rude Greek shall lead thee
          weeping hence,
These free days clouded, and a night of captive violence
Loading thy temples out of which thine eyes must never see,
But spin the Greek wives' webs of task, and their fetch-water
          be
To Argos, from Messeides, or clear Hyperia's spring;
Which howsoever thou abhorr'st, Fate's such a shrewish thing
She will be mistress; whose cursed hands, when they shall
          crush out cries
From thy oppressions (being beheld by other enemies)
Thus they will nourish thy extremes: 'This dame was Hector's
          wife,
A man that at the wars ot Troy did breathe the worthiest life
Of all their army.' This again will rub thy fruitful wounds,
To miss the man that to thy bands could give such narrow
          bounds.
But that day shall not wound mine eyes; the solid heap of
          night
Shall interpose, and stop mine ears against thy plaints and
          plight."
This said, he reached to take his son; who, of his arms afraid,
And then the horse-hair plume, with which he so was overlaid,
Nodded so horribly, he clinged back to his nurse and cried.
Laughter affected his great sire, who doffed and laid aside
His fearful helm, that on the earth cast round about it light;
Then took and kissed his loving son, and, balancing his weight
In dancing him, these loving vows to living Jove he used. . . .

ROBERT SOUTHWELL

(1561?–1595)

The Burning Babe

As I in hoary winter's night
    Stood shivering in the snow,
Surprised I was with sudden heat
    Which made my heart to glow;
And lifting up a fearful eye
    To view what fire was near,

A pretty babe all burning bright
  Did in the air appear;
Who, scorchéd with excessive heat,
  Such floods of tears did shed,
As though His floods should quench His flames,
  Which with His tears were fed.
"Alas!" quoth He, "but newly born
  In fiery heats I fry,
Yet none approach to warm their hearts
  Or feel my fire but I!
My faultless breast the furnace is,
  The fuel wounding thorns;
Love is the fire, and sighs the smoke,
  The ashes shame and scorns;
The fuel Justice layerh on,
  And Mercy blows the coals;
The metal in this furnace wrought
  Are men's defiléd souls.
For which, as now on fire I am,
  To work them to their good,
So will I melt into a bath
  To wash them in My blood."
With this He vanished out of sight,
  And swiftly shrunk away,
And straight I calléd unto mind
  That it was Christmas Day.

The Virgin Mary to Christ on the Cross

What mist hath dimmed that glorious face!
  What seas of grief my sun doth toss!
The golden rays of heavenly grace
  Lies now eclipséd on the cross.

Jesus! my Love, my Son, my God,
  Behold Thy mother washed in tears;
Thy bloody wounds be made a rod
  To chasten these my latter years.

You cruel Jews, come work your ire
　Upon this worthless flesh of mine;
And kindle not eternal fire
　By wounding Him which is divine.

Thou messenger that didst impart
　His first descent into my womb,
Come, help me now to cleave my heart,
　That there I may my Son entomb.

You angels all, that present were
　To show His birth with harmony,
Why are you not now ready here
　To make a mourning symphony?

The cause I know; you wail alone
　And shed your tears in secrecy,
Lest I should movéd be to moan
　By force of heavy company.

But wail, my soul, thy comfort dies;
　My woeful womb, lament thy fruit;
My heart, give tears unto my eyes,
　Let Sorrow string my heavy lute.

FROM *The Image of Death*

The gown which I do use to wear,
　The knife wherewith I cut my meat,
And eke that old and ancient chair
　Which is my only usual seat,
All these do tell me I must die,
And yet my life amend not I.

My ancestors are turned to clay,
　And many of my mates are gone;
My youngers daily drop away,
　And can I think to 'scape alone?
No, no, I know that I must die,
And yet my life amend not I.

Not Solomon, for all his wit,
   Nor Samson, though he were so strong,
No king nor person ever yet
   Could 'scape, but Death laid him along;
Wherefore I know that I must die,
And yet my life amend not I.

Though all the East did quake to hear
   Of Alexander's dreadful name,
And all the West did likewise fear
   To hear of Julius Caesar's fame,
Yet both by Death in dust now lie;
Who then can 'scape, but he must die?

If none can 'scape Death's dreadful dart,
   If rich and poor his beck obey;
If strong, if wise, if all do smart,
   Then I to 'scape shall have no way.
Oh! grant me grace, O God! that I
My life may mend, sith I must die.

HENRY CONSTABLE
(1562?–1613?)

Damelus' Song to His Diaphenia

Diaphenia, like the daffadowndilly,
White as the sun, fair as the lily,
   Heighho, how I do love thee!
I do love thee as my lambs
Are belovéd of their dams:
   How blest were I if thou wouldst prove me!

Diaphenia, like the spreading roses,
That in thy sweets all sweets encloses,
   Fair sweet, how I do love thee!
I do love thee as each flower
Loves the sun's life-giving power;
   For dead, thy breath to life might move me.

Diaphenia, like to all things blesséd,
When all thy praises are expresséd,
   Dear joy, how I do love thee!
As the birds do love the Spring,
Or the bees their careful king:
   Then in requite, sweet virgin, love me!

SAMUEL DANIEL

(1562–1619)

"Love Is a Sickness..."

Love is a sickness full of woes,
   All remedies refusing;
A plant that with most cutting grows,
   Most barren with best using.
           Why so?
More we enjoy it, more it dies,
If not enjoyed, it sighing cries,
           Heigh-ho!

Love is a torment of the mind,
   A tempest everlasting;
And Jove hath made it of a kind
   Not well, nor full nor fasting.
           Why so?
More we enjoy it, more it dies,
If not enjoyed, it sighing cries,
           Heigh-ho!

Ulysses and the Siren

Siren: Come, worthy Greek, Ulysses, come,
        Possess these shores with me;
     The winds and seas are troublesome,
        And here we may be free.
     Here may we sit and view their toil
        That travail in the deep,
     And joy the day in mirth the while,
        And spend the night in sleep.

Ulysses: Fair nymph, if fame or honour were
       To be attained with ease,
   Then would I come and rest with thee,
       And leave such toils as these.
   But here it dwells, and here must I
       With danger seek it forth,
   To spend the time luxuriously
       Becomes not men of worth.

Siren: Ulysses, Oh be not deceived
       With that unreal name;
   This honour is a thing conceived,
       And rests on others' fame;
   Begotten only to molest
       Our peace and to beguile,
   The best thing of our life, our rest,
       And give us up to toil.

Ulysses: Delicious nymph, suppose there were
       Nor honour, nor report,
   Yet manliness would scorn to wear
       The time in idle sport.
   For toil doth give a better touch
       To make us feel our joy;
   And ease finds tediousness as much
       As labour yields annoy.

Siren: Then pleasure likewise seems the shore
       Whereto tends all your toil,
   Which you forgo to make it more,
       And perish oft the while.
   Who may disport them diversely
       Find never tedious day,
   And ease may have variety
       As well as action may.

Ulysses: But natures of the noblest frame
       These toils and dangers please,
   And they take comfort in the same
       As much as you in ease.

And with the thought of actions past
    Are recreated still;
When pleasure leaves a touch at last
    To show that it was ill.

Siren: That doth opinion only cause,
    That's out of custom bred,
Which makes us many other laws
    Than ever Nature did.
No widows wail for our delights,
    Our sports are without blood,
The world we see by warlike wights
    Receives more ill than good.

Ulysses: But yet the state of things require
    These motions of unrest,
And these great Spirits of high desire
    Seem born to turn them best;
To purge the mischiefs that increase
    And all good order mar;
For oft we see a wicked peace
    To be well changed for war.

Siren: Well, well, Ulysses, then I see
    I shall not have thee here,
And therefore I will come to thee,
    And take my fortunes there.
I must be won that cannot win,
    Yet lost were I not won;
For beauty hath created been
    T' undo or be undone.

Sonnets

1.

Fair is my love and cruel as she's fair;
Her brow-shades frown, although her eyes are sunny.
Her smiles are lightning, though her pride despair,
And her disdains are gall, her favours honey;
A modest maid, decked with a blush of honour,
Whose feet do tread green paths of youth and love,

The wonder of all eyes that look upon her,
Sacred on earth, designed a saint above.
Chastity and beauty, which were deadly foes,
Live reconciléd friends within her brow;
And had she pity to conjoin with those,
Then who had heard the plaints I utter now?
For had she not been fair, and thus unkind,
My Muse had slept, and none had known my mind.

2.

Beauty, sweet love, is like the morning dew,
Whose short refresh upon the tender green
Cheers for a time, but till the sun doth show,
And straight 'tis gone as it had never been.
Soon doth it fade that makes the fairest flourish,
Short is the glory of the blushing rose;
The hue which thou so carefully dost nourish,
Yet which at length thou must be forced to lose.
When thou, surcharged with burthen of thy years,
Shall bend thy wrinkles homeward to the earth;
And that, in beauty's lease expired, appears
The date of age, the calends of our death—
But ah, no more!—this must not be foretold,
For women grieve to think they must be old.

3.

Let others sing of knights and paladins
In agéd accents and untimely words,
Paint shadows in imaginary lines,
Which well the reach of their high wit records;
But I must sing of thee, and those fair eyes
Authentic shall my verse in time to come;
When yet th'unborn shall say, Lo, where she lies!
Whose beauty made him speak that else was dumb!
These are the arcs, the trophies I erect,
That fortify thy name against old age;
And these thy sacred virtues must protect
Against the dark and time's consuming rage.
Though th'error of my youth in them appear,
Suffice they show I lived and loved thee dear.

4.

Care-charmer sleep, son of the sable night,
Brother to death, in silent darkness born,
Relieve my languish and restore the light,
With dark forgetting of my cares return.
And let the day be time enough to mourn
The shipwreck of my ill-adventured youth;
Let waking eyes suffice to wail their scorn,
Without the torment of the night's untruth.
Cease, dreams, the images of day desires,
To model forth the passions of the morrow;
Never let rising sun approve you liars,
To add more grief to aggravate my sorrow.
Still let me sleep, embracing clouds in vain,
And never wake to feel the day's disdain.

JOSHUA SYLVESTER

(1563–1618)

Sonnet

Were I as base as is the lowly plain
And you, my love, as high as heav'n above,
Yet should the thoughts of me your humble swain
Ascend to heav'n in honour of my love.
Were I as high as heav'n above the plain,
And you, my love, as humble and as low
As are the deepest bottoms of the main,
Wheresoe'er you were, with you my love should go.
Were you the earth, dear love, and I the skies,
My love should shine on you like to the sun,
And look upon you with ten thousand eyes,
Till heav'n waxed blind and till the world were dun.
Wheresoe'er I am, below or else above you,
Wheresoe'er you are, my heart shall truly love you.

MICHAEL DRAYTON

(1563–1631)

FROM *The Shepherd's Garland*

Batte: Gorbo, as thou cam'st this way
By yonder little hill,
Or as thou through the fields didst stray,
Saw'st thou my Daffodil?

She's in a frock of Lincoln green,
The colour maids delight,
And never hath her beauty seen
But through a veil of white;

Than roses richer to behold
That trim up lovers' bowers,
The pansy and the marigold
Though Phoebus' paramours.

Gorbo: Thou well describ'st the daffodil;
It is not full an hour
Since by the spring near yonder hill
I saw that lovely flower.

Batte: Yet my fair flower thou didst not meet,
Nor news of her didst bring,
And yet my Daffodil's more sweet
Than that by yonder spring.

Gorbo: I saw a shepherd that doth keep
In yonder field of lilies,
Was making, as he fed his sheep,
A wreath of daffodillies.

Batte: Yet, Gorbo, thou delud'st me still;
My flower thou didst not see;
For, know, my pretty Daffodil
Is worn of none but me.

To show itself but near her seat
No lily is so bold,
Except to shade her from the heat
Or keep her from the cold.

Gorbo: Through yonder vale as I did pass,
Descending from the hill,
I met a smirking bonny lass,
They call her Daffodil,

Whose presence as along she went
The pretty flowers did greet,
As though their heads they downward bent
With homage to her feet.

And all the shepherds that were nigh,
From top of every hill,
Unto the valleys low did cry:
"There goes sweet Daffodil!"

Batte: Ay, gentle shepherd, now with joy
Thou all my flocks dost fill,
That's she alone, kind shepherd's boy;
Let us to Daffodil.

To His Coy Love

I pray thee leave, love me no more,
    Call home the heart you gave me,
I but in vain that saint adore,
    That can, but will not save me.
These poor half kisses kill me quite;
    Was ever man thus served?
Amidst an ocean of delight
    For pleasure to be sterved.

Show me no more those snowy breasts
    With azure riverets branchéd,
Where, whilst mine eye with plenty feasts,
    Yet is my thirst not stanchéd.

O Tantalus, thy pains ne'er tell,
    By me thou art prevented,
'Tis nothing to be plagued in hell,
    But thus in heaven tormented.

Clip me no more in those dear arms,
    Nor thy life's comfort call me;
O, these are but too pow'rful charms,
    And do but more enthral me.
But see, how patient I am grown,
    In all this coil about thee;
Come, nice thing, let my heart alone,
    I cannot live without thee.

To the Virginian Voyage

You brave heroic minds,
Worthy your country's name,
    That honour still pursue;
    Go and subduc
Whilst loit'ring hinds
Lurk here at home with shame.

Britons, you stay too long;
Quickly abroad bestow you,
    And with a merry gale
    Swell your stretch'd sail,
With vows as strong
As the winds that blow you.

Your course securely steer,
West and by south forth keep;
    Rocks, lee-shores, nor shoals,
    When Eolus scowls,
You need not fear,
So absolute the deep

And, cheerfully at sea,
Success you still entice,
   To get the pearl and gold,
   And ours to hold,
VIRGINIA,
Earth's only paradise.

Where Nature hath in store
Fowl, venison and fish,
   And the fruitfull'st soil,
   Without your toil,
Three harvests more,
All greater than your wish.

And the ambitious vine
Crowns with his purple mass
   The cedar reaching high
   To kiss the sky,
The cypress, pine,
And useful sassafras.

To whom the golden age
Still Nature's laws doth give,
   No other cares that tend,
   But them to defend
From winter's rage,
That long there doth not live.

When as the luscious smell
Of that delicious land,
   Above the sea's that flows,
   The clear wind throws,
Your hearts to swell
Approaching the dear strand.

In kenning of the shore,
(Thanks to God first given)
   O you, the happiest men,
   Be frolic then,
Let cannons roar,
Frighting the wide heaven.

And as there plenty grows
Of laurel everywhere,
 Apollo's sacred tree.
 You may it see
A poet's brows
To crown, that may sing there.

Thy voyages attend
Industrious Hakluyt,
 Whose reading shall inflame
 Men to seek fame,
And much commend
To after-times thy wit.

FROM *Nimphidia, the Court of Fayrie*

Pigwiggen was this fairy knight,
One wondrous gracious in the sight
Of fair Queen Mab, which day and night
 He amorously observed;
Which made king Oberon suspect
His service took too good effect,
His sauciness and often checkt,
 And could have wished him starved.

Pigwiggen gladly would commend
Some token to queen Mab to send,
If sea or land him aught could lend
 Were worthy of her wearing;
At length this lover doth devise
A bracelet made of emmets' eyes,
A thing he thought that she would prize,
 No whit her state impairing.

And to the queen a letter writes,
Which he most curiously indites,
Conjuring her by all the rites
 Of love she would be pleased

To meet him, her true servant, where
They might without suspect or fear,
Themselves to one another clear,
  And have their poor hearts eased.

At midnight, the appointed hour,
And for the queen a fitting bower
(Quoth he) is that fair cowslip flower
  On Hipcut hill that groweth.
In all your train there's not a fay
That ever went to gather may
But she hath made it in her way,
  The tallest there that groweth.

When by Tom Thumb, a fairy page,
He sent it, and doth him engage
By promise of a mighty wage
  It secretly to carry;
Which done, the queen her maids doth call,
And bids them to be ready all,
She would go see her summer hall,
  She could no longer tarry.

Her chariot ready straight is made,
Each thing therein is fitting laid,
That she by nothing might be stayed,
  For naught must be her letting;
Four nimble gnats the horses were,
Their harnesses of gossamer,
Fly Cranion her charioteer,
  Upon the coach-box getting.

Her chariot of a snail's fine shell,
Which for the colours did excel,
The fair queen Mab becoming well,
  So lively was the limning;
The seat, the soft wool of the bee;
The cover, gallantly to see,
The wing of a pied butterfly,
  I trow 'twas simple trimming.

The wheels compos'd of crickets' bones,
And daintily made for the nones,
For fear of rattling on the stones,
　　　With thistle-down they shod it;
For all her maidens much did fear,
If Oberon had chanced to hear
That Mab his queen should have been there,
　　　He would not have abode it.

She mounts her chariot with a trice,
Nor would she stay for no advice,
Until her maids that were so nice,
　　　To wait on her were fitted;
But run herself away alone,
Which, when they heard, there was not one
But hasted after to be gone,
　　　As she had been diswitted.

Hop and Mop and Drop so clear,
Pip and Trip and Skip that were
To Mab their sovereign ever dear,
　　　Her special maids of honour;
Fib and Tib and Pink and Pin,
Tick and Quick and Jill and Jin,
Tit and Nit and Wap and Win,
　　　The train that wait upon her.

Upon a grasshopper they got,
And what with amble and with trot
For hedge nor ditch they sparéd not,
　　　But after her they hie them.
A cobweb over them they throw
To shield the wind if it should blow,
Themselves they wisely could bestow,
　　　Lest any should espy them.

Sonnets

1.

If chaste and pure devotion of my youth
Or glory of my April-springing years,
Unfeignéd love in naked simple truth,

A thousand vows, a thousand sighs and tears;
Or if a world of faithful service done,
Words, thoughts and deeds devoted to her honour,
Or eyes that have beheld her as their sun,
With admiration ever looking on her;
A life that never joyed but in her love,
A soul that ever hath adored her name,
A faith that time nor fortune could not move.
A Muse that unto heaven hath raised her fame:
Though these, nor these, deserve to be embraced,
Yet, fair unkind, too good to be disgraced.

2.

Sweet secrecy, what tongue can tell thy worth?
What mortal pen sufficiently can praise thee?
What curious pencil serves to limn thee forth?
What Muse hath power above thy height to raise thee?
Strong lock of kindness, closet of love's store,
Heart's mithridate, the soul's preservative,
O virtue! which all virtues do adore,
Chief good, from whom all good things we derive.
O rare effect! true bond of friendship's measure,
Conceit of angels, which all wisdom teachest,
O richest casket of all heavenly treasure,
In secret silence which such wonders preachest.
O purest mirror, wherein men may see
The lively image of divinity.

3.

Into these loves who but for passion looks,
At this first sight here let him lay them by,
And seek elsewhere in turning other books
Which better may his labour satisfy.
No far-fetched sigh shall ever wound my breast,
Love from mine eye a tear shall never wring,
Nor in Ah-mes! my whining sonnets drest,
A libertine fantastic'ly I sing;

My verse is the true image of my mind,
Ever in motion, still desiring change,
To choice of all variety inclined,
And in all humours sportively I range;
My active Muse is of the world's right strain,
That cannot long one fashion entertain.

4.

To nothing fitter can I thee compare
Than to the son of some rich pennyfather,
Who having now brought on his end with care
Leaves to his son all he had heaped together;
This new rich novice, lavish of his chest,
To one man gives, and on another spends,
Then here he riots, yet among the rest
Haps to lend some to one true honest friend.
Thy gifts thou in obscurity dost waste,
False friends thy kindness, born but to deceive thee,
Thy love, that is on the unworthy placed;
Time hath thy beauty which with age will leave thee:
Only that little which to me was lent
I give thee back, when all the rest is spent.

5.

Whilst thus my pen strives to eternise thee,
Age rules my lines with wrinkles in my face,
Where in the map of all my misery
Is modelled out the world of my disgrace;
Whilst in despite of tyrannising times,
Medea-like I make thee young again;
Proudly thou scorn'st my world-outwearing rhymes
And murder'st virtue with thy coy disdain.
And though in youth my youth untimely perish
To keep thee from oblivion and the grave,
Ensuing ages yet my rhymes shall cherish,
Where I entombed my better part shall save;
And though this earthly body fade and die,
My name shall mount upon eternity.

6.

Dear, why should you command me to my rest
When now the night doth summon all to sleep?
Methinks this time becometh lovers best,
Night was ordained together friends to keep.
How happy are all other living things,
Which though the day disjoin by several flight,
The quiet evening yet together brings
And each returns unto his love at night.
O thou that art so courteous unto all,
Why shouldst thou, Night, abuse me only thus,
That every creature to his kind dost call,
And yet 'tis thou dost only sever us?
Well could I wish it would be ever day,
If when night comes you bid me go away.

7.

Since there's no help, come, let us kiss and part.
Nay, I have done. You get no more of me.
And I am glad, yea, glad with all my heart,
That thus so cleanly I myself can free.
Shake hands for ever, cancel all our vows;
And when we meet at any time again,
Be it not seen in either of our brows
That we one jot of former love retain.
Now at the last gasp of Love's latest breath,
When, his pulse failing, Passion speechless lies,
When Faith is kneeling by his bed of death,
And Innocence is closing up his eyes,
Now, if thou would'st, when all have given him over,
From death to life thou might'st him yet recover.

CHRISTOPHER MARLOWE

(1564–1593)

The Passionate Shepherd to His Love

Come live with me, and be my love,
And we will all the pleasures prove
That hills and valleys, dales and fields,
And all the craggy mountains yields.

And we will sit upon the rocks,
Seeing the shepherds feed their flocks
By shallow rivers, to whose falls
Melodious birds sing madrigals.

And I will make thee beds of roses,
And a thousand fragrant posies,
A cap of flowers and a kirtle
Embroider'd all with leaves of myrtle.

A gown made of the finest wool
Which from our pretty lambs we pull,
Fair linéd slippers for the cold,
With buckles of the purest gold;

A belt of straw and ivy-buds,
With coral clasps and amber studs,
And if these pleasures may thee move,
Come live with me, and be my love.

Thy silver dishes for thy meat,
As precious as the gods do eat,
Shall on an ivory table be
Prepar'd each day for thee and me.

The shepherd swains shall dance and sing
For thy delight each May-morning;
If these delights thy mind may move,
Then live with me, and be my love.

Reply

By SIR WALTER RALEIGH

If all the world and love were young,
And truth in every shepherd's tongue,
These pretty pleasures might me move
To live with thee and be thy love.

But Time drives flocks from field to fold
When rivers rage and rocks grow cold,
And Philomel becometh dumb;
The rest complains of cares to come.

The flowers do fade, and wanton fields
To wayward winter reckoning yields;
A honey tongue, a heart of gall,
Is fancy's spring but sorrow's fall.

Thy gowns, thy shoes, the beds of roses,
Thy cap, thy kirtle, and thy posies,
Soon break, soon wither, soon forgotten
In folly ripe, in reason rotten.

Thy belt of straw and ivy-buds,
Thy coral clasps and amber studs,
All these in me no means can move
To come to thee and be thy love.

But could youth last and love still breed,
Had joy no date nor age no need,
Then these delights my mind might move
To live with thee and be thy love.

FROM *Hero and Leander*

On this feast day, O curséd day and hour,
Went Hero thorough Sestos, from her tower
To Venus' temple, where unhappily,
As after chanc'd, they did each other spy.
So fair a church as this, had Venus none:
The walls were of discoloured jasper stone,
Wherein was Proteus carvéd, and o'erhead
A lively vine of green sea-agate spread;
Where by one hand, light-headed Bacchus hung,
And with the other, wine from grapes outwrung.
Of crystal shining fair the pavement was;
The town of Sestos call'd it Venus' glass.
There might you see the gods in sundry shapes,

Committing heady riots, incest, rapes:
For know, that underneath this radiant floor
Was Danae's statue in a brazen tower,
Jove slily stealing from his sister's bed,
To dally with Idalian Ganymed;
And for his love, Europa, bellowing loud,
And tumbling with the Rainbow in a cloud:
Blood-quaffing Mars heaving the iron net
Which limping Vulcan and his Cyclops set:
Love kindling fire, to burn such towns as Troy,
Sylvanus weeping for the lovely boy
That now is turn'd into a cypress tree,
Under whose shade the wood-gods love to be.
And in the midst a silver altar stood;
There Hero sacrificing turtles' blood,
Vail'd to the ground, vailing her eyelids close,
And modestly they opened as she rose:
Thence flew Love's arrow with the golden head,
And thus Leander was enamouréd.
Stone still he stood, and evermore he gazed,
Till with the fire that from his count'nance blazed,
Relenting Hero's gentle heart was strook:
Such force and virtue hath an amorous look.

It lies not in our power to love, or hate,
For will in us is over-rul'd by fate.
When two are stript, long ere the course begin,
We wish that one should lose, the other win;
And one especially do we affect
Of two gold ingots, like in each respect.
The reason no man knows; let it suffice,
What we behold is censur'd by our eyes.
Where both deliberate, the love is slight;
Who ever lov'd, that lov'd not at first sight?

FROM *The First Part of Tamburlaine the Great*

1.

Tamburlaine: Disdains Zenocrate to live with me?
Or you, my lords, to be my followers?
Think you I weigh this treasure more than you?

Not all the wealth in India's wealthy arms
Shall buy the meanest soldier in my train.
Zenocrate, lovelier than the love of Jove,
Brighter than is the silver Rhodope,
Fairer than whitest snow on Scythian hills,
Thy person is more worth to Tamburlaine
Than the possession of the Persian crown,
Which gracious stars have promis'd at my birth.
A hundred Tartars shall attend on thee,
Mounted on steeds swifter than Pegasus.
Thy garments shall be made of Median silk,
Enchas'd with precious jewels of mine own,
More rich and valorous than Zenocrate's.
With milk-white harts upon an ivory sled
Thou shalt be drawn amidst the frozen pools,
And scale the icy mountains' lofty tops,
Which with thy beauty will be soon resolv'd.
My martial prizes, with five hundred men,
Won on the fifty-headed Volga's waves,
Shall we all offer to Zenocrate,
And then myself to fair Zenocrate.

2.

Tamburlaine: The thirst of reign and sweetness of a crown,
That caused the eldest son of heavenly Ops
To thrust his doting father from his chair
And place himself in the imperial heaven,
Mov'd me to manage arms against thy state,
What better precedent than mighty Jove?
Nature, that fram'd us of four elements
Warring within our breasts for regiment,
Doth teach us all to have aspiring minds:
Our souls, whose faculties can comprehend
The wondrous architecture of the world,
And measure every wandering planet's course,
Still climbing after knowledge infinite,
And always moving as the restless spheres,
Wills us to wear ourselves and never rest,
Until we reach the ripest fruit of all,
That perfect bliss and sole felicity,
The sweet fruition of an earthly crown.

3.

Tamburlaine: Those wallèd garrisons will I subdue,
And write myself great lord of Africa.
So from the East unto the furthest West
Shall Tamburlaine extend his puissant arm.
The galleys and those pilling brigandines,
That yearly sail to the Venetian gulf,
And hover in the straits for Christians' wreck,
Shall lie at anchor in the Isle Asant,
Until the Persian fleet and men-of-war,
Sailing along the oriental sea,
Have fetched about the Indian continent,
Even from Persepolis to Mexico,
And thence unto the Straits of Jubalter,
Where they shall meet and join their force in
one
Keeping in awe the bay of Portingale,
And all the ocean by the British shore;
And by this means I'll win the world at last.

4.

Tamburlaine: Ah, fair Zenocrate, divine Zenocrate,
Fair is too foul an epithet for thee,
That in thy passion for thy country's love,
And fear to see thy kingly father's harm,
With hair dishevelled wip'st thy watery cheeks;
And like to Flora in her morning pride,
Shaking her silver tresses in the air,
Rain'st on the earth resolvèd pearl in showers,
And sprinklest sapphires on thy shining face,
Where Beauty, mother to the Muses, sits,
And comments volumes on her ivory pen,
Taking instructions from thy flowing eyes,
Eyes, when that Ebena steps to heaven,
In silence of thy solemn evening's walk,
Making the mantle of the richest night,
The moon, the planets, and the meteors, light.
There angels in their crystal armours fight
A doubtful battle with my tempted thoughts

For Egypt's freedom and the Soldan's life,
His life that so consumes Zenocrate;
Whose sorrows lay more siege unto my soul
Than all my army to Damascus' walls;
And neither Persia's sovereign nor the Turk
Troubled my senses with conceit of foil
So much by much as doth Zenocrate.
What is beauty, saith my sufferings, then?
If all the pens that ever poets held
Had fed the feeling of their masters' thoughts,
And every sweetness that inspir'd their hearts,
Their minds and muses on admiréd themes;
If all the heavenly quintessence they still
From the immortal flowers of poesy,
Wherein as in a mirror we perceive
The highest reaches of a human wit--
If these had made one poem's period,
And all combin'd in beauty's worthiness,
Yet should there hover in their restless heads
One thought, one grace, one wonder, at the
    least,
Which into words no virtue can digest.

FROM *The Second Part of Tamburlaine the Great*

1.

Tamburlaine: Black is the beauty of the brightest day;
    The golden ball of heaven's eternal fire,
    That danc'd with glory on the silver waves,
    Now wants the fuel that inflamed his beams,
    And all with faintness and for foul disgrace,
    He binds his temples with a frowning cloud,
    Ready to darken earth with endless night.
    Zenocrate, that gave him light and life,
    Whose eyes shot fire from their ivory bowers,
    And tempered every soul with lively heat,
    Now by the malice of the angry skies,
    Whose jealousy admits no second mate,
    Draws in the comfort of her latest breath,
    All dazzled with the hellish mists of death.

Now walk the angels on the walls of heaven,
As sentinels to warn th'immortal souls
To entertain divine Zenocrate:
Apollo, Cynthia, and the ceaseless lamps
That gently look'd upon this loathsome earth,
Shine downwards now no more, but deck the
      heavens
To entertain divine Zenocrate:
The crystal springs, whose taste illuminates
Refinéd eyes with an eternal sight,
Like triéd silver run through Paradise
To entertain divine Zenocrate:
The cherubins and holy seraphins,
That sing and play before the King of Kings,
Use all their voices and their instruments
To entertain divine Zenocrate:
And in this sweet and curious harmony,
The god that tunes this music to our souls
Holds out his hand in highest majesty
To entertain divine Zenocrate.

2.

Tamburlaine: Forward, then, ye jades!
Now crouch, ye kings of greatest Asia,
And tremble when ye hear this scourge will
      come
That whips down cities and controlleth crowns,
Adding their wealth and treasure to my store.
The Euxine sea, north to Natolia;
The Terrene, west; the Caspian, north north-
      east;
And on the south, Sinus Arabicus;
Shall all be loaden with the martial spoils
We will convey with us to Persia.
Then shall my native city Samarcanda,
And crystal waves of fresh Jaertis' stream,
The pride and beauty of her princely seat,
Be famous through the furthest continents;
For there my palace royal shall be plac'd,
Whose shining turrets shall dismay the heavens,

And cast the fame of Ilion's tower to hell;
Thorough the streets, with troops of conquered
    kings,
I'll ride in golden armour like the sun;
And in my helm a triple plume shall spring,
Spangled with diamonds, dancing in the air,
To note me emperor of the three-fold world;
Like to an almond tree ymounted high
Upon the lofty and celestial mount
Of ever green Selinus, quaintly decked
With blooms more white than Herycina's
    brows,
Whose tender blossoms tremble every one
At every little breath that thorough heaven
    is blown.
Then in my coach, like Saturn's royal son
Mounted his shining chariot gilt with fire,
And drawn with princely eagles through the
    path
Pav'd with bright crystal and enchas'd with
    stars
Where all the gods stand gazing at his pomp,
So will I ride through Samarcanda streets,
Until my soul, dissevered from this flesh,
Shall mount the milk-white way, and meet him
    there.
To Babylon, my lords, to Babylon!

FROM *The Tragical History of Doctor Faustus*
1.
    (*Enter Helen again, passing over the stage*)

Faustus: Was this the face that launch'd a thousand ships,
And burnt the topless towers of Ilium?—
Sweet Helen, make me immortal with a kiss.—
               (*She kisses him*)
Her lips suck forth my soul: see where it flies!—
Come, Helen, come, give me my soul again.
Here will I dwell, for heaven is in those lips,
And all is dross that is not Helena.

I will be Paris, and for love of thee,
Instead of Troy, shall Wittenberg be sack'd;
And I will combat with meek Menelaus,
And wear thy colours on my pluméd crest:
Yea, I will wound Achilles in the heel,
And then return to Helen for a kiss.
O, thou art fairer than the evening air
Clad in the beauty of a thousand stars;
Brighter art thou than flaming Jupiter
When he appear'd to hapless Semele;
More lovely than the monarch of the sky
In wanton Arethusa's azured arms;
And none but thou shalt be my paramour!

2.

Faustus: Ah, Faustus,
Now hast thou but one bare hour to live,
And then thou must be damn'd perpetually!
Stand still, you ever-moving spheres of heaven,
That time may cease, and midnight never come;
Fair Nature's eye, rise, rise again, and make
Perpetual day; or let this hour be but
A year, a month, a week, a natural day,
That Faustus may repent and save his soul!
O lente, lente currite, noctis equi!
The stars move still, time runs, the clock will
    strike,
The devil will come, and Faustus must be damn'd.
O, I'll leap up to my God!—Who pulls me down?—
See, see, where Christ's blood streams in the firma-
    ment!
One drop would save my soul, half a drop: ah, my
    Christ!—
Ah, rend not my heart for naming of my Christ!
Yet will I call on him: O, spare me, Lucifer!—
Where is it now! 'tis gone: and see, where God
Stretcheth out his arm, and bends his ireful brows!
Mountains and hills, come, come, and fall on me,
And hide me from the heavy wrath of God!

No, no!
Then will I headlong run into the earth:
Earth, gape! O, no, it will not harbour me!
You stars that reign'd at my nativity,
Whose influence hath allotted death and hell,
Now draw up Faustus, like a foggy mist,
Into the entrails of yon lab'ring cloud
That, when you vomit forth into the air,
My limbs may issue from your smoky mouths,
So that my soul may but ascend to heaven!
                                    (*The watch strikes*)
Ah, half the hour is past! 'twill all be passed anon.
O God,
If thou wilt not have mercy on my soul,
Yet for Christ's sake, whose blood hath ransom'd me,
Impose some end to my incessant pain;
Let Faustus live in hell a thousand years,
A hundred thousand, and at last be sav'd!
O, no end is limited to damnéd souls!
Why wert thou not a creature wanting soul?
Or why is this immortal that thou hast?
Ah, Pythagoras' metempsychosis, were that true,
This soul should fly from me, and I be changed
Unto some brutish beast! all beasts are happy,
For, when they die,
Their souls are soon dissolved in elements;
But mine must live still to be plagu'd in hell.
Curs'd be the parents that engendered me!
No, Faustus, curse thyself, curse Lucifer
That hath depriv'd thee of the joys of heaven.
                              (*The clock striketh twelve*)
O, it strikes, it strikes! Now, body, turn to air,
Or Lucifer will bear thee quick to hell!
O soul, be changed into little water-drops,
And fall into the ocean, ne'er be found!
                        (*Thunder and enter the Devils*)
My God, my God, look not so fierce on me!
Adders and serpents, let me breathe a while!
Ugly hell, gape not! come not, Lucifer!
I'll burn my book!—Ah, Mephistophilis!
                              (*The Devils hale him off*)

3.

EPILOGUE

Chorus: Cut is the branch that might have grown full
        straight,
And burnéd is Apollo's laurel-bough,
That sometime grew within this learned man.
Faustus is gone: regard his hellish fall,
Whose fiendful fortune may exhort the wise,
Only to wonder at unlawful things,
Whose deepness doth entice such forward wits
To practise more than heavenly power permits.

FROM *Edward the Second*

Gaveston: I must have wanton poets, pleasant wits,
Musicians, that with touching of a string
May draw the pliant king which way I please.
Music and poetry are his delight;
Therefore I'll have Italian masques by night,
Sweet speeches, comedies, and pleasing shows;
And in the day, when he shall walk abroad,
Like sylvan nymphs my pages shall be clad;
My men, like satyrs grazing on the lawns,
Shall with their goat-feet dance the antic hay.
Sometimes a lovely boy in Dian's shape,
With hair that gilds the water as it glides,
Crownets of pearl about his naked arms,
And in his sportful hands an olive tree
To hide those parts which men delight to see,
Shall bathe him in a spring, and there hard by,
One like Acteon, peeping through the grove,
Shall by the angry goddess be transformed,
And running in the likeness of a hart,
By yelping hounds pulled down, shall seem to die;
Such things as these best please his majesty.

WILLIAM SHAKESPEARE

(1564–1616)

Song

Who is Silvia? what is she,
   That all our swains commend her?
Holy, fair, and wise is she;
   The heaven such grace did lend her,
That she might admiréd be.

Is she kind as she is fair?
   For beauty lives with kindness.
Love doth to her eyes repair,
   To help him of his blindness,
And, being help'd, inhabits there.

Then to Silvia let us sing,
   That Silvia is excelling;
She excels each mortal thing
   Upon the dull earth dwelling:
To her let us garlands bring.

The Two Gentlemen of Verona

Sonnet

Did not the heavenly rhetoric of thine eye,
   'Gainst whom the world cannot hold argument,
Persuade my heart to this false perjury?
   Vows for thee broke deserve not punishment.
A woman I forswore; but I will prove,
   Thou being a goddess, I forswore not thee:
My vow was earthly, thou a heavenly love;
   Thy grace being gain'd cures all disgrace in me.
Vows are but breath, and breath a vapour is:
   Then thou, fair sun, which on my earth dost shine,
Exhalest this vapour-vow; in thee it is:
   If broken then, it is no fault of mine:
If by me broke, what fool is not so wise
To lose an oath to win a paradise?

Love's Labour's Lost

"On a Day—Alack the Day!"

On a day—alack the day!—
Love, whose month is ever May,
Spied a blossom passing fair
Playing in the wanton air:
Through the velvet leaves the wind,
All unseen, can passage find;
That the lover, sick to death,
Wish himself the heaven's breath.
Air, quoth he, thy cheeks may blow;
Air, would I might triumph so!

But, alack, my hand is sworn
Ne'er to pluck thee from thy thorn;
Vow, alack, for youth unmeet,
Youth so apt to pluck a sweet!
Do not call it sin in me,
That I am forsworn for thee;
Thou for whom e'en Jove would swear
Juno but an Ethiop were,
And deny himself for Jove,
Turning mortal for thy love.

Love's Labour's Lost

Spring

When daisies pied and violets blue
   And lady-smocks all silver-white
And cuckoo buds of yellow hue
   Do paint the meadows with delight,
The cuckoo then, on every tree,
Mocks married men; for thus sings he,
      Cuckoo;
Cuckoo, cuckoo: O word of fear,
Unpleasing to a married ear.

When shepherds pipe on oaten straws,
   And merry larks are ploughmen's clocks,
When turtles tread, and rooks, and daws,
   And maidens bleach their summer smocks,

The cuckoo then, on every tree,
Mocks married men; for thus sings he,
  Cuckoo;
Cuckoo, cuckoo; O word of fear,
Unpleasing to a married ear.

Love's Labour's Lost

Winter

When icicles hang by the wall,
 And Dick the shepherd blows his nail,
And Tom bears logs into the hall,
 And milk comes frozen home in pail,
When blood is nipp'd and ways be foul,
Then nightly sings the staring owl,
  Tu-whit;
Tu-who, a merry note,
While greasy Joan doth keel the pot.

When all aloud the wind doth blow,
 And coughing drowns the parson's saw,
And birds sit brooding in the snow,
 And Marion's nose looks red and raw,
When roasted crabs hiss in the bowl,
Then nightly sings the staring owl,
  Tu-whit;
Tu-who, a merry note,
While greasy Joan doth keel the pot.

Love's Labour's Lost

"Over Hill, over Dale"

Over hill, over dale,
 Thorough bush, thorough briar,
Over park, over pale,
 Thorough flood, thorough fire,
I do wander everywhere,
Swifter than the moonë's sphere;

And I serve the fairy queen,
To dew her orbs upon the green.
The cowslips tall her pensioners be:
In their gold coats spots you see;
Those be rubies, fairy favours,
In those freckles live their savours:
I must go seek some dewdrops here,
And hang a pearl in every cowslip's ear.
Farewell, thou lob of spirits; I'll be gone:
Our queen and all her elves come here anon.

A Midsummer-Night's Dream

"You Spotted Snakes..."

First Fairy: You spotted snakes with double tongue,
   Thorny hedgehogs, be not seen;
   Newts and blind-worms, do no wrong,
   Come not near our fairy queen.

Chorus: Philomel, with melody
   Sing in our sweet lullaby;
  Lulla, lulla, lullaby, lulla, lulla, lullaby:
    Never harm,
    Nor spell, nor charm,
   Come our lovely lady nigh;
   So, good night, with lullaby.

First Fairy: Weaving spiders, come not here;
   Hence, you long-legg'd spinners, hence!
   Beetles black, approach not near;
   Worm nor snail, do no offence.

Chorus: Philomel, with melody
   Sing in our sweet lullaby.

A Midsummer-Night's Dream

"The Ousel Cock..."

The ousel cock so black of hue,
   With orange-tawny bill,
The throstle with his note so true,
   The wren with little quill;

The finch, the sparrow, and the lark,
   The plain-song cuckoo gray,
Whose note full many a man doth mark,
   And dares not answer nay.

A Midsummer-Night's Dream

"Now the Hungry Lion Roars"

Now the hungry lion roars,
   And the wolf behowls the moon;
Whilst the heavy ploughman snores,
   All with weary task foredone.
Now the wasted brands do glow,
   Whilst the screech-owl, screeching loud,
Puts the wretch that lies in woe
   In remembrance of a shroud.
Now it is the time of night,
   That the graves, all gaping wide,
Every one lets forth his sprite,
   In the church-way paths to glide:
And we fairies, that do run
   By the triple Hecate's team,
From the presence of the sun,
   Following darkness like a dream,
Now are frolic: not a mouse
Shall disturb this hallow'd house:
I am sent with broom before,
To sweep the dust behind the door.

A Midsummer-Night's Dream

"Tell Me Where Is Fancy Bred"

Tell me where is fancy bred,
Or in the heart or in the head?
How begot, how nourishéd?
    Reply, reply.
It is engender'd in the eyes,
With gazing fed; and fancy dies
In the cradle where it lies.
    Let us all ring fancy's knell;
    I'll begin it—Ding, dong, bell.

All: Ding, dong, bell.

                                The Merchant of Venice

"Sigh No More, Ladies..."

Sigh no more, ladies, sigh no more,
    Men were deceivers ever,
One foot in sea and one on shore,
    To one thing constant never:
Then sigh not so, but let them go,
    And be you blithe and bonny,
Converting all your sounds of woe
    Into Hey nonny, nonny.

Sing no more ditties, sing no moe,
    Of dumps so dull and heavy;
The fraud of men was ever so,
    Since summer first was leafy:
Then sigh not so, but let them go,
    And be you blithe and bonny,
Converting all your sounds of woe
    Into Hey nonny, nonny.

                                Much Ado about Nothing

"Pardon, Goddess of the Night"

Pardon, goddess of the night,
Those that slew thy virgin knight;
For the which, with songs of woe,
Round about her tomb they go.
    Midnight, assist our moan;
    Help us to sigh and groan,
        Heavily, heavily:
    Graves, yawn, and yield your dead,
    Till death be utteréd,
        Heavily, heavily.

Much Ado about Nothing

"Under the Greenwood Tree"

Under the greenwood tree
Who loves to lie with me,
And turn his merry note
Unto the sweet bird's throat,
Come hither, come hither, come hither:
  Here shall he see
  No enemy
But winter and rough weather.

Who doth ambition shun,
And loves to live i' the sun,
Seeking the food he eats,
And pleased with what he gets,
Come hither, come hither, come hither:
  Here shall he see
  No enemy
But winter and rough weather.

As You Like It

"If It Do Come to Pass"

If it do come to pass
That any man turn ass,
Leaving his wealth and ease
A stubborn will to please,
Ducdame, ducdame, ducdame:
Here shall he see
Gross fools as he,
And if he will come to me.

As You Like It

"Blow, Blow, Thou Winter Wind"

Blow, blow, thou winter wind,
Thou art not so unkind
   As man's ingratitude;
Thy tooth is not so keen,
Because thou art not seen,
   Although thy breath be rude.
Heigh-ho! sing, heigh-ho! unto the green holly:
Most friendship is feigning, most loving mere folly:
   Then, heigh-ho, the holly!
   This life is most jolly.

Freeze, freeze, thou bitter sky,
That dost not bite so nigh
   As benefits forgot:
Though thou the waters warp,
Thy sting is not so sharp
   As friends remember'd not.
Heigh-ho! sing, heigh-ho! unto the green holly:
Most friendship is feigning, most loving mere folly:
   Then, heigh-ho, the holly!
   This life is most jolly.

As You Like It

"What Shall He Have..."

What shall he have that kill'd the deer?
His leather skin and horns to wear.
  Then sing him home:
Take thou no scorn to wear the horn;
It was a crest ere thou wast born:
Thy father's father wore it,
And thy father bore it:
The horn, the horn, the lusty horn
Is not a thing to laugh to scorn.

As You Like It

"It Was a Lover and His Lass"

It was a lover and his lass,
  With a hey, and a ho, and hey nonino,
That o'er the green corn-field did pass
  In the spring time, the only pretty ring time,
When birds do sing, hey ding a ding, ding:
Sweet lovers love the spring.

Between the acres of the rye,
  With a hey, and a ho, and a hey nonino,
These pretty country folk would lie,
  In the spring time, the only pretty ring time,
When birds do sing, hey ding a ding, ding:
Sweet lovers love the spring.

This carol they began that hour,
  With a hey, and a ho, and a hey nonino,
How that a life was but a flower
  In the spring time, the only pretty ring time,
When birds do sing, hey ding a ding, ding,
Sweet lovers love the spring.

And therefore take the present time,
    With a hey, and a ho, and a hey nonino,
For love is crowned with the prime
    In the spring time, the only pretty ring time,
When birds do sing, hey ding a ding, ding,
Sweet lovers love the spring.

                                As You Like It

"Wedding Is Great Juno's Crown"

Wedding is great Juno's crown:
    O blessed bond of board and bed!
'Tis Hymen peoples every town:
    High wedlock then be honouréd:
Honour, high honour and renown,
To Hymen, god of every town!

                                As You Like It

"O Mistress Mine..."

O Mistress mine, where are you roaming?
O, stay and hear; your true love's coming,
    That can sing both high and low:
Trip no further, pretty sweeting;
Journeys end in lovers meeting,
    Every wise man's son doth know.

What is love? 'Tis not hereafter;
Present mirth hath present laughter;
    What's to come is still unsure:
In delay there lies no plenty;
Then, come kiss me, sweet and twenty,
    Youth's a stuff will not endure.

                                Twelfth Night

"Come Away, Come Away, Death"

Come away, come away, death,
  And in sad cypress let me be laid;
Fly away, fly away, breath;
  I am slain by a fair cruel maid.
My shroud of white, stuck all with yew,
      O, prepare it!
My part of death, no one so true
      Did share it.

Not a flower, not a flower sweet,
  On my black coffin let there be strown;
Not a friend, not a friend greet
  My poor corpse, where my bones shall be thrown:
A thousand thousand sighs to save,
      Lay me, O, where,
Sad true lover never find my grave,
      To weep there!

Twelfth Night

"When That I Was and a Little Tiny Boy"

When that I was and a little tiny boy,
  With hey, ho, the wind and the rain,
A foolish thing was but a toy,
  For the rain it raineth every day.

But when I came to man's estate,
  With hey, ho, the wind and the rain,
'Gainst knaves and thieves men shut the gate,
  For the rain it raineth every day.

But when I came, alas! to wive,
  With hey, ho, the wind and the rain,
By swaggering could I never thrive,
  For the rain it raineth every day.

But when i came unto my beds,
   With hey, ho, the wind and the rain,
With toss-pots still had drunken heads,
   For the rain it raineth every day.

A great while ago the world begun,
   With hey, ho, the wind and the rain,
But that's all one, our play is done,
   And we'll strive to please you every day.

Twelfth Night

"How Should I Your True Love Know"

How should I your true love know
   From another one?
By his cockle hat and staff
   And his sandal shoon.

He is dead and gone, lady,
   He is dead and gone;
At his head a grass-green turf,
   At his heels a stone.

White his shroud as the mountain snow,
   Larded with sweet flowers;
Which bewept to the grave did go
   With true-love showers.

Hamlet

"To-morrow Is Saint Valentine's Day"

To-morrow is Saint Valentine's day,
   All in the morning betimes,
And I a maid at your window,
   To be your Valentine.

Then up he rose, and donn'd his clothes,
   And dupp'd the chamber-door;
Let in the maid, that out a maid
   Never departed more.

Hamlet

"And Will A' Not Come Again?"

And will a' not come again?
And will a' not come again?
  No, no, he is dead,
  Go to thy death-bed,
He never will come again.

His beard was as white as snow,
All flaxen was his poll:
  He is gone, he is gone,
  And we cast away moan:
God ha' mercy on his soul!

Hamlet

"Fie on Sinful Fantasy!"

Fie on sinful fantasy!
Fie on lust and luxury!
Lust is but a bloody fire,
Kindled with unchaste desire,
Fed in heart, whose flames aspire,
As thoughts do blow them, higher and higher.
Pinch him, fairies, mutually;
Pinch him for his villany;
Pinch him, and burn him, and turn him about,
Till candles and starlight and moonshine be out.

The Merry Wives of Windsor

"For I the Ballad Will Repeat"

For I the ballad will repeat,
  Which men full true shall find;
Your marriage comes by destiny,
  Your cuckoo sings by kind.

All's Well That Ends Well

"Take, O Take Those Lips Away"

Take, O take those lips away,
   That so sweetly were forsworn;
And those eyes, the break of day,
   Lights that do mislead the morn:
But my kisses bring again, bring again;
Seals of love, but seal'd in vain, seal'd in vain.

                              Measure for Measure

"The Cod-Piece That Will House"

The cod-piece that will house
   Before the head has any,
The head and he shall louse;
   So beggars marry many.
The man that makes his toe
   What he his heart should make
Shall of a corn cry woe,
   And turn his sleep to wake.

                              King Lear

"He That Has and a Little Tiny Wit"

He that has and a little tiny wit,—
With hey, ho, the wind and the rain,—
Must make content with his fortune's fit,
For the rain it raineth every day.

                              King Lear

"When Priests Are More in Word..."

When priests are more in word than matter;
When brewers mar their malt with water;
When nobles are their tailors' tutors;
No heretics burn'd, but wenches' suitors;
When every case in law is right;

No squire in debt, nor no poor knight;
When slanders do not live in tongues,
Nor cutpurses come not to throngs;
When usurers tell their gold i' the field,
And bawds and whores do churches build;
Then shall the realm of Albion
Come to great confusion:
Then comes the time, who lives to see't,
That going shall be used with feet.

King Lear

"Come, Thou Monarch..."

Come, thou monarch of the vine,
Plumpy Bacchus with pink eyne!
In thy fats our cares be drown'd,
With thy grapes our hairs be crown'd:
Cup us, till the world go round,
Cup us, till the world go round!

Antony and Cleopatra

"Hark, Hark! the Lark..."

Hark, hark! the lark at heaven's gate sings,
    And Phoebus 'gins arise,
His steeds to water at those springs
    On chaliced flowers that lies;
And winking Mary-buds begin
    To ope their golden eyes;
With every thing that pretty is,
    My lady sweet, arise:
        Arise, arise!

Cymbeline

"*Fear No More...*"

Fear no more the heat o' the sun,
   Nor the furious winter's rages;
Thou thy worldly task hast done,
   Home art gone and ta'en thy wages:
Golden lads and girls all must,
As chimney-sweepers, come to dust.

Fear no more the frown o' the great;
   Thou art past the tyrant's stroke;
Care no more to clothe and eat;
   To thee the reed is as the oak:
The sceptre, learning, physic, must
All follow this and come to dust.

Fear no more the lightning-flash,
   Nor the all-dreaded thunder-stone;
Fear not slander, censure rash;
   Thou hast finish'd joy and moan:
All lovers young, all lovers must
Consign to thee and come to dust.

No exorciser harm thee!
Nor no witchcraft charm thee!
Ghost unlaid forbear thee!
Nothing ill come near thee!
Quiet consummation have;
And renownéd be thy grave!

                                        Cymbeline

"When Daffodils Begin to Peer"

When daffodils begin to peer,
   With heigh! the doxy over the dale,
Why, then comes in the sweet o' the year;
   For the red blood reigns in the winter's pale.

The white sheet bleaching on the hedge,
　With heigh! the sweet birds, O, how they sing!
Doth set my pugging tooth on edge;
　For a quart of ale is a dish for a king.

The lark, that tirra-lyra chants,
　With heigh! with heigh! the thrush and the jay,
Are summer songs for me and my aunts,
　While we lie tumbling in the hay.

The Winter's Tale

"Jog On, Jog On..."

Jog on, jog on, the foot-path way,
　And merrily hent the stile-a:
A merry heart goes all the day,
　Your sad tires in a mile-a.

The Winter's Tale

"Lawn as White as Driven Snow"

Lawn as white as driven snow;
Cypress black as e'er was crow;
Gloves as sweet as damask roses;
Masks for faces and for noses;
Bugle bracelet, necklace amber,
Perfume for a lady's chamber;
Golden coifs and stomachers,
For my lads to give their dears;
Pins and poking-sticks of steel,
What maids lack from head to heel:
Come, buy of me, come; come buy, come buy;
Buy, lads, or else your lasses cry:
Come buy.

The Winter's Tale

"Will You Buy Any Tape"

Will you buy any tape,
  Or lace for your cape,
My dainty duck, my dear-a?
  Any silk, any thread,
  Any toys for your head,
Of the new'st, and finest, finest wear-a?
  Come to the pedlar;
  Money's a medlar,
That doth utter all men's ware-a.

The Winter's Tale

"Come unto These Yellow Sands"

Come unto these yellow sands,
  And then take hands:
Courtsied when you have and kiss'd
  The wild waves whist:
Foot it featly here and there;
And, sweet sprites, the burthen bear.
    Hark, hark!

Bow-wow.
The watch-dogs bark.
Bow-wow.
Hark, hark! I hear
The strain of strutting chanticleer
Cry, cock-a-diddle-dow.

The Tempest

"Full Fathom Five..."

Full fathom five thy father lies;
  Of his bones are coral made;
Those are pearls that were his eyes:
  Nothing of him that doth fade,
But doth suffer a sea-change

Into something rich and strange.
Sea-nymphs hourly ring his knell:
                    Ding-dong.
Hark! now I hear them—Ding-dong, bell.

The Tempest

"No More Dams I'll Make..."

No more dams I'll make for fish;
    Nor fetch in firing
    At requiring;
Nor scrape trencher, nor wash dish:
    'Ban, 'Ban, Ca-Caliban
    Has a new master—get a new man.

The Tempest

"The Master, the Swabber..."

The master, the swabber, the boatswain, and I,
    The gunner, and his mate,
Loved Mall, Meg, and Marian, and Margery,
    But none of us cared for Kate;
    For she had a tongue with a tang,
    Would cry to a sailor, Go hang!
She loved not the savour of tar nor of pitch;
Yet a tailor might scratch her where'er she did itch.
    Then, to sea, boys, and let her go hang!

The Tempest

"You Nymphs, Call'd Naiads..."

You nymphs, call'd Naiads, of the windring brooks,
With your sedged crowns and ever-harmless looks,
Leave your crisp channels, and on this green land
Answer your summons; Juno does command:
Come, temperate nymphs, and help to celebrate
A contract of true love; be not too late.

You sunburn'd sicklemen, of August weary,
Come hither from the furrow, and be merry:
Make holiday; your rye-straw hats put on,
And these fresh nymphs encounter every one
In country footing.

The Tempest

"Where the Bee Sucks..."

Where the bee sucks, there suck I:
In a cowslip's bell I lie;
There I couch when owls do cry.
On the bat's back I do fly
After summer merrily.
Merrily, merrily shall I live now
Under the blossom that hangs on the bough.

The Tempest

Sonnets

VIII

Music to hear, why hear'st thou music sadly?
Sweets with sweets war not, joy delights in joy.
Why lovest thou that which thou receivest not gladly?
Or else receiv'st with pleasure thine annoy?
If the true concord of well tunéd sounds,
By unions married, do offend thine ear,
They do but sweetly chide thee, who confounds
In singleness the parts that thou shouldst bear.
Mark how one string, sweet husband to another,
Strikes each in each by mutual ordering;
Resembling sire and child and happy mother,
Who, all in one, one pleasing note do sing:
Whose speechless song, being many, seeming one,
Sings this to thee: "Thou single wilt prove none."

XII

When I do count the clock that tells the time,
And see the brave day sunk in hideous night;
When I behold the violet past prime,
And sable curls all silver'd o'er with white;
When lofty trees I see barren of leaves,
Which erst from heat did canopy the herd,
And summer's green all girded up in sheaves,
Borne on the bier with white and bristly beard.
Then of thy beauty do I question make,
That thou among the wastes of time must go,
Since sweets and beauties do themselves forsake
And die as fast as they see others grow;
And nothing 'gainst Time's scythe can make defence
Save breed, to brave him when he takes thee hence

XVIII

Shall I compare thee to a summer's day?
Thou art more lovely and more temperate:
Rough winds do shake the darling buds of May,
And summer's lease hath all too short a date:
Sometimes too hot the eye of heaven shines,
And often is his gold complexion dimm'd;
And every fair from fair sometime declines,
By chance or nature's changing course untrimm'd;
But thy eternal summer shall not fade,
Nor lose possession of that fair thou owest;
Nor shall Death brag thou wander'st in his shade,
When in eternal lines to time thou growest:
So long as men can breathe, or eyes can see,
So long lives this, and this gives life to thee.

XXIX

When, in disgrace with fortune and men's eyes,
I all alone beweep my outcast state,
And trouble deaf heaven with my bootless cries.
And look upon myself, and curse my fate,
Wishing me like to one more rich in hope,
Featured like him, like him with friends possessed,
Desiring this man's art and that man's scope,

With what I most enjoy contented least;
Yet in these thoughts myself almost despising,
Haply I think on thee, and then my state,
Like to the lark at break of day arising
From sullen earth, sings hymns at heaven's gate;
For thy sweet love remembered such wealth brings
That then I scorn to change my state with kings.

XXX

When to the sessions of sweet silent thought
I summon up remembrance of things past,
I sigh the lack of many a thing I sought,
And with old woes new wail my dear time's waste:
Then can I drown an eye, unused to flow,
For precious friends hid in death's dateless night,
And weep afresh love's long since cancelled woe,
And moan the expense of many a vanished sight:
Then can I grieve at grievances foregone,
And heavily from woe to woe tell o'er
The sad account of fore-bemoaned moan,
Which I new pay as if not paid before.
But if the while I think on thee, dear friend,
All losses are restored and sorrows end.

XXXIII

Full many a glorious morning have I seen
Flatter the mountain-tops with sovereign eye,
Kissing with golden face the meadows green,
Gilding pale streams with heavenly alchemy;
Anon permit the basest clouds to ride
With ugly rack on his celestial face,
And from the forlorn world his visage hide,
Stealing unseen to west with this disgrace:
Even so my sun one early morn did shine
With all-triumphant splendour on my brow;
But, out, alack! he was but one hour mine,
The region cloud hath masked him from me now.
Yet him for this my love no whit disdaineth;
Suns of the world may stain when heaven's sun staineth.

LIII

What is your substance, whereof are you made,
That millions of fair shadows on you tend?
Since every one hath, every one, one shade,
And you, but one, can every shadow lend.
Describe Adonis, and the counterfeit
Is poorly imitated after you;
On Helen's cheek all art of beauty set,
And you in Grecian tires are painted new:
Speak of the spring and foison of the year,
The one doth shadow of your beauty show,
The other as your bounty doth appear;
And you in every blessed shape we know.
In all external grace you have some part,
But you like none, none you, for constant heart.

LIV

O, how much more doth beauty beauteous seem
By that sweet ornament which truth doth give!
The rose looks fair, but fairer we it deem
For that sweet odour which doth in it live.
The canker-blooms have full as deep a dye
As the perfuméd tincture of the roses,
Hang on such thorns, and play as wantonly
When summer's breath their maskéd buds discloses:
But, for their virtue only is their show,
They live unwoo'd and unrespected fade;
Die to themselves. Sweet roses do not so;
Of their sweet deaths are sweetest odours made:
And so of you, beauteous and lovely youth,
When that shall vade, my verse distils your truth.

LV

Not marble, nor the gilded monuments
Of princes, shall outlive this powerful rhyme;
But you shall shine more bright in these contents
Than unswept stone, besmeared with sluttish time.
When wasteful war shall statues overturn,
And broils root out the work of masonry,
Nor Mars his sword nor war's quick fire shall burn

The living record of your memory.
'Gainst death and all-oblivious enmity
Shall you pace forth; your praise shall still find room
Even in the eyes of all posterity
That wear this world out to the ending doom.
So, till the judgement that yourself arise,
You live in this, and dwell in lovers' eyes.

LVII

Being your slave, what should I do but tend
Upon the hours and times of your desire?
I have no precious time at all to spend,
Nor services to do, till you require.
Nor dare I chide the world-without-end hour
Whilst I, my sovereign, watch the clock for you.
Nor think the bitterness of absence sour
When you have bid your servant once adieu;
Nor dare I question with my jealous thought
Where you may be, or your affairs suppose,
But like a sad slave, stay and think of nought,
Save, where you are how happy you make those.
So true a fool is love that in your will,
Though you do anything, he thinks no ill.

LX

Like as the waves make toward the pebbled shore,
So do our minutes hasten to their end;
Each changing place with that which goes before,
In sequent toil all forwards do contend.
Nativity, once in the main of light,
Crawls to maturity, wherewith being crowned,
Crooked eclipses 'gainst his glory fight,
And Time that gave doth now his gift confound.
Time doth transfix the flourish set on youth
And delves the parallels in beauty's brow,
Feeds on the rarities of nature's truth,
And nothing stands but for his scythe to mow:
And yet to times in hope my verse shall stand,
Praising thy worth, despite his cruel hand.

LXIV

When I have seen by Time's fell hand defac'd
The rich-proud cost of outworn buried age;
When sometime lofty towers I see down-razed,
And brass eternal slave to mortal rage;
When I have seen the hungry ocean gain
Advantage on the kingdom of the shore,
And the firm soil win of the watery main,
Increasing store with loss, and loss with store;
When I have seen such interchange of state,
Or state itself confounded to decay;
Ruin hath taught me thus to ruminate—
That Time will come and take my love away.
This thought is as a death, which cannot choose
But weep to have that which it fears to lose.

LXVI

Tired with all these, for restful death I cry,
As, to behold desert a beggar born,
And needy nothing trimmed in jollity,
And purest faith unhappily forsworn,
And gilded honour shamefully misplaced,
And maiden virtue rudely strumpeted,
And right perfection wrongfully disgraced,
And strength by limping sway disabled,
And art made tongue-tied by authority,
And folly, doctor-like, controlling skill,
And simple truth miscalled simplicity,
And captive good attending captain ill:
Tired with all these, from these would I be gone,
Save that, to die, I leave my love alone.

LXXI

No longer mourn for me when I am dead
Than you shall hear the surly sullen bell
Give warning to the world that I am fled
From this vile world, with vilest worms to dwell:
Nay, if you read this line, remember not
The hand that writ it; for I love you so,
That I in your sweet thoughts would be forgot,

If thinking on me then should make you woe.
O, if, I say, you look upon this verse
When I perhaps compounded am with clay,
Do not so much as my poor name rehearse,
But let your love even with my life decay;
Lest the wise world should look into your moan
And mock you with me after I am gone.

LXXIII

That time of year thou mayst in me behold
When yellow leaves, or none, or few, do hang
Upon those boughs which shake against the cold,
Bare ruined choirs, where late the sweet birds sang
In me thou see'st the twilight of such day
As after sunset fadeth in the west;
Which by and by black night doth take away,
Death's second self, that seals up all in rest.
In me thou see'st the glowing of such fire,
That on the ashes of his youth doth lie,
As the death-bed whereon it must expire,
Consumed with that which it was nourished by.
This thou perceivest, which makes thy love more strong.
To love that well which thou must leave ere long.

LXXXVII

Farewell! thou art too dear for my possessing,
And like enough thou know'st thy estimate:
The charter of thy worth gives thee releasing;
My bonds in thee are all determinate.
For how do I hold thee but by thy granting?
And for that riches where is my deserving?
The cause of this fair gift in me is wanting,
And so my patent back again is swerving.
Thyself thou gavest, thy own worth then not knowing,
Or me, to whom thou gavest it, else mistaking;
So thy great gift, upon misprision growing,
Comes home again, on better judgement making.
Thus have I had thee, as a dream doth flatter,
In sleep a king, but waking no such matter.

XCIV

They that have power to hurt and will do none,
That do not do the thing they most do show;
Who, moving others, are themselves as stone,
Unmovéd, cold and to temptation slow;
They rightly do inherit heaven's graces
And husband nature's riches from expense;
They are the lords and owners of their faces.
Others but stewards of their excellence.
The summer's flower is to the summer sweet,
Though to itself it only live and die,
But if that flower with base infection meet,
The basest weed outbraves his dignity:
For sweetest things turn sourest by their deeds;
Lilies that fester smell far worse than weeds.

XCVIII

From you have I been absent in the spring,
When proud-pied April, dressed in all his trim,
Hath put a spirit of youth in everything,
That heavy Saturn laughed and leaped with him.
Yet nor the lays of birds, nor the sweet smell
Of different flowers in odour and in hue,
Could make me any summer's story tell,
Or from their proud lap pluck them where they grew:
Nor did I wonder at the lily's white,
Nor praise the deep vermilion of the rose;
They were but sweet, but figures of delight,
Drawn after you, you pattern of all those.
Yet seemed it winter still, and, you away,
As with your shadow I with these did play.

CII

My love is strengthened, though more weak in seeming;
I love not less, though less the show appear:
That love is merchandized whose rich esteeming
The owner's tongue doth publish everywhere.
Our love was new, and then but in the spring,
When I was wont to greet it with my lays;
As Philomel in summer's front doth sing,

And stops her pipe in growth of riper days:
Not that the summer is less pleasant now
Than when her mournful hymns did hush the night,
But that wild music burthens every bough,
And sweets grown common lose their dear delight.
Therefore, like her, I sometime hold my tongue,
Because I would not dull you with my song.

CIV

To me, fair friend, you never can be old,
For as you were when first your eye I eyed,
Such seems your beauty still. Three winters cold
Have from the forests shook three summers' pride,
Three beauteous springs to yellow autumn turned
In process of the seasons have I seen,
Three April perfumes in three hot Junes burned,
Since first I saw you fresh, which yet are green.
Ah, yet doth beauty, like a dial-hand,
Steal from his figure, and no pace perceived;
So your sweet hue, which methinks still doth stand,
Hath motion, and mine eye may be deceived:
For fear of which, hear this, thou age unbred;
Ere you were born was beauty's summer dead.

CVI

When in the chronicle of wasted time
I see descriptions of the fairest wights,
And beauty making beautiful old rhyme
In praise of ladies dead and lovely knights,
Then, in the blazon of sweet beauty's best,
Of hand, of foot, of lip, of eye, of brow,
I see their antique pen would have expressed
Even such a beauty as you master now.
So all their praises are but prophecies
Of this our time, all you prefiguring;
And, for they looked but with divining eyes,
They had not skill enough your worth to sing:
For we, which now behold these present days,
Have eyes to wonder, but lack tongues to praise.

CX

Alas, 'tis true I have gone here and there,
And made myself a motley to the view,
Gored mine own thoughts, sold cheap what is most dear,
Made old offences of affections new;
Most true it is that I have looked on truth
Askance and strangely: but, by all above,
These blenches gave my heart another youth,
And worse essays proved thee my best of love.
Now all is done, have what shall have no end:
Mine appetite I never more will grind
On newer proof, to try an older friend,
A god in love, to whom I am confined.
Then give me welcome, next to my heaven the best,
Even to thy pure and most most loving breast.

CXVI

Let me not to the marriage of true minds
Admit impediments. Love is not love
Which alters when it alteration finds,
Or bends with the remover to remove:
O, no! it is an ever-fixéd mark,
That looks on tempests and is never shaken;
It is the star to every wandering bark,
Whose worth's unknown, although his height be taken.
Love's not Time's fool, though rosy lips and cheeks
Within his bending sickle's compass come;
Love alters not with his brief hours and weeks,
And bears it out even to the edge of doom.
If this be error and upon me proved,
I never writ, nor no man ever loved.

CXXIX

Th' expense of spirit in a waste of shame
Is lust in action; and till action, lust
Is perjured, murderous, bloody, full of blame,
Savage, extreme, rude, cruel, not to trust;
Enjoy'd no sooner but despiséd straight;
Past reason hunted; and, no sooner had,
Past reason hated, as a swallow'd bait

On purpose laid to make the taker mad:
Mad in pursuit, and in possession so;
Had, having, and in quest to have, extreme;
A bliss in proof, and proved, a very woe;
Before, a joy proposed; behind, a dream.
All this the world well knows; yet none knows well
To shun the heaven that leads men to this hell.

CXXXVIII

When my love swears that she is made of truth,
I do believe her, though I know she lies,
That she might think me some untutored youth,
Unlearnéd in the world's false subtleties.
Thus vainly thinking that she thinks me young,
Although she knows my days are past the best,
Simply I credit her false-speaking tongue:
On both sides thus is simple truth suppressed.
But wherefore says she not she is unjust?
And wherefore say not I that I am old?
O, love's best habit is in seeming trust,
And age in love loves not to have years told:
Therefore I lie with her and she with me,
And in our faults by lies we flattered be.

CXLVI

Poor soul, the centre of my sinful earth,
Pressed by these rebel powers that thee array,
Why dost thou pine within and suffer dearth,
Painting thy outward walls so costly gay?
Why so large cost, having so short a lease,
Dost thou upon thy fading mansion spend?
Shall worms, inheritors of this excess,
Eat up thy charge? Is this thy body's end?
Then, soul, live thou upon thy servant's loss,
And let that pine to aggravate thy store;
Buy terms divine in selling hours of dross;
Within be fed, without be rich no more:
So shalt thou feed on Death, that feeds on men;
And Death once dead, there's no more dying then.

RICHARD ROWLANDS, *alias* VERSTEGAN
(1565–1630)
"Upon My Lap My Sovereign Sits"

Upon my lap my sovereign sits
And sucks upon my breast;
Meantime his love maintains my life
And gives my sense her rest.
   Sing lullaby, my little boy,
   Sing lullaby, mine only joy!

When thou hast taken thy repast,
Repose, my babe, on me;
So may thy mother and thy nurse
Thy cradle also be.
   Sing lullaby, my little boy,
   Sing lullaby, mine only joy!

I grieve that duty doth not work
All that my wishing would,
Because I would not be to thee
But in the best I should.
   Sing lullaby, my little boy,
   Sing lullaby, mine only joy!

Yet as I am, and as I may,
I must and will be thine,
Though all too little for thyself
Vouchsafing to be mine.
   Sing lullaby, my little boy,
   Sing lullaby, mine only joy!

THOMAS NASHE
(1567–1601)
"Spring, the Sweet Spring..."

Spring, the sweet Spring, is the year's pleasant king;
Then blooms each thing, then maids dance in a ring,
Cold doth not sting, the pretty birds do sing,
Cuckoo, jug, jug, pu we, to witta woo.

The palm and may make country houses gay,
Lambs frisk and play, the shepherds pipe all day,
And we hear aye birds tune this merry lay,
Cuckoo, jug, jug, pu we, to witta woo.

The fields breathe sweet, the daisies kiss our feet,
Young lovers meet, old wives a-sunning sit,
In every street these tunes our ears do greet,
Cuckoo, jug, jug, pu we, to witta woo.
　　　　　Spring, the sweet spring!

Summer's Last Will and Testament, 1600

"Adieu, Farewell Earth's Bliss"

Adieu; farewell earth's bliss,
This world uncertain is:
Fond are life's lustful joys,
Death proves them all but toys.
None from his darts can fly:
I am sick, I must die.
　　Lord have mercy on us!

Rich men, trust not in wealth,
Gold cannot buy you health;
Physic himself must fade;
All things to end are made;
The plague full swift goes by;
I am sick, I must die.
　　Lord have mercy on us!

Beauty is but a flower,
Which wrinkles will devour:
Brightness falls from the air;
Queens have died young and fair;
Dust hath closed Helen's eye;
I am sick, I must die.
　　Lord have mercy on us!

Strength stoops unto the grave:
Worms feed on Hector brave;
Swords may not fight with fate:
Earth still holds ope her gate.
Come, come, the bells do cry;
I am sick, I must die.
    Lord have mercy on us!

Wit with his wantonness,
Tasteth death's bitterness.
Hell's executioner
Hath no ears for to hear
What vain art can reply;
I am sick, I must die.
    Lord have mercy on us!

Haste therefore each degree
To welcome destiny:
Heaven is our heritage,
Earth but a player's stage.
Mount we unto the sky;
I am sick, I must die.
    Lord have mercy on us!

Summer's Last Will and Testament, 1600

WILLIAM ALEXANDER, EARL OF STIRLING
(1567?–1640)

Sonnet

Then whilst that Latmos did contain her bliss
Chaste Phoebe left her church so much admired,
And when her brother from that bounds retired
Would of the sleepy shepherd steal a kiss;
But to no greater grace I crave to climb
Than of my goddess whiles whilst she reposes
That I might kiss the still-selfkissing roses,
And steal of her that which was stol'n of him:
And though I know that this would only prove
A maimed delight, whereof th'one half would want,

Yet whilst the light did Morpheus' power supplant;
If that my theft did her displeasure move,
I render would all that I robbed again
And for each kiss I take would give her twain.

THOMAS CAMPION
(1567–1619)

"Follow Your Saint..."

Follow your saint, follow with accents sweet!
Haste you, sad notes, fall at her flying feet!
There, wrapped in cloud of sorrow, pity move,
And tell the ravisher of my soul I perish for her love:
But, if she scorns my never-ceasing pain,
Then burst with sighing in her sight and ne'er return again.

All that I sang still to her praise did tend,
Still she was first, still she my songs did end;
Yet she my love and music both doth fly,
The music that her echo is and beauty's sympathy.
Then let my notes pursue her scornful flight!
It shall suffice that they were breathed and died for her
      delight.

"Follow Thy Fair Sun..."

Follow thy fair sun, unhappy shadow!
   Though thou be black as night,
   And she made all of light,
Yet follow thy fair sun, unhappy shadow!

Follow her, whose light thy light depriveth!
   Though here thou liv'st disgraced,
   And she in heaven is placed,
Yet follow her whose light the world reviveth!

Follow those pure beams, whose beauty burneth!
   That so have scorchéd thee
   As thou still black must be
Till her kind beams thy black to brightness turneth.

Follow her, while yet her glory shineth!
  There comes a luckless night
  That will dim all her light;
And this the black unhappy shade divineth.

Follow still, since so thy fates ordained!
  The sun must have his shade,
  Till both at once do fade,
The sun still proud, the shadow still disdained.

"Give Beauty All Her Right"

Give Beauty all her right,
  She's not to one form tied;
Each shape yields fair delight
  Where her perfections bide:
Helen, I grant might pleasing be,
And Ros'mund was as sweet as she.

Some the quick eye commends,
  Some swelling lips and red;
Pale looks have many friends,
  Through sacred sweetness bred:
Meadows have flowers that pleasures move,
Though roses are the flowers of love.

Free beauty is not bound
  To one unmovéd clime;
She visits every ground
  And favours every time.
Let the old loves with mine compare,
My sovereign is as sweet and fair.

"Thou Art Not Fair..."

Thou art not fair, for all thy red and white,
  For all those rosy ornaments in thee;
Thou art not sweet, tho' made of mere delight,
  Nor fair, nor sweet—unless thou pity me.
I will not soothe thy fancies, thou shalt prove
That beauty is no beauty without love.

Yet love not me, nor seek not to allure
  My thoughts with beauty were it more divine;
Thy smiles and kisses I cannot endure,
  I'll not be wrapped up in those arms of thine:
Now show it, if thou be a woman right,—
Embrace and kiss and love me in despite.

"Turn All Thy Thoughts..."

Turn all thy thoughts to eyes,
Turn all thy hairs to ears,
Change all thy friends to spies
And all thy joys to fears;
  True love will yet be free
  In spite of jealousy.

Turn darkness into day,
Conjectures into truth,
Believe what th' envious say,
Let age interpret youth:
  True love will yet be free
  In spite of jealousy.

Wrest every word and look,
Rack every hidden thought,
Or fish with golden hook;
True love cannot be caught:
  For that will still be free
  In spite of jealousy.

"Never Love..."

Never love unless you can
Bear with all the faults of man:
Men sometimes will jealous be
Though but little cause they see;
And hang the head as discontent,
And speak what straight they will repent.

Men that but one saint adore
Make a show of love to more;
Beauty must be scorned in none,
Though but truly served in one:
For what is courtship but disguise?
True hearts may have dissembling eyes.

Men, when their affairs require,
Must awhile themselves retire;
Sometimes hunt, and sometimes hawk,
And not ever sit and talk.
If these and such-like you can bear,
Then like, and love, and never fear!

"Thrice Toss These Oaken Ashes..."

Thrice toss these oaken ashes in the air,
Thrice sit thou mute in this enchanted chair,
Then thrice-three times tie up this true love's knot,
And murmur soft "She will or she will not."

Go, burn these poisonous weeds in yon blue fire,
These screech-owl's feathers and this prickling briar,
This cypress gathered at a dead man's grave,
That all my fears and cares an end may have.

Then come, you Fairies! dance with me a round!
Melt her hard heart with your melodious sound!
In vain are all the charms I can devise:
She hath an art to break them with her eyes.

"Love Me or Not..."

Love me or not, love her I must or die;
Leave me or not, follow her needs must I.
O that her grace would my wish'd comforts give!
How rich in her, how happy should I live!

All my desire, all my delight should be
Her to enjoy, her to unite to me;
Envy should cease, her would I love alone:
Who loves by looks is seldom true to one.

Could I enchant, and that it lawful were,
Her would I charm softly that none should hear;
But love enforced rarely yields firm content:
So would I love that neither should repent.

"Shall I Come, Sweet Love..."

Shall I come, sweet Love, to thee
   When the evening beams are set?
Shall I not excluded be,
   Will you find no feignéd let?
Let me not, for pity, more
Tell the long hours at your door.

Who can tell what thief or foe,
   In the covert of the night,
For his prey will work my woe,
   Or through wicked foul despite?
So may I die unredrest
Ere my long love be possest.

But to let such dangers pass,
   Which a lover's thoughts disdain,
'Tis enough in such a place
   To attend love's joys in vain:
Do not mock me in thy bed,
While these cold nights freeze me dead.

"There Is a Garden in Her Face"

There is a garden in her face
Where roses and white lilies grow;
A heavenly paradise is that place
Wherein all pleasant fruits do flow.
   There cherries grow which none may buy,
   Till "Cherry ripe" themselves do cry.

Those cherries fairly do enclose
Of orient pearl a double row,
Which when her lovely laughter shows,
They look like rose-buds filled with snow;
   Yet them nor peer nor prince can buy,
   Till "Cherry ripe" themselves do cry.

Her eyes like angels watch them still,
Her brows like bended bows do stand,
Threatening with piercing frowns to kill
All that attempt, with eye or hand,
   Those sacred cherries to come nigh
   Till "Cherry ripe" themselves do cry.

"When Thou Must Home..."

When thou must home to shades of underground,
And there arrived, a new admiréd guest,
The beauteous spirits do engirt thee round,
White Iope, blithe Helen and the rest,
To hear the stories of thy finished love
From that smooth tongue whose music hell can move;
Then wilt thou speak of banqueting delights,
Of masques and revels which sweet youth did make,
Of tourneys and great challenges of knights,
And all these triumphs for thy beauty's sake:
When thou hast told these honours done to thee,
Then tell, O tell, how thou didst murder me.

"Now Winter Nights..."

Now winter nights enlarge
The number of their hours,
And clouds their storms discharge
Upon the airy towers.
Let now the chimneys blaze,
And cups o'erflow with wine;

Let well-tuned words amaze
With harmony divine.
Now yellow waxen lights
Shall wait on honey love,
While youthful revels, masques and courtly sights
Sleep's leaden spells remove.

This time doth well dispense
With lovers' long discourse;
Much speech hath some defence,
Though beauty no remorse.
All do not all things well;
Some measures comely tread,
Some knotted riddles tell,
Some poems smoothly read
The summer hath his joys
And winter his delights;
Though love and all his pleasures are but toys,
They shorten tedious nights.

"The Man of Life Upright"

The man of life upright,
    Whose guiltless heart is free
From all dishonest deeds,
    Or thought of vanity;

The man whose silent days
    In harmless joys are spent,
Whom hopes cannot delude
    Nor sorrow discontent:

That man needs neither towers
    Nor armour for defence,
Nor secret vaults to fly
    From thunder's violence.

He only can behold
    With unaffrighted eyes
The horrors of the deep
    And terrors of the skies.

Thus scorning all the cares
   That fate or fortune brings,
He makes the heaven his book,
   His wisdom heavenly things;

Good thoughts his only friends,
   His wealth a well-spent age,
The earth his sober inn
   And quiet pilgrimage.

"I Care Not for These Ladies"

I care not for these ladies
That must be wooed and prayed:
Give me kind Amarillis,
The wanton country maid!
Nature, art disdaineth,
Her beauty is her own,
   Her, when we court and kiss,
   She cries, "Forsooth, let go!"
   But when we come where comfort is,
   She never will say, "No!"

If I love Amarillis,
She gives me fruit and flowers:
But if we love these ladies,
We must give golden showers.
Give them gold, they sell love!
Give me the nut-brown lass!
   Who, when we court and kiss,
   She cries, "Forsooth, let go!"
   But when we come where comfort is,
   She never will say, "No!"

These ladies must have pillows
And beds, by strangers wrought;
Give me a bower of willows,
Of moss and leaves unbought!
And fresh Amarillis,

With milk and honey fed!
   Who, when we court and kiss,
   She cries, "Forsooth, let go!"
   But when we come where comfort is,
   She never will say, "No!"

"Rose-Cheek'd Laura, Come"

   Rose-cheek'd Laura, come;
Sing thou smoothly with thy beauty's
Silent music, either other
     Sweetly gracing.

   Lovely forms do flow
From concent divinely framéd:
Heaven is music, and thy beauty's
     Birth is heavenly

   These dull notes we sing
Discords need for helps to grace them;
Only beauty purely loving
     Knows no discord;

   But still moves delight,
Like clear springs renew'd by flowing,
Ever perfect, ever in them-
     selves eternal.

SIR HENRY WOOTTON

(1568–1639)

The Character of a Happy Life

How happy is he born and taught
   That serveth not another's will;
Whose armour is his honest thought,
   And simple truth his utmost skill;

Whose passions not his masters are;
　　Whose soul is still prepared for death,
Untied unto the world by care
　　Of public fame or private breath;

Who envies none that chance doth raise,
　　Nor vice; who never understood
How deepest wounds are given by praise;
　　Nor rules of state, but rules of good;

Who hath his life from rumours freed;
　　Whose conscience is his strong retreat;
Whose state can neither flatterers feed,
　　Nor ruin make oppressors great;

Who God doth late and early pray
　　More of his grace than gifts to lend;
And entertains the harmless day
　　With a religious book or friend.

This man is free from servile bands
　　Of hope to rise or fear to fall:
Lord of himself, though not of lands,
　　And, having nothing, yet hath all.

On His Mistress, the Queen of Bohemia

You meaner beauties of the night,
　　That poorly satisfy our eyes
More by your number than your light,
　　You common people of the skies;
　　What are you when the moon shall rise?

You curious chanters of the wood,
　　That warble forth Dame Nature's lays,
Thinking your passions understood
　　By your weak accents; what's your praise,
　　When Philomel her voice shall raise?

You violets that first appear,
  By your pure purple mantles known
Like the proud virgins of the year,
  As if the spring were all your own;
  What are you when the rose is blown?

So, when my mistress shall be seen
  In form and beauty of her mind,
By virtue first, then choice, a Queen,
  Tell me if she were not designed
  The eclipse and glory of her kind?

Upon the Death of Sir Albert Morton's Wife

He first deceased; she for a little tried
To live without him, liked it not, and died.

SIR JOHN DAVIES

(1569–1626)

FROM The Immortality of the Soul

For why should we the busy soul believe
  When boldly she concludes of that and this,
When of herself she can no judgment give,
  Nor how, nor whence, nor where, nor what she is?

All things without which round about we see,
  We seek to know, and how therewith to do;
But that whereby we reason, live and be
  Within ourselves, we strangers are thereto.

We seek to know the moving of each sphere
  And the strange cause of th'ebbs and floods of Nile
But of that clock within our breasts we bear
  The subtle motions we forget the while.

We that acquaint ourselves with every zone
  And pass both tropics and behold each pole,
When we come home are to ourselves unknown
  And unacquainted still with our own soul.

We study speech, but others we persuade;
　　We leech-craft learn, but others cure with it;
We interpret laws which other men have made,
　　But read not those which in our hearts are writ.

I know my body's of so frail a kind
　　As force without, fevers within can kill;
I know the heavenly nature of my mind,
　　But 'tis corrupted both in wit and will.

I know my soul hath power to know all things,
　　Yet is she blind and ignorant in all;
I know I'm one of Nature's little kings,
　　Yet to the least and vilest things am thrall.

I know my life's a pain and but a span;
　　I know my sense is mocked in everything;
And, to conclude, I know myself a man,
　　Which is a proud and yet a wretched thing.

SIR ROBERT AYTOUN

(1570–1638)

"I Loved Thee Once..."

I loved thee once; I'll love no more.
　　Thine be the grief, as is the blame;
Thou art not what thou wast before,
　　What reason I should be the same?
　　　　He that can love unloved again,
　　　　Hath better store of love than brain;
　　God send me love my debts to pay
　　While unthrifts fool their love away!

Nothing could have my love o'erthrown
　　If thou hadst still continued mine;
Yea, if thou hadst remained thy own,
　　I might perchance have yet been thine.
　　　　But thou thy freedom did recall
　　　　That it thou might elsewhere enthral;
　　And then how could I but disdain
　　A captive's captive to remain?

When new desires had conquered thee
  And changed the object of thy will,
It had been lethargy in me,
    Not constancy, to love thee still.
      Yea, it had been a sin to go
      And prostitute affection so;
    Since we are taught no prayers to say
    To such as must to others pray.

Yet do thou glory in thy choice,
  Thy choice of his good fortune boast;
I'll neither grieve nor yet rejoice
    To see him gain what I have lost;
      The height of my disdain shall be
      To laugh at him, to blush for thee;
    To love thee still, but go no more
    A-begging at a beggar's door.

THOMAS DEKKER

(1570?–1641?)

"O, the Month of May..."

O, the month of May, the merry month of May,
So frolic, so gay, and so green, so green, so green!
O, and then did I unto my true love say,
Sweet Peg, thou shalt be my Summer's Queen.

Now the nightingale, the pretty nightingale,
The sweetest singer in all the forest quire,
Entreats thee, sweet Peggy, to hear thy true love's tale:
Lo, yonder she sitteth, her breast against a brier.

But O, I spy the cuckoo, the cuckoo, the cuckoo;
See where she sitteth; come away, my joy:
Come away, I prithee, I do not like the cuckoo
Should sing where my Peggy and I kiss and toy.

O, the month of May, the merry month of May,
So frolic, so gay, and so green, so green, so green;
And then did I unto my true love say,
Sweet Peg, thou shalt be my Summer's Queen.

The Shoemaker's Holiday, 1600

"Cold's the Wind..."

Cold's the wind, and wet's the rain,
   Saint Hugh be our good speed!
Ill is the weather that bringeth no gain,
   Nor helps good hearts in need.

Troll the bowl, the jolly nut-brown bowl,
   And here, kind mate, to thee!
Let's sing a dirge for Saint Hugh's soul,
   And down it merrily.

Down-a-down, hey, down-a-down,
   Hey derry derry down-a-down!
Ho! well done, to me let come,
   Ring compass, gentle joy!

Cold's the wind, and wet's the rain,
   Saint Hugh be our good speed!
Ill is the weather that bringeth no gain,
   Nor helps good hearts in need.

The Shoemaker's Holiday, 1600

"Art Thou Poor..."

Art thou poor, yet hast thou golden slumbers?
      O, sweet content!
Art thou rich, yet is thy mind perplexed?
      O, punishment!
   Dost thou laugh to see how fools are vexed
To add to golden numbers golden numbers?
      O, sweet content!

Work apace, apace, apace, apace;
Honest labour bears a lovely face;
Then hey noney, noney, hey noney, noney!

Canst drink the waters of the crispéd spring?
O, sweet content!
Swim'st thou in wealth, yet sink'st in thine own tears?
O, punishment!
Then he that patiently want's burden bears,
No burden bears, but is a king, a king!
O, sweet content!

The Pleasant Comedy of Patient Grissill, 1603

"Golden Slumbers..."

Golden slumbers kiss your eyes,
Smiles awake you when you rise.
Sleep, pretty wantons, do not cry,
And I will sing a lullaby:
Rock them, rock them, lullaby.

Care is heavy, therefore sleep you;
You are care, and care must keep you.
Sleep, pretty wantons, do not cry,
And I will sing a lullaby:
Rock them, rock them, lullaby.

The Pleasant Comedy of Patient Grissill, 1603

"Haymakers, Rakers..."

Haymakers, rakers, reapers, and mowers,
Wait on your summer queen.
Dress up with musk-rose her eglantine bowers,
Daffodils strew the green.
Sing, dance, and play,
'Tis holiday.
The sun does bravely shine
On our ears of corn.
Rich as a pearl,
Comes every girl,
This is mine, this is mine, this is mine;
Let us die, ere away they be borne.

Bow to the sun, to our queen, and that fair one,
    Come to behold our sports.
Each bonny lass here is counted a rare one,
    As those in princes' courts.
        These and we
        With country glee,
Will teach the woods to resound
And the hills with echoes hollow;
        Skipping lambs
        Their bleating dams
'Mongst kids shall trip it round;
For joy thus our wenches we follow.

Wind, jolly huntsman, your neat bugles shrilly,
    Hounds make a lusty cry;
Spring up, you falconers, the partridges freely,
    Then let your brave hawks fly.
        Horses amain
        Over ridge, over plain,
The dogs have the stag in chase;
'Tis a sport to content a king:
        So, ho! ho! through the skies
        How the proud bird flies,
And sousing, kills with a grace.
Now the deer falls; hark! how they ring.

The Sun's Darling, 1632–4

FROM *Old Fortunatus*, 1600

1.

Fortune: Behold you not this globe, this golden bowl,
    This toy called world, at our imperial feet?
    This world is Fortune's ball, wherewith she
        sports.
    Sometimes I strike it up into the air,
    And then create I emperors and kings:
    Sometimes I spurn it, at which spurn crawls
        out
    That wild beast Multitude. Curse on, you fools,—
    'Tis I that tumble princes from their thrones,

And gild false brows with glittering diadems.
'Tis I that tread on necks of conquerors,
And when, like demi-gods, they have been drawn
In ivory chariots to the capitol,
Circled about with wonder of all eyes,
The shouts of every tongue, love of all hearts,
Being swoll'n with their own greatness, I have
      pricked
The bladder of their pride, and made them die,
As water-bubbles, without memory.
I thrust base cowards into Honour's chair,
While the true-spirited soldier stands by
Bare-headed, and all bare, whilst at his scars
They scoff, that ne'er durst view the face of
      wars.
I set an idiot's cap on Virtue's head,
Turn Learning out of doors, clothe Wit in rags,
And paint ten thousand images of loam
In gaudy silken colours. On the backs
Of mules and asses I make asses ride,
Only for sport, to see the apish world
Worship such beasts with sound idolatry.
This Fortune does, and when this is done,
She sits and smiles to hear some curse her name,
And some with adoration crown her fame.

2.

Fortune: Stay, Fortunatus, once more hear me speak;
If thou kiss Wisdom's cheek and make her thine,
She'll breathe into thy lips divinity,
And thou like Phoebus shalt speak oracle,
Thy Heaven-inspiréd soul, on Wisdom's wings,
Shall fly up to the Parliament of Jove,
And read the statutes of eternity,
And see what's past and learn what is to come.
If thou lay claim to strength, armies shall quake
To see thee frown: as kings at mine do lie,
So shall thy feet trample on empery.
Make health thine object, thou shalt be strong
      proof

'Gainst the deep searching darts of surfeiting,
Be ever merry, ever revelling.
Wish but for beauty, and within thine eyes
Two naked Cupids amorously shall swim,
And on thy cheeks I'll mix such white and red,
That Jove shall turn away young Ganymede,
And with immortal arms shall circle thee.
Are thy desires long life?—thy vital thread
Shall be stretched out, thou shalt behold the
    change
Of monarchies and see those children die,
Whose great great grandsires now in cradles
    lie.
If through gold's sacred hunger thou dost pine,
Those gilded wantons which in swarms do run,
To warm their tender bodies in the sun,
Shall stand for number of those golden piles,
Which in rich pride shall swell before thy
    feet;
As those are, so shall these be infinite.
Awaken then thy soul's best faculties,
And gladly kiss this bounteous hand of Fate,
Which strives to bless thy name of Fortunate.

3.

Fortunatus: Oh, whither am I rapt beyond myself?
More violent conflict fights in every thought,
Than his whose fatal choice Troy's downfall
    wrought.
Shall I contract myself to wisdom's love?
Then I lose riches: and a wise man poor,
Is like a sacred book that's never read,—
To himself he lives, and to all else seems dead.
This age thinks better of a gilded fool,
Than of a threadbare saint in wisdom's school.
I will be strong: then I refuse long life,
And though mine arm should conquer twenty
    worlds,
There's a lean fellow beats all conquerors:

The greatest strength expires with loss of
    breath;
The mightiest in one minute stoop to death.
Then take long life, or health: should I do so
I might grow ugly, and that tedious scroll
Of months and years, much misery may enroll.
Therefore I'll beg for beauty; yet I will not,
That fairest cheek hath oftentimes a soul
Leprous as sin itself; than hell more foul.
The wisdom of this world is idiotism,
Strength a weak reed: health sickness' enemy,
And it at length will have the victory.
Beauty is but a painting, and long life
Is a long journey in December gone,
Tedious and full of tribulation
Therefore, dread sacred Empress, make me rich,
My choice is store of gold; the rich are wise.
He that upon his back rich garments wears,
Is wise, though on his head grow Midas' ears.
Gold is the strength, the sinews of the world,
The health, the soul, the beauty most divine,
A mask of gold hides all deformities;
Gold is Heaven's physic, life's restorative,
Oh therefore make me rich: not as the wretch,
That only serves lean banquets to his eye,
Has gold, yet starves: is famished in his store:
No, let me ever spend, be never poor.

FROM *The Honest Whore, Part I,* 1604

Candido: Patience, my lord! why, 'tis the soul of peace;
Of all the virtues, 'tis nearest kin to Heaven.
It makes men look like gods. The best of men
That e'er wore earth about him, was a sufferer,
A soft, meek, patient, humble, tranquil spirit,
The first true gentleman that ever breathed.
The stock of patience then cannot be poor;
All it desires, it has; what monarch more?
It is the greatest enemy to law
That can be: for it doth embrace all wrongs,

And so chains up lawyers' and women's tongues.
'Tis the perpetual prisoner's liberty,
His walks and orchards: 'tis the bond slave's freedom,
And makes him seem proud of each iron chain,
As though he wore it more for state than pain:
It is the beggars' music, and thus sings,
Although their bodies beg, their souls are kings.
O my dread liege! It is the sap of bliss
Rears us aloft, makes men and angels kiss.
And last of all, to end a household strife,
It is the honey 'gainst a waspish wife.

THOMAS MIDDLETON

(1570?–1627)

"Love for Such a Cherry Lip"

Love for such a cherry lip
 Would be glad to pawn his arrows;
Venus here to take a sip
 Would sell her doves and teams of sparrows.
  But they shall not so;
   Hey nonny, nonny no!
  None but I this lip must owe,
   Hey nonny, nonny no!

Did Jove see this wanton eye,
 Ganymede must wait no longer;
Phoebe here one night did lie,
 Would change her face and look much younger.
  But they shall not so;
   Hey nonny, nonny no!
  None but I this lip must owe;
   Hey nonny, nonny no!

Blurt, Master Constable, 1602

"O for a Bowl of Fat Canary"

O for a bowl of fat canary,
Rich Aristippus, sparkling sherry!
Some nectar else from Juno's dairy;
O these draughts would make us merry!

O for a wench! I deal in faces,
And in other daintier things;
Tickled am I with her embraces;
Fine dancing in such fairy rings!

O for a plump, fat leg of mutton,
Veal, lamb, capon, pig, and coney!
None is happy but a glutton,
None an ass, but who wants money.

Wines indeed, and girls are good;
But brave victuals feast the blood;
For wenches, wine and lusty cheer,
Jove would come down to surfeit here.

A Mad World, My Masters, 1608

BEN JONSON

(1573–1637)

An Epitaph on Salathiel Pavey, a Child of Queen Elizabeth's Chapel

Weep with me all you that read
    This little story;
And know, for whom a tear you shed,
    Death's self is sorry.
'Twas a child, that so did thrive
    In grace and feature,
As Heaven and Nature seemed to strive
    Which owned the creature.
Years he numbered scarce thirteen
    When Fates turned cruel,
Yet three filled zodiacs had he been
    The stage's jewel;
And did act (what now we moan)
    Old men so duly
As, sooth, the Parcae thought him one,
    He played so truly.
So by error to his fate
    They all consented;

But viewing him since (alas, too late)
   They have repented.
And have sought (to give new birth)
   In baths to steep him;
But, being so much too good for earth,
   Heaven vows to keep him.

Epitaph on Elizabeth, L.H.

Would'st thou hear what man can say
   In a little? Reader, stay.
Underneath this stone doth lie
   As much beauty as could die;
Which in life did harbour give
   To more virtue than doth live.
If at all she had a fault,
   Leave it buried in this vault.
One name was Elizabeth,
   Th' other let it sleep with death;
Fitter, where it died, to tell,
   Than that it lived at all. Farewell.

That Women Are but Men's Shadows

Follow a shadow, it still flies you;
   Seem to fly, it will pursue;
So court a mistress, she denies you;
   Let her alone, she will court you.
Say, are not women truly then
   Styled but the shadows of us men?
At morn and even shades are longest;
   At noon they are or short or none;
So men at weakest, they are strongest,
   But grant us perfect, they're not known.
Say, are not women truly then
   Styled but the shadows of us men?

To Celia

Drink to me only with thine eyes,
　　And I will pledge with mine;
And leave a kiss but in the cup,
　　And I'll not look for wine.

The thirst that from the soul doth rise
　　Doth ask a drink divine,
But might I of Jove's nectar sup
　　I would not change for thine.

I sent thee late a rosy wreath,
　　Not so much honouring thee,
As giving it a hope that there
　　It could not withered be.

But thou thereon did'st only breathe
　　And sent'st it back to me,
Since when it breathes and smells, I swear,
　　Not of itself but thee.

From the Greek of PHILOSTRATUS

Her Triumph

See the chariot at hand here of Love
　　Wherein my lady rideth!
Each that draws is a swan or a dove,
　　And well the car Love guideth;
As she goes all hearts do duty
　　　Unto her beauty;
And enamoured do wish, so they might
　　　But enjoy such a sight,
That they still were to run by her side
Through swords, through seas, whither she would ride.

Do but look on her eyes, they do light
    All that Love's world compriseth!
Do but look on her hair, it is bright
    As Love's star when it riseth!
Do but mark, her forehead's smoother
    Than words that soothe her!
And from her arched brows such a grace
    Sheds itself through her face,
As alone there triumphs to the life
All the gain, all the good, of the elements' strife.

Have you seen but a bright lily grow
    Before rude hands have touched it?
Ha' you marked but the fall o' the snow
    Before the soil hath smutched it?
Ha' you felt the wool of beaver
    Or swan's down ever?
Or have smelt o' the bud o' the briar?
    Or the nard in the fire?
Or have tasted the bag of the bee?
O so white! O so soft! O so sweet is she!

To the Memory of My Beloved, the Author, Mr. William Shakespeare

To draw no envy, Shakespeare, on thy name,
    Am I thus ample to thy book and fame;
While I confess thy writings to be such
    As neither man nor Muse can praise too much.
'Tis true, and all men's suffrage. But these ways
    Were not the paths I meant unto thy praise;
For silliest ignorance on these may light,
    Which, when it sounds at best, but echoes right,
Or blind affection, which doth ne'er advance
    The truth, but gropes and urgeth all by chance;
Or crafty malice might pretend this praise
    And think to ruin where it seemed to praise.
These are as some infamous bawd or whore
    Should praise a matron. What could hurt her more?

But thou art proof against them, and indeed
    Above th' ill fortune of them or the need.
I, therefore, will begin. Soul of the Age!
    The applause, delight, the wonder of our stage!
My Shakespeare, rise. I will not lodge thee by
    Chaucer or Spenser, or bid Beaumont lie
A little further to make thee a room;
    Thou art a monument without a tomb,
And art alive still while thy book doth live,
    And we have wits to read and praise to give.
That I not mix thee so, my brain excuses;
    I mean with great but disproportioned Muses;
For, if I thought my judgment were of years,
    I should commit thee surely with thy peers,
And tell how far thou didst our Lyly outshine,
    Or sporting Kyd or Marlowe's mighty line.
And though thou hadst small Latin and less Greek,
    From thence to honour thee I would not seek
For names, but call forth thundering Aeschylus,
    Euripides and Sophocles to us,
Pacuvius, Accius, him of Cordoba dead,
    To life again, to hear thy buskin tread
And shake a stage; or, when thy socks were on,
    Leave thee alone for the comparison
Of all that insolent Greece or haughty Rome
    Sent forth, or since did from their ashes come.
Triumph, my Britain, thou hast one to show
    To whom all scenes of Europe homage owe.
He was not of an age, but for all time!
    And all the Muses still were in their prime
When like Apollo forth he came to warm
    Our ears, or like a Mercury to charm.
Nature herself was proud of his designs,
    And joyed to wear the dressing of his lines;
Which were so richly spun and woven so fit
    As since she will vouchsafe no other wit.
The merry Greek, tart Aristophanes,
    Neat Terence, witty Plautus, now not please;
But antiquated and deserted lie,
    As they were not of Nature's family.

Yet must I not give Nature all; thy Art,
  My gentle Shakespeare, must enjoy a part.
For though the poet's matter Nature be,
  His art doth give the fashion. And that he
Who casts to write a living line must sweat,
  (Such as thine are) and strike the second heat
Upon the Muses' anvil; turn the same
  (And himself with it) that he thinks to frame;
Or for the laurel he may gain a scorn,
  For a good poet's made as well as born.
And such wert thou. Look, how the father's face
  Lives in his issue, even so the race
Of Shakespeare's mind and manners brightly shines
  In his well-turnéd and true-filéd lines;
In each of which he seems to shake a lance
  As brandished at the eyes of ignorance.
Sweet Swan of Avon! what a sight it were
  To see thee in our waters yet appear,
And make those flights upon the banks of Thames
  That did so take Eliza and our James!
But stay, I see thee in the hemisphere
  Advanced, and make a constellation there.
Shine forth, thou Star of Poets, and with rage
  Or influence chide or cheer the drooping stage,
Which since thy flight from hence hath mourned like night,
  And despairs day but for thy volume's light.

Song

Slow, slow, fresh fount, keep time with my salt tears;
  Yet slower, yet, O faintly gentle springs;
  List to the heavy part the music bears:
    Woe weeps out her division when she sings.
      Droop herbs and flowers,
      Fall grief in showers,
      Our beauties are not ours;
        O, I could still
  (Like melting snow upon some craggy hill)
      Drop, drop, drop, drop,
Since Nature's pride is now a withered daffodil.

Cynthia's Revels, 1616

Song

O, that joy so soon should waste!
   Or so sweet a bliss
      As a kiss
Might not for ever last!
So sugared, so melting, so soft, so delicious,
   The dew that lies on roses,
   When the Morn herself discloses,
      Is not so precious.
O, rather than I would it smother,
Were I to taste such another,
   It should be my wishing
   That I might die kissing.

Cynthia's Revels, 1616

Hymn

Queen and huntress, chaste and fair,
Now the sun is laid to sleep,
Seated in thy silver chair
State in wonted manner keep;
   Hesperus entreats thy light,
   Goddess excellently bright.

Earth, let not thy envious shade
Dare itself to interpose;
Cynthia's shining orb was made
Heaven to clear, when day did close;
   Bless us then with wishéd sight,
   Goddess excellently bright.

Lay thy bow of pearl apart
And thy crystal-shining quiver,
Give unto the flying hart
Space to breathe, how short soever;
   Thou that mak'st a day of night,
   Goddess excellently bright.

Cynthia's Revels, 1616

Song

Still to be neat, still to be dressed,
As you were going to a feast,
Still to be powdered, still perfumed,
Lady, it is to be presumed,
Though art's hid causes are not found,
All is not sweet, all is not sound.

Give me a look, give me a face,
That makes simplicity a grace,
Robes loosely flowing, hair as free;
Such sweet neglect more taketh me
Than all the adulteries of art.
They strike mine eye, but not my heart.

The Silent Woman, 1616

FROM *Volpone or The Fox,* 1605

Volpone: If thou hast wisdom, hear me, Celia.
Thy baths shall be the juice of July-flowers,
Spirit of roses, and of violets,
The milk of unicorns, and panthers' breath
Gathered in bags, and mixt with Cretan wines.
Our drink shall be preparéd gold and amber;
Which we will take, until my roof whirl round
With the vertigo: and my dwarf shall dance,
My eunuch sing, my fool make up the antic,
Whilst we, in changéd shapes, act Ovid's tales,
Thou, like Europa now, and I like Jove,
Then I like Mars, and thou like Erycine:
So, of the rest, till we have quite run through,
And wearied all the fables of the gods.
Then will I have thee in more modern forms,
Attiréd like some sprightly dame of France,
Brave Tuscan lady, or proud Spanish beauty;
Sometimes, unto the Persian sophy's wife;
Or the grand signior's mistress; and, for change,
To one of our most artful courtezans,

Or some quick Negro, or cold Russian;
And I will meet thee in as many shapes:
Where we may so transfuse our wandering souls
Out at our lips, and score up sums of pleasure.

FROM *The Alchemist*, 1610

Sir Epicure   No. I'll have no bawds,
Mammon: But fathers and mothers: they will do it best,
      Best of all others. And my flatterers
      Shall be the pure and gravest of divines,
      That I can get for money. My mere fools,
      Eloquent burgesses, and then my poets
      The same that writ so subtly of the fart,
      Whom I will entertain still for that subject.
      The few that would give out themselves to be
      Court and town-stallions, and, each-where, belie
      Ladies who are known most innocent for them;
      Those will I beg, to make me eunuchs of:
      And they shall fan me with ten estrich tails
      A-piece, made in a plume to gather wind.
      We will be brave, Puffe, now we have the
         med'cine.
      My meat shall all come in, in Indian shells,
      Dishes of agate set in gold, and studded
      With emeralds, sapphires, hyacinths and rubies.
      The tongues of carps, dormice, and camels' heels,
      Boiled in the spirit of sol, and dissolved pearl,
      Apicius' diet, 'gainst the epilepsy:
      And I will eat these broths with spoons of amber,
      Headed with diamond and carbuncle.
      My foot-boy shall eat pheasants, calver'd
         salmons,
      Knots, godwits, lampreys: I myself will have
      The beards of barbels served, instead of salads;
      Oil'd mushrooms; and the swelling unctuous
         paps
      Of a fat pregnant sow, newly cut off,
      Dressed with an exquisite and poignant sauce:

For which I'll say unto my cook, *There's gold,*
Go forth, and be a knight.

. . . My shirts
I'll have of taffeta-sarsnet, soft and light
As cobwebs; and for all my other raiment,
It shall be such as might provoke the Persian,
Were he to teach the world riot anew.
My gloves of fishes' and birds' skins, perfumed
With gums of paradise and eastern air.

JOHN DAY

(15—?—1640?)

FROM *The Parliament of Bees,* 1607?

1.

Polypragmus: I will have one built
Like Pompey's theatre; the ceiling gilt
And interseamed with pearl, to make it shine
Like high Jove's palace: my descent's divine.
My great hall I'll have paved with clouds; which
                    done
By wondrous skill, an artificial sun
Shall roll about, reflecting golden beams,
Like Phoebus dancing on the wanton streams.
And when 'tis night, just as that sun goes down,
I'll have the stars draw up a silver moon
In her full height of glory. Overhead
A roof of woods and forests I'll have spread,
Trees growing downwards, full of fallow-deer;
When of the sudden, listening, you shall hear
A noise of horns and hunting, which shall bring
Actaeon to Diana in the spring,
Where all shall see her naked skin; and there
Actaeon's hounds shall their own master tear,
As emblem of his folly that will keep
Hounds to devour and eat him up asleep.
All this I'll do that men with praise may crown
My fame for turning the world upside-down.

2.

Iltriste: This baseness follows your profession:
You are like common beadles, easily won
To whip poor bees to death, scarce worth the striking,
But fawn with slavish flattery and throw liking
On great drones' vices; you clap hands at those,
Which proves your vices friends and virtues foes;
Where the true poet indeed doth scorn to gild
A coward's tomb with glories, or to build
A sumptuous pyramid of golden verse
Over the ruins of an ignoble hearse.
His lines like his invention are born free,
And both live blameless to eternity:
He holds his reputation so dear
As neither flattering hope nor servile fear
Can bribe his pen to temporize with kings;
The blacker are their crimes, he louder sings.

3.

    Vintager: High steward of thy vines,
           Taster both of grapes and wines,
           In these ripe clusters that present
           Full bounty, on his knees low bent,
           Pays Oberon homage; and in this bowl
           Brimmed with grape blood, tender toll
           Of all thy vintage.

    Oberon: May thy grapes thrive
           In autumn, and the roots survive
           In churlish winter; may thy fence
           Be proof 'gainst wild boars' violence;
           As thou in service true shalt be
           To us and our high royalty.
           —A female bee: thy character?

    Flora: Flora, Oberon's gardener,
           (Housewife both of herbs and flowers,
           To strew thy shrine and trim thy bowers
           With violets, roses, eglantine,

Daffodil and blue columbine)
Hath forth the bosom of the spring
Plucked this nosegay, which I bring
From Eleusis, mine own shrine,
To thee a monarch all divine;
And, as true impost of my grove,
Present it to great Oberon's love.

Oberon: Honey-dew refresh thy meads,
Cowslips spring with golden heads;
July-flowers and carnations wear
Leaves double streaked with maiden-hair;
May thy lilies taller grow,
Thy violets fuller sweetness owe;
And, last of all, may Phoebus love
To kiss thee and frequent thy grove,
As thou in service true shalt be
Unto our crown and royalty.

JOHN DONNE

(1573–1631)

The Good-Morrow

I wonder by my troth what thou and I
Did till we loved? were we not weaned till then?
But sucked on country pleasures childishly?
Or snorted we in the seven sleepers' den?
'Twas so; but this, all pleasures fancies be.
If ever any beauty I did see,
Which I desired and got, 'twas but a dream of thee.

And now good morrow to our waking souls,
Which watch not one another out of fear;
For love all love of other sights controls,
And makes one little room an everywhere.
Let sea-discoverers to new worlds have gone,
Let maps to other worlds on worlds have shown,
Let us possess one world, each hath one, and is one.

My face in thine eye, thine in mine appears,
And true plain hearts do in the faces rest;
Where can we find two better hemispheres
Without sharp North, without declining West?
Whatever dies was not mixt equally;
If our two loves be one, or thou and I
Love so alike that none do slacken, none can die.

Song

Go and catch a falling star,
  Get with child a mandrake root,
Tell me, where all past years are,
  Or who cleft the Devil's foot,
Teach me to hear Mermaids singing,
  Or to keep off envy's stinging.
        And find
        What wind
Serves to advance an honest mind.

If thou be'st born to strange sights,
  Things invisible to see,
Ride ten thousand days and nights,
  Till age snow white hairs on thee;
Thou, when thou return'st, will tell me
All strange wonders that befell thee,
        And swear
        No where
Lives a woman true and fair.

If thou find'st one, let me know,
  Such a Pilgrimage were sweet;
Yet do not, I would not go,
  Though at next door we might meet;
Though she were true when you met her,
And last till you write your letter,
        Yet she
        Will be
False ere I come to two or three.

The Canonization

For God's sake hold your tongue, and let me love;
　Or chide my palsy, or my gout,
My five grey hairs, or ruined fortune flout;
　With wealth your state, your mind with arts improve,
　　Take you a course, get you a place,
　　Observe his Honour, or his Grace,
Or the King's real, or his stamped face
　Contemplate; what you will, approve,
　So you will let me love.

Alas, alas, who's injured by my love?
　What merchant's ships have my sighs drowned?
Who says my tears have overflowed his ground?
　When did my colds a forward spring remove?
　　When did the heats which my veins fill
　　Add one more to the plaguy bill?
Soldiers find wars, and lawyers find out still
　Litigious men, which quarrels move,
　Though she and I do love.

Call us what you will, we are made such by love;
　Call her one, me another fly,
We're tapers too, and at our own cost die,
　And we in us find the Eagle and the Dove.
　　The Phoenix riddle hath more wit
　　By us; we two being one, are it.
So to one neutral thing both sexes fit,
　We die and rise the same, and prove
　Mysterious by this love.

We can die by it, if not live by love,
　And if unfit for tombs and hearse
Our legend be, it will be fit for verse;
　And if no piece of Chronicle we prove,
　　We'll build in sonnets pretty rooms;
　　As well a well-wrought urn becomes
The greatest ashes, as half-acre tombs,
　And by these hymns all shall approve
　Us canonized for Love:

And thus invoke us: You whom reverend love
   Made one another's hermitage;
You, to whom love was peace, that now is rage;
    Who did the whole world's soul contract, and drove
      Into the glasses of your eyes
      (So made such mirrors, and such spies,
That they did all to you epitomise,)
    Countries, Towns, Courts: beg from above
    A pattern of your love!

Song

    Sweetest love, I do not go,
      For weariness of thee,
    Nor in hope the world can show
      A fitter love for me;
        But since that I
    Must die at last, 'tis best
    To use myself in jest
        Thus by feigned deaths to die.

    Yesternight the sun went hence,
      And yet is here to-day;
    He hath no desire nor sense,
      Nor half so short a way;
        Then fear not me,
    But believe that I shall make
    Speedier journeys, since I take
        More wings and spurs than he.

    O how feeble is man's power,
      That if good fortune fall,
    Cannot add another hour
      Nor a lost hour recall!
        But come bad chance,
    And we join to it our strength,
    And we teach it art and length,
        Itself o'er us to advance.

When thou sigh'st, thou sigh'st not wind,
   But sigh'st my soul away;
When thou weep'st, unkindly kind,
   My life's blood doth decay.
     It cannot be
That thou lov'st me, as thou say'st,
If in thine my life thou waste,
   That art the best of me.

Let not thy divining heart
   Forethink me any ill,
Destiny may take thy part,
   And may thy fears fulfil;
     But think that we
Are but turned aside to sleep;
They who one another keep
   Alive, ne'er parted be.

Love's Alchemy

Some that have deeper digged love's mine than I,
Say where his centric happiness doth lie.
   I have loved and got and told,
But should I love, get, tell, till I were old,
I should not find that hidden mystery;
   Oh, 'tis imposture all:
And as no chemic yet the Elixir got,
   But glorifies his pregnant pot,
   If by the way to him befall
Some odoriferous thing, or medicinal,
  So lovers dream a rich and long delight,
  But get a winter-seeming summer's night.

Our ease, our thrift, our honour, and our day,
Shall we, for this vain bubble's shadow pay?
   Ends love in this, that my man
Can be as happy as I can; if he can
Endure the short scorn of a bridegroom's play?
   The loving wretch that swears

'Tis not the bodies marry, but the minds,
    Which he in her angelic finds,
    Would swear as justly that he hears
In that day's rude hoarse minstrelsy, the spheres.
Hope not for mind in women; at their best
    Sweetness and wit they are but mummy possessed.

The Message

Send home my long strayed eyes to me,
Which O! too long have dwelt on thee;
Yet since there they have learned such ill,
        Such forced fashions,
        And false passions,
            That they be
            Made by thee
Fit for no good sight, keep them still.

Send home my harmless heart again,
Which no unworthy thought could stain;
But if it be taught by thine
        To make jestings
        Of protestings,
            And cross both
            Word and oath,
Keep it, for then 'tis none of mine.

Yet send me back my heart and eyes,
That I may know, and see thy lies,
And may laugh and joy, when thou
        Art in anguish
        And dost languish
            For some one
            That will none,
Or prove as false as thou art now.

The Apparition

When by thy scorn, O murd'ress, I am dead,
And that thou think'st thee free
From all solicitations from me,
Then shall my ghost come to thy bed,
And thee, feigned vestal, in worse arms shall see;
Then thy sick taper will begin to wink,
And he, whose thou art then, being tired before,
Will, if thou stir, or pinch to wake him, think
 Thou call'st for more,
And in false sleep will from thee shrink,
And then poor aspen wretch, neglected thou
Bathed in a cold quicksilver sweat wilt lie
 A verier ghost than I;
What I will say, I will not tell thee now,
Lest that preserve thee; and since my love is spent,
I'd rather thou should'st painfully repent,
Than by my threat'nings rest still innocent.

The Ecstasy

Where, like a pillow on a bed,
 A pregnant bank swelled up, to rest
The violet's reclining head,
 Sat we two, one another's best.
Our hands were firmly cemented
 With a fast balm, which thence did spring,
Our eye-beams twisted, and did thread
 Our eyes upon one double string;
So t'intergraft our hands, as yet
 Was all the means to make us one,
And pictures in our eyes to get
 Was all our propagation.
As 'twixt two equal armies, Fate
 Suspends uncertain victory,
Our souls (which to advance their state
 Were gone out,) hung 'twixt her and me.

And whilst our souls negotiate there,
　We like sepulchral statues lay;
All day, the same our postures were,
　And we said nothing all the day.
If any so by love refined
　That he soul's language understood,
And by good love were grown all mind,
　Within convenient distance stood.
He (though he knew not which soul spake,
　Because both meant, not spake the same)
Might thence a new concoction take,
　And part far purer than he came.
This Ecstasy doth unperplex
　(We said) and tell us what we love,
We see by this, it was not sex,
　We see, we saw not what did move:
But as all several souls contain
　Mixture of things, they knew not what,
Love these mixed souls doth mix again,
　And makes both one each this and that.
A single violet transplant,
　The strength, the colour, and the size,
(All which before was poor and scant)
　Redoubles still, and multiplies.
When love, with one another so
　Interinanimates two souls,
That abler soul, which thence doth flow,
　Defects of loneliness controls.
We then, who are this new soul, know
　Of what we are composed and made,
For th'atomies of which we grow
　Are souls, whom no change can invade.
But O alas, so long, so far
　Our bodies why do we forbear?
They are ours, though they are not we. We are
　The intelligences, they the spheres.
We owe them thanks, because they thus
　Did us to us at first convey,
Yielded their forces, sense, to us,
　Nor are dross to us, but allay.

On man heaven's influence works not so,
    But that it first imprints the air,
So soul into the soul may flow,
    Though it to body first repair.
As our blood labours to beget
    Spirits as like souls as it can,
Because such fingers need to knit
    That subtle knot which makes us man:
So must pure lovers' souls descend
    T' affections and to faculties,
Which sense may reach and apprehend,
    Else a great Prince in prison lies.
To our bodies turn we then, that so
    Weak men on love revealed may look;
Love's mysteries in souls do grow,
    But yet the body is his book,
And if some lover such as we
    Have heard this dialogue of one,
Let him still mark us, he shall see
    Small change when we're to bodies gone.

The Relique

When my grave is broke up again
Some second guest to entertain,
(For graves have learned that woman-head
To be to more than one a bed)
    And he that digs it spies
A bracelet of bright hair about the bone,
    Will he not let us alone,
And think that there a loving couple lies,
Who thought that this device might be some way
To make their souls, at the last busy day,
Meet at this grave and make a little stay?

If this fall in a time or land
Where mis-devotion doth command,
Then he that digs us up will bring
Us to the Bishop and the King
    To make us Reliques; then

Thou shalt be Mary Magdalen, and I
    A something else thereby;
All women shall adore us and some men;
And since at such time miracles are sought,
I would have that age by this paper taught
What miracles we harmless lovers wrought

    First, we loved well and faithfully,
    Yet knew not what we loved nor why,
    Difference of sex no more we knew
    Than our Guardian Angels do;
      Coming and going, we
Perchance might kiss, but not between those meals;
    Our hands ne'er touched the seals
Which nature, injured by late law, sets free
These miracles we did; but now, alas,
All measure and all language I should pass,
Should I tell what a miracle she was.

Change

Although thy hand and faith and good works too,
Have sealed thy love which nothing should undo,
Yea, though thou fall back, that apostasy
Confirm thy love; yet much, much I fear thee.
Women are like the Arts, forced unto none,
Open to all searchers, unprized if unknown.
If I have caught a bird and let him fly,
Another fowler using these means, as I,
May catch the same bird; and, as these things be,
Women are made for men, not him, nor me.
Foxes and goats, all beasts change when they please;
Shall women, more hot, wily, wild than these,
Be bound to one man, and did Nature then
Idly make them apter to endure than men?
They're our clogs, not their own; if a man be
Chained to a galley, yet the galley's free;
Who hath a plough-land casts all his seed corn there,
And yet allows his ground more corn should bear;
Though Danube into the sea must flow,

The sea receives the Rhine, Volga, and Po.
By nature, which gave it, this liberty
Thou lov'st, but Oh! canst thou love it and me?
Likeness glues love: and if that thou so do,
To make us like and love, must I change too?
More than thy hate, I hate it, rather let me
Allow her change, than change as oft as she,
And so not teach, but force my opinion
To love not any one, nor every one.
To live in one land is captivity,
To run all countries a wild roguery;
Waters stink soon if in one place they bide,
And in the vast sea are more putrefied:
But when they kiss one bank and, leaving this,
Never look back but the next bank do kiss,
Then are they purest; Change is the nursery
Of music, joy, life and eternity.

The Autumnal

No Spring, nor Summer Beauty hath such grace
    As I have seen in one Autumnal face.
Young Beauties force our love, and that's a rape,
    This doth but counsel, yet you cannot 'scape.
If 'twere a shame to love, here 'twere no shame,
    Affection here takes Reverence's name.
Were her first years the Golden Age; that's true,
    But now she's gold oft-tried and ever new.
That was her torrid and inflaming time,
    This is her tolerable tropic clime.
Fair eyes, who asks more heat than come from hence,
    He in a fever wishes pestilence.
Call not these wrinkles, graves; if graves they were,
    They were Love's graves, for else he is no where.
Yet lies not Love dead here, but here doth sit
    Vowed to this trench like an anachorite.
And here, till hers, which must be his death, come,
    He doth not dig a grave, but build a tomb.
Here dwells he, though he sojourn everywhere
    In Progress, yet his standing house is here.

Here where still evening is, not noon nor night;
 Where no voluptuousness, yet all delight.
In all her words, unto all hearers fit,
 You may at Revels, you at Council, sit.
This is love's timber, youth his underwood;
 There he as wine in June enrages blood,
Which then comes seasonabliest, when our taste
 And appetite to other things is past.
Xerxes' strange Lydian love, the Platane tree,
 Was loved for age, none being so large as she,
Or else because, being young, nature did bless
 Her youth with age's glory, barrenness.
If we love things long sought, Age is a thing
 Which we are fifty years in compassing;
If transitory things which soon decay,
 Age must be loveliest at the latest day.
But name not Winter-faces, whose skin's slack,
 Lank as an unthrift's purse, but a soul's sack;
Whose eyes seek light within, for all here's shade;
 Whose mouths are holes rather worn out than made;
Whose every truth to a several place is gone
 To vex their souls at Resurrection;
Name not these living Death's-heads unto me,
 For these not ancient but antique be.
I hate extremes, yet I had rather stay
 With tombs than cradles to wear out a day.
Since such love's natural lation is, may still
 My love descend, and journey down the hill,
Not panting after growing beauties, so
 I shall ebb out with them who homeward go.

On His Mistress

By our first strange and fatal interview,
By all desires which thereof did ensue,
By our long starving hopes, by that remorse
Which my words' masculine persuasive force
Begot in thee, and by the memory
Of hurts, which spies and rivals threatened me,

Lation, *astronomical motion.*

I calmly beg; but by thy father's wrath,
By all pains, which want and divorcement hath,
I conjure thee, and all the oaths which I
And thou have sworn to seal joint constancy,
Here I unswear, and overswear them thus,
Thou shalt not love by ways so dangerous.
Temper, O fair Love, love's impetuous rage,
Be my true mistress still, not my feigned page;
I'll go, and by thy kind leave, leave behind
Thee, only worthy to nurse in my mind
Thirst to come back; O if thou die before,
My soul from other lands to thee shall soar.
Thy (else Almighty) beauty cannot move
Rage from the seas, nor thy love teach them love,
Nor tame wild Boreas' harshness; thou hast read
How roughly he in pieces shiveréd
Fair Orithea, whom he swore he loved.
Fall ill or good, 'tis madness to have proved
Dangers unurged; feed on this flattery,
That absent lovers one in th'other be.
Dissemble nothing, not a boy, nor change
Thy body's habit, nor mind's; be not strange
To thyself only; all will spy in thy face
A blushing womanly discovering grace;
Richly clothed apes are called apes, and as soon
Eclipsed as bright we call the moon the moon.
Men of France, changeable chameleons,
Spitals of diseases, shops of fashions,
Love's fuellers, and the rightest company
Of players, which upon the world's stage be,
Will quickly know thee, and no less, alas!
Th'indifferent Italian, as we pass
His warm land, well content to think thee page,
Will hunt thee with such lust and hideous rage
As Lot's fair guests were vexed. But none of these
Nor spongy hydroptic Dutch shall thee displease,
If thou stay here. O stay here, for to thee
England is only a worthy gallery,
To walk in expectation, till from thence
Our greatest King call thee to his presence.
When I am gone, dream me some happiness,

Nor let thy looks our long-hid love confess,
Nor praise, nor dispraise me, nor bless nor curse
Openly love's force, nor in bed fright thy nurse
With midnight startings, crying out: Oh, oh,
Nurse, O my love is slain, I saw him go
O'er the white Alps alone; I saw him, I,
Assailed, fight, taken, stabbed, bleed, fall, and die.
Augur me better chance, except great Jove
Think it enough for me to have had thy love.

Love's Progress

Whoever loves, if he do not propose
The right true end of love, he's one that goes
To sea for nothing but to make him sick.
Love is a bear whelp born, if we o'er-lick
Our love, and force it new strange shapes to take,
We err, and of a lump a monster make.
Were not a calf a monster that were grown
Faced like a man, though better than his own?
Perfection is in unity; prefer
One woman first, and then one thing in her.
I, when I value gold, may think upon
The ductileness, the application,
The wholesomeness, the ingenuity,
From rust, from soil, from fire ever free:
But if I love it, 'tis because 'tis made
By our new nature (Use) the soul of trade.

All these in women we might think upon
(If women had them) and yet love but one.
Can men more injure women than to say
They love for that, by which they're not they?
Makes virtue women? Must I cool my blood
Till I both be, and find one, wise and good?
May barren angels love so. But if we
Make love to woman, virtue is not she,
As beauty's not, nor wealth; he that strays thus
From her to hers is more adulterous
Than if he took the maid. Search every sphere

And firmament, our Cupid is not there;
He's an infernal god, and underground
With Pluto dwells, where gold and fire abound;
Men to such gods their sacrificing coals
Did not in altars lay, but pits and holes.
Although we see the celestial bodies move
Above the earth, the earth we till and love;
So we her airs contemplate, words and heart,
And virtues, but we love the centric part.

Nor is the soul more worthy, or more fit
For love than this, as infinite it is.
But in attaining this desiréd place
How much they err that set out at the face.
The hair a forest is of ambushes,
Of springs, snares, fetters and manacles;
The brow becalms us when 'tis smooth and plain,
And when 'tis wrinkled shipwrecks us again.
Smooth, 'tis a paradise where we would have
Immortal stay, and wrinkled 'tis our grave.
The nose (like to the first meridian) runs
Not 'twixt an East and West, but 'twixt two suns;
It leaves a cheek, a rosy hemisphere
On either side, and then directs us where
Upon the Islands Fortunate we fall,
(Not faint Canaries, but ambrosial)
Her swelling lips; to which when we are come,
We anchor there and think ourselves at home,
For they seem all; there sirens' songs and there
Wise Delphic oracles to fill the ear,
There in a creek where chosen pearls do swell,
The remora, her cleaving tongue, doth dwell.
These and the glorious promontory, her chin,
O'erpast, and the strait Hellespont between
The Sestos and Abydos of her breasts,
(Not of two lovers, but two loves the nests)
Succeeds a boundless sea, but yet thine eye
Some island moles may scattered there descry,
And sailing toward her India in that way
Shall at her fair Atlantic navel stay;
Though thence the current be thy pilot made,

Yet ere thou be where thou wouldst be embayed
Thou shalt upon another forest set,
Where many shipwreck and no further get.
When thou art there, consider what this chase
Misspent by thy beginning at the face.

Rather set out below; practise my art,
Some symmetry the foot hath with that part
Which thou dost seek, and is thy map for that
Lovely enough to stoop, but not stay at;
Least subject to disguise and change it is;
Men say the Devil never can change his.
It is the emblem that hath figuréd
Firmness; 'tis the first part that comes to bed.
Civility we see refined; the kiss
Which at the face began, transplanted is,
Since to the hand, since to the Imperial knee,
Now at the Papal foot delights to be.
If kings think that the nearer way, and do
Rise from the foot, lovers may do so too;
For as free spheres move faster far than can
Birds, whom the air resists, so may that man
Which goes this empty and acthereal way,
Than if at beauty's elements he stay.
Rich Nature hath in woman wisely made
Two purses, and their mouths aversely laid;
They then which to the lower tribute owe,
That way which that Exchequer looks must go.
He that doth not, his error is as great
As who by clyster gave the stomach meat.

Satire II

Sir: though (I thank God for it) I do hate
Perfectly all this town, yet there's one state
In all ill things so excellently best
That hate toward them breeds pity toward the rest.
Though poetry indeed be such a sin
As I think that brings dearth and Spaniards in,
Though like the pestilence and old-fashioned love
Riddlingly it catch men, and doth remove

Never till it be starved out, yet their state
Is poor, disarmed, like papists, not worth hate.
One (like a wretch which at Bar judged as dead,
Yet prompts him which stands next, and cannot read,
And saves his life) gives idiot actors means
(Starving himself) to live by his laboured scenes;
As in some organ puppets dance above
And bellows pant below, which them do move.
One would move Love by rhythms; but witchcraft's charms
Bring not now their old fears nor their old harms;
Rams and slings now are silly battery,
Pistolets are the best artillery.
And they who write to Lords, rewards to get,
Are they not like singers at doors for meat?
And they who write, because all write, have still
That excuse for writing and for writing ill;
But he is worst who beggarly doth chaw
Others' wits' fruits, and in his ravenous maw
Rankly digested doth those things out spew
As his own things; and they are his own, 'tis true,
For if one eat my meat, though it be known
The meat was mine, th'excrement is his own.
But these do me no harm, nor they which use
To out-do dildos and out-usure Jews,
To out-drink the sea, to out-swear the litany;
Who with sins all kinds as familiar be
As confessors, and for whose sinful sake
Schoolmen new tenements in hell must make,
Whose strange sins Canonists could hardly tell
In which Commandment's large receipt they dwell.
But these punish themselves. The insolence
Of Coscus only breeds my just offence,
Whom time (which rots all, and makes botches pox,
And, plodding on, must make a calf an ox)
Hath made a Lawyer, which was, alas, of late
But a scarce poet; jollier of this state
Than are now beneficed ministers, he throws
Like nets or lime-twigs wheresoever he goes
His title of Barrister on every wench,
And woos in language of the Pleas and Bench.
A motion, Lady. Speak, Coscus. I have been

In love ever since tricesimo of the Queen,
Continual claims I have made, injunctions got
To stay my rival's suit that he should not
Proceed. Spare me. In Hilary term I went;
You said, if I returned next 'size in Lent
I should be in remitter of your grace;
In th'interim my letters should take place
Of affidavits; words, words, which would tear
The tender labyrinth of a soft maid's ear
More, more than ten Sclavonians scolding, more
Than when winds in our ruined abbeys roar.
When sick with poetry and possessed with Muse
Thou wast and mad, I hoped; but men which choose
Law-practice for mere gain, bold soul, repute
Worse than embrothelled strumpets prostitute.
Now like an owl-like watchman, he must walk
His hand still at a bill, now he must talk
Idly like prisoners, which whole months will swear
That only suretyship hath brought them there,
And to every suitor lie in everything
Like a King's favourite, yea, like a King;
Like a wedge in a block, wring to the bar,
Bearing like asses; and more shameless far
Than carted whores, lie to the grave Judge; for
Bastardy abounds not in King's titles nor
Simony and Sodomy in churchmen's lives,
As these things do in him; by these he thrives.
Shortly (as the sea) he will compass all our land,
From Scots to Wight, from Mount to Dover strand.
And spying heirs melting with luxury,
Satan will not joy at their sins, as he.
For as a thrifty wench scrapes kitchen stuff,
And barrelling the droppings and the snuff
Of wasting candles, which in thirty years
(Relique-like kept) perchance buys wedding gear;
Piecemeal he gets lands, and spends as much time
Wringing each acre as men pulling prime.
In parchments then, large as his fields, he draws
Assurances big as glossed civil laws,
So huge that men (in our time's forwardness)
Are Fathers of the Church for writing less.

These he writes not, nor for those written pays,
Therefore spares no length; as in those first days
When Luther was professed he did desire
Short Pater nosters, saying as a friar
Each day his beads; but having left those laws
Adds to Christ's prayer the Power and glory clause.
And when he sells or changes land he impairs
His writings, and unwatched leaves out "ses heires,"
As slily as any commentator goes by
Hard words or sense; or in divinity
As controverters in vouched texts leave out
Shrewd words, which might against them clear the doubt.
Where are those spread woods which clothed heretofore
Those bought lands? Not built, nor burnt within door.
Where's th'old landlord's troops and alms? In great halls
Carthusian fasts and fulsome bacchanals
Equally I hate; means bless; in rich men's homes
I bid kill some beasts but no hecatombs;
None starve, none surfeit so; but Oh, we allow
Good works as good, but out of fashion now,
Like old rich wardrobes; but my words none draws
Within the vast reach of the huge statute laws.

Holy Sonnets

VII

At the round earth's imagined corners, blow
Your trumpets, Angels, and arise, arise
From death, you numberless infinities
Of souls, and to your scattered bodies go,
All whom the flood did, and fire shall o'erthrow,
All whom war, dearth, age, agues, tyrannies,
Despair, law, chance, hath slain, and you whose eyes
Shall behold God and never taste death's woe.
But let them sleep, Lord, and me mourn a space,
For if above all these my sins abound,
'Tis late to ask abundance of Thy grace,
When we are there; here on this lowly ground,
Teach me how to repent; for that's as good
As if Thou hadst seal'd my pardon with Thy blood.

X

Death, be not proud though some have called thee
Mighty and dreadful, for thou art not so,
For those, whom thou think'st thou dost overthrow,
Die not, poor Death, nor yet canst thou kill me.
From rest and sleep, which but thy pictures be,
Much pleasure, then from thee much more must flow,
And soonest our best men with thee do go,
Rest of their bones and soul's delivery.
Thou art slave to Fate, Chance, kings and desperate men,
And dost with poison, war, and sickness dwell,
And poppy or charms can make us sleep as well,
And better than thy stroke; why swell'st thou then?
One short sleep past, we wake eternally,
And death shall be no more, Death, thou shalt die.

A Hymn to Christ at the Author's Last Going into Germany

In what torn ship soever I embark,
That ship shall be my emblem of Thy Ark;
What sea soever swallow me, that flood
Shall be to me an emblem of Thy blood;
Though Thou with clouds of anger do disguise
Thy face, yet through that mask I know those eyes,
    Which, though they turn away sometimes,
        They never will despise.

I sacrifice this Island unto Thee,
And all whom I loved there and who loved me;
When I have put our seas 'twixt them and me,
Put Thou Thy sea betwixt my sins and Thee.
As the tree's sap doth seek the root below
In winter, in my winter now I go,
    Where none but Thee, th'Eternal root
        Of true Love, I may know.

Nor Thou nor Thy religion dost control
The amorousness of an harmonious soul,
But Thou would'st have that love Thyself; as Thou
Art jealous, Lord, so I am jealous now,

Thou lov'st not till from loving more Thou free
My soul; who ever gives, takes liberty.
   O, if Thou car'st not whom I love,
     Alas, Thou lov'st not me.

Seal then this bill of my Divorce to All,
On whom those fainter beams of love did fall;
Marry those loves, which in youth scattered be
On Fame, Wit, Hopes (false mistresses) to Thee.
Churches are best for prayer that have least light;
To see God only I go out of sight.
   And to 'scape stormy days, I choose
     An everlasting night.

A Hymn to God the Father

Wilt Thou forgive that sin where I begun,
   Which is my sin though it were done before?
Wilt Thou forgive that sin through which I run
   And do run still, though still I do deplore?
     When Thou hast done, Thou hast not done,
      For I have more.

Wilt Thou forgive that sin by which I have won
   Others to sin? and made my sin their door?
Wilt Thou forgive that sin which I did shun
   A year or two, but wallowed in a score?
     When Thou hast done, Thou hast not done,
      For I have more.

I have a sin of fear, that when I have spun
   My last thread I shall perish on the shore;
Swear by Thyself that at my death Thy son
   Shall shine as He shines now and heretofore;
     And having done that Thou hast done,
      I fear no more.

RICHARD BARNEFIELD

(1574–1627)

"As It Fell upon a Day"

As it fell upon a day
In the merry month of May,
Sitting in a pleasant shade
Which a grove of myrtles made,
Beasts did leap and birds did sing,
Trees did grow and plants did spring;
Every thing did banish moan,
Save the nightingale alone:
She, poor bird, as all forlorn,
Lean'd her breast up-till a thorn,
And there sung the dolefull'st ditty,
That to hear it was great pity:
"Fie, fie, fie," now would she cry;
"Tereu, Tereu!" by and by;
That to hear her so complain,
Scarce I could from tears refrain;
For her griefs so lively shown
Made me think upon mine own.
Ah, thought I, thou mourn'st in vain!
None takes pity on thy pain:
Senseless trees they cannot hear thee;
Ruthless beasts they will not cheer thee:
King Pandion he is dead;
All thy friends are lapped in lead;
All thy fellow birds do sing,
Careless of thy sorrowing.
Even so, poor bird, like thee,
None alive will pity me.
Whilst as fickle Fortune smiled,
Thou and I were both beguiled.

Every one that flatters thee
Is no friend to misery.
Words are easy, like the wind;
Faithful friends are hard to find:
Every man will be thy friend

Whilst thou hast wherewith to spend;
But if store of crowns be scant,
No man will supply thy want.
If that one be prodigal,
Bountiful they will him call,
And with such-like flattering,
"Pity but he were a king;"
If he be addict to vice,
Quickly him they will entice;
If to women he be bent,
They have at commandment:
But if Fortune once do frown,
Then farewell his great renown;
They that fawn'd on him before
Use his company no more.
He that is thy friend indeed,
He will help thee in thy need:
If thou sorrow, he will weep;
If thou wake, he cannot sleep;
Thus of every grief in heart
He with thee doth bear a part.
These are certain signs to know
Faithful friend from flattering foe.

The Passionate Pilgrim, 1599

"If Music and Sweet Poetry..."

If music and sweet poetry agree,
As they needs must, the sister and the brother,
Then must the love be great 'twixt thee and me,
Because thou lovest the one and I the other.
Dowland to thee is dear, whose heavenly touch
Upon the lute doth ravish human sense;
Spenser to me, whose deep conceit is such
As passing all conceit needs no defence.
Thou lovest to hear the sweet melodious sound
That Phoebus' lute, the queen of music, makes;
And I in deep delight am chiefly drown'd

Whenas himself to singing he betakes.
One god is god of both, as poets feign;
One knight loves both, and both in thee remain.

The Passionate Pilgrim, 1599

JOSEPH HALL

(1574–1656)

FROM *Vergidemiarum*

1.

PROLOGUE

I first adventure, with foolhardy might,
To tread the steps of perilous despite:
I first adventure; follow me who list,
And be the second English satirist.
Envy waits at my back, Truth on my side;
Envy will be my page, and Truth my guide.
Envy the margent holds, and Truth the line;
Truth doth approve, but Envy doth repine.
For in this smoothing age who durst indite,
Hath made his pen an hired parasite,
To claw the back of him that beastly lives,
And prank base men in proud superlatives.
Whence damnéd vice is shrouded quite from shame
And crowned with Virtue's meed, immortal name;
Infamy dispossest of native due
Ordained of old on looser life to sue:
The world's eye blearéd with those shameless lies,
Masked in the shew of meal-mouthed poesies.
Go, daring Muse, on with thy thankless task,
And do the ugly face of vice unmask;
And if thou canst not thine high flight remit,
So as it may a lowly satire fit,
Let lowly satires rise aloft to thee:
Truth be thy speed, and Truth thy patron be.

2.

A Gentle Squire would gladly entertain
Into his house some trencher-chaplain,
Some willing man that might instruct his sons,
And that would stand to good conditions:

First, that he lie upon the truckle-bed,
While his young master lieth o'er his head;
Secondly, that he do, on no default,
Ever presume to sit above the salt;
Third, that he never charge his trencher twice;
Fourth, that he use all comely courtesies,
Sit bare at meals, and one half rise and wait;
Last, that he never his young master beat,
But he must ask his mother to define
How many yerks she would his breech should line.
All these observed, he would contented be
To give five marks and winter livery.

Book 2, Satire 6

JOHN MARSTON

(1575?–1634)

FROM Antonio and Mellida, 1602

Andrugio: My thoughts are fixed in contemplation
Why this huge earth, this monstrous animal
That eats her children, should not have eyes and
ears.
Philosophy maintains that Nature's wise
And forms no useless nor unperfect thing.
Did Nature make the earth, or the earth Nature?
For earthly dirt makes all things, makes the man,
Moulds me up honour, and, like a cunning Dutch-
man
Paints me a puppet e'en with seeming breath,
And gives a sot appearance of a soul.
Go to, go to; thou liest, Philosophy.
Nature forms things unperfect, useless, vain.
Why made she not the earth with eyes and ears
That she might see desert and hear men's plaints
That when a soul is splitted, sunk with grief,
He might fall thus upon the breast of earth
And in her ear halloo his misery,
Exclaiming thus: O thou all-bearing Earth,
Which men do gape for till thou cramm'st their
mouths

And chok'st their throats with dust, open thy breast,
And let me sink into thee; look who knocks;
Andrugio calls. But O, she's deaf and blind.
A wretch but lean relief on earth can find.

FROM *Antonio's Revenge*, 1602

PROLOGUE

The rawish dank of clumsy winter ramps
The fluent summer's vein; and drizzling sleet
Chilleth the wan bleak cheek of the numbed earth,
While snarling gusts nibble the juiceless leaves
From the nak'd shuddering branch, and pills the skin
From off the soft and delicate aspects.
O now methinks a sullon tragic scene
Would suit the time with pleasing congruence.
May we be happy in our weak devoir,
And all part pleased in most wished content.
But sweat of Hercules can ne'er beget
So blest an issue. Therefore we proclaim,
If any spirit breathes within this round
Uncapable of weighty passion,
(As from his birth being hugged in the arms
And nuzzled 'twixt the breasts of Happiness)
Who winks and shuts his apprehension up
Of common sense of what men were, and are;
Who would not know what men must be; let such
Hurry amain from our black-visaged shows,
We shall affright their eyes. But if a breast
Nailed to the earth with grief, if any heart
Pierced through with anguish pant within this ring,
If there be any blood whose heat is choked
And stifled with true sense of misery;
If aught of these strains fill his consort up,
They arrive most welcome. O that our power
Could lackey or keep wing with our desires,
That with unused poise of style and sense
We might weigh massy in judicious scale!
Yet here's the prop that doth support our hopes;
When our scenes falter or invention halts,
Your favour will give crutches to our faults.

FROM *Satire V*

Ambitious Gorgons, wide-mouthed Lamians,
Shape-changing Proteans, damned Briarians,
Is Minos dead, is Rhadamanth asleep?
That ye thus dare unto Jove's palace creep?
What, hath Rhamnusia spent her knotted whip,
That ye dare strive on Hebe's cup to sip?
Yet know, Apollo's quiver is not spent,
But can abate your daring hardiment.
Python is slain, yet his accurséd race
Dare look divine Astraea in the face;
Chaos returns, and with confusion;
Involves the world with strange disunion;
For Pluto sits in that adoréd chair
Which doth belong unto Minerva's heir.
O hecatombe! O catastrophe!
From Midas' pomp to Irus' beggary!
Prometheus, who celestial fire
Did steal from heaven, therewith to inspire
Our earthly bodies with a senseful mind,
Whereby we might the depth of nature find,
Is dinged to hell, and vulture eats his heart,
Which did such deep philosophy impart
To mortal men; when thieving Mercury,
That even in his new-born infancy
Stole fair Apollo's quiver and Jove's mace,
And would have filched the lightning from his place,
But that he feared he should have burned his wing
And singed his downy feathers' new-come spring;
He that in ghastly shade of night doth lead
Our souls unto the empire of the dead;
When he that better doth deserve a rope
Is a fair planet in our horoscope,
And now hath caduceus in his hand,
Of life and death that hath the sole command.
Thus petty thefts are paid and soundly whipped.
But greater crimes are slightly overslipped;
Nay, he's a god that can do villainy
With a good grace and glib facility.

THOMAS HEYWOOD
(1575?–1650?)

"Pack, Clouds, Away..."

Pack, clouds, away, and welcome, day!
With night we banish sorrow.
Sweet air, blow soft; mount, lark, aloft
To give my love good morrow.
Wings from the wind to please her mind,
Notes from the lark I'll borrow:
Bird, prune thy wing, nightingale, sing,
To give my love good morrow.
To give my love good morrow,
Notes from them all I'll borrow.

Wake from thy nest, robin redbreast!
Sing, birds, in every furrow,
And from each bill let music shrill
Give my fair love good morrow.
Black-bird and thrush in every bush,
Stare, linnet, and cock-sparrow,
You pretty elves, among yourselves
Sing my fair love good morrow.
To give my love good morrow
Sing, birds, in every furrow.

The Rape of Lucrece, 1608

JOHN CHALKHILL
(15—?–16—?)

Coridon's Song

Oh, the sweet contentment
The countryman doth find.
   High trolollie lolly loe,
   High trolollie lee,
That quiet contemplation
Possesseth all my mind:
   Then care away,
   And wend along with me.

For courts are full of flattery,
As hath too oft been tried;
  High trolollie lollie loe,
  High trolollie lee,
The city full of wantonness,
And both are full of pride.
  Then care away,
  And wend along with me.

But oh, the honest countryman
Speaks truly from his heart,
  High trolollie lollie loe,
  High trolollie lee,
His pride is in his tillage,
His horses and his cart:
  Then care away,
  And wend along with me.

Our clothing is good sheepskins,
Grey russet for our wives,
  High trolollie lollie loe,
  High trolollie lee.
'Tis warmth and not gay clothing
That doth prolong our lives;
  Then care away,
  And wend along with me.

The ploughman though he labour hard,
Yet on the holy-day,
  High trolollie lollie loe,
  High trolollie lee,
No emperor so merrily
Does pass his time away;
  Then care away,
  And wend along with me.

To recompense our tillage
The heavens afford us showers;
  High trolollie lollie loe,
  High trolollie lee.

And for our sweet refreshments
The earth affords us bowers:
    Then care away,
    And wend along with me.

The cuckoo and the nightingale
Full merrily do sing,
    High trolollie lollie loe,
    High trolollie lee.
And with their pleasant roundelays
Bid welcome in the spring:
    Then care away,
    And wend along with me.

This is not half the happiness
The countryman enjoys;
    High trolollie lollie loe,
    High trolollie lee.
Though others think they have as much
Yet he that says so lies:
    Then come away, turn
    Countryman with me.

CYRIL TOURNEUR
(1575?–1626)
FROM *The Atheist's Tragedy*, 1611

Borachio: Walking next day upon the fatal shore,
Among the slaughtered bodies of their men
Which the full-stomached sea had cast upon
The sands, it was my unhappy chance to light
Upon a face, whose favour when it lived,
My astonished mind informed me I had seen.
He lay in's armour, as if that had been
His coffin; and the weeping sea, like one
Whose milder temper doth lament the death
Of him whom in his rage he slew, runs up
The shore, embraces him, kisses his cheek,
Goes back again, and forces up the sands
To bury him, and every time it parts

Sheds tears upon him, till at last (as if
It could no longer endure to see the man
Whom it had slain, yet loath to leave him) with
A kind of unresolved unwilling pace,
Winding her waves one in another, like
A man that folds his arms or wrings his hands
For grief, ebbed from the body, and descends
As if it would sink down into the earth,
And hide itself for shame of such a deed.

FROM *The Revenger's Tragedy*, 1607

1.

Vendice (addressing his mistress' skull):
My study's ornament, thou shell of death,
Once the bright face of my betrothéd lady,
When life and beauty naturally filled out
These ragged imperfections;
When two heaven-pointed diamonds were set
In those unsightly rings—then 'twas a face
So far beyond the artificial shine
Of any woman's bought complexion,
That the uprightest man (if such there be,
That sin but seven times a day) broke custom,
And made up eight with looking after her.
O, she was able to ha' made a usurer's son
Melt all his patrimony in a kiss;
And what his father fifty yearës told,
To have consumed, and yet his suit been cold.
But, O accurséd palace!
Thee, when thou wert apparelled in the flesh,
The old duke poisoned,
Because thy purer part would not consent
Unto his palsied lust; for old men lustful
Do show like young men angry, eager, violent,
Outbidden like their limited performances.
O, 'ware an old man hot and vicious!
"Age, as in gold, in lust is covetous."
Vengeance, thou murder's quit-rent, and whereby
Thou show'st thyself tenant to tragedy,

O keep thy day, hour, minute, I beseech,
For those thou hast determined. Hum! who e'er
    knew
Murder unpaid? faith, give revenge her due,
She has kept touch hitherto; be merry, merry,
Advance thee, O thou terror to fat folks,
To have their costly three-piled flesh worn off
As bare as this; for banquets, ease and laughter
Can make great men, as greatness goes by clay;
But wise men little are more great than they.

2.

Vendice: And now methinks I could e'en chide myself
For doating on her beauty, though her death
Shall be revenged after no common action.
Does the silkworm expend her yellow labours
For thee? For thee does she undo herself?
Are lordships sold to maintain ladyships,
For the poor benefit of a bewildering minute?
Why does yon fellow falsify highways,
And put his life between the judge's lips,
To refine such a thing—keeps horse and men
To beat their valours for her?
Surely we are all mad people, and they
Whom we think are, are not; we mistake those;
'Tis we are mad in sense, they but in clothes.

Does every proud and self-affecting dame
Camphire her face for this, and grieve her Maker
In sinful baths of milk, when many an infant starves
For her superfluous outside—all for this?
Who now bids twenty pounds a night? prepares
Music, perfumes, and sweetmeats? All are hushed.
Thou may'st lie chaste now! it were fine, methinks,
To have thee seen at revels, forgetful feasts,
And unclean brothels! sure, 'twould fright the sin-
    ner,
And make him a good coward; put a reveller
Out of his antic amble,
And cloy an epicure with empty dishes.

Here might a scornful and ambitious woman
Look through and through herself. See, ladies, with
        false forms
You deceive men, but cannot deceive worms.

HENRY FARLEY

(15—?–16—?)

"To See a Quaint Outlandish Fowl"

To see a quaint outlandish fowl,
A quaint baboon, an ape, an owl,
A dancing bear, a giant's bone,
A foolish engine move alone,
A morris dance, a puppet-play,
Mad Tom to sing a roundelay,
A woman dancing on a rope,
Bull-baiting also at the *Hope*,
A rimer's jests, a juggler's cheats,
A tumbler showing cunning feats,
Or players acting on the stage—
There goes the bounty of our age:
        But unto any pious motion
        There's little coin and less devotion.

St. Paul's Church, Her Bill for the Parliament, 1621

JOHN FLETCHER

(1579–1625)

"Hold Back Thy Hours..."

Hold back thy hours, dark Night, till we have done;
    The Day will come too soon;
Young maids will curse thee, if thou steal'st away
And leav'st their losses open to the day:
    Stay, stay, and hide
    The blushes of the bride.

Stay, gentle Night, and with thy darkness cover
　　The kisses of her lover;
Stay, and confound her tears and her shrill cryings,
Her weak denials, vows, and often-dyings;
　　Stay, and hide all:
　　But help not, though she call.

The Maid's Tragedy, 1619

"Lay a Garland on My Hearse"

Lay a garland on my hearse
　　Of the dismal yew;
Maidens, willow branches bear;
　　Say, I died true

My love was false, but I was firm
　　From my hour of birth.
Upon my buried body lie
　　Lightly, gentle earth!

The Maid's Tragedy, 1619

"Sing His Praises..."

Sing his praises that doth keep
　　Our flocks from harm,
Pan, the father of our sheep;
　　And arm in arm
Tread we softly in a round,
Whilst the hollow murmuring ground
Fills the music with her sound.

Pan, oh, great god Pan, to thee
　　Thus do we sing!
Thou that keep'st us chaste and free
　　As the young spring;
Ever be thy honour spoke,
From that place the morn is broke,
To that place day doth unyoke!

The Faithful Shepherdess, 1609–10

"Now the Lusty Spring..."

Now the lusty spring is seen;
  Golden yellow, gaudy blue,
  Daintily invite the view.
Everywhere on every green,
Roses blushing as they blow,
  And enticing men to pull,
Lilies whiter than the snow,
  Woodbines of sweet honey full:
    All love's emblems, and all cry,
    "Ladies, if not plucked, we die."

Yet the lusty spring hath stayed;
  Blushing red and purest white
  Daintily to love invite
Every woman, every maid.
Cherries kissing as they grow,
  And inviting men to taste,
Apples even ripe below,
  Winding gently to the waist:
    All love's emblems, and all cry,
    "Ladies, if not plucked, we die."

The Tragedy of Valentinian, 1619?

"Hear, Ye Ladies..."

Hear, ye ladies that despise,
  What the mighty Love has done;
Fear examples, and be wise:
  Fair Callisto was a nun;
Leda, sailing on the stream
  To deceive the hopes of man,
Love accounting but a dream,
  Doted on a silver swan;
    Danaë, in a brazen tower,
    Where no love was, loved a shower.

Hear, ye ladies that are coy,
   What the mighty Love can do;
Fear the fierceness of the boy:
   The chaste moon he makes to woo;
Vesta, kindling holy fires,
   Circled round about with spies,
Never dreaming loose desires,
    Doting at the altar dies;
      Ilion, in a short hour, higher
      He can build, and once more fire.

The Tragedy of Valentinian, 1619?

"Care-Charming Sleep..."

Care-charming Sleep, thou easer of all woes,
Brother to Death, sweetly thyself dispose
On this afflicted prince; fall like a cloud,
In gentle showers; give nothing that is loud,
Or painful to his slumbers; easy, light,
And as a purling stream, thou son of Night,
Pass by his troubled senses; sing his pain,
Like hollow murmuring wind or silver rain;
Into this prince gently, oh, gently slide,
And kiss him into slumbers like a bride.

The Tragedy of Valentinian, 1619?

"God Lyaeus, Ever Young"

God Lyaeus, ever young,
Ever honoured, ever sung,
Stained with blood of lusty grapes,
In a thousand lusty shapes,
Dance upon the mazer's brim,
In the crimson liquor swim;
From thy plenteous hand divine,
Let a river run with wine:
    God of youth, let this day here
    Enter neither care nor fear.

The Tragedy of Valentinian, 1619?

"Cast Our Caps and Cares Away"

Cast our caps and cares away:
This is beggars' holiday!
At the crowning of our king,
Thus we ever dance and sing.
In the world look out and see,
Where so happy a prince as he?
Where the nation lives so free,
And so merry as do we?
Here at liberty we are,
And enjoy our ease and rest:
To the field we are not pressed;
Nor are called into the town,
To be troubled with the gown.
Hang all offices, we cry,
And the magistrate too, by!
When the subsidy's increased,
We are not a penny sessed;
Nor will any go to law
With the beggar for a straw.
All which happiness, he brags,
He doth owe unto his rags.

Beggars' Bush, 1622

"Dearest, Do Not You Delay Me"

Dearest, do not you delay me,
  Since, thou knowest, I must be gone;
Wind and tide, 'tis thought, doth stay me,
  But 'tis wind that must be blown
    From that breath, whose native smell
    Indian odours far excel.

Oh, then speak, thou fairest fair!
  Kill not him that vows to serve thee;
But perfume this neighbouring air,
  Else dull silence, sure, will sterve me:
    'Tis a word that's quickly spoken,
    Which being restrained, a heart is broken.

The Spanish Curate, 1622

"'Tis Late and Cold..."

'Tis late and cold; stir up the fire;
Sit close, and draw the table nigher;
Be merry, and drink wine that's old,
A hearty medicine 'gainst a cold:
Your beds of wanton down the best,
Where you shall tumble to your rest;
I could wish you wenches too,
But I am dead, and cannot do.
Call for the best the house may ring,
Sack, white, and claret, let them bring,
And drink apace, while breath you have;
You'll find but cold drink in the grave:
Plover, partridge, for your dinner,
And a capon for the sinner,
You shall find ready when you're up,
And your horse shall have his sup:
Welcome, welcome, shall fly round,
And I shall smile, though under ground.

The Lovers' Progress, 1623*

"Hence, All You Vain Delights"

Hence, all you vain delights,
As short as are the nights
Wherein you spend your folly!
There's nought in this life sweet,
If man were wise to see't,
　　But only melancholy,
　　Oh, sweetest melancholy!
Welcome, folded arms, and fixéd eyes,
A sight that piercing mortifies,
A look that's fastened to the ground,
A tongue chained up without a sound!

Fountain-heads, and pathless groves,
Places which pale passion loves!
Moonlight walks, when all the fowls

Are warmly housed, save bats and owls!
  A midnight bell, a parting groan!
  These are the sounds we feed upon;
Then stretch our bones in a still gloomy valley,
Nothing's so dainty sweet as lovely melancholy.

The Nice Valour, 16—?

"Beauty Clear and Fair"

Beauty clear and fair,
        Where the air
Rather like a perfume dwells;
        Where the violet and rose
        Their blue veins and blush disclose,
And come to honour nothing else.

Where to live near,
        And planted there,
Is to live, and still live new;
        Where to gain a favour is
        More than light, perpetual bliss—
Make me live by serving you.

Dear, again back recall
        To this light,
A stranger to himself and all;
        Both the wonder and the story
        Shall be yours, and eke the glory:
I am your servant, and your thrall.

The Elder Brother, 1637

"Drink To-day..."

Drink to-day, and drown all sorrow,
You shall perhaps not do't to-morrow.
Best while you have it use your breath;
There is no drinking after death.

Wine works the heart up, wakes the wit,
There is no cure 'gainst age but it.
It helps the head-ache, cough and phthisic,
And is for all diseases physic.

Then let us swill, boys, for our health;
Who drinks well, loves the commonwealth.
And he that will to bed go sober,
Falls with the leaf, still in October.

The Bloody Brother, 1639

"Hide, Oh, Hide Those Hills..."

Hide, oh, hide those hills of snow,
    Which thy frozen bosom bears,
On whose tops the pinks that grow
    Are of those that April wears;
But first set my poor heart free,
Bound in those icy chains by thee.

The Bloody Brother, 1639

"Tell Me, Dearest..."

Tell me, dearest, what is love?
'Tis a lightning from above;
    'Tis an arrow, 'tis a fire,
    'Tis a boy they call Desire.
        'Tis a grave
        Gapes to have
Those poor fools that long to prove.

Tell me more, are women true?
Yes, some are, and some as you.
    Some are willing, some are strange,
    Since you men first taught to change.
        And till troth
        Be in both,
All shall love, to love anew.

Tell me more yet, can they grieve?
Yes, and sicken sore, but live:
    And be wise, and delay,
    When you men are as wise as they.
      Then I see,
      Faith will be,
Never till they both believe.

The Captain, 1613?

"Away, Delights..."

Away, delights; go seek some other dwelling,
    For I must die:
Farewell, false love; thy tongue is ever telling
    Lie after lie.
For ever let me rest now from thy smarts;
    Alas, for pity go,
    And fire their hearts
That have been hard to thee; mine was not so.

Never again deluding Love shall know me,
    For I will die;
And all those griefs that think to overgrow me,
    Shall be as I:
For ever will I sleep, while poor maids cry,
    "Alas, for pity stay,
    And let us die
With thee; men cannot mock us in the clay."

The Captain, 1613?

"Weep No More..."

Weep no more, nor sigh nor groan,
Sorrow calls no time that's gone;
Violets plucked, the sweetest rain
Makes not fresh nor grow again;
Trim thy locks, look cheerfully,

Fate's hidden ends eyes cannot see.
Joys as wingéd dreams fly fast,
Why should sadness longer last?
Grief is but a wound to woe;
Gentlest fair, mourn, mourn no moe.

The Queen of Corinth, 1617?

"Roses Their Sharp Spines..."

Roses their sharp spines being gone,
Not royal in their smells alone,
    But in their hue;
Maiden pinks of odour faint,
Daisies smell-less, yet most quaint,
    And sweet thyme true;

Primrose, first-born child of Ver,
Merry spring-time's harbinger,
    With her bells dim;
Oxlips in their cradles growing,
Marigolds on death-beds blowing,
    Lark-heels trim;

All, dear Nature's children sweet,
Lie 'fore bride and bridegroom's feet,
    Blessing their sense!
Not an angel of the air,
Bird melodious or bird fair,
    Be absent hence!

The crow, the slanderous cuckoo, nor
The boding raven, nor chough hoar,
    Nor chattering pie,
May on our bridehouse perch or sing,
Or with them any discord bring,
    But from it fly.

[Also attributed to WILLIAM SHAKESPEARE]
The Two Noble Kinsmen, 1634

"Orpheus with His Lute..."

Orpheus with his lute made trees,
And the mountain tops that freeze,
   Bow themselves when he did sing:
To his music plants and flowers
Ever sprung, as sun and showers,
   There had made a lasting spring.

Every thing that heard him play,
Even the billows of the sea,
   Hung their heads, and then lay by.
In sweet music is such art,
Killing care and grief of heart
   Fall asleep, or hearing die.

[*Also attributed to* WILLIAM SHAKESPEARE]
King Henry VIII, 1613

FROM *The Faithful Shepherdess*

1.

Here be grapes, whose lusty blood
Is the learned poets' good,
Sweeter yet did never crown
The head of Bacchus; nuts more brown
Than the squirrel's teeth that crack them;
Deign, oh, fairest fair, to take them.
For these black-eyed Dryope
Hath often times commanded me
With my claspéd knee to climb:
See how well the lusty time
Hath decked their rising cheeks in red,
Such as on your lips is spread.
Here be berries for a queen,
Some be red, some be green;
These are of that luscious meat,
The great god Pan himself doth eat:
All these, and what the woods can yield,
The hanging mountain or the field,
I freely offer, and ere long
Will bring you more, more sweet and strong.

2.

   Here be woods as green
As any, air likewise as fresh and sweet
As where smooth Zephyrus plays on the fleet
Face of the curléd streams, with flowers as many
As the young spring gives, and as choice as any;
Here be all new delights, cool streams and wells,
Arbours o'ergrown with woodbines; caves, and dells;
Choose where thou wilt, whilst I sit by and sing,
Or gather rushes, to make thee a ring
For thy pale fingers; tell thee tales of love,
How the pale Phoebe, hunting in a grove,
First saw the boy Endymion, from whose eyes
She took eternal fire that never dies;
How she convey'd him softly in a sleep,
His temples bound with poppy, to the steep
Head of old Latmus, where she stoops each night,
Gilding the mountain with her brother's light,
To kiss her sweetest.

3.

   Shall I stray
In the middle air, and stay
The sailing rack, or nimbly take
Hold by the moon, and gently make
Suit to the pale queen of night
For a beam to give thee light?
Shall I dive into the sea,
And bring thee coral, making way
Through the rising waves that fall
In snowy fleeces? Dearest, shall
I catch thee wanton fawns, or flies
Whose woven wings the summer dyes
Of many colours? get thee fruit,
Or steal from Heaven old Orpheus' lute?
All these I'll venture for, and more,
To do her service all these woods adore.

Holy virgin, I will dance
Round about these woods as quick
As the breaking light, and prick
Down the lawns, and down the vales
Faster than the windmill-sails.
So I take my leave, and pray
All the comforts of the day,
Such as Phoebus' heat doth send
On the earth, may still befriend
Thee and this arbour!

JOHN WEBSTER

(1580–1630?)

"Call for the Robin..."

Call for the robin redbreast and the wren,
Since o'er shady groves they hover,
And with leaves and flowers do cover
The friendless bodies of unburied men.
Call unto his funeral dole
The ant, the field-mouse and the mole,
To rear him hillocks that shall keep him warm,
And (when gay tombs are robbed) sustain no harm;
But keep the wolf far thence, that's foe to men,
For with his nails he'll dig them up again.

The White Devil, 1612

"Hark, Now Everything Is Still"

Hark, now everything is still,
The screech-owl and the whistler shrill,
Call upon our dame aloud,
And bid her quickly don her shroud!
Much you had of land and rent;
Your length in clay's now competent:
A long war disturbed your mind;
Here your perfect peace is signed.
Of what is't fools make such vain keeping?

Sin their conception, their birth weeping,
Their life a general mist of error,
Their death a hideous storm of terror.
Strew your hair with powders sweet,
Don clean linen, bathe your feet,
And (the foul fiend more to check)
A crucifix let bless your neck:
'Tis now full tide 'tween night and day;
End your groan, and come away.

The Duchess of Malfi, 1623

"All the Flowers of the Spring"

All the flowers of the spring
Meet to perfume our burying;
These have but their growing prime,
And man does flourish but his time:
Survey our progress from our birth;
We are set, we grow, we turn to earth.
Courts adieu, and all delights,
All bewitching appetites!
Sweetest breath and clearest eye,
Like perfumes, go out and die;
And consequently this is done
As shadows wait upon the sun.
Vain the ambition of kings
Who seek by trophies and dead things
To leave a living name behind,
And weave but nets to catch the wind.

The Devil's Law Case, 1623

RICHARD CORBET

(1582–1635)

FROM *The Fairies' Farewell*

Farewell, rewards and fairies,
Good housewives now may say,
For now foul sluts in dairies
Do fare as well as they.

And though they sweep their hearths no less
  Than maids were wont to do,
Yet who of late for cleanliness
  Finds sixpence in her shoe?

Lament, lament, old abbeys,
  The fairies' lost command;
They did but change priests' babies,
  But some have changed your land;
And all your children sprung from thence
  Are now grown puritans,
Who live as changelings ever since
  For love of your demesnes.

At morning and at evening both
  You merry were and glad,
So little care of sleep or sloth
  These pretty ladies had;
When Tom came home from labour
  Or Ciss to milking rose,
Then merrily went their tabor
  And nimbly went their toes.

Witness those rings and roundelays
  Of theirs, which yet remain,
Were footed in queen Mary's days
  On many a grassy plain;
But since of late Elizabeth
  And later James came in,
They never danced on any heath
  As when the time hath bin.

PHINEAS FLETCHER

(1582–1650)

FROM *The Purple Island*

But ah! let me under some Kentish hill
Near rolling Medway 'mong my shepherd peers,
With fearless merry-make and piping still,

Securely pass my few and slow-paced years:
  While yet the great Augustus of our nation
  Shuts up old Janus in this long cessation,
Strengthening our pleasing ease, and gives us sure vacation.

There may I, master of a little flock,
Feed my poor lambs, and often change their fare:
My lovely mate shall tend my sparing stock,
And nurse my little ones with pleasing care;
  Whose love and look shall speak their father plain.
  Health be my feast, Heaven hope, content my gain:
So in my little house my lesser heart shall reign.

The beech shall yield a cool safe canopy,
While down I sit, and chant to th'echoing wood:
Ah, singing might I live and singing die!
So by fair Thames or silver Medway's flood,
  The dying swan, when years her temples pierce,
  In music-strains breathes out her life and verse;
And chanting her own dirge rides on her wat'ry hearse.

What shall I then need seek a patron out,
Or beg a favour from a mistress' eyes,
To fence my song against the vulgar rout,
Or shine upon me with her Geminis?
  What care I, if they praise my slender song?
  Or reck I, if they do me right or wrong?
A shepherd's bliss nor stands nor falls to ev'ry tongue.

FROM *Elisa, or an Elegy upon the Unripe Decease of Sir Antony Irby*

My dearest Betty, my more lovéd heart,
I leave thee now; with thee all earthly joying:
Heaven knows, with thee alone I sadly part:
All other earthly sweets have had their cloying;
  Yet never full of thy sweet love's enjoying,
  Thy constant loves, next Heaven I did refer them:
Had not much grace prevailed 'fore Heaven I should prefer
    them.

I leave them now the trumpet calls away;
In vain thine eyes beg for some time's reprieving;
Yet in my children here immortal stay:
In one I die, in many ones am living:
   In them and for them stay thy too much grieving:
   Look but on them, in them thou still wilt see
Married with thee again thy twice-two Antony.

And when with little hands they stroke thy face,
As in thy lap they sit (ah careless) playing,
And stammering ask a kiss, give them a brace;
The last from me: and then a little staying
   And in their face some part of me surveying,
   In them give me a third, and with a tear
Show thy dear love to him who loved thee ever dear.

And now our falling house leans all on thee;
This little nation to thy care commend them:
In thee it lies that hence they want not me;
Themselves yet cannot, thou the more, defend them;
   And when green age permits to goodness bend them:
   A mother were you once, now both you are:
Then with this double style double your love and care.

Turn their unwary steps into the way:
What first the vessel drinks, it long retaineth;
No bars will hold when they have used to stray:
And when for me one asks and weeping plaineth,
   Point thou to Heaven, and say, he there remaineth:
   And if they live in grace, grow and persever,
There shall they live with me: else shall they see me never.

My God, oh, in Thy fear here let them live;
Thy wards are they, take them to Thy protection:
Thou gav'st them first, now back to Thee I give;
Direct then Thou, and help her weak direction;
   That reunited by Thy strong election,
   Thou now in them, they then may live in Thee;
And seeing here Thy will, may there Thy glory see.

Betty, let these last words long with thee dwell:
If yet a second hymen do expect thee,
Though well he love thee, once I loved as well:
Yet if his presence make thee less respect me,
　Ah, do not in my children's good neglect me:
　Let me this faithful hope departing have;
More easy shall I die, and sleep in careless grave.

Farewell, farewell; I feel my long long rest,
And iron sleep my leaden heart oppressing:
Night after day, sleep after labour's best;
Port after storms, joy after long distressing:
　So weep thy loss, as knowing 'tis my blessing:
　Doth as a widow and a Christian grieve:
Still live I in thy thoughts, but as in Heaven I live.

SIR JOHN BEAUMONT
(1583–1627)

FROM Of My Dear Son, Gervase Beaumont

Can I, who have for others oft compiled
The songs of Death, forget my sweetest child,
Which like a flower crushed, with a blast is dead,
And ere full time hangs down his smiling head,
Expecting with clear hope to live anew,
Among the angels fed with heavenly dew?

Dear Lord, receive my son, whose winning love
To me was like a friendship, far above
The course of nature or his tender age,
Whose looks could all my bitter griefs assuage;
Let his pure soul ordained sev'n years to be
In that frail body, which was part of me,
Remain my pledge in Heav'n, as sent to show
How to this port at ev'ry step I go.

LORD HERBERT OF CHERBURY

(1583–1648)

Sonnet

Thus ends my love, but this doth grieve me most
    That so it ends; but that ends too; this yet
Besides the wishes, hopes and time I lost
    Troubles my mind awhile, that I am set
Free, worse than denied. I can neither boast
    Choice nor success, as my case is, nor get
Pardon from myself that I loved not
    A better mistress, or her worse. This debt
Only's her due still, that she be forgot
    Ere changed lest I love none; this done, the taint
    Of foul inconstancy is cleared at least
In me. There only rests but to unpaint
    Her form in my mind, that so dispossest
It be a temple, but without a saint.

Madrigal

How should I love my best?
What though my love unto that height be grown
    That taking joy in you alone
    I utterly this world detest;
Should I not love it as the only place
    Where beauty hath his perfect grace
    And is possest?

But I beauties despise;
You universal beauty seem to me,
    Giving and showing form and degree
    To all the rest in your fair eyes;
Yet should I not love them as parts whereon
    Your beauty, their perfection
    And top, doth rise?

But even myself I hate;
So far my love is from the least delight
That at my very self I spite,
Senseless of any happy state;
Yet may I not with justest reason fear
How hating her I truly her
Can celebrate?

Thus unresolvéd still
Although world, life, nay what is fair beside
I cannot for your sake abide,
Methinks I love not to my fill;
Yet if a greater love you can devise
In love you some other wise,
Believe't, I will.

Kissing

Come hither Womankind and all their worth,
Give me thy kisses as I call them forth.
Give me the billing-kiss, that of the dove,
A kiss of love;
The melting-kiss, a kiss that doth consume
To a perfume;
The extract-kiss, of every sweet a part,
A kiss of art;
The kiss which ever stirs some new delight,
A kiss of might;
The twaching smacking kiss, and when you cease
A kiss of peace;
The music-kiss, crotchet and quaver time,
The kiss of rhyme;
The kiss of eloquence, which doth belong
Unto the tongue;
The kiss of all the sciences in one,
The Kiss alone.
So 'tis enough.

Elegy over a Tomb

Must I then see, alas! eternal night
   Sitting upon those fairest eyes,
And closing all those beams, which once did rise
   So radiant and bright,
That light and heat in them to us did prove
   Knowledge and Love?

Oh, if you did delight no more to stay
   Upon this low and earthly stage,
But rather chose an endless heritage,
   Tell us at least, we pray,
Where all the beauties that those ashes owed
   Are now bestowed?

Doth the Sun now his light with yours renew?
   Have Waves the curling of your hair?
Did you restore unto the Sky and Air,
   The red and white and blue?
Have you vouchsafed to flowers since your death
   That sweetest breath?

Had not Heaven's Lights else in their houses slept,
   Or to some private life retired?
Must not the Sky and Air have else conspired,
   And in their Regions wept?
Must not each flower else the earth could breed
   Have been a weed?

But thus enriched, may we not yield some cause
   Why they themselves lament no more?
That must have changed the course they held before,
   And broke their proper laws,
Had not your beauties given this second birth
   To Heaven and Earth?

Tell us, for Oracles must still ascend,
   For those that crave them at your tomb;
Tell us, where are those beauties now become,
   And what they now intend;
Tell us, alas, that cannot tell our grief,
   Or hope relief.

FROM *An Ode upon a Question Moved,*
Whether Love Should Continue for Ever?

O no, beloved, I am most sure
  Those virtuous habits we acquire,
  As being with the Soul entire,
Must with it evermore endure.

For if where sins and vice reside
  We find so foul a guilt remain,
  As never dying in his stain
Still punished in the Soul doth bide;

Much more that true and real joy
  Which in a virtuous love is found
  Must be more solid in its ground
Than Fate or Death can e'er destroy.

Else should our Souls in vain elect,
  And vainer yet were Heaven's laws,
  When to an everlasting Cause
They gave a perishing Effect.

Nor here on earth, then, nor above,
  Our good affection can impair;
  For where God doth admit the fair,
Think you that he excludeth Love?

WILLIAM BASSE

(1583?–1653?)

On Mr. Wm. Shakespeare

Renowned Spenser lie a thought more nigh
To learned Chaucer, and rare Beaumont lie
A little nearer Spenser, to make room
For Shakespeare in your threefold, fourfold tomb.
To lodge all four in one bed make a shift
Until doomsday, for hardly will a fift
Betwixt this day and that by Fate be slain,
For whom your curtains may be drawn again.

If your precedency in death doth bar
A fourth place in your sacred sepulchre,
Under this carvéd marble of thine own,
Sleep, rare tragedian, Shakespeare, sleep alone;
Thy unmolested peace, unsharéd cave,
Possess as Lord, not tenant, of thy grave,
That unto us and others it may be
Honour hereafter to be laid by thee.

PHILIP MASSINGER

(1583–1640)

Song

The blushing rose and purple flower,
    Let grow too long, are soonest blasted;
Dainty fruit, though sweet, will sour,
    And rot in ripeness, left untasted.
Yet here is one more sweet than these;
The more you taste, the more she'll please.

Beauty that's enclosed with ice,
    Is a shadow chaste as rare;
Then how much those sweets entice,
    That have issue full as fair!
Earth cannot yield from all her powers
One equal for dame Venus' bowers.

The Picture, 1629

Song

Why art thou slow, thou rest of trouble, Death,
    To stop a wretch's breath,
That calls on thee, and offers her sad heart
    A prey unto thy dart?
I am nor young nor fair; be, therefore, bold;
    Sorrow hath made me old,
Deformed and wrinkled; all that I can crave
    Is, quiet in my grave.

Such as live happy hold long life a jewel;
   But to me thou art cruel,
If thou end not my tedious misery;
   And I soon cease to be.
Strike, and strike home, then; pity unto me
   In one short hour's delay, is tyranny.

The Emperor of the East, 1631

FRANCIS BEAUMONT
(1584–1616)

"Shake Off Your Heavy Trance!"

Shake off your heavy trance!
   And leap into a dance
Such as no mortals use to tread:
   Fit only for Apollo
To play to, for the moon to lead,
   And all the stars to follow!

The Masque of the Inner Temple, 1612–3

"Ye Should Stay Longer..."

Ye should stay longer if we durst:
   Away! Alas that he that first
Gave Time wild wings to fly away—
Hath now no power to make him stay!
And though these games must needs be played,
I would this pair, when they are laid,
   And not a creature nigh 'em,
Could catch his scythe, as he doth pass,
And clip his wings, and break his glass,
   And keep him ever by 'em.

The Masque of the Inner Temple, 1612–3

On the Marriage of a Beauteous Young Gentlewoman with an Ancient Man

Fondly, too curious Nature, to adorn
Aurora with the blushes of the morn:
Why do her rosy lips breathe gums and spice
Unto the East, and sweet to Paradise?
Why do her eyes open the day? her hand
And voice entrance the panther, and command
Incensèd winds; her breasts, the tents of love,
Smooth as the godded swan or Venus' dove,
Soft as the balmy dew whose every touch
Is pregnant—but why those rich spoils, when such
Wonder and perfection must be led
A bridal captive unto Tithon's bed?
Aged and deformèd Tithon! Must thy twine
Circle and blast at once what care and time
Had made for wonder? Must pure beauty have
No other foil but ruin and a grave?
So have I seen the pride of Nature's store,
The orient pearl, chained to the sooty Moor;
So hath the diamond's bright ray been set
In night and wedded to the negro jet.
See, see, how thick those showers of pearl do fall
To weep her ransom or her funeral;
Whose every treasured drop congealed might bring
Freedom and ransom to a fettered king;
While tyrant Wealth stands by, and laughs to see
How he can wed love and antipathy.
Hymen, thy pine burns with adulterate fire.
Thou and thy quivered boy did once conspire
To mingle equal flames, and then no shine
Of gold, but beauty dressed the Paphian shrine.
Roses and lilies kissed; the amorous vine
Did with the fair and straight-limbed elm entwine.

On the Tombs in Westminster Abbey

Mortality, behold and fear,
What a change of flesh is here!
Think how many royal bones
Sleep within this heap of stones;
Here they lie had realms and lands,
Who now want strength to stir their hands;
Where, from their pulpits sealed with dust,
They preach: "In greatness is no trust."
Here's an acre sown indeed
With the richest royalest seed
That the earth did e'er suck in
Since the first man died for sin.
Here the bones of birth have cried:
"Though gods they were, as men they died."
Here are sands, ignoble things,
Dropt from the ruined sides of kings.
Here's a world of pomp and state
Buried in dust, once dead by fate.

FROM Mr. Francis Beaumont's Letter to Ben Jonson

The sun, which doth the greatest comfort bring
To absent friends, because the self-same thing
They know they see, however absent, is
Here our best hay-maker—forgive me this!
It is our country style. In this warm shine
I lie and dream of your full Mermaid wine.

Methinks the little wit I had is lost
Since I saw you; for wit is like a rest
Held up at tennis, which men do the best
With the best gamesters. What things have we seen
Done at the Mermaid! Heard words that have been
So nimble and so full of subtle flame
As if that every one from whence they came
Had meant to put his whole wit in a jest,
And had resolved to live a fool the rest

Of his dull life. Then when there hath been thrown
Wit able enough to justify the town
For three days past, wit that might warrant be
For the whole city to talk foolishly
Till that were cancelled, and when that was gone
We left an air behind us which alone
Was able to make the two next companies
Right witty, though but downright fools mere wise.

WILLIAM DRUMMOND OF HAWTHORNDEN
(1585–1649)

Madrigal

Like the Idalian Queen,
Her hair about her eyne,
With neck and breasts' ripe apples to be seen,
At first glance of the Morn
In Cyprus' gardens gathering those fair flowers
Which of her blood were born,
I saw, but fainting saw, my paramours.
The Graces naked danced about the place,
The winds and trees amazed
With silence on her gazed,
The flowers did smile, like those upon her face,
And as their aspen stalks those fingers band,
That she might read my case,
A hyacinth I wished me in her hand.

Sonnet

Dear quirister, who from those shadows sends,
Ere that the blushing dawn dare show her light,
Such sad lamenting strains that night attends
Become all ear, stars stay to hear thy plight;
If one whose grief even reach of thought transcends,
Who ne'er, not in a dream, did taste delight,
May thee importune who like case pretends
And seems to joy in woe, in woe's despite;

Tell me, so may thou Fortune milder try
And long, long sing, for what thou thus complains?
Sith, winter gone, the sun in dappled sky
Now smiles on meadows, mountains, woods and plains?
The bird, as if my questions did her move,
With trembling wings sobbed forth, *I love, I love.*

Song

Phoebus, arise,
And paint the sable skies
With azure, white and red:
Rouse Memnon's mother from her Tithon's bed
That she thy cariere may with roses spread,
The nightingales thy coming each where sing,
Make an eternal spring,
Give life to this dark world which lieth dead.
Spread forth thy golden hair
In larger locks than thou wast wont before,
And emperor-like decore
With diadem of pearl thy temples fair;
Chase hence the ugly night
Which serves but to make dear thy glorious light.
This is that happy morn,
That day, long-wished day,
Of all my life so dark,
(If cruel stars have not my ruin sworn,
And fates not hope betray)
Which, only white, deserves
A diamond for ever should it mark:
This is the morn should bring into this grove
My love to hear and recompense my love.
Fair king, who all preserves,
But show thy blushing beams,
And thou two sweeter eyes
Shalt see than those which by Peneus' streams
Did once thy heart surprise,
Nay, suns which shine as clear
As thou when two thou did to Rome appear.
Now, Flora, deck thyself in fairest guise;

If that ye, winds, would hear
A voice surpassing far Amphion's lyre,
Your stormy chiding stay,
Let zephyr only breathe
And with her tresses play,
Kissing sometimes those purple ports of death.
The winds all silent are,
And Phoebus in his chair,
Ensaffroning sea and air,
Makes vanish every star:
Night like a drunkard reels
Beyond the hills to shun his flaming wheels.
The fields with flowers are decked in every hue,
The clouds bespangle with bright gold their blue:
Here is the pleasant place
And everything save Her who all should grace.

Sonnet

My lute, be as thou wast when thou didst grow
With thy green mother in some shady grove,
When immelodious winds but made thee move,
And birds on thee their ramage did bestow.
Sith that dear voice which did thy sounds approve,
Which used in such harmonious strains to flow,
Is reft from earth to tune those spheres above,
What art thou but a harbinger of woe?
Thy pleasing notes, be pleasing notes no more,
But orphan wailings to the fainting ear,
Each stop a sigh, each sound draws forth a tear,
Be therefore silent as in woods before;
Or if that any hand to touch thee deign,
Like widowed turtle still her loss complain.

Sonnet

A passing glance, a lightning long the skies
That ush'ring thunder dies straight to our sight,
A spark, of contraries which doth arise,

Then drowns in the huge depths of day and night,
Is this small Small called life, held in such price
Of blinded wights who nothing judge aright:
Of Parthian shaft so swift is not the flight
As life, that wastes itself and living dies.
Oh, what is human greatness, valour, wit?
What fading beauty, riches, honour, praise?
To what doth serve in golden thrones to sit,
Thrall earth's vast round, triumphal arches raise?
All is a dream, learn in this prince's fall,
In whom, save death, naught mortal was at all.

GILES EARLE

(15—?–16—?)

Tom o' Bedlam's Song

From the hag and hungry goblin
That into rags would rend ye,
  And the spirit that stands
  By the naked man
In the book of moons defend ye,
That of your five sound senses
You never be forsaken,
  Nor wander from
  Yourselves with Tom
Abroad to beg your bacon.

    While I do sing, "Any food, any feeding,
     Feeding, drink or clothing?
      Come, dame or maid,
       Be not afraid,
     Poor Tom will injure nothing."

Of thirty bare years have I
Twice twenty been enragéd,
  And of forty been
  Three times fifteen
In durance sadly cagéd

On the lordly lofts of Bedlam
With stubble soft and dainty.
  Brave bracelets strong,
  Sweet whips, ding-dong,
With wholesome hunger plenty.

    And now I do sing, &c.

With a thought I took for Maudlin,
And a cruse of cockle pottage,
  With a thing thus tall,
  Sky bless you all!
I befell into this dotage.
I slept not since the conquest,
Till then I never wakéd,
  Till the roguish boy
  Of love where I lay
Me found and stript me naked.

    And now I do sing, &c.

When I short have shorn my sow's face
And swigged my horny barrel
  In an oaken inn
  I pound my skin
As a suit of gilt apparel.
The moon's my constant mistress
And the lowly owl my morrow;
  The flaming drake
  And the night-crow make
Me music to my sorrow.

    While I do sing, &c.

The palsy plagues my pulses
When I prig your pigs or pullen,
  Your culvers take,
  Or matchless make
Your chanticleer or sullen—

When I want provant with Humphrey
I sup, and when benighted,
  I repose in Paul's
  With waking souls
Yet never am affrighted.

  But I do sing, &c.

I know more than Apollo,
For oft, when he lies sleeping,
  I see the stars
  At bloody wars
In the wounded welkin weeping,
The moon embrace her shepherd
And the queen of love her warrior,
  While the first doth horn
  The star of the morn
And the next the heavenly farrier.

  While I do sing, &c.

The gipsy Snap, and Pedro,
Are none of Tom's comradoes;
  The punk I scorn
  And the cutpurse sworn
And the roaring-boys' bravadoes;
The meek, the white, the gentle,
Me handle, touch, and spare not,
  But those that cross
  Tom Rhinoceros
Do what the panther dare not.

  Although I do sing, &c.

With a heart of furious fancies
Whereof I am commander,
  With a burning spear
  And a horse of air
To the wilderness I wander;

By a knight of ghosts and shadows
I summoned am to tourney
  Ten leagues beyond
  The wide world's end
—Methinks it is no journey.

Yet will I sing, "Any food, any feeding,
  Feeding, drink or clothing?
   Come, dame or maid,
    Be not afraid,
   Poor Tom will injure nothing."

JOHN FORD

(1586–1639)

"Fly Hence, Shadows..."

Fly hence, shadows, that do keep
Watchful sorrows, charmed in sleep!
Though the eyes be overtaken,
Yet the heart doth ever waken
Thoughts, chained up in busy snares
Of continual woes and cares;
Love and griefs are so expressed,
As they rather sigh than rest.
Fly hence, shadows, that do keep
Watchful sorrows, charmed in sleep.

The Lover's Melancholy, 1628

"Can You Paint a Thought?..."

Can you paint a thought? or number
Every fancy in a slumber?
Can you count soft minutes roving
From a dial's point by moving?
Can you grasp a sigh? or, lastly,
Rob a virgin's honour chastely?
No, oh no! yet you may
  Sooner do both that and this,
  This and that, and never miss,

Than by any praise display
  Beauty's beauty; such a glory
  As beyond all fate, all story,
    All arms, all arts,
    All loves, all hearts,
Greater than those or they,
Do, shall, and must obey.

The Broken Heart, 1639

"Oh, No More, No More..."

Oh, no more, no more, too late
  Sighs are spent; the burning tapers
Of a life as chaste as fate,
  Pure as are unwritten papers,
Are burned out; no heat, no light
Now remains; 'tis ever night.

Love is dead; let lovers' eyes,
  Locked in endless dreams,
  Th' extremes of all extremes,
Ope no more, for now Love dies.
Now Love dies—implying
Love's martyrs must be ever, ever dying.

The Broken Heart, 1639

"Glories, Pleasures..."

Glories, pleasures, pomps, delights and ease
    Can but please
The outward senses, when the mind
Is or untroubled or by peace refined.

Crowns may flourish and decay,
Beauties shine, but fade away.

Youth may revel, but it must
Lie down in a bed of dust.

Earthly honours flow and waste,
Time alone doth change and last.

Sorrows mingled with contents, prepare
          Rest for care;
Love only reigns in death; though art
Can find no comfort for a broken heart.

The Broken Heart, 1639

"Pleasures, Beauty ..."

Pleasures, beauty, youth attend ye,
    Whilst the Spring of nature lasteth;
Love and melting thoughts befriend ye,
    Use the time ere Winter hasteth.
        Active blood and free delight
        Place and privacy invite.
Do, do! be kind as fair,
Lose not opportunity for air.

She is cruel that denies it,
    Bounty best appears in granting,
Stealth of sport as soon supplies it,
    Whilst the dues of love are wanting.
        Here's the sweet exchange of bliss
        When each whisper proves a kiss.
In the game are felt no pains,
For in all the loser gains.

The Lady's Trial, 1638

SIR FRANCIS KYNASTON
(1587–1642)

To Cynthia
(ON CONCEALMENT OF HER BEAUTY)

Do not conceal thy radiant eyes,
The star-light of serenest skies,
Lest wanting of their heavenly light,
They turn to Chaos' endless night.

Do not conceal those tresses fair,
The silken snares of thy curled hair,
Lest finding neither gold nor ore
The curious silkworm work no more.

Do not conceal those breasts of thine,
More snow-white than the Apennine,
Lest if there be like cold or frost
The lily be for ever lost.

Do not conceal that fragrant scent,
Thy breath, which to all flowers hath lent
Perfumes, lest it being supprest
No spices grow in all the East.

Do not conceal thy heavenly voice,
Which makes the hearts of gods rejoice,
Lest Music hearing no such thing
The nightingale forget to sing.

Do not conceal nor yet eclipse
Thy pearly teeth with coral lips,
Lest that the seas cease to bring forth
Gems which from thee have all their worth.

Do not conceal no beauty-grace,
That's either in thy mind or face,
Lest virtue overcome by vice
Make men believe no Paradise.

GEORGE WITHER

(1588–1667)

The Author's Resolution

Shall I wasting in despair
Die because a woman's fair?
Or make pale my cheeks with care
'Cause another's rosy are?
Be she fairer than the day,
Or the flowery meads in May,
　　If she think not well of me
　　What care I how fair she be?

Shall my silly heart be pined
'Cause I see a woman kind?
Or a well-disposéd nature
Joinéd with a lovely feature?
Be she meeker, kinder than
Turtle-dove or pelican,
   If she be not so to me
   What care I how kind she be?

Shall a woman's virtues move
Me to perish for her love?
Or her well-deservings known
Make me quite forget mine own?
Be she with that goodness blessed
Which may merit name of best,
   If she be not such to me
   What care I how good she be?

'Cause her fortune seems too high,
Shall I play the fool and die?
She that bears a noble mind,
If not outward helps she find,
Thinks what with them he would do
That without them dares her woo;
   And unless that mind I see
   What care I how great she be?

Great, or good, or kind, or fair,
I will ne'er the more despair;
If she loves me, this believe,
I will die, ere she shall grieve;
If she slight me when I woo
I can scorn and let her go,
   For if she be not for me
   What care I for whom she be?

A Love Sonnet

I loved a lass, a fair one,
   As fair as e'er was seen;
She was indeed a rare one,
   Another Sheba queen.

But fool as then I was,
   I thought she loved me too;
But now, alas! sh' 'as left me,
   Falero, lero, loo.

Her hair like gold did glister,
   Each eye was like a star;
She did surpass her sister,
   Which passed all others far.
She would me honey call;
   She'd, O she'd kiss me too;
But now, alas! sh' 'as left me,
   Falero, lero, loo.

In summer time to Medley,
   My love and I would go;
The boatmen there stood ready,
   My love and I to row.
For cream there would we call,
   For cakes, and for prunes too;
But now, alas! sh' 'as left me,
   Falero, lero, loo.

Many a merry meeting
   My love and I have had;
She was my only sweeting,
   She made my heart full glad.
The tears stood in her eyes,
   Like to the morning dew;
But now, alas! sh' 'as left me,
   Falero, lero, loo.

And as abroad we walked,
   As lovers' fashion is,
Oft as we sweetly talked
   The sun should steal a kiss.
The wind upon her lips
   Likewise most sweetly blew;
But now, alas! sh' 'as left me,
   Falero, lero, loo.

Her cheeks were like the cherry,
    Her skin as white as snow;
When she was blithe and merry,
    She angel-like did show.
Her waist exceeding small,
    The fives did fit her shoe;
But now, alas! sh' 'as left me,
    Falero, lero, loo.

In summer time or winter
    She had her heart's desire;
I still did scorn to stint her
    From sugar, sack, or fire.
The world went round about,
    No cares we ever knew;
But now, alas! sh' 'as left me,
    Falero, lero, loo.

As we walked home together
    At midnight through the town,
To keep away the weather
    O'er her I'd cast my gown.
No cold my love should feel,
    Whate'er the heavens could do;
But now, alas! sh' 'as left me,
    Falero, lero, loo.

Like doves we would be billing,
    And clip and kiss so fast;
Yet she would be unwilling
    That I should kiss the last.
They're Judas-kisses now,
    Since that they proved untrue;
For now, alas! sh' 'as left me,
    Falero, lero, loo.

To maidens' vows and swearing
    Henceforth no credit give;
You may give them the hearing,
    But never them believe.

They are as false as fair,
    Unconstant, frail, untrue;
For mine, alas! has left me,
    Falero, lero, loo.

'Twas I that paid for all things,
    'Twas others drank the wine;
I cannot now recall things,
    Live but a fool to pine.
'Twas I that beat the bush,
    The bird to others flew;
For she, alas! hath left me,
    Falero, lero, loo.

If ever that dame Nature,
    For this false lover's sake,
Another pleasing creature
    Like unto her would make,
Let her remember this,
    To make the other true;
For this, alas! hath left me,
    Falero, lero, loo.

No riches now can raise me,
    No want make me despair;
No misery amaze me,
    Not yet for want I care.
I have lost a world itself.
    My earthly heaven, adieu,
Since she, alas! hath left me,
    Falero, lero, loo.

A Christmas Carol

So now is come our joyful'st feast;
Let every man be jolly.
Each room with ivy-leaves is dressed,
And every post with holly.
    Though some churls at our mirth repine
    Round your foreheads garlands twine,
    Drown sorrow in a cup of wine,
And let us all be merry.

Now all our neighbours' chimneys smoke,
And Christmas blocks are burning;
The ovens they with baked meats choke,
And all their spits are turning.
  Without the door let sorrow lie,
  And if for cold it hap to die,
  We'll bury 't in a Christmas pie,
And evermore be merry.

Now every lad is wondrous trim,
And no man minds his labour;
Our lasses have provided them
A bag-pipe and a tabor.
  Young men, and maids, and girls and boys,
  Give life to one another's joys,
  And you anon shall by their noise
Perceive that they are merry.

Rank misers now do sparing shun,
Their hall of music soundeth,
And dogs thence with whole shoulders run,
So all things there aboundeth.
  The country-folk themselves advance,
  For crowdy-mutton's come out of France;
  And Jack shall pipe, and Jill shall dance,
And all the town be merry.

Ned Swash hath fetched his bands from pawn,
And all his best apparel;
Brisk Nell hath bought a ruff of lawn
With droppings of the barrel;
  And those that hardly all the year
  Had bread to eat or rags to wear,
  Will have both clothes and dainty fare,
And all the day be merry.

Now poor men to the justices
With capons make their arrants,
And if they hap to fail of these
They plague them with their warrants.

But now they feed them with good cheer,
And what they want they take in beer,
For Christmas comes but once a year,
And then they shall be merry.

Good farmers in the country nurse
The poor, that else were undone.
Some landlords spend their money worse,
On lust and pride in London.
    There the roysters they do play,
    Drab and dice their land away,
    Which may be ours another day;
And therefore let's be merry.

The client now his suit forbears,
The prisoner's heart is eased,
The debtor drinks away his cares,
And for the time is pleased.
    Though others' purses be more fat,
    Why should we pine or grieve at that?
    Hang sorrow, care will kill a cat,
And therefore let's be merry.

Hark how the wags abroad do call
Each other forth to rambling;
Anon you'll see them in the hall
For nuts and apples scrambling.
    Hark how the roofs with laughters sound!
    Anon they'll think the house goes round,
    For they the cellar's depths have found,
And there they will be merry.

The wenches with their wassail bowls
About the streets are singing,
The boys are come to catch the owls,
The wild mare in is bringing.
    Our kitchen-boy hath broke his box,
    And to the dealing of the ox
    Our honest neighbours come by flocks,
And here they will be merry.

Now kings and queens poor sheepcotes have,
And mate with everybody;
The honest now may play the knave,
And wise men play at noddy.
　　Some youths will now a-mumming go,
　　Some others play at rowland-hoe,
　　And twenty other gameboys moe,
Because they will be merry.

Then wherefore in these merry days
Should we, I pray, be duller?
No; let us sing our roundelays
To make our mirth the fuller.
　　And, whilst thus inspired we sing,
　　Let all the streets with echoes ring;
　　Woods, and hills, and everything,
Bear witness we are merry.

GILES FLETCHER THE YOUNGER
(1588?–1623)

FROM Christ's Victory in Heaven
(JUSTICE)

She was a Virgin of austere regard,
Not as the world esteems her, deaf and blind,
But as the eagle, that hath oft compared
Her eye with Heav'n's, so, and more brightly shined
Her lamping sight: for she the same could wind
　　Into the solid heart, and with her ears
　　The silence of the thought loud speaking hears,
And in one hand a pair of even scales she wears.

The wingéd Lightning is her Mercury,
And round about her mighty thunders sound:
Impatient of himself lies pining by
Pale Sickness, with his kerchered head upwound,
And thousand noisome plagues attend her round,
　　But if her cloudy brow but once grow foul,
　　The flints do melt and rocks to water roll,
And aery mountains shake and frighted shadows howl.

Upon two stony tables spread before her
She leaned her bosom, more than stony hard,
There slept th' impartial judge and strict restorer
Of wrong or right, with pain or with reward,
There hung the score of all our debts, the card
   Where good and bad, and life and death were painted:
   Was never heart of mortal so untainted,
But when that scroll was read with thousand terrors fainted.

Witness the thunder that Mount Sinai heard,
When all the hill with fiery clouds did flame,
And wandering Israel, with the sight afeared,
Blinded with seeing, durst not touch the same,
But like a wood of shaking leaves became.
   On this dead Justice, she, the living law,
   Bowing herself with a majestic awe,
All Heaven, to hear her speech, did into silence draw.

FROM *Christ's Victory on Earth*

Love is the blossom where there blows
Everything that lives or grows,
Love doth make the heavens to move,
And the Sun doth burn in love;
Love the strong and weak doth yoke,
And makes the ivy climb the oak,
Under whose shadows lions wild,
Softened by love, grow tame and mild;
Love no medicine can appease,
He burns the fishes in the seas,
Not all the skill his wounds can stanch,
Not all the sea his fire can quench;
Love did make the bloody spear
Once a leafy coat to wear,
While in his leaves there shrouded lay
Sweet birds, for love that sing and play;
And of all Love's joyful flame
I the bud and blossom am.
   Only bend thy knee to me,
   Thy wooing shall thy winning be.

See, see the flowers that below
Now as fresh as morning blow,
And of all the virgin rose,
That as bright Aurora shows,
How they all unleavéd die,
Losing their virginity:
Like unto a summer shade,
But now born, and now they fade.
Everything doth pass away,
There is danger in delay,
Come, come gather then the rose,
Gather it, or it you lose.
All the sand of Tagus' shore
Into my bosom casts his ore;
All the valley's swimming corn
To my house is yearly borne;
Every grape of every vine
Is gladly bruised to make me wine.
While ten thousand kings, as proud
To carry up my train have bowed,
And a world of ladies send me
In my chambers to attend me:
All the stars in heaven that shine
And ten thousand more are mine:
   Only bend thy knee to me,
   Thy wooing shall thy winning be.

WILLIAM BROWNE OF TAVISTOCK
(1591–1643?)

FROM *Britannia's Pastorals*

1.

Gentle nymphs, be not refusing,
Love's neglect is time's abusing,
   They and beauty are but lent you,
Take the one and keep the other;
Love keeps fresh what age doth smother;
   Beauty gone, you will repent you.

'Twill be said when ye have proved,
Never swains more truly loved;
 Oh then, fly all nice behaviour.
Pity fain would, as her duty,
Be attending still on beauty,
 Let her not be out of favour.

2.

So shuts the marigold her leaves
 At the departure of the sun;
So from the honeysuckle sheaves
 The bee goes when the day is done;
So sits the turtle when she is but one,
And so all woe, as I, since she is gone.

To some few birds kind Nature hath
 Made all the summer as one day;
Which once enjoyed, cold winter's wrath
 As night they sleeping pass away.
Those happy creatures are that know not yet
The pain to be deprived or to forget.

I oft have heard men say there be
 Some that with confidence profess
The helpful Art of Memory;
 But could they teach forgetfulness
I'd learn, and try what further art could do
To make me love her and forget her too.

FROM *The Inner Temple Masque*

1.

Steer hither, steer your wingéd pines,
 All beaten mariners,
Here lie Love's undiscovered mines,
 A prey to passengers;
Perfumes far sweeter than the best
Which make the Phoenix' urn and nest.
 Fear not your ships,
Nor any to oppose you save our lips,
 But come on shore,
Where no joy dies till love hath gotten more.

2.

> Son of Erebus and Night,
> Hie away; and aim thy flight
> Where consort none other fowl
> Than the bat and sullen owl;
> Where upon thy limber grass
> Poppy and mandragoras,
> With like simples not a few,
> Hang for ever drops of dew.
> Where flows Lethe without coil
> Softly like a stream of oil,
> Hie thee thither, gentle Sleep;
> With this Greek no longer keep.
> Thrice I charge thee by my wand,
> Thrice with moly from my hand
> Do I touch Ulysses' eyes,
> And with the jaspis. Then arise,
> Sagest Greek . . .

"Shall I Love Again..."

Shall I love again, and try
   If I still must love to lose,
And make weak mortality
   Give new birth unto my woes?
No, let me ever live from Love's enclosing,
Rather than love to live in fear of losing.

One whom hasty Nature gives
   To the world without his sight,
Not so discontented lives,
   As a man deprived of light;
'Tis knowledge that gives vigour to our woe,
And not the want but loss that pains us so.

With the Arabian bird then be
   Both the lover and beloved;
Be thy lines thy progeny
   By some gracious fair approved;
So may'st thou live, and be beloved of many,
Without the fear of loss or want of any.

"Welcome, Welcome, Do I Sing"

Welcome, welcome, do I sing,
　　Far more welcome than the spring;
He that parteth from you never
　　Shall enjoy a spring for ever.

Love, that to the voice is near,
　　Breaking from your iv'ry pale,
Need not walk abroad to hear
　　The delightful nightingale.
　　　　　　　　Welcome, welcome, then I sing, &c.

Love, that looks still on your eyes
　　Though the winter have begun
To benumb our arteries,
　　Shall not want the summer's sun.
　　　　　　　　Welcome, welcome, then I sing, &c.

Love, that still may see your cheeks
　　Where all rareness still reposes,
Is a fool if e'er he seeks
　　Other lilies, other roses.
　　　　　　　　Welcome, welcome, then I sing, &c.

Love, to whom your soft lips yields,
　　And perceives your breath in kissing,
All the odours of the fields
　　Never, never shall be missing.
　　　　　　　　Welcome, welcome, then I sing, &c.

Love, that question would anew
　　What fair Eden was of old,
Let him rightly study you
　　And a brief of that behold.
　　　　　　　　Welcome, welcome, then I sing, &c.

A Round

Now that the Spring hath filled our veins
　　With kind and active fire,
And made green liveries for the plains,
　　And every grove a choir;

Sing we a song of merry glee,
  And Bacchus fill the bowl.
Then here's to thee! And thou to me
  And every thirsty soul.

Nor care nor sorrow e'er paid debt,
  Nor never shall do mine;
I have no cradle going yet,
  Not I, by this good wine.

No wife at home to send for me,
  No hogs are in my ground,
No suit at law to pay a fee;
  Then round, old jockey, round!

Shear sheep that have them, cry we still,
  But see that no man 'scape
    To drink of the sherry
    That makes us so merry,
  And plump as the lusty grape.

FROM *Visions*

A rose, as fair as ever saw the north,
Grew in a little garden all alone;
A sweeter flower did Nature ne'er put forth,
Nor fairer garden yet was never known.
The maidens danced about it more and more,
And learned bards of it their ditties made;
The nimble fairies by the pale-faced moon
Watered the root and kissed her pretty shade.
But well-a-day, the gardener careless grew,
The maids and fairies both were kept away,
And in a drought the caterpillars threw
Themselves upon the bud and every spray.
God shield the stock! if Heaven send no supplies,
The fairest blossom of the garden dies.

On the Dowager Countess of Pembroke

Underneath this sable hearse
Lies the subject of all verse,
Sidney's sister, Pembroke's mother;
Death, ere thou hast slain another
Fair and learn'd and good as she,
Time shall throw a dart at thee.

ROBERT HERRICK

(1591–1674)

The Argument of His Book

I sing of Brooks, of Blossoms, Birds and Bowers:
Of April, May, of June, and July-Flowers.
I sing of May-poles, Hock-carts, Wassails, Wakes,
Of Bride-grooms, Brides, and of their Bridal-cakes.
I write of Youth, of Love, and have access
By these, to sing of cleanly-Wantonness.
I sing of Dews, of Rains, and piece by piece
Of Balm, of Oil, of Spice and Ambergris.
I sing of Times trans-shifting; and I write
How Roses first came red, and Lilies white.
I write of Groves, of Twilights, and I sing
The Court of Mab, and of the Fairy-King.
I write of Hell; I sing (and ever shall)
Of Heaven, and hope to have it after all.

Delight in Disorder

A sweet disorder in the dress
Kindles in clothes a wantonness:
A Lawn about the shoulders thrown
Into a fine distraction:
An erring lace, which here and there
Enthralls the crimson stomacher:
A cuff neglectful, and thereby
Ribbons to flow confusedly:

A winning wave (deserving note)
In the tempestuous petticoat:
A careless shoe-string, in whose tie
I see a wild civility:
Do more bewitch me, than when art
Is too precise in every part.

To His Mistress

Choose me your Valentine;
    Next, let us marry:
Love to the death will pine,
    If we long tarry.

Promise, and keep your vows,
    Or vow ye never:
Love's doctrine disallows
    Troth-breakers ever.

You have broke promise twice
    (Dear) to undo me;
If you prove faithless thrice,
    None then will woo ye.

To Dianeme

Sweet, be not proud of those two eyes,
Which star-like sparkle in their skies:
Nor be you proud, that you can see
All hearts your captives; yours, yet free:
Be you not proud of that rich hair,
Which wantons with the love-sick air:
When as that ruby, which you wear,
Sunk from the tip of your soft ear,
Will last to be a precious stone,
When all your world of beauty's gone.

To Violets

Welcome Maids of Honour,
    You do bring
    In the Spring;
And wait upon her.

She has virgins many,
    Fresh and fair;
    Yet you are
More sweet than any.

Y'are the maiden posies,
    And so grac'd,
    To be plac'd,
'Fore damask roses.

Yet though thus respected,
    By and by
    Ye do lie
Poor girls, neglected.

The Primrose

Ask me why I send you here
This sweet Infanta of the year?
Ask me why I send to you
This Primrose, thus bepearl'd with dew?
I will whisper in your ears,
The sweets of love are mixed with tears.

Ask me why this flower does show
So yellow-green, and sickly too?
Ask me why the stalk is weak,
And bending, (yet it doth not break?)
I will answer, These discover
What fainting hopes are in a lover.

Upon Julia's Clothes

Whenas in silks my Julia goes,
Then, then, methinks, how sweetly flows
The liquefaction of her clothes!

Next, when I cast mine eyes and see
That brave vibration each way free,
—O how that glittering taketh me!

To the Virgins, to Make Much of Time

Gather ye rose-buds while ye may,
    Old Time is still a-flying:
And this same flower that smiles to-day,
    To-morrow will be dying.

The glorious lamp of Heaven, the sun,
    The higher he's a-getting;
The sooner will his race be run,
    And nearer he's to setting.

That age is best, which is the first,
    When youth and blood are warmer;
But being spent, the worse, and worst
    Times, still succeed the former.

Then be not coy, but use your time;
    And while ye may, go marry:
For having lost but once your prime,
    You may for ever tarry.

FROM The Hock-Cart or Harvest Home

Come sons of Summer, by whose toil,
We are the lords of wine and oil:
By whose tough labours, and rough hands,
We rip up first, then reap our lands.

Crown'd with the ears of corn, now come,
And, to the pipe, sing harvest home.
Come forth, my lord, and see the cart
Dressed up with all the country art.
See, here a mankin, there a sheet,
As spotless pure, as it is sweet:
The horses, mares, and frisking fillies,
Clad, all, in linen, white as Lilies.
The harvest swains, and wenches bound
For joy, to see the Hock-cart crowned.
About the cart, hear, how the rout
Of rural younglings raise the shout;
Pressing before, some coming after,
Those with a shout, and these with laughter.
Some bless the cart; some kiss the sheaves;
Some prank them up with oaken leaves:
Some cross the fill horse; some with great
Devotion, stroke the home-borne wheat:
While other rustics, less attent
To prayers, than to merriment,
Run after with their breeches rent.
Well, on, brave boys, to your lord's hearth,
Glitt'ring with fire; where for your mirth,
Ye shall see first the large and chief
Foundation of your feast, fat beef:
With upper stories, mutton, veal
And bacon, (which makes full the meal)
With sev'ral dishes standing by,
As here a custard, there a pie,
And here all-tempting frumenty.
And for to make the merry cheer,
If smirking wine be wanting here,
There's that, which drowns all care, stout beer.

To Primroses Fill'd with Morning-Dew

Why do ye weep, sweet babes? Can tears
          Speak grief in you,
          Who were but born
       Just as the modest Morn
       Teem'd her refreshing dew?

Alas, you have not known that shower,
      That mars a flower;
      Nor felt th'unkind
  Breath of a blasting wind;
  Nor are ye worn with years;
      Or warped, as we,
  Who think it strange to see,
Such pretty flowers, (like to orphans young)
To speak by tears, before ye have a tongue.

Speak, whimp'ring younglings, and make known
      The reason, why
      Ye droop, and weep;
  Is it for want of sleep?
  Or childish lullaby?
Or that ye have not seen as yet
      The violet?
      Or brought a kiss
  From that sweetheart, to this?
  No, no, this sorrow shown
      By your tears shed,
  Would have this lecture read,
The things of greatest, so of meanest worth,
Conceiv'd with grief are, and with tears brought forth.

FROM *Oberon's Feast*

A little mushroom table spread,
After short prayers, they set on bread;
A moon-parch'd grain of purest wheat,
With some small glitt'ring grit, to eat
His choice bits with; then in a trice
They make a feast less great than nice.
But all this while his eye is serv'd,
We must not think his ear was starv'd:
But that there was in place to stir
His spleen, the chirring grasshopper;
The merry cricket, puling fly,
The piping gnat for minstrelsy.

And now, we must imagine first,
The elves present to quench his thirst
A pure seed-pearl of infant dew,
Brought and besweetened in a blue
And pregnant violet; which done,
His kitling eyes begin to run
Quite through the table, where he spys
The horns of papery butterflies,
Of which he eats, and tastes a little
Of that we call the cuckoo's spittle.
A little fuzz-ball pudding stands
By, yet not blessed by his hands,
That was too coarse; but then forthwith
He ventures boldly on the pith
Of sugared rush, and eats the sag
And well bestrutted bee's sweet bag:
Gladding his palate with some store
Of emmit's eggs; what would he more?

To Virgins

Hear ye virgins, and I'll teach,
What the times of old did preach.
Rosamund was in a bower
Kept, as Danaë in a tower:
But yet Love (who subtle is)
Crept to that, and came to this.

Be ye locked up like to these,
Or the rich Hesperides;
Or those babies in your eyes,
In their crystal nunneries;
Notwithstanding Love will win,
Or else force a passage in:
And as coy be, as you can,
Gifts will get ye, or the man.

To Daffodils

Fair daffodils, we weep to see
  You haste away so soon:
As yet the early-rising sun
  Has not attain'd his noon.
      Stay, stay,
    Until the hasting day
       Has run
    But to the even-song;
And, having pray'd together, we
    Will go with you along.

We have short time to stay, as you.
  We have as short a Spring;
As quick a growth to meet decay,
  As you, or any thing.
      We die,
    As your hours do, and dry
       Away,
    Like to the Summer's rain;
Or as the pearls of morning's dew
    Ne'er to be found again.

To the Most Fair and Lovely Mistress, Anne Soame, Now Lady Abdie

So smell those odours that do rise
From out the wealthy spiceries:
So smells the flower of blooming clove;
Or roses smother'd in the stove:
So smells the air of spicéd wine;
Or essences of jessamine:
So smells the breath about the hives,
When all the work of honey thrives;
And all the basic factors come
Laden with wax and honey home:
So smell those neat and woven bowers,
All over-arched with orange flowers;

And almond blossoms, that do mix
To make rich these aromatics:
So smell those bracelets, and those bands
Of amber chaf'd between the hands,
When thus enkindled they transpire
A noble perfume from the fire.
The wine of cherries, and to these
The cooling breath of respasses;
The smell of morning's milk, and cream;
Butter of cowslips mixed with them;
Of roasted warden, or bak'd pear,
These are not to be reckon'd here;
When as the meanest part of her,
Smells like the maiden-pomander.
Thus sweet she smells, or what can be
More lik'd by her, or lov'd by me.

The Mad Maid's Song

Good morrow to the day so fair;
   Good morrow Sir to you:
Good morrow to mine own torn hair
   Bedabbled with the dew.

Good morrow to this primrose too;
   Good morrow to each maid;
That will with flowers the tomb bestrew,
   Wherein my love is laid.

Ah woe is me, woe, woe is me,
   Alack and well-a-day!
For pity, Sir, find out that bee,
   Which bore my love away.

I'll seek him in your bonnet brave;
   I'll seek him in your eyes;
Nay, now I think they've made his grave
   I' th' bed of strawberries.

I'll seek him there; I know, ere this,
　　The cold, cold earth doth shake him;
But I will go, or send a kiss
　　By you, Sir, to awake him.

Pray hurt him not; though he be dead,
　　He knows well who do love him,
And who with green turfs rear his head,
　　And who do rudely move him.

He's soft and tender (pray take heed)
　　With bands of cowslips bind him;
And bring him home, but 'tis decreed,
　　That I shall never find him.

Upon the Nipples of Julia's Breast

Have ye beheld (with much delight)
A red rose peeping through a white?
Or else a cherry (double grac'd)
Within a lily? Centre plac'd?
Or ever mark'd the pretty beam,
A strawberry shows half drown'd in cream?
Or seen rich rubies blushing through
A pure smooth pearl, and orient too?
So like to this, nay all the rest,
Is each neat niplet of her breast.

To the Water Nymphs, Drinking at the Fountain

Reach, with your whiter hands, to me,
　　Some crystal of the spring;
And I, about the cup shall see
　　Fresh lilies flourishing.

Or else sweet nymphs do you but this;
　　To th' glass your lips incline;
And I shall see by that one kiss,
　　The water turn'd to wine.

Upon Her Feet

Her pretty feet
Like snails did creep
A little out, and then,
As if they started at bo-peep,
Did soon draw in again.

To Anthea, Who May Command Him in Anything

Bid me to live, and I will live
    Thy Protestant to be:
Or bid me love, and I will give
    A loving heart to thee.

A heart as soft, a heart as kind,
    A heart as sound and free,
As in the whole world thou canst find,
    That heart I'll give to thee.

Bid that heart stay, and it will stay,
    To honour thy decree:
Or bid it languish quite away,
    And 't shall do so for thee.

Bid me to weep, and I will weep,
    While I have eyes to see:
And having none, yet I will keep
    A heart to weep for thee.

Bid me despair, and I'll despair
    Under that cypress tree:
Or bid me die, and I will dare
    E'en death to die for thee.

Thou art my life, my love, my heart,
    The very eyes of me:
And hast command of every part,
    To live and die for thee.

To Meadows

Ye have been fresh and green,
　Ye have been fill'd with flowers:
And ye the walks have been
　Where maids have spent their hours.

You have beheld, how they
　With wicker arks did come
To kiss, and bear away
　The richer cowslips home.

Y'ave heard them sweetly sing,
　And seen them in a round:
Each virgin, like a Spring,
　With honeysuckles crown'd.

But now, we see, none here,
　Whose silv'ry feet did tread,
And with dishevell'd hair,
　Adorn'd this smoother mead.

Like unthrifts, having spent
　Your stock, and needy grown,
Y'are left here to lament
　Your poor estate, alone.

Grace for a Child

Here a little child I stand,
Heaving up my either hand;
Cold as paddocks though they be,
Here I lift them up to Thee,
For a benison to fall
On our meat, and on us all. *Amen.*

A *Thanksgiving to God, for His House*

Lord, Thou hast given me a cell
    Wherein to dwell,
A little house, whose humble roof
    Is weather-proof;
Under the spars of which I lie
    Both soft, and dry;
Where Thou my chamber for to ward
    Hast set a guard
Of harmless thoughts, to watch and keep
    Me, while I sleep.
Low is my porch, as is my fate,
    Both void of state;
And yet the threshold of my door
    Is worn by th' poor,
Who thither come, and freely get
    Good words, or meat:
Like as my parlour, so my hall
    And kitchen's small:
A little buttery, and therein
    A little bin,
Which keeps my little loaf of bread
    Unchipp'd, unflead:
Some brittle sticks of thorn or briar
    Make me a fire,
Close by whose living coal I sit,
    And glow like it.
Lord, I confess too, when I dine,
    The pulse is thine,
And all those other bits, that be
    There plac'd by thee;
The worts, the purslain, and the mess
    Of water-cress,
Which of Thy kindness Thou has sent;
    And my content
Makes those, and my beloved beet,
    To be more sweet.
'Tis Thou that crown'st my glittering hearth
    With guiltless mirth;

And giv'st me wassail bowls to drink,
    Spic'd to the brink.
Lord, 'tis Thy plenty-dropping hand,
    That soils my land;
And giv'st me, for my bushel sown,
    Twice ten for one:
Thou mak'st my teeming hen to lay
    Her egg each day:
Besides my healthful ewes to bear
    Me twins each year:
The while the conduits of my kine
    Run cream, (for wine.)
All these, and better Thou dost send
    Me, to this end,
That I should render, for my part,
    A thankful heart;
Which, fir'd with incense, I resign,
    As wholly Thine;
But the acceptance, that must be,
    My Christ, by Thee.

HENRY KING

(1592–1669)

"Sonnet"

Tell me no more how fair she is,
    I have no mind to hear
The story of that distant bliss
    I never shall come near:
By sad experience I have found
That her perfection is my wound.

And tell me not how fond I am
    To tempt a daring fate,
From whence no triumph ever came,
    But to repent too late:
There is some hope ere long I may
In silence dote myself away.

I ask no pity, Love, from thee,
　　Nor will thy justice blame,
So that thou wilt not envy me
　　The glory of my flame:
Which crowns my heart whene'er it dies,
In that it falls her sacrifice.

FROM *The Exequy*

(ON HIS WIFE'S DEATH)

Accept, thou shrine of my dead saint,
Instead of dirges this complaint;
And for sweet flowers to crown thy hearse,
Receive a strew of weeping verse
From thy grieved friend, whom thou might'st see
Quite melted into tears for thee.

Sleep on, my Love, in thy cold bed,
Never to be disquieted!
My last good night! Thou wilt not wake
Till I thy fate shall overtake:
Till age or grief or sickness must
Marry my body to that dust
It so much loves; and fill the room
My heart keeps empty in thy tomb.
Stay for me there; I will not fail
To meet thee in that hollow vale;
And think not much of my delay;
I am already on the way,
And follow thee with all the speed
Desire can make or sorrows breed.
Each minute is a short degree,
And ev'ry hour a step towards thee.
At night, when I betake to rest,
Next morn I rise nearer my West
Of Life, almost by eight hours' sail
Than when sleep breathed his drowsy gale.

The thought of this bids me go on,
And wait my dissolution
With hope and comfort. Dear (forgive
The crime) I am content to live
Divided, with but half a heart,
Till we shall meet and never part.

GEORGE HERBERT

(1593–1633)

Man's Medley

Hark, how the birds do sing,
    And woods do ring!
All creatures have their joy, and man hath his.
    Yet if we rightly measure,
    Man's joy and pleasure
Rather hereafter than in present is.

To this life things of sense
    Make their pretence;
In th' other angels have a right by birth.
    Man ties them both alone,
    And makes them one,
With th' one hand touching Heav'n, with th' other earth.

In soul he mounts and flies,
    In flesh he dies.
He wears a stuff whose thread is coarse and round,
    But trimmed with curious lace,
    And should take place
After the trimming, not the stuff and ground.

Not that he may not here
    Taste of the cheer;
But as birds drink and straight lift up their head,
    So must he sip and think
    Of better drink
He may attain to after he is dead.

But as his joys are double,
    So is his trouble.
He hath two winters, other things but one.
    Both frosts and thoughts do nip
    And bite his lip,
And he of all things fears two deaths alone.

Yet ev'n the greatest griefs
    May be reliefs,
Could he but take them right and in their ways.
    Happy is he whose heart
    Hath found the art
To turn his double pains to double praise.

The Collar

I struck the board, and cried, No more!
    I will abroad.
What? Shall I ever sigh and pine?
My lines and life are free, free as the road,
    Loose as the wind, as large as store.
    Shall I be still in suit?
Have I no harvest but a thorn
To let me blood, and not restore
What I have lost with cordial fruit?
    Sure there was wine
Before my sighs did dry it. There was corn
Before my tears did drown it.
Is the year only lost to me?
    Have I no bays to crown it?
No flowers, no garlands gay? All blasted?
    All wasted?
Not so, my heart! But there is fruit,
    And thou hast hands.
Recover all thy sigh-blown age
On double pleasures. Leave thy cold dispute
Of what is fit and not. Forsake thy cage,
    Thy rope of sands,

Which petty thoughts have made, and made to thee
  Good cable, to enforce and draw,
      And be thy law,
While thou didst wink and wouldst not see.
      Away! Take heed!
      I will abroad.
Call in thy death's head there. Tie up thy fears.
      He that forbears
  To suit and serve his need
  Deserves his load.
But as I raved and grew more fierce and wild
      At every word,
  Methought I heard one calling, *Child!*
  And I replied, *My Lord.*

Discipline

    Throw away Thy rod,
    Throw away Thy wrath.
      O my God,
    Take the gentle path.

    For my heart's desire
    Unto Thine is bent.
      I aspire
    To a full consent.

    Not a word or look
    I affect to own,
      But by book,
    And Thy book alone.

    Though I fail, I weep.
    Though I halt in pace,
      Yet I creep
    To the throne of grace.

    Then let wrath remove.
    Love will do the deed:
      For with love
    Stony hearts will bleed.

Love is swift of foot.
Love's a man of war,
  And can shoot,
And can hit from far.

Who can 'scape his bow?
That which wrought on Thee,
  Brought Thee low,
Needs must work on me.

Throw away Thy rod,
Though man frailties hath,
  Thou art God.
Throw away Thy wrath.

Virtue

Sweet day, so cool, so calm, so bright,
 The bridal of the earth and sky;
The dew shall weep thy fall to night,
  For thou must die.

Sweet rose, whose hue angry and brave
 Bids the rash gazer wipe his eye;
Thy root is ever in its grave,
  And thou must die.

Sweet spring, full of sweet days and roses,
 A box where sweets compacted lie;
My music shows ye have your closes,
  And all must die.

Only a sweet and virtuous soul,
 Like seasoned timber, never gives;
But though the whole world turn to coal,
  Then chiefly lives.

Sin

Lord, with what care hast Thou begirt us round!
   Parents first season us; then schoolmasters
Deliver us to laws; they send us bound
   To rules of reason, holy messengers,
Pulpits and Sundays, sorrow dogging sin,
   Afflictions sorted, anguish of all sizes,
Fine nets and stratagems to catch us in.
   Bibles laid open, millions of surprises,
Blessings beforehand, ties of gratefulness,
   The sound of glory ringing in our ears;
Without, our shame; within, our consciences;
   Angels and grace, eternal hopes and fears.
Yet all these fences and their whole array
One cunning bosom-sin blows quite away.

Love

Love bade me welcome; yet my soul drew back,
         Guilty of dust and sin.
But quick-eyed Love, observing me grow slack
         From my first entrance in,
Drew nearer to me, sweetly questioning
         If I lacked any thing.

A guest, I answered, worthy to be here.
         Love said, You shall be he.
I, the unkind, ungrateful? Ah, my dear,
         I cannot look on thee.
Love took my hand and smiling did reply,
         Who made the eyes but I?

Truth, Lord, but I have marred them; let my shame
         Go where it doth deserve.
And know you not, says Love, who bore the blame?
         My dear, then I will serve
You must sit down, says Love, and taste my meat.
         So I did sit and eat.

Mortification

How soon doth man decay!
When clothes are taken from a chest of sweets
　To swaddle infants, whose young breath
　　Scarce knows the way,
　Those clouts are little winding sheets,
Which do consign and send them unto death.

　When boys go first to bed,
They step into their voluntary graves;
　Sleep binds them fast; only their breath
　　Makes them not dead.
　Successive nights, like rolling waves,
Convey them quickly who are bound for death.

　When youth is frank and free,
And calls for music, while his veins do swell,
　All day exchanging mirth and breath
　　In company,
　That music summons to the knell
Which shall befriend him at the house of death.

　When man grows staid and wise,
Getting a house and home, where he may move
　Within the circle of his breath,
　　Schooling his eyes,
　That dumb inclosure maketh love
Unto the coffin that attends his death.

　When age grows low and weak,
Marking his grave, and thawing ev'ry year,
　Till all do melt and drown his breath
　　When he would speak,
　A chair or litter shows the bier
Which shall convey him to the house of death.

　Man, ere he is aware,
Hath put together a solemnity,
　And drest his hearse, while he has breath
　　As yet to spare;
　Yet, Lord, instruct us so to die,
That all these dyings may be life in death.

The Pulley

When God at first made man,
Having a glass of blessings standing by,
"Let us," said he, "pour on him all we can;
Let the world's riches, which dispersèd lie,
  Contract into a span."

So strength first made a way,
Then beauty flowed, then wisdom, honour, pleasure;
When almost all was out, God made a stay,
Perceiving that, alone of all his treasure,
  Rest in the bottom lay.

"For if I should," said he,
"Bestow this jewel also on my creature,
He would adore my gifts instead of me,
And rest in Nature, not the God of Nature;
  So both should losers be.

Yet let him keep the rest,
But keep them with repining, restlessness;
Let him be rich and weary, that at least,
If goodness lead him not, yet weariness
  May toss him to my breast."

THOMAS MAY?

(1595–1650)

"Dear, Do Not Your Fair Beauty Wrong"

Dear, do not your fair beauty wrong
In thinking still you are too young;
The rose and lily in your cheek
Flourish, and no more ripening seek;
Inflaming beams shot from your eye
Do show Love's midsummer is nigh;
Your cherry lip, red, soft and sweet,
Proclaims such fruit for taste is meet;
Love is still young, a buxom boy,
And younglings are allowed to toy:
Then lose no time, for love hath wings,
  And flies away from aged things.

JAMES SHIRLEY

(1596–1666)

"You Virgins..."

You virgins, that did late despair
  To keep your wealth from cruel men,
Tie up in silk your careless hair:
  Soft peace is come again.

Now lovers' eyes may gently shoot
  A flame that will not kill;
The drum was angry, but the lute
  Shall whisper what you will.

Sing Io, Io! for his sake
  That hath restored your drooping heads;
With choice of sweetest flowers make
  A garden where he treads;

Whilst we whole groves of laurel bring,
  A petty triumph for his brow,
Who is the master of our spring
  And all the bloom we owe.

                          The Imposture, 1640?

"The Glories of Our Blood..."

The glories of our blood and state
  Are shadows, not substantial things;
There is no armour against Fate;
  Death lays his icy hand on kings:
      Sceptre and crown
      Must tumble down,
And in the dust be equal made
With the poor crooked scythe and spade.

Some men with swords may reap the field,
  And plant fresh laurels where they kill;
But their strong nerves at last must yield;
  They tame but one another still:

Early or late,
They stoop to fate,
And must give up their murmuring breath,
When they, pale captives, creep to death.

The garlands wither on your brow,
   Then boast no more your mighty deeds;
Upon Death's purple altar now
   See where the victor-victim bleeds:
         Your heads must come
         To the cold tomb;
Only the actions of the just
Smell sweet and blossom in the dust.

The Contention of Ajax and Ulysses, 1659

THOMAS CAREW

(1598?–1639?)

FROM *Persuasions to Love*

For that lovely face will fail,
Beauty's sweet, but beauty's frail;
'Tis sooner past, 'tis sooner done
Than summer's rain or winter's sun,
Most fleeting when it is most dear;
'Tis gone, while we but say 'tis here.
These curious locks so aptly twined,
Whose every hair a soul doth bind,
Will change their auburn hue and grow
White and cold as winter's snow.
That eye which now is Cupid's nest
Will prove his grave, and all the rest
Will follow; in the cheek, chin, nose,
Nor lily shall be found nor rose;
And what will then become of all
Those whom now you servants call?
Like swallows, when your summer's done
They'll fly and seek some warmer sun.

For when the storms of time have moved
Waves on that cheek that was beloved,
When a fair lady's face is pined

And yellow spread where red once shined,
When beauty, youth and all sweets leave her,
Love may return, but lovers never.

Oh, love me then, and now begin it,
Let us not lose this present minute.

Song

Give me more love or more disdain,
    The torrid or the frozen zone
Bring equal ease unto my pain,
    The temperate affords me none;
Either extreme of love or hate
Is sweeter than a calm estate.

Give me a storm; if it be love,
    Like Danaë in that golden shower
I swim in pleasure; if it prove
    Disdain, that torrent will devour
My vulture hopes; and he's possessed
Of heaven that's but from hell released.

Then crown my joys or cure my pain,
Give me more love or more disdain.

FROM Disdain Returned

He that loves a rosy cheek
    Or a coral lip admires,
Or from star-like eyes doth seek
    Fuel to maintain his fires;
As old Time makes these decay,
So his flames must waste away.

But a smooth and stedfast mind,
    Gentle thoughts and calm desires,
Hearts with equal love combined,
    Kindle never-dying fires.
Where these are not, I despise
Lovely cheeks or lips or eyes.

Song

Ask me no more where Jove bestows
When June is past, the fading rose;
For in your beauties' orient deep
These flowers as in their causes sleep.

Ask me no more whither do stray
The golden atoms of the day;
For in pure love Heaven did prepare
These powders to enrich your hair.

Ask me no more whither doth haste
The nightingale when May is past;
For in your sweet dividing throat
She winters and keeps warm her note.

Ask me no more where those stars light
That downwards fall in dead of night;
For in your eyes they sit and there
Fixéd become, as in their sphere.

Ask me no more if east or west
The phoenix builds her spicy nest;
For unto you at last she flies
And in your fragrant bosom dies.

Epitaph on the Lady Mary Villiers

The Lady Mary Villiers lies
Under this stone; with weeping eyes
The parents that first gave her breath,
And their sad friends, laid her in earth.
If any of them, reader, were
Known unto thee, shed a tear.
Or if thyself possess a gem
As dear to thee as this to them,
Though a stranger to this place
Bewail in theirs thine own hard case,
For thou perhaps at thy return
May'st find thy darling in an urn.

FROM A *Rapture*

I will enjoy thee now, my Celia, come,
And fly with me to Love's Elysium.
The giant, Honour, that keeps cowards out
Is but a masquer, and the servile rout
Of baser subjects only bend in vain
To the vast idol; whilst the nobler train
Of valiant lovers daily sail between
The huge Colossus' legs, and pass unseen
Unto the blissful shore. Be bold and wise,
And we shall enter; the grim Swiss denies
Only to tame fools a passage, that not know
He is but form and only frights in show
The duller eyes that look from far; draw near
And thou shalt scorn what we were wont to fear.
We shall see how the stalking pageant goes
With borrow'd legs, a heavy load to those
That made and bear him; not, as we once thought,
The seed of gods, but a weak model wrought
By greedy men, that seek to enclose the common,
And within private arms empale free woman.

Come, then, and mounted on the wings of Love
We'll cut the flitting air and soar above
The monster's head, and in the noblest seats
Of those blest shades quench and renew our heats.
There shall the queens of love and innocence,
Beauty and Nature, banish all offence
From our close ivy-twines; there I'll behold
Thy baréd snow and thy unbraided gold;
There my enfranchised hand on every side
Shall o'er thy naked polish'd ivory slide.
No curtain there, though of transparent lawn,
Shall be before thy virgin-treasure drawn;
But the rich mine, to the enquiring eye
Exposed, shall ready still for mintage lie,
And we will coin young Cupids. There a bed
Of roses and fresh myrtles shall be spread,
Under the cooler shades of cypress groves;
Our pillows of the down of Venus' doves.

Whereon our panting limbs we'll gently lay,
In the faint respites of our active play;
That so our slumbers may in dreams have leisure
To tell the nimble fancy our past pleasure,
And so our souls, that cannot be embraced,
Shall the embraces of our bodies taste.
Meanwhile the bubbling stream shall court the shore,
Th' enamour'd chirping wood-choir shall adore
In varied tunes the deity of love;
The gentle blasts of western winds shall move
The trembling leaves, and through their close boughs breathe
Still music, whilst we rest ourselves beneath
Their dancing shade; till a soft murmur, sent
From souls entranced in amorous languishment,
Rouse us, and shoot into our veins fresh fire,
Till we in their sweet ecstasy expire.

Then, as the empty bee that lately bore
Into the common treasure all her store,
Flies 'bout the painted field with nimble wing,
Deflow'ring the fresh virgins of the spring,
So will I rifle all the sweets that dwell
In my delicious paradise, and swell
My bag with honey, drawn forth by the power
Of fervent kisses from each spicy flower.
I'll seize the rose-buds in their perfumed bed,
The violet knots, like curious mazes spread
O'er all the garden, taste the ripen'd cherry,
The warm firm apple, tipp'd with coral berry;
Then will I visit with a wand'ring kiss
The vales of lilies and the bower of bliss;
And where the beauteous region doth divide
Into two milky ways, my lips shall slide
Down those smooth alleys, wearing as they go
A track for lovers on the printed snow;
Thence climbing o'er the swelling Apennine,
Retire into thy grove of eglantine,
Where I will all those ravish'd sweets distill
Through Love's alembic, and with chemic skill
From the mix'd mass one sovereign balm derive,
Then bring that great elixir to thy hive.

ANONYMOUS

(17TH CENTURY)

"Art Thou That She..."

"Art thou that she than whom no fairer is,
   Art thou that she desire so strives to kiss?"
         "Say I am: how then?
         Maids may not kiss
      Such wanton-humour'd men."

"Art thou that she the world commends for wit?
   Art thou so wise and makest no use of it?"
         "Say I am: how then?
         My wit doth teach me shun
      Such foolish foolish men."

ANONYMOUS

(17TH CENTURY)

"Hey Nonny No!"

Hey nonny no!
Men are fools that wish to die!
Is't not fine to dance and sing
When the bells of death do ring?
Is't not fine to swim in wine,
And turn upon the toe
And sing hey nonny no,
When the winds blow and the seas flow?
Hey nonny no!

ANONYMOUS

(17TH CENTURY)

"Yet If His Majesty..."

Yet if his majesty our sovereign lord
Should of his own accord
Friendly himself invite,
And say "I'll be your guest to morrow night",

How should we stir ourselves, call and command
All hands to work! "Let no man idle stand.
Set me fine Spanish tables in the hall,
See they be fitted all;
Let there be room to eat,
And order taken that there want no meat.
See every sconce and candlestick made bright,
That without tapers they may give a light.
Look to the presence: are the carpets spread,
The dais o'er the head,
The cushions in the chairs,
And all the candles lighted on the stairs?
Perfume the chambers, and in any case
Let each man give attendance in his place."
Thus if the king were coming would we do,
And 'twere good reason too;
For 'tis a duteous thing
To show all honour to an earthly king,
And after all our travail and our cost,
So he be pleased, to think no labour lost.
But at the coming of the King of Heaven
All's set at six and seven:
We wallow in our sin,
Christ cannot find a chamber in the inn.
We entertain Him always like a stranger,
And as at first still lodge Him in the manger.

ANONYMOUS

(17TH CENTURY)

"Daphnis Came on a Summer's Day"

Daphnis came on a summer's day
  Where fair Phyllis sleeping lay,
  With breast half naked bare:
  He ran and gathered stores of lilies,
  Wherewith he covered his fair Phyllis,
  She being nought aware.
  Fond youth, why dost thou mar
  Those lily bowers and lose the pain!
  Her lily breast doth stain
  All flowers and lilies far.

ANONYMOUS
(17TH CENTURY)

"On a Fair Morning..."

On a fair morning, as I came by the way,
Met I with a merry maid in the merry month of May,
When a sweet love song sings his lovely lay
And every bird upon the bush bechirps it up so gay,
With a heave and ho! with a heave and ho!
Thy wife shall be thy master, I trow.
Sing, care away, care away, let the world go!
Hey, lustily all in a row, all in a row,
Sing, care away, care away, let the world go!

Thomas Morley's *Madrigals to Four Voices*, 1600

ANONYMOUS
(17TH CENTURY)

"I Saw My Lady Weep"

I saw my lady weep,
And Sorrow proud to be advancéd so
In those fair eyes where all perfections keep.
    Her face was full of woe,
But such a woe (believe me) as wins more hearts
Than Mirth can do with her enticing parts.

Sorrow was there made fair,
And Passion wise; Tears a delightful thing;
Silence beyond all speech, a wisdom rare;
    She made her sighs to sing,
And all things with so sweet a sadness move
As made my heart at once both grieve and love.

O fairer than aught else
The world can show, leave off in time to grieve.
Enough, enough; your joyful look excels:
    Tears kill the heart, believe.
O strive not to be excellent in woe,
Which only breeds your beauty's overthrow.

John Dowland's *Second Book of Songs or Airs*,

ANONYMOUS

(17TH CENTURY)

"Fine Knacks for Ladies..."

Fine knacks for ladies, cheap choice, brave and new,
Good pennyworths—but money cannot move:
I keep a fair but for the Fair to view,—
    A beggar may be liberal of love.
Though all my wares be trash, the heart is true,
                    The heart is true.

Great gifts are guiles and look for gifts again,
    My trifles come as treasures from my mind;
It is a precious jewel to be plain;
    Sometimes in shell the orient'st pearls we find:
Of others take a sheaf, of me a grain!
                Of me a grain.

Within this pack pins, points, laces, and gloves,
    And divers toys fitting a country fair,
But my heart, wherein duty serves and loves,
    Turtles and twins, court's brood, a heavenly pair—
Happy the heart that thinks of no removes!
                Of no removes!

John Dowland's *Second Book of Songs or Airs,* 1600

ANONYMOUS

(17TH CENTURY)

"My Love in Her Attire..."

My love in her attire doth show her wit,
    It doth so well become her:
For every season she hath dressings fit,
    For winter, spring, and summer.
    No beauty she doth miss,
    When all her robes are on:
    But Beauty's self she is,
    When all her robes are gone.

Davison's *Poetical Rhapsody,* 1602

ANONYMOUS
(17TH CENTURY)

"Flow Not so Fast..."

Flow not so fast, ye fountains,
What needeth all this haste?
Swell not above your mountains,
Nor spend your time in waste!
  Gentle springs! freshly your salt tears
  Must still fall, dropping from their spheres.

Weep not apace, whom Reason
Or lingering Time can ease;
My sorrow can no season,
Nor ought beside appease.
  Gentle springs! freshly your salt tears
  Must still fall, dropping from their spheres.

Time can abate the terror
Of every common pain:
But common grief is error,
True grief will still remain.
  Gentle springs! freshly your salt tears
  Must still fall, dropping from their spheres.

John Dowland's *Third and Last Book of Songs or Airs*, 1603

ANONYMOUS
(17TH CENTURY)

"Weep You No More..."

Weep you no more, sad fountains;
  What need you flow so fast?
Look how the snowy mountains
  Heaven's sun doth gently waste!
But my sun's heavenly eyes,
  View not your weeping,
  That now lies sleeping
Softly, now softly lies
        Sleeping.

Sleep is a reconciling,
   A rest that peace begets;
Doth not the sun rise smiling
   When fair at ev'n he sets?
Rest you then, rest, sad eyes!
   Melt not in weeping,
   While she lies sleeping
Softly, now softly lies
     Sleeping.

John Dowland's *Third and Last Book of Songs or Airs*, 1603

ANONYMOUS
(17TH CENTURY)
"*Fain Would I Change* ..."

Fain would I change that note
To which fond love hath charm'd me
Long long to sing by rote,
Fancying that that harm'd me:
Yet when this thought doth come,
"Love is the perfect sum
Of all delight,"
I have no other choice
Either for pen or voice
To sing or write.

O Love, they wrong thee much
That say thy sweet is bitter,
When thy rich fruit is such
As nothing can be sweeter.
Fair house of joy and bliss,
Where truest pleasure is,
I do adore thee;
I know thee what thou art,
I serve thee with my heart,
And fall before thee.

Captain Tobias Hume's *The First Part of Airs*, 1605

ANONYMOUS

(17TH CENTURY)

"Ye Little Birds..."

Ye little birds that sit and sing
    Amidst the shady valleys,
And see how Phyllis sweetly walks
    Within her garden-alleys;
Go, pretty birds, about her bower;
Sing, pretty birds, she may not lower;
Ah me! methinks I see her frown!
    Ye pretty wantons, warble.

Go, tell her through your chirping bills,
    As you by me are bidden,
To her is only known my love,
    Which from the world is hidden.
Go, pretty birds, and tell her so;
See that your notes strain not too low,
For still, methinks, I see her frown;
    Ye pretty wantons, warble.

Go, tune your voices' harmony,
    And sing, I am her lover;
Strain loud and sweet, that every note
    With sweet content may move her:
And she that hath the sweetest voice,
Tell her I will not change my choice;
Yet still, methinks, I see her frown!
    Ye pretty wantons, warble.

Oh, fly! make haste! see, see, she falls
    Into a pretty slumber.
Sing round about her rosy bed,
    That waking, she may wonder.
So to her, 'tis her lover true
That sendeth love to you, to you;
And when you hear her kind reply,
    Return with pleasant warblings.

Fair Maid of the Exchange, 1607 [THOMAS HEYWOOD?]

ANONYMOUS

(17TH CENTURY)

"Ha Ha! Ha Ha! This World..."

Ha ha! ha ha! this world doth pass
　Most merrily, I'll be sworn;
For many an honest Indian ass
　Goes for an Unicorn.
　　　　　Fara diddle dino;
　　　　　This is idle fino.

Ty hye! ty hye! O sweet delight!
　He tickles this age that can
Call Tullia's ape a marmosyte
　And Leda's goose a swan.
　　　　　Fara diddle dino;
　　　　　This is idle fino.

So so! so so! fine English days!
　When false play's no reproach;
For he that doth the coachman praise,
　May safely use the coach.
　　　　　Fara diddle dino;
　　　　　This is idle fino.

Thomas Weelkes's *Airs or Fantastic Spirits*, 1608

ANONYMOUS

(17TH CENTURY)

"Love Not Me..."

Love not me for comely grace,
For my pleasing eye or face,
Nor for any outward part:
No, nor for a constant heart!
For these may fail or turn to ill:
　So thou and I shall sever.
Keep therefore a true woman's eye,
And love me still, but know not why!
So hast thou the same reason still
　To doat upon me ever.

John Wilbye's *Second Set of Madrigals*, 1609

ANONYMOUS
(17TH CENTURY)

"The Sea Hath Many Thousand Sands"

The sea hath many thousand sands,
The sky hath motes as many;
The sky is full of stars, and love
As full of woes as any:
Believe me, that do know the elf,
And make no trial by thyself.

It is in truth a pretty toy
For babes to play withal;
But O the honies of our youth
Are oft our age's gall!
Self-proof in time will make thee know
He was a prophet told thee so:

A prophet that, Cassandra-like,
Tells truth without belief;
For headstrong youth will run his race,
Although his goal be grief:
Love's martyr, when his heat is past,
Proves Care's confessor at the last.

Robert Jones's *The Muses' Garden of Delights*, 1610

ANONYMOUS
(17TH CENTURY)

"Sweet, Let Me Go!"

Sweet, let me go! sweet, let me go!
What do you mean to vex me so?
Cease your pleading force!
Do you think thus to extort remorse?
Now, now! no more! alas, you overbear me,
And I would cry—but some would hear, I fear me.

William Corkine's *Airs*, 1610

ANONYMOUS

(17TH CENTURY)

"Sweet Cupid, Ripen Her Desire"

Sweet Cupid, ripen her desire,
Thy joyful harvest may begin;
If age approach a little nigher,
'Twill be too late to get it in.

Cold winter storms lay standing corn,
Which once too ripe will never rise,
And lovers wish themselves unborn,
When all their joys lie in their eyes.

Then, sweet, let us embrace and kiss:
Shall beauty shale upon the ground?
If age bereave us of this bliss,
Then will no more such sport be found.

William Corkine's *Airs*, 1610

ANONYMOUS

(17TH CENTURY)

"On a Time the Amorous Silvy"

On a time the amorous Silvy
Said to her shepherd, "Sweet, how do you?
Kiss me this once and then God be wi' you,
My sweetest dear!
Kiss me this once and then God be wi' you,
For now the morning draweth near."

With that her fairest bosom showing,
Opening her lips, rich perfumes blowing,
She said, "Now kiss me and be going,
My sweetest dear!
Kiss me this once and then be going,
For now the morning draweth near."

With that the shepherd waked from sleeping,
And, spying where the day was peeping,
He said, "Now take my soul in keeping,
                    My sweetest dear!
Kiss me, and take my soul in keeping,
Since I must go, now day is near."

                    John Attye's *First Book of Airs*, 1622

ANONYMOUS

(17TH CENTURY)

"Love in Thy Youth..."

Love in thy youth, fair maid; be wise,
    Old Time will make thee colder,
And though each morning new arise
    Yet we each day grow older.

Thou as heaven art fair and young,
    Thine eyes like twin stars shining:
But ere another day be sprung,
    All these will be declining.

Then winter comes with all his fears
    And all thy sweets shall borrow;
Too late then wilt thou shower thy tears,
    And I too late shall sorrow.

                    Walter Porter's *Madrigals and Airs*, 1632

ANONYMOUS

(17TH CENTURY)

Phillada Flouts Me

O! what a plague is love!
    How shall I bear it?
She will inconstant prove,
    I greatly fear it.
She so torments my mind,
    That my strength faileth,

And wavers with the wind,
　As a ship saileth.
Please her the best I may,
She loves still to gainsay:
Alack and well a day!
　　　Phillada flouts me.

At the fair yesterday,
　She did pass by me;
She looked another way,
　And would not spy me.
I wooed her for to dine,
　But could not get her.
Will had her to the wine—
　He might intreat her.
With Daniel she did dance,
On me she looked askance.
O thrice unhappy chance!
　　　Phillada flouts me.

Fair maid, be not so coy,
　Do not disdain me:
I am my mother's joy,
　Sweet, entertain me.
She'll give me when she dies
　All that is fitting,
Her poultry and her bees
　And her geese sitting.
A pair of mattress beds,
And a bag full of shreds.
And yet for all this guedes,
　　　Phillada flouts me.

She hath a clout of mine
　Wrought with blue Coventry,
Which she keeps for a sign
　Of my fidelity.
But i' faith, if she flinch,
　She shall not wear it;

Guedes, *goods*.

To Tibb, my t'other wench,
  I mean to bear it.
And yet it grieves my heart,
So soon from her to part.
Death strikes me with his dart!
    Phillada flouts me.

Thou shalt eat curds and cream,
  All the year lasting:
And drink the crystal stream,
  Pleasant in tasting;
Whig and whey whilst thou lust
  And bramble-berries;
Pie-lid and pasty-crust,
  Pears, plums and cherries.
Thy raiment shall be thin,
Made of a weaver's skin:
Yet all's not worth a pin,
    Phillada flouts me.

In the last month of May
  I made her posies;
I heard her often say
  That she loved roses.
Cowslips and gillyflowers
  And the white lily
I brought to deck the bowers
  For my sweet Philly.
But she did all disdain,
And threw them back again;
Therefore 'tis flat and plain
    Phillada flouts me.

Fair maiden, have a care,
  And in time take me;
I can have those as fair
  If you forsake me.
For Doll the dairy-maid
  Laughed on me lately,

And wanton Winifred
  Favours me greatly.
One throws milk on my clothes,
T'other plays with my nose;
What wanton signs are those?
  Phillada flouts me.

I cannot work nor sleep
  At all in season;
Love wounds my heart so deep
  Without all reason.
I gin to pine away,
  In my love's shadow,
Like as a fat beast may,
  Penned in a meadow.
I shall be dead, I fear,
Within this thousand year:
And all for that my dear
  Phillada flouts me.

Wit Restored, 1658, but written much earlier

ANONYMOUS

(17TH CENTURY)

FROM *The New Jerusalem*

Hierusalem, my happy home,
  When shall I come to thee?
When shall my sorrows have an end?
  Thy joys when shall I see?

O happy harbour of the saints,
  O sweet and pleasant soil,
In thee no sorrow may be found,
  No grief, no care, no toil.

In thee no sickness may be seen,
  No hurt, no ache, no sore,
There is no death nor ugly devil,
  There is life for evermore.

No dampish mist is seen in thee,
   No cold nor darksome night,
There every soul shines as the sun,
   There God Himself gives light.

There lust and lucre cannot dwell,
   There envy bears no sway,
There is no hunger, heat nor cold,
   But pleasure every way.

Hierusalem, Hierusalem,
   God grant I once may see
Thy endless joys and of the same
   Partaker aye to be.

Thy walls are made of precious stones,
   Thy bulwarks diamonds square,
Thy gates are of right orient pearl
   Exceeding rich and rare.

Thy turrets and thy pinnacles
   With carbuncles do shine,
Thy very streets are paved with gold
   Surpassing clear and fine.

Thy houses are of ivory,
   Thy windows crystal clear,
Thy tiles are made of beaten gold—
   O God, that I were there!

Ah! my sweet home, Hierusalem,
   Would God I were in thee,
Would God my woes were at an end,
   Thy joys that I might see.

Thy saints are crowned with glory great,
   They see God face to face,
They triumph still, they still rejoice,
   Most happy is their case.

Thy vineyards and thy orchards are
   Most beautiful and fair,
Full furnishéd with trees and fruits
   Most wonderful and rare.

Thy gardens and thy gallant walks
   Continually are green,
There grows such sweet and pleasant flowers
   As nowhere else are seen.

There is nectar and ambrosia made,
   There is musk and civet sweet,
There many a fair and dainty drug
   Are trodden under feet.

There cinnamon, there sugar grows,
   There nard and balm abound;
What tongue can tell or heart conceive
   The joys that there are found.

Quiet through the streets with silver sound
   The flood of life does flow,
Upon whose bank at every side
   The wood of life doth grow.

There trees for evermore bear fruit
   And evermore do spring,
There evermore the angels sit
   And evermore do sing.

Hierusalem, my happy home,
   Would God I were in thee,
Would God my woes were at an end
   Thy joys that I might see.

ANONYMOUS

(17TH CENTURY)

The Old and Young Courtier

An old song made by an agéd old pate,
Of an old worshipful gentleman, who had a great estate,
That kept a brave old house at a bountiful rate,
And an old porter to relieve the poor at his gate;
      Like an old courtier of the Queen's,
      And the Queen's old courtier.

With an old lady, whose anger one word assuages;
They every quarter paid their old servants their wages,
And never knew what belonged to coachman, footmen, nor
    pages,
But kept twenty old fellows with blue coats and badges;
      Like an old courtier &c.

With an old study filled full of learnéd old books,
With an old reverend chaplain, you might know him by his
    looks.
With an old buttery hatch quite worn off the hooks,
And an old kitchen, that maintained half a dozen old cooks:
      Like an old courtier &c.

With an old hall hung about with pikes, guns and bows,
With old swords, and bucklers, that had borne many shrewd
    blows,
And an old frieze coat to cover his worship's trunk hose,
And a cup of old sherry, to comfort his copper nose:
      Like an old courtier &c.

With a good old fashion, when Christmas was come,
To call in all his neighbours with bagpipe and drum,
With good cheer enough to furnish every old room,
And old liquor able to make a cat speak, and man dumb,
      Like an old courtier &c.

With an old falconer, huntsman, and a kennel of hounds,
That never hawked, nor hunted, but in his own grounds,
Who, like a wise man, kept himself within his own bounds,
And when he died gave every child a thousand good pounds:
      Like an old courtier &c.

But to his eldest son his house and lands he assigned,
Charging him in his will to keep the old bountiful mind,
To be good to his old tenants, and to his neighbours be kind:
But in the ensuing ditty you shall hear how he was inclined;
  Like a young courtier of the King's,
  And the King's young courtier.

Like a flourishing young gallant, newly come to his land,
Who keeps a brace of painted madams at his command,
And takes up a thousand pound upon his father's land,
And gets drunk in a tavern, till he can neither go nor stand;
  Like a young courtier &c.

With a new-fangled lady, that is dainty, nice, and spare,
Who never knew what belonged to good housekeeping, or
  care,
Who buys gaudy-coloured fans to play with wanton air,
And seven or eight different dressings of other women's hair;
  Like a young courtier &c.

With a new-fashioned hall, built where the old one stood,
Hung round with new pictures, that do the poor no good,
With a fine marble chimney, wherein burns neither coal nor
  wood,
And a new smooth shovelboard, whereon no victuals ne'er
  stood;
  Like a young courtier &c.

With a new study, stuffed full of pamphlets, and plays,
And a new chaplain, that swears faster than he prays,
With a new buttery hatch, that opens once in four or five days,
And a new French cook, to devise fine kickshaws, and toys;
  Like a young courtier &c.

With a new fashion, when Christmas is drawing on,
On a new journey to London straight we all must begone,
And leave none to keep house, but our new porter John,
Who relieves the poor with a thump on the back with a stone;
  Like a young courtier &c.

With a new gentleman-usher, whose carriage is complete,
With a new coachman, footmen, and pages to carry up the
    meat,
With a waiting-gentlewoman, whose dressing is very neat,
Who when her lady has dined, lets the servants not eat;
        Like a young courtier &c.

With new titles of honour bought with his father's old gold,
For which sundry of his ancestors' old manors are sold;
And this is the course most of our new gallants hold,
Which makes that good house-keeping is now grown so cold,
        Among the young courtiers of the King,
        Or the King's young courtiers.

ANONYMOUS

(17TH CENTURY?)

Robin Goodfellow

From Oberon, in fairy land,
   The king of ghosts and shadows there,
Mad Robin I, at his command,
   Am sent to view the night-sports here.
      What revel rout
      Is kept about,
  In every corner where I go,
      I will o'ersee,
      And merry be,
And make good sport, with ho, ho, ho!

More swift than lightning can I fly
   About this airy welkin soon,
And, in a minute's space, descry
   Each thing that's done beneath the moon.
      There's not a hag
      Or ghost shall wag,
  Or cry, 'ware goblins! where I go;
      But Robin I
      Their feats will spy,
And send them home with ho, ho, ho!

Whene'er such wanderers I meet,
　As from their night-sports they trudge home,
With counterfeiting voice I greet,
　And call them on with me to roam:
　　Through woods, through lakes,
　　Through bogs, through brakes;
　Or else, unseen, with them I go,
　　All in the nick,
　　To play some trick,
And frolic it, with ho, ho, ho!

Sometimes I meet them like a man,
　Sometimes an ox, sometimes a hound;
And to a horse I turn me can,
　To trip and trot about them round.
　　But if to ride
　　My back they stride,
More swift than wind away I go:
　　O'er hedge and lands,
　　Through pools and ponds
I hurry laughing, ho, ho, ho!

When lads and lasses merry be,
　With possets and with junkets fine;
Unseen of all the company,
　I eat their cakes and sip their wine!
　　And, to make sport,
　　I puff and snort:
And out the candles I do blow:
　　The maids I kiss,
　　They shriek—Who's this?
I answer nought but ho, ho, ho!

Yet now and then, the maids to please,
　At midnight I card up their wool;
And, while they sleep and take their ease,
　With wheel to threads their flax I pull.
　　I grind at mill
　　Their malt up still;

I dress their hemp; I spin their tow;
 If any wake,
 And would me take,
I wend me laughing, ho, ho, ho!

When any need to borrow aught,
 We lend them what they do require:
And for the use demand we nought;
 Our own is all we do desire.
  If to repay
  They do delay,
 Abroad amongst them then I go,
  And night by night
  I them affright
 With pinchings, dreams, and ho, ho, ho!

When lazy queans have nought to do,
 But study how to cheat and lie:
To make debate and mischief too,
 'Twixt one another secretly:
  I mark their gloze,
  And it disclose
 To them whom they have wrongéd so:
  When I have done,
  I get me gone,
 And leave them scolding, ho, ho, ho!

When men do traps and engines set
 In loop-holes, where the vermin creep,
Who from their folds and houses get
 Their ducks and geese, and lambs and sheep;
  I spy the gin,
  And enter in,
 And seem a vermin taken so;
  But when they there
  Approach me near,
 I leap out laughing, ho, ho, ho!

By wells and rills, in meadows green,
 We nightly dance our heyday guise;
And to our fairy king and queen

We chant our moonlight minstrelsies.
 When larks 'gin sing,
 Away we fling;
And babes newborn steal as we go;
 And elf in bed
 We leave instead,
And wend us laughing, ho, ho, ho!

From hag-bred Merlin's time, have I
 Thus nightly revelled to and fro;
And for my pranks men call me by
 The name of Robin Goodfellow.
  Fiends, ghosts, and sprites,
  Who haunt the nights,
The hags and goblins do me know;
  And beldames old
  My feats have told,
So vale, vale; ho, ho, ho!

ANONYMOUS

(17TH CENTURY)

The Queen of Fairies

 Come follow, follow me,
 You, fairy elves that be,
 Which circle on the green;
 Come follow me, your queen.
Hand in hand, let's dance a round,
For this place is fairy ground.

 When mortals are at rest,
 And snoring in their nest;
 Unheard and unespied,
 Through key-holes we do glide;
Over tables, stools, and shelves,
We trip it with our fairy elves.

 And, if the house be foul,
 Or platter, dish, or bowl,
 Up stairs we nimbly creep,

And find the sluts asleep:
There we pinch their arms and thighs—
None escapes; nor none espies.

    But if the house be swept,
    And from uncleanness kept,
    We praise the household maid,
    And surely she is paid:
For we do use before we go,
To drop a tester in her shoe.

    Upon a mushroom's head,
    Our table we do spread;
    A grain of rye, or wheat,
    Is manchet, which we eat;
Pearly drops of dew we drink
In acorn cups filled to the brink.

    The brains of nightingales,
    With unctuous dew of snails,
    Between two nutshells stewed,
    Is meat that's easily chewed;
And the beards of little mice
Do make a feast of wondrous price.

    On tops of dewy grass,
    So nimbly do we pass,
    The young and tender stalk
    Ne'er bends where we do walk;
Yet in the morning may be seen
Where we, the night before, have been.

    The grasshopper, gnat and fly,
    Serve for our minstrelsy;
    Grace said, we dance a while,
    And so the time beguile:
And when the moon doth hide her head,
The glow-worm lights us home to bed.

ANONYMOUS

(17TH CENTURY)

In Praise of Ale

When the chill Charoko blows,
    And Winter tells a heavy tale,
And pyes and daws and rooks and crows
Do sit and curse the frosts and snows;
        Then give me ale.

Ale in a Saxon rumkin then,
    Such as will make grim Malkin prate;
Bids valour burgeon in tall men,
Quickens the poet's wits and pen,
        Despises fate.

Ale, that the absent battle fights,
    And forms the march of Swedish drum,
Disputes the princes' laws, and rights,
What's past and done tells mortal wights,
        And what's to come.

Ale, that the plowman's heart up-keeps,
    And equals it to tyrant's thrones,
That wipes the eye that ever weeps,
And lulls in sweet and dainty sleeps
        Their very bones.

Grandchild of Ceres, Bacchus' daughter,
    Wine's emulous neighbour, though but stale,
Ennobling all the nymphs of water,
And filling each man's heart with laughter—
        Ha! Ha! give me ale!

ANONYMOUS

(17TH CENTURY)

The Farewell

It was a' for our rightfu' King
  We left fair Scotland's strand;
It was a' for our rightfu' King
  We e'er saw Irish land,
     My dear—
  We e'er saw Irish land.

Now a' is done that men can do,
  And a' is done in vain;
My love and native land, farewell!
  For I maun cross the main,
     My dear—
  For I maun cross the main.

He turned him right and round about
  Upon the Irish shore;
And gave his bridle-reins a shake,
  With Adieu for evermore,
     My dear—
  With Adieu for evermore!

The sodger frae the wars returns,
  The sailor frae the main;
But I hae parted frae my love,
  Never to meet again,
     My dear—
  Never to meet again.

When day is gane, and night is come,
  And a' folk bound to sleep,
I think on him that's far awa',
  The lee-lang night, and weep,
     My dear—
  The lee-lang night, and weep.

[*Also attributed to* ROBERT BURNS]

WILLIAM HABINGTON
(1605–1654)

To Roses in the Bosom of Castara

Ye blushing virgins happy are
In the chaste nunnery of her breasts,
For he'd profane so chaste a fair
Who e'er should call them Cupid's nests.

Transplanted thus, how bright ye grow,
How rich a perfume do ye yield!
In some close garden cowslips so
Are sweeter than i' th' open field.

In these white cloisters live secure
From the rude blasts of wanton breath,
Each hour more innocent and pure,
Till you shall wither into death.

Then that which living gave you room,
Your glorious sepulchre shall be;
There wants no marble for a tomb,
Whose breast hath marble been to me.

THOMAS RANDOLPH
(1605–1635)

An Ode to Mr. Anthony Stafford to Hasten Him into the Country

Come, spur away,
I have no patience for a longer stay;
But must go down
And leave the chargeable noise of this great town.
I will the country see,
Where old simplicity,
Though hid in grey,
Doth look more gay
Than foppery in plush and scarlet clad.
Farewell, you City wits, that are
Almost at civil war;
'Tis time that I grow wise, when all the world grows mad.

More of my days
I will not spend to gain an idiot's praise;
            Or to make sport
For some slight puisne of the Inns of Court.
        Then worthy Stafford, say
        How shall we spend the day,
            With what delights
            Shorten the nights?
When from the tumult we are got secure;
    Where mirth with all her freedom goes,
        Yet shall no finger lose;
Where every word is thought, and every thought is pure.

There from the tree
We'll cherries pluck, and pick the strawberry.
            And every day
Go see the wholesome country girls make hay;
        Whose brown hath lovelier grace
        Than any painted face
            That I do know
            Hyde Park can show.
Where I had rather gain a kiss than meet
    (Though some of them in greater state
        Might court my love with plate)
The beauties of the Cheap and wives of Lombard Street.

But think upon
Some other pleasures, these to me are none.
            Why do I prate
Of women, that are things against my fate?
        I never mean to wed
        That torture to my bed.
            My Muse is she
            My love shall be.
Let clowns get wealth and heirs; when I am gone,
    And the great bugbear, grisly death,
        Shall take this idle breath,
If I a poem leave, that poem is my son.

Of this, no more;
We'll rather taste the bright Pomona's store.
No fruit shall 'scape
Our palates, from the damson to the grape.
Then full we'll seek a shade
And hear what music's made;
How Philomel
Her tale doth tell;
And how the other birds do fill the choir;
The thrush and blackbird lend their notes,
Warbling melodious notes;
We will all sports enjoy which others but desire.

Ours is the sky,
Where at what fowl we please our hawk shall fly;
Nor will we spare
To hunt the crafty fox or timorous hare;
But let our hounds run loose
In any ground they choose,
The buck shall fall,
The stag and all.
Our pleasures must from our own warrants be,
For to my Muse, if not to me,
I'm sure all game is free;
Heaven, earth are all but parts of her great royalty.

And when we mean
To taste of Bacchus' blessings now and then,
And drink by stealth
A cup or two to noble Berkeley's health.
I'll take my pipe and try
The Phrygian melody,
Which he that hears
Lets through his ears
A madness to distemper all the brain.
Then I another pipe will take
And Doric music make
To civilize with graver notes our wits again.

To One Admiring Herself in a Looking Glass

Fair lady, when you see the grace
Of beauty in your looking glass:
A stately forehead smooth and high
And full of princely majesty;
A sparkling eye, no gem so fair,
Whose lustre dims the Cyprian star;
A glorious cheek divinely sweet
Wherein both roses kindly meet;
A cherry lip that would entice
Even gods to kiss at any price;
You think no beauty is so rare
That with your shadow might compare,
That your reflection is alone
The thing that men most dote upon.
Madam, alas, your glass doth lie,
And you are much deceived; for I
A beauty know of richer grace.
Sweet, be not angry—'tis your face.
Hence then, oh learn more mild to be,
And leave to lay your blame on me;
If me your real substance move
When you so much your shadow love.
Wise nature would not let your eye
Look on her own bright majesty,
Which had you once but gazed upon,
You could except yourself love none.
What then you cannot love, let me,
That face I can, you cannot see.
Now you have what to love, you'll say,
What then is left for me, I pray?
My face, sweetheart, if it please thee;
That which you can, I cannot see.
So either love shall gain his due;
Yours, sweet, in me, and mine in you.

FROM A *Pastoral Courtship*

Being set, let's sport a while, my fair;
I will tie love-knots in thy hair.
See, Zephyr through the leaves doth stray
And has free liberty to play,
And braids thy locks; and shall I find
Less favour than a saucy wind?
Now let me sit and fix my eyes
On thee that art my paradise.
Thou art my all. The Spring remains
In the fair violets of thy veins;
And that it is a Summer's day,
Ripe cherries in thy lips display;
And when for Autumn I would seek,
'Tis in the apples of thy cheek;
But that which only moves my smart,
Is to see Winter in thy heart.
Strange, when at once in one appear
All the four seasons of the year!
I'll clasp that neck, where should be set
A rich and orient carcanet;
But swains are poor; admit of, then,
More natural chains, the arms of men.
Come, let me touch those breasts that swell
Like two fair mountains, and may well
Be styled the Alps, but that I fear
The snow has less of whiteness there.
But stay, my love; a fault I spy.
Why are these two fair fountains dry?
Which, if they run, no Muse would please
To taste of any spring but these.
And Ganymede employed should be
To fetch his Jove nectar from thee.
Thou shalt be nurse, fair Venus swears,
To the next Cupid that she bears.
Were it not then discreetly done
To ope one spring to let two run?
Fie, fie, this belly, beauty's mint,
Blushes to see no coin stamped in't.

Employ it then, for though it be
Our wealth, it is your royalty;
And beauty will have current grace
That bears the image of your face.
How to the touch the ivory thighs
Vail gently, and again do rise,
As pliable to impression
As virgin wax or Parian stone
Dissolved to softness, plump and full,
More white and soft than Cotswold wool,
Or cotton from the Indian tree,
Or pretty silkworm's housewifery.
These on two marble pillars raised,
Make me in doubt which should be praised,
They or their columns, most; but when
I view those feet which I have seen
So nimbly trip it o'er the lawns
That all the satyrs and the fawns
Have stood amazed when they would pass
Over the leas, and not a grass
Would feel the weight, nor rush nor bent,
Drooping betray which way you went;
Oh then I felt my hot desires
Burn more and flame with double fires.

Now let us kiss. Would you be gone?
Manners at least allows me one.
Blush you at this, pretty one? Stay,
And I will take that kiss away
Thus, with a second, and that too
A third wipes off; so will we go
To numbers that the stars outrun
And all the atoms in the sun.
For though we kiss till Phoebus' ray
Sink in the seas, and kissing stay
Till his bright beams return again,
There can of all but one remain;
And if for one good manners call.
In one good manners grant me all.

SIR WILLIAM DAVENANT

(1606–1668)

"The Lark Now Leaves..."

The lark now leaves his watery nest,
  And climbing shakes his dewy wings;
He takes this window for the East,
  And to implore your light he sings—
Awake, awake, the morn will never rise
Till she can dress her beauty at your eyes.

The merchant bows unto the seaman's star,
  The ploughman from the sun his season takes;
But still the lover wonders what they are
  Who look for day before his mistress wakes.
Awake, awake! break through your veils of lawn!
Then draw your curtains, and begin the dawn!

FROM *Song*

Roses and pinks will be strewn where you go;
Whilst I walk in shades of willow, willow.
  When I am dead let him that did slay me
  Be but so good as kindly to lay me
  There where neglected lovers mourn,
  Where lamps and hallowed tapers burn,
  Where clerks in choirs sad dirges sing,
  Where sweetly bells at burials ring.

  My rose of youth is gone,
  Withered as soon as blown.
  Lovers, go ring my knell.
  Beauty and love, farewell.
  And lest virgins forsaken
  Should perhaps be mistaken
In seeking my grave, alas! let them know
I lie near a shade of willow, willow.

The Unfortunate Lovers, 1638

EDMUND WALLER

(1606–1687)

To a Very Young Lady

Why came I so untimely forth
Into a world which, wanting thee,
Could entertain us with no worth
Or shadow of felicity,
That time should me so far remove
From that which I was born to love?

Yet, fairest blossom! do not slight
That age which you may know so soon;
The rosy morn resigns her light,
And milder glory, to the noon;
And then what wonders shall you do,
Whose dawning beauty warms us so?

Hope waits upon the flowery prime;
And summer, though it be less gay,
Yet is not looked on as a time
Of declination or decay;
For with a full hand that doth bring
All that was promised by the spring.

On a Girdle

That which her slender waist confined,
Shall now my joyful temples bind;
No monarch but would give his crown,
His arms might do what this has done.

It was my heaven's extremest sphere,
The pale which held that lovely deer.
My joy, my grief, my hope, my love,
Did all within this circle move!

A narrow compass! and yet there
Dwelt all that's good and all that's fair;
Give me but what this ribband bound,
Take all the rest the sun goes round.

Go, Lovely Rose!

Go, lovely Rose!
Tell her that wastes her time and me
That now she knows,
When I resemble her to thee,
How sweet and fair she seems to be.

Tell her that's young,
And shuns to have her graces spied,
That hadst thou sprung
In deserts, where no men abide,
Thou must have uncommended died.

Small is the worth
Of beauty from the light retired;
Bid her come forth,
Suffer herself to be desired,
And not blush so to be admired.

Then die! that she
The common fate of all things rare
May read in thee;
How small a part of time they share
That are so wondrous sweet and fair!

Of the Last Verses in the Book

When we for age could neither read nor write,
The subject made us able to indite;
The soul, with nobler resolutions decked,
The body stooping, does herself erect.
No mortal parts are requisite to raise
Her that, unbodied, can her Maker praise.

The seas are quiet when the winds give o'er;
So, calm are we when passions are no more!
For then we know how vain it was to boast
Of fleeting things, so certain to be lost.
Clouds of affection from our younger eyes
Conceal that emptiness which age descries.

The soul's dark cottage, battered and decayed,
Lets in new light through chinks that time has made;
Stronger by weakness, wiser men become,
As they draw near to their eternal home.
Leaving the old, both worlds at once they view,
That stand upon the threshold of the new.

JOHN MILTON

(1608–1674)

Sonnet

O Nightingale, that on yon bloomy spray
Warbl'st at eve, when all the woods are still,
Thou with fresh hope the lover's heart dost fill,
While the jolly hours lead on propitious May,
Thy liquid notes that close the eye of Day,
First heard before the shallow cuckoo's bill
Portend success in love: O if Jove's will
Have linked that amorous power to thy soft lay,
Now timely sing, ere the rude bird of hate
Foretell my hopeless doom in some grove nigh:
As thou from year to year hast sung too late
For my relief; yet hadst no reason why,
Whether the Muse, or Love call thee his mate,
Both them I serve, and of their train am I.

An Epitaph on the Admirable Dramatic Poet William Shakespeare

What needs my Shakespeare for his honoured bones
The labour of an age in piléd stones,
Or that his hallowed relics should be hid
Under a star-ypointing pyramid?
Dear son of memory, great heir of fame,
What need'st thou such weak witness of thy name?
Thou in our wonder and astonishment
Hast built thyself a live-long monument.
For whilst to th' shame of slow-endeavouring art,

Thy easy numbers flow, and that each heart
Hath from the leaves of thy unvalued book
Those Delphic lines with deep impression took,
Then thou our fancy of itself bereaving,
Dost make us marble with too much conceiving:
And so sepulchred in such pomp dost lie,
That kings for such a tomb would wish to die.

Sonnet

How soon hath Time the subtle thief of youth,
Stol'n on his wing my three and twentieth year!
My hasting days fly on with full career,
But my late spring no bud or blossom shew'th.
Perhaps my semblance might deceive the truth,
That I to manhood am arriv'd so near,
And inward ripeness doth much less appear,
That some more timely-happy spirits endu'th.
Yet be it less or more, or soon or slow,
It shall be still in strictest measure ev'n,
To that same lot, however mean, or high,
Toward which Time leads me, and the will of Heav'n;
All is, if I have grace to use it so,
As ever in my great Task-Master's eye.

FROM *Arcades*

SECOND SONG

O'er the smooth enamelled green
Where no print of step hath been,
    Follow me as I sing,
    And touch the warbled string.
Under the shady roof
Of branching elm star-proof,
    Follow me;
I will bring you where she sits
Clad in splendour as befits
    Her deity.
Such a rural queen
All Arcadia hath not seen.

THIRD SONG

Nymphs and shepherds dance no more
    By sandy Ladon's lilied banks.
On old Lycaeus or Cyllene hoar
    Trip no more in twilight ranks.
Though Erymanth your loss deplore
    A better soil shall give ye thanks.
From the stony Maenalus
Bring your flocks, and live with us,
Here ye shall have greater grace,
To serve the Lady of this place.
Though Syrinx your Pan's mistress were,
Yet Syrinx well might wait on her.
      Such a rural queen
All Arcadia hath not seen.

L'Allegro

Hence loathéd Melancholy
    Of Cerberus and blackest midnight born,
In Stygian cave forlorn
    'Mongst horrid shapes, and shrieks, and sights unholy,
Find out some uncouth cell,
    Where brooding darkness spreads his jealous wings,
And the night-raven sings;
    There under ebon shades, and low-browed rocks,
As ragged as thy locks,
    In dark Cimmerian desert ever dwell.
But come thou goddess fair and free,
In Heaven yclept Euphrosyne,
And by men, heart-easing Mirth,
Whom lovely Venus at a birth
With two sister Graces more
To ivy-crownéd Bacchus bore;
Or whether (as some sager sing)
The frolic wind that breathes the spring,
Zephyr with Aurora playing,
As he met her once a-maying,
There on beds of violets blue,

And fresh-blown roses washed in dew,
Filled her with thee a daughter fair,
So buxom, blithe, and debonair.
Haste thee nymph and bring with thee
Jest and youthful jollity,
Quips and cranks, and wanton wiles,
Nods, and becks, and wreathéd smiles,
Such as hang on Hebe's cheek,
And love to live in dimple sleek;
Sport that wrinkled care derides,
And laughter holding both his sides.
Come, and trip it as ye go
On the light fantastic toe,
And in thy right hand lead with thee,
The mountain nymph, sweet Liberty;
And if I give thee honour due,
Mirth, admit me of thy crew
To live with her, and live with thee,
In unreprovéd pleasures free;
To hear the lark begin his flight,
And singing startle the dull night,
From his watch-tower in the skies,
Till the dappled dawn doth rise;
Then to come in spite of sorrow,
And at my window bid good morrow,
Through the sweet-briar, or the vine,
Or the twisted eglantine;
While the cock with lively din,
Scatters the rear of darkness thin,
And to the stack, or the barn door,
Stoutly struts his dames before;
Oft listening how the hounds and horn
Cheerly rouse the slumbering morn,
From the side of some hoar hill,
Through the high wood echoing shrill.
Some time walking not unseen
By hedge-row elms, on hillocks green,
Right against the eastern gate,
Where the great sun begins his state,
Robed in flames, and amber light,
The clouds in thousand liveries dight.

While the ploughman near at hand,
Whistles o'er the furrowed land,
And the milkmaid singeth blithe,
And the mower whets his scythe,
And every shepherd tells his tale
Under the hawthorn in the dale.

Straight mine eye hath caught new pleasures
While the landskip round it measures,
Russet lawns, and fallows gray,
Where the nibbling flocks do stray;
Mountains on whose barren breast
The labouring clouds do often rest;
Meadows trim with daisies pied,
Shallow brooks, and rivers wide.
Towers, and battlements it sees
Bosomed high in tufted trees,
Where perhaps some beauty lies,
The cynosure of neighbouring eyes.
Hard by, a cottage chimney smokes,
From betwixt two aged oaks,
Where Corydon and Thyrsis met,
Are at their savoury dinner set
Of herbs, and other country messes,
Which the neat-handed Phyllis dresses;
And then in haste her bower she leaves,
With Thestylis to bind the sheaves;
Or if the earlier season lead
To the tanned haycock in the mead.

Sometimes with secure delight
The upland hamlets will invite,
When the merry bells ring round,
And the jocund rebecks sound
To many a youth, and many a maid
Dancing in the chequered shade;
And young and old come forth to play
On a sunshine holiday,
Till the live-long daylight fail;
Then to the spicy nut-brown ale,
With stories told of many a feat,

How Faery Mab the junkets eat;
She was pinched, and pulled she said,
And he by friar's lanthorn led;
Tells how the drudging goblin sweat,
To earn his cream-bowl duly set,
When in one night, ere glimpse of morn,
His shadowy flail hath threshed the corn
That ten day-labourers could not end;
Then lies him down the lubber fiend,
And stretched out all the chimney's length,
Basks at the fire his hairy strength;
And crop-full out of doors he flings,
Ere the first cock his matin rings.
Thus done the tales, to bed they creep,
By whispering winds soon lulled asleep.

Towered cities please us then,
And the busy hum of men,
Where throngs of knights and barons bold,
In weeds of peace high triumphs hold,
With store of ladies, whose bright eyes
Rain influence, and judge the prize
Of wit, or arms, while both contend
To win her grace, whom all commend.
There let Hymen oft appear
In saffron robe, with taper clear,
And pomp, and feast, and revelry,
With mask, and antique pageantry,
Such sights as youthful poets dream
On summer eves by haunted stream.
Then to the well-trod stage anon,
If Jonson's learned sock be on,
Or sweetest Shakespeare, fancy's child,
Warble his native wood-notes wild.
And ever against eating cares,
Lap me in soft Lydian airs,
Married to immortal verse,
Such as the meeting soul may pierce
In notes, with many a winding bout
Of linkéd sweetness long drawn out,
With wanton heed, and giddy cunning,

The melting voice through mazes running;
Untwisting all the chains that tie
The hidden soul of harmony:
That Orpheus' self may heave his head
From golden slumber on a bed
Of heaped Elysian flowers, and hear
Such strains as would have won the ear
Of Pluto, to have quite set free
His half-regained Eurydice.
These delights if thou canst give,
Mirth, with thee I mean to live.

Il Penseroso

Hence, vain deluding joys,
   The brood of folly without father bred,
How little you bested,
   Or fill the fixéd mind with all your toys;
Dwell in some idle brain,
   And fancies fond with gaudy shapes possess,
As thick and numberless
   As the gay motes that people the sun-beams,
Or likest hovering dreams
   The fickle pensioners of Morpheus' train.
But hail thou goddess, sage and holy,
Hail divinest Melancholy,
Whose saintly visage is too bright
To hit the sense of human sight;
And therefore to our weaker view,
O'er-laid with black, staid wisdom's hue:
Black, but such as in esteem
Prince Memnon's sister might beseem,
Or that starred Ethiop queen that strove
To set her beauty's praise above
The sea nymphs, and their power offended.
Yet thou art higher far descended,
Thee bright-haired Vesta long of yore,
To solitary Saturn bore;
His sister she (in Saturn's reign,
Such mixture was not held a stain).

Oft in glimmering bowers and glades
He met her, and in secret shades
Of woody Ida's inmost grove,
While yet there was no fear of Jove.
Come pensive nun, devout and pure,
Sober, stedfast, and demure,
All in a robe of darkest grain,
Flowing with majestic train,
And sable stole of cypress lawn,
Over thy decent shoulders drawn.
Come, but keep thy wonted state,
With even step and musing gait,
And looks commercing with the skies,
Thy rapt soul sitting in thine eyes:
There held in holy passion still,
Forget thyself to marble, till
With a sad leaden downward cast,
Thou fix them on the earth as fast.
And join with thee calm peace, and quiet,
Spare fast, that oft with gods doth diet,
And hears the Muses in a ring,
Aye round about Jove's altar sing.
And add to these retiréd leisure,
That in trim gardens takes his pleasure;
But first, and chiefest, with thee bring
Him that yon soars on golden wing,
Guiding the fiery-wheeléd throne,
The cherub, contemplation;
And the mute silence hist along,
'Less Philomel will deign a song,
In her sweetest, saddest plight,
Smoothing the rugged brow of night,
While Cynthia checks her dragon yoke,
Gently o'er th' accustomed oak;
Sweet bird that shunn'st the noise of folly,
Most musical, most melancholy!
Thee chauntress oft the woods among,
I woo to hear thy even-song;
And missing thee, I walk unseen
On the dry smooth-shaven green,
To behold the wandering moon,

Riding near her highest noon,
Like one that hath been led astray
Through the heav'ns wide pathless way;
And oft, as if her head she bowed,
Stooping through a fleecy cloud.
Oft on a plat of rising ground,
I hear the far-off curfew sound,
Over some wide-watered shore,
Swinging slow with sullen roar;
Or if the air will not permit,
Some still removéd place will fit,
Where glowing embers through the room
Teach light to counterfeit a gloom,
Far from all resort of mirth,
Save the cricket on the hearth,
Or the bellman's drowsy charm,
To bless the doors from nightly harm:
Or let my lamp at midnight hour
Be seen in some high lonely tower,
Where I may oft out-watch the Bear,
With thrice-great Hermes, or unsphere
The spirit of Plato to unfold
What worlds, or what vast regions hold
The immortal mind that hath forsook
Her mansion in this fleshly nook:
And of those daemons that are found
In fire, air, flood, or under ground,
Whose power hath a true consent
With planet or with element.
Sometimes let gorgeous tragedy
In sceptered pall come sweeping by,
Presenting Thebes', or Pelops' line,
Or the tale of Troy divine,
Or what (though rare) of later age,
Ennobled hath the buskined stage.

But, O sad virgin, that thy power
Might raise Musaeus from his bower,
Or bid the soul of Orpheus sing
Such notes as warbled to the string
Drew iron tears down Pluto's cheek,

And made hell grant what love did seek.
Or call up him that left half told
The story of Cambuscan bold,
Of Camball, and of Algarsife,
And who had Canace to wife,
That owned the virtuous ring and glass,
And of the wond'rous horse of brass,
On which the Tartar king did ride;
And if aught else, great bards beside,
In sage and solemn tunes have sung,
Of tourneys and of trophies hung;
Of forests, and enchantments drear,
Where more is meant than meets the ear.
Thus night oft see me in thy pale career,
Till civil-suited morn appear,
Not tricked and frounced as she was wont,
With the Attic boy to hunt,
But kerchiefed in a comely cloud,
While rocking winds are piping loud,
Or ushered with a shower still,
When the gust hath blown his fill,
Ending on the rustling leaves,
With minute drops from off the eaves.
And when the sun begins to fling
His flaring beams, me goddess bring
To archéd walks of twilight groves,
And shadows brown that Sylvan loves
Of pine, or monumental oak,
Where the rude axe with heavéd stroke,
Was never heard the nymphs to daunt,
Or fright them from their hallowed haunt.
There in close covert by some brook,
Where no profaner eye may look,
Hide me from day's garish eye,
While the bee with honied thigh,
That at her flower work doth sing,
And the waters murmuring
With such consort as they keep,
Entice the dewy-feathered sleep;
And let some strange mysterious dream,
Wave at his wings in airy stream,

Of lively portraiture displayed,
Softly on my eye-lids laid.
And as I wake, sweet music breathe
Above, about, or underneath,
Sent by some spirit to mortals good,
Or th' unseen genius of the wood.

But let my due feet never fail
To walk the studious cloisters pale,
And love the high embowéd roof,
With antic pillars massy proof,
And storied windows richly dight,
Casting a dim religious light.
There let the pealing organ blow,
To the full-voiced choir below,
In service high, and anthems clear,
As may with sweetness, through mine ear,
Dissolve me into ecstasies,
And bring all heav'n before mine eyes.
And may at last my weary age
Find out the peaceful hermitage,
The hairy gown and mossy cell,
Where I may sit and rightly spell
Of every star that heav'n doth show,
And every herb that sips the dew;
Till old experience do attain
To something like prophetic strain.
These pleasures, Melancholy, give,
And I with thee will choose to live.

FROM A Mask Presented at Ludlow Castle
(Comus)

1.

Comus: The star that bids the shepherd fold,
Now the top of heav'n doth hold,
And the gilded car of day
His glowing axle doth allay
In the steep Atlantic stream,
And the slope sun his upward beam

Shoots against the dusky pole,
Pacing toward the other goal
Of his chamber in the east.
Meanwhile, welcome joy, and feast,
Midnight shout, and revelry,
Tipsy dance, and jollity.
Braid your locks with rosy twine
Dropping odours, dropping wine.
Rigour now is gone to bed,
And advice with scrupulous head,
Strict age, and sour severity,
With their grave saws in slumber lie.
We that are of purer fire
Imitate the starry choir,
Who in their nightly watchful spheres
Lead in swift round the months and years.
The sounds and seas with all their finny drove
Now to the moon in wavering morris move,
And on the tawny sands and shelves
Trip the pert fairies and the dapper elves;
By dimpled brook and fountain brim
The wood nymphs decked with daisies trim
Their merry wakes and pastimes keep:
What hath night to do with sleep?
Night hath better sweets to prove,
Venus now wakes, and wakens Love.
Come, let us our rites begin,
'Tis only daylight that makes sin
Which these dun shades will ne'er report.
Hail goddess of nocturnal sport,
Dark-veiled Cotytto, t' whom the secret flame
Of midnight torches burns; mysterious dame
That ne'er art called but when the dragon womb
Of Stygian darkness spits her thickest gloom,
And makes one blot of all the air,
Stay thy cloudy ebon chair,
Wherein thou rid'st with Hecat', and befriend
Us thy vowed priests, till utmost end
Of all thy dues be done, and none left out,
Ere the blabbing eastern scout,
The nice morn on the Indian steep

From her cabined loop-hole peep,
And to the tell-tale sun descry
Our concealed solemnity.
Come, knit hands, and beat the ground,
In a light fantastic round.

2.   SONG
   Sweet Echo, sweetest nymph that liv'st unseen
            Within thy airy shell
         By slow Meander's margent green,
   And in the violet-embroidered vale
            Where the love-lorn nightingale
   Nightly to thee her sad song mourneth well,
   Canst thou not tell me of a gentle pair
            That likest thy Narcissus are?
               O if thou have
            Hid them in some flowery cave,
               Tell me but where,
   Sweet queen of parley, daughter of the sphere,
   So mayst thou be transplanted to the skies,
And give resounding grace to all Heav'n's harmonies.

3.

Comus: O foolishness of men! that lend their ears
         To those budge doctors of the Stoic fur,
         And fetch their precepts from the Cynic tub,
         Praising the lean and sallow abstinence.
         Wherefore did Nature pour her bounties forth,
         With such a full and unwithdrawing hand,
         Covering the earth with odours, fruits and flocks,
         Thronging the seas with spawn innumerable,
         But all to please and sate the curious taste?
         And set to work millions of spinning worms,
         That in their green shops weave the smooth-haired
               silk
         To deck her sons, and that no corner might
         Be vacant of her plenty, in her own loins
         She hutched th'all-worshipped ore, and precious gems

To store her children with; if all the world
Should in a pet of temperance feed on pulse,
Drink the clear stream, and nothing wear but frieze,
Th'all-giver would be unthanked, would be un-
　　　praised,
Not half his riches known, and yet despised,
And we should serve him as a grudging master,
As a penurious niggard of his wealth,
And live like Nature's bastards, not her sons,
Who would be quite surcharged with her own
　　　weight,
And strangled with her waste fertility;
Th'earth cumbered, and the winged air darked with
　　　plumes,
The herds would over-multitude their lords,
The sea o'erfraught would swell, and th'unsought
　　　diamonds
Would so emblaze the forehead of the deep,
And so bestud with stars, that they below
Would grow inured to light, and come at last
To gaze upon the sun with shameless brows.

4.　　　　　　　　　　SONG
Sabrina fair
　　Listen where thou art sitting
Under the glassy, cool, translucent wave,
　　In twisted braids of lilies knitting
The loose train of thy amber-dropping hair;
　　Listen for dear honour's sake,
　　Goddess of the silver lake,
　　　　　　　　　　　Listen and save.

Listen and appear to us
In name of great Oceanus,
By the earth-shaking Neptune's mace,
And Tethys' grave majestic pace,
By hoary Nereus' wrinkled look,
And the Carpathian wizard's hook,
By scaly Triton's winding shell,
And old sooth-saying Glaucus' spell,

By Leucothea's lovely hands,
And her son that rules the strands,
By Thetis' tinsel-slippered feet,
And the song of sirens sweet,
By dead Parthenope's dear tomb,
And fair Ligea's golden comb,
Wherewith she sits on diamond rocks
Sleeking her soft alluring locks,
By all the nymphs that nightly dance
Upon thy streams with wily glance,
Rise, rise, and heave thy rosy head
From thy coral-paven bed,
And bridle in thy headlong wave,
Till thou our summons answered have.
Listen and save.

5.   "TO THE OCEAN NOW I FLY"

Spirit: To the ocean now I fly,
And those happy climes that lie
Where day never shuts his eye,
Up in the broad fields of the sky:
There I suck the liquid air
All amidst the gardens fair
Of Hesperus, and his daughters three
That sing about the golden tree:
Along the crispéd shades and bowers
Revels the spruce and jocund Spring,
The Graces, and the rosy-bosomed Hours,
Thither all their bounties bring.
There eternal Summer dwells,
And west winds, with musky wing
About the cedarn alleys fling
Nard, and cassia's balmy smells.
Iris there with humid bow
Waters the odorous banks that blow
Flowers of more mingled hue
Than her purfled scarf can show,
And drenches with Elysian dew
(List mortals, if your ears be true)

Beds of hyacinth and roses
Where young Adonis oft reposes,
Waxing well of his deep wound
In slumber soft, and on the ground
Sadly sits th' Assyrian queen;
But far above in spangled sheen
Celestial Cupid, her famed son advanced,
Holds his dead Psyche sweet entranced
After her wandering labours long,
Till free consent the gods among
Make her his eternal bride,
And from her fair unspotted side
Two blissful twins are to be born,
Youth and Joy; so Jove has sworn.

But now my task is smoothly done,
I can fly, or I can run
Quickly to the green earth's end,
Where the bowed welkin slow doth bend,
And from thence can soar as soon
To the corners of the moon.

Mortals that would follow me,
Love virtue, she alone is free,
She can teach ye how to climb
Higher than the sphery chime;
Or if Virtue feeble were,
Heaven itself would stoop to her.

Lycidas

Yet once more, O ye laurels, and once more
Ye myrtles brown, with ivy never sere,
I come to pluck your berries harsh and crude,
And with forced fingers rude,
Shatter your leaves before the mellowing year.
Bitter constraint, and sad occasion dear,
Compels me to disturb your season due:
For Lycidas is dead, dead ere his prime
Young Lycidas, and hath not left his peer:

Who would not sing for Lycidas? he knew
Himself to sing, and build the lofty rhyme.
He must not float upon his watery bier
Unwept, and welter to the parching wind,
Without the meed of some melodious tear.
Begin then, Sisters of the sacred well,
That from beneath the seat of Jove doth spring,
Begin, and somewhat loudly sweep the string.
Hence with denial vain, and coy excuse,
So may some gentle Muse
With lucky words favour my destined urn,
And as he passes turn,
And bid fair peace be to my sable shroud.
For we were nursed upon the self-same hill,
Fed the same flock, by fountain, shade, and rill.

Together both, ere the high lawns appeared
Under the opening eye-lids of the morn,
We drove afield, and both together heard
What time the gray-fly winds her sultry horn,
Battening our flocks with the fresh dews of night,
Oft till the star that rose at evening, bright
Toward heaven's descent had sloped his westering wheel.
Meanwhile the rural ditties were not mute,
Tempered to th' oaten flute,
Rough satyrs danced, and fauns with cloven heel,
From the glad sound would not be absent long,
And old Damaetas loved to hear our song.

But O the heavy change, now thou art gone,
Now thou art gone, and never must return!
Thee shepherd, thee the woods and desert caves,
With wild thyme and the gadding vine o'ergrown,
And all their echoes mourn.
The willows, and the hazel copses green,
Shall now no more be seen,
Fanning their joyous leaves to thy soft lays.
As killing as the canker to the rose,
Or taint-worm to the weanling herds that graze,
Or frost to flowers, that their gay wardrobe wear,
When first the white thorn blows;
Such, Lycidas, thy loss to shepherd's ear.

Where were ye, nymphs, when the remorseless deep

Closed o'er the head of your loved Lycidas?
For neither were ye playing on the steep,
Where your old bards, the famous Druids lie,
Nor on the shaggy top of Mona high,
Nor yet where Deva spreads her wizard stream:
Ay me, I fondly dream!
Had ye been there—for what could that have done?
What could the Muse herself that Orpheus bore,
The Muse herself, for her enchanting son
Whom universal Nature did lament,
When by the rout that made the hideous roar,
His gory visage down the stream was sent,
Down the swift Hebrus to the Lesbian shore?
 Alas! What boots it with incessant care
To tend the homely slighted shepherd's trade,
And strictly meditate the thankless Muse?
Were it not better done as others use,
To sport with Amaryllis in the shade,
Or with the tangles of Neaera's hair?
Fame is the spur that the clear spirit doth raise
(That last infirmity of noble mind)
To scorn delights, and live laborious days;
But the fair guerdon when we hope to find,
And think to burst out into sudden blaze,
Comes the blind Fury with th' abhorréd shears,
And slits the thin spun life. But not the praise,
Phoebus replied, and touched my trembling ears;
Fame is no plant that grows on mortal soil,
Nor in the glistering foil
Set off to th' world, nor in broad rumour lies,
But lives and spreads aloft by those pure eyes,
And perfect witness of all judging Jove;
As He pronounces lastly on each deed,
Of so much fame in Heav'n expect thy meed.
 O fountain Arethuse, and thou honoured flood,
Smooth-sliding Mincius, crowned with vocal reeds,
That strain I heard was of a higher mood:
But now my oat proceeds,
And listens to the herald of the sea,
That came in Neptune's plea.
He asked the waves, and asked the felon winds,

What hard mishap hath doomed this gentle swain?
And questioned every gust of rugged wings
That blows from off each beakéd promontory,
They knew not of his story,
And sage Hippotades their answer brings,
That not a blast was from his dungeon strayed,
The air was calm, and on the level brine
Sleek Panope with all her sisters played.
It was that fatal and perfidious bark
Built in th' eclipse, and rigged with curses dark,
That sunk so low that sacred head of thine.
    Next Camus, reverend sire, went footing slow,
His mantle hairy, and his bonnet sedge,
Inwrought with figures dim, and on the edge
Like to that sanguine flower inscribed with woe.
Ah! Who hath reft (quoth he) my dearest pledge?
Last came, and last did go,
The pilot of the Galilean lake,
Two massy keys he bore of metals twain,
(The golden opes, the iron shuts amain)
He shook his mitred locks, and stern bespake:
How well could I have spared for thee, young swain,
Enow of such as for their belly's sake
Creep and intrude, and climb into the fold?
Of other care they little reckoning make,
Than how to scramble at the shearers' feast,
And shove away the worthy bidden guest.
Blind mouths! that scarce themselves know how to hold
A sheep-hook, or have learned aught else the least
That to the faithful herdman's art belongs!
What recks it them? What need they? They are sped;
And when they list, their lean and flashy songs
Grate on their scrannel pipes of wretched straw.
The hungry sheep look up, and are not fed,
But swoll'n with wind, and the rank mist they draw,
Rot inwardly, and foul contagion spread:
Beside what the grim wolf with privy paw
Daily devours apace, and nothing said,
But that two-handed engine at the door,
Stands ready to smite once, and smite no more.
    Return, Alpheus, the dread voice is past,

That shrunk thy streams; return, Sicilian Muse,
And call the vales, and bid them hither cast
Their bells and flow'rets of a thousand hues.
Ye valleys low, where the mild whispers use
Of shades and wanton winds and gushing brooks,
On whose fresh lap the swart star sparely looks,
Throw hither all your quaint enameled eyes,
That on the green turf suck the honied showers,
And purple all the ground with verna! showers.
Bring the rathe primrose that forsaken dies,
The tufted crow-toe, and pale jessamine,
The white pink, and the pansy freaked with jet,
The glowing violet,
The musk-rose, and the well-attired woodbine,
The cowslips wan that hang the pensive head,
And every flower that sad embroidery wears:
Bid Amaranthus all his beauty shed,
And daffadillies fill their cups with tears,
To strew the laureate hearse where Lycid lies.
For so to interpose a little ease,
Let our frail thoughts dally with false surmise.
Ay me! Whilst thee the shores and sounding seas
Wash far away, where'er thy bones are hurled,
Whether beyond the stormy Hebrides,
Where thou perhaps under the whelming tide
Visit'st the bottom of the monstrous world;
Or whether thou to our moist vows denied,
Sleep'st by the fable of Bellerus old,
Where the great vision of the guarded mount
Looks toward Namancos and Bayona's hold;
Look homeward Angel now, and melt with ruth,
And, O ye dolphins, waft the hapless youth.
   Weep no more, woeful shepherds, weep no more,
For Lycidas your sorrow is not dead,
Sunk though he be beneath the watery floor,
So sinks the day-star in the ocean bed,
And yet anon repairs his drooping head,
And tricks his beams, and with new spangled ore
Flames in the forehead of the morning sky:
So Lycidas sunk low, but mounted high,
Through the dear might of him that walked the waves,

Where other groves, and other streams along,
With nectar pure his oozy locks he laves,
And hears the unexpressive nuptial song,
In the blest kingdoms meek of joy and love.
There entertain him all the saints above,
In solemn troops, and sweet societies
That sing, and singing in their glory move,
And wipe the tears for ever from his eyes.
Now Lycidas the shepherds weep no more;
Henceforth thou art the genius of the shore,
In thy large recompense, and shalt be good
To all that wander in that perilous flood.
    Thus sang the uncouth swain to th' oaks and rills,
While the still morn went out with sandals gray,
He touched the tender stops of various quills,
With eager thought warbling his Doric lay:
And now the sun had stretched out all the hills,
And now was dropped into the western bay;
At last he rose, and twitched his mantle blue:
To morrow to fresh woods, and pastures new.

To the Lord General Cromwell

Cromwell, our chief of men, who through a cloud
Not of war only, but detractions rude,
Guided by faith and matchless fortitude,
To peace and truth thy glorious way hast plough'd,
And on the neck of crownéd Fortune proud
Hast rear'd God's trophies, and His work pursu'd,
While Darwen stream with blood of Scots imbru'd,
And Dunbar field resounds thy praises loud,
And Worcester's laureate wreath; yet much remains
To conquer still; peace hath her victories
No less renown'd than war, new foes arise
Threat'ning to bind our souls with secular chains:
Help us to save free Conscience from the paw
Of hireling wolves whose Gospel is their maw.

On the Late Massacre in Piedmont

Avenge O Lord Thy slaughtered saints, whose bones
Lie scattered on the Alpine mountains cold,
Ev'n them that kept Thy truth so pure of old
When all our fathers worshipped stocks and stones,
Forget not: in Thy book record their groans
Who were Thy sheep and in their ancient fold
Slain by the bloody Piedmontese that rolled
Mother with infant down the rocks. Their moans
The vales redoubled to the hills, and they
To Heav'n. Their martyred blood and ashes sow
O'er all th' Italian fields where still doth sway
The triple tyrant; that from these may grow
A hundred-fold, who having learnt Thy way
Early may fly the Babylonian woe.

"When I Consider..."

When I consider how my light is spent,
Ere half my days, in this dark world and wide,
And that one talent which is death to hide,
Lodged with me useless, though my soul more bent
To serve therewith my Maker, and present
My true account, lest He returning chide:
Doth God exact day-labour, light denied,
I fondly ask; but patience to prevent
That murmur, soon replies, God doth not need
Either man's works or His own gifts; who best
Bear His mild yoke, they serve Him best; His state
Is kingly; thousands at His bidding speed
And post o'er land and ocean without rest:
They also serve who only stand and wait.

FROM *Paradise Lost*

1.

Hail holy light, offspring of Heav'n's first-born,
Or of th' Eternal co-eternal beam,
May I express thee unblamed? since God is light,

And never but in unapproachéd light
Dwelt from Eternity, dwelt then in thee,
Bright effluence of bright essence increate.
Or hear'st thou rather pure ethereal stream,
Whose fountain who shall tell? before the sun,
Before the heavens thou wert, and at the voice
Of God, as with a mantle didst invest
The rising world of waters dark and deep,
Won from the void and formless infinite.
Thee I revisit now with bolder wing,
Escaped the Stygian pool, though long detained
In that obscure sojourn, while in my flight
Through utter and through middle darkness borne,
With other notes than to th' Orphean lyre
I sung of Chaos and Eternal Night,
Taught by the heavenly Muse to venture down
The dark descent, and up to reascend,
Though hard and rare; thee I revisit safe,
And feel thy sovereign vital lamp; but thou
Revisit'st not these eyes, that roll in vain
To find thy piercing ray, and find no dawn;
So thick a drop serene hath quenched their orbs,
Or dim suffusion veiled. Yet not the more
Cease I to wander where the Muses haunt
Clear spring, or shady grove, or sunny hill,
Smit with the love of sacred song; but chief
Thee, Sion, and the flowery brooks beneath
That wash thy hallowed feet, and warbling flow,
Nightly I visit: nor sometimes forget
Those other two equalled with me in fate,
So were I equalled with them in renown,
Blind Thamyris and blind Maeonides,
And Tiresias and Phineus prophets old:
Then feed on thoughts, that voluntary move
Harmonious numbers; as the wakeful bird
Sings darkling, and in shadiest covert hid
Tunes her nocturnal note. Thus with the year
Seasons return, but not to me returns
Day, or the sweet approach of ev'n or morn,
Or sight of vernal bloom, or summer's rose,
Or flocks, or herds, or human face divine;

But cloud instead, and ever-during dark
Surrounds me, from the cheerful ways of men
Cut off, and from the book of knowledge fair
Presented with a universal blank
Of Nature's works to me expunged and razed,
And wisdom at one entrance quite shut out.
So much the rather thou celestial light
Shine inward, and the mind through all her powers
Irradiate, there plant eyes, all mist from thence
Purge and disperse, that I may see and tell
Of things invisible to mortal sight.

2.

Southward through Eden went a river large,
Nor changed his course, but through the shaggy hill
Passed underneath engulfed, for God had thrown
That mountain as His garden mould high raised
Upon the rapid current, which through veins
Or porous earth with kindly thirst updrawn,
Rose a fresh fountain, and with many a rill
Watered the garden; thence united fell
Down the steep glade, and met the nether flood,
Which from his darksome passage now appears,
And now divided into four main streams,
Runs diverse, wand'ring many a famous realm
And country whereof here needs no account,
But rather to tell how, if art could tell,
How from that sapphire fount the crispéd brooks,
Rolling on orient pearl and sands of gold,
With mazy error under pendant shades
Ran nectar, visiting each plant, and fed
Flowers worthy of Paradise which not nice art
In beds and curious knots, but Nature boon
Poured forth profuse on hill and dale and plain,
Both where the morning sun first warmly smote
The open field, and where the unpierced shade
Embrowned the noontide bow'rs: Thus was this place
A happy rural seat of various view:
Groves whose rich trees wept odorous gums and balm,
Others whose fruit burnished with golden rind

Hung amiable, Hesperian fables true,
If true, here only, and of delicious taste:
Betwixt them lawns, or level downs, and flocks
Grazing the tender herb, were interposed,
Or palmy hillock, or the flowery lap
Of some irriguous valley spread her store,
Flowers of all hue, and without thorn the rose:
Another side, umbrageous grots and caves
Of cool recess, o'er which the mantling vine
Lays forth her purple grape, and gently creeps
Luxuriant; meanwhile murmuring waters fall
Down the slope hills, dispersed, or in a lake,
That to the fringéd bank with myrtle crowned,
Her crystal mirror holds, unito their streams.
The birds their choir apply; airs, vernal airs,
Breathing the smell of field and grove, attune
The trembling leaves, while universal Pan
Knit with the Graces and the Hours in dance
Led on th' eternal spring. Not that fair field
Of Enna, where Proserpin gathering flowers
Herself a fairer flower by gloomy Dis
Was gathered, which cost Ceres all that pain
To seek her through the world; nor that sweet grove
Of Daphne by Orontes, and th' inspired
Castalian spring might with this Paradise
Of Eden strive; nor that Nyseian isle
Girt with the river Triton, where old Cham,
Whom gentiles Ammon call and Lybian Jove,
Hid Amalthea and her florid son
Young Bacchus from his stepdame Rhea's eye;
Nor where Abassin kings their issue guard,
Mount Amara, though this by some supposed
True Paradise under the Ethiop line
By Nilus' head, enclosed with shining rock,
A whole day's journey high, but wide remote
From this Assyrian garden, where the fiend
Saw undelighted all delight, all kind
Of living creatures new to sight and strange:
Two of far nobler shape erect and tall,
Godlike erect, with native honour clad
In naked majesty seemed lords of all,

And worthy seemed, for in their looks divine
The image of their glorious Maker shone,
Truth, wisdom, sanctitude severe and pure,
Severe, but in true filial freedom placed;
Whence true authority in men; though both
Not equal, as their sex not equal seemed;
For contemplation he and valour formed,
For softness she and sweet attractive grace,
He for God only, she for God in him:
His fair large front and eye sublime declared
Absolute rule; and hyacinthine locks
Round from his parted forelock manly hung
Clust'ring, but not beneath his shoulders broad:
She as a veil down to the slender waist
Her unadornéd golden tresses wore
Dishevelled, but in wanton ringlets waved
As the vine curls her tendrils, which implied
Subjection, but required with gentle sway,
And by her yielded, by him best received,
Yielded with coy submission, modest pride,
And sweet reluctant amorous delay.

FROM *Paradise Regained*

Look once more ere we leave this specular Mount
Westward, much nearer by southwest, behold
Where on the Aegean shore a city stands
Built nobly, pure the air, and light the soil,
Athens the eye of Greece, mother of arts
And eloquence, native to famous wits
Or hospitable, in her sweet recess,
City or suburban, studious walks and shades;
See there the olive grove of Academe,
Plato's retirement, where the Attic bird
Trills her thick-warbled notes the summer long;
There flowery hill Hymettus with the sound
Of bees' industrious murmur, oft invites
To studious musing; there Ilissus rolls
His whispering stream; within the walls then view
The schools of ancient sages; his who bred

Great Alexander to subdue the world,
Lyceum there, and painted Stoa next;
There shalt thou hear and learn the secret power
Of harmony in tones and numbers hit
By voice or hand, and various-measured verse,
Aeolian charms and Dorian lyric odes,
And his who gave them breath, but higher sung,
Blind Melesigenes thence Homer called,
Whose poem Phoebus challenged for his own.
Thence what the lofty grave tragedians taught
In chorus or iambic, teachers best
Of moral prudence, with delight received
In brief sententious precepts, while they treat
Of fate, and chance, and change in human life;
High actions, and high passions best describing:
Thence to the famous orators repair,
Those ancient, whose resistless eloquence
Wielded at will that fierce democracy,
Shook the Arsenal and fulmined over Greece,
To Macedon, and Artaxerxes' throne;
To sage philosophy next lend thine ear,
From Heaven descended to the low-roofed house
Of Socrates, see there his tenement,
Whom well inspired the oracle pronounced
Wisest of men; from whose mouth issued forth
Mellifluous streams that watered all the schools
Of Academics old and new, with those
Surnamed Peripatetics, and the sect
Epicurean, and the Stoic severe;
These here revolve, or, as thou lik'st, at home,
Till time mature thee to a kingdom's weight;
These rules will render thee a king complete
Within thyself, much more with empire joined.

FROM *Samson Agonistes*

Samson: A little onward lend thy guiding hand
          To these dark steps, a little further on;
          For yonder bank hath choice of sun or shade,
          There I am wont to sit, when any chance

Relieves me from my task of servile toil,
Daily in the common prison else enjoined me,
Where I a prisoner chained, scarce freely draw
The air imprisoned also, close and damp,
Unwholesome draught: but here I feel amends
The breath of heaven fresh-blowing, pure and
        sweet,
With day-spring born; here leave me to respire.
This day a solemn feast the people hold
To Dagon their sea-idol, and forbid
Laborious works, unwillingly this rest
Their superstition yields me; hence with leave
Retiring from the popular noise, I seek
This unfrequented place to find some ease,
Ease to the body some, none to the mind
From restless thoughts, that like a deadly swarm
Of hornets armed, no sooner found alone,
But rush upon me thronging, and present
Times past, what once I was, and what am now.
O wherefore was my birth from Heaven foretold
Twice by an angel, who at last in sight
Of both my parents all in flames ascended
From off the altar, where an offering burned,
As in a fiery column charioting
His Godlike presence, and from some great act
Or benefit revealed to Abraham's race?
Why was my breeding ordered and prescribed
As of a person separate to God,
Designed for great exploits; if I must die
Betrayed, captive, and both my eyes put out,
Made of my enemies the scorn and gaze;
To grind in brazen fetters under task
With this heaven-gifted strength? O glorious
        strength
Put to the labour of a beast, debased
Lower than bondslave! Promise was that I
Should Israel from Philistian yoke deliver;
Ask for this great deliverer now, and find him
Eyeless in Gaza at the mill with slaves,
Himself in bonds under Philistian yoke;
Yet stay, let me not rashly call in doubt

Divine prediction; what if all foretold
Had been fulfilled but through mine own default,
Whom have I to complain of but myself?
Who this high gift of strength committed to me,
In what part lodged, how easily bereft me,
Under the seal of silence could not keep,
But weakly to a woman must reveal it
O'ercome with importunity and tears.
O impotence of mind, in body strong!
But what is strength without a double share
Of wisdom? vast, unwieldy, burdensome,
Proudly secure, yet liable to fall
By weakest subtleties, not made to rule,
But to subserve where wisdom bears command.
God, when He gave me strength, to show withal
How slight the gift was, hung it in my hair.
But peace, I must not quarrel with the will
Of highest dispensation, which herein
Haply had ends above my reach to know:
Suffices that to me strength is my bane,
And proves the source of all my miseries;
So many, and so huge, that each apart
Would ask a life to wail, but chief of all,
O loss of sight, of thee I most complain!
Blind among enemies, O worse than chains,
Dungeon, or beggary, or decrepit age!
Light the prime work of God to me is extinct,
And all her various objects of delight
Annulled, which might in part my grief have eased,
Inferior to the vilest now become
Of man or worm; the vilest here excel me,
They creep, yet see, I dark in light exposed
To daily fraud, contempt, abuse and wrong,
Within doors, or without, still as a fool,
In power of others, never in my own;
Scarce half I seem to live, dead more than half.
O dark, dark, dark, amid the blaze of noon,
Irrecoverably dark, total eclipse
Without all hope of day!
O first created beam, and thou great Word,
Let there be light, and light was over all;

Why am I thus bereaved thy prime decree?
The sun to me is dark
And silent as the moon,
When she deserts the night
Hid in her vacant interlunar cave.
Since light so necessary is to life,
And almost life itself, if it be true
That light is in the soul,
She all in every part; why was the sight
To such a tender ball as th' eye confined?
So obvious and so easy to be quenched,
And not as feeling through all parts diffused,
That she might look at will through every pore?
Then had I not been thus exiled from light;
As in the land of darkness yet in light,
To live a life half dead, a living death,
And buried; but O yet more miserable!
Myself my sepulchre, a moving grave,
Buried, yet not exempt
By privilege of death and burial
From worst of other evils, pains and wrongs,
But made hereby obnoxious more
To all the miseries of life,
Life in captivity
Among inhuman foes.

SIR JOHN SUCKLING

(1609–1642)

The Siege

'Tis now, since I sat down before
    That foolish fort, a heart,—
Time strangely spent—a year or more,
    And still I did my part,

Made my approaches, from her hand
    Unto her lip did rise,
And did already understand
    The language of her eyes;

Proceeded on with no less art—
   My tongue was engineer;
I thought to undermine the heart
   By whispering in the ear.

When this did nothing, I brought down
   Great cannon-oaths, and shot
A thousand thousand to the town;
   And still it yielded not.

I then resolved to starve the place
   By cutting off all kisses,
Praising and gazing on her face,
   And all such little blisses.

To draw her out and from her strength,
   I drew all batteries in;
And brought myself to lie at length
   As if no siege had been.

When I had done what man could do
   And thought the place mine own,
The enemy lay quiet too
   And smiled at all was done.

I sent to know from whence and where
   These hopes and this relief?
A spy informed Honour was there,
   And did command in chief.

March, march, quoth I; the word straight give;
   Let's lose no time, but leave her:
That giant upon air will live
   And hold it out for ever.

To such a place our camp remove,
   As will no siege abide:
I hate a fool that starves her love
   Only to feed her pride.

A Ballad upon a Wedding

I tell thee, Dick, where I have been;
Where I the rarest things have seen,
   O, things without compare!
Such sights again cannot be found
In any place on English ground,
   Be it at wake or fair.

At Charing Cross, hard by the way
Where we, thou know'st, do sell our hay,
   There is a house with stairs;
And there did I see coming down
Such folks as are not in our town,
   Forty at least in pairs.

Amongst the rest one pest'lent fine,
His beard no bigger though than thine,
   Walked on before the rest:
Our landlord looks like nothing to him:
The King, God bless him!, 'twould undo him,
   Should he go still so dressed.

At Course-a-Park without all doubt
He should have first been taken out
   By all the maids i' th' town:
Though lusty Roger there had been,
Or little George upon the Green,
   Or Vincent of the Crown.

But wot you what? the youth was going
To make an end of all his wooing;
   The parson for him staid:
Yet by his leave, for all his haste,
He did not so much wish all past,
   Perchance, as did the maid.

The maid—and thereby hangs a tale;
For such a maid no Whitson-ale
   Could ever yet produce:

No grape, that's kindly ripe, could be
So round, so plump, so soft as she,
    Nor half so full of juice.

Her finger was so small, the ring
Would not stay on, which they did bring;
    It was too wide a peck:
And to say truth, for out it must,
It looked like the great collar, just,
    About our young colt's neck.

Her feet beneath her petticoat
Like little mice stole in and out,
    As if they feared the light:
But O, she dances such a way!
No sun upon an Easter-day
    Is half so fine a sight.

He would have kissed her once or twice;
But she would not, she was so nice,
    She would not do't in sight:
And then she looked as who should say,
"I will do what I list to-day,
    And you shall do't at night."

Her cheeks so rare a white was on,
No daisy makes comparison;
    Who sees them is undone:
For streaks of red were mingled there
Such as are on a Catherine pear,
    The side that's next the sun.

Her lips were red; and one was thin
Compared to that was next her chin,
    Some bee had stung it newly:
But, Dick, her eyes so guard her face
I durst no more upon them gaze
    Than on the sun in July.

Her mouth so small, when she does speak
Thou'dst swear her teeth her words did break
    That they might passage get;
But she so handled still the matter
They came as good as ours, or better,
    And are not spent a whit.

If wishing should be any sin,
The parson himself had guilty been,
    She looked that day so purely;
And, did the youth so oft the feat
At night, as some did in conceit,
    It would have spoiled him surely.

Just in the nick the cook knocked thrice,
And all the waiters in a trice
    His summons did obey:
Each serving-man, with dish in hand,
Marched boldly up, like our trained band,
    Presented, and away.

The business of the kitchen's great,
For it is fit that man should eat;
    Nor was it there denied—
Passion o' me, how I run on!
There's that that would be thought upon,
    I trow, besides the bride.

Now hats fly off and youths carouse,
Healths first go round and then the house:
    The bride's came thick and thick;
And, when 'twas named another's health,
Perhaps he made it hers by stealth;
    And who could help it, Dick?

O' th' sudden up they rise and dance;
Then sit again and sigh and glance;
    Then dance again and kiss:
Thus several ways the time did pass,
Whilst every woman wished her place,
    And every man wished his.

By this time all were stolen aside
To counsel and undress the bride;
 But that he must not know:
But yet 'twas thought he guessed her mind,
And did not mean to stay behind
 Above an hour or so.

When in he came, Dick, there she lay
Like new-fallen snow melting away;
 'Twas time, I trow, to part:
Kisses were now the only stay,
Which soon she gave, as one would say,
 Good-bye with all my heart.

But, just as Heavens would have, to cross it,
In came the bridesmaids with the posset;
 The bridegroom ate in spite:
For, had he left the women to't,
It would have cost two hours to do't,
 Which were too much that night.

At length the candle's out; and now
All that they had not done they do;
 What that is, who can tell?
But I believe it was no more
Than thou and I have done before
 With Bridget and with Nell.

A Poem

Out upon it! I have loved
 Three whole days together;
And am like to love three more,
 If it prove fair weather.

Time shall moult away his wings,
 Ere he shall discover
In the whole wide world again
 Such a constant lover.

But the spite on't is, no praise
   Is due at all to me;
Love with me had made no stays,
   Had it any been but she.

Had it any been but she,
   And that very face,
There had been at least ere this
   A dozen dozen in her place.

Song

I prithee send me back my heart,
   Since I cannot have thine;
For if from yours you will not part,
   Why then shouldst thou have mine?

Yet now I think on't, let it lie;
   To find it were in vain,
For th' hast a thief in either eye
   Would steal it back again.

Why should two hearts in one breast lie,
   And yet not lodge together?
O love, where is thy sympathy,
   If thus our breasts thou sever?

But love is such a mystery,
   I cannot find it out;
For when I think I'm best resolved,
   I then am most in doubt.

Then farewell care, and farewell woe,
   I will no longer pine;
For I'll believe I have her heart
   As much as she hath mine.

Song

Why so pale and wan, fond lover?
    Prithee, why so pale?
Will, when looking well can't win her,
    Looking ill prevail?
    Prithee, why so pale?

Why so dull and mute, young sinner?
    Prithee, why so mute?
Will, when speaking well can't win her,
    Saying nothing do't?
    Prithee, why so mute?

Quit, quit for shame, this will not move;
    This cannot take her.
If of herself she will not love,
    Nothing can make her;
    The devil take her!

Aglaura, 1646

WILLIAM CARTWRIGHT

(1611–1643)

To Chloe,
Who Wished Herself Young Enough for Me

Chloe, why wish you that your years
    Would backward run, till they meet mine,
That perfect likeness which endears
    Things unto things might us combine?
Our ages so in date agree
That twins do differ more than we.

There are two births; the one when light
    First strikes the new awakened sense;
The other when two souls unite;
    And we must count our life from thence.
When you loved me and I loved you,
The both of us were born anew.

Love then to us did new souls give,
 And in those souls did plant new powers;
Since when another life we live,
 The breath we breathe is his, not ours;
Love makes those young whom age doth chill,
And whom he finds young, keeps young still.

Love, like that angel that shall call
 Our bodies from the silent grave,
Unto one age doth raise us all,
 None too much, none too little have.
Nay, that the difference may be none,
He makes two not alike, but one.

And now since you and I are such,
 Tell me what's yours, and what is mine?
Our eyes, our ears, our taste, smell, touch,
 Do, like our souls, in one combine.
So by this, I as well may be
Too old for you as you for me.

JAMES GRAHAM, Marquess of Montrose

(1612–1650)

Montrose to His Mistress

My dear and only love, I pray
 This noble world of thee,
Be governed by no other sway
 But purest monarchy.
For if confusion have a part,
 Which virtuous souls abhor,
And hold a synod in thy heart,
 I'll never love thee more.

Like Alexander I will reign,
 And I will reign alone,
My thoughts shall evermore disdain
 A rival on my throne.

He either fears his fate too much,
   Or his deserts are small,
That puts it not unto the touch,
   To win or lose it all.

But I must rule, and govern still,
   And always give the law,
And have each subject at my will,
   And all to stand in awe.
But 'gainst my battery if I find
   Thou shun'st the prize so sore,
As that thou set'st me up a blind,
   I'll never love thee more.

Or in the empire of thy heart,
   Where I should solely bo,
Another do pretend a part,
   And dares to vie with me,
Or if committees thou erect,
   And go on such a score,
I'll sing and laugh at thy neglect,
   And never love thee more.

But if thou wilt be constant then,
   And faithful of thy word,
I'll make thee glorious by my pen,
   And famous by my sword.
I'll serve thee in such noble ways
   Was never heard before:
I'll crown and deck thee all with bays,
   And love thee evermore.

His Metrical Vow
(ON THE DEATH OF KING CHARLES I)

Great, Good and Just, could I but rate
My grief to thy too rigid fate!
I'd weep the world in such a strain,
As it would once deluge again:

But since thy loud-tongued blood demands supplies,
More from Briareus' hands than Argus' eyes,
I'll tune thy elegies to trumpet-sounds,
And write thy epitaph in blood and wounds.

SAMUEL BUTLER

(1612–1680)

FROM *Hudibras*

1.

When civil dudgeon first grew high,
And men fell out, they knew not why;
When hard words, jealousies, and fears,
Set folks together by the ears,
And made them fight, like mad or drunk,
For Dame Religion, as for punk;
Whose honesty they all durst swear for,
Though not a man of them knew wherefore;
When Gospel-trumpeter, surrounded
With long-eared rout, to battle sounded;
And pulpit, drum ecclesiastic,
Was beat with fist instead of a stick:
Then did Sir Knight abandon dwelling,
And out he rode a-colonelling.
A wight he was whose very sight would
Entitle him Mirror of Knighthood,
That never bowed his stubborn knee
To any thing but chivalry,
Nor put up blow, but that which laid
Right Worshipful on shoulder-blade;
Chief of domestic knights and errant,
Either for chartel or for warrant;
Great on the bench, great in the saddle,
That could as well bind o'er as swaddle.
Mighty he was at both of these,
And styled of War, as well as Peace
(So some rats of amphibious nature,
Are either for the land or water):
But here our authors make a doubt
Whether he was more wise or stout:
Some hold the one, and some the other;

But, howso'er they make a pother,
The diff'rence was so small, his brain
Outweighed his rage but half a grain;
Which made some take him for a tool
That knaves do work with, called a Fool.
For 't has been held by many, that
As Montaigne, playing with his cat,
Complains she thought him but an ass,
Much more she would Sir Hudibras
(For that's the name our valiant Knight
To all his challenges did write):
But they're mistaken very much,
'Tis plain enough he was no such.
We grant, although he had much wit,
H'was very shy of using it,
As being loath to wear it out,
And therefore bore it not about,
Unless on holidays or so,
As men their best apparel do.
Beside, 'tis known he could speak Greek
As naturally as pigs squeak;
That Latin was no more difficile,
Than to a blackbird 'tis to whistle.
Being rich in both, he never scanted
His bounty unto such as wanted;
But much of either could afford
To many that had not one word.
For Hebrew roots, although they're found
To flourish most in barren ground,
He had such plenty as sufficed
To make some think him circumcised:
And truly so perhaps he was,
'Tis many a pious Christian's case.

2.

For his religion, it was fit
To match his learning and his wit:
'Twas Presbyterian true blue;
For he was of that stubborn crew
Of errant Saints, whom all men grant

To be the true Church Militant;
Such as do build their faith upon
The holy text of pike and gun;
Decide all controversies by
Infallible artillery;
And prove their doctrine orthodox
By apostolic blows and knocks;
Call fire, sword, and desolation,
A godly, thorough Reformation,
Which always must be carried on,
And still be doing, never done;
As if Religion were intended
For nothing else but to be mended:
A sect whose chief devotion lies
In odd perverse antipathies;
In falling out with that or this,
And finding somewhat still amiss:
More peevish, cross, and splenetic,
Than dog distract, or monkey sick;
That with more care kept holiday
The wrong, than others the right way;
Compound for sins they are inclined to,
By damning those they have no mind to.
Still so perverse and opposite,
As if they worshipped God for spite:
The self-same thing they will abhor
One way, and long another for.
Free-will they one way disavow,
Another, nothing else allow:
All piety consists therein
In them, in other men all sin:
Rather than fail, they will defy
That which they love most tenderly;
Quarrel with minced-pies, and disparage
Their best and dearest friend, plum-porridge;
Fat pig and goose itself oppose,
And blaspheme custard through the nose.
Th'apostles of this fierce religion,
Like Mahomet's, were ass and widgeon,
To whom our Knight, by fast instinct
Of wit and temper, was so linked,

As if hypocrisy and nonsense
Had got th'advowson of his conscience.

3.

This sturdy Squire, he had, as well
As the bold Trojan Knight, seen hell,
Not with a counterfeited pass
Of golden bough, but true gold lace:
His knowledge was not far behind
The Knight's, but of another kind,
And he another way came by't:
Some call it Gifts, and some New-Light;
A lib'ral art, that cost no pains
Of study, industry, or brains.
His wit was sent him for a token,
But in the carriage cracked and broken;
Like commendation ninepence crooked,
With—To and from my Love—it looked.
He ne'er considered it, as loath
To look a gift-horse in the mouth,
And very wisely would lay forth
No more upon it than 'twas worth;
But as he got it freely, so
He spent it frank and freely too:
For Saints themselves will sometimes be
Of gifts that cost them nothing, free.
By means of this, with hem and cough,
Prolongers to enlightened stuff,
He could deep mysteries unriddle,
As easily as thread a needle;
For as of vagabonds we say,
That they are ne'er beside their way;
Whate'er men speak by this new light,
Still they are sure to be i' th' right.
'Tis a dark lantern of the spirit,
Which none sees by but those that bear it;
A light that falls down from on high,
For spiritual trades to cozen by;
An *ignis fatuus,* that bewitches
And leads men into pools and ditches,

To make them dip themselves, and sound
For Christendom in dirty pond;
To dive, like wild-fowl, for salvation,
And fish to catch regeneration.
This light inspires and plays upon
The nose of Saint, like bagpipe drone,
And speaks through hollow empty soul,
As through a trunk, or whisp'ring hole,
Such language as no mortal ear
But spiritual eaves-droppers can hear:
So Phoebus, or some friendly Muse,
Into small poets song infuse,
Which they at second-hand rehearse,
Through reed or bagpipe, verse for verse.

RICHARD CRASHAW

(1613?–1649)

FROM *Epithalamium*

Come, virgin tapers of pure wax,
    Made in the hive of love, all white
As snow and yet as cold, where lacks
    Hymen's holy heat and light;
        Where blooming kisses
            Their beds yet keep,
        And steep their blisses
            In rosy sleep;
Where sister buds yet wanting brothers
Kiss their own lips in lieu of others;
Help me to mourn a matchless maidenhead
        That now is dead.

A fine thin negative thing it was,
    A nothing with a dainty name,
Which pruned her plumes in self-love's glass,
    Made up of fancy and fond fame;
        Within the shade
            Of its own wing

It sate and played
    A self-crowned King;
A froward flower, whose peevish pride
Within itself itself did hide,
Flying all fingers, and even thinking much
     Of its own touch.

The bird indeed the phoenix was
    Late chased by Love's revengeful arrows,
Whose wars now left the wonted pass
    And spared the little lives of sparrows;
      To hunt this fool,
        Whose froward pride
    Love's noble school
      And courts denied,
And froze the fruits of fair desire
Which flourisheth in mutual fire,
'Gainst Nature, who 'mong all the webs she spun
     Ne'er wove a Nun.

She of Cupid's shafts afraid
    Left her own balm-breathing East,
And in a western bosom made
    A softer and a sweeter nest:
      There did she rest
        In the sweet shade
      Of a soft breast,
        Whose beauties made
Thames oft stand still and lend a glass
While in her own she saw heaven's face,
And sent him full of her fair name's report
     To Thetis' Court.

And now poor Love was at a stand.
    The crystal castle which she kept
Was proof against the proudest hand;
    There in safest hold she slept;
      His shafts' expence
        Left there no smart,

But bounding thence
Broached his own heart;
At length a fort he did devise
Built in noble Brampston's eyes,
And aiming thence this matchless maidenhead
Was soon found dead.

Yet Love in death did wait upon her,
Granting leave she should expire
In her fumes, and have the honour
T'exhale in flames of his own fire.
Her funeral pile
The marriage bed,
In a sighed smile
She vanishéd.
So rich a dress of death ne'er famed
The cradles where her kindred flamed;
So sweet her mother phoenixes of th'East
Ne'er spiced their nest.

FROM *Wishes. To His Supposed Mistress*

Whoe'er she be,
That not impossible she
That shall command my heart and me;

Where'er she lie,
Locked up from mortal eye
In shady leaves of Destiny:

Till that ripe birth
Of studied fate stand forth,
And teach her fair steps to our earth;

Till that divine
Idea take a shrine
Of crystal flesh through which to shine:

Meet you her my wishes,
Bespeak her to me blisses,
And be ye called my absent kisses.

I wish her Beauty
That owes not all his duty
To gaudy tire or glist'ring shoe-tie.

Something more than
Taffata or tissue can,
Or rampant feather or rich fan.

More than the spoil
Of shop or silkworms' toil,
Or a bought blush or a set smile.

A Face that's best
By its own beauty drest,
And can alone commend the rest.

A Face made up
Out of no other shop
Than what Nature's white hand sets ope.

A Cheek where youth
And blood with pen of truth
Write what the reader sweetly ru'th.

A Cheek where grows
More than a morning rose,
Which to no box his being owes.

Lips, where all day
A lover's kiss may play,
Yet carry nothing thence away.

Looks that oppress
Their richest tires, but dress
And clothe their simplest nakedness.

Eyes, that displaces
The neighbour diamond, and outfaces
That sunshine by their own sweet graces

Tresses, that wear
Jewels but to declare
How much themselves more precious are;

Whose native ray
Can tame the wanton day
Of gems, that in their bright shades play.

Each ruby there,
Or pearl that dare appear,
Be its own blush, be its own tear.

A well tamed Heart,
For whose more noble smart
Love may be long choosing a dart.

Eyes, that bestow
Full quivers on Love's bow,
Yet pay less arrows than they owe.

Smiles, that can warm
The blood, yet teach a charm
That chastity shall take no harm.

Blushes, that bin
The burnish of no sin,
Nor flames of aught too hot within.

Joys, that confess
Virtue, their mistress,
And have no other head to dress.

Fears, fond and slight,
As the coy bride's, when night
First does the longing lover right.

Tears, quickly fled,
And vain, as those are shed
For a dying maidenhead.

Days, that need borrow
No part of their good morrow
From a forespent night of sorrow.

Days, that in spite
Of darkness, by the light
Of a clear mind are day all night.

Nights, sweet as they
Made short by lovers' play,
Yet long by th'absence of the day.

Life, that dares send
A challenge to his end,
And when it comes say, Welcome friend.

I wish her store
Of worth may leave her poor
Of wishes; and I wish—no more.

A Song

Lord, when the sense of Thy sweet grace
Sends up my soul to seek Thy face,
Thy blessed eyes breed such desire
I die in love's delicious fire.
O Love, I am thy Sacrifice.
Be still triumphant, blessed eyes.
Still shine on me, fair suns! that I
Still may behold, though still I die.

Though still I die, I live again,
Still longing so to be still slain;
So gainful is such loss of breath,
I die even in desire of death.
Still live in me this loving strife
Of living Death and dying Life.
For while Thou sweetly slayest me,
Dead to myself I live in Thee.

For Hope

Dear hope! Earth's dowry and heav'n's debt!
The entity of those that are not yet.
Subtlest, but surest being! Thou by whom
Our nothing has a definition!
Substantial shade! whose sweet allay
Blends both the noons of night and day.
Fates cannot find out a capacity
Of hurting thee.
From Thee their lean dilemma with blunt horn
Shrinks, as the sick moon from the wholesome morn.
Rich hope! Love's legacy under lock
Of faith! still spending and still growing stock!
Our crown-land lies above, yet each meal brings
A seemly portion for the sons of kings.
Nor will the virgin joys we wed
Come less unbroken to our bed
Because that from the bridal cheek of bliss
Thou steal'st us down a distant kiss.
Hope's chaste stealth harms no more joy's maidenhead
Than spousal rites prejudge the marriage bed.
Fair hope! Our earlier heav'n, by thee
Young time is taster to eternity.
Thy generous wine with age grows strong, not sour.
Nor does it kill the fruit to smell the flower.
Thy golden, growing head never hangs down,
Till in the lap of love's full noon
It falls, and dies! O no, it melts away
As does the dawn into the day,
As lumps of sugar lose themselves and twine
Their supple essence with the soul of wine.
Fortune? Alas, above the world's low wars,
Hope walks, and kicks the curl'd heads of conspiring stars.
Her keel cuts not the waves where these winds stir;
Fortune's whole lottery is one blank to her.
Her shafts and she fly far above
And forage in the fields of light and love.
Sweet hope! Kind cheat! Fair fallacy! By thee
We are not Where nor What we be,

But What and Where we would be. Thus art thou
Our absent Presence and our future Now.
Faith's sister! Nurse of fair desire!
Fear's antidote! A wise and well-stay'd fire!
Temper 'twixt chill despair and torrid joy!
Queen Regent in young Love's minority!
Though the vext chymick vainly chases
His fugitive gold through all her faces,
Though Love's more fierce, more fugitive fires assay
One face more fugitive than all they,
True hope's a glorious hunter, and her chase
The God of Nature in the fields of grace.

FROM A *Hymn of the Nativity*

Gloomy Night embraced the place
    Where the noble Infant lay;
The Babe looked up, and shewed his face,
    In spite of darkness it was day.
It was thy day, sweet, and did rise
Not from the East, but from thy eyes.

Winter chid the world, and sent
    The angry North to wage his wars;
The North forgot his fierce intent,
    And left perfumes instead of scars;
By those sweet eyes' persuasive powers
Where he meant frosts he scattered flowers.

We see thee in thy balmy nest,
    Bright Dawn of our eternal day;
We saw thine eyes break from the East
    And chase the trembling shades away;
We saw thee (and we blessed the sight)
We saw thee by thine own sweet light.

I saw the curled drops soft and slow
    Come hovering o'er the place's head,
Off'ring their whitest sheets of snow
    To furnish the fair Infant's bed.
Forbear, (said I) be not too bold,
Your fleece is white, but 'tis too cold.

I saw th'officious angels bring
   The down that their soft breasts did strow,
For well they now can spare their wings,
   When Heaven itself lies here below.
Fair youth, (said I) be not too rough,
Thy down though soft's not soft enough.

The Babe no sooner 'gan to seek
   Where to lay his lovely head,
But straight his eyes advised his cheek
   'Twixt Mother's breasts to go to bed.
Sweet choice (said I) no way but so
Not to lie cold, yet sleep in snow.

Welcome to our wondering sight,
   Eternity shut in a span!
Summer in winter! Day in night!
   Heaven in earth! and God in man!
Great little one, whose glorious birth
Lifts earth to Heaven, stoops Heaven to earth.

FROM *The Weeper*

Hail Sister Springs!
Parents of silver-forded rills!
   Ever bubbling things!
Thawing crystal! Snowy hills!
Still spending, never spent; I mean
Thy fair eyes, sweet Magdalene.

   Heavens thy fair eyes be,
Heavens of ever-falling stars;
   'Tis seed-time still with thee,
And stars thou sowest, whose harvest dares
Promise the earth to countershine
Whatever makes Heaven's forehead fine.

   But we are deceived all,
Stars they are indeed too true,
   For they but seem to fall

As Heaven's other spangles do;
It is not for our earth and us
To shine in things so precious.

Upwards thou dost weep;
Heaven's bosom drinks the gentle stream.
   Where the milky rivers meet
Thine crawls above and is the cream.
Heaven, of such fair floods as this
Heaven the crystal ocean is.

The dew no more will weep,
The primrose's pale cheek to deck;
   The dew no more will sleep,
Nuzzled in the lily's neck.
Much rather would it tremble here,
And leave them both to be thy tear.

Not the soft gold which
Steals from the amber-weeping tree,
   Makes Sorrow half so rich
As the drops distilled from thee.
Sorrow's best jewels lie in these
Caskets, of which Heaven keeps the keys.

Not in the Evening's eyes
When they red with weeping are
   For the sun that dies,
Sits Sorrow with a face so fair.
Nowhere but here did ever meet
Sweetness so sad, sadness so sweet.

Well does the May that lies
Smiling in thy cheeks, confess
   The April in thine eyes;
Mutual sweetness they express.
No April e'er lent softer showers
Nor May returnéd fairer flowers.

Whither away so fast?
O whither? for the sluttish earth
   Your sweetness cannot taste,

Nor does the dust deserve your birth.
Whither haste ye then? O say
Why ye trip so fast away?

We go not to seek
The darlings of Aurora's bed,
    The rose's modest cheek
Nor the violet's humble head.
No such thing; we go to meet
A worthier object, Our Lord's feet.

JOHN CLEVELAND

(1613–1658)

Mark Antony

When as the nightingale chanted her vespers,
    And the wild forester couched on the ground,
Venus invited me in th'evening whispers
    Unto a fragrant field with roses crowned,
        Where she before had sent
        My wishes' compliment;
        Unto my heart's content
        Played with me on the green.
            Never Mark Antony
            Dallied more wantonly
            With the fair Egyptian Queen.

First on her cherry cheeks I mine eye feasted,
    Thence fear of surfeiting made me retire;
Next on her warmer lips, which, when I tasted,
    My duller spirits were active as fire.
        Then we began to dart,
        Each at another's heart,
        Arrows that know no smart,
        Sweet lips and smiles between.
            Never Mark Antony
            Dallied more wantonly
            With the fair Egyptian Queen.

Wanting a glass to plait her amber tresses
  Which like a bracelet rich deckéd mine arm,
Gaudier than Juno wears when as she graces
  Jove with embraces more stately than warm,
      Then did she peep in mine
      Eyes' humor crystalline;
      I in her eyes was seen
      As if we one had been.
        Never Mark Antony
        Dallied more wantonly
        With the fair Egyptian Queen.

Mystical grammar of amorous glances;
  Feeling of pulses, the physic of love;
Rhetorical courtings and musical dances;
  Numbering of kisses arithmetic prove;
      Eyes like astronomy;
      Straight-limbed geometry;
      In her art's ingeny
      Our wits were sharp and keen.
        Never Mark Antony
        Dallied more wantonly
        With the fair Egyptian Queen.

FROM *The Rebel Scot*

Come, keen iambics, with your badger's feet
And badger-like bite till your teeth do meet.
Help, ye tart satirists, to imp my rage
With all the scorpions that should whip this age.
Scots are like witches; do but whet your pen,
Scratch till the blood come, they'll not hurt you then.
Now, as the martyrs were enforced to take
The shapes of beasts, like hypocrites at stake,
I'll bait my Scot so, yet not cheat your eyes;
A Scot within a beast is no disguise.
  No more let Ireland brag her harmless nation
Fosters no venom since the Scot's plantation:
Nor can ours feigned antiquity maintain;
Since they came in, England hath wolves again.

The Scot that kept the Tower might have shown
Within the grate of his own breast alone,
The leopard and the panther, and engrossed
What all those wild collegiates had cost
The honest high-shoes in their termly fees;
First to the salvage lawyer, next to these.
Nature herself doth Scotchmen beasts confess,
Making their country such a wilderness:
A land that brings in question and suspense
God's omnipresence, but that Charles came thence,
But that Montrose and Crawford's loyal band
Atoned their sins and christened half the land.
Nor is it all the nation hath these spots;
There is a Church as well as Kirk of Scots.
As in a picture where the squinting paint
Shows fiend on this side, and on that side saint.
He, that saw Hell in's melancholy dream
And in the twilight of his fancy's theme,
Scared from his sins, repented in a fright,
Had he viewed Scotland, had turned proselyte.
A land where one may pray with cursed intent,
"Oh may they never suffer banishment!"
Had Cain been Scot, God would have changed his doom;
Not forced him wander but confined him home!

SIR JOHN DENHAM

(1615–1669)

FROM Cooper's Hill

My eye descending from the Hill, surveys
Where Thames amongst the wanton valleys strays.
Thames, the most loved of all the Ocean's sons,
By his old sire to his embraces runs,
Hastening to pay his tribute to the sea,
Like mortal life to meet Eternity.
Though with those streams he no resemblance hold,
Whose foam is amber and their gravel gold;
His genuine and less guilty wealth t' explore,
Search not his bottom, but survey his shore;
O'er which he kindly spreads his spacious wing

And hatches plenty for th' ensuing spring.
Nor then destroys it with too fond a stay,
Like mothers which their infants overlay.
Nor with a sudden and impetuous wave,
Like profuse kings, resumes the wealth he gave.
No unexpected inundations spoil
The mower's hopes nor mock the ploughman's toil,
But God-like his unwearied bounty flows,
First loves to do, then loves the good he does.
Nor are his blessings to his banks confined,
But free and common as the sea or wind;
When he to boast or to disperse his stores
Full of the tributes of his grateful shores,
Visits the world, and in his flying towers
Brings home to us, and makes both Indies ours;
Finds wealth where 'tis, bestows it where it wants,
Cities in deserts, woods in cities plants.
So that to us no thing, no place is strange,
While his fair bosom is the world's exchange.
Oh, could I flow like thee, and make thy stream
My great example, as it is my theme!
Though deep, yet clear, though gentle, yet not dull,
Strong without rage, without o'er-flowing full.

RICHARD LOVELACE

(1618–1658)

The Rose

Sweet serene sky-like flower,
Haste to adorn her bower:
    From thy long cloudy bed
    Shoot forth thy damask head.

New-startled blush of Flora!
The grief of pale Aurora,
    Who will contest no more;
    Haste, haste, to strew her floor.

Vermilion ball that's given
From lip to lip in Heaven;
    Love's couch's coverlet;
    Haste, haste, to make her bed.

Dear offspring of pleased Venus
And jolly, plump Silenus:
    Haste, haste to deck the hair
    Of the only, sweetly fair.

See! rosy is her bower,
Her floor is all this flower;
    Her bed a rosy nest
    By a bed of roses prest.

But early as she dresses,
Why fly you her bright tresses?
    Ah! I have found, I fear—
    Because her cheeks are near.

To Amarantha

Amarantha sweet and fair,
Ah, braid no more that shining hair!
As my curious hand or eye
Hovering round thee, let it fly!

Let it fly as unconfined
As its calm ravisher the wind,
Who hath left his darling, th' East,
To wanton o'er that spicy nest.

Every tress must be confest,
But neatly tangled at the best;
Like a clue of golden thread
Most excellently ravelléd.

Do not then wind up that light
In ribbands, and o'ercloud in night
Like the sun in's early ray;
But shake your head, and scatter day!

To Lucasta, Going beyond the Seas

If to be absent were to be
　　Away from thee;
　Or that when I am gone,
　　You or I were alone;
Then, my Lucasta, might I crave
Pity from blustering wind, or swallowing wave.

But I'll not sigh one blast or gale
　　To swell my sail,
　Or pay a tear t' assuage
　　The foaming blue god's rage;
For whether he will let me pass
Or no, I'm still as happy as I was.

Though seas and land betwixt us both,
　　Our faith and troth,
　Like separated souls,
　　All time and space controls;
Above the highest sphere we meet
Unseen, unknown, and greet as angels greet.

So then we do anticipate
　　Our after-fate,
　And are alive i' the skies,
　　If thus our lips and eyes
Can speak like spirits unconfined
In Heaven, their earthly bodies left behind.

To Althea from Prison

When Love with unconfinéd wing
　　Hovers within my gates;
And my divine Althea brings
　　To whisper at the grates;
When I lie tangled in her hair,
　　And fettered to her eye;
The birds that wanton in the air
　　Know no such liberty.

When flowing cups run swiftly round
    With no allaying Thames,
Our careless heads with roses bound,
    Our hearts with loyal flames;
When thirsty grief in wine we steep,
    When healths and draughts go free,
Fishes that tipple in the deep
    Know no such liberty.

When, like committed linnets, I
    With shriller voice shall sing
The sweetness, mercy, majesty
    And glories of my King;
When I shall voice aloud, how good
    He is, how great should be;
Enlargéd winds that curl the flood
    Know no such liberty.

Stone walls do not a prison make,
    Nor iron bars a cage;
Minds innocent and quiet take
    That for an Hermitage;
If I have freedom in my love,
    And in my soul am free;
Angels alone that soar above
    Enjoy such liberty.

To Lucasta, Going to the Wars

Tell me not, sweet, I am unkind
    That from the nunnery
Of thy chaste breast and quiet mind
    To wars and arms I fly.

True, a new mistress now I chase:
    The first foe in the field;
And with a stronger faith embrace
    A sword, a horse, a shield.

Yet this inconstancy is such
   As you too shall adore;
I could not love thee, dear, so much,
   Loved I not honour more.

ABRAHAM COWLEY
(1618–1667)

FROM On the Death of Mr. William Hervey

It was a dismal and a fearful night,
Scarce could the morn drive on th'unwilling light,
When sleep, death's image, left my troubled breast,
    By something liker death possest.
My eyes with tears did uncommanded flow,
    And on my soul hung the dull weight
    Of some intolerable Fate.
What bell was that? Ah me! Too much I know.

My sweet companion and my gentle peer,
Why hast thou left me thus unkindly here,
Thy end for ever and my life to moan?
    Oh, thou hast left me all alone!
Thy soul and body when death's agony
    Besieged around thy noble heart,
    Did not with more reluctance part
Than I, my dearest friend, do part from thee.

My dearest friend, would I had died for thee!
Life and this world henceforth will tedious be.
Nor shall I know hereafter what to do
    If once my griefs prove tedious too.
Silent and sad I walk about all day,
    As sullen ghosts stalk speechless by
    Where their hidden treasures lie;
Alas, my treasure's gone, why do I stay?

He was my friend, the truest friend on earth;
A strong and mighty influence joined our birth.
Nor did we envy the most sounding name
    By friendship given of old to fame.

None but his brethren he, and sisters knew,
      Whom the kind youth preferred to me;
      And even in that we did agree,
For much above myself I loved them too.

Say, for you saw us, ye immortal lights,
How oft unwearied have we spent the nights?
Till the Ledaean stars so famed for love
      Wondered at us from above.
We spent them not in toys, in lusts or wine;
      But search of deep philosophy,
      Wit, eloquence, and poetry,
Arts which I loved, for they, my friend, were thine.

Ye fields of Cambridge, our dear Cambridge, say
Have ye not seen us walking every day?
Was there a tree about which did not know
      The love betwixt us two?
Henceforth, ye gentle trees, for ever fade;
      Or your sad branches thicker join,
      And into darksome shades combine,
Dark as the grave wherein my friend is laid.

On the Death of Mr. Crashaw

Poet and saint! to thee alone are given
The two most sacred names of Earth and Heaven.
The hard and rarest union which can be
Next that of Godhead with humanity.
Long did the Muses banished slaves abide,
And built vain pyramids to mortal pride;
Like Moses thou, though spells and charms withstand,
Hast brought them nobly home back to their Holy Land.

Ah wretched we, poets of Earth! but thou
Wert living the same poet which thou'rt now.
Whilst angels sing to thee their airs divine,
And joy in an applause so great as thine.
Equal society with them to hold,
Thou need'st not make new songs, but say the old.

And they, kind spirits! shall all rejoice to see
How little less than they exalted man may be.
Still the old heathen gods in numbers dwell,
The heav'nliest thing on Earth still keeps up Hell.
Nor have we yet quite purged the Christian land;
Still idols here, like calves at Bethel stand.
And though Pan's death long since all oracles broke,
Yet still in rhyme the fiend Apollo spoke:
Nay, with the worst of heathen dotage we,
Vain men! the monster woman deify;
Find stars, and tie our fates there in a face,
And Paradise in them by whom we lost it place.
What different faults corrupt our Muses thus?
Wanton as girls, as old wives fabulous!

Thy spotless Muse, like Mary, did contain
The boundless Godhead; she did well disdain
That her eternal verse employed should be
On a less subject than eternity;
And for a sacred mistress scorned to take
But her whom God Himself scorned not his spouse to make.
It, in a kind, her miracle did do;
A fruitful mother was and virgin too.

How well, blest swan, did Fate contrive thy death;
And made thee render up thy tuneful breath
In thy great Mistress' arms! thou most divine
And richest offering of Loretto's shrine!
Where like some holy sacrifice t' expire,
A fever burns thee, and love lights the fire.
Angels, they say, brought the famed chapel there,
And bore the sacred load in triumph through the air.
'Tis surer much they brought thee there, and they
And thou, their charge, went singing all the way.

Pardon, my Mother Church, if I consent
That angels led him when from thee he went,
For even in error sure no danger is
When joined with so much piety as his.
Ah, mighty God, with shame I speak't and grief,
Ah, that our greatest faults were in belief!

And our weak reason were ev'n weaker yet,
Rather than thus our wills too strong for it.
His faith perhaps in some nice tenets might
Be wrong; his life, I'm sure, was in the right.
And I myself a Catholic will be,
So far at least, great saint, to pray to thee.

Hail, bard triumphant! and some care bestow
On us, the poets militant below!
Opposed by our old en'my, adverse chance,
Attacked by envy and by ignorance,
Enchained by beauty, tortured by desires,
Exposed by tyrant love to savage beasts and fires.
Thou from low earth in nobler flames didst rise,
And, like Elijah, mount alive the skies.
Elisha-like (but with a wish much less,
More fit thy greatness and my littleness)
Lo here I beg (I whom thou once didst prove
So humble to esteem, so good to love)
Not that thy spirit might on me doubled be,
I ask but half thy mighty spirit for me.
And when my Muse soars with so strong a wing,
'Twill learn of things divine, and first of thee to sing.

The Wish

Well then, I now do plainly see
This busy world and I shall ne'er agree;
The very honey of all earthly joy
Does of all meats the soonest cloy,
And they methinks deserve my pity
Who for it can endure the stings,
The crowd and buzz and murmurings
Of this great hive, the city.

Ah, yet, ere I descend to th' grave
May I a small house and large garden have!
And a few friends and many books, both true,
Both wise and both delightful too!

And since love ne'er will from me flee,
A mistress moderately fair,
And good as guardian-angels are,
  Only beloved and loving me!

  O fountains, when in you shall I
Myself eased of unpeaceful thoughts espy?
O fields, O woods, when, when shall I be made
  The happy tenant of your shade?
  Here's the spring-head of pleasure's flood;
Here's wealthy Nature's treasury,
Where all the riches lie that she
  Has coined and stamped for good.

  Pride and ambition here
Only in far-fetched metaphors appear;
Here nought but winds can hurtful murmurs scatter,
  And nought but echo flatter.
  The gods when they descended hither
From heaven did always choose their way;
And therefore we may boldly say,
  That 'tis the way too thither.

  How happy here should I
And one dear she live and embracing die!
She who is all the world, and can exclude
  In deserts solitude.
  I should have then this only fear,
Lest men, when they my pleasures see,
Should hither throng to live like me,
  And so make a city here.

FROM *Essay on Solitude*

Hail, old patrician trees, so great and good!
  Hail, ye plebeian underwood!
  Where the poetic birds rejoice
And for their quiet nests and plenteous food,
  Pay with their grateful voice.

Hail, the poor Muse's richest manor seat!
    Ye country houses and retreat,
    Which all the happy gods so love,
That for you oft they quit their bright and great
    Metropolis above.

Here Nature does a house for me erect,
    Nature, the wisest architect,
    Who those fond artists does despise
That can the fair and living trees neglect,
    Yet the dead timber prize.

Here let me careless and unthoughtful lying
    Hear the soft winds above me flying,
    With all their wanton boughs dispute,
And the more tuneful birds to both replying,
    Nor be myself too mute.

Ah wretched and too solitary he
    Who loves not his own company!
    He'll feel the weight of 't many a day
Unless he call in sin or vanity
    To help to bear 't away.

Whilst this hard truth I teach, methinks I see
    The monster London laugh at me,
    I should at thee too, foolish city,
If it were fit to laugh at misery,
    But thy estate I pity.

Let but thy wicked men from out thee go,
    And all the fools that crowd thee so,
    Even thou who dost thy millions boast,
A village less than Islington wilt grow,
    A solitude almost.

The Chronicle

Margarita first possessed,
If I remember well, my breast;
   Margarita first of all!
But when awhile the wanton maid
With my restless heart had played,
   Martha took the flying ball.

Martha soon did it resign
To the beauteous Catherine,
   Beauteous Catherine gave place
(Though loath and angry she to part
With the possession of my heart)
   To Eliza's conquering face.

Eliza to this hour might reign,
Had not she evil counsels ta'en.
   Fundamental laws she broke;
And still new favourites she chose,
Till up in arms my passions rose,
   And cast away her yoke.

Mary then and gentle Anne
Both to reign at once began.
   Alternately they swayed;
And sometimes Mary was the fair,
And sometimes Anne the crown did wear;
   And sometimes both I obeyed.

Another Mary then arose
And did the rigorous laws impose;
   A mighty tyrant she!
Long, alas, should I have been
Under that iron-sceptered queen,
   Had not Rebecca set me free.

When fair Rebecca set me free,
'Twas then a golden time with me.
   But soon these pleasures fled,

For the gracious princess died
In her youth and beauty's pride,
   And Judith reigned in her stead.

But when Isabella came,
Armed with a resistless flame
   And the artillery of her eye,
Whilst she proudly marched about
Greater conquests to find out,
   She beat out Susan by the bye.

But in her place I then obeyed
Black-eyed Bess, her viceroy maid,
   To whom ensued a vacancy.
Thousand worse passions then possessed
The interregnum of my breast;
   Bless me from such an anarchy!

Gentle Henrietta then,
And a third Mary next began;
   Then Joan and Jane and Audria,
And then a pretty Thomasine,
And then another Katherine,
   And then a long et cetera.

But should I now to you relate
The strength and riches of their state,
   The powder, patches, and the pins,
The ribands, jewels, and the rings,
The lace, the paint and warlike things
   That make up all their magazines;

If I should tell the politic arts
To take and keep men's hearts,
   The letters, embassies and spies,
The frowns, and smiles and flatteries,
The quarrels, tears, and perjuries
   Numberless, nameless, mysteries;

And all the little lime-twigs laid
By Machiavel, the waiting-maid,
   I more voluminous should grow

(Chiefly if I, like them, should tell
All change of weathers that befell)
    Than Holinshed or Stow.

But I will briefer with them be,
Since few of them were long with me.
    A higher and a nobler strain
My present Emperess doth claim:
Eleonora first o' th' name,
    Whom God grant long to reign.

ANDREW MARVELL

(1621 1678)

Bermudas

Where the remote Bermudas ride
In th' ocean's bosom unespied,
From a small boat that rowed along
The listening winds received this song:
    What should we do but sing His praise
Who led us through the watery maze,
Unto an isle so long unknown,
And yet far kinder than our own?
Where He the huge sea-monsters wracks
That lift the deep upon their backs.
He lands us on a grassy stage,
Safe from the storms and prelate's rage.
He gave us this eternal spring
Which here enamels every thing;
And sends the fowls to us in care
On daily visits through the air.
He hangs in shades the orange bright,
Like golden lamps in a green night;
And does in the pomegranates close
Jewels more rich than Ormus shows.
He makes the figs our mouths to meet,
And throws the melons at our feet;
But apples plants of such a price
No tree could ever bear them twice.

With cedars chosen by His hand
From Lebanon He stores the land;
And makes the hollow seas that roar
Proclaim the ambergris on shore.
He cast (of which we rather boast)
The gospel's pearl upon our coast,
And in these rocks for us did frame
A temple, where to sound His name.
Oh, let our voice His praise exalt
Till it arrive at Heaven's vault,
Which then perhaps rebounding may
Echo beyond the Mexique bay.
  Thus sung they in the English boat
A holy and a cheerful note,
And all the way to guide their chime
With falling oars they kept the time.

To His Coy Mistress

Had we but world enough and time,
This coyness, lady, were no crime.
We would sit down, and think which way
To walk, and pass our long love's day.
Thou by the Indian Ganges' side
Should'st rubies find; I by the tide
Of Humber would complain. I would
Love you ten years before the flood;
And you should if you please refuse
Till the conversion of the Jews.
My vegetable love should grow
Vaster than empires and more slow.
A hundred years should go to praise
Thine eyes, and on thy forehead gaze.
Two hundred to adore each breast;
But thirty thousand to the rest.
An age at least to every part,
And the last age should show your heart.
For, lady, you deserve this state,
Nor would I love at lower rate.

But at my back I always hear
Time's wingéd chariot hurrying near;
And yonder all before us lie
Deserts of vast eternity.
Thy beauty shall no more be found,
Nor in thy marble vault shall sound
My echoing song; then worms shall try
That long preserved virginity,
And your quaint honour turn to dust,
And into ashes all my lust.
The grave's a fine and private place,
But none I think do there embrace.
    Now therefore while the youthful hue
Sits on thy skin like morning dew,
And while thy willing soul transpires
At every pore with instant fires,
Now let us sport us while we may;
And now like amorous birds of prey
Rather at once our time devour
Than languish in his slow-chapped power.
Let us roll all our strength and all
Our sweetness up into one ball,
And tear our pleasures with rough strife
Thorough the iron gates of life.
Thus, though we cannot make our sun
Stand still, yet we will make him run.

The Garden

How vainly men themselves amaze
To win the palm, the oak, or bays;
And their incessant labours see
Crowned from some single herb or tree,
Whose short and narrow-vergéd shade
Does prudently their toils upbraid;
While all flow'rs and all trees do close
To weave the garlands of repose.

Fair quiet, have I found thee here,
And innocence, thy sister dear!
Mistaken long, I sought you then
In busy companies of men.
Your sacred plants, if here below,
Only among the plants will grow.
Society is all but rude,
To this delicious solitude.

No white nor red was ever seen
So amorous as this lovely green.
Fond lovers, cruel as their flame,
Cut in these trees their mistress' name.
Little, alas, they know or heed
How far these beauties hers exceed!
Fair trees! wheres'e'er your barks I wound,
No name shall but your own be found.

When we have run our passions' heat,
Love hither makes his best retreat.
The gods, that mortal beauty chase,
Still in a tree did end their race.
Apollo hunted Daphne so,
Only that she might laurel grow;
And Pan did after Syrinx speed,
Not as a nymph, but for a reed.

What wond'rous life is this I lead!
Ripe apples drop about my head;
The luscious clusters of the vine
Upon my mouth do crush their wine;
The nectarine and curious peach
Into my hands themselves do reach;
Stumbling on melons as I pass,
Ensnared with flow'rs, I fall on grass.

Meanwhile the mind, from pleasure less,
Withdraws into its happiness;
The mind, that ocean where each kind
Does straight its own resemblance find;

Yet it creates, transcending these,
Far other worlds and other seas;
Annihilating all that's made
To a green thought in a green shade.

Here at the fountain's sliding foot
Or at some fruit-tree's mossy root,
Casting the body's vest aside,
My soul into the boughs does glide;
There like a bird it sits and sings,
Then whets and combs its silver wings;
And, till prepared for longer flight,
Waves in its plumes the various light.

Such was that happy garden-state,
While Man there walked without a mate.
After a place so pure and sweet,
What other help could yet be meet!
But 'twas beyond a mortal's share
To wander solitary there;
Two paradises 'twere in one
To live in Paradise alone.

How well the skilful gardener drew
Of flow'rs and herbs this dial new,
Where from above the milder sun
Does through a fragrant zodiac run;
And as it works th' industrious bee
Computes its time as well as we.
How could such sweet and wholesome hours
Be reckoned but with herbs and flowers!

FROM *A Horatian Ode upon Cromwell*

So restless Cromwell could not cease
In the inglorious arts of peace,
    But through adventurous war
    Urged his active star.
And, like the three-forked lightning, first
Breaking the clouds where it was nursed,

Did thorough his own side
His fiery way divide.
'Tis madness to resist or blame
The force of angry Heaven's flame;
And if we would speak true
Much to the man is due.
What field of all the civil wars
Where his were not the deepest scars?
And Hampton shows what part
He had of wiser art.
Where, twining subtle fears with hope,
He wove a net of such a scope
That Charles himself might chase
To Carisbrooke's narrow case.
That thence the royal actor borne,
The tragic scaffold might adorn;
While round the arméd bands
Did clap their bloody hands.
He nothing common did or mean
Upon that memorable scene;
But with his keener eye
The axe's edge did try:
Nor called the gods with vulgar spite
To vindicate his helpless right,
But bowed his comely head
Down as upon a bed.

FROM *A Poem upon the Death of Oliver Cromwell*

I saw him dead, a leaden slumber lies
And mortal sleep over those wakeful eyes;
Those gentle rays under the lids were fled,
Which through his looks that piercing sweetness shed;
That port which so majestic was and strong,
Loose and deprived of vigour, stretched along,
All withered, all discoloured, pale and wan,
How much another thing, no more that man!
O human glory vain, O death, O wings,
O worthless world, O transitory things!

Yet dwelt that greatness in his shape decayed
That still, though dead, greater than death he laid;
And in his altered face you something feign
That threatens death he yet will live again.

FROM *The Loyal Scot*

But who considers well will find indeed
'Tis Holy Island parts us, not the Tweed.
Nothing but clergy could us two seclude,
No Scotch was ever like a Bishop's feud.
All litanies in this have wanted faith;
There's no "deliver us from a Bishop's wrath."
Never shall Calvin pardoned be for sales,
Never for Burnet's sake the Lauderdales,
For Becket's sake Kent always shall have tails.
Who sermons e'er can pacify and prayers?
Or to the joint stools reconcile the chairs?
Nothing, not bogs, not sands, not seas, not alps,
Separate the world so as the Bishops' scalps.
Stretch for your Line their circingle alone,
'Twill make a more inhabitable zone.
The friendly loadstone hath not more combined
Than Bishops cramped the commerce of mankind.
A Bishop will like Mahomet tear the moon
And slip one half into his sleeve as soon.
The juggling prelate on his hocus calls,
Shows you first one, then makes that one two balls.
Instead of all the plagues, had Bishops come,
Pharaoh at first would have sent Israel home.
From church they need not censure men away,
A Bishop's self is an anathema.
Where foxes dung their earths, the badgers yield;
At Bishops' dung the foxes quit the field.
Their rank ambition all this heat hath stirred;
A Bishop's rennet makes the strongest curd.
How reverend things are Lord, lawn sleeves and ease!
How a clean laundress and no sermons please!
They wanted zeal and learning, so mistook
The Bible and grammar for the service book.

Religion has the world too long depraved,
A shorter way's to be by clergy saved.
Believe but only as the Church believes,
And learn to pin your faith upon their sleeves.
Ah! like Lot's wife they still look back and halt,
And surpliced show like pillars too of salt.
Who that is wise would pulpit toil endure?
A Bishopric is a great sinecure.
Enough for them, God knows, to count their wealth,
To excommunicate, and study health;
A higher work is to their Court annexed:
The nation they divide, their curates text.
No Bishop rather than it should be so!
No Church, no trade, no king, no people, no!
All mischiefs moulded by those state divines;
Aaron casts calves, but Moses them calcines.
The legion devil did but one man possess,
One Bishop fiend spirits a whole diocese.
That power alone can loose this spell that ties,
For only Kings can Bishops exorcise.
Will you be treated princes? Here fall to,
Fish and flesh Bishops are the ambigu;
Howe'er insipid, yet the sauce will mend 'em;
Bishops are very good when in commendum.
If wealth or vice can tempt your appetites,
These Templar Lords exceed the Templar Knights,
And in a Baron Bishop you have both
Leviathan served up and Behemoth.

HENRY VAUGHAN

(1622–1695)

A Song to Amoret

If I were dead, and in my place
    Some fresher youth designed
To warm thee with new fires, and grace
    Those arms I left behind;

Were he as faithful as the sun,
    That's wedded to the sphere;

His blood as chaste and temp'rate run,
　　As April's mildest tear;

Or were he rich, and with his heaps
　　And spacious share of earth,
Could make divine affection cheap,
　　And court his golden birth:

For all these arts I'd not believe,
　　No, though he should be thine—
The mighty amorist could not give
　　So rich a heart as mine.

Fortune and beauty thou might'st find,
　　And greater men than I;
But my true resolvéd mind
　　They never shall come nigh.

For I not for an hour did love,
　　Or for a day desire,
But with my soul had from above
　　This endless, holy fire.

FROM *To His Retired Friend*

Come! leave this sullen state, and let not wine
And precious wit lie dead for want of thine.
Shall the dull market-landlord with his rout
Of sneaking tenants dirtily swill out
This harmless liquor? shall they knock and beat
For sack, only to talk of rye and wheat?
Oh, let not such prepost'rous tippling be
In our metropolis; may I ne'er see
Such tavern-sacrilege, nor lend a line
To weep the rapes and tragedy of wine!

Here lives that chymic quick fire which betrays
Fresh spirits to the blood, and warms our lays.
I have reserved 'gainst thy approach a cup
That were thy Muse stark dead, shall raise her up,
And teach her yet more charming words and skill
Than ever Celia, Chloris, Astrophil,
Or any of the threadbare names inspired
Poor rhyming lovers with a mistress fired.
Come then! and while the slow icicle hangs
At the stiff thatch, and winter's frosty pangs
Benumb the year, blithe—as of old—let us
'Midst noise and war, of peace and mirth discuss.
This portion thou wert born for; why should we
Vex at the time's ridiculous misery?
An age that thus hath fooled itself, and will
—Spite of thy teeth and mine—persist so still.
Let's sit then at this fire, and while we steal
A revel in the town, let others seal,
Purchase or cheat, and who can let them pay,
Till those black deeds bring on the darksome day.
Innocent spenders we! a better use
Shall wear out our short lease, and leave th' obtuse
Rout to their husks; they and their bags at best
Have cares in earnest; we care for a jest.

FROM *The Waterfall*

With what deep murmurs, through Time's silent stealth,
Doth thy transparent, cool and watery wealth
          Here flowing fall,
          And chide and call,
As if his liquid, loose retinue stayed
Lingering, and were of this steep place afraid,
          The common pass,
          Where clear as glass,
          All must descend
          Not to an end,
But quickened by this deep and rocky grave,
Rise to a longer course more bright and brave.

The Shower

'Twas so; I saw thy birth. That drowsy lake
From her faint bosom breathed thee, the disease
Of her sick waters and infectious ease.
            But now at even,
            Too gross for Heaven,
Thou fall'st in tears, and weep'st for thy mistake.

Ah! it is so with me. Oft have I pressed
Heaven with a lazy breath, but fruitless this
Pierced not; love only can with quick access
            Unlock the way,
            When all else stray,
The smoke and exhalations of the breast.

Yet, if as thou dost melt, and with thy train
Of drops make soft the Earth, my eyes could weep
O'er my hard heart, that's bound up and asleep;
            Perhaps, at last,
            Some such showers past,
My God would give a sunshine after rain.

The Morning-Watch

O joys! infinite sweetness! with what flowers
And shoots of glory my soul breaks and buds!
            All the long hours
            Of night and rest,
            Through the still shrouds
            Of sleep and clouds,
        This dew fell on my breast.
            Oh, how it bloods
And spirits all my earth! hark! in what rings
And hymning circulations the quick world
            Awakes and sings!
            The rising winds,
            And falling springs,
            Birds, beasts, all things
        Adore Him in their kinds.
            Thus all is hurled

In sacred hymns and order; the great chime
And symphony of Nature. Prayer is
      The world in tune,
      A spirit-voice,
      And vocal joys,
    Whose echo is Heaven's bliss.
      Oh, let me climb
When I lie down! The pious soul by night
Is like a clouded star, whose beams, though said
      To shed their light
      Under some cloud,
      Yet are above,
      And shine and move
    Beyond that misty shroud.
      So in my bed,
That curtained grave, though sleep like ashes hide
My lamp and life, both shall in Thee abide.

The Retreat

Happy those early days when I
Shined in my angel-infancy!
Before I understood this place
Appointed for my second race,
Or taught my soul to fancy ought
But a white, celestial thought;
When yet I had not walked above
A mile, or two, from my first love,
And looking back (at that short space,)
Could see a glimpse of his bright face;
When on some gilded cloud or flower
My gazing soul would dwell an hour,
And in those weaker glories spy
Some shadows of eternity;
Before I taught my tongue to wound
My conscience with a sinful sound,
Or had the black art to dispense
A sev'ral sin to ev'ry sense;
But felt through all this fleshly dress
Bright shoots of everlastingness.

O how I long to travel back
And tread again that ancient track!
That I might once more reach that plain,
Where first I left my glorious train,
From whence th'enlightened spirit sees
That shady city of palm trees;
But (ah!) my soul with too much stay
Is drunk, and staggers in the way.
Some men a forward motion love,
But I by backward steps would move,
And when this dust falls to the urn,
In that state I came, return.

The World

I saw Eternity the other night,
Like a great ring of pure and endless light,
    All calm, as it was bright;
And round beneath it, Time in hours, days, years,
    Driven by the spheres
Like a vast shadow moved; in which the world
    And all her train were hurled.
The doting lover in his quaintest strain
    Did there complain;
Near him, his lute, his fancy, and his flights,
    Wit's sour delights;
With gloves, and knots, the silly snares of pleasure,
    Yet his dear treasure,
All scattered lay, while he his eyes did pour
    Upon a flower.

The darksome statesman, hung with weights and woe,
Like a thick midnight-fog, moved there so slow,
    He did not stay, nor go;
Condemning thoughts—like sad eclipses—scowl
    Upon his soul,
And clouds of crying witnesses without
    Pursued him with one shout.

Yet digged the mole, and lest his ways be found,
　　Worked underground,
Where he did clutch his prey; but one did see
　　That policy.
Churches and altars fed him; perjuries
　　Were gnats and flies;
It rained about him blood and tears, but he
　　Drank them as free.

The fearful miser on a heap of rust
Sat pining all his life there, did scarce trust
　　His own hands with the dust,
Yet would not place one piece above, but lives
　　In fear of thieves.
Thousands there were as frantic as himself,
　　And hugged each one his pelf;
The downright epicure placed heav'n in sense,
　　And scorned pretence;
While others, slipped into a wide excess,
　　Said little less;
The weaker sort slight, trivial wares enslave,
　　Who think them brave;
And poor, despiséd Truth sat counting by
　　Their victory.

Yet some, who all this while did weep and sing,
And sing and weep, soared up into the ring;
　　But most would use no wing.
Oh, fools—said I—thus to prefer dark night
　　Before true light!
To live in grots and caves, and hate the day
　　Because it shows the way;
The way, which from this dead and dark abode
　　Leads up to God;
A way where you might tread the sun, and be
　　More bright than he!
But as I did their madness so discuss,
　　One whispered thus,
"This ring the Bridegroom did for none provide,
　　But for His bride."

"They Are All Gone ..."

They are all gone into the world of light!
    And I alone sit lingering here;
Their very memory is fair and bright,
    And my sad thoughts doth clear.

It glows and glitters in my cloudy breast,
    Like stars upon some gloomy grove,
Or those faint beams in which this hill is dressed,
    After the sun's remove.

I see them walking in an air of glory,
    Whose light doth trample on my days;
My days, which are at best but dull and hoary,
    Mere glimmering and decays.

O holy Hope! and high Humility!
    High as the heavens above!
These are your walks, and you have showed them me,
    To kindle my cold love.

Dear beauteous Death! the jewel of the just,
    Shining nowhere but in the dark;
What mysteries do lie beyond thy dust,
    Could man outlook that mark!

He that hath found some fledged bird's nest may know
    At first sight if the bird be flown;
But what fair well or grove he sings in now,
    That is to him unknown.

And yet, as angels in some brighter dreams
    Call to the soul when man doth sleep,
So some strange thoughts transcend our wonted themes,
    And into glory peep.

If a star were confined into a tomb,
    Her captive flames must needs burn there;
But when the hand that locked her up gives room,
    She'll shine through all the sphere.

O Father of eternal life, and all
   Created glories under Thee!
Resume Thy spirit from this world of thrall
   Into true liberty.

Either disperse these mists, which blot and fill
   My perspective still as they pass;
Or else remove me hence unto that hill
   Where I shall need no glass.

THOMAS STANLEY

(1625–1678)

Song

When I lie burning in thine eye,
   Or freezing in thy breast,
What martyrs, in wished flames that die,
   Are half so pleased or blest?

When thy soft accents through mine ear
   Into my soul do fly,
What angel would not quit his sphere
   To hear such harmony?

Or when the kiss thou gav'st me last
   My soul stole in its breath,
What life would sooner be embraced
   Than so desired a death?

When I commanded am by thee,
   Or by thine eye or hand,
What monarch would not prouder be
   To serve than to command?

Then think no freedom I desire,
   Or would my fetters leave,
Since Phoenix-like I from this fire
   Both life and youth receive.

Song

I prithee let my heart alone,
   Since now 'tis raised above thee,
Not all the beauty thou dost own,
   Again can make me love thee:

He that was shipwrecked once before
   By such a siren's call,
And yet neglects to shun that shore,
   Deserves his second fall.

Each flatt'ring kiss, each tempting smile,
   Thou dost in vain bestow,
Some other lovers might beguile,
   Who not thy falsehood know.

But I am proof against all art,
   No vows shall e'er persuade me
Twice to present a wounded heart
   To her that hath betrayed me.

Could I again be brought to love
   Thy form, though more divine,
I might thy scorn as justly move,
   As now thou sufferest mine.

JOHN HALL

(1627–1656)

The Call

   Romira, stay
And run not thus like a young roe away;
   No enemy
Pursues thee, foolish girl! 'tis only I:
   I'll keep off harms,
If thou'll be pleased to garrison mine arms;
   What, dost thou fear
I'll turn a traitor? may these roses here

To paleness shred,
And lilies stand disguiséd in new red,
If that I lay
A snare wherein thou wouldst not gladly stay.
See, see, the sun
Does slowly to his azure lodging run;
Come, sit but here,
And presently he'll quit our hemisphere:
So, still among
Lovers, time is too short or else too long;
Here will we spin
Legends for them that have love-martyrs been;
Here on this plain
We'll talk Narcissus to a flower again.
Come here, and choose
On which of these proud plats thou would repose;
Here may'st thou shame
The rusty violets with the crimson flame
Of either cheek,
And primroses white as thy fingers seek;
Nay, thou may'st prove
That man's most noble passion is to love.

CHARLES COTTON

(1630–1687)

FROM *To Mr. Izaak Walton*

Farewell, thou busy world, and may
We never meet again;
Here I can eat, and sleep, and pray,
And do more good in one short day,
Than he who his whole age out-wears
Upon thy most conspicuous theatres,
Where naught but vice and vanity do reign.

Good God! how sweet are all things here!
How beautiful the fields appear!
How cleanly do we feed and lie!
Lord! what good hours do we keep!

How quietly we sleep!
What peace! what unanimity!
How innocent from the lewd fashion
Is all our business, all our conversation!

Oh, how happy here's our leisure!
Oh, how innocent our pleasure!
O ye valleys, O ye mountains,
O ye groves and crystal fountains,
    How I love at liberty
By turn to come and visit ye!

O Solitude, the soul's best friend,
That man acquainted with himself dost make,
And all his Maker's wonders to intend;
    With thee I here converse at will,
    And would be glad to do so still;
For it is thou alone that keep'st the soul awake.

How calm and quiet a delight
    It is alone
To read, and meditate, and write,
By none offended, nor offending none;
To walk, ride, sit, or sleep at one's own ease,
And pleasing a man's self, none other to displease!

O my beloved nymph, fair Dove,
Princess of rivers, how I love
    Upon thy flowery banks to lie,
    And view thy silver stream
    When gilded by a summer's beam,
    And in it all thy wanton fry
        Playing at liberty,
    And with my angle upon them
        The all of treachery
I ever learned to practise and to try!

O my beloved rocks, that rise
To awe the earth and brave the skies,
From some aspiring mountain's crown

How dearly do I love,
Giddy with pleasure, to look down,
And from the vales to view the noble heights above!

Lord! would men let me alone,
What an over-happy one
Should I think myself to be,
Might I in this desert place,
Which most men by their voice disgrace,
Live but undisturbed and free!
Here in this despised recess,
Would I maugre winter's cold
And the summer's worst excess,
Try to live out to sixty full years old,
And all the while
Without an envious eye
On any thriving under Fortune's smile,
Contented live, and then contented die.

FROM *Old Tityrus to Eugenia*

Eugenia, young and fair and sweet,
The glories of the plains,
In thee alone the graces meet
To conquer all the swains;
Tall as the poplar of the grove,
Straight as the wingéd shaft of Love,
As the spring's early blossoms white,
Soft as the kisses of the light,
Serene and modest as the morn,
Ere vapours do from fens arise
To dim the glory of the skies,
Untainted, or with pride or scorn,
T' oblige the world, bright nymph, thou sure wast born

Ode

Good night, my Love, may gentle rest
   Charm up your senses till the light,
Whilst I with care and woe opprest
   Go to inhabit endless night.

There, whilst your eyes shall grace the day,
   I must in the despairing shade,
Sigh such a woeful time away,
   As never yet poor lover had.

Yet to this endless solitude
   There is one dangorous step to pass,
To one that loves your sight, so rude,
   As flesh and blood is loath to pass.

But I will take it to express
   I worthily your favours wore,
Your merits, sweet, can claim no less,
   Who dies for you can do no more.

Sonnet

Chloris, whilst thou and I were free,
Wedded to naught but liberty,
How sweetly happy did we live,
How free to promise, free to give!

Then, monarchs of ourselves, we might
Love here or there, to change delight,
And tied to none, with all dispense,
Paying each Love its recompense.

But in that happy freedom, we
Were so improvidently free,
To give away our liberties;

And now in fruitful sorrow pine
At what we are, what might have been,
Had thou or I or both been wise.

Song

Join once again, my Celia, join
Thy rosy lips to these of mine,
   Which, though they be not such,
Are full as sensible of bliss,
That is, as soon can taste a kiss,
   As thine of softer touch.

Each kiss of thine creates desire,
Thy odorous breath inflames Love's fire,
   And wakes the sleeping coal;
Such a kiss to be I find
The conversation of the mind,
   And whisper of the soul.

Thanks, sweetest, now thou'rt perfect grown,
For by this last kiss I'm undone;
   Thou breathest silent darts;
Henceforth each little touch will prove
A dangerous stratagem in love,
   And thou wilt blow up hearts.

Laura Sleeping

Winds, whisper gently whilst she sleeps,
   And fan her with your cooling wings;
Whilst she her drops of beauty weeps
   From pure and yet unrivalled springs.

Glide over beauty's field, her face,
   To kiss her lip and cheek be bold,
But with a calm and stealing pace,
   Neither too rude nor yet too cold.

Play in her beams and crisp her hair
   With such a gale as wings soft Love,
And with so sweet, so rich an air
   As breathes from the Arabian grove.

A breath as hushed as lover's sigh,
　　Or that unfolds the morning door;
Sweet as the winds that gently fly
　　To sweep the spring's enamelled floor.

Murmur soft music to her dreams,
　　That pure and unpolluted run,
Like to the new-born crystal streams
　　Under the bright enamoured sun.

But when she waking shall display
　　Her light, retire within your bar;
Her breath is life, her eyes are day,
　　And all mankind her creatures are.

from Ode

Without the evening dew and showers
　　The Earth would be a barren place,
Of trees and plants, or herbs and flowers,
　　To crown her now enamelled face;

Nor can wit spring or fancies grow
　　Unless we dew our heads in wine,
Plump autumn's wealthy overflow
　　And sprightly issue of the vine.

Wine is the cure of cares and sloth
　　That rust the metal of the mind,
The juice that man to man does both
　　In freedom and in friendship bind.

This clears the monarch's cloudy brows
　　And cheers the hearts of sullen swains,
To wearied souls repose allows,
　　And makes slaves caper in their chains.

Wine, that distributes to each part
　　Its heat and motion, is the spring,
The poet's head, the subject's heart,
　　'Twas wine made old Anacreon sing.

Then let us quaff it, whilst the night
   Serves but to hide such guilty souls,
As fly the beauty of the light
   Or dare not pledge our loyal bowls.

JOHN DRYDEN

(1631–1700)

Song

Sylvia the fair, in the bloom of fifteen,
Felt an innocent warmth as she lay on the green;
She had heard of a pleasure, and something she guessed
By the towsing and tumbling and touching her breast;
She saw the men eager, but was at a loss
What they meant by their sighing and kissing so close;
     By their praying and whining,
     And clasping and twining,
     And panting and wishing,
     And sighing and kissing,
     And sighing and kissing so close.

Ah, she cried, ah, for a languishing maid
In a country of Christians to die without aid!
Not a Whig or a Tory or Trimmer at least,
Or a Protestant parson or Catholic priest,
To instruct a young virgin that is at a loss
What they meant by their sighing and kissing so close;
     By their praying &c.

Cupid in shape of a swain did appear;
He saw the sad wound, and in pity drew near,
Then showed her his arrow and bid her not fear,
For the pain was no more than a maiden may bear;
When the balm was infused, she was not at a loss
What they meant by their sighing and kissing so close;
     By their praying &c.

Rondelay

Chloe found Amyntas lying
  All in tears upon the plain,
Sighing to himself and crying:
  Wretched I to love in vain!
Kiss me, dear, before my dying;
  Kiss me once, and ease my pain.

Sighing to himself and crying:
  Wretched I to love in vain!
Ever scorning and denying
  To reward your faithful swain.
Kiss me, dear, before my dying;
  Kiss me once, and ease my pain!

Ever scorning and denying
  To reward your faithful swain.
Chloe, laughing at his crying,
  Told him that he loved in vain.
Kiss me, dear, before my dying;
  Kiss me once, and ease my pain!

Chloe, laughing at his crying,
  Told him that he loved in vain;
But repenting, and complying,
  When he kissed, she kissed again;
Kissed him up, before his dying;
  Kissed him up, and eased his pain.

"Ah, Fading Joy..."

Ah, fading joy, how quickly art thou past!
  Yet we thy ruin haste;
As if the cares of human life were few,
  We seek out new,
And follow fate that does too fast pursue

See how on ev'ry bough the birds express
In their sweet notes their happiness.
They all enjoy and nothing spare;
But on their mother Nature lay their care.
Why then should Man, the lord of all below,
Such troubles choose to know,
As none of all his subjects undergo?

Hark, hark, the waters fall, fall, fall,
And with a murmuring sound
Dash, dash upon the ground,
To gentle slumbers call.

The Indian Emperor, 1665

"After the Pangs of a Desperate Lover"

After the pangs of a desperate lover,
When day and night I have sighed all in vain;
Ah, what a pleasure it is to discover
In her eyes pity, who causes my pain!

When with unkindness our love at a stand is,
And both have punished ourselves with the pain,
Ah, what a pleasure the touch of her hand is,
Ah, what a pleasure to press it again!

When the denial comes fainter and fainter,
And her eyes give what her tongue does deny,
Ah, what a trembling I feel when I venture,
Ah, what a trembling does usher my joy!

When with a sigh she accords me the blessing,
And her eyes twinkle 'twixt pleasure and pain,
Ah, what a joy 'tis beyond all expressing,
Ah, what a joy to hear: Shall we again?

An Evening's Love, 1668

"Ah, How Sweet It Is to Love"

Ah, how sweet it is to love,
Ah, how gay is young desire!
And what pleasing pains we prove
When we first approach Love's fire.
    Pains of Love be sweeter far
    Than all other pleasures are.

Sighs which are from lovers blown,
Do but gently heave the heart;
Ev'n the tears they shed alone
Cure like trickling balm their smart.
    Lovers when they lose their breath
    Bleed away in easy death.

Love and time with reverence use,
Treat them like a parting friend,
Nor the golden gifts refuse
Which in youth sincere they send;
    For each year their price is more,
    And they less simple than before.

Love, like spring-tides full and high,
Swells in ev'ry youthful vein;
But each tide does less supply,
Till they quite shrink in again.
    If a flow in age appear,
    'Tis but rain, and runs not clear.

Tyrannic Love, 1669

"Why Should a Foolish Marriage Vow"

Why should a foolish marriage vow
    Which long ago was made
Oblige us to each other now,
    When passion is decayed?
We loved, and we loved, as long as we could,
    Till our love was loved out in us both;
But our marriage is dead when the pleasure is fled;
    'Twas pleasure first made it an oath.

> If I have pleasures for a friend
>   And further love in store,
> What wrong has he whose joys did end,
>   And who could give no more?
> 'Tis a madness that he
> Should be jealous of me,
> Or that I should bar him of another;
> For all we can gain is to give ourselves pain
> When neither can hinder the other.

Marriage a-la-Mode, 1672

"*Long betwixt Love and Fear...*"

Long betwixt love and fear Phillis tormented
Shunned her own wish, yet at last she consented;
But loath that day should her blushes discover:
    Come gentle night, she said,
    Come quickly to my aid,
    And a poor shamefaced maid
    Hide from her lover.

Now cold as ice I am, now hot as fire,
I dare not tell myself my own desire,
But let day fly away and let night haste her.
    Grant, ye kind powers above,
    Slow hours to parting love,
    But when to bliss we move,
    Bid them fly faster.

How sweet it is to love when I discover
That fire which burns my heart warming my lover;
'Tis pity love so true should be mistaken.
    But if this night he be
    False or unkind to me,
    Let me die ere I see
    That I'm forsaken.

The Assignation, 1673

"Can Life Be a Blessing"

Can life be a blessing
　　Or worth the possessing,
Can life be a blessing if love were away?
　Ah no! though our love all night keep us waking,
And though he torment us with cares all the day,
　　Yet he sweetens, he sweetens our pains in the taking,
There's an hour at the last, there's an hour to repay.

　　In ev'ry possessing
　　The ravishing blessing,
In ev'ry possessing the fruit of our pain,
　Poor lovers forget long ages of anguish,
Whate'er they have suffered and done to obtain;
　　'Tis a pleasure, a pleasure to sigh and to languish,
When we hope, when we hope to be happy again.

Troilus and Cressida, 1679

"Farewell, Ungrateful Traitor"

Farewell, ungrateful traitor,
　　Farewell, my perjured swain;
Let never injured creature
　　Believe a man again.
The pleasure of possessing
Surpasses all expressing,
But 'tis too short a blessing,
　　And love too long a pain.

'Tis easy to deceive us
　　In pity of your pain,
But when we love you leave us
　　To rail at you in vain.
Before we have described it,
There is no bliss beside it,
But she that once has tried it,
　　Will never love again.

The passion you pretended
Was only to obtain,
But when the charm is ended
The charmer you disdain.
Your love by ours we measure
Till we have lost our treasure,
But dying is a pleasure,
When living is a pain.

The Spanish Friar, 1681

"Fair Iris and Her Swain"

Thyrsis: Fair Iris and her swain
Were in a shady bower,
Where Thyrsis long in vain
Had sought the shepherd's hour.
At length his hand advancing upon her snowy
breast,
He said, Oh kiss me longer,
And longer yet and longer,
If you will make me blest.

Iris: An easy trusting maid
By trusting is undone;
Our sex is oft betrayed
By granting love too soon.
If you desire to gain me, your sufferings to redress,
Prepare to love me longer,
And longer yet, and longer,
Before you shall possess.

Thyrsis: The little care you show
Of all my sorrows past
Makes death appear too slow,
And life too long to last.
Fair Iris, kiss me kindly, in pity of my fate;
And kindly still, and kindly,
Before it is too late.

Iris: You fondly court your bliss
           And no advances make;
         'Tis not for maids to kiss,
           But 'tis for men to take.
So you may kiss me kindly, and I will not rebel;
         But kindly still, and kindly,
           But kiss me not and tell.

Chorus: Thus at the height we love and live,
         And fear not to be poor;
We give, and give, and give, and give,
         Till we can give no more:
But what to day will take away
         To morrow will restore.
Thus at the hoight we love and live,
         And fear not to be poor.

                               Amphitryon, 1690

"How Happy the Lover"

How happy the lover,
     How easy his chain,
     How pleasing his pain!
How sweet to discover
     He sighs not in vain.
For love ev'ry creature
Is formed by his nature;
No joys are above
The pleasures of love.

In vain are our graces,
     In vain are your eyes,
     If love you despise;
When age furrows faces,
     'Tis time to be wise.
Then use the short blessing,
That flies in possessing:
No joys are above
The pleasures of love.

                              King Arthur, 1691

"No, No, Poor Suffering Heart..."

No, no, poor suffering heart, no change endeavour;
Choose to sustain the smart rather than leave her;
My ravished eyes behold such charms about her,
I can die with her, but not live without her.
One tender sigh of hers to see me languish
Will more than pay the price of my past anguish;
Beware, O cruel fair, how you smile on me,
'Twas a kind look of yours that has undone me.

Love has in store for me one happy minute,
And she will end my pain who did begin it;
Then no day void of bliss or pleasure leaving
Ages shall slide away without perceiving:
Cupid shall guard the door the more to please us,
And keep out time and death when they would seize us;
Time and death shall depart and say in flying
Love has found out a way to live by dying.

Cleomenes, 1692

FROM *Annus Mirabilis*

Yet London, empress of the northern clime,
By an high fate thou greatly didst expire;
Great as the world's, which, at the death of time,
Must fall and rise a nobler frame by fire.

As when some dire usurper Heav'n provides
To scourge his country with a lawless sway,
His birth perhaps some petty village hides,
And sets his cradle out of Fortune's way.

Till fully ripe his swelling fate breaks out,
And hurries him to mighty mischiefs on;
His prince, surprised at first, no ill could doubt,
And wants the power to meet it when 'tis known.

Such was the rise of this prodigious fire,
Which in mean buildings first obscurely bred,
From thence did soon to open streets aspire,
And straight to palaces and temples spread.

The diligence of trades and noiseful gain,
And luxury, more late, asleep were laid;
All was the night's, and in her silent reign
No sound the rest of Nature did invade.

In this deep quiet, from what source unknown,
Those seeds of fire their fatal birth disclose;
And first, few scatt'ring sparks about were blown,
Big with the flames that to our ruin rose.

Then in some close pent room it crept along,
And, smould'ring as it went, in silence fed;
Till th' infant monster, with devouring strong
Walked boldly upright with exalted head.

At length the crackling noise and dreadful blaze
Called up some waking lover to the sight;
And long it was ere he the rest could raise,
Whose heavy eyelids yet were full of night.

The next to danger, hot pursued by fate,
Half-clothed, half-naked, hastily retire;
And frighted mothers strike their breasts too late
For helpless infants left amidst the fire.

Their cries soon waken all the dwellers near;
Now murmuring noises rise in every street;
The more remote run stumbling with their fear,
And in the dark men justle as they meet.

A key of fire ran all along the shore,
And lightened all the river with a blaze;
The wakened tides began again to roar,
And wondering fish in shining waters gaze.

Old Father Thames raised up his reverend head,
But feared the fate of Simois would return;
Deep in his ooze he sought his sedgy bed,
And shrunk his waters back into his urn.

The Fire meantime walks in a broader gross;
To either hand his wings he opens wide;
He wades the streets, and straight he reaches cross,
And plays his longing flames on th' other side.

To every nobler portion of the town
The curling billows roll their restless tide;
In parties now they straggle up and down,
As armies unopposed for prey divide.

One mighty squadron with a side-wind sped
Through narrow lanes his cumbered fire does haste;
By powerful charms of gold and silver led,
The Lombard bankers and the Change to waste.

Another backward to the Tower would go,
And slowly eats his way against the wind;
But the main body of the marching foe
Against th' imperial palace is designed.

Those who have homes, when home they do repair,
To a last lodging call their wand'ring friends;
Their short uneasy sleeps are broke with care,
To look how near their own destruction tends.

Those who have none, sit round where once it was,
And with full eyes each wonted room require;
Haunting the yet warm ashes of the place,
As murdered men walk where they did expire.

The most in fields like herded beasts lie down,
To dews obnoxious on the grassy floor;
And while their babes in sleep their sorrows drown,
Sad parents watch the remnants of their store.

FROM *Absalom and Achitophel*

1.

Of these the false Achitophel was first,
A name to all succeeding ages curst.
For close designs and crooked counsels fit,
Sagacious, bold, and turbulent of wit,
Restless, unfixed in principles and place,
In power unpleased, impatient of disgrace;
A fiery soul, which working out its way,
Fretted the pygmy body to decay;
And o'er-informed the tenement of clay.
A daring pilot in extremity,
Pleased with the danger when the waves went high
He sought the storms; but for a calm unfit
Would steer too nigh the sands to boast his wit.
Great wits are sure to madness near allied,
And thin partitions do their bounds divide;
Else why should he, with wealth and honours blest,
Refuse his age the needful hours of rest?
And all to leave what with his toil he won
To that unfeathered two-legged thing, a son;
Got while his soul did huddled notions try,
And born a shapeless lump like anarchy.
In friendship false, implacable in hate,
Resolved to ruin or to rule the State.

2.

In the first rank of these did Zimri stand;
A man so various that he seemed to be
Not one, but all mankind's epitome.
Stiff in opinions, always in the wrong,
Was everything by starts, and nothing long,
But in the course of one revolving moon
Was chymist, fiddler, statesman and buffoon,
Then all for women, painting, rhyming, drinking,
Besides ten thousand freaks that died in thinking.
Blest madman, who could every hour employ
With something new to wish or to enjoy!
Railing and praising were his usual themes,
And both (to show his judgment) in extremes;

So over violent or over civil
That every man with him was God or Devil.
In squandering wealth was his peculiar art,
Nothing went unrewarded but desert.
Beggared by fools, whom still he found too late,
He had his jest, and they had his estate.

FROM MacFlecknoe

All human things are subject to decay,
And when fate summons monarchs must obey;
This Flecknoe found, who like Augustus young
Was called to empire, and had governed long,
In prose and verse was owned without dispute
Through all the realms of Nonsense absolute.
This aged prince now flourishes in peace
And blest with issue of a large increase,
Worn out with business did at length debate
To settle the succession of the State;
And pondered which of all his sons was fit
To reign and wage immortal war with wit,
Cried: 'Tis resolved, for nature pleads that he
Should only rule who most resembles me;
Shadwell alone my perfect image bears,
Mature in dullness from his tender years,
Shadwell alone of all my sons is he
Who stands confirmed in full stupidity.
The rest to some faint meaning make pretence,
But Shadwell never deviates into sense.
Some beams of wit on other souls may fall,
Strike through and make a lucid interval,
But Shadwell's genuine night admits no ray,
His rising fogs prevail upon the day;
Besides, his goodly fabric fills the eye
And seems designed for thoughtless majesty;
Thoughtless as monarch oaks that shade the plain
And, spread in solemn state, supinely reign.

FROM *Religio Laici*

Dim, as the borrowed beams of moon and stars
To lonely, weary, wandering travellers
Is Reason to the soul; and as on high
Those rolling fires discover but the sky
Not light us here; so Reason's glimmering ray
Was lent, not to assure our doubtful way,
But guide us upward to a better day.
And as those nightly tapers disappear
When day's bright lord ascends our hemisphere;
So pale grows Reason at Religion's sight,
So dies, and so dissolves in supernatural light.
Some few whose lamp shone brighter have been led
From cause to cause to Nature's secret head;
And found that one first principle must be.
But what or who that universal He,
Whether some soul encompassing this ball,
Unmade, unmoved, yet making, moving all;
Or various atoms' interfering dance
Leapt into form (the noble work of chance)
Or this great All was from eternity;
Not ev'n the Stagirite himself could see,
And Epicurus guessed as well as he.

To the Memory of Mr. Oldham

Farewell, too little and too lately known,
Whom I began to think and call my own;
For sure our souls were near allied, and thine
Cast in the same poetic mould with mine.
One common note on either lyre did strike,
And knaves and fools we both abhorred alike.
To the same goal did both our studies drive,
The last set out the soonest did arrive.
Thus Nisus fell upon the slippery place,
Whilst his young friend performed and won the race.
Oh, early ripe! to thy abundant store
What could advancing age have added more?

It might (what Nature never gives the young)
Have taught the numbers of thy native tongue.
But satire needs not those, and wit will shine
Through the harsh cadence of a rugged line.
A noble error, and but seldom made,
When poets are by too much force betrayed.
Thy generous fruits, though gathered ere their prime,
Still shewed a quickness; and maturing time
But mellows what we write to the dull sweets of rhyme.
Once more, hail and farewell! farewell, thou young,
But ah! too short, Marcellus of our tongue!
Thy brow's with ivy and with laurels bound;
But fate and gloomy night encompass thee around.

FROM *Tyrannic Love,* 1669

PROLOGUE

Self-love (which never rightly understood)
Makes poets still conclude their plays are good,
And malice in all critics reigns so high,
That for small errors, they whole plays decry;
So that to see this fondness, and that spite,
You'd think that none but madmen judge or write.
Therefore our Poet, as he thinks not fit
T'impose upon you what he writes for wit
So hopes that, leaving you your censures free,
You equal judges of the whole will be:
They judge but half, who only faults will see.
Poets, like lovers, should be bold and dare,
They spoil their business with an over-care;
And he, who servilely creeps after sense,
Is safe, but ne'er will reach an excellence.
Hence 'tis, our Poet, in his conjuring,
Allow'd his fancy the full scope and swing.
But when a tyrant for his theme he had,
He loos'd the reins, and bid his Muse run mad;
And though he stumbles in a full career,
Yet rashness is a better fault than fear.

He saw his way; but in so swift a pace,
To choose the ground might be to lose the race.
They then, who of each trip th' advantage take,
Find but those faults, which they want wit to make.

EPILOGUE

*Spoken by Mrs. Ellen [i.e., Nell Gwynn] when she was to be
carried off by the Bearers*

To the Bearer:

    Hold! are you mad? you damned, confounded dog!
    I am to rise, and speak the epilogue.

To the Audience:

    I come, kind gentlemen, strange news to tell ye;
    I am the ghost of poor departed Nelly.
    Sweet ladies, be not frightened; I'll be civil;
    I'm what I was, a little harmless devil.
    For, after death, we sprites have just such natures,
    We had, for all the world, when human creatures;
    And, therefore, I, that was an actress here,
    Play all my tricks in Hell, a goblin there.
    Gallants, look to 't, you say there are no sprites;
    But I'll come dance about your beds at nights;
    And faith you'll be in a sweet kind of taking,
    When I surprise you between sleep and waking.
    To tell you true, I walk, because I die
    Out of my calling, in a tragedy.
    O poet, damned dull poet, who could prove
    So senseless, to make Nelly die for love!
    Nay, what's yet worse, to kill me in the prime
    Of Easter-term, in tart and cheese-cake time!
    I'll fit the fop; for I'll not one word say,
    T' excuse his godly, out of fashion play;
    A play, which, if you dare but twice sit out,
    You'll all be slandered, and be thought devout.
    But farewell, gentlemen, make haste to me,
    I'm sure ere long to have your company.
    As for my epitaph when I am gone,
    I'll trust no poet, but will write my own:
    "Here Nelly lies, who, though she lived a slater'n,
    Yet died a princess, acting in S. Cathar'n.

FROM *The Secular Masque*

CHORUS

All, all of a piece throughout:
  Thy chase had a beast in view;
Thy wars brought nothing about;
  Thy lovers were all untrue.
'Tis well an old age is out,
  And time to begin a new.

KATHERINE PHILIPS

(1631–1664)

Friendship's Mystery
(TO MY DEAREST LUCASIA)

Come, my Lucasia, since we see
  That miracles men's faith do move,
By wonder and by prodigy
  To the dull angry world let's prove
  There's a religion in our love.

For though we were designed t' agree,
  That Fate no liberty destroys,
But our election is as free
  As angels', who with greedy choice
  Are yet determined to their joys.

Our hearts are doubled by the loss;
  Here mixture is addition grown;
We both diffuse, and both engross:
  And we whose minds are so much one,
  Never, yet ever are alone.

We court our own captivity
  Than thrones more great and innocent:
'Twere banishment to be set free,
  Since we wear fetters whose intent
  Not bondage is but ornament.

Divided joys are tedious found,
  And griefs united easier grow:
We are ourselves but by rebound,
  And all our titles shuffled so,
  Both princes, and both subjects too.

Our hearts are mutual victims laid,
  While they (such power in friendship lies)
Are altars, priests and off'rings made:
  And each heart which thus kindly dies,
  Grows deathless by the sacrifice.

SIR GEORGE ETHEREGE

(1635?–1691)

Song

Ye happy swains, whose hearts are free
  From love's imperial chain,
Take warning and be taught by me,
  T' avoid th' enchanting pain.
Fatal the wolves to trembling flocks,
  Fierce winds to blossoms prove,
To careless seamen hidden rocks,
  To human quiet love.

Fly the fair sex, if bliss you prize;
  The snake's beneath the flower:
Whoever gazed on beauteous eyes
  That tasted quiet more?
How faithless is the lover's joy!
  How constant is their care,
The kind with falsehood to destroy,
  The cruel with despair!

Upon the Downs...

Upon the downs when shall I breathe at ease,
Have nothing else to do but what I please?
In a fresh cooling shade upon the brink
Of Arden's spring have time to read and think.

And stretch, and sleep, when all my care shall be
For health, and pleasure my philosophy?
When shall I rest from business, noise, and strife,
Lay down the soldier's and the courtier's life,
And in a little melancholy seat
Begin at last to live and to forget
The nonsense and the farce of what the fools call great?

To a Lady, Asking Him How Long He Would Love Her

It is not, Celia, in our power
To say how long our love will last;
It may be we within this hour
May lose those joys we now do taste;
The blessed, that immortal be,
From change in love are only free.

Then, since we mortal lovers are,
Ask not how long our love will last;
But while it does, let us take care
Each minute be with pleasure passed:
Were it not madness to deny
To live because we're sure to die?

To a Very Young Lady

Sweetest bud of beauty, may
No untimely frost decay
Th' early glories which we trace
Blooming in thy matchless face!
But kindly opening like the rose
Fresh beauties every day disclose,
Such as by nature are not shown
In all the blossoms she has blown.
And then what conquests shall you make
Who hearts already daily take!

Scorched in the morning with thy beams,
How shall he bear those sad extremes,
Which must attend thy threatening eyes
When thou shalt to thy noon arise!

SIR CHARLES SEDLEY

(1639–1701)

Song

Not, Celia, that I juster am,
    Or better than the rest,
For I would change each hour like them,
    Were not my heart at rest.

But I am tied to very thee
    By every thought I have,
Thy face I only care to see,
    Thy heart I only crave.

All that in Woman is adored
    In thy dear self I find,
For the whole sex can but afford
    The handsome and the kind.

Why then should I seek farther store,
    And still make love anew?
When change itself can give no more,
    'Tis easy to be true.

Song

Love still has something of the sea
    From whence his mother rose;
No time his slaves from doubt can free,
    Nor give their thoughts repose.

They are becalmed in clearest days,
    And in rough weather tost;
They wither under cold delays,
    Or are in tempests lost.

One while they seem to touch the port,
    Then straight into the main,
Some angry wind in cruel sport
    The vessel drives again.

At first disdain and pride they fear,
    Which if they chance to 'scape,
Rivals and falsehood soon appear
    In a more dreadful shape.

By such degrees to joy they come,
    And are so long withstood,
So slowly they receive the sum,
    It hardly does them good.

'Tis cruel to prolong a pain,
    And to defer a joy,
Believe me, gentle Celimene,
    Offends the wingéd boy.

An hundred thousand oaths your fears
    Perhaps would not remove;
And if I gazed a thousand years
    I could no deeper love.

Song

Ah Chloris! that I now could sit
    As unconcerned, as when
Your infant beauty could beget
    No pleasure nor no pain.

When I the dawn used to admire,
    And praised the coming day;
I little thought the growing fire
    Must take my rest away.

Your charms in harmless childhood lay,
    Like metals in the mine,
Age from no face took more away
    Than youth concealed in thine.

But as your charms insensibly
    To their perfections prest,
Fond Love as unperceived did fly
    And in my bosom rest.

My passion with your beauty grew,
    And Cupid in my heart
Still as his mother favoured you
    Threw a new flaming dart.

Each gloried in their wanton part;
    To make a lover he
Employed the utmost of his art,
    To make a beauty she.

Though now I slowly bend to love
    Uncertain of my fate,
If your fair self my chains approve
    I shall my freedom hate.

Lovers, like dying men, may well
    At first disordered be,
Since none alive can truly tell
    What fortune they must see.

The Mulberry Garden, 1668

APHRA BEHN

(1640–1689)

The Coquet

Melinda, who had never been
Esteemed a beauty at fifteen,
Always amorous was and kind;
    To every swain she lent an ear,
Free as air but false as wind;
    Yet none complained she was severe.
She eased more than she made complain,
Was always singing, pert, and vain.

Where-e'er the throng was, she was seen,
And swept the youths along the green;
With equal grace she flattered all;
    And fondly proud of all address,
Her smiles invite, her eyes do call,
    And her vain heart her looks confess.
She rallies this, to that she bowed,
Was talking ever, laughing loud.

On every side she makes advance,
And everywhere a confidence;
She tells for secrets all she knows,
    And all to know she does pretend.
Beauty in maids she treats as foes,
    But every handsome youth as friend.
Scandal still passes off for truth,
And noise and nonsense, wit and youth.

Coquet all o'er and every part,
Yet wanting beauty even of art,
Herds with the ugly and the old,
    And plays the critic on the rest;
Of men the bashful and the bold
    Either and all by turns likes best;
Even now, though youth be languished, she
Sets up for love and gallantry.

The Willing Mistress

Amyntas led me to a grove
    Where all the trees did shade us;
The sun itself though it had strove
    It could not have betrayed us.
The place secured from human eyes
    No other fear allows,
But when the winds that gently rise
    Do kiss the yielding boughs.

Down there we sat upon the moss,
   And did begin to play
A thousand amorous tricks, to pass
   The heat of all the day.
A many kisses he did give,
   And I returned the same,
Which made me willing to receive
   That which I dare not name.

His charming eyes no aid required
   To tell their softening tale;
On her that was already fired
   'Twas easy to prevail.
He did but kiss and clasp me round,
   Whilst those his thoughts exprest;
And laid me gently on the ground:
   Ah, who can guess the rest?

Song

Love in fantastic triumph sate
   Whilst bleeding hearts around him flow'd,
For whom fresh pains he did create
   And strange tyrannic power he show'd:
From thy bright eyes he took his fires,
   Which round about in sport he hurl'd;
But 'twas from mine he took desires
   Enough t' undo the amorous world.

From me he took his sighs and tears,
   From thee his pride and cruelty;
From me his languishments and fears,
   And every killing dart from thee.
Thus thou and I the god have arm'd
   And set him up a deity;
But my poor heart alone is harm'd,
   Whilst thine the victor is, and free!

Abdelazer, 1676

THOMAS SHADWELL
(1642?–1692)

Song

The fringéd vallance of your eyes advance,
Shake off your canopied and downy trance;
Phoebus already quaffs the morning dew,
Each does his daily lease of life renew.

He darts his beams on the lark's mossy house,
And from his quiet tenement does rouse
The little charming and harmonious fowl,
Which sings its lump of body to a soul;
Swiftly it clambers up in the steep air
With warbling throat, and makes each note a stair.

This the solicitous lover straight alarms,
Who too long slumbered in his Celia's arms.
And now the swelling spunges of the night
With aching heads stagger from their delight;
Slovenly tailors to their needles haste;
Already now the moving shops are placed
By those who crop the treasures of the fields,
And all those gems the ripening summer yields.

JOHN WILMOT, EARL OF ROCHESTER
(1647–1680)

FROM *The Mistress*

An age in her embraces past
    Would seem a winter's day,
Where life and light with envious haste
    Are torn and snatched away.

But oh! how slowly minutes roll
    When absent from her eyes;
That fed my love, which is my soul,
    It languishes and dies.

For then no more a soul, but shade,
　　It mournfully does move,
And haunts my breast by absence made
　　The living tomb of love.

A Song

Absent from thee I languish still;
　　Then ask me not, when I return?
The straying fool 'twill plainly kill
　　To wish all day, all night to mourn.

Dear, from thine arms then let me fly,
　　That my fantastic mind may prove
The torments it deserves to try,
　　That tears my fixed heart from my love.

When wearied with a world of woe,
　　To thy safe bosom I retire,
Where love and peace and truth do flow,
　　May I contented there expire.

Lest once more wandering from that heaven
　　I fall on some base heart unblest,
Faithless to thee, false, unforgiven,
　　And lose my everlasting rest.

Love and Life

All my past life is mine no more,
　　The flying hours are gone;
Like transitory dreams given o'er,
Whose images are kept in store
　　By memory alone.

The time that is to come is not;
　　How can it then be mine?
The present moment's all my lot,
And that as fast as it is got,
　　Phyllis, is only thine.

Then talk not of inconstancy,
   False hearts and broken vows;
If I by miracle can be
This live-long minute true to thee,
   'Tis all that Heaven allows.

Upon His Leaving His Mistress

'Tis not that I am weary grown
Of being yours, and yours alone,
But with what face can I incline
To damn you to be only mine?
You, whom some kinder power did fashion
By merit and by inclination
The joy at least of a whole nation.

Let meaner spirits of your sex
With humble aims their thoughts perplex,
And boast if by their arts they can
Contrive to make one happy man;
While moved by an impartial sense
Favours, like Nature, you dispense
With universal influence.

See the kind seed-receiving earth
To every grain affords a birth:
On her no showers unwelcome fall,
Her willing womb retains 'em all,
And shall my Cælia be confined?
No, live up to thy mighty mind,
And be the mistress of Mankind!

Upon Nothing

Nothing! Thou elder brother ev'n to shade,
Thou hadst a being ere the world was made,
And well-fixed art alone of ending not afraid.

Ere time and place were, time and place were not,
With primitive Nothing something straight begot,
Then all proceeded from the great united—what?

Something, the general attribute of all,
Severed from thee, its sole original,
Into thy boundless self must undistinguished fall.

Yet something did thy mighty power command,
And from thy fruitful emptiness's hand
Snatched men, beasts, birds, fire, air and land.

Matter, the wicked'st offspring of thy race,
By Form assisted flew from thy embrace,
And rebel Light obscured thy reverend dusky face.

With Form and Matter, Time and Place did join,
Body, thy foe, with thee did leagues combine,
To spoil thy peaceful realm, and ruin all thy line.

But turn-coat Time assists the foe in vain,
And bribed by thee assists thy short-lived reign,
And to thy hungry womb drives back thy slaves again.

Though mysteries are barred from laic eyes,
And the divine alone with warrant pries
Into thy bosom, where the truth in private lies;

Yet this of thee the wise may freely say,
Thou from the virtuous nothing tak'st away,
And to be part with thee the wicked wisely pray.

Great Negative, how vainly would the wise
Enquire, define, distinguish, teach, devise,
Didst thou not stand to point their dull philosophies!

Is or is not, the two great ends of Fate,
And, true or false, the subject of debate,
That perfect or destroy the vast designs of Fate,

When they have racked the politician's breast
Within thy bosom most securely rest,
And when reduced to thee are least unsafe and best.

But, Nothing, why does Something still permit
That sacred monarchs should at council sit,
With persons highly thought at best for nothing fit?

Whilst weighty something modestly abstains
From princes' coffers and from statesmen's brains,
And nothing there like stately Nothing reigns?

Nothing, who dwell'st with fools in grave disguise,
For whom they reverend shapes and forms devise,
Lawn sleeves and furs and gowns, when they like thee look
        wise.

French truth, Dutch prowess, British policy,
Hibernian learning, Scotch civility,
Spaniards' despatch, Danes' wit, are mainly seen in thee.

The great man's gratitude to his best friend,
Kings' promises, whores' vows towards thee they bend,
Flow swiftly into thee, and in thee ever end.

King Charles II

Here lies our sovereign lord the King,
    Whose word no man relies on,
Who never said a foolish thing
    And never did a wise one.

THOMAS OTWAY

(1652–1685)

The Enchantment

I did but look and love awhile,
    'Twas but for one half-hour;
Then to resist I had no will,
    And now I have no power.

To sigh and wish is all my ease;
    Sighs which do heat impart
Enough to melt the coldest ice
    Yet cannot warm your heart.

O would your pity give my heart
    One corner of your breast,
'Twould learn of yours the winning art
    And quickly steal the rest.

JOHN OLDHAM

(1653–1683)

FROM A Satire

(The ghost of Spenser speaks)

But, grant thy poetry should find success,
And, which is rare, the squeamish critics please;
Admit it read, and praised, and courted be
By this nice age and all posterity;
If thou expectest aught but empty fame,
Condemn thy hopes and labours to the flame.
The rich have now learned only to admire;
He, who to greater favours does aspire,
Is mercenary thought, and writes for hire.

"Bless me! how great his genius! how each line
Is big with sense! how glorious a design
Does through the whole and each proportion shine!
How lofty all his thoughts and how inspired!
Pity, such wondrous thoughts are not preferred,"
Cries a gay wealthy sot, who would not bail
For bare five pounds the author out of jail
Should he starve there and rot; who if a brief
Came out the needy poets to relieve
To the whole tribe would scarce a tester give.

But fifty guineas for a punk—good hap!
The peer's well used, and comes off wondrous cheap;
A poet would be dear, and out o' th' way,
Should he expect above a coachman's pay.
For this will any dedicate, and lie,
And daub the gaudy ass with flattery?
For this will any prostitute his sense
To coxcombs void of bounty as of brains?
Yet such is the hard fate of writers now,
They're forced for alms to each great name to bow;
Fawn, like her lap-dog, on her tawdry Grace,
Commend her beauty, and belie her glass,
By which she every morning primes her face;
Sneak to his Honour, call him witty, brave,
And just, though a known coward, fool or knave;
And praise his lineage and nobility
Whose arms at first came from the Company.

'Tis so, 'twas ever so, since heretofore
The blind old bard, with dog and bell before
Was fain to sing for bread from door to door;
The needy Muses all turned gipsies then,
And of the begging trade e'er since have been.

My own hard usage here I need not press,
Where you have every day before your face
Plenty of fresh resembling instances.
Great Cowley's muse the same ill treatment had,
Whose verse shall live for ever to upbraid
The ungrateful world that left such worth unpaid.
Waller himself may thank inheritance
For what he else had never got by sense.
On Butler who can think without just rage,
The glory and the scandal of the age?
Fair stood his hopes when first he came to town,
Met everywhere with welcomes of renown,
Courted, and loved by all, with wonder read,
And promises of princely favour fed;
But what reward for all had he at last,
After a life in dull expectance passed?

The wretch at summing up his misspent days
Found nothing left but poverty and praise;
Of all his gains by verse he could not save
Enough to purchase flannel and a grave;
Reduced to want, he in due time fell sick,
Was fain to die, and be interred on tick;
And well might bless the fever that was sent
To rid him hence, and his worse fate prevent.

All trades and all professions here abound,
And yet encouragement for all is found;
Here a vile empiric, who by license kills,
Who every week helps to increase the bills,
Wears velvet, keeps his coach, and jade beside,
For what less villains must to Tyburn ride.
There a dull trading sot, in wealth o'ergrown
By thriving knavery, can call his own
A dozen manors, and, if fate still bless,
Expects as many counties to possess.
Punks, panders, bawds, all their due pensions gain,
And every day the great men's bounty drain;
Lavish expense on wit, has never yet
Been taxed among the grievances of state.

Then be advised, the slighted Muse forsake,
And Coke and Dalton for thy study take;
For fees each term sweat in the crowded hall,
And there for charters and cracked titles bawl;
Or else to orders and the church betake
Thyself, and that thy future refuge make;
There fawn on some proud patron to engage
The advowson of cast punk and parsonage.
Or soothe the Court, and preach up kingly right,
To gain a prebend or a mitre by 't.
In fine, turn pettifogger, canonist,
Civilian, pedant, mountebank or priest,
Soldier or merchant, fiddler, painter, fencer,
Jack-pudding, juggler, player or rope-dancer;
Preach, plead, cure, fight, game, pimp, beg, cheat or thieve;
Be all but poet, and there's way to live.

ANNE FINCH, Countess of Winchelsea

(1661?–1720)

A Song

If for a woman I would die,
    It should for Gloriana be;
But lovers, you that talk so high,
Inform, whilst in the grave I lie,
    What reward shall reach to me?

If I my freedom would resign,
    That freedom she alone should have;
But tell me, you that can define,
If I by marriage make her mine
    Which may be called the greater slave?

Then Gloriana, since 'tis plain,
    Love with these two can ne'er agree,
Since death and marriage are his bane,
Those melancholy thoughts we'll flee,
    And cheerful lovers always be.

RICHARD BENTLEY

(1662–1742)

Verses

Who strives to mount Parnassus hill
    And thence poetic laurels bring,
Must first acquire due force and skill,
    Must fly with swan's or eagle's wing.

Who Nature's treasures would explore,
    Her mysteries and arcana know,
Must high as lofty Newton soar,
    Must stoop as searching Woodward low.

Who studies ancient laws and rites,
    Tongues, arts, and arms, all history,
Must drudge like Selden days and nights,
    And in the endless labour die.

Who travels in religious jars,
  (Truth mixed with errors, shade with rays),
Like Whiston, wanting Pyx and stars
  In ocean wide or sinks, or stays.

But grant our hero's hopes long toil
  And comprehensive genius crown;
All sciences, all arts, his spoil,
  Yet what reward or what renown?

Envy, innate in vulgar souls,
  Envy steps in and stops his rise;
Envy with poisoned tarnish fouls
  His lustre, and his worth decries.

Inglorious, or by wants enthralled,
  To College and old books confined,
A pedant for his learning called,
  Dunces advanced, he's left behind;
Yet left content, a genuine Stoic he,
Great without patron, rich without South-Sea.

WILLIAM WALSH

(1663–1708)

Song

Of all the torments, all the cares,
  With which our lives are cursed;
Of all the plagues a lover bears,
  Sure rivals are the worst!
By partners, in each other kind,
  Afflictions easier grow;
In love alone we hate to find
  Companions of our woe.

Sylvia, for all the pangs you see
  Are labouring in my breast;
I beg not you would favour me,
  Would you but slight the rest!

How great so e'er your rigours are,
    With them alone I'll cope;
I can endure my own despair,
    But not another's hope.

Sonnet on Death

What has this bugbear Death that's worth our care?
After a life in pain and sorrow past,
After deluding hope and dire despair,
Death only gives us quiet at the last.
How strangely are our love and hate misplaced!
Freedom we seek, and yet from freedom flee;
Courting those tyrant-sins that chain us fast,
And shunning Death that only sets us free.
'Tis not a foolish fear of future pains—
Why should they fear who keep their souls from stains?—
That makes me dread thy terrors, Death, to see;
'Tis not the loss of riches or of fame,
Or the vain toys the vulgar pleasures name:
'Tis nothing, Celia, but the losing thee.

MATTHEW PRIOR
(1664–1721)

An Ode

The merchant, to secure his treasure,
    Conveys it in a borrowed name;
Euphelia serves to grace my measure,
    But Cloe is my real flame.

My softest verse, my darling lyre,
    Upon Euphelia's toilet lay;
When Cloe noted her desire,
    That I should sing, that I should play.

My lyre I tune, my voice I raise;
  But with the numbers mix my sighs;
And whilst I sing Euphelia's praise,
  I fix my soul on Cloe's eyes.

Fair Cloe blushed; Euphelia frowned;
  I sung and gazed, I played and trembled;
And Venus to the Loves around
  Remarked, how ill we all dissembled.

Cupid's Mistaken

As after noon, one summer's day,
  Venus stood bathing in a river,
Cupid a-shooting went that way,
  New strung his bow, new filled his quiver.

With skill he chose his sharpest dart,
  With all his might his bow he drew;
Swift to his beauteous parent's heart
  The too well-guided arrow flew.

I faint! I die! the goddess cried,
  O cruel, couldst thou find none other
To wreck thy spleen on? Parricide!
  Like Nero, thou hast slain thy mother.

Poor Cupid sobbing scarce could speak;
  Indeed, mamma, I did not know ye;
Alas! how easy my mistake,
  I took you for your likeness, Cloe.

The Lady Who Offers Her Looking Glass

Venus, take my votive glass,
Since I am not what I was;
What from this day I shall be,
Venus, let me never see.

From the Greek of PLATO

To Cloe Jealous, a Better Answer

Dear Cloe, how blubber'd is that pretty face;
   Thy cheek all on fire, and thy hair all uncurl'd:
Prythee quit this caprice; and (as old Falstaff says)
   Let us e'en talk a little like folks of this world.

How canst thou presume, thou hast leave to destroy
   The beauties, which Venus but lent to thy keeping?
Those looks were design'd to inspire love and joy:
   More ord'nary eyes may serve people for weeping.

To be vex'd at a trifle or two that I writ,
   Your judgment at once, and my passion you wrong:
You take that for fact, which will scarce be found wit:
   Odds life! must one swear to the truth of a song?

What I speak, my fair Cloe, and what I write, shows
   The difference there is betwixt nature and art:
I court others in verse; but I love thee in prose:
   And they have my whimsies, but thou hast my heart.

The god of us verse-men (you know, child) the sun,
   How after his journeys he sets up his rest:
If at morning o'er earth 'tis his fancy to run;
   At night he declines on his Thetis's breast.

So when I am wearied with wandering all day,
   To thee, my delight, in the evening I come:
No matter what beauties I saw in my way;
   They were all but my visits, but thou art my home.

Then finish, dear Cloe, this pastoral war;
   And let us, like Horace and Lydia, agree:
For thou art a girl as much brighter than her,
   As he was a poet sublimer than me.

JONATHAN SWIFT

(1667–1745)

A Description of the Morning

Now hardly here and there a hackney coach
Appearing, showed the ruddy morn's approach.
Now Betty from her master's bed had flown,
And softly stole to discompose her own;
The slip-shod 'prentice from his master's door
Had pared the dirt and sprinkled round the floor.
Now Moll had whirled her mop with dext'rous airs,
Prepared to scrub the entry and the stairs.
The youth with broomy stumps began to trace
The kennel's edge, where wheels had worn the place.
The small-coal man was heard with cadence deep,
Till drowned in shriller notes of chimney-sweep:
Duns at his lordship's gate began to meet;
And brickdust Moll had screamed through half the street.
The turnkey now his flock returning sees,
Duly let out a-nights to steal for fees:
The watchful bailiffs take their silent stands,
And schoolboys lag with satchels in their hands.

FROM A Description of a City Shower

Ah! where must needy poet seek for aid,
When dust and rain at once his coat invade?
Sole coat! where dust cemented by the rain
Erects the nap, and leaves a cloudy stain!
Now in contiguous drops the flood comes down,
Threatening with deluge this *devoted* town.
To shops in crowds the daggled females fly,
Pretend to cheapen goods, but nothing buy.
The Templar spruce, while every spout's abroach,
Stays till 'tis fair, yet seems to call a coach.
The tucked-up sempstress walks with hasty strides,
While streams run down her oiled umbrella's sides.
Here various kinds, by various fortunes led,
Commence acquaintance underneath a shed.

Triumphant Tories and desponding Whigs
Forget their feuds, and join to save their wigs.
Boxed in a chair the beau impatient sits,
While spouts run clattering o'er the roof by fits,
And ever and anon with frightful din
The leather sounds; he trembles from within.

FROM *On the Death of Doctor Swift*

1.

The time is not remote when I
Must by the course of nature die;
When I foresee, my special friends
Will try to find their private ends:
And, though 'tis hardly understood
Which way my death can do them good,
Yet thus, methinks, I hear them speak:
"See, how the dean begins to break!
Poor gentleman, he droops apace!
You plainly find it in his face.
That old vertigo in his head
Will never leave him till he's dead.
Besides, his memory decays;
He recollects not what he says;
He cannot call his friends to mind;
Forgets the place where last he dined;
Plies you with stories o'er and o'er;
He told them fifty times before.
How does he fancy we can sit
To hear his out-of-fashion wit?
But he takes up with younger folks,
Who for his wine will bear his jokes.
Faith! he must make his stories shorter,
Or change his comrades once a quarter;
In half the time he talks them round,
There must another set be found.
For poetry he's past his prime;
He takes an hour to find a rhyme;
His fire is out, his wit decayed,
His fancy sunk, his Muse a jade.

I'd have them throw away his pen—
But there's no talking to some men."
And then their tenderness appears
By adding largely to my years:
"He's older than he would be reckoned,
And well remembers Charles the Second.
He hardly drinks a pint of wine;
And that, I doubt, is no good sign.
His stomach too begins to fail;
Last year we thought him strong and hale;
But now he's quite another thing;
I wish he may hold out till spring!"
They hug themselves, and reason thus:
"It is not yet so bad with us!"

2.

Behold the fatal day arrive!
"How is the dean?" "He's just alive."
Now the departing prayer is read.
"He hardly breathes." "The dean is dead."
Before the passing bell begun,
The news through half the town is run.
"O! may we all for death prepare!
What has he left? and who's his heir?"
"I know no more than what the news is;
'Tis all bequeathed to public uses."
"To public uses! There's a whim!
What had the public done for him?
Mere envy, avarice, and pride;
He gave it all—but first he died.
And had the dean in all the nation
No worthy friend, no poor relation?
So ready to do strangers good,
Forgetting his own flesh and blood!"

3.

From Dublin soon to London spread,
'Tis told at Court, "the dean is dead."
And Lady Suffolk, in the spleen,
Runs laughing up to tell the Queen.

The Queen, so gracious, mild, and good,
Cries: "Is he gone? 'Tis time he should.
He's dead, you say; then let him rot;
I'm glad the medals were forgot.
I promised him, I own; but when?
I only was the Princess then;
But now, as consort of the King,
You know 'tis quite another thing."
Now Chartres, at Sir Robert's levee,
Tells with a sneer the tidings heavy:
"Why, if he died without his shoes,"
Cries Bob, "I'm sorry for the news;
Oh, were the wretch but living still,
And in his place my good friend Will!
Or had a mitre on his head,
Provided Bolingbroke were dead!"
Now Curll his shop from rubbish drains;
Three genuine tomes of Swift's remains!
And then to make them pass the glibber,
Revised by Tibbalds, Moore, and Cibber.
He'll treat me as he does my betters,
Publish my will, my life, my letters;
Revive the libels born to die;
Which Pope must bear as well as I.

4.

My female friends, whose tender hearts
Have better learned to act their parts,
Receive the news in doleful dumps:
"The dean is dead—pray what is trumps?—
The Lord have mercy on his soul!
—Ladies, I'll venture for the vole.—
Six deans, they say, must bear the pall—
I wish I knew what king to call.—
Madam, your husband will attend
The funeral of so good a friend?
No, madam, 'tis a shocking sight,
And he's engaged to-morrow night;
My Lady Club will take it ill
If he should fail her at quadrille.

He loved the dean—I lead a heart—
But dearest friends, they say, must part.
His time was come, he ran his race;
We hope he's in a better place."

5.

"He gave the little wealth he had
To build a house for fools and mad;
And showed by one satiric touch
No nation wanted it so much.
That kingdom he had left his debtor,
I wish it soon may have a better."

WILLIAM CONGREVE

(1670–1729)

Song

False though she be to me and love,
    I'll ne'er pursue revenge;
For still the charmer I approve,
    Though I deplore her change.

In hours of bliss we oft have met;
    They could not always last;
And though the present I regret,
    I'm grateful for the past.

Amoret

Fair Amoret is gone astray;
    Pursue and seek her, every lover;
I'll tell the signs by which you may
    The wandering shepherdess discover.

Coquet and coy at once her air,
    Both studied, though both seem neglected;
Careless she is with artful care,
    Affecting to seem unaffected.

With skill her eyes dart every glance,
    Yet change so soon you'd ne'er suspect them;
For she'd persuade they wound by chance,
    Though certain aim and art direct them.

She likes herself, yet others hates
    For that which in herself she prizes;
And, while she laughs at them, forgets
    She is the thing that she despises.

FROM *The Mourning Bride,* 1697

Almeria: Music has charms to soothe a savage breast,
    To soften rocks, or bend a knotted oak.
    I've read that things inanimate have moved,
    And, as with living souls, have been informed,
    By magic numbers and persuasive sound.
    What then am I? O force of constant woe!
    'Tis not in harmony to calm my griefs . . .
    Why do I live to say you are no more?

SIR RICHARD STEELE

(1672–1729)

Song

Why, lovely charmer, tell me why,
So very kind, so very shy?
Why does that cold forbidding air
Give damps of sorrow and despair?
Or why that smile my soul subdue,
And kindle up my flames anew?

In vain you strive with all your art,
By turns to freeze and fire my heart:
When I behold a face so fair,
So sweet a look, so soft an air,
My ravished soul is charmed all o'er,
I cannot love thee less nor more.

The Tender Husband, 1705

ABEL EVANS
(1679–1737)

Epitaph on Sir John Vanbrugh

Under this stone, reader, survey
Dead Sir John Vanbrugh's house of clay.
Lie heavy on him, Earth! for he
Laid many heavy loads on thee!

EDWARD YOUNG
(1683–1765)

Extempore to Voltaire Criticising Milton

You are so witty, profligate and thin,
At once we think you Milton, death, and sin.

GEORGE BERKELEY
(1685–1753)

Verses on the Prospect of Planting Arts and Learning in America

The Muse, disgusted at an age and clime
    Barren of every glorious theme,
In distant lands now waits a better time,
    Producing subjects worthy fame:

In happy climes, where from the genial sun
    And virgin earth such scenes ensue,
The force of art by nature seems outdone,
    And fancied beauties by the true:

In happy climes, the seat of innocence,
    Where nature guides and virtue rules,
Where men shall not impose for truth and sense
    The pedantry of courts and schools:

There shall be sung another golden age,
   The rise of empire and of arts,
The good and great inspiring epic rage,
   The wisest heads, and noblest hearts.

Not such as Europe breeds in her decay;
   Such as she bred when fresh and young,
When heavenly flame did animate her clay,
   By future poets shall be sung.

Westward the course of empire takes its way;
   The first four acts already past,
A fifth shall close the drama with the day;
   Time's noblest offspring is the last.

JOHN GAY

(1685–1732)

Ballad

'Twas when the seas were roaring
   With hollow blasts of wind;
A damsel lay deploring,
   All on a rock reclined.
Wide o'er the rolling billows
   She cast a wistful look;
Her head was crowned with willows
   That tremble o'er the brook.

Twelve months are gone and over,
   And nine long tedious days.
Why didst thou, vent'rous lover,
   Why didst thou trust the seas?
Cease, cease, thou cruel ocean,
   And let my lover rest;
Ah! what's thy troubled motion
   To that within my breast?

The merchant robbed of pleasure
    Sees tempests in despair;
But what's the loss of treasure
    To losing of my dear?
Should you some coast be laid on
    Where gold and di'monds grow,
You'd find a richer maiden,
    But none that loves you so.

How can they say that nature
    Has nothing made in vain,
Why then beneath the water
    Should hideous rocks remain?
No eyes the rocks discover,
    That lurk beneath the deep,
To wreck the wand'ring lover,
    And leave the maid to weep.

All melancholy lying,
    Thus wailed she for her dear;
Repaid each blast with sighing,
    Each billow with a tear;
When, o'er the white wave stooping,
    His floating corpse she spied;
Then like a lily drooping,
    She bowed her head, and died.

                    The What D'ye Call It, 1715

Love in Her Eyes Sits Playing

Love in her eyes sits playing,
    And sheds delicious death;
Love in her lips sits straying,
    And warbling in her breath.
Love on her breast sits panting,
    And swells with soft desire;
No grace, no charm is wanting
    To set the heart on fire.

                    Acis and Galatea, 1732

O Ruddier Than the Cherry

O ruddier than the cherry,
O sweeter than the berry,
　O Nymph more bright
　Than moonshine night,
Like kidlings blithe and merry.
Ripe as the melting cluster,
No lily has such lustre,
　Yet hard to tame
　As raging flame,
And fierce as storms that bluster.

Acis and Galatea, 1732

Air XXXV

How happy could I be with either,
　Were t'other dear charmer away!
But while you thus tease me together,
　To neither a word will I say:
　　But tol de rol.

The Beggar's Opera, 1728

Air XXIII

　Sleep, O sleep,
With thy rod of incantation,
Charm my imagination.
Then, only then, I cease to weep.
　By thy power,
The virgin, by time o'ertaken,
For years forlorn, forsaken,
Enjoys the happy hour.
　What's to sleep?
'Tis a visionary blessing;
A dream that's past expressing;
Our utmost wish possessing;
　So may I always keep.

Polly, 1729

FROM *The Fan*

Rise, happy youth, this bright machine survey,
Whose rattling sticks my busy fingers sway,
This present shall thy cruel charmer move,
And in her fickle bosom kindle love.
The fan shall flutter in all female hands,
And various fashions learn from various lands.
For this shall elephants their ivory shed,
And polished sticks the waving engine spread;
His clouded mail the tortoise shall resign,
And round the rivet pearly circles shine.
On this shall Indians all their art employ,
And with bright colours stain the gaudy toy;
Their paint shall here in wildest fancies flow,
Their dress, their customs, their religion show,
So shall the British fair their minds improve,
And on the fan to distant climates rove.
Here China's ladies shall their pride display,
And silver figures gild their loose array;
This boasts her little feet and winking eyes;
That tunes the fife, or tinkling cymbal plies;
Here cross-legged nobles in rich state shall dine,
There in bright mail distorted heroes shine.
The peeping fan in modern times shall rise
Through which unseen the female ogle flies;
This shall in temples the sly maid conceal,
And shelter love beneath devotion's veil.
Gay France shall make the fan her artist's care,
And with the costly trinket arm the fair.
As learned orators that touch the heart,
With various actions raise their soothing art,
Both head and hand affect the listening throng,
And humour each expression of the tongue.
So shall each passion by the fan be seen,
From noisy anger to the sullen spleen.

His Own Epitaph

Life is a jest, and all things show it;
I thought so once, and now I know it.

ALLAN RAMSAY

(1686–1758)

FROM "An Thou Were My Ain Thing"

An thou were my ain thing,
I wou'd love thee, I wou'd love thee;
An thou were my ain thing,
    How dearly wou'd I love thee!

Like bees that suck the morning dew,
Frae flow'rs of sweetest scent and hue,
Sae would I dwell upon thy mow,
    And gar the gods envy me.

Sae lang's I had the use of light
I'd on thy beauties feast my sight,
Syne in saft whispers through the night
    I'd tell how much I love thee.

Time's on the wing and will not stay,
In shining youth let's make our hay;
Since love admits of no delay,
    O, let nae scorn undo thee.

An thou were my ain thing,
I wou'd love thee, I wou'd love thee;
And thou were my ain thing,
    How dearly wou'd I love thee.

Peggy

My Peggy is a young thing,
    Just entered in her teens,
Fair as the day, and sweet as May,
Fair as the day, and always gay.

Mow, mouth. Gar, make.

My Peggy is a young thing,
    And I'm not very auld,
Yet well I like to meet her at
    The wauking of the fauld.

My Peggy speaks sae sweetly,
    Whene'er we meet alane,
I wish nae mair to lay my care,
I wish nae mair of a' that's rare.
    My Peggy speaks sae sweetly,
        To a' the lave I'm cauld;
    But she gars a' my spirits glow
        At wauking of the fauld.

My Peggy smiles sae kindly,
    Whene'er I whisper love,
That I look doun on a' the toun,
That I look doun upon a croun.
    My Peggy smiles sae kindly,
        It makes me blythe and bauld,
    And naething gi'es me sic delight
        As wauking of the fauld.

My Peggy sings sae saftly,
    When on my pipe I play;
By a' the rest it is confessed,
By a' the rest, that she sings best.
    My Peggy sings sae saftly,
        And in her sangs are tald,
    With innocence, the wale of sense,
        At wauking of the fauld.

HENRY CAREY

(1687–1743)

Sally in Our Alley

Of all the girls that are so smart
    There's none like pretty Sally;
She is the darling of my heart,
    And she lives in our alley.

Wauking, watching. The lave, the rest. Bauld, bold. Wale, pick.

There's ne'er a lady in the land
    That's half so sweet as Sally;
She is the darling of my heart,
    And she lives in our alley.

Her father he makes cabbage-nets,
    And thro' the street does cry 'em;
Her mother she sells laces long
    To such as please to buy 'em;
But sure such folks could ne'er beget
    So sweet a girl as Sally;
She is the darling of my heart,
    And she lives in our alley.

When she is by I leave my work,
    I love her so sincerely:
My master comes like any Turk
    And bangs me most severely;
But let him bang his bellyful,
    I'll bear it all for Sally;
She is the darling of my heart,
    And she lives in our alley.

Of all the days that's in the week
    I dearly love but one day,
And that's the day that comes betwixt
    A Saturday and Monday,
For then I'm dressed in all my best
    To walk abroad with Sally;
She is the darling of my heart,
    And she lives in our alley.

My master carries me to church,
    And often am I blamed
Because I leave him in the lurch
    As soon as text is named;
I leave the church in sermon time
    And slink away to Sally;
She is the darling of my heart,
    And she lives in our alley.

When Christmas comes about again,
  O, then I shall have money;
I'll hoard it up, and box and all,
  I'll give it to my honey;
And would it were ten thousand pounds,
  I'd give it all to Sally;
She is the darling of my heart,
  And she lives in our alley.

My master and the neighbours all
  Make game of me and Sally,
And, but for her, I'd better be
  A slave, and row a galley;
But when my seven long years are out,
  O, then I'll marry Sally;
O, then we'll wed, and then we'll bed,
  But not in our alley.

ALEXANDER POPE

(1688–1744)

Ode on Solitude

Happy the man whose wish and care
  A few paternal acres bound,
Content to breath his native air,
    In his own ground.

Whose herds with milk, whose fields with bread,
  Whose flocks supply him with attire,
Whose trees in summer yield him shade,
    In winter fire.

Blest, who can unconcern'dly find
  Hours, days, and years slide soft away,
In health of body, peace of mind,
    Quiet by day,

Sound sleep by night; study and ease,
  Together mixt; sweet recreation;
And Innocence, which most does please
    With meditation.

Thus let me live, unseen, unknown,
Thus unlamented, let me die,
Steal from the world, and not a stone
Tell where I lie.

FROM An Essay on Criticism

'Tis with our judgments as our watches, none
Go just alike, yet each believes his own.
In poets as true genius is but rare,
True taste as seldom is the critic's share;
Both must alike from Heav'n derive their light,
These born to judge, as well as those to write.
Let such teach others who themselves excel,
And censure freely who have written well.
Authors are partial to their wit, 'tis true,
But are not critics to their judgment too?

Yet if we look more closely, we shall find
Most have the seeds of judgment in their mind:
Nature affords at least a glimm'ring light;
The lines, though touched but faintly, are drawn right.
But as the slightest sketch, if justly traced,
Is by ill-colouring but the more disgraced,
So by false learning is good sense defaced:
Some are bewildered in the maze of schools,
And some made coxcombs Nature meant but fools.
In search of wit these lose their common sense,
And then turn critics in their own defence:
Each burns alike, who can, or cannot write,
Or with a rival's, or an eunuch's spite.
All fools have still an itching to deride,
And fain would be upon the laughing side.
If Maevius scribble in Apollo's spite,
There are who judge still worse than he can write.

Some have at first for wits, then poets past,
Turned critics next, and proved plain fools at last.
Some neither can for wits nor critics pass,
As heavy mules are neither horse nor ass.

Those half-learn'd witlings, num'rous in our isle,
As half-formed insects on the banks of Nile;
Unfinished things, one knows not what to call,
Their generation's so equivocal:
To tell 'em, would a hundred tongues require,
Or one vain wit's, that might a hundred tire.

FROM *The Rape of the Lock*

Not with more glories, in th'etherial plain,
The Sun first rises o'er the purpled main,
Than, issuing forth, the rival of his beams
Launched on the bosom of the silver Thames.
Fair nymphs and well-drest youths around her shone
But ev'ry eye was fixed on her alone.
On her white breast a sparkling cross she wore,
Which Jews might kiss, and infidels adore.
Her lively looks a sprightly mind disclose,
Quick as her eyes, and as unfixed as those:
Favours to none, to all she smiles extends;
Oft she rejects, but never once offends.
Bright as the sun, her eyes the gazers strike,
And, like the sun, they shine on all alike.
Yet graceful ease, and sweetness void of pride,
Might hide her faults, if belles had faults to hide:
If to her share some female errors fall,
Look on her face, and you'll forget 'em all.

This Nymph, to the destruction of mankind,
Nourished two locks, which graceful hung behind
In equal curls, and well conspired to deck
With shining ringlets the smooth iv'ry neck.
Love in these labyrinths his slaves detains,
And mighty hearts are held in slender chains.
With hairy springes we the birds betray,
Slight lines of hair surprise the finny prey,
Fair tresses man's imperial race ensnare,
And beauty draws us with a single hair.

2.

    Ye Sylphs and Sylphids, to your chief give ear!
Fays, Fairies, Genii, Elves, and Daemons, hear!
Ye know the spheres and various tasks assigned
By laws eternal to th'aërial kind.
Some in the fields of purest aether play,
And bask and whiten in the blaze of day.
Some guide the course of wand'ring orbs on high,
Or roll the planets through the boundless sky.
Some less refined, beneath the moon's pale light
Pursue the stars that shoot athwart the night,
Or suck the mists in grosser air below,
Or dip their pinions in the painted bow,
Or brew fierce tempests on the wintry main,
Or o'er the glebe distil the kindly rain.
Others on earth o'er human race preside,
Watch all their ways, and all their actions guide:
Of these the chief the care of Nations own,
And guard with Arms divine the British Throne.

    Our humbler province is to tend the Fair,
Not a less pleasing, though less glorious care;
To save the powder from too rude a gale,
Nor let th'imprisoned essences exhale;
To draw fresh colours from the vernal flowers;
To steal from rainbows ere they drop in showers
A brighter wash; to curl their waving hairs,
Assist their blushes, and inspire their airs;
Nay oft, in dreams, invention we bestow,
To change a Flounce, or add a Furbelow.

    This day, black Omens threat the brightest Fair,
That ere deserved a watchful spirit's care;
Some dire disaster, or by force, or sleight;
But what, or where, the fates have wrapped in night.
Whether the nymph shall break Diana's law,
Or some frail China jar receive a flaw;
Or stain her honour or her new brocade;
Forget her pray'rs, or miss a masquerade;
Or lose her heart, or necklace, at a ball;
Or whether Heav'n has doomed that Shock must fall.

Haste, then, ye spirits! to your charge repair:
The flutt'ring fan be Zephyretta's care;
The drops to thee, Brillante, we consign;
And, Momentilla, let the watch be thine;
Do thou, Crispissa, tend her fav'rite lock;
Ariel himself shall be the guard of Shock.

To fifty chosen Sylphs, of special note,
We trust th'important charge, the Petticoat:
Oft have we known that seven-fold fence to fail,
Though stiff with hoops, and armed with ribs of whale;
Form a strong line about the silver bound,
And guard the wide circumference around.

Whatever spirit, careless of his charge,
His post neglects, or leaves the fair at large,
Shall feel sharp vengeance soon o'ertake his sins,
Be stopped in vials, or transfixed with pins;
Or plunged in lakes of bitter washes lie,
Or wedged whole ages in a bodkin's eye:
Gums and Pomatums shall his flight restrain,
While clogged he beats his silken wings in vain;
Or Alum styptics with contracting power
Shrink his thin essence like a rivel'd flower:
Or, as Ixion fixed, the wretch shall feel
The giddy motion of the whirling Mill,
In fumes of burning Chocolate shall glow,
And tremble at the sea that froths below!

3.

For lo! the board with cups and spoons is crowned,
The berries crackle, and the mill turns round;
On shining altars of Japan they raise
The silver lamp; the fiery spirits blaze:
From silver spouts the grateful liquors glide,
While China's earth receives the smoking tide:
At once they gratify their scent and taste,
And frequent cups prolong the rich repast.
Straight hover round the Fair her airy band;
Some, as she sipped, the fuming liquor fanned,

Some o'er her lap their careful plumes displayed,
Trembling, and conscious of the rich brocade.
Coffee (which makes the politician wise,
And see through all things with his half-shut eyes)
Sent up in vapours to the Baron's brain
New stratagems the radiant Lock to gain.
Ah cease, rash youth! desist ere 'tis too late,
Fear the just Gods, and think of Scylla's fate!
Changed to a bird, and sent to flit in air,
She dearly pays for Nisus' injured hair!

But when to mischief mortals bend their will,
How soon they find fit instruments of ill!
Just then, Clarissa drew with tempting grace
A two-edged weapon from her shining case:
So ladies in Romance assist their knight,
Present the spear, and arm him for the fight.
He takes the gift with rev'rence, and extends
The little engine on his fingers' ends;
This just behind Belinda's neck he spread,
As o'er the fragrant steams she bends her head.
Swift to the Lock a thousand sprites repair,
A thousand wings, by turns, blow back the hair;
And thrice they twitched the diamond in her ear;
Thrice she looked back, and thrice the foe drew near.
Just in that instant, anxious Ariel sought
The close recesses of the Virgin's thought;
As on the nosegay in her breast reclined,
He watched th'Ideas rising in her mind,
Sudden he viewed, in spite of all her art,
An earthly Lover lurking at her heart.
Amazed, confused, he found his pow'r expired,
Resigned to fate, and with a sigh retired.

The Peer now spreads the glitt'ring forfex wide,
T'enclose the Lock; now joins it, to divide.
Ev'n then, before the fatal engine closed,
A wretched Sylph too fondly interposed;
Fate urged the shears, and cut the Sylph in twain,
(But airy substance soon unites again)

The meeting points the sacred hair dissever
From the fair head, for ever and for ever!
Then flashed the living lightning from her eyes,
And screams of horror rend th'affrighted skies.
Not louder shrieks to pitying heav'n are cast,
When husbands, or when lapdogs breathe their last;
Or when rich China vessels fall'n from high,
In glitt'ring dust and painted fragments lie!

FROM *Eloisa to Abelard*

How oft, when pressed to marriage, have I said,
Curse on all laws but those which love has made?
Love, free as air, at sight of human ties,
Spreads his light wings, and in a moment flies.
Let wealth, let honour, wait the wedded dame,
August her deed, and sacred be her fame;
Before true passion all those views remove,
Fame, wealth, and honour! what are you to Love?
The jealous God, when we profane his fires,
Those restless passions in revenge inspires,
And bids them make mistaken mortals groan,
Who seek in love for aught but love alone.
Should at my feet the world's great master fall,
Himself, his throne, his world, I'd scorn 'em all:
Not Caesar's empress would I deign to prove;
No, make me mistress to the man I love;
If there be yet another name more free,
More fond than mistress, make me that to thee!
Oh! happy state! when souls each other draw,
When love is liberty, and nature law:
All then is full, possessing, and possessed,
No craving void left aching in the breast:
Ev'n thought meets thought, ere from the lips it part,
And each warm wish springs mutual from the heart,
This sure is bliss (if bliss on earth there be)
And once the lot of Abelard and me.

FROM *Essay on Man*

1.

Heav'n from all creatures hides the book of Fate,
All but the page prescribed, their present state:
From brutes what men, from men what spirits know:
Or who could suffer Being here below?
The lamb thy riot dooms to bleed to-day,
Had he thy Reason, would he skip and play?
Pleased to the last, he crops the flow'ry food,
And licks the hand just raised to shed his blood.
Oh blindness to the future! kindly giv'n,
That each may fill the circle marked by Heav'n:
Who sees with equal eye, as God by all,
A hero perish, or a sparrow fall,
Atoms or systems into ruin hurled,
And now a bubble burst and now a world.

Hope humbly then; with trembling pinions soar;
Wait the great teacher Death; and God adore.
What future bliss, He gives not thee to know,
But gives that Hope to be thy blessing now.
Hope springs eternal in the human breast:
Man never Is, but always To be blest:
The soul, uneasy and confined from home,
Rests and expatiates in a life to come.

2.

Know then thyself, presume not God to scan;
The proper study of Mankind is Man.
Placed on this isthmus of a middle state,
A Being darkly wise, and rudely great:
With too much knowledge for the Sceptic side,
With too much weakness for the Stoic's pride,
He hangs between; in doubt to act, or rest;
In doubt to deem himself a God, or Beast;
In doubt his Mind or Body to prefer;
Born but to die, and reas'ning but to err;
Alike in ignorance, his reason such,
Whether he thinks too little, or too much:

Chaos of Thought and Passion, all confused;
Still by himself abused, or disabused;
Created half to rise, and half to fall;
Great lord of all things, yet a prey to all;
Sole judge of Truth, in endless Error hurled:
The glory, jest, and riddle of the world!

3.

For Forms of Government let fools contest;
Whate'er is best administered is best:
For Modes of Faith let graceless zealots fight;
He can't be wrong whose life is in the right:
In Faith and Hope the world will disagree,
But all Mankind's concern is Charity,
All must be false that thwart this One great End;
And all of God, that bless Mankind or mend.

4.

What's Fame? a fancied life in others' breath,
A thing beyond us, ev'n before our death.
Just what you hear, you have, and what's unknown
The same (my Lord) if Tully's, or your own.
All that we feel of it begins and ends
In the small circle of our foes or friends;
To all beside as much an empty shade
As Eugene living, as a Caesar dead;
Alike or when, or where, they shone, or shine,
Or on the Rubicon, or on the Rhine.
A Wit's a feather, and a Chief a rod;
An honest Man's the noblest work of God.
Fame but from death a villain's name can save,
As Justice tears his body from the grave;
When what t'oblivion better were resigned,
Is hung on high, to poison half mankind.
All fame is foreign, but of true desert;
Plays round the head, but comes not to the heart:
One self-approving hour whole years out-weighs
Of stupid starers, and of loud huzzas;
And more true joy Marcellus exiled feels,
Than Caesar with a senate at his heels.

In Parts superior what advantage lies?
Tell (for You can) what is it to be wise?
'Tis but to know how little can be known;
To see all others' faults, and feel our own:
Condemned in business or in arts to drudge,
Without a second, or without a judge:
Truths would you teach, or save a sinking land,
All fear, none aid you, and few understand.
Painful pre-eminence! yourself to view
Above life's weakness, and its comforts too.

Bring then these blessings to a strict account;
Make fair deductions; see to what they mount:
How much of other each is sure to cost;
How each for other oft is wholly lost;
How inconsistent greater goods with these;
How sometimes life is risked, and always ease:
Think, and if still the things thy envy call,
Say, would'st thou be the Man to whom they fall?
To sigh for ribbands if thou art so silly,
Mark how they grace Lord Umbra, or Sir Billy:
Is yellow dirt the passion of thy life?
Look but on Gripus, or on Gripus' wife:
If Parts allure thee, think how Bacon shined,
The wisest, brightest, meanest of mankind:
Or ravished with the whistling of a name,
See Cromwell damned to everlasting fame!

5.

Search then the Ruling Passion: there, alone,
The Wild are constant, and the Cunning known;
The Fool consistent, and the False sincere;
Priests, Princes, Women, no dissemblers here.
This clue once found, unravels all the rest,
The prospect clears, and Wharton stands confest.
Wharton, the scorn and wonder of our days,
Whose ruling passion was the lust of praise:
Born with whate'er could win it from the wise,
Women and fools must like him or he dies;
Though wond'ring Senates hung on all he spoke,

The Club must hail him master of the joke.
Shall parts so various aim at nothing new?
He'll shine a Tully and a Wilmot too.
Then turns repentant, and his God adores
With the same spirit that he drinks and whores;
Enough if all around him but admire,
And now the Punk applaud, and now the Friar.
Thus with each gift of nature and of art,
And wanting nothing but an honest heart;
Grown all to all, from no one vice exempt;
And most contemptible, to shun contempt:
His passion still, to covet gen'ral praise,
His life, to forfeit it a thousand ways;
A constant bounty which no friend has made;
An angel tongue, which no man can persuade;
A fool with more of wit than half mankind,
Too rash for thought, for action too refined.
A tyrant to the wife his heart approves;
A rebel to the very king he loves;
He dies, sad outcast of each church and state,
And harder still! flagitious, yet not great.
Ask you why Wharton broke through ev'ry rule?
'Twas all for fear the knaves should call him Fool.

FROM *Epistle to Dr. Arbuthnot*

1.

Why did I write? what sin to me unknown
Dipt me in ink, my parents', or my own?
As yet a child, not yet a fool to fame,
I lisped in numbers, for the numbers came.
I left no calling for this idle trade,
No duty broke, no father disobeyed.
The Muse but served to ease some friend, not wife,
To help me through this long disease, my life . . .

2.

Peace to all such! but were there One whose fires
True genius kindles, and fair fame inspires;
Blest with each talent and each art to please,
And born to write, converse, and live with ease:

Should such a man, too fond to rule alone,
Bear, like the Turk, no brother near the throne;
View him with scornful, yet with jealous eyes,
And hate for arts that caused himself to rise;
Damn with faint praise, assent with civil leer,
And without sneering, teach the rest to sneer;
Willing to wound, and yet afraid to strike,
Just hint a fault, and hesitate dislike;
Alike reserved to blame, or to commend,
A tim'rous foe, and a suspicious friend;
Dreading ev'n fools, by flatterers besieged,
And so obliging, that he ne'er obliged;
Like Cato, give his little Senate laws,
And sit attentive to his own applause;
While wits and Templars ev'ry sentence raise,
And wonder with a foolish face of praise—
Who but must laugh, if such a man there be?
Who would not weep, if Atticus were he?

Let Sporus tremble—A. What? that thing of silk,
Sporus, that mere white curd of ass's milk?
Satire or sense, alas! can Sporus feel?
Who breaks a butterfly upon a wheel?
P. Yet let me flap this bug with gilded wings,
This painted child of dirt, that stinks and stings;
Whose buzz the witty and the fair annoys,
Yet wit ne'er tastes, and beauty ne'er enjoys:
So well-bred spaniels civilly delight
In mumbling of the game they dare not bite.
Eternal smiles his emptiness betray,
As shallow streams run dimpling all the way.
Whether in florid impotence he speaks,
And, as the prompter breathes, the puppet squeaks;
Or at the ear of Eve, familiar Toad,
Half froth, half venom, spits himself abroad,
In puns, or politics, or tales, or lies,
Or spite, or smut, or rhymes, or blasphemies.
His wit all see-saw, between *that* and *this*,
Now high, now low, now master up, now miss,
And he himself one vile Antithesis.

Amphibious thing! that acting either part,
The trifling head or the corrupted heart,
Fop at the toilet, flatt'rer at the board,
Now trips a Lady, and now struts a Lord.
Eve's tempter thus the rabbins have exprest,
A cherub's face, a reptile all the rest;
Beauty that shocks you, parts that none will trust;
Wit that can creep, and pride that licks the dust.

FROM *The Dunciad*

In vain, in vain—the all-composing hour
Resistless falls: the Muse obeys the Power.
She comes! she comes! the sable throne behold
Of Night primaeval and of Chaos old!
Before her, Fancy's gilded clouds decay,
And all its varying rainbows die away.
Wit shoots in vain its momentary fires,
The meteor drops, and in a flash expires.
As one by one, at dread Medea's strain,
The sickening stars fade off th'ethereal plain;
As Argus' eyes by Hermes' wand opprest,
Closed one by one to everlasting rest;
Thus at her felt approach, and secret might,
Art after Art goes out, and all is Night.
See skulking Truth to her old cavern fled,
Mountains of Casuistry heaped o'er her head!
Philosophy, that leaned on Heav'n before,
Shrinks to her second cause, and is no more.
Physic of Metaphysic begs defence,
And Metaphysic calls for aid on Sense!
See Mystery to Mathematics fly!
In vain! they gaze, turn giddy, rave, and die.
Religion blushing veils her sacred fires,
And unaware Morality expires.
Nor public flame, nor private, dares to shine;
Nor human spark is left, nor glimpse divine!
Lo! thy dread empire, Chaos, is restored;
Light dies before thy uncreating word;
Thy hand, great Anarch! lets the curtain fall,
And universal darkness buries all.

Epitaph on Sir Isaac Newton

Nature and Nature's laws lay hid in night;
God said: "Let Newton be", and all was light.

THOMAS WARTON THE ELDER
(1688–1745)

FROM *Retirement, an Ode*

Joy, rose-lipped dryad, loves to dwell
In sunny field or mossy cell,
Delights on echoing hills to hear
The reaper's song or lowing steer;
Or view with tenfold plenty spread
The crowded cornfield, blooming mead;
While beauty, health, and innocence
Transport the eye, the soul, the sense.

Nymphs of the grove in green arrayed,
Conduct me to your thickest shade,
Deep in the bosom of the vale,
Where haunts the lonesome nightingale;
Where Contemplation, maid divine,
Leans against some aged pine,
Wrapped in steadfast thought profound,
Her eyes fixed steadfast on the ground.

O Virtue's nurse! retired Queen,
By saints alone and virtues seen,
Beyond vain mortals' wishes wise,
Teach me St. James's to despise;
For what are courts, but schools
For fops, or hospitals for fools?
Where slaves and madmen, young and old,
Meet to adore some Calf of Gold.

JOHN BYROM

(1692–1763)

A Toast

God bless the King!—I mean the Faith's defender;
God bless—no harm in blessing—the Pretender!
But who Pretender is, or who is King—
God bless us all! that's quite another thing.

WILLIAM OLDYS

(1696–1761)

On a Fly Drinking Out of His Cup

Busy, curious, thirsty fly!
Drink with me and drink as I;
Freely welcome to my cup,
Couldst thou sip and sip it up:
Make the most of life you may,
Life is short and wears away.

Just alike, both mine and thine,
Hasten quick to their decline:
Thine's a summer, mine no more,
Though repeated to three-score.
Three-score summers, when they're gone,
Will appear as short as one!

ROBERT BLAIR

(1699–1746)

FROM The Grave

See yonder hallowed fane, the pious work
Of names once famed, now dubious or forgot,
And buried midst the wreck of things which were:
There lie interred the more illustrious dead.
The wind is up: hark how it howls! Methinks
Till now I never heard a sound so dreary.
Doors creak, and windows clap, and night's foul bird,

Rooked in the spire, screams loud. The gloomy aisles,
Black-plaistered, and hung round with shreds of 'scutcheons
And tattered coats of arms, send back the sound,
Laden with heavier airs, from the low vaults,
The mansions of the dead. Roused from their slumbers,
In grim array the grisly spectres rise,
Grin horribly, and obstinately sullen
Pass and repass, hushed as the foot of night.
Again the screech owl shrieks– ungracious sound.
I'll hear no more; it makes one's blood run chill.
Quite round the pile, a row of reverend elms,
Co-eval near with that, all ragged show,
Long lashed by the rude winds; some rift half down
Their branchless trunks, others so thin atop
That scarce two crows could lodge in the same tree.
Strange things, the neighbours say, have happened here.
Wild shrieks have issued from the hollow tombs;
Dead men have come again, and walked about;
And the great bell has tolled unrung, untouched.
Such tales their cheer, at wake or gossiping,
When it draws near the witching time of night.

JOHN DYER

(1700?–1758)

FROM Grongar Hill

Old castles on the cliff arise,
Proudly towering in the skies.
Rushing from the woods, the spires
Seem from hence ascending fires.

Below me, trees unnumbered rise,
Beautiful in various dyes:
The gloomy pine, the poplar blue,
The yellow beech, the sable yew,
The slender fir that taper grows,
The sturdy oak with broad-spread boughs.
And beyond the purple grove,
Haunt of Phyllis, queen of love,

Gaudy as the opening dawn,
Lies a long and level lawn,
On which a dark hill, steep and high,
Holds and charms the wandering eye.
Deep are his feet in Towy's flood,
His sides are clothed with waving wood,
And ancient towers crown his brow,
That cast an aweful look below;
Whose ragged walls the ivy creeps,
And with her arms from falling keeps.

Yet time has seen that lifts the low,
And level lays the lofty brow,
Has seen this broken pile complete,
Big with the vanity of state.
But transient is the smile of fate;
A little rule, a little sway,
A sunbeam in a winter's day,
Is all the proud and mighty have
Between the cradle and the grave.

JAMES THOMSON THE ELDER
(1700–1748)

FROM *The Castle of Indolence*

I.

In lowly dale, fast by a river's side,
With woody hill o'er hill encompassed round,
A most enchanting wizard did abide,
Than whom a fiend more fell is nowhere found.
It was, I ween, a lovely spot of ground;
And there a season atween June and May,
Half prankt with spring, with summer half imbrowned,
A listless climate made, where, sooth to say,
No living wight could work, ne caréd even for play.

Was nought around but images of rest:
Sleep-soothing groves, and quiet lawns between;
And flowery beds that slumbrous influence kest,
From poppies breathed; and beds of pleasant green,
Where never yet was creeping creature seen.

Meantime unnumbered glittering streamlets played,
And hurléd everywhere their waters sheen;
That, as they bickered through the sunny glade,
Though restless still themselves, a lulling murmur made.

Joined to the prattle of the purling rills,
Were heard the lowing herds along the vale,
And flocks loud-bleating from the distant hills,
And vacant shepherds piping in the dale:
And now and then sweet Philomel would wail,
Or stock-droves plain amid the forest deep,
That drowsy rustled to the sighing gale;
And still a coil the grasshopper did keep:
Yet all these sounds yblent inclinéd all to sleep.

Full in the passage of the vale, above,
A sable, silent, solemn forest stood;
Where nought but shadowy forms were seen to move,
As Idless fancied in her dreaming mood.
And up the hills, on either side, a wood
Of blackening pines, ay waving to and fro,
Sent forth a sleepy horror through the blood;
And where this valley winded out, below,
The murmuring main was heard, and scarcely heard, to flow

A pleasing land of drowsyhed it was:
Of dreams that wave before the half-shut eye;
And of gay castles in the clouds that pass,
For ever flushing round a summer sky:
There eke the soft delights, that witchingly
Instil a wanton sweetness through the breast,
And the calm pleasures always hovered nigh;
But whate'er smacked of noyance, or unrest,
Was far far off expelled from this delicious nest.

The landskip such, inspiring perfect ease;
Where Indolence (for so the wizard hight)
Close-hid his castle mid embowering trees,
That half shut out the beams of Phoebus bright,
And made a kind of checkered day and night.

2.

    The doors that knew no shrill alarming bell,
    Ne curséd knocker plied by villain's hand,
    Self-opened into halls, where, who can tell
    What elegance and grandeur wide expand
    The pride of Turkey and of Persia land?
    Soft quilts on quilts, on carpets carpets spread,
    And couches stretched around in seemly band;
    And endless pillows rise to prop the head;
So that each spacious room was one full-swelling bed.

    And everywhere huge covered tables stood,
    With wines high-flavoured and rich viands crowned;
    Whatever sprightly juice or tasteful food
    On the green bosom of this Earth are found,
    And all old Ocean genders in his round—
    Some hand unseen these silently displayed,
    Even undemanded by a sign or sound;
    You need but wish, and instantly obeyed,
Fair-ranged the dishes rose, and thick the glasses played.

    Here freedom reigned without the least alloy;
    Nor gossip's tale, nor ancient maiden's gall,
    Nor saintly spleen durst murmur at our joy,
    And with envenomed tongues our pleasures pall.
    For why? there was but one great rule for all;
    To wit, that each should work his own desire,
    And eat, drink, study, sleep, as it may fall,
    Or melt the time in love, or wake the lyre,
And carol what, unbid, the Muses might inspire.

    The rooms with costly tapestry were hung,
    Where was inwoven many a gentle tale,
    Such as of old the rural poets sung
    Or of Arcadian or Sicilian vale:
    Reclining lovers, in the lonely dale,
    Poured forth at large the sweetly tortured heart;
    Or, looking tender passion, swelled the gale,
    And taught charmed echo to resound their smart;
While flocks, woods, streams around, repose and peace impart.

Those pleased the most, where, by a cunning hand,
Depeinten was the patriarchal age;
What time Dan Abraham left the Chaldee land,
And pastured on from verdant stage to stage,
Where fields and fountains fresh could best engage.
Toil was not then. Of nothing took they heed,
But with wild beasts the sylvan war to wage,
And o'er vast plains their herds and flocks to feed:
Blest sons of nature they! true golden age indeed!

Sometimes the pencil, in cool airy halls,
Bade the gay bloom of vernal landskips rise,
Or Autumn's varied shades imbrown the walls:
Now the black tempest strikes the astonished eyes;
Now down the steep the flashing torrent flies;
The trembling sun now plays o'er ocean blue,
And now rude mountains frown amid the skies;
Whate'er Lorrain light-touched with softening hue,
Or savage Rosa dashed, or learnéd Poussin drew.

Each sound too here to languishment inclined,
Lulled the weak bosom, and inducéd ease.
Aërial music in the warbling wind,
At distance rising oft, by small degrees,
Nearer and nearer came, till o'er the trees
It hung, and breathed such soul-dissolving airs
As did, alas! with soft perdition please:
Entangled deep in its enchanting snares,
The listening heart forgot all duties and all cares.

A certain music, never known before,
Here soothed the pensive melancholy mind;
Full easily obtained. Behoves no more,
But sidelong to the gently-waving wind
To lay the well-tuned instrument reclined;
From which, with airy flying fingers light,
Beyond each mortal touch the most refined,
The god of winds drew sounds of deep delight:
Whence, with just cause, the Harp of Æolus it hight.

Ah me! what hand can touch the strings so fine?
Who up the lofty diapason roll
Such sweet, such sad, such solemn airs divine,
Then let them down again into the soul?
Now rising love they fanned; now pleasing dole
They breathed, in tender musings, through the heart;
And now a graver sacred strain they stole,
As when seraphic hands an hymn impart:
Wild warbling Nature all, above the reach of Art!

FROM *Spring*

At length the finished garden to the view
Its vistas opens and its alleys green.
Snatched through the verdant maze, the hurried eye
Distracted wanders; now the bowery walk
Of covert close, where scarce a speck of day
Falls on the lengthened gloom, protracted sweeps;
Now meets the bending sky, the river now
Dimpling along, the breezy ruffled lake,
The forest darkening round, the glittering spire,
The ethereal mountain, and the distant main.
But why so far excursive? when at hand,
Along these blushing borders bright with dew,
And in yon mingled wilderness of flowers,
Fair-handed Spring unbosoms every grace—
Throws out the snow-drop and the crocus first,
The daisy, primrose, violet darkly blue,
And polyanthus of unnumbered dyes;
The yellow wall-flower, stained with iron brown,
And lavish stock, that scents the garden round:
From the soft wing of vernal breezes shed,
Anemones, auriculas, enriched
With shining meal o'er all their velvet leaves;
And full ranunculus of glowing red.
Then comes the tulip-race, where beauty plays
Her idle freaks: from family diffused
To family, as flies the father-dust,
The varied colours run; and, while they break,
On the charmed eye, the exulting florist marks

With secret pride the wonders of his hand.
No gradual bloom is wanting—from the bud
First-born of Spring to Summer's musky tribes;
Nor hyacinths, of purest virgin white,
Low bent and blushing inward; nor jonquils,
Of potent fragrance; nor narcissus fair,
As o'er the fabled fountain hanging still;
Nor broad carnations, nor gay-spotted pinks;
Nor, showered from every bush, the damask-rose:
Infinite numbers, delicacies, smells.
With hues on hues expression cannot paint,
The breath of Nature, and her endless bloom.

FROM Winter

The keener tempests come: and, fuming dun
From all the livid east or piercing north,
Thick clouds ascend, in whose capacious womb
A vapoury deluge lies, to snow congealed.
Heavy they roll their fleecy world along,
And the sky saddens with the gathered storm.
Through the hushed air the whitening shower descends,
At first thin-wavering; till at last the flakes
Fall broad and wide and fast, dimming the day
With a continual flow. The cherished fields
Put on their winter-robe of purest white.
'Tis brightness all; save where the new snow melts
Along the mazy current. Low the woods
Bow their hoar head; and, ere the languid sun
Faint from the west emits his evening ray,
Earth's universal face, deep-hid and chill,
Is one wild dazzling waste, that buries wide
The works of man. Drooping, the labourer-ox
Stands covered o'er with snow, and then demands
The fruit of all his toil. The fowls of heaven,
Tamed by the cruel season, crowd around
The winnowing store, and claim the little boon
Which Providence assigns them. One alone,
The redbreast, sacred to the household gods,
Wisely regardful of the embroiling sky,

In joyless fields and thorny thickets leaves
His shivering mates, and pays to trusted man
His annual visit. Half afraid, he first
Against the window beats; then brisk alights
On the warm hearth; then, hopping o'er the floor,
Eyes all the smiling family askance,
And pecks, and starts, and wonders where he is—
Till, more familiar grown, the table-crumbs
Attract his slender feet. The foodless wilds
Pour forth their brown inhabitants. The hare,
Though timorous of heart, and hard beset
By death in various forms, dark snares, and dogs,
And more unpitying men, the garden seeks,
Urged on by fearless want. The bleating kind
Eye the bleak heaven, and next the glistening earth,
With looks of dumb despair; then, sad-dispersed,
Dig for the withered herb through heaps of snow.

HENRY FIELDING

(1707–1754)

"A-Hunting We Will Go"

The dusky night rides down the sky,
    And ushers in the morn;
The hounds all join in glorious cry;
    The huntsman winds his horn.
    And a-hunting we will go.

The wife around her husband throws
    Her arms, and begs his stay;
"My dear, it rains, and hails, and snows!
    You will not hunt to-day!"
    But a-hunting we will go!

A brushing fox in yonder wood,
    Secure to find we seek;
For why, I carried sound and good,
    A cartload there last week!
    And a-hunting we will go!

Away he goes! He flies the rout!
   Their steeds all spur and switch!
Some are thrown in, and some thrown out,
   And some thrown in the ditch!
   But a-hunting we will go!

At length, his strength to faintness worn,
   Poor Reynard ceases flight,
Then hungry homeward we return,
   To feast away the night.
   Then a-drinking we will go!

SAMUEL JOHNSON

(1709–1784)

FROM *The Vanity of Human Wishes*

On what foundations stands the warrior's pride,
How just his hopes, let Swedish Charles decide.
A frame of adamant, a soul of fire,
No dangers fright him, and no labours tire;
O'er love, o'er fear, extends his wide domain,
Unconquered lord of pleasure and of pain;
No joys to him pacific sceptres yield,
War sounds the trump, he rushes to the field.
Behold surrounding kings their powers combine,
And one capitulate, and one resign:
Peace courts his hand, but spreads her charms in vain;
"Think nothing gained," he cries, "till nought remain,
On Moscow's walls till Gothic standards fly,
And all be mine beneath the polar sky."
The march begins, in military state,
And nations on his eye suspended wait;
Stern Famine guards the solitary coast,
And Winter barricades the realms of Frost;
He comes, nor want nor cold his course delay!—
Hide, blushing glory, hide Pultowa's day:
The vanquished hero leaves his broken bands,
And shows his miseries in distant lands;
Condemned a needy suppliant to wait,
While ladies interpose, and slaves debate.

But did not Chance at length her error mend?
Did no subverted empire mark his end?
Did rival monarchs give the fatal wound?
Or hostile millions press him to the ground?
His fall was destined to a barren strand,
A petty fortress, and a dubious hand;
He left the name at which the world grew pale,
To point a moral, or adorn a tale.

FROM *London*

By numbers here from shame or censure free,
All crimes are safe, but hated poverty.
This, only this the rigid law pursues,
This, only this provokes the snarling muse.
The sober trader at a tattered cloak
Wakes from his dream, and labours for a joke;
With brisker air the silken courtiers gaze,
And turn the varied taunt a thousand ways.
Of all the griefs that harass the distressed,
Sure the most bitter is a scornful jest;
Fate never wounds more deep the generous heart,
Than when a blockhead's insult points the dart.
Has Heaven reserved, in pity to the poor,
No pathless waste, or undiscovered shore?
No secret island in the boundless main?
No peaceful desert yet unclaimed by Spain?
Quick, let us rise, the happy seats explore,
And bear oppression's insolence no more.
This mournful truth is everywhere confest:
Slow rises worth by poverty depressed.

FROM *On the Death of Mr. Robert Levet,*
a Practiser in Physic

In Misery's darkest cavern known,
 His useful care was ever nigh,
Where hopeless Anguish poured his groan,
 And lonely Want retired to die.

No summons mocked by chill delay,
  No petty gain disdained by pride,
The modest wants of every day
  The toil of every day supplied.

His virtues walked their narrow round,
  Nor made a pause, nor left a void;
And sure th' Eternal Master found
  The single talent well employed.

FROM On the Coming of Age of a Rich Extravagant Young Man

Wealth, my lad, was made to wander,
  Let it wander as it will;
Call the jockey, call the pander,
  Bid them come and take their fill.

When the bonny blade carouses,
  Pockets full, and spirits high—
What are acres? what are houses?
  Only dirt, or wet or dry.

Should the guardian friend or mother
  Tell the woes of wilful waste;
Scorn their counsel, scorn their pother—
  You can hang or drown at last.

"Hermit Hoar..."

Hermit hoar, in solemn cell,
  Wearing out life's evening gray,
Smite thy bosom, sage, and tell,
  What is bliss? and which the way?

Thus I spoke; and speaking sighed;
  Scarce repressed the starting tear;
When the smiling sage replied:
  "Come, my lad, and drink some beer."

Boswell's *Life of Johnson*

WILLIAM THOMPSON
(1712?–1766?)

FROM *The Happy Life*

A book, a friend, a song, a glass,
A chaste, yet laughter-loving lass,
To mortals various joys impart,
Inform the sense, and warm the heart.

Thrice happy they, who careless laid
Beneath a kind-embowering shade,
With rosy wreaths their temples crown,
In rosy wine their sorrow drown.

Begone, ambition, riches, toys,
And splendid cares, and guilty joys—
Give me a book, a friend, a glass,
And a chaste, laughter-loving lass.

RICHARD GLOVER
(1712–1785)

Admiral Hosier's Ghost

As near Porto-Bello lying
    On the gently swelling flood,
At midnight with streamers flying,
    Our triumphant navy rode:
There while Vernon sat all-glorious
    From the Spaniards' late defeat;
And his crews, with shouts victorious,
    Drank success to England's fleet:

On a sudden shrilly sounding,
    Hideous yells and shrieks were heard;
Then each heart with fear confounding,
    A sad troop of ghosts appeared,

All in dreary hammocks shrouded,
    Which for winding-sheets they wore,
And with looks by sorrow clouded,
    Frowning on that hostile shore.

On them gleamed the moon's wan lustre,
    When the shade of Hosier brave
His pale bands was seen to muster,
    Rising from their watery grave:
O'er the glimmering wave he hied him,
    Where the Burford reared her sail,
With three thousand ghosts beside him,
    And in groans did Vernon hail:

"Heed, O heed, our fatal story,
    I am Hosier's injured ghost,
You, who now have purchased glory
    At this place where I was lost;
Though in Porto-Bello's ruin
    You now triumph free from fears,
When you think on our undoing,
    You will mix your joy with tears.

"See these mournful spectres, sweeping
    Ghastly o'er this hated wave,
Whose wan cheeks are stained with weeping;
    These were England's captains brave:
Mark those numbers pale and horrid,
    Those were once my sailors bold,
Lo! each hangs his drooping forehead,
    While his dismal tale is told.

"I, by twenty sail attended,
    Did this Spanish town affright:
Nothing then its wealth defended
    But my orders not to fight:
Oh! that in this rolling ocean
    I had cast them with disdain,
And obeyed my heart's warm motion,
    To have quelled the pride of Spain.

"For resistance I could fear none,
   But with twenty ships had done
What thou, brave and happy Vernon,
   Hast achieved with six alone.
Then tho Bastimentos never
   Had our foul dishonour seen,
Nor the sea the sad receiver
   Of this gallant train had been.

"Thus, like thee, proud Spain dismaying,
   And her galleons leading home,
Though condemned for disobeying,
   I had met a traitor's doom;
To have fallen, my country crying,
   He has played an English part,
Had been better far than dying
   Of a grieved and broken heart.

"Unrepining at thy glory,
   Thy successful arms we hail;
But remember our sad story,
   And let Hosier's wrongs prevail.
Sent in this foul clime to languish,
   Think what thousands fell in vain,
Wasted with disease and anguish,
   Not in glorious battle slain.

"Hence, with all my train attending
   From their oozy tombs below,
Through the hoary foam ascending,
   Here I feed my constant woe:
Here the Bastimentos viewing,
   We recall our shameful doom,
And our plaintive cries renewing,
   Wander through the midnight gloom.

"O'er these waves for ever mourning
   Shall we roam deprived of rest,
If to Britain's shores returning,
   You neglect my just request.

After this proud foe subduing,
    When your patriot friends you see,
Think on vengeance for my ruin,
    And for England shamed in me."

WILLIAM SHENSTONE

(1714–1763)

Written at an Inn at Henley

To thee, fair freedom, I retire
    From flattery, cards, and dice, and din;
Nor art thou found in mansions higher
    Than the low cot, or humble inn.

'Tis here with boundless power I reign;
    And every health which I begin,
Converts dull port to bright champagne;
    Such freedom crowns it at an inn.

I fly from pomp, I fly from plate,
    I fly from falsehood's specious grin!
Freedom I love, and form I hate,
    And choose my lodgings at an inn.

Here, waiter, take my sordid ore,
    Which lackeys else might hope to win;
It buys, what courts have not in store;
    It buys me freedom at an inn.

Whoe'er has travelled life's dull round,
    Where'er his stages may have been,
May sigh to think he still has found
    The warmest welcome at an inn.

THOMAS GRAY

(1716–1771)

Elegy Written in a Country Churchyard

The curfew tolls the knell of parting day,
  The lowing herd winds slowly o'er the lea,
The ploughman homeward plods his weary way,
  And leaves the world to darkness and to me.

Now fades the glimmering landscape on the sight,
  And all the air a solemn stillness holds,
Save where the beetle wheels his droning flight,
  And drowsy tinklings lull the distant folds.

Save that from yonder ivy-mantled tower,
  The moping owl does to the moon complain
Of such as, wandering near her secret bower,
  Molest her ancient solitary reign.

Beneath these rugged elms, that yew-tree's shade,
  Where heaves the turf in many a mould'ring heap,
Each in his narrow cell for ever laid,
  The rude forefathers of the hamlet sleep.

The breezy call of incense-breathing morn,
  The swallow twittering from the straw-built shed,
The cock's shrill clarion, or the echoing horn,
  No more shall rouse them from their lowly bed.

For them no more the blazing hearth shall burn,
  Or busy housewife ply her evening-care;
No children run to lisp their sire's return,
  Or climb his knees the envied kiss to share.

Oft did the harvest to their sickle yield,
  Their furrow oft the stubborn glebe has broke:
How jocund did they drive their team afield!
  How bowed the woods beneath their sturdy stroke!

Let not Ambition mock their useful toil,
  Their homely joys and destiny obscure;
Nor Grandeur hear with a disdainful smile,
  The short and simple annals of the poor.

The boast of heraldry, the pomp of power,
  And all that beauty, all that wealth e'er gave,
Awaits alike th' inevitable hour.
  The paths of glory lead but to the grave.

Nor you, ye proud, impute to these the fault,
  If Memory o'er their tomb no trophies raise,
Where through the long-drawn aisle, and fretted vault,
  The pealing anthem swells the note of praise.

Can storied urn, or animated bust,
  Back to its mansion call the fleeting breath?
Can Honour's voice provoke the silent dust,
  Or flattery soothe the dull cold ear of Death?

Perhaps in this neglected spot is laid
  Some heart once pregnant with celestial fire;
Hands, that the rod of empire might have swayed,
  Or waked to ecstasy the living lyre.

But Knowledge to their eyes her ample page,
  Rich with the spoils of Time, did ne'er unroll;
Chill penury repressed their noble rage,
  And froze the genial current of the soul.

Full many a gem of purest ray serene
  The dark unfathomed caves of ocean bear;
Full many a flower is born to blush unseen,
  And waste its sweetness on the desert air.

Some village Hampden, that with dauntless breast
  The little tyrant of his fields withstood,
Some mute inglorious Milton here may rest,
  Some Cromwell, guiltless of his country's blood.

Th' applause of listening senates to command,
  The threats of pain and ruin to despise,
To scatter plenty o'er a smiling land,
  And read their history in a nation's eyes,

Their lot forbade: nor circumscribed alone
  Their growing virtues, but their crimes confined;
Forbade to wade through slaughter to a throne,
  And shut the gates of Mercy on mankind,

The struggling pangs of conscious truth to hide,
  To quench the blushes of ingenuous shame,
Or heap the shrine of luxury and pride
  With incense kindled at the Muse's flame.

Far from the madding crowd's ignoble strife,
  Their sober wishes never learned to stray;
Along the cool sequestered vale of life
  They kept the noiseless tenor of their way.

Yet ev'n these bones from insult to protect
  Some frail memorial still erected nigh,
With uncouth rhymes and shapeless sculpture decked,
  Implores the passing tribute of a sigh.

Their name, their years, spelt by th' unlettered Muse,
  The place of fame and elegy supply:
And many a holy text around she strews,
  That teach the rustic moralist to die.

For who, to dumb Forgetfulness a prey,
  This pleasing anxious being e'er resigned,
Left the warm precincts of the cheerful day,
  Nor cast one longing, ling'ring look behind?

On some fond breast the parting soul relies,
  Some pious drops the closing eye requires;
Ev'n from the tomb the voice of Nature cries,
  Ev'n in our ashes live their wonted fires.

For thee, who, mindful of th' unhonoured dead,
  Dost in these lines their artless tale relate;
If chance, by lonely Contemplation led,
  Some kindred spirit shall inquire thy fate,—

Haply some hoary-headed swain may say,
  "Oft have we seen him at the peep of dawn
Brushing with hasty steps the dews away,
  To meet the sun upon the upland lawn;

"There at the foot of yonder nodding beech,
  That wreathes its old fantastic roots so high,
His listless length at noon-tide would he stretch,
  And pore upon the brook that babbles by.

"Hard by yon wood, now smiling as in scorn,
  Mutt'ring his wayward fancies would he rove;
Now drooping, woeful-wan, like one forlorn,
  Or crazed with care, or crossed in hopeless love.

"One morn I missed him from the customed hill,
  Along the heath, and near his fav'rite tree;
Another came; nor yet beside the rill,
  Nor up the lawn, nor at the wood was he;

"The next, with dirges due in sad array
  Slow through the church-way path we saw him borne,—
Approach and read, for thou canst read, the lay
  Graved on the stone beneath yon agéd thorn."

THE EPITAPH

Here rests his head upon the lap of earth
  A youth to Fortune and to Fame unknown:
Fair Science frowned not on his humble birth,
  And Melancholy marked him for her own.

Large was his bounty, and his soul sincere,
  Heaven did a recompense as largely send:
He gave to Misery (all he had) a tear,
  He gained from Heaven ('twas all he wished) a friend.

No farther seek his merits to disclose,
  Or draw his frailties from their dread abode,
(There they alike in trembling hope repose,)
  The bosom of his Father and his God.

Stanzas Cancelled from the Elegy

Hark! how the sacred calm that breathes around,
  Bids every fierce tumultuous passion cease;
In still small accents whispering from the ground,
  A grateful earnest of eternal peace.

Him have we seen the greenwood-side along,
  While o'er the heath we hied, our labour done,
What time the wood-lark piped her farewell song,
  With wistful eyes pursue tho setting sun.

There scattered oft, the earliest of the year,
  By hands unseen are showers of violets found;
The red-breast loves to build and warble there,
  And little footsteps lightly print the ground.

Ode on a Distant Prospect of Eton College

Ye distant spires, ye antique towers,
  That crown the wat'ry glade,
Where grateful Science still adores
  Her Henry's holy shade;
And ye, that from the stately brow
Of Windsor's heights th' expanse below
  Of grove, of lawn, of mead survey,
Whose turf, whose shade, whose flowers among
Wanders the hoary Thames along
  His silver-winding way:

Ah, happy hills! ah, pleasing shade!
  Ah, fields beloved in vain!
Where once my careless childhood strayed,
  A stranger yet to pain!

I feel the gales that from ye blow
A momentary bliss bestow,
   As, waving fresh their gladsome wing,
My weary soul they seem to soothe,
And, redolent of joy and youth,
   To breathe a second spring.

Say, Father Thames, for thou hast seen
   Full many a sprightly race
Disporting on thy margent green
   The paths of pleasure trace;
Who foremost now delight to cleave,
With pliant arm, thy glassy wave?
   The captive linnet which enthrall?
What idle progeny succeed
To chase the rolling circle's speed,
   Or urge the flying ball?

While some, on earnest business bent,
   Their murm'ring labours ply
'Gainst graver hours, that bring constraint
   To sweeten liberty:
Some bold adventurers disdain
The limits of their little reign,
   And unknown regions dare descry:
Still as they run they look behind,
They hear a voice in every wind,
   And snatch a fearful joy.

Gay hope is theirs, by Fancy fed,
   Less pleasing when possest;
The tear forgot as soon as shed,
   The sunshine of the breast:
Their buxom health of rosy hue,
Wild wit, invention ever new,
   And lively cheer of vigour born;
The thoughtless day, the easy night,
The spirits pure, the slumbers light,
   That fly th'approach of morn.

Alas! regardless of their doom,
 The little victims play!
No sense have they of ills to come,
 Nor care beyond to-day:
Yet see, how all around them wait
The ministers of human fate,
 And black Misfortune's baleful train!
Ah, show them where in ambush stand,
To seize their prey, the murd'rous band!
 Ah, tell them, they are men!

These shall the fury Passions tear,
 The vultures of the mind,
Disdainful Anger, pallid Fear,
 And Shame that skulks behind;
Or pining Love shall waste their youth,
Or Jealousy, with rankling tooth,
 That inly gnaws the secret heart;
And Envy wan, and faded Care,
Grim-visaged comfortless Despair,
 And Sorrow's piercing dart.

Ambition this shall tempt to rise,
 Then whirl the wretch from high,
To bitter Scorn a sacrifice,
 And grinning Infamy.
The strings of Falsehood those shall try,
And hard Unkindness' altered eye,
 That mocks the tear it forced to flow;
And keen Remorse with blood defiled,
And moody Madness laughing wild,
 Amid severest woe.

Lo! in the vale of years beneath
 A grisly troop are seen,
The painful family of Death,
 More hideous than their Queen:
This racks the joints, this fires the veins,
That every labouring sinew strains,
 Those in the deeper vitals rage:

Lo! Poverty, to fill the band,
That numbs the soul with icy hand,
    And slow-consuming Age.

To each his sufferings: all are men,
    Condemned alike to groan;
The tender for another's pain,
    Th' unfeeling for his own.
Yet, ah! why should they know their fate,
Since sorrow never comes too late,
    And happiness too swiftly flies.
Thought would destroy their paradise.
No more—where ignorance is bliss,
    'Tis folly to be wise.

The Progress of Poesy

Awake, Æolian lyre, awake,
And give to rapture all thy trembling strings.
From Helicon's harmonious springs
    A thousand rills their mazy progress take:
The laughing flowers, that round them blow,
Drink life and fragrance as they flow.
Now the rich stream of Music winds along,
Deep, majestic, smooth, and strong,
    Through verdant vales, and Ceres' golden reign;
Now rolling down the steep amain,
Headlong, impetuous, see it pour;
The rocks and nodding groves re-bellow to the roar.

Oh! Sovereign of the willing soul,
Parent of sweet and solemn-breathing airs,
Enchanting shell! the sullen Cares
    And frantic Passions hear thy soft control.
On Thracia's hills the Lord of War
Has curbed the fury of his car,
And dropt his thirsty lance at thy command.
Perching on the sceptred hand

Of Jove, thy magic lulls the feathered king
With ruffled plumes and flagging wing:
Quenched in dark clouds of slumber lie
The terror of his beak, and lightnings of his eye.

Thee, the voice, the dance, obey,
Tempered to thy warbled lay.
O'er Idalia's velvet-green
The rosy-crownéd Loves are seen
On Cytherea's day
With antic Sports and blue-eyed Pleasures.
Frisking light in frolic measures;
Now pursuing, now retreating,
　　Now in circling troops they meet:
To brisk notes in cadence beating,
　　Glance their many-twinkling feet.
Slow melting strains their Queen's approach declare:
　　Where'er she turns, the Graces homage pay.
With arms sublime, that float upon the air,
　　In gliding state she wins her easy way:
O'er her warm cheek and rising bosom move
The bloom of young Desire and purple light of Love.

Man's feeble race what ills await!
Labour and Penury, the racks of Pain,
Disease, and Sorrow's weeping train,
　　And Death, sad refuge from the storms of Fate!
The fond complaint, my song, disprove,
And justify the laws of Jove.
Say, has he given in vain the heavenly Muse?
Night and all her sickly dews,
Her spectres wan, and birds of boding cry,
He gives to range the dreary sky:
Till down the eastern cliffs afar
Hyperion's march they spy, and glittering shafts of war.

In climes beyond the solar road,
Where shaggy forms o'er ice-built mountains roam,
The Muse has broke the twilight-gloom
　　To cheer the shivering native's dull abode.
And oft, beneath the odorous shade
Of Chili's boundless forests laid,

She deigns to hear the savage youth repeat,
In loose numbers wildly sweet,
Their feather-cinctured chief and dusky loves.
Her track, where'er the goddess roves,
Glory pursue and generous Shame,
Th' unconquerable Mind, and Freedom's holy flame.

Woods, that wave o'er Delphi's steep,
Isles, that crown th'Ægean deep,
   Fields, that cool Ilissus laves,
   Or where Maeander's amber waves
In lingering lab'rinths creep,
   How do your tuneful Echoes languish,
   Mute, but to the voice of Anguish!
Where each old poetic mountain
   Inspiration breathed around;
Ev'ry shade and hallowed fountain
   Murmured deep a solemn sound:
Till the sad Nine, in Greece's evil hour,
   Left their Parnassus for the Latin plains.
Alike they scorn the pomp of tyrant Power,
   And coward Vice, that revels in her chains.
When Latium had her lofty spirit lost,
They sought, oh Albion! next thy sea-encircled coast.

Far from the sun and summer-gale,
In thy green lap was Nature's darling laid,
What time, where lucid Avon strayed,
   To him the mighty mother did unveil
Her awful face: the dauntless child
Stretched forth his little arms and smiled.
"This pencil take (she said), whose colours clear
Richly paint the vernal year:
Thine too these golden keys, immortal Boy!
This can unlock the gates of Joy;
Of Horror that, and thrilling Fears,
Or ope the sacred source of sympathetic tears."

Nor second he, that rode sublime
Upon the seraph-wings of ecstasy,
The secrets of th'abyss to spy.
   He passed the flaming bounds of place and time:

The living throne, the sapphire-blaze,
Where angels tremble while they gaze,
He saw; but, blasted with excess of light,
Closed his eyes in endless night.
Behold, where Dryden's less presumptuous car,
Wide o'er the fields of glory bear
Two coursers of ethereal race,
With necks in thunder clothed, and long-resounding pace.

Hark, his hands the lyre explore!
Bright-eyed Fancy, hovering o'er,
Scatters from her pictured urn
Thoughts that breathe, and words that burn.
But ah! 'tis heard no more—
Oh! Lyre divine, what daring Spirit
Wakes thee now? Though he inherit
Nor the pride, nor ample pinion
That the Theban eagle bear,
Sailing with supreme dominion
Through the azure deep of air:
Yet oft before his infant eyes would run
Such forms as glitter in the Muse's ray,
With orient hues, unborrowed of the sun:
Yet shall he mount, and keep his distant way
Beyond the limits of a vulgar fate,
Beneath the Good how far—but far above the Great.

Sonnet on the Death of Mr. Richard West

In vain to me the smiling mornings shine,
And redd'ning Phoebus lifts his golden fire:
The birds in vain their amorous descant join;
Or cheerful fields resume their green attire:
These ears, alas! for other notes repine,
A different object do these eyes require:
My lonely anguish melts no heart but mine;
And in my breast the imperfect joys expire.
Yet morning smiles the busy race to cheer,
And new-born pleasure brings to happier men:

The fields to all their wonted tribute bear:
To warm their little loves the birds complain:
I fruitless mourn to him that cannot hear,
And weep the more, because I weep in vain.

FRANCIS FAWKES

(1720–1777)

The Brown Jug

Dear Tom, this brown jug that now foams with mild ale,
(In which I will drink to sweet Nan of the Vale,)
Was once Toby Fillpot, a thirsty old soul
As e'er drank a bottle, or fathomed a bowl;
In boosing about 'twas his praise to excel,
And among jolly topers he bore off the bell.

In chanced as in dog-days he sat at his ease
In his flower-woven arbour as gay as you please,
With a friend and a pipe puffing sorrows away,
And with honest old stingo was soaking his clay,
His breath-doors of life on a sudden were shut,
And he died full as big as a Dorchester butt.

His body, when long in the ground it had lain,
And time into clay had resolved it again,
A potter found out in its covert so snug,
And with part of fat Toby he formed this brown jug,
Now sacred to friendship, and mirth, and mild ale;
So here's to my lovely sweet Nan of the Vale.

From the Latin of AMALTHEUS

JAMES GRAINGER

(1721–1767)

FROM *Ode to Solitude*

O solitude, romantic maid!
Whether by nodding towers you tread,
Or hunt the desert's trackless gloom,
Or hover o'er the yawning tomb,

Or climb the Andes' clifted side,
Or by the Nile's coy source abide,
Or starting from your half-year's sleep
From Hecla view the thawing deep,
Or, at the purple dawn of day,
Tadmor's marble wastes survey,
You, recluse, again I woo,
And again your steps pursue.

With you roses brighter bloom,
Sweeter every sweet perfume,
Purer every fountain flows,
Stronger every wilding grows.
Let those toil for gold who please,
Or for fame renounce their ease.
What is fame? an empty bubble.
Gold? a transient shining trouble.
Let them for their country bleed,
What was Sidney's, Raleigh's meed?
Man's not worth a moment's pain,
Base, ungrateful, fickle, vain.
Then let me, sequestered fair,
To your sibyl grot repair;
On yon hanging cliff it stands,
Scooped by nature's savage hands,
Bosomed in the gloomy shade
Of cypress not with age decayed.
Where the owl still-hooting sits,
Where the bat incessant flits,
There in loftier strains I'll sing
Whence the changing seasons spring,
Tell how storms deform the skies,
Whence the waves subside and rise,
Trace the comet's blazing tail,
Weigh the planets in a scale;
Bend, great God, before thy shrine,
The bournless macrocosm's thine.

WILLIAM COLLINS

(1721-1759)

Ode

How sleep the brave, who sink to rest
By all their country's wishes blessed!
When Spring with dewy fingers cold
Returns to deck their hallowed mould,
She there shall dress a sweeter sod
Than Fancy's feet have ever trod.

By fairy hands their knell is rung;
By forms unseen their dirge is sung;
There Honour comes, a pilgrim gray,
To bless the turf that wraps their clay;
And Freedom shall awhile repair,
To dwell a weeping hermit there.

Ode to Evening

If aught of oaten stop, or pastoral song,
May hope, chaste Eve, to soothe thy modest ear,
    Like thy own brawling springs,
    Thy springs, and dying gales;

O Nymph reserved, while now the bright-haired sun
Sits in yon western tent, whose cloudy skirts,
    With brede ethereal wove,
    O'erhang his wavy bed:

Now air is hushed, save where the weak-eyed bat
With short shrill shriek flits by on leathern wing;
    Or where the beetle winds
    His small but sullen horn,

As oft he rises midst the twilight path,
Against the pilgrim borne in heedless hum:
    Now teach me, maid composed,
    To breathe some softened strain,

Whose numbers, stealing through thy darkening vale,
May not unseemly with its stillness suit;
   As, musing slow, I hail
   Thy genial loved return.

For when thy folding-star arising shows
His paly circlet, at his warning lamp
   The fragrant Hours, and Elves
   Who slept in buds the day,

And many a Nymph who wreathes her brows with sedge,
And sheds the freshening dew, and, lovelier still,
   The pensive Pleasures sweet,
   Prepare thy shadowy car;

Then let me rove some wild and heathy scene;
Or find some ruin, midst its dreary dells,
   Whose walls more awful nod
   By thy religious gleams.

Or, if chill blustering winds, or driving rain,
Prevent my willing feet, be mine the hut,
   That, from the mountain's side,
   Views wilds, and swelling floods,

And hamlets brown, and dim-discovered spires;
And hears their simple bell, and marks o'er all
   Thy dewy fingers draw
   The gradual dusky veil.

While Spring shall pour his showers, as oft he wont,
And bathe thy breathing tresses, meekest Eve!
   While Summer loves to sport
   Beneath thy lingering light;

While sallow Autumn fills thy lap with leaves;
Or Winter, yelling through the troublous air,
   Affrights thy shrinking train,
   And rudely rends thy robes;

So long, regardful of thy quiet rule,
Shall Fancy, Friendship, Science, smiling Peace,
   Thy gentlest influence own,
   And love thy favourite name!

Dirge in Cymbeline

To fair Fidele's grassy tomb
   Soft maids and village hinds shall bring
Each opening sweet of earliest bloom,
   And rifle all the breathing spring.

No wailing ghost shall dare appear
   To vex with shrieks this quiet grove;
But shepherd lads assemble here,
   And melting virgins own their love.

No withered witch shall here be seen;
   No goblins lead their nightly crew:
The female fays shall haunt the green,
   And dress thy grave with pearly dew.

The redbreast oft, at evening hours,
   Shall kindly lend his little aid,
With hoary moss, and gathered flowers,
   To deck the ground where thou art laid.

When howling winds, and beating rain,
   In tempests shake the sylvan cell;
Or midst the chase, on every plain,
   The tender thought on thee shall dwell;

Each lonely scene shall thee restore;
   For thee the tear be duly shed;
Beloved till life can charm no more,
   And mourned till Pity's self be dead.

CHRISTOPHER SMART

(1722–1771)

FROM Song to David

O servant of God's holiest charge,
The minister of praise at large,
   Which thou mayst now receive;
From thy blest mansion hail and hear,
From topmost eminence appear
   To this the wreath I weave.

His muse, bright angel of his verse,
Gives balm for all the thorns that pierce,
   For all the pangs that rage;
Blest light, still gaining on the gloom,
The more than Michal of his bloom,
   The Abishag of his age.

He sang of God—the mighty source
Of all things—the stupendous force
   On which all strength depends;
From whose right arm, beneath whose eyes,
All period, power and enterprise
   Commences, reigns and ends.

The world—the clustering spheres he made,
The glorious light, the soothing shade,
   Dale, champaign, grove, and hill;
The multitudinous abyss,
Whose secrecy remains in bliss,
   And wisdom hides her skill.

Trees, plants and flowers—of virtuous root;
Gem yielding blossom, yielding fruit,
   Choice gums and precious balm;
Bless ye the nosegay in the vale,
And with the sweetness of the gale
   Enrich the thankful psalm.

Of fowl—even every beak and wing
Which cheer the winter, hail the spring,
  That live in peace, or prey;
They that make music, or that mock,
The quail, the brave domestic cock,
  The raven, swan, and jay.

Of beasts—the beaver plods his task;
While the sleek tigers roll and bask,
  Nor yet the shades arouse;
Her cave the mining coney scoops;
Where o'er the mead the mountain stoops,
  The kids exult and browse.

Of gems—their virtue and their price,
Which, hid in earth from man's device,
  Their darts of lustre sheath;
The jasper of the master's stamp,
The topaz blazing like a lamp,
  Among the mines beneath.

The pillars of the Lord are seven,
Which stand from earth to topmost heaven;
  His wisdom drew the plan;
His word accomplished the design,
From brightest gem to deepest mine,
  From Christ enthroned to man.

Alpha, the cause of causes, first
In station, fountain, whence the burst
  Of light and blaze of day;
Whence bold attempt, and brave advance,
Have motion, life and ordinance,
  And heaven itself its stay.

Gamma supports the glorious arch
On which angelic legions march,
  And is with sapphires paved;
Thence the fleet clouds are sent adrift,
And thence the painted folds that lift
  The crimson veil, are waved.

Eta with living sculpture breathes,
With verdant carvings, flowery wreaths
   Of never-wasting bloom;
In strong relief his goodly base
All instruments of labour grace,
   The trowel, spade, and loom.

Next Theta stands to the supreme—
Who formed in number, sign and scheme,
   The illustrious lights that are;
And one addressed his saffron robe,
And one, clad in a silver globe,
   Held rule with every star.

Iota's tuned to choral hymns
Of those that fly, while he that swims
   In thankful safety lurks;
And foot, and chapiter, and niche,
The various histories enrich
   Of God's recorded works.

Sigma presents the social droves
With him that solitary roves,
   And man of all the chief;
Fair on whose face, and stately frame,
Did God impress his hallowed name,
   For ocular belief.

Omega! greatest and the best,
Stands sacred to the day of rest,
   For gratitude and thought;
Which blessed the world upon his pole,
And gave the universe his goal,
   And closed the infernal draught.

O David, scholar of the Lord!
Such is thy science, whence reward,
   And infinite degree;
O strength, O sweetness, lasting ripe!
God's harp thy symbol, and thy type
   The lion and the bee!

For Adoration all the ranks
Of angels yield eternal thanks,
   And David in the midst;
With God's good poor, which, last and least,
In man's esteem, thou to thy feast,
   O blessed bridegroom, bidst.

For Adoration seasons change,
And order, truth, and beauty range,
   Adjust, attract, and fill:
The grass the polyanthus checks;
And polished porphyry reflects,
   By the descending rill.

Rich almonds colour to the prime
For Adoration; tendrils climb,
   And fruit-trees pledge their gems;
And Ivis, with her gorgeous vest,
Builds for her eggs her cunning nest,
   And bell-flowers bow their stems.

The spotted ounce and playsome cubs
Run rustling 'mongst the flowering shrubs,
   And lizards feed the moss;
For Adoration beasts embark,
While waves upholding halcyon's ark
   No longer roar and toss.

While Israel sits beneath his fig,
With coral root and amber sprig
   The weaned adventurer sports;
Where to the palm the jasmine cleaves,
For Adoration 'mong the leaves
   The gale his peace reports.

The wealthy crop of whitening rice
'Mongst thyine woods and groves of spice,
   For Adoration grow;
And, marshalled in the fencéd land,
The peaches and pomegranates stand,
   Where wild carnations blow.

The laurels with the winter strive;
The crocus burnishes alive
    Upon the snow-clad earth;
For Adoration myrtles stay
To keep the garden from dismay,
    And bless the sight from dearth.

The pheasant shows his pompous neck;
And ermine, jealous of a speck,
    With fear eludes offence;
The sable, with his glossy pride,
For Adoration is descried,
    Where frosts and waves condense.

For Adoration, beyond match,
The scholar bullfinch aims to catch
    The soft flute's ivory touch;
And careless, on the hazel spray
The daring redbreast keeps at bay
    The damsel's greedy clutch.

For Adoration, in the skies,
The Lord's philosopher espies
    The dog, the ram, the rose;
The planets' ring, Orion's sword;
Nor is his greatness less adored
    In the vile worm that glows.

For Adoration, on the strings
The western breezes work their wings,
    The captive ear to soothe—
Hark! 'tis a voice—how still, and small—
That makes the cataracts to fall,
    Or bids the sea be smooth!

For Adoration, incense comes
From bezoar, and Arabian gums,
    And from the civet's fur;
But as for prayer, or e'er it faints,
Far better is the breath of saints
    Than galbanum or myrrh.

For Adoration, in the dome
Of Christ, the sparrows find a home,
    And on his olives perch:
The swallow also dwells with thee,
O man of God's humility,
    Within his Saviour's church.

Sweet is the dew that falls betimes,
And drops upon the leafy limes;
    Sweet Hermon's fragrant air:
Sweet is the lily's silver bell,
And sweet the wakeful tapers' smell
    That watch for early prayer.

Sweet the young Nurse, with love intense,
Which smiles o'er sleeping innocence;
    Sweet when the lost arrive:
Sweet the musician's ardour beats,
While his vague mind's in quest of sweets,
    The choicest flowers to hive.

Sweeter, in all the strains of love,
The language of thy turtle-dove,
    Paired to thy swelling chord;
Sweeter, with every grace endued,
The glory of thy gratitude,
    Respired unto the Lord.

Strong is the horse upon his speed;
Strong in pursuit the rapid glede,
    Which makes at once his game:
Strong the tall ostrich on the ground;
Strong through the turbulent profound
    Shoots xiphias to his aim.

Strong is the lion—like a coal
His eyeball—like a bastion's mole
    His chest against the foes:
Strong the gier-eagle on his sail,
Strong against tide the enormous whale
    Emerges as he goes.

But stronger still in earth and air,
And in the sea the man of prayer,
   And far beneath the tide:
And in the seat to faith assigned,
Where ask is have, where seek is find,
   Where knock is open wide.

Beauteous the fleet before the gale;
Beauteous the multitudes in mail,
   Ranked arms, and crested heads;
Beauteous the garden's umbrage mild,
Walk, water, meditated wild,
   And all the bloomy beds.

Beauteous the moon full on the lawn;
And beauteous when the veil's withdrawn,
   The virgin to her spouse:
Beauteous the temple, decked and filled,
When to the heaven of heavens they build
   Their heart-directed vows.

Beauteous, yea beauteous more than these,
The Shepherd King upon his knees,
   For his momentous trust;
With wish of infinite conceit,
For man, beast, mute, the small and great,
   And prostrate dust to dust.

Precious, the bounteous widow's mite;
And precious, for extreme delight,
   The largess from the churl:
Precious the ruby's blushing blaze,
And alba's blest imperial rays,
   And pure cerulean pearl.

Precious the penitential tear;
And precious is the sigh sincere;
   Acceptable to God:
And precious are the winning flowers,
In gladsome Israel's feast of bowers,
   Bound on the hallowed sod.

More precious that diviner part
Of David, even the Lord's own heart,
  Great, beautiful, and new:
In all things, where it was intent,
In all extremes, in each event,
  Proof—answering true to true.

Glorious the sun in mid career;
Glorious the assembled fires appear;
  Glorious the comet's train:
Glorious the trumpet and alarm;
Glorious the Almighty's stretched-out arm;
  Glorious the enraptured main:

Glorious the northern lights astream;
Glorious the song, when God's the theme;
  Glorious the thunder's roar:
Glorious hosannah from the den;
Glorious the catholic amen;
  Glorious the martyr's gore:

Glorious—more glorious is the crown
Of Him that brought salvation down,
  By meekness called thy Son;
Thou that stupendous truth believed,
And now the matchless deed's achieved,
  Determined, Dared, and Done.

JANE ELLIOT

(1727–1805)

Lament for Flodden

I've heard them lilting at our ewe-milking,
  Lasses a-lilting before dawn o' day;
But now they are moaning on ilka green loaning:
  The flowers of the forest are a' wede away.

Lilting, *singing*. Ilka, *every*. Loaning, *field-track*. Wede, *weeded*.

At bughts, in the morning, nae blythe lads are scorning,
   Lassies are lonely and dowie and wae;
Nae daffing, nae gabbing, but sighing and sabbing,
   Ilk ane lifts her leglin and hies her away.

In hairst, at the shearing, nae youths now are jeering,
   Bandsters are lyart, and runkled, and gray;
At fair or at preaching, nae wooing, nae fleeching:
   The flowers of the forest are a' wede away.

At e'en, in the gloaming, nae swankies are roaming
   'Bout stacks wi' the lasses at bogle to play;
But ilk ane sits eerie, lamenting her dearie:
   The flowers of the forest are a' wede away.

Dool and wae for the order sent our lads to the Border!
   The English, for ance, by guile wan the day;
The flowers of the forest, that fought aye the foremost,
   The prime of our land, lie cauld in the clay.

We'll hear nae mair lilting at our ewe-milking;
   Women and bairns are heartless and wae;
Sighing and moaning on ilka green loaning:
   The flowers of the forest are a' wede away.

THOMAS WARTON THE YOUNGER

(1728–1790)

Sonnet, to the River Loddon

Ah! what a weary race my feet have run,
Since first I trod thy banks with alders crowned,
And thought my way was all through fairy ground,
Beneath thy azure sky and golden sun,
Where first my Muse to lisp her notes begun.
While pensive memory traces back the round,
Which fills the varied interval between,
Much pleasure, more of sorrow, mark the scene.
Sweet native stream, those skies and suns so pure

Bughts, *sheepfolds.* Dowie, *low-spirited.* Wae, *woe.* Daffing, *joking.* Gabbing, *prattling.* Leglin, *milk-pail.* Hairst, *harvest.* Shearing, *reaping.* Bandsters, *binders.* Lyart, *grizzled.* Runkled, *wrinkled.* Fleeching, *coaxing.* Swankies, *lusty lads.* Bogle, *hide-and-seek.* Dool, *mourning.*

No more return to cheer my evening road.
Yet still one joy remains; that not obscure
Nor useless all my vacant days have flowed,
From youth's gay dawn to manhood's prime mature,
Nor with the Muse's laurel unbestowed.

OLIVER GOLDSMITH

(1728?–1774)

FROM *The Traveller*

Remote, unfriended, melancholy, slow,
Or by the lazy Scheldt or wandering Po;
Or onward where the rude Carinthian boor
Against the homeless stranger shuts the door;
Or where Campania's plain forsaken lies,
A weary waste expanding to the skies;
Where'er I roam, whatever realms to see,
My heart untravelled fondly turns to thee;
Still to my brother turns, with ceaseless pain,
And drags at each remove a lengthening chain.
Eternal blessings crown my earliest friend,
And round his dwelling guardian saints attend;
Blessed be that spot, where cheerful guests retire
To pause from toil, and trim their evening fire;
Blessed that abode where want and pain repair,
And every stranger finds a ready chair;
Blessed be those feasts with simple plenty crowned,
Where all the ruddy family around
Laugh at the jests or pranks that never fail,
Or sigh with pity at some mournful tale;
Or press the bashful stranger to his food,
And learn the luxury of doing good.
But me, not destined such delights to share,
My prime of life in wandering spent and care;
Impelled with steps unceasing to pursue
Some fleeting good, that mocks me with the view;
That, like the circle bounding earth and skies,
Allures from far, yet as I follow flies;
My fortune leads to traverse realms alone,
And find no spot of all the world my own.

FROM *The Deserted Village*

Sweet Auburn! loveliest village of the plain,
Where health and plenty cheered the labouring swain,
Where smiling spring its earliest visit paid,
And parting summer's lingering blooms delayed;
Dear lovely bowers of innocence and ease.
Seats of my youth, when every sport could please!
How often have I loitered o'er thy green,
Where humble happiness endeared each scene!
How often have I paused on every charm,
The sheltered cot, the cultivated farm,
The never failing brook, the busy mill,
The decent church that topped the neighbouring hill,
The hawthorn bush with seats beneath the shade,
For talking age and whispering lovers made!
How often have I blessed the coming day,
When toil remitting lent its turn to play,
And all the village train, from labour free,
Led up their sports beneath the spreading tree;
While many a pastime circled in the shade,
The young contending as the old surveyed;
And many a gambol frolicked o'er the ground,
And sleights of art and feats of strength went round;
And still, as each repeated pleasure tired,
Succeeding sports the mirthful band inspired;
The dancing pair that simply sought renown,
By holding out, to tire each other down;
The swain mistrustless of his smutted face,
While secret laughter tittered round the place;
The bashful virgin's sidelong looks of love,
The matron's glance that would those looks reprove:
These were thy charms, sweet village! sports like these,
With sweet succession, taught e'en toil to please;
These round thy bowers their cheerful influence shed,
These were thy charms—but all these charms are fled.

Sweet smiling village, loveliest of the lawn!
Thy sports are fled, and all thy charms withdrawn;
Amidst thy bowers the tyrant's hand is seen,

And desolation saddens all thy green.
One only master grasps thy whole domain,
And half a tillage stints thy smiling plain;
No more thy glassy brook reflects the day,
But choked with sedges works its weedy way;
Along thy glades, a solitary guest,
The hollow-sounding bittern guards its nest;
Amidst thy desert-walks the lapwing flies,
And tires their echoes with unvaried cries.
Sunk are thy bowers in shapeless ruin all,
And the long grass o'ertops the mouldering wall;
And, trembling, shrinking from the spoiler's hand,
Far, far away thy children leave the land.

Ill fares the land, to hastening ills a prey,
Where wealth accumulates, and men decay.
Princes and lords may flourish or may fade;
A breath can make them, as a breath has made;
But a bold peasantry, their country's pride,
When once destroyed, can never be supplied.

Song

When lovely woman stoops to folly,
    And finds too late that men betray,
What charm can soothe her melancholy?
    What art can wash her guilt away?

The only art her guilt to cover,
    To hide her shame from every eye,
To give repentance to her lover,
    And wring his bosom, is—to die.

The Vicar of Wakefield, 1765

Song

O memory! thou fond deceiver,
    Still importunate and vain;
To former joys recurring ever,
    And turning all the past to pain;

Thou, like the world, the oppressed oppressing,
  Thy smiles increase the wretch's woe!
And he who wants each other blessing,
  In thee must ever find a foe.

Song

Let schoolmasters puzzle their brains
  With grammar and nonsense and learning;
Good liquor, I stoutly maintain,
  Gives genius a better discerning.
Let them brag of their heathenish gods,
  Their Lethes, their Styxes and Stygians;
Their quis and their quaes and their quods,
  They're all but a parcel of pigeons.
    Toroddle, toroddle, toroll.

When methodist preachers come down,
  A-preaching that drinking is sinful,
I wager the rascals a crown,
  They always preach best with a skinful.
But when you come down with your pence
  For a slice of their scurvy religion,
I'll leave it to all men of sense,
  But you, my good friend, are the pigeon.
    Toroddle, toroddle, toroll.

Then come, put the jorum about,
  And let us be merry and clever;
Our hearts and our liquors are stout;
  Here's the Three Jolly Pigeons for ever.
Let some cry up woodcock or hare,
  Your bustards, your ducks, and your widgeons;
But of all the birds in the air,
  Here's a health to the Three Jolly Pigeons.
    Toroddle, toroddle, toroll.

She Stoops to Conquer, 1773

JOHN SCOTT OF AMWELL

(1730–1783)

The Drum

I hate that drum's discordant sound,
Parading round, and round, and round:
To thoughtless youth it pleasure yields,
And lures from cities and from fields,
To sell their liberty for charms
Of tawdry lace, and glittering arms;
And when ambition's voice commands,
To march, to fight, and fall in foreign lands.

I hate that drum's discordant sound,
Parading round, and round, and round;
To me it talks of ravaged plains,
And burning towns, and ruined swains,
And mangled limbs, and dying groans,
And widow's tears, and orphan's moans,
And all that Misery's hand bestows,
To fill the catalogue of human woes.

WILLIAM COWPER

(1731–1800)

John Gilpin

John Gilpin was a citizen
    Of credit and renown,
A train-band captain eke was he
    Of famous London town.

John Gilpin's spouse said to her dear:
    "Though wedded we have been
These twice ten tedious years, yet we
    No holiday have seen.

"To-morrow is our wedding-day,
    And we will then repair
Unto the Bell at Edmonton
    All in a chaise and pair.

"My sister, and my sister's child,
    Myself, and children three,
Will fill the chaise; so you must ride
    On horseback after we."

He soon replied: "I do admire
    Of womankind but one,
And you are she, my dearest dear,
    Therefore it shall be done.

"I am a linen-draper bold,
    As all the world doth know,
And my good friend the calender
    Will lend his horse to go."

Quoth Mrs. Gilpin: "That's well said;
    And, for that wine is dear,
We will be furnished with our own,
    Which is both bright and clear."

John Gilpin kissed his loving wife;
    O'erjoyed was he to find
That, though on pleasure she was bent,
    She had a frugal mind.

The morning came, the chaise was brought,
    But yet was not allowed
To drive up to the door, lest all
    Should say that she was proud.

So three doors off the chaise was stayed,
    Where they did all get in;
Six precious souls, and all agog
    To dash through thick and thin!

Smack went the whip, round went the wheels,
    Were never folk so glad,
The stones did rattle underneath,
    As if Cheapside were mad.

John Gilpin at his horse's side
  Seized fast the flowing mane,
And up he got, in haste to ride,
  But soon came down again;

For saddle-tree scarce reached had he,
  His journey to begin,
When, turning round his head, he saw
  Three customers come in.

So down he came; for loss of time,
  Although it grieved him sore,
Yet loss of pence, full well he knew,
  Would trouble him much more.

'Twas long before his customers
  Were suited to their mind,
When Betty screaming came downstairs:
  "The wine is left behind!"

"Good lack!" quoth he, "yet bring it me,
  My leathern belt likewise,
In which I bear my trusty sword
  When I do exercise."

Now mistress Gilpin (careful soul!)
  Had two stone bottles found,
To hold the liquor that she loved,
  And keep it safe and sound.

Each bottle had a curling ear,
  Through which the belt he drew,
And hung a bottle on each side,
  To make his balance true.

Then, over all, that he might be
  Equipped from top to toe,
His long red cloak, well brushed and neat,
  He manfully did throw.

Now see him mounted once again
 Upon his nimble steed,
Full slowly pacing o'er the stones,
 With caution and good heed!

But, finding soon a smoother road
 Beneath his well-shod feet,
The snorting beast began to trot,
 Which galled him in his seat.

So, "Fair and softly," John he cried,
 But John he cried in vain;
The trot became a gallop soon,
 In spite of curb and rein.

So stooping down, as needs he must
 Who cannot sit upright,
He grasped the mane with both his hands,
 And eke with all his might.

His horse, who never in that sort
 Had handled been before,
What thing upon his back had got
 Did wonder more and more.

Away went Gilpin, neck or nought;
 Away went hat and wig!
He little dreamt, when he set out,
 Of running such a rig!

The wind did blow, the cloak did fly,
 Like streamer long and gay,
Till, loop and button failing both,
 At last it flew away.

Then might all people well discern
 The bottles he had slung;
A bottle swinging at each side,
 As hath been said or sung.

The dogs did bark, the children screamed,
　　Up flew the windows all;
And every soul cried out: "Well done!"
　　As loud as he could bawl.

Away went Gilpin—Who but he?
　　His fame soon spread around—
"He carries weight!" "He rides a race!"
　　" 'Tis for a thousand pound!"

And still, as fast as he drew near,
　　'Twas wonderful to view
How in a trice the turnpike men
　　Their gates wide open threw.

And now, as he went bowing down
　　His reeking head full low,
The bottles twain behind his back
　　Were shattered at a blow.

Down ran the wine into the road,
　　Most piteous to be seen,
Which made his horse's flanks to smoke
　　As they had basted been.

But still he seemed to carry weight,
　　With leathern girdle braced;
For all might see the bottle-necks
　　Still dangling at his waist.

Thus all through merry Islington
　　These gambols he did play,
And till he came unto the Wash
　　Of Edmonton so gay.

And there he threw the wash about
　　On both sides of the way,
Just like unto a trundling mop,
　　Or a wild goose at play.

At Edmonton his loving wife
　　From the balcóny spied
Her tender husband, wond'ring much
　　To see how he did ride.

"Stop, stop, John Gilpin! Here's the house!"
　　They all at once did cry;
"The dinner waits, and we are tired."
　　Said Gilpin: "So am I!"

But yet his horse was not a whit
　　Inclined to tarry there;
For why?—his owner had a house
　　Full ten miles off, at Ware.

So like an arrow swift he flew,
　　Shot by an archer strong;
So did he fly—which brings me to
　　The middle of my song.

Away went Gilpin, out of breath,
　　And sore against his will,
Till at his friend the calender's
　　His horse at last stood still.

The calender, amazed to see
　　His neighbour in such trim,
Laid down his pipe, flew to the gate,
　　And thus accosted him:

"What news? what news? your tidings tell;
　　Tell me you must and shall—
Say why bare-headed you are come,
　　Or why you come at all?"

Now Gilpin had a pleasant wit,
　　And loved a timely joke;
And thus unto the calender
　　In merry guise he spoke:

"I came because your horse would come;
   And, if I well forebode,
My hat and wig will soon be here—
   They are upon the road."

The calender, right glad to find
   His friend in merry pin,
Returned him not a single word,
   But to the house went in;

Whence straight he came with hat and wig;
   A wig that flowed behind,
A hat not much the worse for wear,
   Each comely in its kind.

He held them up, and, in his turn,
   Thus showed his ready wit:
"My head is twice as big as yours,
   They therefore needs must fit.

"But let me scrape the dirt away
   That hangs upon your face;
And stop and eat, for well you may
   Be in a hungry case."

Said John: "It is my wedding-day,
   And all the world would stare,
If wife should dine at Edmonton
   And I should dine at Ware!"

So, turning to his horse, he said:
   "I am in haste to dine;
'Twas for your pleasure you came here,
   You shall go back for mine."

Ah, luckless speech, and bootless boast!
   For which he paid full dear;
For, while he spake, a braying ass
   Did sing most loud and clear;

Whereat his horse did snort, as he
    Had heard a lion roar,
And galloped ·off with all his might,
    As he had done before.

Away went Gilpin, and away
    Went Gilpin's hat and wig!
He lost them sooner than at first—
    For why?—they were too big!

Now, mistress Gilpin, when she saw
    Her husband posting down
Into the country far away,
    She pulled out half a crown;

And thus unto the youth she said
    That drove them to the Bell—
"This shall be yours when you bring back
    My husband safe and well."

The youth did ride, and soon did meet
    John coming back amain;
Whom in a trice he tried to stop
    By catching at the rein;

But, not performing what he meant,
    And gladly would have done,
The frightened steed he frighted more,
    And made him faster run.

Away went Gilpin, and away
    Went post-boy at his heels!
The post-boy's horse right glad to miss
    The lumb'ring of the wheels.

Six gentlemen upon the road,
    Thus seeing Gilpin fly,
With post-boy scamp'ring in the rear,
    They raised the hue and cry:

"Stop thief, stop thief!—a highwayman!"
  Not one of them was mute;
And all and each that passed that way
  Did join in the pursuit.

And now the turnpike gates again
  Flew open in short space;
The toll-men thinking, as before,
  That Gilpin rode a race.

And so he did—and won it too!
  For he got first to town;
Nor stopped till where he had got up
  He did again get down.

Now let us sing Long live the King,
  And Gilpin long live he;
And, when he next doth ride abroad,
  May I be there to see!

SAMUEL BISHOP

(1731–1795)

To His Wife on the Fourteenth Anniversary of Her Wedding-Day, with a Ring

"Thee, Mary, with this ring I wed,"
So fourteen years ago I said.
Behold another ring! "For what?"
To wed thee o'er again—why not?

With the first ring I married youth,
Grace, beauty, innocence, and truth;
Taste long admired, sense long revered,
And all my Molly then appeared.

If she, by merit since disclosed,
Prove twice the woman I supposed,
I plead that double merit now,
To justify a double vow.

Here then, to-day, with faith as sure,
With ardour as intense and pure,
As when amidst the rites divine
I took thy troth, and plighted mine,
To thee, sweet girl, my second ring,
A token and a pledge I bring;
With this I wed, till death us part,
Thy riper virtues to my heart;
Those virtues which, before untried,
The wife has added to the bride—
Those virtues, whose progressive claim,
Endearing wedlock's very name,
My soul enjoys, my song approves,
For conscience' sake as well as love's.

For why? They show me every hour
Honour's high thought, affection's power,
Discretion's deed, sound judgment's sentence,
And teach me all things—but repentance.

SIR BROOKE BOOTHBY

(1734–1824)

Sonnet on Life

What art thou, Life? The shadow of a dream:
The past and future dwell in thought alone;
The present, ere we note its flight, is gone;
And all ideal, vain, fantastic, seem.
Whence is thy source? And whither dost thou tend?
So short thy period, and thy form so frail;
Poor prisoner! pent in Death's surrounding vale,
Born but to breathe, to suffer, and to end.
Why, Shadow, bring'st thou on thy raven wing
Dark trains of grief and visions of the night,
Rather than graces robed in purple light,
Elysian flowers and love's unclouded spring,
Since sad or gay, whatever be thy theme,
Death surely ends at once the dreamer and the dream?

JAMES BEATTIE

(1735–1803)

FROM *The Minstrel*

But who the melodies of morn can tell?
The wild brook babbling down the mountain side;
The lowing herd; the sheepfold's simple bell;
The pipe of early shepherd dim descried
In the lone valley; echoing far and wide
The clamorous horn along the cliffs above;
The hollow murmur of the ocean-tide;
The hum of bees, the linnet's lay of love,
And the full choir that wakes the universal grove.

The cottage curs at early pilgrim bark;
Crowned with her pail the tripping milkmaid sings;
The whistling ploughman stalks afield; and hark!
Down the rough slope the ponderous wagon rings;
Through rustling corn the hare astonished springs;
Slow tolls the village clock the drowsy hour;
The partridge bursts away on whirring wings;
Deep mourns the turtle in sequestered bower,
And shrill lark carols clear from her aërial tower.

ISAAC BICKERSTAFFE

(1735?–1812?)

FROM *Love in a Village*

There was a jolly miller once,
    Lived on the river Dee;
He worked and sung, from morn till night,
    No lark more blithe than he.
And this the burthen of his song
    For ever used to be:
"I care for nobody, not I,
    If no one cares for me."

WILLIAM JULIUS MICKLE

(1735–1788)

FROM *Cumnor Hall*

The dews of summer night did fall,
The moon, sweet regent of the sky,
Silvered the walls of Cumnor Hall,
And many an oak that grew thereby.

Now nought was heard beneath the skies,
The sounds of busy life were still,
Save an unhappy lady's sighs,
That issued from that lonely pile.

Thus sore and sad that lady grieved
In Cumnor Hall so lone and drear;
And many a heartfelt sigh she heaved,
And let fall many a bitter tear.

And ere the dawn of day appeared,
In Cumnor Hall, so lone and drear,
Full many a piercing scream was heard,
And many a cry of mortal fear.

The death-bell thrice was heard to ring,
An aërial voice was heard to call,
And thrice the raven flapped his wings
Around the towers of Cumnor Hall.

The mastiff howled at village door,
The oaks were shattered on the green;
Woe was the hour, for never more
That hapless Countess e'er was seen.

And in that manor, now no more
Is cheerful feast or sprightly ball;
For ever since that dreary hour
Have spirits haunted Cumnor Hall.

The village maids, with fearful glance,
Avoid the ancient moss-grown wall;
Nor ever lead the merry dance
   Among the groves of Cumnor Hall.

Full many a traveller has sighed,
   And pensive wept the Countess' fall,
As wandering onwards they've espied
   The haunted towers of Cumnor Hall.

The Mariner's Wife

But are ye sure the news is true?
   And are ye sure he's weel?
Is this a time to think o' wark?
   Ye jauds, fling by your wheel.
     For there's nae luck about the house,
      There's nae luck at a',
     There's nae luck about the house,
      When our gudeman's awa.

Is this a time to think o' wark,
   When Colin's at the door?
Rax down my cloak—I'll to the quay,
   And see him come ashore.

Rise up and make a clean fireside,
   Put on the mickle pot;
Gie little Kate her cotton goun,
   And Jock his Sunday's coat.

And mak their shoon as black as slaes,
   Their stockins white as snaw;
It's a' to pleasure our gudeman—
   He likes to see them braw.

Jauds, jades. Rax, take. Braw, handsome.

There are twa hens into the crib,
  Hae fed this month and mair;
Mak haste and thraw their necks about,
  That Colin weel may fare.

My Turkey slippers I'll put on,
  My stockins pearl blue—
It's a' to pleasure our gudeman,
  For he's baith leal and true.

Sae sweet his voice, sae smooth his tongue;
  His breath's like caller air;
His very fit has music in't,
  As he comes up tho stair.

And will I see his face again?
  And will I hear him speak?
I'm downright dizzy wi' the thought:
  In troth I'm like to greet.
    For there's nae luck about the house,
      There's nae luck at a',
    There's nae luck about the house,
      When our gudeman's awa.

MICHAEL BRUCE

(1746-1767)

To the Cuckoo

Hail, beauteous stranger of the grove!
  Thou messenger of Spring!
Now Heaven repairs thy rural seat,
  And woods thy welcome ring.

What time the daisy decks the green,
  Thy certain voice we hear:
Hast thou a star to guide thy path,
  Or mark the rolling year?

Thraw, twist. Caller, fresh. Fit, foot. Greet, weep.

Delightful visitant! with thee
  I hail the time of flowers,
And hear the sound of music sweet
  From birds among the bowers.

The schoolboy, wand'ring through the wood,
  To pull the primrose gay,
Starts, the new voice of Spring to hear,
  And imitates thy lay.

What time the pea puts on the bloom,
  Thou fly'st thy vocal vale,
An annual guest in other lands,
  Another Spring to hail.

Sweet bird! thy bower is ever green,
  Thy sky is ever clear;
Thou hast no sorrow in thy song,
  No winter in thy year.

O could I fly, I'd fly with thee!
  We'd make, with joyful wing,
Our annual visit o'er the globe,
  Companions of the Spring.

CHARLOTTE SMITH

(1749–1806)

The Gossamer

O'er faded heath-flowers spun or thorny furze,
The filmy gossamer is lightly spread;
Waving in every sighing air that stirs,
As fairy fingers had entwined the thread:
A thousand trembling orbs of lucid dew
Spangle the texture of the fairy loom,
As if soft Sylphs, lamenting as they flew,
Had wept departed summer's transient bloom:
But the wind rises, and the turf receives
The glittering web: so, evanescent, fade

Bright views that youth with sanguine heart believes;
So vanish schemes of bliss by Fancy made;
Which, fragile as the fleeting dreams of morn,
Leave but the withered heath and barren thorn.

LADY ANNE LINDSAY

(1750–1825)

Auld Robin Gray

When the sheep are in the fauld, and the kye at hame,
And a' the warld to rest are gane,
The waes o' my heart fa' in showers frae my e'e,
While my gudeman lies sound by me.

Young Jamie lo'ed me weel, and sought me for his bride;
But saving a croun he had naething else beside:
To make the croun a pund, young Jamie gaed to sea;
And the croun and the pund were baith for me.

He hadna been awa' a week but only twa,
When my father brak his arm, and the cow was stown awa';
My mother she fell sick—and my Jamie at the sea—
And auld Robin Gray came a-courtin' me.

My father couldna work, and my mother couldna spin;
I toiled night and day, but their bread I couldna win;
Auld Rob maintained them baith, and wi' tears in his e'e
Said, "Jennie, for their sakes, O, marry me!"

My heart it said nay; I looked for Jamie back;
But the wind it blew high, and the ship it was a wrack;
His ship it was a wrack—why didna Jamie dee?
Or why do I live to cry, Wae's me!

My father urged me sair; my mother didna speak;
But she looked in my face till my heart was like to break;
They gi'ed him my hand, though my heart was in the sea;
Sae auld Robin Gray he was gudeman to me.

Fauld, *fold.* Kye, *cows.* Waes, *woes.* Stown, *stolen.*

I hadna been a wife a week but only four,
When mournfu' as I sat on the stane at the door,
I saw my Jamie's wraith—for I couldna think it he,
Till he said, "I'm come hame to marry thee."

O sair, sair did we greet, and muckle did we say;
We took but ae kiss, and we tore ourselves away;
I wish that I were dead, but I'm no like to dee;
And why was I born to say, Wae's me!

I gang like a ghaist, and I carena to spin;
I daurna think of Jamie, for that wad be a sin;
But I'll do my best a gude wife to be,
For auld Robin Gray he is kind unto me.

JOHN PHILPOT CURRAN

(1750–1817)

The Deserter

If sadly thinking
With spirits sinking,
Could more than drinking
    My cares compose,
A cure for sorrow
From sighs I'd borrow,
And hope to-morrow
    Would end my woes.
But as in wailing
There's nought availing,
And Death unfailing
    Will strike the blow,
Then for that reason,
And for a season,
Let us be merry
    Before we go.
To joy a stranger,
A way-worn ranger,

Greet, *weep.*

In every danger
   My course I've run;
Now hope all ending,
And Death befriending,
His last aid lending,
   My cares are done:
No more a rover,
Or hapless lover,
My griefs are over,
   My glass runs low;
Then for that reason,
And for a season,
Let us be merry
   Before we go!

RICHARD BRINSLEY SHERIDAN
(1751–1816)

Song

Here's to the maiden of bashful fifteen!
   Here's to the widow of fifty!
Here's to the flaunting extravagant quean;
   And here's to the housewife that's thrifty!
      Let the toast pass,
      Drink to the lass!
      I'll warrant she'll prove an excuse for the glass!

Here's to the charmer, whose dimples we prize!
   Now to the maid who has none, sir!
Here's to the girl with a pair of blue eyes;
   And here's to the nymph with but one, sir!
      Let the toast pass, &c.

Here's to the maid with a bosom of snow!
   Now to her that's as brown as a berry!
Here's to the wife with a face full of woe,
   And now to the girl that is merry!
      Let the toast pass, &c.

For let them be clumsy, or let them be slim,
Young or ancient, I care not a feather!
So fill a pint bumper, quite up to the brim,
And let us e'en toast them together!
Let the toast pass,
Drink to the lass!
I'll warrant she'll prove an excuse for the glass!

The School for Scandal, 1777

PHILIP FRENEAU

(1752–1832)

Song of Thyrsis

The turtle on yon withered bough,
That lately mourned her murdered mate,
Has found another comrade now—
Such changes all await!
Again her drooping plume is drest,
Again she's willing to be blest
And takes her lover to her nest.
If nature has decreed it so
With all above, and all below,
Let us like them forget our woe,
And not be killed with sorrow.
If I should quit your arms to-night
And chanced to die before 'twas light—
I would advise you—and you might—
Love again to-morrow.

THOMAS CHATTERTON

(1752–1770)

FROM Aella

The budding floweret blushes at the light,
The meads are sprinkled with the yellow hue;
In daisied mantles is the mountain dight,
The nesh young cowslip bendeth with the dew;
The trees enleaféd, unto heaven straught,
When gentle winds do blow, to whistling din are brought.

Nesh, *tender*. Straught, *extended?*

The evening comes, and brings the dew along:
The ruddy welkin shineth to the eyne;
Around the ale-stake minstrels sing the song,
Young ivy round the doorpost doth entwine;
  I lay me on the grass; yet, to my will,
Albeit all is fair, there lacketh something still.

So Adam thought when once, in Paradise,
All heaven and earth did homage to his mind;
In woman only man's chief solace lies,
As instruments of joy are those of kind.
  Go, take a wife unto thine arms, and see
Winter and barren hills will have a charm for thee.

When Autumn sere and sunburnt doth appear,
With his gold hand gilding the falling leaf,
Bringing up Winter to fulfil the year,
Bearing upon his back the ripened sheaf,
  When all the hills with woody seed are white,
When lightning-fires and gleams do meet from far the sight;

When the fair apples, red as evening sky,
Do bend the tree unto the fruitful ground,
When juicy pears, and berries of black dye,
Do dance in air, and call the eyes around;
  Then, be the evening foul, or be it fair,
Methinks my heart's delight is mingled with some care.

Angels are wrought to be of neither kind,
Angels alone from hot desire are free;
There is a somewhat ever in the mind,
That, without woman, cannot stilléd be;
  No saint in cell but having blood and tere
Doth find the spright to joy in sight of woman fair.

Kind, *nature.* Tere, *muscle.*

ANONYMOUS

(18TH CENTURY)

The Vicar of Bray

In good King Charles's golden days,
When loyalty no harm meant;
A furious High-Church man was I,
And so I got preferment.
Unto my flock I daily preached
Kings are by God appointed,
And damned are those who dare resist
Or touch the Lord's anointed.
   And this is law, I will maintain
   Unto my dying day, Sir,
   That whatsoever king shall reign,
   I will be Vicar of Bray, Sir.

When royal James possessed the crown,
And Popery came in fashion;
The penal laws I hooted down,
And read the Declaration:
The Church of Rome, I found, would fit
Full well my constitution,
And I had been a Jesuit
But for the Revolution.
   And this is law, I will maintain
   Unto my dying day, Sir,
   That whatsoever king shall reign,
   I will be Vicar of Bray, Sir.

When William our deliverer came,
To heal the nation's grievance,
I turned the Cat in Pan again,
And swore to him allegiance:
Old principles I did revoke,
Set conscience at a distance,
Passive obedience is a joke,
A jest is non-resistance.
   And this is law, I will maintain,
   Unto my dying day, Sir,
   That whatsoever king shall reign,
   I will be Vicar of Bray, Sir.

When glorious Anne became our Queen,
The Church of England's glory,
Another face of things was seen,
And I became a Tory:
Occasional-Conformists base
I damned, and moderation,
And thought the Church in danger was
From such prevarication.
    And this is law, I will maintain,
    Unto my dying day, Sir,
    That whatsoever king shall reign,
    I will be Vicar of Bray, Sir.

When George in pudding-time came o'er,
And mod'rate men looked big, Sir,
My principles I changed once more,
And I became a Whig, Sir:
And thus preferment I procured
From our faith's great Defender,
And almost every day abjured
The Pope and the Pretender.
    And this is law, I will maintain,
    Unto my dying day, Sir,
    That whatsoever king shall reign,
    I will be Vicar of Bray, Sir.

Th' illustrious house of Hanover
And Protestant succession,
To these I lustily will swear
While they can keep possession:
For in my faith and loyalty
I never once will falter,
But George my lawful king shall be
Except the times shall alter.
    And this is law, I will maintain,
    Unto my dying day, Sir,
    That whatsoever king shall reign,
    I will be Vicar of Bray, Sir.

ANONYMOUS

(18TH CENTURY)

Verses Copied from the Window of an Obscure Lodging-House, in the Neighbourhood of London

Stranger! whoe'er thou art, whose restless mind,
Like me within these walls is cribbed, confined;
Learn how each want that heaves our mutual sigh
A woman's soft solicitudes supply.
From her white breast retreat all rude alarms,
Or fly the magic circle of her arms;
While souls exchanged alternate grace acquire,
And passions catch from passion's glorious fire:
What though to deck this roof no arts combine,
Such forms as rival every fair but mine;
No nodding plumes, our humble couch above,
Proclaim each triumph of unbounded love;
No silver lamp with sculptured Cupids gay,
O'er yielding beauty pours its midnight ray;
Yet Fanny's charms could Time's slow flight beguile,
Soothe every care, and make each dungeon smile:
In her, what kings, what saints have wished, is given.
Her heart is empire, and her love is heaven.

WILLIAM BLAKE

(1757–1827)

Song

How sweet I roam'd from field to field
And tasted all the summer's pride,
Till I the Prince of Love beheld
Who in the sunny beams did glide!

He show'd me lilies for my hair,
And blushing roses for my brow;
He led me through his gardens fair
Where all his golden pleasures grow.

With sweet May dews my wings were wet,
And Phoebus fir'd my vocal rage;
He caught me in his silken net,
And shut me in his golden cage.

He loves to sit and hear me sing,
Then, laughing, sports and plays with me;
Then stretches out my golden wing,
And mocks my loss of liberty.

To the Muses

Whether on Ida's shady brow
    Or in the chambers of the East,
The chambers of the sun, that now
    From ancient melody have ceas'd;

Whether in Heav'n ye wander fair,
    Or the green corners of the earth,
Or the blue regions of the air,
    Where the melodious winds have birth;

Whether on crystal rocks ye rove,
    Beneath the bosom of the sea
Wand'ring in many a coral grove,
    Fair Nine, forsaking Poetry!

How have you left the ancient love
    That bards of old enjoy'd in you!
The languid strings do scarcely move!
    The sound is forc'd, the notes are few!

Introduction to Songs of Innocence

Piping down the valleys wild,
Piping songs of pleasant glee,
On a cloud I saw a child,
And he laughing said to me:

"Pipe a song about a Lamb!"
So I piped with merry cheer.
"Piper, pipe that song again;"
So I piped: he wept to hear.

"Drop thy pipe, thy happy pipe;
Sing thy songs of happy cheer:"
So I sang the same again,
While he wept with joy to hear.

"Piper, sit thee down and write
In a book, that all may read."
So he vanish'd from my sight,
And I pluck'd a hollow reed,

And I made a rural pen,
And I stain'd the water clear,
And I wrote my happy songs
Every child may joy to hear.

A Cradle Song

Sweet dreams, form a shade
O'er my lovely infant's head;
Sweet dreams of pleasant streams
By happy, silent, moony beams.

Sweet sleep, with soft down
Weave thy brows and infant crown.
Sweet sleep, Angel mild,
Hover o'er my happy child.

Sweet smiles, in the night
Hover over my delight;
Sweet smiles, mother's smiles,
All the livelong night beguiles.

Sweet moans, dovelike sighs,
Chase not slumber from thy eyes.
Sweet moans, sweeter smiles.
All the dovelike moans beguiles.

Sleep, sleep, happy child,
All creation slept and smil'd;
Sleep, sleep, happy sleep,
While o'er thee thy mother weep.

Sweet babe, in thy face
Holy image I can trace.
Sweet babe, once like thee,
Thy Maker lay and wept for me,

Wept for me, for thee, for all,
When He was an infant small.
Thou His image ever see,
Heavenly face that smiles on thee,

Smiles on thee, on me, on all;
Who became an infant small.
Infant smiles are His own smiles;
Heaven and earth to peace beguiles.

The Divine Image

To Mercy, Pity, Peace, and Love
All pray in their distress;
And to these virtues of delight
Return their thankfulness.

For Mercy, Pity, Peace, and Love
Is God, our Father dear,
And Mercy, Pity, Peace, and Love
Is man, His child and care.

For Mercy has a human heart,
Pity a human face,
And Love, the human form divine,
And Peace, the human dress.

Then every man, of every clime,
That prays in his distress,
Prays to the human form divine,
Love, Mercy, Pity, Peace.

And all must love the human form,
In heathen, Turk, or Jew;
Where Mercy, Love, and Pity dwell
There God is dwelling too.

Infant Joy

"I have no name:
"I am but two days old."
What shall I call thee?
"I happy am,
"Joy is my name."
Sweet joy befall thee!

Pretty joy!
Sweet joy but two days old,
Sweet joy I call thee:
Thou dost smile,
I sing the while,
Sweet joy befall thee!

On Another's Sorrow

Can I see another's woe,
And not be in sorrow too?
Can I see another's grief,
And not seek for kind relief?

Can I see a falling tear,
And not feel my sorrow's share?
Can a father see his child
Weep, nor be with sorrow fill'd?

Can a mother sit and hear
An infant groan an infant fear?
No, no! never can it be!
Never, never can it be!

And can he who smiles on all
Hear the wren with sorrows small,
Hear the small bird's grief and care,
Hear the woes that infants bear,

And not sit beside the nest,
Pouring pity in their breast;
And not sit the cradle near,
Weeping tear on infant's tear;

And not sit both night and day,
Wiping all our tears away?
O, no! never can it be!
Never, never can it be!

He doth give his joy to all;
He becomes an infant small;
He becomes a man of woe;
He doth feel the sorrow too.

Think not thou canst sigh a sigh
And thy maker is not by;
Think not thou canst weep a tear
And thy maker is not near.

O! he gives to us his joy
That our grief he may destroy;
Till our grief is fled and gone
He doth sit by us and moan.

The Clod and the Pebble

"Love seeketh not Itself to please,
"Nor for itself hath any care,
"But for another gives its ease,
"And builds a Heaven in Hell's despair."

So sung a little Clod of Clay
Trodden with the cattle's feet,
But a Pebble of the brook
Warbled out these metres meet:

"Love seeketh only Self to please,
"To bind another to Its delight,
"Joys in another's loss of ease,
"And builds a hell in Heaven's despite."

The Tiger

Tiger! Tiger! burning bright
In the forests of the night,
What immortal hand or eye
Could frame thy fearful symmetry?

In what distant deeps or skies
Burnt the fire of thine eyes?
On what wings dare he aspire?
What the hand dare seize the fire?

And what shoulder, and what art,
Could twist the sinews of thy heart?
And when thy heart began to beat,
What dread hand? and what dread feet?

What the hammer? what the chain?
In what furnace was thy brain?
What the anvil? what dread grasp
Dare its deadly terrors clasp?

When the stars threw down their spears,
And water'd heaven with their tears,
Did he smile his work to see?
Did he who made the Lamb make thee?

Tiger! Tiger! burning bright
In the forests of the night,
What immortal hand or eye,
Dare frame thy fearful symmetry?

The Sick Rose

O Rose, thou art sick!
The invisible worm,
That flies in the night,
In the howling storm,

Has found out thy bed
Of crimson joy;
And his dark secret love
Does thy life destroy.

"Ah! Sun-Flower!..."

Ah! Sun-flower! weary of time,
Who countest the steps of the sun;
Seeking after that sweet golden clime,
Where the traveller's journey is done;

Where the Youth pined away with desire,
And the pale Virgin shrouded in snow,
Arise from their graves, and aspire
Where my Sun-flower wishes to go.

The Garden of Love

I went to the Garden of Love
And I saw what I never had seen:
A Chapel was built in the midst,
Where I used to play on the green.

And the gates of this Chapel were shut,
And "Thou shalt not" writ over the door;
So I turn'd to the Garden of Love
That so many sweet flowers bore;

And I saw it was filled with graves,
And tomb-stones where flowers should be;
And Priests in black gowns were walking their rounds,
And binding with briars my joys and desires.

London

I wander thro' each charter'd street,
Near where the charter'd Thames doth flow,
And mark in every face I meet
Marks of weakness, marks of woe.

In ev'ry cry of every Man,
In ev'ry Infant's cry of fear,
In every voice, in every ban,
The mind-forg'd manacles I hear.

How the Chimney-sweeper's cry
Every black'ning Church appalls;
And the hapless Soldier's sigh
Runs in blood down Palace walls.

But most thro' midnight streets I hear
How the youthful Harlot's curse
Blasts the new born Infant's tear
And blights with plagues the Marriage hearse.

A Little Boy Lost

"Nought loves another as itself,
"Nor venerates another so,
"Nor is it possible to thought
"A greater than itself to know:

"And Father, how can I love you
"Or any of my brothers more?
"I love you like the little bird
"That picks up crumbs around the door."

The Priest sat by and heard the child,
In trembling zeal he seiz'd his hair:
He led him by his little coat,
And all admir'd the Priestly care.

And standing on the altar high,
"Lo! what a fiend is here!" said he,
"One who sets reason up for judge
"Of our most holy Mystery."

The weeping child could not be heard,
The weeping parents wept in vain;
They strip'd him to his little shirt,
And bound him in an iron chain;

And burn'd him in a holy place,
Where many had been burn'd before:
The weeping parents wept in vain.
Are such things done on Albion's shore?

FROM *Poems from MSS.*

1.

Never seek to tell thy love
Love that never told can be;
For the gentle wind does move
Silently, invisibly.

I told my love, I told my love,
I told her all my heart,
Trembling, cold, in ghastly fears—
Ah, she doth depart.

Soon as she was gone from me
A traveller came by
Silently, invisibly—
O, was no deny.

2.

I laid me down upon a bank
Where love lay sleeping.
I heard among the rushes dank
Weeping, Weeping.

3.

I asked a thief to steal me a peach:
He turn'd up his eyes.
I ask'd a lithe lady to lie her down:
Holy and meek she cries.

As soon as I went an angel came:
He wink'd at the thief
And smil'd at the dame,
And without one word spoke
Had a peach from the tree,
And 'twixt earnest and joke
Enjoy'd the Lady.

4.

Love to faults is always blind,
Always is to joy inclin'd,
Lawless, wing'd, and unconfin'd,
And breaks all chains from every mind.

Deceit to secresy confin'd,
Lawful, cautious, and refin'd;
To every thing but interest blind,
And forges fetters for the mind.

5.

Abstinence sows sand all over
The ruddy limbs and flaming hair,
But Desire Gratified
Plants fruits of life and beauty there.

The Question Answer'd

What is it men in women do require?
The lineaments of Gratified Desire.
What is it women do in men require?
The lineaments of Gratified Desire.

FROM *Auguries of Innocence*

To see a World in a Grain of Sand
And a Heaven in a Wild Flower,
Hold Infinity in the palm of your hand
And Eternity in an hour.

FROM *Visions of the Daughters of Albion*

"Father of Jealousy, be thou accursed from the earth!
Why hast thou taught my Theotormon this accursed thing?
Till beauty fades from off my shoulders, darken'd and cast out,
A solitary shadow wailing on the margin of non-entity.

"I cry: Love! Love! Love! happy happy Love! free as the
      mountain wind!
Can that be Love that drinks another as a sponge drinks water,
That clouds with jealousy his nights, with weeping all the day,
To spin a web of age around him, grey and hoary, dark,
Till his eyes sicken at the fruit that hangs before his sight?
Such is self-love that envies all, a creeping skeleton
With lamplike eyes watching around the frozen marriage bed."

FROM *Vala, or the Four Zoas*

1.

The Cities send to one another saying: "My sons are Mad
With wine of cruelty. Let us plait a scourge, O Sister City."
Children are nourish'd for the Slaughter; once the Child was
      fed
With Milk, but wherefore now are Children fed with blood?

The Horse is of more value than the Man. The Tiger fierce
Laughs at the Human form; the Lion mocks and thirsts for
      blood.
They cry, "O Spider, spread thy web! Enlarge thy bones and,
      fill'd
With marrow, sinews and flesh, Exalt thyself, attain a voice.

"Call to thy dark arm'd hosts; for all the sons of Men muster
together
To desolate their cities! Man shall be no more! Awake, O
Hosts!"

2.

O Lord, wilt thou not look upon our sore afflictions
Amongst these flames incessant labouring? our hard masters
laugh
At all our sorrow. We are made to turn the wheel for water,
To carry the heavy basket on our scorched shoulders, to sift
The sand and ashes, and to mix the clay with tears and re-
pentance.
The times are now return'd upon us; we have given ourselves
To scorn, and now are scorned by the slaves of our enemies.
Our beauty is cover'd over with clay and ashes, and our backs
Furrow'd with whips, and our flesh bruised with the heavy
basket.
Forgive us, O thou piteous one whom we have offended!
forgive
The weak remaining shadow of Vala that returns in sorrow
to thee.

FROM *Milton*

And did those feet in ancient time
Walk upon England's mountains green?
And was the Holy Lamb of God
On England's pleasant pastures seen?

And did the Countenance Divine
Shine forth upon our clouded hills?
And was Jerusalem builded here
Among these dark Satanic Mills?

Bring me my Bow of burning gold:
Bring me my Arrows of desire:
Bring me my Spear: O clouds unfold!
Bring me my Chariot of fire.

I will not cease from Mental Fight,
Nor shall my Sword sleep in my hand
Till we have built Jerusalem
In England's green and pleasant Land.

FROM *Jerusalem*

The Rhine was red with human blood,
The Danube roll'd a purple tide,
  On the Euphrates Satan stood,
And over Asia stretch'd his pride.

He wither'd up sweet Zion's Hill
From every Nation of the Earth;
  He wither'd up Jerusalem's Gates
And in a dark Land gave her birth.

He wither'd up the Human Form
By laws of sacrifice for sin,
  Till it became a Mortal Worm,
But O! translucent all within.

The Divine Vision still was seen,
Still was the Human Form Divine,
  Weeping in weak and mortal clay,
O Jesus, still the Form was thine.

And thine the Human Face, and thine
The Human Hands and Feet and Breath,
  Entering thro' the Gates of Birth
And passing thro' the Gates of Death.

And O thou Lamb of God, whom I
Slew in my dark self-righteous pride,
  Art thou return'd to Albion's Land?
And is Jerusalem thy Bride?

Come to my arms and never more
Depart but dwell for ever here:
  Create my Spirit to thy Love:
Subdue my Spectre to thy Fear.

Spectre of Albion! warlike Fiend!
In clouds of blood and ruin roll'd,
  I here reclaim thee as my own,
My Selfhood! Satan! arm'd in gold.

  Is this thy soft Family-Love,
Thy cruel Patriarchal pride,
  Planting thy Family alone,
Destroying all the World beside?

  A man's worst enemies are those
Of his own house and family;
  And he who makes his law a curse,
By his own law shall surely die.

  In my Exchanges every Land
Shall walk, and mine in every Land,
  Mutual shall build Jerusalem,
Both heart in heart and hand in hand.

To the Accuser Who Is the God of This World

  Truly, my Satan, thou art but a Dunce,
  And dost not know the Garment from the Man.
  Every Harlot was a Virgin once,
  Nor canst thou ever change Kate into Nan.

  Tho' thou art Worship'd by the Names Divine
  Of Jesus and Jehovah, thou art still
  The Son of Morn in weary Night's decline,
  The lost Traveller's Dream under the Hill.

ROBERT BURNS

(1759–1796)

A Poet's Welcome to His Love-Begotten Daughter

Thou's welcome, wean; mishanter fa' me,
If thoughts o' thee, or yet thy mammie,
Shall ever daunton me or awe me,
    My sweet wee lady,
Or if I blush when thou shalt ca' me
    Tyta or daddie.

Tho' now they ca' me fornicator,
An' tease my name wi' countra clatter,
The mair they talk, I'm kend the better,
    E'en let them clash;
An auld wife's tongue's a feckless matter
    To gie ane fash.

Welcome! my bonie, sweet, wee dochter,
Tho' ye come here a wee unsought for,
And tho' your comin' I hae fought for,
    Baith kirk and queir;
Yet, by my faith, ye're no unwrought for,
    That I shall swear!

Sweet fruit o' monie a merry dint,
My funny toil is no a' tint,
Tho' thou cam to the warl' asklent,
    Which fools may scoff at;
In my last plack thy part's be in't
    The better ha'f o't.

Tho' I should be the waur bestead,
Thou's be as braw and bienly clad,
And thy young years as nicely bred
    Wi' education,
As onie brat o' wedlock's bed,
    In a' thy station.

Mishanter, *mishap.* Clash, *gossip.* Fash, *trouble.* Tint, *lost.* Plack, *a coin.*
Bienly, *comfortably.*

Wee image o' my bonie Betty,
As fatherly I kiss and daut thee,
As dear and near my heart I set thee
        Wi' as gude will
As a' the priests had seen me get thee
        That's out o' hell.

Lord grant that thou may aye inherit
Thy mither's person, grace, an' merit,
An' thy poor, worthless daddy's spirit,
        Without his failins,
'Twill please me more to see thee heir it,
        Than stockit mailens.

For if thou be what I wad hae thee,
And tak the counsel I shall gie thee,
I'll never rue my trouble wi' thee—
        The cost nor shame o't,
But be a loving father to thee,
        And brag the name o't.

Holy Willie's Prayer

And send the godly in a pet to pray.—POPE

O Thou, that in the heavens dost dwell,
Wha, as it pleases best Thysel',
Sends ane to heaven an ten to hell,
        A' for Thy glory,
And no for onie guid or ill
        They've done afore Thee!

I bless and praise Thy matchless might,
When thousands Thou hast left in night,
That I am here afore Thy sight,
        For gifts an' grace
A burning and a shining light
        To a' this place.

Daut, *pet.* Mailens, *farms.*

What was I, or my generation,
That I should get sic exaltation,
I wha deserv'd most just damnation
    For broken laws,
Sax thousand years ere my creation,
      Thro' Adam's cause.

When from my mither's womb I fell,
Thou might hae plung'd me deep in hell,
To gnash my gooms, and weep and wail,
    In burnin lakes,
Where damnéd devils roar and yell,
      Chain'd to their stakes.

Yet I am here a chosen sample,
To show Thy grace is great and ample;
I'm here a pillar o' Thy temple,
    Strong as a rock,
A guide, a buckler, and example,
      To a' Thy flock.

O Lord, Thou kens what zeal I bear,
When drinkers drink, an' swearers swear,
An' singing here, an' dancing there,
    Wi' great and sma';
For I am keepit by Thy fear
      Free frae them a'.

But yet, O Lord! confess I must,
At times I'm fash'd wi' fleshly lust:
An' sometimes, too, in warldly trust,
    Vile self gets in;
But Thou remembers we are dust,
      Defil'd wi' sin.

O Lord! yestreen, Thou kens, wi' Meg—
Thy pardon I sincerely beg;
O! may't ne'er be a livin plague
    To my dishonour,
An' I'll ne'er lift a lawless leg
      Again upon her.

Besides, I farther maun allow,
Wi' Leezie's lass, three times I trow—
But Lord, that Friday I was fou,
        When I cam near her;
Or else, Thou kens, Thy servant true
        Wad never steer her.

Maybe Thou lets this fleshly thorn
Buffet Thy servant e'en and morn,
Lest owre proud and high shou'd turn,
        That he's sae gifted:
If sae, Thy han' maun e'en be borne,
        Until Thou lift it.

Lord, bless Thy chosen in this place,
For here Thou has a chosen race:
But God confound their stubborn face
        An' blast their name,
Wha bring Thy elders to disgrace
        An' public shame.

Lord, mind Gaw'n Hamilton's deserts;
He drinks, an' swears, an' plays at cartes,
Yet has sae mony takin arts,
        Wi' great and sma',
Frae God's ain priest the people's hearts
        He steals awa.

An' when we chasten'd him therefor,
Thou kens how he bred sic a splore,
An' set the warld in a roar
        O' laughing at us;—
Curse Thou his basket and his store,
        Kail an' potatoes.

Lord, hear my earnest cry and pray'r,
Against that Presbyt'ry o' Ayr;
Thy strong right hand, Lord, make it bare
        Upo' their heads;
Lord, visit them, an' dinna spare,
        For their misdeeds.

Fou, drunk. Steer, *stir.* Splore, *uproar.* Kail, *broth.*

O Lord, my God! that glib-tongu'd Aiken,
My vera heart and flesh are quakin,
To think how we stood sweatin, shakin,
      An' p——'d wi' dread,
While he, wi' hingin lip an' snakin,
      Held up his head.

Lord, in Thy day o' vengeance try him,
Lord, visit them wha did employ him,
And pass not in Thy mercy by them,
      Nor hear their pray'r,
But for Thy people's sake destroy them,
      An' dinna spare.

But, Lord, remember me an' mine
Wi' mercies temporal and divine,
That I for grace and gear may shine,
      Excell'd by nane,
And a' the glory shall be Thine,
      Amen, Amen!

To a Louse on Seeing One on a Lady's Bonnet at Church

Ha! whaur ye gaun, ye crowlin ferlie?
Your impudence protects you sairly;
I canna say but ye strunt rarely,
      Owre gauze and lace;
Tho', faith! I fear ye dine but sparely
      On sic a place.

Ye ugly, creepin, blastit wonner,
Detested, shunn'd by saunt an' sinner,
How daur ye set your fit upon her—
      Sae fine a lady?
Gae somewhere else and seek your dinner
      On some poor body.

Snakin, *sneering*. Gear, *money*.

Crowlin ferlie, *crawling wonder*. Strunt, *strut*. Fit, *feet*.

Swith! in some beggar's haffet squattle;
There ye may creep, and sprawl, and sprattle,
Wi' ither kindred, jumping cattle,
          In shoals and nations;
Whaur horn nor bane ne'er daur unsettle
          Your thick plantations.

Now haud you there, ye're out o' sight,
Below the fatt'rels, snug and tight;
Na, faith ye yet; ye'll no be right,
          Till ye've got on it—
The verra tapmost, tow'rin height
          O' Miss's bonnet.

My sooth! right bauld ye set your nose out,
As plump and grey as ony groset:
O for some rank, mercurial rozet,
          Or fell, red smeddum,
I'd gie you sic a hearty dose o't,
          Wad dress your droddum.

I wad na be surpris'd to spy
You on an auld wife's flainen toy;
Or aiblins some bit duddie boy,
          On's wyliecoat;
But Miss's fine Lunardi! fye!
          How daur ye do't?

O Jeany, dinna toss your head,
An' set your beauties a' abroad!
Ye little ken what cursed speed
          The blastie's makin:
Thae winks an' finger-ends, I dread,
          Are notice takin.

Haffet, *temple.* Squattle, *sprawl.* Sprattle, *struggle.* Fatt'rels, *trimmings.*
Bauld, *bold.* Groset, *gooseberry.* Rozet, ? . Smeddum, *powder.* Drod-
dum, *breech.* Flainen, *flannel.* Aiblins, *perhaps.* Duddie, *ragged.* Wyliecoat,
vest. Lunardi, *balloon-bonnet.* Abread, *abroad.*

O wad some Power the giftie gie us
To see oursels as ithers see us!
It wad frae mony a blunder free us,
    An' foolish notion:
What airs in dress an' gait wad lea'e us,
    An' ev'n devotion!

Address to the Unco Guid or the Rigidly Righteous

O ye wha are sae guid yoursel',
    Sae pious and sae holy,
Ye've nought to do but mark and tell
    Your neibours' fauts and folly!
Whase life is like a wool gaun mill,
    Supplied wi' store o' water;
The heapéd happer's ebbing still,
    An' still the clap plays clatter.

Hear me, ye venerable core,
    As counsel for poor mortals
That frequent pass douce Wisdom's door
    For glaikit Folly's portals:
I, for their thoughtless, careless sakes,
    Would here propone defences—
Their donsie tricks, their black mistakes,
    Their failings and mischances.

Ye see your state wi' theirs compared,
    And shudder at the niffer;
But cast a moment's fair regard,
    What makes the mighty differ?
Discount what scant occasion gave,
    That purity ye pride in;
And (what's aft mair than a' the lave)
    Your better art o' hidin.

Happer, hopper. Clap, clapper. Douce, sedate. Glaikit, giddy. Donsie, vicious. Niffer, exchange. Lave, rest.

Think, when your castigated pulse
    Gies now and then a wallop,
What ragings must his veins convulse,
    That still eternal gallop!
Wi' wind and tide fair i' your tail,
    Right on ye scud your sea-way;
But in the teeth o' baith to sail,
    It makes an unco lee-way.

See Social Life and Glee sit down,
    All joyous and unthinking,
Till quite transmugrified, they're grown
    Debauchery and Drinking:
O would they stay to calculate
    Th' eternal consequences;
Or your more dreaded hell to state,
    Damnation of expenses!

Ye high, exalted, virtuous dames,
    Tied up in godly laces,
Before ye gie poor Frailty names,
    Suppose a change o' cases;
A dear-lov'd lad, convenience snug,
    A treach'rous inclination—
But let me whisper i' your lug,
    Ye're aiblins no temptation.

Then gently scan your brother man,
    Still gentler sister woman;
Tho' they may gang a kennin wrang,
    To step aside is human;
One point must still be greatly dark—
    The moving *Why* they do it;
And just as lamely can ye mark
    How far perhaps they rue it.

Who made the heart, 'tis He alone
    Decidely can try us;
He knows each chord, its various tone,
    Each spring, its various bias:

Lug, ear. Aiblins, *perhaps.* Kennin, *a very little.*

Then at the balance let's be mute,
   We never can adjust it;
What's done we partly may compute,
   But know not what's resisted.

Address to a Haggis

Fair fa' your honest, sonsie face,
Great chieftain o' the pudding-race!
Aboon them a' ye take your place,
     Painch, tripe, or thairm:
Weel are ye wordy o' a grace
     As lang's my arm.

The groaning trenchers there ye fill,
Your hurdies like a distant hill,
Your pin wad help to mend a mill
     In time o' need,
While thro' your pores the dews distil
     Like amber bead.

His knife see rustic Labour dight,
An' cut you up wi' ready sleight,
Trenching your gushing entrails bright,
     Like ony ditch;
And then, O what a glorious sight,
     Warm-reekin, rich!

Then, horn for horn, they stretch an strive:
Deil tak the hindmost! on they drive,
Till a' their weel-swall'd kytes belyve,
     Are bent lyke drums;
Then auld Guidman, maist like to rive,
     "Bethankit!" hums.

Sonsie, *jolly.* Painch, *paunch.* Thairm, *gut.* Hurdies, *buttocks.* Weel-swall'd kytes belyve, *well-swollen bellies soon.* Rive, *burst.*

Is there that owre his French *ragout*
Or *olio* that wad staw a sow,
Or fricassee wad mak her spew
          Wi' perfect sconner,
Looks down wi' sneering, scornfu' view
          On sic a dinner?

Poor devil! see him owre his trash,
As feckless as a wither'd rash,
His spindle shank, a guid whip-lash,
          His nieve a nit;
Thro' bloody flood or field to dash,
          O how unfit!

But mark the Rustic, haggis fed,
The trembling earth resounds his tread.
Clap in his walie nieve a blade,
          He'll mak it whissle;
An' legs an' arms, an' heads will send,
          Like taps o' thrissle.

Ye Pow'rs wha mak mankind your care,
And dish them out their bill o' fare,
Auld Scotland wants nae skinking ware
          That jaups in luggies;
But, if ye wish her gratefu' prayer,
          Gie her a haggis!

Tam o' Shanter
(A TALE)

When chapman billies leave the street,
And drouthy neibors neibors meet;
As market days are wearing late,
And folk begin to tak the gate,

Staw, *surfeit*. Sconner, *disgust*. Rash, *rush*. Nieve, *fist*. Nit, *nut*. Walie, *stout*. Taps o' thrissle, *thistle tops*. Skinking, *watery*. Jaups, *splashes*. Luggies, *wooden bowls*.

Chapman billies, *fellow pedlars*. Drouthy, *thirsty*. Gate, *way*.

While we sit bousing at the nappy,
An' getting fou and unco happy,
We think na on the lang Scots miles,
The mosses, waters, slaps and stiles,
That lie between us and our hame,
Where sits our sulky, sullen dame,
Gathering her brows like gathering storm,
Nursing her wrath to keep it warm.

This truth fand honest TAM O' SHANTER,
As he frae Ayr ae night did canter:
(Auld Ayr, wham ne'er a town surpasses,
For honest men and bonie lasses).

O Tam! had'st thou but been sae wise,
As taen thy ain wife Kate's advice!
She tauld thee weel thou was a skellum,
A blethering, blustering, drunken blellum;
That frae November till October,
Ae market-day thou was na sober;
That ilka melder wi' the Miller,
Thou sat as lang as thou had siller;
That ev'ry naig was ca'd a shoe on
The Smith and thee gat roarin fou on;
That at the Lord's house, ev'n on Sunday,
Thou drank wi' Kirkton Jean till Monday;
She prophesied that late or soon,
Thou wad be found, deep drown'd in Doon,
Or catch'd wi' warlocks in the mirk,
By Alloway's auld, haunted kirk.

Ah, gentle dames! it gars me greet,
To think how mony counsels sweet,
How mony lengthen'd, sage advices,
The husband frae the wife despises!

Bousing at the nappy, *drinking ale.* Fou, *drunk.* Slaps, *hedge gaps.* Skellum,
rascal. Blellum, *babbler.* Melder, *grinding of corn.* Naig, *nag.* Shoe on,
appetiser. Warlocks, *wizards.* Gars me greet, *makes me cry.*

But to our tale:—Ae market night,
Tam had got planted unco right,
Fast by an ingle, bleezing finely,
Wi' reaming swats that drank divinely;
And at his elbow, Souter Johnie,
His ancient, trusty, drouthy crony:
Tam lo'ed him like a very brither;
They had been fou for weeks thegither.
The night drave on wi' sangs an' clatter;
And aye the ale was growing better:
The Landlady and Tam grew gracious,
Wi' favours secret, sweet and precious:
The Souter tauld his queerest stories;
The Landlord's laugh was ready chorus:
The storm without might rair and rustle,
Tam did na mind the storm a whistle.

Care, mad to see a man sae happy,
E'en drowned himsel among the nappy.
As bees flee hame wi' lades o' treasure,
The minutes wing'd their way wi' pleasure:
Kings may be blest, but Tam was glorious,
O'er a' the ills o' life victorious!

But pleasures are like poppies spread,
You seize the flow'r, its bloom is shed;
Or like the snow falls in the river,
A moment white—then melts for ever;
Or like the Borealis race,
That flit ere you can point their place;
Or like the Rainbow's lovely form
Evanishing amid the storm.—
Nae man can tether Time nor Tide,
The hour approaches Tam maun ride;
That hour, o' night's black arch the key-stane,
That dreary hour he mounts his beast in;
And sic a night he taks the road in,
As ne'er poor sinner was abroad in.

Reaming swats, *frothing ale.* Souter, *cobbler.* Rair, *roar.* Lades, *loads.*

The wind blew as 'twad blawn its last;
The rattling showers rose on the blast;
The speedy gleams the darkness swallow'd;
Loud, deep, and lang the thunder bellow'd:
That night, a child might understand,
The deil had business on his hand.

Weel-mounted on his grey mare Meg,
A better never lifted leg.
Tam skelpit on thro' dub and mire,
Despising wind, and rain, and fire;
Whiles holding fast his gude blue bonnet,
Whiles crooning o'er some auld Scots sonnet,
Whiles glow'rin round wi' prudent cares,
Lest bogles catch him unawares;
Kirk-Alloway was drawing nigh,
Where ghaists and houlets nightly cry.

By this time he was cross the ford,
Where in the snaw the chapman smoor'd;
And past the birks and meikle stane,
Where drunken Charlie brak's neck-bane;
And thro' the whins, and by the cairn,
Where hunters fand the murder'd bairn;
And near the thorn, aboon the well,
Where Mungo's mither hang'd hersel'.
Before him Doon pours all his floods,
The doubling storm roars thro' the woods,
The lightnings flash from pole to pole,
Near and more near the thunders roll,
When, glimmering thro' the groaning trees,
Kirk-Alloway seem'd in a bleeze,
Thro' ilka bore the beams were glancing,
And loud resounded mirth and dancing.

Skelpit, hurried. Dub, puddle. Bogles, hobgoblins. Houlets, owls. Smoor'd,
smothered. Birks, birch trees. Meikle, big. Whins, gorse. Bore, chink.

Inspiring bold John Barleycorn!
What dangers thou canst make us scorn!
Wi' tipenny, we fear nae evil;
Wi' usquabae, we'll face the devil!
The swats sae ream'd in Tammie's noddle,
Fair play, he car'd na deils a boddle,
But Maggie stood, right sair astonish'd,
Till, by the heel and hand admonish'd,
She ventur'd forward on the light;
And, wow! Tam saw an unco sight!

Warlocks and witches in a dance:
Nae cotillon, brent new frae France,
But hornpipes, jigs, strathspeys, and reels,
Put life and mettle in their heels.
A winnock-bunker in the east,
There sat auld Nick, in shape o' beast;
A tousie tyke, black, grim, and large,
To gie them music was his charge:
He screw'd the pipes, and gart them skirl,
Till roof and rafters a' did dirl.—
Coffins stood round, like open presses,
That shaw's the Dead in their last dresses;
And (by some devilish cantraip sleight)
Each in its cauld hand held a light.
By which heroic Tam was able
To note upon the haly table,
A murderer's banes, in gibbet-airns;
Two span-lang, wee, unchristened bairns;
A thief, new-cutted frae a rape,
Wi' his last gasp his gab did gape;
Five tomahawks, wi' blude red-rusted;
Five scimitars, wi' murder crusted;
A garter which a babe had strangled;
A knife, a father's throat had mangled,
Whom his ain son of life bereft,
The grey hairs yet stack to the heft;
Wi' mair of horrible and awfu',
Which even to name wad be unlawfu'.

Tipenny, *twopenny ale.* Boddle, *twopence Scots.* Winnock-bunker, *window seat.* Tousie tyke, *shaggy dog.* Gart, *made.* Skirl, *squeal.* Dirl, *rattle.* Cantraip, *magic.* Haly table, *altar.*

As Tammie glowr'd, amaz'd and curious,
The mirth and fun grew fast and furious;
The piper loud and louder blew,
The dancers quick and quicker flew,
They reel'd, they set, they cross'd, they cleekit,
Till ilka carlin swat and reekit,
And coost her duddies to the wark,
And linkit at it in her sark!

Now Tam, O Tam! had they been queans,
A' plump and strapping in their teens!
Their sarks, instead of creeshie flainen,
Been snaw-white seventeen-hunder linen!—
Thir breeks o' mine, my only pair,
That aince were plush, o' guid blue hair,
I wad hae gien them off my hurdies,
For ae blink o' the bonie burdies!
But wither'd beldams, auld and droll,
Rigwoodie hags wad spean a foal,
Louping an' flinging on a crummock,
I wonder did na turn thy stomach.

But Tam kent what was what fu' brawlie:
There was ae winsome wench and waulie
That night enlisted in the core,
Lang after ken'd on Carrick shore
(For mony a beast to dead she shot,
And perish'd mony a bonie boat,
And shook baith meikle corn and bear,
And kept the country-side in fear);
Her cutty sark, o' Paisley harn,
That while a lassie she had worn,
In longitude tho' sorely scanty,
It was her best, and she was vauntie.

Cleekit, *joined hands.* Ilka carlin, *each old woman.* Reekit, *smoked.* Coost, *cast.* Duddies, *clothes.* Wark, *work.* Linkit, *tripped.* Sark, *chemise.* Queans, *girls.* Creeshie flainen, *greasy flannel.* Hurdies, *buttocks.* Blink, *glimpse.* Burdies, *girls.* Rigwoodie, *bony.* Spean, *wean.* Louping an' flinging, *leaping and kicking out.* Crummock, *staff.* Brawlie, *very well.* Waulie, *jolly.* Bear, *barley.* Cutty, *short.* Harn, *coarse cloth.* Vauntie, *proud.*

Ah! little ken'd thy reverend grannie,
That sark she coft for her wee Nannie,
Wi' twa pund Scots ('twas a' her riches),
Wad ever grac'd a dance of witches!

But here my Muse her wing maun cour,
Sic flights are far beyond her power;
To sing how Nannie lap and flang
(A souple jade she was and strang),
And how Tam stood, like ane bewitch'd,
And thought his very een enrich'd:
Even Satan glowr'd, and fidg'd fu' fain,
And hotch'd and blew wi' might and main:
Till first ae caper, syne anither,
Tam tint his reason a' thegither,
And roars out, "Weel done, Cutty-Sark!"
And in an instant all was dark:
And scarcely had he Maggie rallied,
When out the hellish legion sallied.

As bees bizz out wi' angry fyke,
When plundering herds assail their byke ;
As open pussie's mortal foes,
When, pop! she starts before their nose;
As eager runs the market-crowd,
When "Catch the thief!" resounds aloud;
So Maggie runs, the witches follow,
Wi' mony an eldritch skreich and hollo.

Ah, Tam! Ah, Tam! thou'll get thy fairin!
In hell they'll roast thee like a herrin!
In vain thy Kate awaits thy comin!
Kate soon will be a woefu' woman!
Now, do thy speedy utmost, Meg,
And win the key-stane o' the brig;
There, at them thou thy tail may toss,
A running stream they dare na cross,

Coft, bought. Lap and flang, *leaped and kicked.* Fidg'd, *wriggled.* Hotch'd,
jerked. Fyke, *bustle.* Byke, *hive.* Pussie, *hare.* Eldritch, *unearthly.* Fairin,
reward. Brig, *bridge.*

But ere the key-stane she could make,
The fient a tail she had to shake!
For Nannie, far before the rest,
Hard upon noble Maggie prest,
And flew at Tam wi' furious ettle;
But little wist she Maggie's mettle!
Ae spring brought off her master hale,
But left behind her ain grey tail:
The carlin claught her by the rump,
And left poor Maggie scarce a stump.

Now, wha this tale o' truth shall read,
Ilk man, and mother's son, take heed:
Whene'er to Drink you are inclin'd,
Or Cutty-Sarks rin in your mind,
Think ye may buy the joys o'er dear;
Remember Tam o' Shanter's mare.

The Rigs o' Barley

It was upon a Lammas night,
    When corn rigs are bonie,
Beneath the moon's unclouded light,
    I held awa to Annie;
The time flew by, wi' tentless heed,
    Till, 'tween the late and early,
Wi' sma' persuasion she agreed
    To see me thro' the barley.

Corn rigs, an' barley rigs,
    An' corn rigs are bonie:
I'll ne'er forget that happy night
    Amang the rigs wi' Annie.

Fient a, *not a*. Ettle, *intent*. Claught, *clutched*.

Rig, *a ridge of land*. Tentless, *careless*.

The sky was blue, the wind was still,
   The moon was shining clearly;
I set her down, wi' right good will,
   Amang the rigs o' barley:
I ken't her heart was a' my ain;
   I lov'd her most sincerely;
I kiss'd her owre and owre again,
   Amang the rigs o' barley.
         Corn rigs, an' barley rigs, etc.

I lock'd her in my fond embrace;
   Her heart was beating rarely:
My blessings on that happy place,
   Amang the rigs o' barley!
But by the moon and stars so bright,
   That shone that hour so clearly!
She aye shall bless that happy night
   Amang the rigs o' barley.
         Corn rigs, an' barley rigs, etc.

I hae been blythe wi' comrades dear;
   I hae been merry drinking;
I hae been joyfu' gath'rin gear;
   I hae been happy thinking;
But a' the pleasures e'er I saw,
   Tho' three times doubl'd fairly,
That happy night was worth them a'
   Amang the rigs o' barley.
         Corn rigs, an' barley rigs, etc.

Green Grow the Rashes

Green grow the rashes, O;
   Green grow the rashes, O;
The sweetest hours that e'er I spend,
   Are spent amang the lasses, O.

Rashes, *rushes.*

There's nought but care on ev'ry han',
  In ev'ry hour that passes, O:
What signifies the life o' man,
  An 'twere na for the lasses, O.
      Green grow, etc.

The war'ly race may riches chase,
  An' riches still may fly them, O;
An' tho' at last they catch them fast,
  Their hearts can ne'er enjoy them, O
      Green grow, etc.

But gie me a cannie hour at e'en,
  My arms about my dearie, O;
An' war'ly cares, an' war'ly men,
  May a' gang tapsalteerie, O!
      Green grow, etc.

For you sae douce, ye sneer at this;
  Ye're nought but senseless asses, O:
The wisest man that warl' e'er saw,
  He dearly lov'd the lasses, O.
      Green grow, etc.

Auld Nature swears, the lovely dears
  Her noblest work she classes, O;
Her prentice han' she try'd on man,
  An' then she made the lasses, O.
      Green grow, etc.

The Birks of Aberfeldy

Bonie lassie, will ye go,
Will ye go, will ye go,
Bonie lassie, will ye go
  To the birks of Aberfeldy!

War'ly, *worldly*. Cannie, *gentle*. Tapsalteerie, *topsy-turvy*. Douce, *sober*.
Birks, *birch trees*.

Now Simmer blinks on flowery braes,
And o'er the crystal streamlets plays;
Come let us spend the lightsome days
   In the birks of Aberfeldy.
        Bonie lassie, etc.

The little birdies blythely sing,
While o'er their heads the hazels hing,
Or lightly flit on wanton wing
   In the birks of Aberfeldy.
        Bonie lassie, etc.

The braes ascend like lofty wa's,
The foamy stream deep-roaring fa's,
O'erhung wi' fragrant spreading shaws—
   The birks o' Aberfeldy.
        Bonie lassie, etc.

The hoary cliffs are crown'd wi' flowers,
White o'er the linns the burnie pours,
And rising, weets wi' misty showers
   The birks o' Aberfeldy.
        Bonie lassie, etc.

Let Fortune's gifts at random flee,
They ne'er shall draw a wish frae me;
Supremely blest wi' love and thee,
   In the birks o' Aberfeldy.
        Bonie lassie, etc.

I'm O'er Young to Marry Yet

I'm o'er young, I'm o'er young,
   I'm o'er young to marry yet;
I'm o'er young, 'twad be a sin
   To tak me frae my mammy yet.

Blinks, *beams.* Braes, *slopes.* Shaws, *woods.* Linns, *waterfalls.* Burnie, *stream.*

I am my mammy's ae bairn,
    Wi' unco folk I weary, sir;
And lying in a man's bed,
    I'm fley'd it mak me eerie, sir.
        I'm o'er young, etc.

Hallowmass is come and gane,
    The nights are lang in winter, sir,
And you and I in ae bed,—
    In trowth, I dare na venture, sir.
        I'm o'er young, etc.

Fu' loud an' shill the frosty wind
    Blaws thro' the leafless timmer, sir;
But if ye come this gate again,
    I'll aulder be gin simmer, sir.
        I'm o'er young, etc.

Of A' the Airts the Wind Can Blaw

Of a' the airts the wind can blaw,
    I dearly like the west,
For there the bonie lassic lives,
    The lassie I lo'e best;
There's wild-woods grow, and rivers row,
    And mony a hill between:
But day and night my fancy's flight
    Is ever wi' my Jean.

I see her in the dewy flowers,
    I see her sweet and fair:
I hear her in the tunefu' birds,
    I hear her charm the air:
There's not a bonie flower that springs,
    By fountain, shaw, or green;
There's not a bonie bird that sings,
    But minds me o' my Jean.

Unco, *strange.* Fley'd, *scared.* Eerie, *frightened.* Shill, *shrill.* Simmer, *summer.*

Airts, *directions.* Row, *flow.* Shaw, *wood.*

My Bonie Mary

Go, fetch to me a pint o' wine,
    And fill it in a silver tassie;
That I may drink before I go
    A service to my bonie lassie.
The boat rocks at the pier o' Leith;
    Fu' loud the wind blaws frae the Ferry;
The ship rides by the Berwick-law,
    And I maun leave my bonie Mary.

The trumpets sound, the banners fly,
    The glittering spears are rankéd ready;
The shouts o' war are heard afar,
    The battle closes deep and bloody;
It's not the roar o' sea or shore,
    Wad mak me langer wish to tarry,
Nor shouts o' war that's heard afar—
    It's leaving thee, my bonie Mary!

John Anderson, My Jo

John Anderson, my jo, John,
    When we were first acquent,
Your locks were like the raven,
    Your bonie brow was brent;
But now your brow is beld, John,
    Your locks are like the snow;
But blessings on your frosty pow,
    John Anderson, my jo.

John Anderson, my jo, John,
    We clamb the hill thegither;
And mony a cantie day, John,
    We've had wi' ane anither:
Now we maun totter down, John,
    And hand in hand we'll go,
And sleep thegither at the foot,
    John Anderson, my jo.

Tassie, *goblet.*

Jo, *sweetheart.* Brent, *smooth.* Beld, *bald.* Pow, *head.* Cantie, *merry.*

My Love, She's but a Lassie Yet

My love, she's but a lassie yet,
My love, she's but a lassie yet;
We'll let her stand a year or twa,
She'll no be half sae saucy yet.

I rue the day I sought her O!
I rue the day I sought her O!
Wha gets her needs na say he's woo'd,
But he may say he has bought her O.

Come draw a drap o' the best o't yet,
Come draw a drap o' the best o't yet,
Gae seek for pleasure whare you will,
But here I never miss'd it yet.

We're a' dry wi' drinkin o't,
We're a' dry wi' drinkin o't;
The minister kiss'd the fiddler's wife ;
He could na preach for thinkin o't.

Willie Brew'd a Peck o' Maut

O Willie brew'd a peck o' maut,
And Rob and Allen cam to see;
Three blyther hearts, that lee-lang night,
Ye wadna found in Christendie.

We are na fou, we're nae that fou,
But just a drappie in our ee;
The cock may craw, the day may daw,
And aye we'll taste the barley bree.

Here are we met, three merry boys,
Three merry boys I trow are we;
And mony a night we've merry been,
And mony may we hope to be!
We are na fou, etc.

Maut, malt. Fou, drunk. Drappie, drop. Bree, juice. Lift, sky.

It is the moon, I ken her horn,
  That's blinkin' in the lift sae hie;
She shines sae bright to wile us hame,
  But, by my sooth, she'll wait a wee!
    We are na fou, etc.

Wha first shall rise to gang awa,
  A cuckold, cowardly loun is he!
Wha first beside his chair shall fa',
  He is the King amang us three.
    We are na fou, etc.

The Banks o' Doon

Ye banks and braes o' bonie Doon,
  How can ye bloom sae fresh and fair?
How can ye chant, ye little birds,
  And I sae weary fu' o' care!
Thou'll break my heart, thou warbling bird,
  That wantons thro' the flowering thorn:
Thou minds me o' departed joys,
  Departed never to return.

Aft hae I rov'd by Bonie Doon,
  To see the rose and woodbine twine:
And ilka bird sang o' its luve,
  And fondly sae did I o' mine.
Wi' lightsome heart I pu'd a rose,
  Fu' sweet upon its thorny tree!
And my fause luver staw my rose,
  But ah! he left the thorn wi' me.

Ae Fond Kiss, and Then We Sever

Ae fond kiss, and then we sever;
Ae fareweel, and then for ever!
Deep in heart-wrung tears I'll pledge thee,
Warring sighs and groans I'll wage thee.

Loun, *fellow.*

Who shall say that Fortune grieves him,
While the star of hope she leaves him?
Me, nae cheerful twinkle lights me;
Dark despair around benights me.

I'll ne'er blame my partial fancy,
Naething could resist my Nancy:
But to see her was to love her;
Love but her, and love for ever.
Had we never lov'd sae kindly,
Had we never lov'd sae blindly,
Never met—or never parted,
We had ne'er been broken-hearted.

Fare thee-weel, thou first and fairest!
Fare-thee-weel, thou best and dearest!
Thine be ilka joy and treasure,
Peace, Enjoyment, Love and Pleasure.
Ae fond kiss, and then we sever!
Ae fareweel, alas, for ever!
Deep in heart-wrung tears I'll pledge thee,
Warring sighs and groans I'll wage thee.

The Deil's Awa wi' the Exciseman

The deil cam fiddlin thro' the town,
    And danc'd awa wi' th' Exciseman,
And ilka wife cries, "Auld Mahoun,
    I wish you luck o' the prize, man."

        The deil's awa, the deil's awa,
            The deil's awa wi' the Exciseman,
        He's danced awa, he's danced awa,
            He's danced awa wi' the Exciseman.

We'll mak our maut, and we'll brew our drink,
    We'll laugh, sing, and rejoice, man,
And mony braw thanks to the meikle black deil,
    That's danced awa wi' the Exciseman,
        The deil's awa, etc.

There's threesome reels, there's foursome reels.
There's hornpipes and strathspeys, man,
But the ae best dance ere came to the land
    Was "The deil's awa wi' th' Exciseman."
        The deil's awa, etc.

Highland Mary

Ye banks and braes and streams around
    The castle o' Montgomery!
Green be your woods, and fair your flowers,
    Your waters never drumlie:
There Simmer first unfald her robes,
    And there the langest tarry;
For there I took the last fareweel
    O' my sweet Highland Mary.

How sweetly bloom'd the gay, green birk,
    How rich the hawthorn's blossom,
As underneath their fragrant shade,
    I clasp'd her to my bosom!
The golden hours on angel wings,
    Flew o'er me and my dearie;
For dear to me, as light and life,
    Was my sweet Highland Mary.

Wi' mony a vow, and lock'd embrace,
    Our parting was fu' tender;
And, pledging aft to meet again,
    We tore oursels asunder;
But, O, fell Death's untimely frost,
    That nipt my flower sae early!
Now green's the sod, and cauld's the clay
    That wraps my Highland Mary!

O pale, pale now, those rosy lips,
    I aft hae kiss'd sae fondly!
And clos'd for aye, the sparkling glance
    That dwelt on me sae kindly!

Drumlie, *turbid.*

And mouldering now in silent dust,
    That heart that lo'ed me dearly!
But still within my bosom's core
    Shall live my Highland Mary.

Whistle an' I'll Come to Ye, My Lad

O whistle an' I'll come to ye, my lad,
O whistle and I'll come to ye, my lad,
Tho' father an' mother an' a' should gae mad,
O whistle an' I'll come to ye, my lad.

But warily tent when ye come to court me,
And come nae unless the back-yett be a-jee,
Syne up the back-stile, and let naebody see,
And come as ye were na comin to me,
And come as ye were na comin to me.
            O whistle an' I'll come, etc.

At kirk, or at market, whene'er ye meet me,
Gang by me as tho' that ye car'd not a flie;
But steal me a blink o' your bonie black e'e,
Yet look as ye were na lookin to me,
Yet look as ye were na lookin to me.
            O whistle an' I'll come, etc.

Aye vow and protest that ye care na for me,
And whiles ye may lightly my beauty a-wee;
But court na anither, tho' jokin ye be,
For fear that she wile your fancy frae me,
For fear that she wile your fancy frae me.
            O whistle an' I'll come, etc.

A Red, Red Rose

O my luve is like a red, red rose,
    That's newly sprung in June:
O my luve is like the melodie,
    That's sweetly play'd in tune.

Tent, take care. Back-yett, back-gate.

As fair art thou, my bonie lass,
　　So deep in luve am I;
And I will luve thee still, my dear,
　　Till a' the seas gang dry.

Till a' the seas gang dry, my dear,
　　And the rocks melt wi' the sun;
And I will love thee still, my dear,
　　While the sands o' life shall run.

And fare-thee-weel, my only luve!
　　And fare-thee-weel a while!
And I will come again, my luve,
　　Though it were ten thousand mile.

Charlie, He's My Darling

'Twas on a Monday morning,
　　Right early in the year,
That Charlie came to our town,
　　The young Chevalier.

　　　　An' Charlie, he's my darling,
　　　　My darling, my darling,
　　　　Charlie, he's my darling,
　　　　　The young Chevalier.

As he was walking up the street,
　　The city for to view,
O there he spied a bonie lass
　　The window looking through.
　　　　An' Charlie, etc.

Sae light's he jumped up the stair,
　　And tirl'd at the pin;
And wha sae ready as hersel'
　　To let the laddie in.
　　　　An' Charlie, etc.

He sets his Jenny on his knee,
   All in his Highland dress;
For brawlie weel he ken'd the way
   To please a bonie lass.
          An' Charlie, etc.

It's up yon heathery mountain,
   An' down yon scroggie glen,
We daur na gang a milking,
   For Charlie and his men.
          An' Charlie, etc.

A Man's a Man for A' That

Is there for honest poverty
   That hings his head, an' a' that;
The coward slave we pass him by,
   We dare be poor for a' that!
For a' that, an' a' that,
   Our toils obscure an' a' that,
The rank is but the guinea's stamp,
   The man's the gowd for a' that.

What though on hamely fare we dine,
   Wear hoddin grey, an' a' that?
Gie fools their silks, and knaves their wine,
   A man's a man for a' that.
For a' that, an' a' that,
   Their tinsel show an' a' that,
The honest man, tho' e'er sae poor,
   Is king o' men for a' that.

Ye see yon birkie ca'd a lord,
   Wha struts, an' stares, an' a' that;
Tho' hundreds worship at his word,
   He's but a coof for a' that.
For a' that, an' a' that,
   His ribband, star, an' a' that,
The man o' independent mind
   He looks an' laughs at a' that.

Birkie, *fellow.* Coof, *fool.*

A prince can mak a belted knight,
    A marquis, duke, an' a' that;
But an honest man's aboon his might,
    Gude faith, he maunna fa' that!
For a' that, an' a' that,
    Their dignities an' a' that,
The pith o' sense, an' pride o' worth,
    Are higher rank than a' that.

Then let us pray that come it may,
    (As come it will for a' that,)
That Sense and Worth, o'er a' the earth,
    Shall bear the gree, an' a' that.
For a' that, an' a' that,
    It's coming yet for a' that,
That man to man, the world o'er,
    Shall brithers be for a' that.

WILLIAM LISLE BOWLES
(1762–1850)

At Dover Cliffs, July 20, 1787

On these white cliffs, that calm above the flood
Uplift their shadowing heads, and, at their feet,
Scarce hear the surge that has for ages beat,
Sure many a lonely wanderer has stood;
And, whilst the lifted murmur met his ear,
And o'er the distant billows the still Eve
Sailed slow, has thought of all his heart must leave
To-morrow; of the friends he loved most dear;
Of social scenes, from which he wept to part;
But if, like me, he knew how fruitless all
The thoughts that would full fain the past recall,
Soon would he quell the risings of his heart,
And brave the wild winds and unhearing tide,
The world his country, and his God his guide.

Fa', *deserve*. Gree, *prize*.

WILLIAM WORDSWORTH

(1770–1850)

"My Heart Leaps Up..."

My heart leaps up when I behold
   A rainbow in the sky;
So was it when my life began;
So is it now I am a man;
So be it when I shall grow old.
   Or let me die!
The Child is father of the Man;
And I could wish my days to be
Bound each to each by natural piety.

"Strange Fits of Passion..."

Strange fits of passion have I known:
And I will dare to tell,
But in the Lover's ear alone,
What once to me befell.

When she I loved looked every day
Fresh as a rose in June,
I to her cottage bent my way,
Beneath an evening-moon.

Upon the moon I fixed my eye,
All over the wide lea;
With quickening pace my horse drew nigh
Those paths so dear to me.

And now we reached the orchard plot;
And, as we climbed the hill,
The sinking moon to Lucy's cot
Came near, and nearer still.

In one of those sweet dreams I slept,
Kind Nature's gentlest boon!
And all the while my eyes I kept
On the descending moon.

My horse moved on; hoof after hoof
He raised, and never stopped:
When down behind the cottage roof,
At once, the bright moon dropped.

What fond and wayward thoughts will slide
Into a Lover's head!
"O mercy!" to myself I cried,
"If Lucy should be dead!"

"She Dwelt among the Untrodden Ways"

She dwelt among the untrodden ways
    Beside the springs of Dove,
A Maid whom there were none to praise
    And very few to love:

A violet by a mossy stone
    Half hidden from the eye!
—Fair as a star, when only one
    Is shining in the sky.

She lived unknown, and few could know
    When Lucy ceased to be;
But she is in her grave, and, oh,
    The difference to me!

"She Was a Phantom ..."

She was a Phantom of delight
When first she gleamed upon my sight;
A lovely Apparition, sent
To be a moment's ornament;
Her eyes as stars of Twilight fair;
Like Twilight's, too, her dusky hair;
But all things else about her drawn
From May-time and the cheerful Dawn;
A dancing Shape, an Image gay,
To haunt, to startle, and way-lay.

I saw her upon nearer view,
A Spirit, yet a Woman too!
Her household motions light and free,
And steps of virgin-liberty;
A countenance in which did meet
Sweet records, promises as sweet;
A Creature not too bright or good
For human nature's daily food;
For transient sorrows, simple wiles,
Praise, blame, love, kisses, tears, and smiles.

And now I see with eye serene
The very pulse of the machine;
A Being breathing thoughtful breath,
A Traveller between life and death;
The reason firm, the temperate will,
Endurance, foresight, strength, and skill;
A perfect Woman, nobly planned,
To warn, to comfort, and command;
And yet a Spirit still, and bright
With something of angelic light.

"A Slumber Did My Spirit Seal"

A slumber did my spirit seal;
    I had no human fears:
She seemed a thing that could not feel
    The touch of earthly years.

No motion has she now, no force;
    She neither hears nor sees;
Rolled round in earth's diurnal course,
    With rocks, and stones, and trees.

"I Wandered Lonely..."

I wandered lonely as a cloud
That floats on high o'er vales and hills,
When all at once I saw a crowd,

A host, of golden daffodils;
Beside the lake, beneath the trees,
Fluttering and dancing in the breeze.

Continuous as the stars that shine
And twinkle on the milky way,
They stretched in never-ending line
Along the margin of a bay:
Ten thousand saw I at a glance,
Tossing their heads in sprightly dance.

The waves beside them danced; but they
Out-did the sparkling waves in glee:
A poet could not but be gay,
In such a jocund company:
I gazed—and gazed—but little thought
What wealth the show to me had brought:

For oft, when on my couch I lie
In vacant or in pensive mood,
They flash upon that inward eye
Which is the bliss of solitude;
And then my heart with pleasure fills,
And dances with the daffodils.

Sonnets

1.

Nuns fret not at their convent's narrow room;
And hermits are contented with their cells;
And students with their pensive citadels;
Maids at the wheel, the weaver at his loom,
Sit blithe and happy; bees that soar for bloom,
High as the highest peak of Furness-fells,
Will murmur by the hour in foxglove bells:
In truth the prison, unto which we doom
Ourselves, no prison is: and hence for me,
In sundry moods, 'twas pastime to be bound
Within the Sonnet's scanty plot of ground;
Pleased if some Souls (for such there needs must be)
Who have felt the weight of too much liberty,
Should find brief solace there, as I have found.

2.   TO SLEEP

A flock of sheep that leisurely pass by,
One after one; the sound of rain, and bees
Murmuring; the fall of rivers, winds and seas,
Smooth fields, white sheets of water, and pure sky;
I have thought of all by turns, and yet do lie
Sleepless! and soon the small birds' melodies
Must hear, first uttered from my orchard trees;
And the first cuckoo's melancholy cry.
Even thus last night, and two nights more, I lay
And could not win thee, Sleep! by any stealth:
So do not let me wear to-night away:
Without Thee what is all the morning's wealth?
Come, blessed barrier between day and day,
Dear mother of fresh thoughts and joyous health!

3.

Surprised by joy—impatient as the Wind
I turned to share the transport—Oh! with whom
But Thee, deep buried in the silent tomb,
That spot which no vicissitude can find?
Love, faithful love, recalled thee to my mind—
But how could I forget thee? Through what power,
Even for the least division of an hour,
Have I been so beguiled as to be blind
To my most grievous loss!—That thought's return
Was the worst pang that sorrow ever bore,
Save one, one only, when I stood forlorn,
Knowing my heart's best treasure was no more;
That neither present time, nor years unborn
Could to my sight that heavenly face restore.

4.

It is a beauteous evening, calm and free,
The holy time is quiet as a Nun
Breathless with adoration; the broad sun
Is sinking down in its tranquillity;
The gentleness of heaven broods o'er the Sea:

Listen! the mighty Being is awake,
And doth with his eternal motion make
A sound like thunder—everlastingly.
Dear Child! dear Girl! that walkest with me here,
If thou appear untouched by solemn thought,
Thy nature is not therefore less divine:
Thou liest in Abraham's bosom all the year;
And worshipp'st at the Temple's inner shrine,
God being with thee when we know it not.

5.

The world is too much with us; late and soon,
Getting and spending, we lay waste our powers:
Little we see in Nature that is ours;
We have given our hearts away, a sordid boon!
This Sea that bares her bosom to the moon;
The winds that will be howling at all hours,
And are up-gathered now like sleeping flowers;
For this, for everything, we are out of tune;
It moves us not.—Great God! I'd rather be
A Pagan suckled in a creed outworn;
So might I, standing on this pleasant lea,
Have glimpses that would make me less forlorn;
Have sight of Proteus rising from the sea;
Or hear old Triton blow his wreathéd horn.

6.   WESTMINSTER BRIDGE, SEPTEMBER 3, 1802

Earth has not anything to show more fair:
Dull would he be of soul who could pass by
A sight so touching in its majesty:
This City now doth, like a garment, wear
The beauty of the morning; silent, bare,
Ships, towers, domes, theatres, and temples lie
Open unto the fields, and to the sky;
All bright and glittering in the smokeless air.
Never did sun more beautifully steep
In his first splendour, valley, rock, or hill;

Ne'er saw I, never felt, a calm so deep!
The river glideth at his own sweet will:
Dear God! the very houses seem asleep;
And all that mighty heart is lying still!

7. ON THE EXTINCTION OF THE VENETIAN REPUBLIC

Once did She hold the gorgeous east in fee;
And was the safeguard of the west: the worth
Of Venice did not fall below her birth,
Venice, the eldest Child of Liberty.
She was a maiden City, bright and free;
No guile seduced, no force could violate;
And, when she took unto herself a Mate,
She must espouse the everlasting Sea.
And what if she had seen those glories fade,
Those titles vanish, and that strength decay;
Yet shall some tribute of regret be paid
When her long life hath reached its final day:
Men are we, and must grieve when even the Shade
Of that which once was great is passed away.

8.

England! the time is come when thou shouldst wean
Thy heart from its emasculating food;
The truth should now be better understood;
Old things have been unsettled; we have seen
Fair seed-time, better harvest might have been
But for thy trespasses; and, at this day,
If for Greece, Egypt, India, Africa,
Aught good were destined, thou wouldst step between.
England! all nations in this charge agree:
But worse, more ignorant in love and hate,
Far—far more abject, is thine Enemy:
Therefore the wise pray for thee, though the freight
Of thy offences be a heavy weight:
Oh grief that Earth's best hopes rest all with Thee!

Ode

(INTIMATIONS OF IMMORTALITY
FROM RECOLLECTIONS OF EARLY CHILDHOOD)

The child is father of the Man;
And I could wish my days to be
Bound each to each by natural piety.

There was a time when meadow, grove, and stream,
The earth and every common sight,
  To me did seem
  Apparelled in celestial light,
The glory and the freshness of a dream.
It is not now as it hath been of yore;—
  Turn wheresoe'er I may,
   By night or day,
The things which I have seen I now can see no more.

  The Rainbow comes and goes,
  And lovely is the Rose,
  The Moon doth with delight
 Look round her when the heavens are bare,
  Waters on a starry night
  Are beautiful and fair;
  The sunshine is a glorious birth;
  But yet I know, where'er I go,
That there hath passed away a glory from the earth.

Now, while the birds thus sing a joyous song,
 And while the young lambs bound
  As to the tabor's sound,
To me alone there came a thought of grief:
A timely utterance gave that thought relief,
  And I again am strong:
The cataracts blow their trumpets from the steep;
No more shall grief of mine the season wrong;
I hear the Echoes through the mountains throng,
The Winds come to me from the fields of sleep,
  And all the earth is gay;
   Land and sea
  Give themselves up to jollity,
   And with the heart of May

Doth every beast keep holiday—
    Thou child of Joy,
Shout round me, let me hear thy shouts, thou
    happy Shepherd-boy!

Ye blessèd Creatures, I have heard the call
    Ye to each other make; I see
The heavens laugh with you in your jubilee;
    My heart is at your festival,
    My head hath its coronal,
The fullness of your bliss, I feel—I feel it all.
        Oh evil day! if I were sullen
        While earth itself is adorning,
            This sweet May morning,
        And the children are culling
            On every side,
        In a thousand valleys far and wide,
        Fresh flowers; while the sun shines warm,
And the babe leaps up in his mother's arm—
    I hear, I hear, with joy I hear!
    —But there's a tree, of many, one,
A single field which I have looked upon,
Both of them speak of something that is gone:
        The pansy at my feet
        Doth the same tale repeat:
Whither is fled the visionary gleam?
Where is it now, the glory and the dream?

Our birth is but a sleep and a forgetting:
The Soul that rises with us, our life's Star,
        Hath had elsewhere its setting,
            And cometh from afar:
        Not in entire forgetfulness,
            And not in utter nakedness,
But trailing clouds of glory do we come
        From God, who is our home:
Heaven lies about us in our infancy!
Shades of the prison-house begin to close
        Upon the growing Boy,
But He beholds the light, and whence it flows,
        He sees it in his joy;

The Youth, who daily farther from the east
    Must travel, still is Nature's Priest,
    And by the vision splendid
    Is on his way attended;
At length the Man perceives it die away,
And fade into the light of common day.

Earth fills her lap with pleasures of her own;
Yearnings she hath in her own natural kind,
And, even with something of a Mother's mind,
    And no unworthy aim,
To make her Foster-child, her Inmate Man,
    Forget the glories he hath known,
And that imperial palace whence he came.
Behold the Child among his new-born blisses,
A six years' Darling of a pygmy size!
Fretted by sallies of his mother's kisses,
With light upon him from his father's eyes!
See, at his feet, some little plan or chart,
Some fragment from his dream of human life,
Shaped by himself with newly-learnéd art;
    A wedding or a festival,
    A mourning or a funeral;
      And this hath now his heart,
    And unto this he frames his song:
      Then will he fit his tongue
To dialogues of business, love, or strife;
    But it will not be long
    Ere this be thrown aside,
    And with new joy and pride
The little Actor cons another part;
Filling from time to time his "humorous stage"
With all the Persons, down to palsied Age,
That Life brings with her in her equipage;
    As if his whole vocation
    Were endless imitation.

Thou, whose exterior semblance doth belie
    Thy Soul's immensity;
Thou best Philosopher, who yet dost keep
Thy heritage, thou Eye among the blind,

That, deaf and silent, read'st the eternal deep,
Haunted for ever by the eternal mind—
    Mighty Prophet! Seer blest!
    On whom those truths do rest,
Which we are toiling all our lives to find,
In darkness lost, the darkness of the grave;
Thou, over whom thy Immortality
Broods like the Day, a Master o'er a Slave,
A Presence which is not to be put by;
    To whom the grave
Is but a lonely bed without the sense or sight
    Of day or the warm light,
A place of thought where we in waiting lie;
Thou little Child, yet glorious in the might
Of heaven-born freedom on thy being's height,
Why with such earnest pains dost thou provoke
The years to bring the inevitable yoke,
Thus blindly with thy blessedness at strife?
Full soon thy Soul shall have her earthly freight,
And custom lie upon thee with a weight,
Heavy as frost, and deep almost as life!

    O joy! that in our embers
    Is something that doth live,
    That nature yet remembers
    What was so fugitive!
The thought of our past years in me doth breed
Perpetual benediction: not indeed
For that which is most worthy to be blest;
Delight and liberty, the simple creed
Of Childhood, whether busy or at rest,
With new-fledged hope still fluttering in his breast—
    Not for these I raise
    The song of thanks and praise;
  But for those obstinate questionings
    Of sense and outward things,
    Fallings from us, vanishings;
    Blank misgivings of a Creature
Moving about in worlds not realised,
High instincts before which our mortal Nature
Did tremble like a guilty Thing surprised:

But for those first affections,
    Those shadowy recollections,
        Which, be they what they may,
Are yet the fountain-light of all our day,
Are yet a master-light of all our seeing;
    Uphold us, cherish, and have power to make
Our noisy years seem moments in the being
Of the eternal Silence: truths that wake,
        To perish never:
Which neither listlessness, nor mad endeavour,
        Nor Man nor Boy,
Nor all that is at enmity with joy,
Can utterly abolish or destroy!
    Hence in a season of calm weather
        Though inland far we be,
Our Souls have sight of that immortal sea
        Which brought us hither,
        Can in a moment travel thither,
And see the Children sport upon the shore,
And hear the mighty waters rolling evermore.

Then sing, ye Birds, sing, sing a joyous song!
        And let the young Lambs bound
        As to the tabor's sound!
We in thought will join your throng,
        Ye that pipe and ye that play,
        Ye that through your hearts to-day
        Feel the gladness of the May!
What though the radiance which was once so bright
Be now for ever taken from my sight,
    Though nothing can bring back the hour
Of splendour in the grass, of glory in the flower;
        We will grieve not, rather find
        Strength in what remains behind;
        In the primal sympathy
        Which having been must ever be;
        In the soothing thoughts that spring
        Out of human suffering;
        In the faith that looks through death,
In years that bring the philosophic mind.

And O, ye Fountains, Meadows, Hills, and Groves,
Forebode not any severing of our loves!
Yet in my heart of hearts I feel your might;
I only have relinquished one delight
To live beneath your more habitual sway.
I love the Brooks which down their channels fret,
Even more than when I tripped lightly as they;
The innocent brightness of a new-born Day
      Is lovely yet;
The Clouds that gather round the setting sun
Do take a sober colouring from an eye
That hath kept watch o'er man's mortality;
Another race hath been, and other palms are won.
Thanks to the human heart by which we live,
Thanks to its tenderness, its joys, and fears,
To me the meanest flower that blows can give
Thoughts that do often lie too deep for tears.

FROM *Tintern Abbey*

And now, with gleams of half-extinguished thought,
With many recognitions dim and faint,
And somewhat of a sad perplexity,
The picture of the mind revives again:
While here I stand, not only with the sense
Of present pleasure, but with pleasing thoughts
That in this moment there is life and food
For future years. And so I dare to hope,
Though changed, no doubt, from what I was when first
I came among these hills; when like a roe
I bounded o'er the mountains, by the sides
Of the deep rivers, and the lonely streams,
Wherever nature led: more like a man
Flying from something that he dreads than one
Who sought the thing he loved. For nature then
(The coarser pleasures of my boyish days,
And their glad animal movements all gone by)
To me was all in all.—I cannot paint
What then I was. The sounding cataract
Haunted me like a passion: the tall rock,

The mountain, and the deep and gloomy wood,
Their colours and their forms, were then to me
An appetite; a feeling and a love,
That had no need of a remoter charm,
By thought supplied, nor any interest
Unborrowed from the eye.—That time is past,
And all its aching joys are now no more,
And all its dizzy raptures. Not for this
Faint I, nor mourn nor murmur; other gifts
Have followed; for such loss, I would believe,
Abundant recompense. For I have learned
To look on nature, not as in the hour
Of thoughtless youth; but hearing oftentimes
The still, sad music of humanity,
Nor harsh, nor grating, though of ample power
To chasten and subdue. And I have felt
A presence that disturbs me with the joy
Of elevated thoughts; a sense sublime
Of something far more deeply interfused,
Whose dwelling is the light of setting suns,
And the round ocean and the living air,
And the blue sky, and in the mind of man:
A motion and a spirit, that impels
All thinking things, all objects of all thought,
And rolls through all things. Therefore am I still
A lover of the meadows and the woods,
And mountains; and of all that we behold
From this green earth; of all the mighty world
Of eye, and ear—both what they half create,
And what perceive; well pleased to recognise
In nature and the language of the sense
The anchor of my purest thoughts, the nurse,
The guide, the guardian of my heart, and soul
Of all my moral being.

FROM *The Prelude*

One summer evening (led by her) I found
A little boat tied to a willow tree
Within a rocky cave, its usual home.

Straight I unloosed her chain, and stepping in
Pushed from the shore. It was an act of stealth
And troubled pleasure, nor without the voice
Of mountain-echoes did my boat move on;
Leaving behind her still, on either side,
Small circles glittering idly in the moon,
Until they melted all into one track
Of sparkling light. But now, like one who rows,
Proud of his skill, to reach a chosen point
With an unswerving line, I fixed my view
Upon the summit of a craggy ridge,
The horizon's utmost boundary; far above
Was nothing but the stars and the grey sky.
She was an elfin pinnace; lustily
I dipped my oars into the silent lake,
And, as I rose upon the stroke, my boat
Went heaving through the water like a swan;
When, from behind that craggy steep till then
The horizon's bound, a huge peak, black and huge,
As if with voluntary power instinct
Upreared its head. I struck and struck again,
And growing still in stature the grim shape
Towered up between me and the stars, and still,
For so it seemed, with purpose of its own
And measured motion like a living thing,
Strode after me. With trembling oars I turned,
And through the silent water stole my way
Back to the covert of the willow tree;
There in her mooring-place I left my bark—
And through the meadows homeward went, in grave
And serious mood; but after I had seen
That spectacle, for many days, my brain
Worked with a dim and undetermined sense
Of unknown modes of being; o'er my thoughts
There hung a darkness, call it solitude
Or blank desertion. No familiar shapes
Remained, no pleasant images of trees,
Of sea or sky, no colours of green fields;
But huge and mighty forms, that do not live
Like living men, moved slowly through the mind
By day, and were a trouble to my dreams.

SIR WALTER SCOTT

(1771–1832)

FROM *The Lay of the Last Minstrel*

In peace, Love tunes the shepherd's reed;
In war, he mounts the warrior's steed;
In halls, in gay attire is seen;
In hamlets, dances on the green.
Love rules the court, the camp, the grove,
And men below, and saints above;
For love is heaven, and heaven is love.

FROM *Marmion*

SONG

Where shall the lover rest,
　Whom the fates sever
From his true maiden's breast,
　Parted for ever?
Where, through groves deep and high,
　Sounds the far billow,
Where early violets die,
　Under the willow.

Chorus:
Eleu loro, &c. Soft shall be his pillow.

There, through the summer day
　Cool streams are laving;
There, while the tempests sway
　Scarce are boughs waving.
There thy rest thou shalt take,
　Parted for ever,
Never again to wake,
　Never, O never!

Chorus:
Eleu loro, &c. Never, O never!

Where shall the traitor rest,
   He, the deceiver,
Who could win maiden's breast,
   Ruin, and leave her?
In the lost battle,
   Borne down by the flying,
Where mingles war's rattle
   With groans of the dying.

Chorus:
Eleu loro, &c. There shall he be lying.

Her wing shall the eagle flap
   O'er the false-hearted;
His warm blood the wolf shall lap,
   Ere life be parted.
Shame and dishonour sit
   By his grave ever;
Blessing shall hallow it—
   Never, O never.

Chorus:
Eleu loro, &c. Never, O never.

FROM *The Lady of the Lake*

1.

Harp of the North! that mouldering long hast hung
   On the witch-elm that shades Saint Fillan's spring,
And down the fitful breeze thy numbers flung,
   Till envious ivy did around thee cling,
Muffling with verdant ringlet every string—
   O minstrel harp, still must thine accents sleep?
Mid rustling leaves and fountains murmuring,
   Still must thy sweeter sounds their silence keep,
Nor bid a warrior smile, nor teach a maid to weep?

Not thus, in ancient days of Caledon,
   Was thy voice mute amid the festal crowd,
When lay of hopeless love, or glory won,
   Aroused the fearful, or subdued the proud.
At each according pause, was heard aloud
   Thine ardent symphony sublime and high.
Fair dames and crested chiefs attention bowed;
   For still the burden of thy minstrelsy
Was Knighthood's dauntless deed, and Beauty's matchless
     eye.

O wake once more! how rude soe'er the hand
   That ventures o'er thy magic maze to stray;
O wake once more! though scarce my skill command
   Some feeble echoing of thine earlier lay:
Though harsh and faint, and soon to die away,
   And all unworthy of thy nobler strain,
Yet if one heart throb higher at its sway,
   The wizard note has not been touched in vain,
Then silent be no more! Enchantress, wake again!

2.

Time rolls his ceaseless course. The race of yore,
   Who danced our infancy upon their knee,
And told our marvelling boyhood legends store
   Of their strange ventures happed by land or sea,
How are they blotted from the things that be!
   How few, all weak and withered of their force,
Wait on the verge of dark eternity,
   Like stranded wrecks, the tide returning hoarse,
To sweep them from our sight. Time rolls his ceaseless
     course.

3.   CORONACH

    He is gone on the mountain,
      He is lost to the forest,
    Like a summer-dried fountain,
      When our need was the sorest.

The font, reappearing,
  From the rain-drops shall borrow,
But to us comes no cheering,
  To Duncan no morrow.
The hand of the reaper
  Takes the ears that are hoary,
But the voice of the weeper
  Wails manhood in glory.
The autumn winds rushing
  Waft the leaves that are searest,
But our flower was in flushing
  When blighting was nearest.

Fleet foot on the correi,
  Sage counsel in cumber,
Red hand in the foray,
  How sound is thy slumber!
Like the dew on the mountain,
  Like the foam on the river,
Like the bubble on the fountain,
  Thou art gone, and for ever!

4.

The rose is fairest when 'tis budding new,
  And hope is brightest when it dawns from fears,
The rose is sweetest washed in morning dew,
  And love is loveliest when embalmed in tears.
O wilding rose, whom fancy thus endears,
  I bid your blossoms in my bonnet wave,
Emblem of hope and love through future years.

5.   SOLDIER'S SONG

Our vicar still preaches that Peter and Poule
Laid a swinging long curse on the bonny brown bowl,
That there's wrath and despair in the jolly black-jack,
And the seven deadly sins in a flagon of sack;
Yet whoop! Barnaby, off with thy liquor,
Drink upsees out, and a fig for the vicar!

Correi, *hollow of the hill, where game lies.*

Our vicar he calls it damnation to sip
The ripe ruddy dew of a woman's dear lip,
Says that Beelzebub lurks in her kerchief so sly,
And Apollyon shoots darts from her merry black eye;
Yet whoop! Jack, kiss Gillian the quicker,
Till she bloom like a rose, and a fig for the vicar!

Our vicar thus preaches—and why should he not?
For the dues of his cure are the placket and pot;
And 'tis right of his office poor laymen to lurch,
Who infringe the domains of our good Mother Church.
Yet whoop! bully-boys, off with your liquor
Sweet Marjorie's the word, and a fig for the vicar!

6.

Harp of the North, farewell! The hills grow dark,
    On purple peaks a deeper shade descending;
In twilight copse the glow-worm lights her spark,
    The deer, half-seen, are to the covert wending.
Resume thy wizard elm, the fountain lending
    And the wild breeze thy wilder minstrelsy;
Thy numbers sweet with nature's vespers blending,
    With distant echo from the fold and lea,
And herd-boy's evening pipe, and hum of housing bee.

Yet, once again, farewell, thou Minstrel harp.
    Yet, once again, forgive my feeble sway,
And little reck I of the censure sharp
    May idly cavil at an idle lay.
Much have I owed thy strains on life's long way,
    Through secret woes the world has never known,
When on the weary night dawned wearier day,
    And bitterer was the grief devoured alone.
That I o'erlive such woes, Enchantress, is thine own.

Hark! as my lingering footsteps slow retire,
    Some Spirit of the Air has waked thy string!
'Tis now a seraph bold, with touch of fire,
    'Tis now the brush of Fairy's frolic wing.

Receding now, the dying numbers ring
   Fainter and fainter down the rugged dell,
And now the mountain breezes scarcely bring
   A wandering witch-note of the distant spell—
And now 'tis silent all—Enchantress, fare thee well!

FROM *Rokeby*

SONG

A weary lot is thine, fair maid,
   A weary lot is thine.
To pull the thorn thy brow to braid,
   And press the rue for wine.
A lightsome eye, a soldier's mien,
   A feather of the blue,
A doublet of the Lincoln green—
   No more of me you knew,
         My love,
No more of me you knew.

This morn in merry June, I trow,
   The rose is budding fain;
But she shall bloom in winter snow,
   Ere we two meet again.
He turned his charger as he spake,
   Upon the river shore,
He gave his bridle-reins a shake,
   Said: Adieu for evermore,
         My love!
And adieu for evermore.

"False Love..."

False love, and hast thou played me this
   In summer among the flowers?
I will repay thee back again
   In winter among the showers.

Unless again, again, my love,
  Unless you turn again;
As you with other maidens rove,
  I'll smile on other men.

Waverley

"Hie Away..."

Hie away, hie away,
Over bank and over brae,
Where the copsewood is the greenest,
Where the fountains glisten sheenest,
Where the lady-fern grows strongest,
Where the morning dew lies longest,
Where the black-cock sweetest sips it,
Where the fairy latest trips it:
Hie to haunts right seldom seen,
Lovely, lonesome, cool, and green,
Over bank and over brae,
Hie away, hie away.

Waverley

"When Israel..."

When Israel, of the Lord beloved,
  Out from the land of bondage came,
Her fathers' God before her moved,
  An awful guide in smoke and flame.
By day, along the astonished lands
  The cloudy pillar glided slow;
By night, Arabia's crimsoned sands
  Returned the fiery column's glow.

There rose the choral hymn of praise,
  And trump and timbrel answered keen,
And Zion's daughters poured their lays,
  With priest's and warrior's voice between.
No portents now our foes amaze,
  Forsaken Israel wanders lone;
Our fathers would not know Thy ways,
  And Thou hast left them to their own.

But present still, though now unseen!
   When brightly shines the prosperous day,
Be thoughts of Thee a cloudy screen
   To temper the deceitful ray.
And oh, when stoops on Judah's path
   In shade and storm the frequent night,
Be Thou, long-suffering, slow to wrath,
   A burning and a shining light!

Our harps we left by Babel's streams,
   The tyrant's jest, the Gentile's scorn;
No censer round our altar beams,
   And mute are timbrel, harp, and horn.
But Thou hast said, The blood of goat,
   The flesh of rams I will not prize;
A contrite heart, a humble thought,
   Are Mine accepted sacrifice.

Ivanhoe

"Anna-Marie, Love, Up Is the Sun"

Knight: Anna-Marie, love, up is the sun,
       Anna-Marie, love, morn is begun,
       Mists are dispersing, love, birds singing free,
       Up in the morning, love, Anna-Marie.
       Anna-Marie, love, up in the morn,
       The hunter is winding blithe sounds on his horn,
       The echo rings merry from rock and from tree.
       'Tis time to arouse thee, love, Anna-Marie.

Wamba: O Tybalt, love, Tybalt, awake me not yet,
       Around my soft pillow while softer dreams flit;
       For what are the joys that in waking we prove,
       Compared with these visions, O Tybalt! my love?
       Let the birds to the rise of the mist carol shrill,
       Let the hunter blow out his loud horn on the hill,
       Softer sounds, softer pleasures, in slumber I prove,
       But think not I dream of thee, Tybalt, my love.

Ivanhoe

"March, March..."

March, march, Ettrick and Teviotdale,
　Why the deil dinna ye march forward in order!
March, march, Eskdale and Liddesdale,
　All the blue bonnets are bound for the Border.
　　Many a banner spread
　　Flutters above your head,
　Many a crest that is famous in story.
　　Mount and make ready then,
　　Sons of the mountain glen,
　Fight for the Queen and our old Scottish glory.

Come from the hills where your hirsels are grazing,
　Come from the glen of the buck and the roe;
Come to the crag where the beacon is blazing,
　Come with the buckler, the lance, and the bow.
　　Trumpets are sounding,
　　War-steeds are bounding,
　Stand to your arms, and march in good order,
　　England shall many a day
　　Tell of the bloody fray,
　When the Blue Bonnets came over the Border.

The Monastery

"Woman's Faith..."

　Woman's faith, and woman's trust—
　Write the characters in dust;
　Stamp them on the running stream,
　Print them on the moon's pale beam,
　And each evanescent letter
　Shall be clearer, firmer, better,
　And more permanent, I ween,
　Than the thing those letters mean.

　I have strained the spider's thread
　'Gainst the promise of a maid;
　I have weighed a grain of sand
　'Gainst her plight of heart and hand;

I told my true love of the token,
How her faith proved light, and her word was broken:
Again her word and truth she plight,
And I believed them again ere night.

The Betrothed

SAMUEL TAYLOR COLERIDGE

(1772–1834)

The Rime of the Ancient Mariner

PART I

An ancient
mariner meet
eth three gal-
lants bidden
to a wedding-
feast, and de-
taineth one.

It is an ancient Mariner,
And he stoppeth one of three.
"By thy long grey beard and glittering eye,
Now wherefore stopp'st thou me?

The Bridegroom's doors are opened wide,
And I am next of kin;
The guests are met, the feast is set:
May'st hear the merry din."

He holds him with his skinny hand,
"There was a ship," quoth he.
"Hold off! unhand me, grey-beard loon!"
Eftsoons his hand dropt he.

The Wedding-
Guest is spell-
bound by the
eye of the old
seafaring man,
and con-
strained to
hear his tale.

He holds him with his glittering eye—
The Wedding-Guest stood still,
And listens like a three years' child:
The Mariner hath his will.

The Wedding-Guest sat on a stone:
He cannot choose but hear;
And thus spake on that ancient man,
The bright-eyed Mariner.

The Mariner
tells how the
ship sailed
southward
with a good

"The ship was cheered, the harbour cleared,
Merrily did we drop
Below the kirk, below the hill,
Below the lighthouse top.

wind and fair weather, till it reached the line.

The Sun came up upon the left,
Out of the sea came he!
And he shone bright, and on the right
Went down into the sea.

Higher and higher every day,
Till over the mast at noon—"
The Wedding-Guest here beat his breast,
For he heard the loud bassoon.

The Wedding-Guest heareth the bridal music; but the Mariner continueth his tale.

The bride hath paced into the hall,
Red as a rose is she;
Nodding their heads before her goes
The merry minstrelsy.

The Wedding-Guest he beat his breast,
Yet he cannot choose but hear;
And thus spake on that ancient man,
The bright-eyed Mariner.

The ship driven by a storm toward the south pole.

"And now the STORM-BLAST came, and he
Was tyrannous and strong:
He struck with his o'ertaking wings,
And chased us south along.

With sloping masts and dipping prow,
As who pursued with yell and blow
Still treads the shadow of his foe,
And forward bends his head,
The ship drove fast, loud roared the blast,
And southward aye we fled.

And now there came both mist and snow,
And it grew wondrous cold:
And ice, mast-high, came floating by,
As green as emerald.

The land of ice, and of fearful sounds where no living thing was to be seen.

And through the drifts the snowy clifts
Did send a dismal sheen:
Nor shapes of men nor beasts we ken—
The ice was all between.

The ice was here, the ice was there,
The ice was all around:
It cracked and growled, and roared and howled,
Like noises in a swound!

Till a great
sea-bird,
called the
Albatross,
came through
the snow-fog,
and was
received with
great joy and
hospitality.

At length did cross an Albatross,
Thorough the fog it came;
As if it had been a Christian soul,
We hailed it in God's name.

It ate the food it ne'er had eat,
And round and round it flew.
The ice did split with a thunder-fit;
The helmsman steered us through.

And lo! the
Albatross
proveth a bird
of good omen,
and followeth
the ship as it
returned
northward
through fog
and floating
ice. The
ancient
Mariner
inhospitably
killeth the
pious bird of
good omen.

And a good south wind sprung up behind;
The Albatross did follow,
And every day, for food or play,
Came to the mariner's hollo!

In mist or cloud, or mast or shroud,
It perched for vespers nine;
Whiles all the nights, through fog-smoke white,
Glimmered the white Moon-shine."

"God save thee, ancient Mariner!
From the fiends, that plague thee thus!—
Why look'st thou so?"—With my cross-bow
I shot the ALBATROSS.

PART II

The Sun now rose upon the right:
Out of the sea came he,
Still hid in mist, and on the left
Went down into the sea.

And the good south wind still blew behind,
But no sweet bird did follow,
Nor any day for food or play
Came to the mariners' hollo!

*His shipmates
cry out against
the ancient
Mariner, for
killing the
bird of good
luck.*

And I had done a hellish thing,
And it would work 'em woe:
For all averred, I had killed the bird
That made the breeze to blow.
Ah wretch! said they, the bird to slay,
That made the breeze to blow!

*But when the
fog cleared
off, they
justify the
same, and
thus make
themselves
accomplices
in the crime.
The fair
breeze con-
tinues; the ship
enters the
Pacific Ocean,
and sails north-
ward, even
till it reaches
the Line.
The ship hath
been suddenly
becalmed.*

Nor dim nor red, like God's own head,
The glorious Sun uprist:
Then all averred, I had killed the bird
That brought the fog and mist.
'Twas right, said they, such birds to slay,
That bring the fog and mist.

The fair breeze blew, the white foam flew,
The furrow followed free;
We were the first that ever burst
Into that silent sea.

Down dropt the breeze, the sails dropt down,
'Twas sad as sad could be;
And we did speak only to break
The silence of the sea!

All in a hot and copper sky,
The bloody Sun, at noon,
Right up above the mast did stand
No bigger than the Moon.

Day after day, day after day,
We stuck, nor breath nor motion;
As idle as a painted ship
Upon a painted ocean.

*And the Alba-
tross begins to
be avenged.*

Water, water, every where,
And all the boards did shrink;
Water, water, every where,
Nor any drop to drink.

The very deep did rot: O Christ!
That ever this should be!

Yea, slimy things did crawl with legs
Upon the slimy sea.

About, about, in reel and rout,
The death fires danced at night;
The water, like a witch's oils,
Burnt green, and blue and white.

A Spirit had
followed
them; one of
the invisible
inhabitants of
this planet,
neither do
And some in dreams assuréd were
Of the Spirit that plagued us so;
Nine fathom deep he had followed us
From the land of mist and snow.

parted souls nor angels, concerning whom the learned Jew, Josephus, and
the Platonic Constantinopolitan, Michael Psellus, may be consulted. They
are very numerous, and there is no climate or element without one or more.

And every tongue, through utter drought,
Was withered at the root;
We could not speak, no more than if
We had been choked with soot.

The shipmates
in their sore
distress, would
fain throw the
whole guilt on
Ah! well-a-day! what evil looks
Had I from old and young!
Instead of the cross, the Albatross
About my neck was hung.

the ancient Mariner; in sign whereof they hang the dead sea-bird round
his neck.

PART III

There passed a weary time. Each throat
Was parched, and glazed each eye.
A weary time! A weary time!
The ancient
Mariner be-
holdeth a sign
in the element
afar off.
How glazed each weary eye,
When looking westward, I beheld
A something in the sky.

At first it seemed a little speck,
And then it seemed a mist;
It moved and moved, and took at last
A certain shape, I wist.

A speck, a mist, a shape, I wist!
And still it neared and neared:
As if it dodged a water-sprite,
It plunged and tacked and veered.

At its nearer approach, it seemeth him to be a ship; and at a dear ransom he freeth his speech from the bonds of thirst.

With throats unslaked, with black lips baked,
We could not laugh nor wail;
Through utter drought all dumb we stood!
I bit my arm, I sucked the blood,
And cried, A sail! a sail!

With throats unslaked, with black lips baked,
Agape they heard me call:
Gramercy! they for joy did grin,
And all at once their breath drew in,
As they were drinking all.

A flash of joy;

See! See! (I cried) she tacks no more!
Hither to work us weal;
Without a breeze, without a tide,
She steadies with upright keel!

And horror follows. For can it be a ship that comes onward without wind or tide?

The western wave was all a-flame.
The day was well nigh done!
Almost upon the western wave
Rested the broad bright Sun;
When that strange shape drove suddenly
Betwixt us and the Sun.

And straight the Sun was flecked with bars,
(Heaven's Mother send us grace!)
As if through a dungeon-grate he peered
With broad and burning face.

It seemeth him but the skeleton of a ship.

Alas! (thought I, and my heart beat loud)
How fast she nears and nears!
Are those *her* sails that glance in the Sun,
Like restless gossameres?

And its ribs are seen as bars on the face of the setting Sun.

Are those *her* ribs through which the Sun
Did peer, as through a grate?

The Spectre-Woman and her Death-

mate, and no other on board the skeleton ship.

And is that Woman all her crew?
Is that a DEATH? and are there two?
Is DEATH that woman's mate?

Like vessel, like crew! Death and Life-in-Death have diced for the ship's crew, and she (the latter) winneth the ancient Mariner.

Her lips were red, *her* looks were free,
Her locks were yellow as gold.
Her skin was white as leprosy,
The Night-mare LIFE-IN-DEATH was she,
Who thicks man's blood with cold.

The naked hulk alongside came,
And the twain were casting dice;
'The game is done! I've won! I've won!'
Quoth she, and whistles thrice.

No twilight within the courts of the Sun.

The Sun's rim dips; the stars rush out.
At one stride comes the dark;
With far-off whisper, o'er the sea,
Off shot the spectre-bark.

At the rising of the Moon,

We listened and looked sideways up!
Fear at my heart, as at a cup,
My life-blood seemed to sip!
The stars were dim, and thick the night,
The steersman's face by his lamp gleamed
          white;
From the sails the dew did drip—
Till clomb above the eastern bar
The hornéd Moon, with one bright star
Within the nether tip.

One after another,

One after one, by the star-dogged Moon,
Too quick for groan or sigh,
Each turned his face with a ghastly pang,
And cursed me with his eye.

His shipmates drop down dead.

Four times fifty living men,
(And I heard nor sigh nor groan)
With heavy thump, a lifeless lump,
They dropped down one by one.

But Life-in-
Death begins
her work on
the ancient
Mariner.

The souls did from their bodies fly,—
They fled to bliss or woe!
And every soul, it passed me by,
Like the whizz of my cross-bow!

PART IV

The Wedding-
Guest feareth
that a Spirit
is talking to
him;

"I fear thee, ancient Mariner!
I fear thy skinny hand!
And thou art long, and lank, and brown,
As is the ribbed sea-sand.

I fear thee and thy glittering eye,
And thy skinny hand, so brown."—
Fear not, fear not, thou Wedding-Guest!
This body dropt not down.

But the an-
cient Mariner
assureth him
of his bodily
life, and pro-
ceedeth to re-
late his horri-
ble penance.

Alone, alone, all, all alone,
Alone on a wide wide sea!
And never a saint took pity on
My soul in agony.

He despiseth
the creatures
of the calm,

The many men, so beautiful!
And they all dead did lie:
And a thousand thousand slimy things
Lived on; and so did I.

And envieth
that they
should live,
and so many
lie dead.

I looked upon the rotting sea,
And drew my eyes away;
I looked upon the rotting deck,
And there the dead men lay.

I looked to heaven, and tried to pray;
But or ever a prayer had gusht,
A wicked whisper came, and made
My heart as dry as dust.

I closed my lids, and kept them close,
And the balls like pulses beat;
For the sky and the sea, and the sea and the
        sky
Lay like a load on my weary eye,
And the dead were at my feet.

But the curse
liveth for him
in the eye of
the dead men.

The cold sweat melted from their limbs,
Nor rot nor reek did they:
The look with which they looked on me
Had never passed away.

An orphan's curse would drag to hell
A spirit from on high;
But oh! more horrible than that
Is the curse in a dead man's eye!
Seven days, seven nights, I saw that curse,
And yet I could not die.

In his lone-
liness and
fixedness he
yearneth to-
wards the
journeying
Moon, and
the stars that
still sojourn,
yet still move
onward; and
everywhere
the blue sky
belongs to

The moving Moon went up the sky,
And no where did abide:
Softly she was going up,
And a star or two beside—

Her beams bemocked the sultry main,
Like April hoar-frost spread;
But where the ship's huge shadow lay,
The charmèd water burnt alway
A still and awful red.

them, and is their appointed rest, and their native country and their own
natural homes, which they enter unannounced, as lords that are certainly
expected and yet there is a silent joy at their arrival.

By the light
of the Moon
he beholdeth
God's crea-
tures of the
great calm.

Beyond the shadow of the ship,
I watched the water-snakes:
They moved in tracks of shining white,
And when they reared, the elfish light
Fell off in hoary flakes.

Within the shadow of the ship
I watched their rich attire:
Blue, glossy green, and velvet black,
They coiled and swam; and every track
Was a flash of golden fire.

Their beauty
and their
happiness.
He blesseth

O happy living things! no tongue
Their beauty might declare:
A spring of love gushed from my heart,

them in his heart.

And I blessed them unaware:
Sure my kind saint took pity on me,
And I blessed them unaware.

The spell begins to break.

The self-same moment I could pray;
And from my neck so free
The Albatross fell off, and sank
Like lead into the sea.

PART V

Oh sleep! it is a gentle thing,
Beloved from pole to pole!
To Mary Queen the praise be given!
She sent the gentle sleep from Heaven,
That slid into my soul.

By grace of the holy Mother, the ancient Mariner is refreshed with rain.

The silly buckets on the deck,
That had so long remained,
I dreamt that they were filled with dew;
And when I awoke, it rained.

My lips were wet, my throat was cold,
My garments all were dank;
Sure I had drunken in my dreams,
And still my body drank.

I moved, and could not feel my limbs:
I was so light—almost
I thought that I had died in sleep,
And was a blessèd ghost.

He heareth sounds and seeth strange sights and commotions in the sky and the element.

And soon I heard a roaring wind:
It did not come anear;
But with its sound it shook the sails,
That were so thin and sere.

The upper air burst into life!
And a hundred fire-flags sheen,
To and fro they were hurried about!
And to and fro, and in and out,
The wan stars danced between.

And the coming wind did roar more loud,
And the sails did sigh like sedge;
And the rain poured down from one black
    cloud;
The Moon was at its edge.

The thick black cloud was cleft, and still
The Moon was at its side:
Like waters shot from some high crag,
The lightning fell with never a jag,
A river steep and wide.

The bodies of
the ship's crew
are inspired
and the ship
moves on;

The loud wind never reached the ship,
Yet now the ship moved on!
Beneath the lightning and the Moon
The dead men gave a groan.

They groaned, they stirred, they all uprose,
Nor spake, nor moved their eyes;
It had been strange, even in a dream,
To have seen those dead men rise.

The helmsman steered, the ship moved on;
Yet never a breeze up-blew;
The mariners all 'gan work the ropes,
Where they were wont to do;
They raised their limbs like lifeless tools—
We were a ghastly crew.

The body of my brother's son
Stood by me, knee to knee:
The body and I pulled at one rope,
But he said nought to me.

But not by the
souls of the
men, nor by
daemons of
earth or
middle air,
but by a
blessed troop
of angelic
spirits sent
down by the

"I fear thee, ancient Mariner!"
Be calm, thou Wedding-Guest!
'Twas not those souls that fled in pain,
Which to their corses came again,
But a troop of spirits blest:

For when it dawned—they dropped their arms
And clustered round the mast;

*invocation of
the guardian
saint.*
Sweet sounds rose slowly through their mouths,
And from their bodies passed.

Around, around, flew each sweet sound,
Then darted to the Sun;
Slowly the sounds came back again,
Now mixed, now one by one.

Sometimes, a-dropping from the sky
I heard the sky-lark sing;
Sometimes all little birds that are,
How they seemed to fill the sea and air
With their sweet jargoning!

And now 'twas like all instruments,
Now like a lonely flute;
And now it is an angel's song,
That makes the heavens be mute.

It ceased; yet still the sails made on
A pleasant noise till noon,
A noise like of a hidden brook
In the leafy month of June,
That to the sleeping woods all night
Singeth a quiet tune.

Yet noon we quietly sailed on,
Yet never a breeze did breathe:
Slowly and smoothly went the ship,
Moved onward from beneath.

*The lonesome
Spirit from
the south pole
carries on the
ship as far as
the Line, in
obedience to
the angelic
troop, but still
requireth
vengeance.*
Under the keel nine fathom deep,
From the land of mist and snow,
The spirit slid: and it was he
That made the ship to go.
The sails at noon left off their tune,
And the ship stood still also.

The Sun, right up above the mast,
Had fixed her to the ocean:
But in a minute she 'gan stir,

With a short uneasy motion—
Backwards and forwards half her length
With a short uneasy motion.

Then like a pawing horse let go,
She made a sudden bound:
It flung the blood into my head,
And I fell down in a swound.

The Polar Spirit's fellow daemons, the invisible inhabitants of the element, take part in his wrong; and two of them relate, one to the other, that penance long and heavy for the ancient Mariner hath been accorded to the Polar Spirit, who returneth southward.

How long in that same fit I lay,
I have not to declare;
But ere my living life returned,
I heard and in my soul discerned
Two voices in the air.

"Is it he?" quoth one, "Is this the man?
By him who died on cross,
With his cruel bow he laid full low
The harmless Albatross.

The spirit who bideth by himself
In the land of mist and snow,
He loved the bird that loved the man
Who shot him with his bow."

The other was a softer voice,
As soft as honey-dew:
Quoth he: "The man hath penance done,
And penance more will do."

PART VI

First Voice:

"But tell me, tell me! speak again,
Thy soft response renewing—
What makes that ship drive on so fast?
What is the ocean doing?

Second Voice:

"Still as a slave before his lord,
The ocean hath no blast;

His great bright eye most silently
Up to the Moon is cast—

If he may know which way to go;
For she guides him smooth or grim.
See, brothers, see! how graciously
She looketh down on him."

First Voice:

"But why drives on that ship so fast,
Without or wave or wind?"

Second Voice:

"The air is cut away before,
And closes from behind.

Fly, brother, fly! more high, more high!
Or we shall be belated:
For slow and slow that ship will go,
When the Mariner's trance is abated."

I woke, and we were sailing on
As in a gentle weather:
'Twas night, calm night, the moon was high;
The dead men stood together.

All stood together on the deck,
For a charnel-dungeon fitter:
All fixed on me their stony eyes,
That in the Moon did glitter.

The pang, the curse, with which they died,
Had never passed away:
I could not draw my eyes from theirs,
Nor turn them up to pray.

And now this spell was snapt: once more
I viewed the ocean green,
And looked far forth, yet little saw
Of what had else been seen—

Like one, that on a lonesome road
Doth walk in fear and dread,
And having once turned round walks on,
And turns no more his head;
Because he knows, a frightful fiend
Doth close behind him tread.

But soon there breathed a wind on me,
Nor sound nor motion made:
Its path was not upon the sea,
In ripple or in shade.

It raised my hair, it fanned my cheek
Like a meadow-gale of spring—
It mingled strangely with my fears,
Yet it felt like a welcoming.

Swiftly, swiftly flew the ship,
Yet she sailed softly too:
Sweetly, sweetly blew the breeze—
On me alone it blew.

*And the
ancient
Mariner be-
holdeth his
native
country.*

Oh! dream of joy! is this indeed
The light-house top I see?
Is this the hill? is this the kirk?
Is this mine own countree?

We drifted o'er the harbour-bar,
And I with sobs did pray—
O let me be awake, my God!
Or let me sleep alway.

The harbour-bay was clear as glass,
So smoothly it was strewn!
And on the bay the moonlight lay,
And the shadow of the Moon.

The rock shone bright, the kirk no less,
That stands above the rock:
The moonlight steeped in silentness
The steady weathercock.

And the bay was white with silent light,
Till rising from the same,
Full many shapes, that shadows were,
In crimson colours came.

The angelic
spirits leave
the dead
bodies,

A little distance from the prow
Those crimson shadows were:
I turned my eyes upon the deck—
Oh, Christ! what saw I there!

And appear in
their own
forms of light.

Each corse lay flat, lifeless and flat,
And, by the holy rood!
A man all light, a seraph-man,
On every corse there stood.

This seraph-band, each waved his hand:
It was a heavenly sight!
They stood as signals to the land,
Each one a lovely light;

This seraph-band, each waved his hand,
No voice did they impart—
No voice; but oh! the silence sank
Like music on my heart.

But soon I heard the dash of oars,
I heard the Pilot's cheer;
My head was turned perforce away
And I saw a boat appear.

The Pilot and the Pilot's boy,
I heard them coming fast:
Dear Lord in Heaven! it was a joy
The dead men could not blast.

I saw a third—I heard his voice:
It is the Hermit good!
He singeth loud his godly hymns
That he makes in the wood.
He'll shrieve my soul, he'll wash away
The Albatross's blood.

PART VII

The Hermit
of the Wood,

This Hermit good lives in that wood
Which slopes down to the sea.
How loudly his sweet voice he rears!
He loves to talk with marineres
That come from a far countree.

He kneels at morn, and noon, and eve—
He hath a cushion plump:
It is the moss that wholly hides
The rotted old oak-stump.

The skiff-boat neared: I heard them talk,
"Why, this is strange, I trow!
Where are those lights so many and fair,
That signal made but now?"

Approacheth
the ship with
wonder.

"Strange, by my faith!" the Hermit said—
"And they answered not our cheer!
The planks look warped! and see those sails!
How thin they are and sere!
I never saw aught like to them,
Unless perchance it were

Brown skeletons of leaves that lag
My forest-brook along;
When the ivy-tod is heavy with snow,
And the owlet whoops to the wolf below,
That eats the she-wolf's young."

"Dear Lord! it hath a fiendish look—
(The Pilot made reply)
I am a-feared"—"Push on, push on!"
Said the Hermit cheerily.

The boat came closer to the ship,
But I nor spake nor stirred;
The boat came close beneath the ship,
And straight a sound was heard.

The ship suddenly sinketh.

Under the water it rumbled on,
Still louder and more dread:
It reached the ship, it split the bay;
The ship went down like lead.

The ancient Mariner is saved in the Pilot's boat.

Stunned by that loud and dreadful sound,
Which sky and ocean smote,
Like one that hath been seven days drowned
My body lay afloat;
But swift as dreams, myself I found
Within the Pilot's boat.

Upon the whirl, where sank the ship,
The boat spun round and round;
And all was still, save that the hill
Was telling of the sound.

I moved my lips—the Pilot shrieked
And fell down in a fit;
The holy Hermit raised his eyes,
And prayed where he did sit.

I took the oars: the Pilot's boy,
Who now doth crazy go,
Laughed loud and long, and all the while
His eyes went to and fro.
"Ha! ha!" quoth he, "full plain I see,
The Devil knows how to row."

And now, all in my own countree,
I stood on the firm land!
The Hermit stepped forth from the boat,
And scarcely he could stand.

The ancient Mariner earnestly entreateth the Hermit to shrieve him; and the penance of life falls on him.

"O shrieve me, shrieve me, holy man!"
The Hermit crossed his brow.
"Say quick," quoth he, "I bid thee say—
What manner of man art thou?

Forthwith this frame of mine was wrenched
With a woful agony,

Which forced me to begin my tale;
And then it left me free.

*And ever and
anon through
out his future
life an agony
constraineth
him to travel
from land to
land;*

Since then, at an uncertain hour,
That agony returns:
And till my ghastly tale is told,
This heart within me burns.

I pass, like night, from land to land;
I have strange power of speech;
That moment that his face I see,
I know the man that must hear me:
To him my tale I teach.

What loud uproar bursts from that door!
The wedding-guests are there;
But in the garden-bower the bride
And bride-maids singing are:
And hark the little vesper bell.
Which biddeth me to prayer!

O Wedding-Guest! this soul hath been
Alone on a wide wide sea:
So lonely 'twas, that God himself
Scarce seeméd there to be.

O sweeter than the marriage-feast,
'Tis sweeter far to me,
To walk together to the kirk
With a goodly company!—

To walk together to the kirk,
And all together pray,
While each to his great Father bends,
Old men, and babes, and loving friends
And youths and maidens gay!

*And to teach,
by his own
example, love
and reverence
to all things
that God made
and loveth.*

Farewell, farewell! but this I tell
To thee, thou Wedding-Guest!
He prayeth well, who loveth well
Both man and bird and beast.

He prayeth best, who loveth best
All things both great and small;
For the dear God who loveth us,
He made and loveth all.

The Mariner, whose eye is bright,
Whose beard with age is hoar,
Is gone: and now the Wedding-Guest
Turned from the bridegroom's door.

He went like one that hath been stunned,
And is of sense forlorn:
A sadder and a wiser man,
He rose the morrow morn.

FROM *Christabel*

A little child, a limber elf,
Singing, dancing to itself,
A fairy thing with red round cheeks,
That always finds, and never seeks,
Makes such a vision to the sight
As fills a father's eyes with light;
And pleasures flow in so thick and fast
Upon his heart, that he at last
Must needs express his love's excess
With words of unmeant bitterness.
Perhaps 'tis pretty to force together
Thoughts so all unlike each other;
To mutter and mock a broken charm,
To dally with wrong that does no harm.
Perhaps 'tis tender too and pretty
At each wild word to feel within
A sweet recoil of love and pity.
And what, if in a world of sin
(O sorrow and shame should this be true!)
Such giddiness of heart and brain
Comes seldom save from rage and pain,
So talks as it's most used to do.

Kubla Khan

In Xanadu did Kubla Khan
A stately pleasure-dome decree:
Where Alph, the sacred river, ran
Through caverns measureless to man
   Down to a sunless sea.
So twice five miles of fertile ground
With walls and towers were girdled round:
And there were gardens bright with sinuous rills,
Where blossomed many an incense-bearing tree;
And here were forests ancient as the hills,
Enfolding sunny spots of greenery.

But oh! that deep romantic chasm which slanted
Down the green hill athwart a cedarn cover!
A savage place! as holy and enchanted
As e'er beneath a waning moon was haunted
By woman wailing for her demon-lover!
And from this chasm, with ceaseless turmoil seething,
As if this earth in fast thick pants were breathing,
A mighty fountain momently was forced:
Amid whose swift half-intermitted burst
Huge fragments vaulted like rebounding hail,
Or chaffy grain beneath the thresher's flail:
And 'mid these dancing rocks at once and ever
It flung up momently the sacred river.
Five miles meandering with a mazy motion
Through wood and dale the sacred river ran,
Then reached the caverns measureless to man,
And sank in tumult to a lifeless ocean:
And 'mid this tumult Kubla heard from far
Ancestral voices prophesying war!
   The shadow of the dome of pleasure
   Floated midway on the waves;
   Where was heard the mingled measure
   From the fountain and the caves.
It was a miracle of rare device,
A sunny pleasure-dome with caves of ice!

A damsel with a dulcimer
In a vision once I saw:
It was an Abyssinian maid,
And on her dulcimer she played,
Singing of Mount Abora.
Could I revive within me
Her symphony and song,
To such a deep delight 'twould win me,
That with music loud and long,
I would build that dome in air,
That sunny dome! those caves of ice!
And all who heard should see them there,
And all should cry, Beware! Beware!
His flashing eyes, his floating hair!
Weave a circle round him thrice,
And close your eyes with holy dread,
For he on honey-dew hath fed,
And drunk the milk of Paradise.

"Hear, Sweet Spirit..."

Hear, sweet spirit, hear the spell,
Lest a blacker charm compel!
So shall the midnight breezes swell
With thy deep long-lingering knell.

And at evening evermore,
In a chapel on the shore,
Shall the chaunter, sad and saintly,
Yellow tapers burning faintly,
Doleful masses chaunt for thee,
    Miserere Domine!

Hark! the cadence dies away
    On the quiet moonlight sea:
The boatmen rest their oars and say,
    Miserere Domine!

Remorse

JOSEPH BLANCO WHITE
(1775–1841)

To Night

Mysterious Night! when our first parent knew
Thee from report divine, and heard thy name,
Did he not tremble for this lovely frame,
This glorious canopy of light and blue?
Yet 'neath a curtain of translucent dew,
Bathed in the rays of the great setting flame,
Hesperus with the host of heaven came,
And lo! Creation widened in man's view.
Who could have thought such darkness lay concealed
Within thy beams, O sun! or who could find,
Whilst fly and leaf and insect stood revealed,
That to such countless orbs thou mad'st us blind!
Why do we then shun death with anxious strife?
If Light can thus deceive, wherefore not Life?

CHARLES LAMB
(1775–1834)

The Old Familiar Faces

I have had playmates, I have had companions,
In my days of childhood, in my joyful school-days—
All, all are gone, the old familiar faces.

I have been laughing, I have been carousing,
Drinking late, sitting late, with my bosom cronies—
All, all are gone, the old familiar faces.

I loved a Love once, fairest among women:
Closed are the doors on me, I must not see her—
All, all are gone, the old familiar faces.

I have a friend, a kinder friend has no man:
Like an ingrate, I left my friend abruptly;
Left him, to muse on the old familiar faces.

Ghost-like I paced round the haunts of my childhood,
Earth seemed a desert I was bound to traverse,
Seeking to find the old familiar faces.

Friend of my bosom, thou more than a brother,
Why wert not thou born in my father's dwelling?
So might we talk of the old familiar faces—

How some they have died, and some they have left me,
And some are taken from me; all are departed—
All, all are gone, the old familiar faces.

WALTER SAVAGE LANDOR

(1775–1864)

Proem to Hellenics

Come back, ye wandering Muses, come back home,
Ye seem to have forgotten where it lies:
Come, let us walk upon the silent sands
Of Simois, where deep footmarks show long strides;
Thence we may mount perhaps to higher ground,
Where Aphrodite from Athene won
The golden apple, and Here too,
And happy Ares shouted far below.

Or would ye rather choose the grassy vale
Where flows Anapos through anemones,
Hyacinths, and narcissuses, that bend
To show their rival beauty in the stream?

Bring with you each her lyre, and each in turn
Temper a graver with a lighter song.

To Robert Browning

There is delight in singing, though none hear
Beside the singer; and there is delight
In praising, though the praiser sit alone
And see the praised far off him, far above.

Shakespeare is not *our* poet, but the world's,
Therefore on him no speech; and short for thee,
Browning! Since Chaucer was alive and hale,
No man hath walked along our roads with step
So active, so inquiring eye, or tongue
So varied in discourse. But warmer climes
Give brighter plumage, stronger wing; the breeze
Of Alpine heights thou playest with, borne on
Beyond Sorrento and Amalfi, where
The Siren waits thee, singing song for song.

On Catullus

Tell me not what too well I know
About the bard of Sirmio . . .
   Yes, in Thalia's son
Such stains there are . . . as when a Grace
Sprinkles another's laughing face
   With nectar, and runs on.

To Shelley

Shelley! whose song so sweet was sweetest here,
We knew each other little; now I walk
Along the same green path, along the shore
Of Lerici, along the sandy plain
Trending from Lucca to the Pisan pines,
Under whose shadow scattered camels lie,
The old and young, and rarer deer uplift
Their knotty branches o'er high-feathered fern.
Regions of happiness! I greet ye well;
Your solitudes, and not your cities, stayed
My steps among you; for with you alone
Conversed I, and with those ye bore of old.
He who beholds the skies of Italy
Sees ancient Rome reflected, sees beyond,
Into more glorious Hellas, nurse of Gods
And godlike men: dwarfs people other lands.
Frown not, maternal England! thy weak child
Kneels at thy feet, and owns in shame a lie.

Dying Speech of an Old Philosopher

I strove with none, for none was worth my strife:
  Nature I loved, and next to Nature, Art:
I warmed both hands before the fire of Life;
  It sinks; and I am ready to depart.

FROM "In Clementina's Artless Mien"

In Clementina's artless mien
  Lucilla asks me what I see,
And are the roses of sixteen
  Enough for me?

Lucilla asks, if that be all,
  Have I not culled as sweet before . . .
Ah yes, Lucilla! and their fall
  I still deplore.

"Fate! I Have Asked..."

Fate! I have asked few things of thee,
  And fewer have to ask.
Shortly, thou knowest, I shall be
  No more . . . then con thy task.

If one be left on earth so late
  Whose love is like the past,
Tell her in whispers, gentle Fate,
  Not even love must last.

Tell her, I leave the noisy feast
  Of life, a little tired;
Amidst its pleasures few possest
  And many undesired.

Tell her, with steady pace to come
  And, where my laurels lie,
To throw the freshest on the tomb
  When it has caught her sigh.

Tell her, to stand some steps apart
   From others, on that day,
And check the tear (if tear should start)
   Too precious for dull clay.

"Sweet Was the Song..."

Sweet was the song that Youth sang once,
And passing sweet was the response;
But there are accents sweeter far
When Love leaps down our evening star,
Holds back the blighting wings of Time,
Melts with his breath the crusty rime,
And looks into our eyes, and says,
"Come, let us talk of former days."

"Years, Many Parti-Coloured Years"

Years, many parti-coloured years,
   Some have crept on, and some have flown,
Since first before me fell those tears
   I never could see fall alone.

Years, not so many, are to come,
   Years not so varied, when from you
One more will fall: when, carried home,
   I see it not, nor hear *adieu!*

"Ah, What Avails..."

Ah, what avails the sceptred race,
   Ah, what the form divine!
What every virtue, every grace!
   Rose Aylmer, all were thine.
Rose Aylmer, whom these wakeful eyes
   May weep, but never see,
A night of memories and sighs
   I consecrate to thee.

"Past Ruined Ilion..."

Past ruined Ilion Helen lives,
　　Alcestis rises from the shades;
Verse calls them forth; 'tis verse that gives
　　Immortal youth to mortal maids.

Soon shall Oblivion's deepening veil
　　Hide all the peopled hills you see,
The gay, the proud, while lovers hail
　　In distant ages you and me.

The tear for fading beauty check,
　　For passing glory cease to sigh;
One form shall rise above the wreck,
　　One name, Ianthe, shall not die.

Ianthe's Troubles

From you, Ianthe, little troubles pass
　　Like little ripples down a sunny river;
Your pleasures spring like daisies in the grass,
　　Cut down, and up again as blithe as ever.

"Twenty Years Hence..."

Twenty years hence my eyes may grow
If not quite dim, yet rather so,
Still yours from others they shall know
　　　　Twenty years hence.
Twenty years hence though it may hap
That I be called to take a nap
In a cool cell where thunder-clap
　　　　Was never heard;
There breathe but o'er my arch of grass
A not too sadly sighed *Alas,*
And I shall catch, ere you can pass,
　　　　That wingéd word.

"Proud Word You Never Spoke..."

Proud word you never spoke, but you will speak
    Four not exempt from pride some future day.
Resting on one white hand a warm wet cheek
    Over my open volume you will say,
    "This man loved *me!*" then rise and trip away.

"Do You Remember Me?..."

"Do you remember me? or are you proud?"
Lightly advancing through her star-trimmed crowd,
    Ianthe said, and looked into my eyes.
"A *yes,* a *yes,* to both: for Memory
Where you but once have been must ever be,
    And at your voice Pride from his throne must rise."

"Well I Remember..."

Well I remember how you smiled
    To see me write your name upon
The soft sea-sand . . . "O! *what a child!*
    You think you're writing upon stone!"
I have since written what no tide
    Shall ever wash away, what men
Unborn shall read o'er ocean wide
    And find Ianthe's name again.

Dirce

Stand close around, ye Stygian set,
    With Dirce in one boat conveyed!
Or Charon, seeing, may forget,
    That he is old and she a shade.

A Foreign Ruler

He says, *My reign is peace,* so slays
    A thousand in the dead of night.
Are you all happy now? he says,
    And those he leaves behind cry *quite.*
He swears he will have no contention,
    And sets all nations by the ears;
He shouts aloud, *No intervention!*
    Invades, and drowns them all in tears.

FROM Regeneration

We are what suns and winds and waters make us;
The mountains are our sponsors, and the rills
Fashion and win their nursling with their smiles.
But where the land is dim from tyranny,
There tiny pleasures occupy the place
Of glories and of duties; as the feet
Of fabled faeries when the sun goes down
Trip o'er the grass where wrestlers strove by day.
Then Justice, called the eternal one above,
Is more inconstant than the buoyant form
That bursts into existence from the froth
Of ever-varying ocean: what is best
Then becomes worst; what loveliest, most deformed.
The heart is hardest in the softest climes,
The passions flourish, the affections die.

FROM Corinna to Tanagra

Tanagra! think not I forget
    Thy beautifully-storied streets:
Be sure my memory bathes yet
    In clear Thermodon, and yet greets
The blithe and liberal shepherd-boy,
Whose sunny bosom swells with joy
When we accept his matted rushes
Upheaved with sylvan fruit; away he bounds, and blushes.

I promise to bring back with me
 What thou with transport wilt receive,
The only proper gift for thee,
 Of which no mortal shall bereave
In later times thy mouldering walls,
Until the last old turret falls;
A crown, a crown from Athens won,
A crown no God can wear, beside Latona's son.

FROM *Pericles and Aspasia*

1.

Beauty! thou art a wanderer on the earth,
 And hast no temple in the fairest isle
Or city over-sea, where wealth and mirth
 And all the Graces, all the Muses, smile.

Thou art a wanderer, Beauty! like the rays
 That now upon the platan, now upon
The sleepy lake, glance quick or idly gaze,
 And now are manifold and now are none.

In more than one bright form hast thou appeared,
 In more than one sweet dialect hast thou spoken:
Beauty! thy spells the heart within me heard,
 Grieved that they bound it, grieves that they are broken.

2.

"Artemidora! Gods invisible,
While thou art lying faint along the couch,
Have tied the sandal to thy veinéd feet,
And stand beside thee, ready to convey
Thy weary steps where other rivers flow.
Refreshing shades will waft thy weariness
Away, and voices like thine own come nigh
Soliciting, nor vainly, thy embrace."

Artemidora sighed, and would have pressed
The hand now pressing hers, but was too weak.
Fate's shears were over her dark hair unseen
While thus Elpenor spake: he looked into
Eyes that had given light and life erewhile
To those above them, those now dim with tears
And watchfulness. Again he spake of joy
Eternal. At that word, that sad word, *joy*,
Faithful and fond her bosom heaved once more,
Her head fell back: one sob, one loud deep sob
Swelled through the darkened chamber; 'twas not hers:
With her that old boat incorruptible,
Unwearied, undiverted in its course,
Had plashed the water up the farther strand.

To Poets

My children! speak not ill of one another;
   I do not ask you not to hate;
Cadets must envy every elder brother,
   The little poet must the great.

"Leaf after Leaf..."

Leaf after leaf drops off, flower after flower,
Some in the chill, some in the warmer hour:
Alike they flourish and alike they fall,
And earth who nourished them receives them all.
Should we, her wiser sons, be less content
To sink into her lap when life is spent?

THOMAS MOORE
(1779–1852)

"The Harp That Once..."

The harp that once through Tara's halls
   The soul of music shed,
Now hangs as mute on Tara's walls
   As if the soul were fled.

So sleeps the pride of former days,
  So glory's thrill is o'er,
And hearts, that once beat high for praise,
  Now feel that pulse no more.

No more to chiefs and ladies bright
  The harp of Tara swells:
The chord alone, that breaks at night,
  Its tale of ruin tells.
Thus Freedom now so seldom wakes,
  The only throb she gives,
Is when some heart indignant breaks,
  To show that still she lives.

"At the Mid Hour of Night..."

At the mid hour of night, when stars are weeping, I fly
To the lone vale we loved, when life shone warm in thine eye;
  And I think oft, if spirits can steal from the regions of air
  To revisit past scenes of delight, thou wilt come to me there,
And tell me our love is remembered even in the sky.

Then I sing the wild song it once was rapture to hear,
When our voices commingling breathed like one on the ear;
  And as Echo far off through the vale my sad orison rolls,
  I think, O my love! 'tis thy voice from the Kingdom of Souls
Faintly answering still the notes that once were so dear.

Child's Song

I have a garden of my own,
  Shining with flowers of every hue;
I loved it dearly while alone,
  But I shall love it more with you:
And there the golden bees shall come,
  In summer time at break of morn,
And wake us with their busy hum
  Around the Siha's fragrant thorn.

I have a fawn from Aden's land,
  On leafy buds and berries nursed;
And you shall feed him from your hand,
  Though he may start with fear at first,
And I will lead you where he lies
  For shelter in the noon-tide heat;
And you may touch his sleeping eyes,
  And feel his little silvery feet.

JAMES HENRY LEIGH HUNT

(1784–1859)

The Nile

It flows through old hushed Egypt and its sands,
  Like some grave mighty thought threading a dream,
  And times and things, as in that vision, seem
Keeping along it their eternal stands,—
Caves, pillars, pyramids, the shepherd bands
  That roamed through the young world, the glory extreme
  Of high Sesostris, and that southern beam,
The laughing queen that caught the world's great hands.

Then comes a mightier silence, stern and strong,
As of a world left empty of its throng,
  And the void weighs on us; and then we wake,
And hear the fruitful stream lapsing along
  Twixt villages, and think how we shall take
  Our own calm journey on for human sake.

The Fish, the Man, and the Spirit

TO A FISH

You strange, astonished-looking, angle-faced,
  Dreary-mouthed, gaping wretches of the sea,
  Gulping salt water everlastingly,
Cold-blooded, though with red your blood be graced,
And mute, though dwellers in the roaring waste;
  And you, all shapes beside, that fishy be,—
  Some round, some flat, some long, all devilry,
Legless, unloving, infamously chaste:—

O scaly, slippery, wet, swift, staring wights,
　　What is't ye do? What life lead? eh, dull goggles?
How do ye vary your vile days and nights?
　　How pass your Sundays? Are ye still but joggles
In ceaseless wash? Still nought but gapes, and bites,
　　And drinks, and stares, diversified with boggles?

A FISH ANSWERS

Amazing monster! that, for aught I know,
　　With the first sight of thee didst make our race
　　For ever stare! O flat and shocking face,
Grimly divided from the breast below!
Thou that on dry land horribly dost go
　　With a split body and most ridiculous pace,
　　Prong after prong, disgracer of all grace,
Long-useless-finned, haired, upright, unwet, slow!

O breather of unbreathable, sword-sharp air,
　　How canst exist? How bear thyself, thou dry
And dreary sloth? What particle canst share
　　Of the only blessed life, the watery?
I sometimes see of ye an actual *pair*
　　Go by! linked fin by fin! most odiously.

THE FISH TURNS INTO A MAN, AND THEN
INTO A SPIRIT, AND AGAIN SPEAKS

Indulge thy smiling scorn, if smiling still,
　　O man! and loathe, but with a sort of love;
　　For difference must its use by difference prove,
And, in sweet clang, the spheres with music fill.
One of the spirits am I, that at his will
　　Live in whate'er has life—fish, eagle, dove—
　　No hate, no pride, beneath nought, nor above,
A visitor of the rounds of God's sweet skill.

Man's life is warm, glad, sad, 'twixt loves and graves,
　　Boundless in hope, honoured with pangs austere,
Heaven-gazing; and his angel-wings he craves:—
　　The fish is swift, small-needling, vague yet clear,
A cold, sweet, silver life, wrapped in round waves,
　　Quickened with touches of transporting fear.

Rondeau

Jenny kissed me when we met,
 Jumping from the chair she sat in;
Time, you thief, who love to get
 Sweets into your list, put that in:
Say I'm weary, say I'm sad,
 Say that health and wealth have missed me,
Say I'm growing old, but add
 Jenny kissed me.

THOMAS LOVE PEACOCK

(1785–1866)

Song

In his last bin Sir Peter lies,
 Who knew not what it was to frown:
Death took him mellow, by surprise,
 And in his cellar stopped him down.
Through all our land we could not boast
 A knight more gay, more prompt than he,
To rise and fill a bumper toast,
 And pass it round with three times three.

None better knew the feast to sway,
 Or keep Mirth's boat in better trim;
For Nature had but little clay
 Like that of which she moulded him.
The meanest guest that graced his board
 Was there the freest of the free,
His bumper toast when Peter poured,
 And passed it round with three times three.

He kept at true good humour's mark
 The social flow of pleasure's tide:
He never made a brow look dark,
 Nor caused a tear, but when he died.
No sorrow round his tomb should dwell:
 More pleased his gay old ghost would be,
For funeral song, and passing bell,
 To hear no sound but three times three.

Headlong Hall

A Catch

Seamen three! What men be ye?
Gotham's three wise men we be.
Whither in your bowl so free?
To rake the moon from out the sea.
The bowl goes trim. The moon doth shine.
And our ballast is old wine;
And your ballast is old wine.

Who art thou, so fast adrift?
I am he they call Old Care.
Here on board we will thee lift.
No: I may not enter there.
Wherefore so? 'Tis Jove's decree,
In a bowl Care may not be;
In a bowl Care may not be.

Fear ye not the waves that roll?
No: in charméd bowl we swim.
What the charm that floats the bowl?
Water may not pass the brim.
The bowl goes trim. The moon doth shine.
And our ballast is old wine;
And your ballast is old wine.

Nightmare Abbey

Song

It was a friar of orders free,
A friar of Rubygill:
At the greenwood-tree a vow made he,
But he kept it very ill:
A vow made he of chastity,
But he kept it very ill.
He kept it, perchance, in the conscious shade
Of the bounds of the forest wherein it was made:
But he roamed where he listed, as free as the wind,
And he left his good vow in the forest behind:
For its woods out of sight were his vow out of mind,
With the friar of Rubygill.

In lonely hut himself he shut,
The friar of Rubygill;
Where the ghostly elf absolved himself,
To follow his own good will:
And he had no lack of canary sack,
To keep his conscience still.
And a damsel well knew, when at lonely midnight
It gleamed on the waters, his signal-lamp-light:
"Over! Over!" she warbled with nightingale throat,
And the friar sprung forth at the magical note,
And she crossed the dark stream in his trim ferry-boat,
With the friar of Rubygill.

Maid Marian

"Not Drunk Is He..."

Not drunk is he, who from the floor
Can rise alone, and still drink more;
But drunk is he, who prostrate lies,
Without the power to drink or rise.

The Misfortunes of Elphin

FROM *The War-Song of Dinas Vawr*

The mountain sheep are sweeter,
But the valley sheep are fatter;
We therefore deemed it meeter
To carry off the latter.

The Misfortunes of Elphin

Chorus

If I drink water while this doth last,
May I never again drink wine:
For how can a man, in his life of a span,
Do anything better than dine?
We'll dine and drink, and say if we think
That anything better can be;
And when we have dined, wish all mankind
May dine as well as we.

And though a good wish will fill no dish,
And brim no cup with sack,
Yet thoughts will spring, as the glasses ring,
To illume our studious track.
On the brilliant dreams of our hopeful schemes
The light of the flask shall shine;
And we'll sit till day, but we'll find the way
To drench the world with wine.

Crotchet Castle

Love and Age

I played with you 'mid cowslips blowing,
When I was six and you were four;
When garlands weaving, flower-balls throwing,
Were pleasures soon to please no more.
Through groves and meads, o'er grass and heather,
With little playmates, to and fro,
We wandered hand in hand together;
But that was sixty years ago.

You grew a lovely roseate maiden,
And still our early love was strong;
Still with no care our days were laden,
They glided joyously along;
Then I did love you, very dearly,
How dearly words want power to show;
I thought your heart was touched as nearly;
But that was fifty years ago.

Then other lovers came around you,
Your beauty grew from year to year,
And many a splendid circle found you
The centre of its glittering sphere.
I saw you then, first vows forsaking,
On rank and wealth your hand bestow;
Oh, then I thought my heart was breaking,—
But that was forty years ago.

And I loved on, to wed another:
No cause she gave me to repine;
And when I heard you were a mother,
I did not wish the children mine.
My own young flock, in fair progression,
Made up a pleasant Christmas row:
My joy in them was past expression;—
But that was thirty years ago.

You grew a matron plump and comely,
You dwelt in fashion's brightest blaze;
My earthly lot was far more homely;
But I too had my festal days.
No merrier eyes have ever glistened
Around the hearth-stone's wintry glow,
Than when my youngest child was christened:—
But that was twenty years ago.

Time passed. My eldest girl was married,
And I am now a grandsire grey;
One pet of four years old I've carried
Among the wild-flowered meads to play.
In our old fields of childish pleasure,
Where now, as then, the cowslips blow,
She fills her basket's ample measure,—
And that is not ten years ago.

But though first love's impassioned blindness
Has passed away in colder light,
I still have thought of you with kindness,
And shall do, till our last good-night.
The ever-rolling silent hours
Will bring a time we shall not know,
When our young days of gathering flowers
Will be an hundred years ago.

Gryll Grange

Glee—The Ghosts

In life three ghostly friars were we,
And now three friarly ghosts we be.
Around our shadowy table placed,
The spectral bowl before us floats;
With wine that none but ghosts can taste,
We wash our unsubstantial throats.
Three merry ghosts—three merry ghosts—three merry ghosts
      are we:
Let the ocean be Port, and we'll think it good sport
To be laid in that Red Sea.

With songs that jovial spectres chaunt,
Our old refectory still we haunt.
The traveller hears our midnight mirth:
"O list!" he cries, "the haunted choir!
The merriest ghost that walks the earth,
Is sure the ghost of a ghostly friar."
Three merry ghosts—three merry ghosts—three merry ghosts
      are we:
Let the ocean be Port, and we'll think it good sport
To be laid in that Red Sea.

Melincourt

GEORGE NOEL GORDON, Lord Byron
(1788–1824)
FROM *To Woman*

Woman! experience might have told me,
That all must love thee who behold thee:
Surely experience might have taught
Thy finest promises are nought:
But, placed in all thy charms before me,
All I forget but to adore thee.
Oh memory! thou choicest blessing
When joined with hope, when still possessing;
But how much cursed by every lover
When hope is fled and passion's over.

"Farewell! If Ever Fondest Prayer"

Farewell! if ever fondest prayer
  For other's weal availed on high,
Mine will not all be lost in air,
  But waft thy name beyond the sky.
'Twere vain to speak, to weep, to sigh:
  Oh! more than tears of blood can tell,
When wrung from guilt's expiring eye,
  Are in that word—Farewell!—Farewell!

These lips are mute, these eyes are dry;
  But in my breast and in my brain,
Awake the pangs that pass not by,
  The thoughts that ne'er shall sleep again.
My soul nor deigns nor dares complain,
  Though grief and passion there rebel:
I only know we loved in vain—
  I only feel—Farewell!—Farewell!

"When We Two Parted"

When we two parted
  In silence and tears,
Half broken-hearted
  To sever for years,
Pale grew thy cheek and cold,
  Colder thy kiss;
Truly that hour foretold
  Sorrow to this.

The dew of the morning
  Sunk chill on my brow—
It felt like the warning
  Of what I feel now.
Thy vows are all broken,
  And light is thy fame;
I hear thy name spoken,
  And share in its shame.

They name thee before me,
  A knell to mine ear;
A shudder comes o'er me—
  Why wert thou so dear?
They know not I knew thee,
  Who knew thee too well—
Long, long shall I rue thee,
  Too deeply to tell.

In secret we met—
  In silence I grieve
That thy heart could forget,
  Thy spirit deceive.
If I should meet thee
  After long years,
How should I greet thee?
  With silence and tears.

"Remember Thee! Remember Thee!"

Remember thee! remember thee!
  Till Lethe quench life's burning stream
Remorse and shame shall cling to thee,
  And haunt thee like a feverish dream!

Remember thee! Aye, doubt it not.
  Thy husband too shall think of thee:
By neither shalt thou be forgot,
  Thou false to him, thou fiend to me!

FROM Stanzas

Could Love for ever
Run like a river,
And Time's endeavour
  Be tried in vain—
No other pleasure
With this could measure

And like a treasure
  We'd hug the chain.
But since our sighing
Ends not in dying,
And, formed for flying,
  Love plumes his wing;
Then for this reason
Let's love a season:
But let that season be only Spring.

When lovers parted
Feel broken-hearted,
And, all hopes thwarted,
  Expect to die;
A few years older,
Ah! how much colder
They might behold her
  For whom they sigh!
When linked together
In every weather
They pluck Love's feather
  From out his wing—
He'll stay for ever
But sadly shiver
Without his plumage when past the Spring.

Wait not, fond lover!
Till years are over,
And then recover,
  As from a dream.
While each bewailing
The other's failing,
With wrath and railing,
  All hideous seem—
While first decreasing,
Yet not quite ceasing,
Wait not till teasing
  All passion blight:
If once diminished
Love's reign is finished—
Then part in friendship—and bid good-night.

"So We'll Go No More a Roving"

So we'll go no more a roving
　So late into the night,
Though the heart be still as loving,
　And the moon be still as bright.

For the sword outwears the sheath,
　And the soul wears out the breast,
And the heart must pause to breathe,
　And Love itself have rest.

Though the night was made for loving,
　And the day returns too soon,
Yet we'll go no more a roving
　By the light of the moon.

FROM *Childe Harold's Pilgrimage*

1.

There was a sound of revelry by night,
And Belgium's capital had gathered then
Her beauty and her chivalry, and bright
The lamps shone o'er fair women and brave men;
A thousand hearts beat happily; and when
Music arose with its voluptuous swell,
Soft eyes looked love to eyes which spake again,
And all went merry as a marriage bell—
But hush! hark! a deep sound strikes like a rising knell!

Did ye not hear it? No, 'twas but the wind,
Or the car rattling o'er the stony street;
On with the dance! let joy be unconfined;
No sleep till morn, when youth and pleasure meet
To chase the glowing hours with flying feet—
But hark!—that heavy sound breaks in once more
As if the clouds its echo would repeat;
And nearer, clearer, deadlier than before!
Arm! Arm! it is—it is—the cannon's opening roar!

Ah! then and there was hurrying to and fro,
And gathering tears, and tremblings of distress,
And cheeks all pale, which but an hour ago
Blushed at the praise of their own loveliness;
And there were sudden partings, such as press
The life from out young hearts, and choking sighs
Which ne'er might be repeated; who could guess
If ever more should meet those mutual eyes,
Since upon night so sweet such awful morn could rise!

And there was mounting in hot haste: the steed,
The mustering squadron, and the clattering car,
Went pouring forward with impetuous speed,
And swiftly forming in the ranks of war;
And the deep thunder peel on peel afar;
And near, the beat of the alarming drum
Roused up the soldier ere the morning star;
While thronged the citizens with terror dumb,
Or whispering with white lips—"The foe! They come! they
      come!"

And Ardennes waves above them her green leaves,
Dewy with nature's tear-drops, as they pass,
Grieving, if aught inanimate e'er grieves,
Over the unreturning brave—alas!
Ere evening to be trodden like the grass
Which now beneath them, but above shall grow
In its next verdure, when this fiery mass
Of living valour, rolling on the foe
And burning with high hope, shall moulder cold and low.

Last noon beheld them full of lusty life,
Last eve in Beauty's circle proudly gay,
The midnight brought the signal-sound of strife,
The morn the marshalling in arms—the day
Battle's magnificently-stern array!
The thunder-clouds close o'er it, which when rent
The earth is covered thick with other clay,
Which her own clay shall cover, heaped and pent,
Rider and horse—friend, foe—in one red burial blent!

2.

The castled crag of Drachenfels
Frowns o'er the wide and winding Rhine,
Whose breast of waters broadly swells
Between the banks which bear the vine;
And hills all rich with blossomed trees,
And fields which promise corn and wine,
And scattered cities crowning these,
Whose far white walls along them shine,
Have strewed a scene, which I should see
With double joy wert thou with me.

And peasant girls, with deep blue eyes
And hands which offer early flowers,
Walk smiling o'er this paradise;
Above, the frequent feudal towers
Through green leaves lift their walls of gray;
And many a rock which steeply lowers,
And noble arch in proud decay,
Look o'er this vale of vintage-bowers;
But one thing want these banks of Rhine—
Thy gentle hand to clasp in mine.

I send the lilies given to me;
Though long before thy hand they touch,
I know that they must withered be,
But yet reject them not as such;
For I have cherished them as dear,
Because they yet may meet thine eye,
And guide thy soul to mine even here,
When thou behold'st them, drooping nigh,
And know'st them gathered by the Rhine,
And offered from my heart to thine!

The river nobly foams and flows,
The charm of this enchanted ground,
And all its thousand turns disclose
Some fresher beauty varying round:
The haughtiest breast its wish might bound

Through life to dwell delighted here;
Nor could on earth a spot be found
To nature and to me so dear,
Could thy dear eyes in following mine
Still sweeten more these banks of Rhine!

3.

I stood in Venice on the Bridge of Sighs,
A palace and a prison on each hand;
I saw from out the wave her structures rise
As from the stroke of the enchanter's wand:
A thousand years their cloudy wings expand
Around me, and a dying glory smiles
O'er the far times, when many a subject land
Looked to the wingéd Lion's marble piles,
Where Venice sat in state, throned on her hundred isles!

She looks a sea Cybele, fresh from ocean,
Rising with her tiara of proud towers
At airy distance, with majestic motion,
A ruler of the waters and their powers.
And such she was—her daughters had their dowers
From spoils of nations, and the exhaustless East
Poured in her lap all gems in sparkling showers:
In purple was she robed, and of her feast
Monarchs partook, and deemed their dignity increased.

In Venice Tasso's echoes are no more,
And silent rows the songless gondolier;
Her palaces are crumbling to the shore,
And music meets not always now the ear;
Those days are gone, but beauty still is here;
States fall, arts fade, but Nature doth not die,
Nor yet forget how Venice once was dear,
The pleasant place of all festivity,
The revel of the earth, the masque of Italy!

4.

Egeria, sweet creation of some heart
Which found no mortal resting-place so fair
As thine ideal breast! whate'er thou art
Or wert—a young Aurora of the air,

The nympholepsy of some fond despair,
Or, it might be, a beauty of the earth,
Who found a more than common votary there
Too much adoring; whatsoe'er thy birth,
Thou wert a beautiful thought, and softly bodied forth.

The mosses of thy fountain still are sprinkled
With thine Elysian water-drops; the face
Of thy cave-guarded spring, with years unwrinkled,
Reflects the meek-eyed genius of the place,
Whose green, wild margin now no more erase
Art's works; nor must the delicate waters sleep
Prisoned in marble, bubbling from the base
Of the cleft statue, with a gentle leap
The rill runs o'er, and round, fern, flowers, and ivy creep,

Fantastically tangled. The green hills
Are clothed with early blossoms, through the grass
The quick-eyed lizard rustles, and the bills
Of summer-birds sing welcome as ye pass;
Flowers fresh in hue, and many in their class,
Implore the pausing step, and with their dyes
Dance in the soft breeze in a fairy mass;
The sweetness of the violet's deep blue eyes,
Kissed by the breath of heaven, seems coloured by its skies.

5.

Oh Love! no habitant of earth thou art—
An unseen seraph, we believe in thee,
A faith whose martyrs are the broken heart,
But never yet hath seen, nor e'er shall see
The naked eye, thy form, as it should be;
The mind hath made thee, as it peopled heaven,
Even with its own desiring phantasy,
And to a thought such shape and image given,
As haunts the unquenched soul—parched—wearied—wrung—
    and riven.

Of its own beauty is the mind diseased,
And fevers into false creation—where,
Where are the forms the sculptor's soul hath seized?
In him alone. Can Nature show so fair?
Where are the charms and virtues which we dare
Conceive in boyhood and pursue as men,
The unreached paradise of our despair,
Which o'er-informs the pencil and the pen,
And overpowers the page where it would bloom again?

Who loves, raves—'tis youth's frenzy; but the cure
Is bitterer still. As charm by charm unwinds
Which robed our idols, and we see too sure
Nor worth nor beauty dwells from out the mind's
Ideal shape of such; yet still it binds
The fatal spell, and still it draws us on,
Reaping the whirlwind from the oft-sown winds;
The stubborn heart, its alchemy begun,
Seems ever near the prize—wealthiest when most undone.

We wither from our youth, we gasp away—
Sick—sick—unfound the boon—unslaked the thirst,
Though to the last, in verge of our decay,
Some phantom lures, such as we sought at first—
But all too late—so are we doubly cursed.
Love, fame, ambition, avarice—'tis the same,
Each idle, and all ill, and none the worst—
For all are meteors with a different name,
And Death the sable smoke where vanishes the flame.

6.

There is a pleasure in the pathless woods,
There is a rapture on the lonely shore,
There is society where none intrudes,
By the deep Sea, and music in its roar:
I love not Man the less, but Nature more,
From these our interviews, in which I steal
From all I may be or have been before,
To mingle with the universe, and feel
What I can ne'er express, yet can not all conceal.

Roll on, thou deep and dark blue ocean, roll!
Ten thousand fleets sweep over thee in vain;
Man marks the earth with ruin, his control
Stops with the shore; upon the watery plain
The wrecks are all thy deed, nor doth remain
A shadow of man's ravage, save his own,
When, for a moment, like a drop of rain,
He sinks into thy depths with bubbling groan,
Without a grave, unknelled, uncoffined, and unknown.

FROM *Don Juan*

1.

. . . 'Tis sweet to hear
At midnight on the blue and moonlit deep
The song and oar of Adria's gondolier,
By distance mellowed, o'er the waters sweep;
'Tis sweet to see the evening star appear;
'Tis sweet to listen as the night-winds creep
From leaf to leaf; 'tis sweet to view on high
The rainbow, based on ocean, span the sky.

'Tis sweet to hear the watch-dog's honest bark
Bay deep-mouthed welcome as we draw near home;
'Tis sweet to know there is an eye will mark
Our coming, and look brighter when we come;
'Tis sweet to be awakened by the lark,
Or lulled by falling waters; sweet the hum
Of bees, the voice of girls, the song of birds,
The lisp of children, and their earliest words.

Sweet is the vintage, when the showering grapes
In Bacchanal profusion reel to earth,
Purple and gushing; sweet are our escapes
From civic revelry to rural mirth;
Sweet to the miser are his glittering heaps,
Sweet to the father is his first-born's birth,
Sweet is revenge—especially to women,
Pillage to soldiers, prize-money to seamen.

But sweeter still than this, than these, than all,
　Is first and passionate love—it stands alone,
Like Adam's recollection of his fall;
　The tree of knowledge has been plucked—all's known—
And life yields nothing further to recall
　Worthy of this ambrosial sin, so shown,
No doubt in fable, as the unforgiven
Fire which Prometheus filched for us from heaven.

2.

　　They tell me 'tis decided; you depart:
　　　'Tis wise—'tis well, but not the less a pain;
　　I have no further claim on your young heart,
　　　Mine is the victim, and would be again;
　　To love too much has been the only art
　　　I used—I write in haste, and if a stain
　　Be on this sheet, 'tis not what it appears;
　　My eyeballs burn and throb, but have no tears.

　　I loved, I love you, for this love have lost
　　　State, station, heaven, mankind's, my own esteem,
　　And yet can not regret what it hath cost,
　　　So dear is still the memory of that dream;
　　Yet, if I name my guilt, 'tis not to boast,
　　　None can deem harshlier of me than I deem:
　　I trace this scrawl because I cannot rest—
　　I've nothing to reproach, or to request.

　　Man's love is of man's life a thing apart,
　　　'Tis woman's whole existence; man may range
　　The court, camp, church, the vessel, and the mart;
　　　Sword, gown, gain, glory, offer in exchange
　　Pride, fame, ambition, to fill up his heart,
　　　And few there are whom these cannot estrange;
　　Men have all these resources, we but one,
　　To love again, and be again undone.

　　You will proceed in pleasure, and in pride,
　　　Beloved and loving many; all is o'er
　　For me on earth, except some years to hide
　　　My shame and sorrow deep in my heart's core;

These I could bear, but cannot cast aside
    The passion which still rages as before—
And so farewell—forgive me, love me—No,
That word is idle now—but let it go.

My breast has been all weakness, is so yet;
    But still I think I can collect my mind;
My blood still rushes where my spirit's set,
    As roll the waves before the settled wind;
My heart is feminine, nor can forget—
    To all, except one image, madly blind;
So shakes the needle, and so stands the pole,
As vibrates my fond heart to my fixed soul.

I have no more to say, but linger still,
    And dare not set my seal upon this sheet,
And yet I may as well the task fulfil,
    My misery can scarce be more complete:
I had not lived till now, could sorrow kill;
    Death shuns the wretch who fain the blow would meet,
And I must even survive this last adieu,
And bear with life, to love and pray for you!

3.

    'Tis pleasing to be schooled in a strange tongue
        By female lips and eyes—that is, I mean,
    When both the teacher and the taught are young,
        As was the case, at least, where I have been;
    They smile so when one's right, and when one's wrong
        They smile still more, and then there intervene
    Pressure of hands, perhaps even a chaste kiss—
    I learned the little that I know by this.

4.

    It was the cooling hour, just when the rounded
        Red sun sinks down behind the azure hill,
    Which then seems as if the whole earth it bounded,
        Circling all nature, hushed, and dim, and still,

With the far mountain-crescent half surrounded
   On one side, and the deep sea calm and chill
Upon the other, and the rosy sky,
With one star sparkling through it like an eye.

And thus they wandered forth, and hand in hand,
   Over the shining pebbles and the shells,
Glided along the smooth and hardened sand,
   And in the worn and wild receptacles
Worked by the storms, yet worked as it were planned
   In hollow halls, with sparry roofs and cells,
They turned to rest; and, each clasped by an arm,
Yielded to the deep twilight's purple charm.

They looked up to the sky, whose floating glow
   Spread like a rosy ocean, vast and bright;
They gazed upon the glittering sea below,
   Whence the broad moon rose circling into sight;
They heard the wave's splash, and the wind so low,
   And saw each other's dark eyes darting light
Into each other—and, beholding this,
Their lips drew near, and clung into a kiss;

A long, long kiss, a kiss of youth, and love,
   And beauty, all concentrating like rays
Into one focus, kindled from above;
   Such kisses as belong to early days,
Where heart, and soul, and sense, in concert move,
   And the blood's lava, and the pulse a blaze,
Each kiss a heart-quake—for a kiss's strength,
I think, it must be reckoned by its length.

By length I mean duration; theirs endured
   Heaven knows how long—no doubt they never reckoned;
And if they had, they could not have secured
   The sum of their sensations to a second:
They had not spoken; but they felt allured,
   As if their souls and lips each other beckoned,
Which, being joined, like swarming bees they clung—
Their hearts the flowers from whence the honey sprung.

They were alone, but not alone as they
  Who shut in chambers think it loneliness;
The silent ocean, and the starlight bay,
  The twilight glow which momently grew less,
The voiceless sands and dropping caves, that lay
  Around them, made them to each other press,
As if there were no life beneath the sky
Save theirs, and that their life could never die.

They feared no eyes nor ears on that lone beach,
  They felt no terrors from the night, they were
All in all to each other: though their speech
  Was broken words, they *thought* a language there—
And all the burning tongues the passions teach
  Found in one sigh the best interpreter
Of nature's oracle—first love—that all
Which Eve has left her daughters since her fall.

Haidée spoke not of scruples, asked no vows,
  Nor offered any; she had never heard
Of plight and promises to be a spouse,
  Or perils by a loving maid incurred;
She was all which pure ignorance allows,
  And flew to her young mate like a young bird;
And, never having dreamed of falsehood, she
Had not one word to say of constancy.

She loved and was belovéd—she adored
  And she was worshipped; after nature's fashion
Their intense souls, into each other poured,
  If souls could die, had perished in that passion—
But by degrees their senses were restored,
  Again to be o'ercome, again to dash on;
And, beating 'gainst his bosom, Haidée's heart
Felt as if never more to beat apart.

Alas! they were so young, so beautiful,
  So lonely, loving, helpless, and the hour
Was that in which the heart is always full,
  And, having o'er itself no further power,

Prompts deeds eternity can not annul,
  But pays off moments in an endless shower
Of hell-fire—all prepared for people giving
Pleasure or pain to one another living.

Alas! for Juan and Haidée! they were
  So loving and so lovely—till then never,
Excepting our first parents, such a pair
  Had run the risk of being damned for ever;
And Haidée, being devout as well as fair,
  Had, doubtless, heard about the Stygian river,
And hell and purgatory—but forgot
Just in the very crisis she should not.

They look upon each other, and their eyes
  Gleam in the moonlight; and her white arm clasps
Round Juan's head, and his around her lies
  Half buried in the tresses which it grasps;
She sits upon his knee, and drinks his sighs,
  He hers, until they end in broken gasps;
And thus they form a group that's quite antique,
Half naked, loving, natural, and Greek.

And when those deep and burning moments passed,
  And Juan sunk to sleep within her arms,
She slept not, but all tenderly, though fast,
  Sustained his head upon her bosom's charms;
And now and then her eye to heaven is cast,
  And then on the pale cheek her breast now warms,
Pillowed on her o'erflowing heart, which pants
With all it granted, and with all it grants.

An infant when it gazes on the light,
  A child the moment when it drains the breast,
A devotee when soars the Host in sight,
  An Arab with a stranger for a guest,
A sailor when the prize has struck in fight,
  A miser filling his most hoarded chest,
Feel rapture; but not such true joy are reaping
As they who watch o'er what they love while sleeping.

For there it lies so tranquil, so beloved,
    All that it hath of life with us is living;
So gentle, stirless, helpless and unmoved,
    And all unconscious of the joy 'tis giving;
All it hath felt, inflicted, passed and proved,
    Hushed into depths beyond the watcher's diving;
There lies the thing we love with all its errors
And all its charms, like death without its terrors.

5.

    The isles of Greece, the isles of Greece!
      Where burning Sappho loved and sung,
    Where grew the arts of war and peace,
      Where Delos rose, and Phoebus sprung!
    Eternal summer gilds them yet,
    But all, except their sun, is set.

    The Scian and the Teian muse,
      The hero's harp, the lover's lute,
    Have found the fame your shores refuse;
      Their place of birth alone is mute
    To sounds which echo further west
    Than your sires' "Islands of the Blest."

    The mountains look on Marathon,
      And Marathon looks on the sea;
    And musing there an hour alone,
      I dreamed that Greece might still be free;
    And standing on the Persians' grave,
    I could not deem myself a slave.

    A king sate on the rocky brow
      Which looks o'er sea-born Salamis;
    And ships, by thousands, lay below,
      And men in nations—all were his!
    He counted them at break of day—
    And when the sun set where were they?

And where are they? and where art thou,
  My country? On thy voiceless shore
The heroic lay is tuneless now—
  The heroic bosom beats no more!
And must thy lyre, so long divine,
Degenerate into hands like mine?

'Tis something, in the dearth of fame,
  Though linked among a fettered race,
To feel at least a patriot's shame,
  Even as I sing, suffuse my face;
For what is left the poet here?
For Greeks a blush—for Greece a tear.

Must we but weep o'er days more blest?
  Must we but blush? Our fathers bled.
Earth! render back from out thy breast
  A remnant of our Spartan dead!
Of the three hundred grant but three
To make a new Thermopylae!

What, silent still? and silent all?
  Ah! no—the voices of the dead
Sound like a distant torrent's fall,
  And answer, "Let one living head,
But one arise—we come, we come!"
'Tis but the living who are dumb.

In vain—in vain: strike other chords;
  Fill high the cup with Samian wine!
Leave battles to the Turkish hordes,
  And shed the blood of Scio's vine!
Hark! rising to the ignoble call—
How answers each bold Bacchanal!

You have the Pyrrhic dance as yet,
  Where is the Pyrrhic phalanx gone?
Of two such lessons, why forget
  The nobler and the manlier one?
You have the letters Cadmus gave—
Think ye he meant them for a slave?

Fill high the bowl with Samian wine!
  We will not think of themes like these!
It made Anacreon's song divine:
  He served—but served Polycrates—
A tyrant; but our masters then
Were still, at least, our countrymen.

The tyrant of the Chersonese
  Was freedom's best and bravest friend;
That tyrant was Miltiades!
  Oh! that the present hour would lend
Another despot of the kind!
Such chains as his were sure to bind.

Fill high the bowl with Samian wine!
  On Suli's rock, and Parga's shore,
Exists the remnant of a line
  Such as the Doric mothers bore;
And there, perhaps, some seed is sown,
The Heracleidan blood might own.

Trust not for freedom to the Franks—
  They have a king who buys and sells:
In native swords, and native ranks,
  The only hope of courage dwells;
But Turkish force, and Latin fraud,
Would break your shield, however broad.

Fill high the bowl with Samian wine!
  Our virgins dance beneath the shade—
I see their glorious black eyes shine;
  But gazing on each glowing maid,
My own the burning tear-drop laves,
To think such breasts must suckle slaves.

Place me on Sunium's marbled steep,
  Where nothing, save the waves and I,
May hear our mutual murmurs sweep;
  There, swan-like, let me sing and die;
A land of slaves shall ne'er be mine—
Dash down yon cup of Samian wine!

On This Day I Complete My Thirty-Sixth Year

'Tis time this heart should be unmoved,
　　Since others it hath ceased to move;
Yet, though I cannot be beloved,
　　　　Still let me love!

My days are in the yellow leaf;
　　The flowers and fruits of love are gone;
The worm, the canker, and the grief
　　　　Are mine alone!

The fire that on my bosom preys
　　Is lone as some volcanic isle;
No torch is kindled at its blaze—
　　　　A funeral pile.

The hope, the fear, the jealous care,
　　The exalted portion of the pain
And power of love, I cannot share,
　　　　But wear the chain.

But 'tis not thus—and 'tis not here—
　　Such thoughts should shake my soul, nor now,
Where glory decks the hero's bier,
　　　　Or binds his brow.

The sword, the banner, and the field,
　　Glory and Greece, around me see!
The Spartan, borne upon his shield,
　　　　Was not more free.

Awake! (not Greece—she is awake!)
　　Awake, my spirit! Think through whom
Thy life-blood tracks its parent lake,
　　　　And then strike home!

Tread those reviving passions down,
　　Unworthy manhood! unto thee
Indifferent should the smile or frown
　　　　Of beauty be.

If thou regret'st thy youth, why live?
  The land of honourable death
Is here—up to the field, and give
      Away thy breath!

Seek out—less often sought than found—
  A soldier's grave, for thee the best;
Then look around, and choose thy ground,
      And take thy rest.

Missolonghi, January 22, 1824

CHARLES WOLFE

(1791–1823)

To Mary

If I had thought thou couldst have died,
  I might not weep for thee;
But I forgot, when by thy side,
  That thou couldst mortal be:
It never through my mind had past
  The time would e'er be o'er,
And I on thee should look my last,
  And thou shouldst smile no more!

And still upon that face I look,
  And think 'twill smile again;
And still the thought I will not brook,
  That I must look in vain.
But when I speak—thou dost not say
  What thou ne'er left'st unsaid;
And now I feel; as well I may,
  Sweet Mary, thou art dead!

If thou wouldst stay, e'en as thou art,
  All cold and all serene—
I still might press thy silent heart,
  And where thy smiles have been.

While e'en thy chill, bleak corse I have,
   Thou seemest still mine own;
But there—I lay thee in the grave,
   And now I am alone!

I do not think, where'er thou art,
   Thou hast forgotten me;
And I, perhaps, may soothe this heart
   In thinking too of thee:
Yet there was round thee such a dawn
   Of light ne'er seen before,
As fancy never could have drawn,
   And never can restore!

PERCY BYSSHE SHELLEY

(1792–1822)

FROM *Prometheus Unbound*

1.

Fourth Spirit:

On a poet's lips I slept
Dreaming like a love-adept
In the sound his breathing kept;
Nor seeks nor finds he mortal blisses,
But feeds on the aërial kisses
Of shapes that haunt thought's wildernesses.
He will watch from dawn to gloom
The lake-reflected sun illume
The yellow bees in the ivy-bloom,
Nor heed nor see, what things they be;
But from these create he can
Forms more real than living man,
Nurslings of immortality!

2.

Semichorus I of Spirits:

The path through which that lovely twain
   Have passed, by cedar, pine, and yew,
   And each dark tree that ever grew,
    Is curtained out from Heaven's wide blue;

Nor sun, nor moon, nor wind, nor rain
 Can pierce its interwoven bowers,
 Nor aught, save where some cloud of dew,
Drifted along the earth-creeping breeze,
Between the trunks of the hoar trees,
 Hangs each a pearl in the pale flowers
 Of the green laurel, blown anew;
And bends, and then fades silently,
One frail and fair anemone:
Or when some star of many a one
That climbs and wanders through steep night,
Has found the cleft through which alone
Beams fall from high those depths upon
Ere it is borne away, away,
By the swift Heavens that cannot stay,
It scatters drops of golden light,
Like lines of rain that ne'er unite:
And the gloom divine is all around,
And underneath is the mossy ground.

Semichorus II:

There the voluptuous nightingales,
 Are awake through all the broad noonday.
When one with bliss or sadness fails,
 And through the windless ivy-boughs,
 Sick with sweet love, droops dying away
On its mate's music-panting bosom;
Another from the swinging blossom,
 Watching to catch the languid close
 Of the last strain, then lifts on high
 The wings of the weak melody,
'Till some new strain of feeling bear
 The song, and all the woods are mute;
When there is heard through the dim air
The rush of wings, and rising there
 Like many a lake-surrounded flute,
Sounds overflow the listener's brain
So sweet, that joy is almost pain.

3.

Voice in the Air, Singing:

Life of Life! thy lips enkindle
    With their love the breath between them;
And thy smiles before they dwindle
    Make the cold air fire; then screen them
In those looks, where whoso gazes
Faints, entangled in their mazes.

Child of Light! thy limbs are burning
    Through the vest which seems to hide them;
As the radiant lines of morning
    Through the clouds ere they divide them;
And this atmosphere divinest
Shrouds thee wheresoe'er thou shinest.

Fair are others; none beholds thee,
    But thy voice sounds low and tender
Like the fairest, for it folds thee
    From the sight, that liquid splendour,
And all feel, yet see thee never,
As I feel now, lost for ever!

Lamp of Earth! where'er thou movest
    Its dim shapes are clad with brightness,
And the souls of whom thou lovest
    Walk upon the winds with lightness,
Till they fail, as I am failing,
Dizzy, lost, yet unbewailing!

Asia:

My soul is an enchanted boat,
    Which, like a sleeping swan, doth float
Upon the silver waves of thy sweet singing;
    And thine doth like an angel sit
    Beside a helm conducting it,
Whilst all the winds with melody are ringing.
    It seems to float ever, for ever,
    Upon that many-winding river,
    Between mountains, woods, abysses,
    A paradise of wildernesses!

Till, like one in slumber bound,
Borne to the ocean, I float down, around,
Into a sea profound, of ever ever-spreading sound:

Meanwhile thy spirit lifts its pinions
In music's most serene dominions;
Catching the winds that fan that happy heaven.
And we sail on, away, afar,
Without a course, without a star,
But, by the instinct of sweet music driven;
Till through Elysian garden islets
By thee, most beautiful of pilots,
Where never mortal pinnace glided,
The boat of my desire is guided:
Realms where the air we breathe is love,
Which in the winds and on the waves doth move,
Harmonizing this earth with what we feel above.

We have passed Age's icy caves,
And Manhood's dark and tossing waves,
And Youth's smooth ocean, smiling to betray:
Beyond the glassy gulfs we flee
Of shadow-peopled Infancy,
Through Death and Birth, to a diviner day;
A paradise of vaulted bowers,
Lit by downward-gazing flowers,
And watery paths that wind between
Wildernesses calm and green,
Peopled by shapes too bright to see,
And rest, having beheld; somewhat like thee;
Which walk upon the sea, and chant melodiously!

FROM *Lines Written among the Euganean Hills*

'Mid the mountains Euganean
I stood listening to the paean
With which the legioned rooks did hail
The sun's uprise majestical;
Gathering round with wings all hoar,

Through the dewy mist they soar
Like gray shades, till the eastern heaven
Bursts, and then, as clouds of even,
Flecked with fire and azure, lie
In the unfathomable sky,
So their plumes of purple grain,
Starred with drops of golden rain,
Gleam above the sunlight woods,
As in silent multitudes
On the morning's fitful gale
Through the broken mist they sail,
And the vapours cloven and gleaming
Follow, down the dark steep streaming,
Till all is bright, and clear, and still,
Round the solitary hill.

Beneath is spread like a green sea
The waveless plain of Lombardy,
Bounded by the vaporous air,
Islanded by cities fair;
Underneath Day's azure eyes
Ocean's nursling, Venice lies,
A peopled labyrinth of walls,
Amphitrite's destined halls,
Which her hoary sire now paves
With his blue and beaming waves.
Lo! the sun upsprings behind,
Broad, red, radiant, half-reclined
On the level quivering line
Of the waters crystalline;
And before that chasm of light,
As within a furnace bright,
Column, tower, and dome, and spire,
Shine like obelisks of fire,
Pointing with inconstant motion
From the altar of dark ocean
To the sapphire-tinted skies;
As the flames of sacrifice
From the marble shrines did rise,
As to pierce the dome of gold
Where Apollo spoke of old.

Stanzas Written in Dejection, near Naples

The sun is warm, the sky is clear,
　The waves are dancing fast and bright,
Blue isles and snowy mountains wear
　The purple noon's transparent might,
　The breath of the moist earth is light,
Around its unexpanded buds;
　Like many a voice of one delight,
The winds, the birds, the ocean floods,
The City's voice itself, is soft like Solitude's.

I see the Deep's untrampled floor
　With green and purple seaweeds strown;
I see the waves upon the shore,
　Like light dissolved in star-showers, thrown:
　I sit upon the sands alone,—
The lightning of the noontide ocean
　Is flashing round me, and a tone
Arises from its measured motion,
How sweet! did any heart now share in my emotion.

Alas! I have nor hope nor health,
　Nor peace within nor calm around,
Nor that content surpassing wealth
　The sage in meditation found,
　And walked with inward glory crowned—
Nor fame, nor power, nor love, nor leisure.
　Others I see whom these surround—
Smiling they live, and call life pleasure;—
To me that cup has been dealt in another measure.

Yet now despair itself is mild,
　Even as the winds and waters are;
I could lie down like a tired child,
　And weep away the life of care
　Which I have borne and yet must bear,
Till death like sleep might steal on me,
　And I might feel in the warm air
My cheek grow cold, and hear the sea
Break o'er my dying brain its last monotony.

Some might lament that I were cold,
  As I, when this sweet day is gone,
Which my lost heart, too soon grown old,
  Insults with this untimely moan;
  They might lament—for I am one
Whom men love not,—and yet regret
  Unlike this day, which, when the sun
Shall on its stainless glory set,
Will linger, though enjoyed, like joy in memory yet.

Song to the Men of England

Men of England, wherefore plough
For the lords who lay ye low?
Wherefore weave with toil and care
The rich robes your tyrants wear?

Wherefore feed, and clothe, and save,
From the cradle to the grave,
Those ungrateful drones who would
Drain your sweat—nay, drink your blood?

Wherefore, Bees of England, forge
Many a weapon, chain, and scourge,
That these stingless drones may spoil
The forced produce of your toil?

Have ye leisure, comfort, calm,
Shelter, food, love's gentle balm?
Or what is it ye buy so dear
With your pain and with your fear?

The seed ye sow, another reaps;
The wealth ye find, another keeps;
The robes ye weave, another wears;
The arms ye forge, another bears.

Sow seed,—but let no tyrant reap;
Find wealth,—let no impostor heap;
Weave robes,—let not the idle wear;
Forge arms,—in your defence to bear.

Shrink to your cellars, holes, and cells;
In halls ye deck another dwells.
Why shake the chains ye wrought? Ye see
The steel ye tempered glance on ye.

With plough and spade, and hoe and loom,
Trace your grave, and build your tomb,
And weave your winding-sheet, till fair
England be your sepulchre.

FROM *To the Lord Chancellor*

Oh, let a father's curse be on thy soul,
    And let a daughter's hope be on thy tomb;
Be both, on thy gray head, a leaden cowl
    To weigh thee down to thine approaching doom!

I curse thee by a parent's outraged love,
    By hopes long cherished and too lately lost,
By gentle feelings thou couldst never prove,
    By griefs which thy stern nature never crossed;

By those infantine smiles of happy light,
    Which were a fire within a stranger's hearth,
Quenched even when kindled, in untimely night
    Hiding the promise of a lovely birth:

By those unpractised accents of young speech,
    Which he who is a father thought to frame
To gentlest lore, such as the wisest teach—
    Thou strike the lyre of mind!—oh, grief and shame!

By all the happy see in children's growth—
    That undeveloped flower of budding years—
Sweetness and sadness interwoven both,
    Source of the sweetest hopes and saddest fears—

By all the days, under an hireling's care,
    Of dull constraint and bitter heaviness,—
O wretched ye if any ever were,—
    Sadder than orphans, yet not fatherless!

By the false cant which on their innocent lips
  Must hang like poison on an opening bloom,
By the dark creeds which cover with eclipse
  Their pathway from the cradle to the tomb—

By all the hate which checks a father's love—
  By all the scorn which kills a father's care—
By those most impious hands which dared remove
  Nature's high bounds—by thee—and by despair—

I curse thee—though I hate thee not.—O slave!
  If thou couldst quench the earth-consuming Hell
Of which thou art a daemon, on thy grave
  This curse should be a blessing. Fare thee well!

Ode to the West Wind

I

O wild West Wind, thou breath of Autumn's being,
Thou, from whose unseen presence the leaves dead
Are driven, like ghosts from an enchanter fleeing,

Yellow, and black, and pale, and hectic red,
Pestilence-stricken multitudes: O thou,
Who chariotest to their dark wintry bed

The wingéd seeds, where they lie cold and low,
Each like a corpse within its grave, until
Thine azure sister of the Spring shall blow

Her clarion o'er the dreaming earth, and fill
(Driving sweet buds like flocks to feed in air)
With living hues and odours plain and hill:

Wild Spirit, which art moving everywhere;
Destroyer and preserver; hear, oh, hear!

II

Thou on whose stream, mid the steep sky's commotion,
Loose clouds like earth's decaying leaves are shed,
Shook from the tangled boughs of Heaven and Ocean,

Angels of rain and lightning: there are spread
On the blue surface of thine aëry surge,
Like the bright hair uplifted from the head

Of some fierce Maenad, even from the dim verge
Of the horizon to the zenith's height,
The locks of the approaching storm. Thou dirge

Of the dying year, to which this closing night
Will be the dome of a vast sepulchre,
Vaulted with all thy congregated might

Of vapours, from whose solid atmosphere
Black rain, and fire, and hail will burst: oh, hear!

III

Thou who didst waken from his summer dreams
The blue Mediterranean, where he lay,
Lulled by the coil of his crystálline streams,

Beside a pumice isle in Baiae's bay,
And saw in sleep old palaces and towers
Quivering within the wave's intenser day,

All overgrown with azure moss and flowers
So sweet, the sense faints picturing them! Thou
For whose path the Atlantic's level powers

Cleave themselves into chasms, while far below
The sea-blooms and the oozy woods which wear
The sapless foliage of the ocean, know

Thy voice, and suddenly grow gray with fear,
And tremble and despoil themselves: oh, hear!

IV

If I were a dead leaf thou mightest bear;
If I were a swift cloud to fly with thee;
A wave to pant beneath thy power, and share

The impulse of thy strength, only less free
Than thou, O uncontrollable! If even
I were as in my boyhood, and could be

The comrade of thy wanderings over Heaven,
As then, when to outstrip thy skiey speed
Scarce seemed a vision; I would ne'er have striven

As thus with thee in prayer in my sore need.
Oh, lift me as a wave, a leaf, a cloud!
I fall upon the thorns of life! I bleed!

A heavy weight of hours has chained and bowed
One too like thee: tameless, and swift, and proud.

V

Make me thy lyre, even as the forest is;
What if my leaves are falling like its own!
The tumult of thy mighty harmonies

Will take from both a deep, autumnal tone,
Sweet though in sadness. Be thou, Spirit fierce,
My spirit! Be thou me, impetuous one!

Drive my dead thoughts over the universe
Like withered leaves to quicken a new birth!
And, by the incantation of this verse,

Scatter, as from an unextinguished hearth
Ashes and sparks, my words among mankind!
Be through my lips to unawakened earth

The trumpet of a prophecy! O, Wind,
If Winter comes, can Spring be far behind?

The Indian Serenade

I arise from dreams of thee
In the first sweet sleep of night.
When the winds are breathing low,
And the stars are shining bright:
I arise from dreams of thee,
And a spirit in my feet
Hath led me—who knows how?
To thy chamber window, Sweet!

The wandering airs they faint
On the dark, the silent stream—
The Champak odours fail
Like sweet thoughts in a dream;
The nightingale's complaint,
It dies upon her heart;—
As I must on thine,
Oh, belovéd as thou art!

Oh lift me from the grass!
I die! I faint! I fail!
Let thy love in kisses rain
On my lips and eyelids pale.
My cheek is cold and white, alas!
My heart beats loud and fast;—
Oh! press it to thine own again,
Where it will break at last.

Love's Philosophy

The fountains mingle with the river
    And the rivers with the Ocean,
The winds of Heaven mix for ever
    With a sweet emotion;
Nothing in the world is single;
    All things by a law divine
In one another's being mingle.
    Why not I with thine?—

See the mountains kiss high Heaven
   And the waves clasp one another;
No sister flower would be forgiven
   If it disdained its brother;
And the sunlight clasps the earth
   And the moonbeams kiss the sea:
What are all these kissings worth
   If thou kiss not me?

The Cloud

I bring fresh showers for the thirsting flowers,
   From the seas and the streams;
I bear light shade for the leaves when laid
   In their noonday dreams.
From my wings are shaken the dews that waken
   The sweet buds every one,
When rocked to rest on their mother's breast,
   As she dances about the sun.
I wield the flail of the lashing hail,
   And whiten the green plains under,
And then again I dissolve it in rain,
   And laugh as I pass in thunder.

I sift the snow on the mountains below,
   And their great pines groan aghast;
And all the night 'tis my pillow white,
   While I sleep in the arms of the blast.
Sublime on the towers of my skiey bowers,
   Lightning my pilot sits;
In a cavern under is fettered the thunder,
   It struggles and howls at fits;
Over earth and ocean, with gentle motion,
   This pilot is guiding me,
Lured by the love of the genii that move
   In the depths of the purple sea;
Over the rills, and the crags, and the hills,
   Over the lakes and the plains,

Wherever he dream, under mountain or stream,
    The Spirit he loves remains;
And I all the while bask in Heaven's blue smile,
    Whilst he is dissolving in rains.

The sanguine Sunrise, with his meteor eyes,
    And his burning plumes outspread,
Leaps on the back of my sailing rack,
    When the morning star shines dead;
As on the jag of a mountain crag,
    Which an earthquake rocks and swings,
An eagle alit one moment may sit
    In the light of its golden wings.
And when Sunset may breathe, from the lit sea beneath,
    Its ardours of rest and of love,
And the crimson pall of eve may fall
    From the depth of Heaven above,
With wings folded I rest, on mine aëry nest,
    As still as a brooding dove.

That orbéd maiden with white fire laden,
    Whom mortals call the Moon,
Glides glimmering o'er my fleece-like floor,
    By the midnight breezes strewn;
And whenever the beat of her unseen feet,
    Which only the angels hear,
May have broken the woof of my tent's thin roof,
    The stars peep behind her and peer;
And I laugh to see them whirl and flee,
    Like a swarm of golden bees,
When I widen the rent in my wind-built tent,
    Till the calm rivers, lakes, and seas,
Like strips of the sky fallen through me on high,
    Are each paved with the moon and these.

I bind the Sun's throne with a burning zone,
    And the Moon's with a girdle of pearl;
The volcanoes are dim, and the stars reel and swim,
    When the whirlwinds my banner unfurl.
From cape to cape, with a bridge-like shape,
    Over a torrent sea,

Sunbeam-proof, I hang like a roof,—
    The mountains its columns be.
The triumphal arch through which I march
    With hurricane, fire, and snow,
When the Powers of the air are chained to my chair,
    Is the million-coloured bow;
The sphere-fire above its soft colours wove,
    While the moist Earth was laughing below.

I am the daughter of Earth and Water,
    And the nursling of the Sky;
I pass through the pores of the ocean and shores;
    I change, but I cannot die.
For after the rain when with never a stain
    The pavilion of Heaven is bare,
And the winds and sunbeams with their convex gleams
    Build up the blue dome of air,
I silently laugh at my own cenotaph,
    And out of the caverns of rain,
Like a child from the womb, like a ghost from the tomb,
    I arise and unbuild it again.

To ——

I fear thy kisses, gentle maiden,
    Thou needest not fear mine;
My spirit is too deeply laden
    Ever to burthen thine.

I fear thy mien, thy tones, thy motion,
    Thou needest not fear mine;
Innocent is the heart's devotion
    With which I worship thine.

To the Moon

Art thou pale for weariness
Of climbing heaven and gazing on the earth,
    Wandering companionless
Among the stars that have a different birth,—
And ever changing, like a joyless eye
That finds no object worth its constancy?

The World's Wanderers

Tell me, thou Star, whose wings of light
Speed thee in thy fiery flight,
In what cavern of the night
   Will thy pinions close now?

Tell me, Moon, thou pale and gray
Pilgrim of Heaven's homeless way,
In what depth of night or day
   Seekest thou repose now?

Weary Wind, who wanderest
Like the world's rejected guest,
Hast thou still some secret nest
   On the tree or billow?

Good-Night

Good-night? ah! no; the hour is ill
 Which severs those it should unite;
Let us remain together still,
 Then it will be *good* night.

How can I call the lone night good,
 Though thy sweet wishes wing its flight?
Be it not said, thought, understood—
 Then it will be—*good* night.

To hearts which near each other move
 From evening close to morning light,
The night is good; because, my love,
 They never *say* good-night.

To Night

Swiftly walk o'er the western wave,
   Spirit of Night!
Out of the misty eastern cave
Where, all the long and lone daylight,

Thou wovest dreams of joy and fear,
Which make thee terrible and dear,—
  Swift be thy flight.

Wrap thy form in a mantle gray,
  Star-inwrought!
Blind with thine hair the eyes of Day;
Kiss her until she be wearied out,
Then wander o'er city, and sea, and land,
Touching all with thine opiate wand—
  Come, long-sought!

When I arose and saw the dawn,
  I sighed for thee;
When light rode high, and the dew was gone,
And noon lay heavy on flower and tree,
And the weary Day turned to his rest,
Lingering like an unloved guest,
  I sighed for thee.

Thy brother Death came, and cried,
  Wouldst thou me?
Thy sweet child Sleep, the filmy-eyed,
Murmured like a noontide bee,
Shall I nestle near thy side?
Wouldst thou me?—And I replied,
  No, not thee!

Death will come when thou art dead,
  Soon, too soon—
Sleep will come when thou art fled;
Of neither would I ask the boon
I ask of thee, belovéd Night—
Swift be thine approaching flight,
  Come soon, soon!

To ——

Music, when soft voices die,
Vibrates in the memory—
Odours, when sweet violets sicken,
Live within the sense they quicken.

Rose leaves, when the rose is dead,
Are heaped for the belovéd's bed;
And so thy thoughts, when thou art gone,
Love itself shall slumber on.

Mutability

The flower that smiles to-day
        To-morrow dies;
All that we wish to stay
        Tempts and then flies.
What is the world's delight?
Lightning that mocks the night,
        Brief even as bright.

Virtue, how frail it is!
        Friendship how rare!
Love, how it sells poor bliss
        For proud despair!
But we, though soon they fall,
Survive their joy, and all
        Which ours we call.

Whilst skies are blue and bright,
        Whilst flowers are gay,
Whilst eyes that change ere night
        Make glad the day;
Whilst yet the calm hours creep,
Dream thou—and from thy sleep
        Then wake to weep.

To ——

One word is too often profaned
    For me to profane it,
One feeling too falsely disdained
    For thee to disdain it;
One hope is too like despair
    For prudence to smother,
And pity from thee more dear
    Than that from another.

I can give not what men call love,
    But wilt thou accept not
The worship the heart lifts above
    And the heavens reject not,—
The desire of the moth for the star,
    Of the night for the morrow,
The devotion to something afar
    From the sphere of our sorrow?

Lines: "When the Lamp Is Shattered"

When the lamp is shattered
The light in the dust lies dead—
    When the cloud is scattered
The rainbow's glory is shed.
    When the lute is broken,
Sweet tones are remembered not;
    When the lips have spoken,
Loved accents are soon forgot.

    As music and splendour
Survive not the lamp and the lute,
    The heart's echoes render
No song when the spirit is mute:—
    No song but sad dirges,
Like the wind through a ruined cell,
    Or the mournful surges
That ring the dead seaman's knell.

When hearts have once mingled
Love leaves the well-built nest;
　The weak one is singled
To endure what it once possessed.
　O Love! who bewailest
The frailty of all things here,
　Why choose you the frailest
For your cradle, your home, and your bier?

　Its passions will rock thee
As the storms rock the ravens on high;
　Bright reason will mock thee,
Like the sun from a wintry sky.
　From thy nest every rafter
Will rot, and thine eagle home
　Leave thee naked to laughter,
When leaves fall and cold winds come.

To Stella

Thou wert the morning star among the living
　Ere thy fair light had fled;
Now, having died, thou art as Hesperus, giving
　New splendour to the dead.

From the Greek of PLATO

FROM Adonais

I weep for Adonais—he is dead!
O, weep for Adonais! though our tears
Thaw not the frost which binds so dear a head!
And thou, sad Hour, selected from all years
To mourn our loss, rouse thy obscure compeers,
And teach them thine own sorrow, say: "With me
Died Adonais; till the Future dares
Forget the Past, his fate and fame shall be
An echo and a light unto eternity!"

Where wert thou, mighty Mother, when he lay,
When thy Son lay, pierced by the shaft which flies
In darkness? where was lorn Urania
When Adonais died? With veiléd eyes,
'Mid listening Echoes, in her Paradise
She sate, while one, with soft enamoured breath,
Rekindled all the fading melodies,
With which, like flowers that mock the corse beneath,
He had adorned and hid the coming bulk of Death.

Oh, weep for Adonais—he is dead!
Wake, melancholy Mother, wake and weep!
Yet wherefore? Quench within their burning bed
Thy fiery tears, and let thy loud heart keep
Like his, a mute and uncomplaining sleep;
For he is gone, where all things wise and fair
Descend;—oh, dream not that the amorous Deep
Will yet restore him to the vital air;
Death feeds on his mute voice, and laughs at our despair.

Most musical of mourners, weep again!
Lament anew, Urania!—He died,
Who was the Sire of an immortal strain,
Blind, old, and lonely, when his country's pride,
The priest, the slave, and the liberticide,
Trampled and mocked with many a loathéd rite
Of lust and blood; he went, unterrified,
Into the gulf of death; but his clear Sprite
Yet reigns o'er earth; the third among the sons of light.

Most musical of mourners, weep anew!
Not all to that bright station dared to climb;
And happier they their happiness who knew,
Whose tapers yet burn through that night of time
In which suns perished; others more sublime,
Struck by the envious wrath of man or god,
Have sunk, extinct in their refulgent prime;
And some yet live, treading the thorny road
Which leads, through toil and hate, to Fame's serene abode.

But now, thy youngest, dearest one, has perished—
The nursling of thy widowhood, who grew
Like a pale flower by some sad maiden cherished,
And fed with true-love tears, instead of dew;
Most musical of mourners, weep anew!
The extreme hope, the loveliest and the last,
The bloom, whose petals nipped before they blew
Died on the promise of the fruit, is waste;
The broken lily lies—the storm is overpast.

All he had loved, and moulded into thought,
From shape, and hue, and odour, and sweet sound,
Lamented Adonais. Morning sought
Her eastern watch-tower, and her hair unbound,
Wet with the tears which should adorn the ground,
Dimmed the aërial eyes that kindle day;
Afar the melancholy thunder moaned,
Pale Ocean in unquiet slumber lay,
And the wild Winds flew round, sobbing in their dismay.

Lost Echo sits amid the voiceless mountains,
And feeds her grief with his remembered lay,
And will no more reply to winds or fountains,
Or amorous birds perched on the young green spray,
Or herdsman's horn, or bell at closing day;
Since she can mimic not his lips, more dear
Than those for whose disdain she pined away
Into a shadow of all sounds:—a drear
Murmur, between their songs, is all the woodmen hear.

Grief made the young Spring wild, and she threw down
Her kindling buds, as if she Autumn were,
Or they dead leaves; since her delight is flown,
For whom should she have waked the sullen year?
To Phoebus was not Hyacinth so dear
Nor to himself Narcissus, as to both
Thou, Adonais: wan they stand and sere
Amid the faint companions of their youth,
With all dew turned to tears; odour, to sighing ruth.

Peace, peace! he is not dead, he doth not sleep—
He hath awakened from the dream of life—
'Tis we, who lost in stormy visions, keep
With phantoms and unprofitable strife,
And in mad trance, strike with our spirit's knife
Invulnerable nothings.—We decay
Like corpses in a charnel; fear and grief
Convulse us and consume us day by day,
And cold hopes swarm like worms within our living clay.

He has outsoared the shadow of our night;
Envy and calumny and hate and pain,
And that unrest which men miscall delight,
Can touch him not and torture not again;
From the contagion of the world's slow stain
He is secure, and now can never mourn
A heart grown cold, a head grown gray in vain;
Nor, when the spirit's self has ceased to burn,
With sparkless ashes load an unlamented urn.

He lives, he wakes—'tis Death is dead, not he;
Mourn not for Adonais.—Thou young Dawn,
Turn all thy dew to splendour, for from thee
The spirit thou lamentest is not gone;
Ye caverns and ye forests, cease to moan!
Cease, ye faint flowers and fountains, and thou Air,
Which like a mourning veil thy scarf hadst thrown
O'er the abandoned Earth, now leave it bare
Even to the joyous stars which smile on its despair!

He is made one with Nature: there is heard
His voice in all her music, from the moan
Of thunder, to the song of night's sweet bird;
He is a presence to be felt and known
In darkness and in light, from herb and stone,
Spreading itself where'er that Power may move
Which has withdrawn his being to its own;
Which wields the world with never-wearied love,
Sustains it from beneath, and kindles it above.

He is a portion of that loveliness
Which once he made more lovely: he doth bear
His part, while the one Spirit's plastic stress
Sweeps through the dull dense world, compelling there,
All new successions to the forms they wear;
Torturing th'unwilling dross that checks its flight
To its own likeness, as each mass may bear;
And bursting in its beauty and its might
From trees and beasts and men into the Heaven's light.

Go thou to Rome,—at once the Paradise,
The grave, the city, and the wilderness;
And where its wrecks like shattered mountains rise,
And flowering weeds, and fragrant copses dress
The bones of Desolation's nakedness
Pass, till the spirit of the spot shall lead
Thy footsteps to a slope of green access
Where, like an infant's smile, over the dead
A light of laughing flowers along the grass is spread;

And grey walls moulder round, on which dull Time
Feeds, like slow fire upon a hoary brand;
And one keen pyramid with wedge sublime,
Pavilioning the dust of him who planned
This refuge for his memory, doth stand
Like flame transformed to marble; and beneath,
A field is spread, on which a newer band
Have pitched in Heaven's smile their camp of death,
Welcoming him we lose with scarce extinguished breath.

Here pause: these graves are all too young as yet
To have outgrown the sorrow which consigned
Its charge to each; and if the seal is set,
Here, on one fountain of a mourning mind,
Break it not thou! too surely shalt thou find
Thine own well full, if thou returnest home,
Of tears and gall. From the world's bitter wind
Seek shelter in the shadow of the tomb.
What Adonais is, why fear we to become?

The One remains, the many change and pass;
Heaven's light forever shines, Earth's shadows fly;
Life, like a dome of many-coloured glass,
Stains the white radiance of Eternity,
Until Death tramples it to fragments.—Die,
If thou wouldst be with that which thou dost seek!
Follow, where all is fled!—Rome's azure sky,
Flowers, ruins, statues, music, words are weak
The glory they transfuse with fitting truth to speak.

The breath whose might I have invoked in song
Descends on me; my spirit's bark is driven,
Far from the shore, far from the trembling throng
Whose sails were never to the tempest given;
The massy earth and spheréd skies are riven!
I am borne darkly, fearfully afar;
Whilst, burning through the inmost veil of Heaven,
The soul of Adonais, like a star,
Beacons from the abode where the Eternal are.

JOHN CLARE

(1793–1864)

Written in Northampton County Asylum

I am! yet what I am who cares, or knows?
    My friends forsake me like a memory lost.
I am the self-consumer of my woes;
    They rise and vanish, an oblivious host,
Shadows of life, whose very soul is lost.
And yet I am—I live—though I am tossed

Into the nothingness of scorn and noise,
    Into the living sea of waking dream,
Where there is neither sense of life, nor joys,
    But the huge shipwreck of my own esteem
And all that's dear. Even those I loved the best
Are strange—nay, they are stranger than the rest

I long for scenes where man has never trod—
   For scenes where woman never smiled or wept—
There to abide with my Creator, God,
   And sleep as I in childhood sweetly slept,
Full of high thoughts, unborn. So let me lie,—
The grass below; above, the vaulted sky.

WILLIAM CULLEN BRYANT
(1794–1878)

Thanatopsis

To him who in the love of Nature holds
Communion with her visible forms, she speaks
A various language; for his gayer hours
She has a voice of gladness, and a smile
And eloquence of beauty, and she glides
Into his darker musings, with a mild
And healing sympathy, that steals away
Their sharpness, ere he is aware. When thoughts
Of the last bitter hour come like a blight
Over thy spirit, and sad images
Of the stern agony, and shroud, and pall,
And breathless darkness, and the narrow house,
Make thee to shudder, and grow sick at heart;—
Go forth, under the open sky, and list
To Nature's teachings, while from all around—
Earth and her waters, and the depths of air—
Comes a still voice—Yet a few days, and thee
The all-beholding sun shall see no more
In all his course; nor yet in the cold ground,
Where thy pale form was laid, with many tears,
Nor in the embrace of ocean, shall exist
Thy image. Earth, that nourished thee, shall claim
Thy growth, to be resolved to earth again,
And, lost each human trace, surrendering up
Thine individual being, shalt thou go
To mix for ever with the elements,
To be a brother to the insensible rock
And to the sluggish clod, which the rude swain

Turns with his share, and treads upon. The oak
Shall send his roots abroad, and pierce thy mould.

Yet not to thine eternal resting-place
Shalt thou retire alone, nor couldst thou wish
Couch more magnificent. Thou shalt lie down
With patriarchs of the infant world—with kings,
The powerful of the earth—the wise, the good,
Fair forms, and hoary seers of ages past,
All in one mighty sepulchre. The hills
Rock-ribbed and ancient as the sun,—the vales
Stretching in pensive quietness between;
The venerable woods—rivers that move
In majesty, and the complaining brooks
That make the meadows green; and, poured round all,
Old Ocean's gray and melancholy waste,—
Are but the solemn decorations all
Of the great tomb of man. The golden sun,
The planets, all the infinite host of heaven,
Are shining on the sad abodes of death,
Through the still lapse of ages. All that tread
The globe are but a handful to the tribes
That slumber in its bosom.—Take the wings
Of morning, pierce the Barcan wilderness,
Or lose thyself in the contiguous woods
Where rolls the Oregon, and hears no sound,
Save his own dashings—yet the dead are there:
And millions in those solitudes, since first
The flight of years began, have laid them down
In their last sleep—the dead reign there alone.
So shalt thou rest, and what if thou withdraw
In silence from the living, and no friend
Take note of thy departure? All that breathe
Will share thy destiny. The gay will laugh
When thou art gone, the solemn brood of care
Plod on, and each one as before will chase
His favorite phantom; yet all these shall leave
Their mirth and their employments, and shall come
And make their bed with thee. As the long train
Of ages glide away, the sons of men,
The youth in life's green spring, and he who goes

In the full strength of years, matron and maid,
The speechless babe, and the gray-headed man—
Shall one by one be gathered to thy side,
By those, who in their turn shall follow them.

So live, that when thy summons comes to join
The innumerable caravan, which moves
To that mysterious realm, where each shall take
His chamber in the silent halls of death,
Thou go not, like the quarry-slave at night,
Scourged to his dungeon, but, sustained and soothed,
By an unfaltering trust, approach thy grave,
Like one who wraps the drapery of his couch
About him, and lies down to pleasant dreams.

"Oh Fairest of the Rural Maids!"

Oh fairest of the rural maids!
Thy birth was in the forest shades;
Green boughs, and glimpses of the sky,
Were all that met thine infant eye.

Thy sports, thy wanderings, when a child,
Were ever in the sylvan wild;
And all the beauty of the place
Is in thy heart and on thy face.

The twilight of the trees and rocks
Is in the light shade of thy locks;
Thy step is as the wind, that weaves
Its playful way among the leaves.

Thine eyes are springs, in whose serene
And silent waters heaven is seen;
Their lashes are the herbs that look
On their young figures in the brook.

The forest depths, by foot unpressed,
Are not more sinless than thy breast;
The holy peace, that fills the air
Of those calm solitudes, is there.

Dante

Who, mid the grasses of the field,
    That spring beneath our careless feet,
First found the shining stems that yield
    The grains of life-sustaining wheat:

Who first, upon the furrowed land,
    Strewed the bright grains to sprout, and grow
And ripen for the reaper's hand—
    We know not, and we cannot know.

But well we know the hand that brought
    And scattered, far as sight can reach,
The seeds of free and living thought
    On the broad field of modern speech.

Mid the white hills that round us lie,
    We cherish that Great Sower's fame,
And, as we pile the sheaves on high,
    With awe we utter Dante's name.

Six centuries, since the poet's birth,
    Have come and flitted o'er our sphere:
The richest harvest reaped on earth
    Crowns the last century's closing year.

JOHN KEATS

(1795–1821)

Dedication
(TO LEIGH HUNT, ESQ.)

Glory and Loveliness have passed away;
    For if we wander out in early morn,
    No wreathèd incense do we see upborne
Into the east to meet the smiling day:
No crowd of nymphs soft-voiced and young and gay,
    In woven baskets bringing ears of corn,
    Roses, and pinks, and violets, to adorn

The shrine of Flora in her early May.
But there are left delights as high as these,
    And I shall ever bless my destiny,
That in a time when under pleasant trees
    Pan is no longer sought, I feel a free,
A leafy luxury, seeing I could please,
    With these poor offerings, a man like thee.

On First Looking into Chapman's Homer

Much have I travelled in the realms of gold,
    And many goodly states and kingdoms seen;
    Round many western islands have I been
Which bards in fealty to Apollo hold.
Oft of one wide expanse had I been told,
    That deep-browed Homer ruled as his demesne:
    Yet did I never breathe its pure serene
Till I heard Chapman speak out loud and bold:
Then felt I like some watcher of the skies
    When a new planet swims into his ken;
Or like stout Cortez when with eagle eyes
    He stared at the Pacific—and all his men
Look'd at each other with a wild surmise—
    Silent, upon a peak in Darien.

To a Nightingale

My heart aches, and a drowsy numbness pains
    My sense, as though of hemlock I had drunk,
Or emptied some dull opiate to the drains
    One minute past, and Lethe-wards had sunk:
'Tis not through envy of thy happy lot,
    Being but too happy in thy happiness,—
        That thou, light-wingéd Dryad of the trees,
            In some melodious plot
Of beechen green, and shadows numberless,
    Singest of summer in full-throated ease.

O for a draught of vintage, that hath been
   Cooled a long age in the deep-delvéd earth,
Tasting of Flora and the country-green,
   Dance, and Provençal song, and sun-burnt mirth!
O for a beaker full of the warm South,
   Full of the true, the blushful Hippocrene,
     With beaded bubbles winking at the brim,
       And purple-stainéd mouth;
   That I might drink and leave the world unseen,
     And with thee fade away into the forest dim:

Fade far away, dissolve, and quite forget
   What thou among the leaves hast never known,
The weariness, the fever, and the fret
   Here, where men sit and hear each other groan;
Where palsy shakes a few, sad, last grey hairs,
   Where youth grows pale, and spectre-thin, and dies;
     Where but to think is to be full of sorrow
       And leaden-eyed despairs;
   Where beauty cannot keep her lustrous eyes,
     Or new Love pine at them beyond to-morrow.

Away! away! for I will fly to thee,
   Not charioted by Bacchus and his pards,
But on the viewless wings of Poesy,
   Though the dull brain perplexes and retards:
Already with thee! tender is the night,
   And haply the Queen-Moon is on her throne,
     Clustered around by all her starry Fays;
       But here there is no light,
   Save what from heaven is with the breezes blown
     Through verdurous glooms and winding mossy ways.

I cannot see what flowers are at my feet,
   Nor what soft incense hangs upon the boughs,
But, in embalméd darkness, guess each sweet
   Wherewith the seasonable month endows
The grass, the thicket, and the fruit-tree wild;

White hawthorn, and the pastoral eglantine;
  Fast-fading violets covered up in leaves;
    And mid-May's eldest child,
The coming musk-rose, full of dewy wine,
  The murmurous haunt of flies on summer eves.

Darkling I listen; and for many a time
  I have been half in love with easeful Death,
Called him soft names in many a muséd rhyme,
  To take into the air my quiet breath;
Now more than ever seems it rich to die,
  To cease upon the midnight with no pain,
    While thou art pouring forth thy soul abroad
      In such an ecstasy!
Still wouldst thou sing, and I have ears in vain—
  To thy high requiem become a sod.

Thou wast not born for death, immortal Bird!
  No hungry generations tread thee down;
The voice I hear this passing night was heard
  In ancient days by emperor and clown:
Perhaps the self-same song that found a path
  Through the sad heart of Ruth, when sick for home,
    She stood in tears amid the alien corn;
      The same that oft-times hath
Charmed magic casements, opening on the foam
  Of perilous seas, in faery lands forlorn.

Forlorn! the very word is like a bell
  To toll me back from thee to my sole self.
Adieu! the fancy cannot cheat so well
  As she is famed to do, deceiving elf.
Adieu! adieu! thy plaintive anthem fades
  Past the near meadows, over the still stream,
    Up the hill-side; and now 'tis buried deep
      In the next valley-glades:
Was it a vision, or a waking dream?
  Fled is that music:—do I wake or sleep?

On a Grecian Urn

Thou still unravished bride of quietness!
  Thou foster-child of Silence and slow Time,
Sylvan historian, who canst thus express
  A flowery tale more sweetly than our rhyme:
What leaf-fringed legend haunts about thy shape
  Of deities or mortals, or of both,
    In Tempe or the dales of Arcady?
  What men or gods are these? What maidens loath?
What mad pursuit? What struggle to escape?
  What pipes and timbrels? What wild ecstasy?

Heard melodies are sweet, but those unheard
  Are sweeter; therefore, ye soft pipes, play on;
Not to the sensual ear, but, more endeared,
  Pipe to the spirit ditties of no tone:
Fair youth, beneath the trees, thou canst not leave
  Thy song, nor ever can those trees be bare;
    Bold Lover, never, never canst thou kiss,
Though winning near the goal—yet, do not grieve;
    She cannot fade, though thou hast not thy bliss,
  For ever wilt thou love, and she be fair!

Ah, happy, happy boughs! that cannot shed
  Your leaves, nor ever bid the Spring adieu;
And, happy melodist, unweariéd,
  For ever piping songs for ever new;
More happy love! more happy, happy love!
  For ever warm and still to be enjoyed,
    For ever panting and for ever young;
All breathing human passion far above,
    That leaves a heart high sorrowful and cloyed,
  A burning forehead, and a parching tongue.

Who are these coming to the sacrifice?
  To what green altar, O mysterious priest,
Lead'st thou that heifer lowing at the skies,
  And all her silken flanks with garlands drest?

What little town by river or sea-shore,
  Or mountain-built with peaceful citadel,
    Is emptied of its folk, this pious morn?
And, little town, thy streets for evermore
  Will silent be; and not a soul to tell
    Why thou art desolate, can e'er return.

O Attic shape! Fair attitude! with brede
  Of marble men and maidens overwrought,
With forest branches and the trodden weed;
  Thou, silent form! dost tease us out of thought
As doth eternity: Cold Pastoral!
  When old age shall this generation waste,
    Thou shalt remain, in midst of other woe
  Than ours, a friend to man, to whom thou say'st,
"Beauty is truth, truth beauty,"—that is all
    Ye know on earth, and all ye need to know.

To Psyche

O Goddess! hear these tuneless numbers, wrung
  By sweet enforcement and remembrance dear,
And pardon that thy secrets should be sung,
  Even into thy own soft-conchéd ear:
Surely I dreamt to-day, or did I see
  The wingéd Psyche with awakened eyes?
I wandered in a forest thoughtlessly,
  And, on the sudden, fainting with surprise,
Saw two fair creatures, couchéd side by side
  In deepest grass, beneath the whispering roof
  Of leaves and trembled blossoms, where there ran
    A brooklet, scarce espied:
'Mid hushed, cool-rooted flowers fragrant-eyed,
  Blue, silver-white, and budded Tyrian,
They lay calm-breathing on the bedded grass;
  Their arms embracéd, and their pinions too;
  Their lips touched not, but had not bade adieu
As if disjoinéd by soft-handed slumber,

And ready still past kisses to outnumber
  At tender eye-dawn of aurorean love:
      The wingéd boy I knew;
  But who wast thou, O happy, happy dove?
      His Psyche true!

O latest-born and loveliest vision far
  Of all Olympus' faded hierarchy!
Fairer than Phoebe's sapphire-regioned star,
  Or Vesper, amorous glow-worm of the sky;
Fairer than these, though temple thou hast none,
  Nor altar heaped with flowers;
Nor Virgin-choir to make delicious moan
  Upon the midnight hours;
No voice, no lute, no pipe, no incense sweet
  From chain-swung censer teeming;
No shrine, no grove, no oracle, no heat
  Of pale-mouthed prophet dreaming.
O brightest! though too late for antique vows,
  Too, too late for the fond believing lyre,
When holy were the haunted forest boughs,
  Holy the air, the water, and the fire;
Yet even in these days so far retired
  From happy pieties, thy lucent fans,
  Fluttering among the faint Olympians,
I see, and sing, by my own eyes inspired.
  So let me be thy choir, and make a moan
      Upon the midnight hours!
Thy voice, thy lute, thy pipe, thy incense sweet
  From swingéd censer teeming:
Thy shrine, thy grove, thy oracle, thy heat
  Of pale-mouthed prophet dreaming.

Yes, I will be thy priest, and build a fane
  In some untrodden region of my mind,
Where branchéd thoughts, new-grown with pleasant pain,
  Instead of pines shall murmur in the wind:
Far, far around shall those dark-clustered trees
  Fledge the wild-ridgéd mountains steep by steep;
And there by zephyrs, streams, and birds, and bees,
  The moss-lain Dryads shall be lulled to sleep;

And in the midst of this wide quietness
  A rosy sanctuary will I dress
With the wreathed trellis of a working brain,
  With buds, and bells, and stars without a name,
With all the gardener Fancy e'er could feign,
  Who breeding flowers, will never breed the same:
And there shall be for thee all soft delight
  That shadowy thought can win,
A bright torch, and a casement ope at night,
  To let the warm Love in!

To the Poets

Bards of Passion and of Mirth,
Ye have left your souls on earth!
Have ye souls in heaven too,
Double-lived in regions new?
Yes, and those of heaven commune
With the spheres of sun and moon;
With the noise of fountains wondrous,
And the parle of voices thund'rous;
With the whisper of heaven's trees
And one another, in soft ease
Seated on Elysian lawns
Browsed by none but Dian's fawns;
Underneath large blue-bells tented,
Where the daisies are rose-scented,
And the rose herself has got
Perfume which on earth is not;
Where the nightingale doth sing
Not a senseless, trancéd thing,
But divine, melodious truth,
Philosophic numbers smooth;
Tales and golden histories
Of heaven and its mysteries.

Thus ye live on high, and then
On the earth ye live again;
And the souls ye left behind you
Teach us, here, the way to find you,

Where your other souls are joying
Never slumbered, never cloying.
Here, your earth-born souls still speak
To mortals, of their little week;
Of their sorrows and delights;
Of their passions and their spites;
Of their glory and their shame;
What does strengthen, and what maim
Thus ye teach us, every day,
Wisdom, though fled far away.

Bards of Passion and of Mirth,
Ye have left your souls on earth!
Ye have souls in heaven too,
Double-lived in regions new!

Lines on the Mermaid Tavern

Souls of poets dead and gone,
What Elysium have ye known,
Happy field or mossy cavern,
Choicer than the Mermaid Tavern?
Have ye tippled drink more fine
Than mine host's Canary wine?
Or are fruits of Paradise
Sweeter than those dainty pies
Of venison? O generous food!
Drest as though bold Robin Hood
Would, with his maid Marian,
Sup and bowse from horn and can.

I have heard that on a day
Mine host's sign-board flew away,
Nobody knew whither, till
An Astrologer's old quill
To a sheepskin gave the story—
Said he saw you in your glory,
Underneath a new old-sign
Sipping beverage divine,
And pledging with contented smack
The Mermaid in the Zodiac.

Souls of poets dead and gone,
What Elysium have ye known,
Happy field or mossy cavern,
Choicer than the Mermaid Tavern?

To Autumn

Season of mists and mellow fruitfulness!
  Close bosom-friend of the maturing sun;
Conspiring with him how to load and bless
  With fruit the vines that round the thatch-eaves run;
To bend with apples the mossed cottage-trees,
  And fill all fruit with ripeness to the core;
    To swell the gourd, and plump the hazel shells
  With a sweet kernel; to set budding more,
And still more, later flowers for the bees,
Until they think warm days will never cease,
    For Summer has o'er-brimmed their clammy cells.

Who hath not seen thee oft amid thy store?
  Sometimes whoever seeks abroad may find
Thee sitting careless on a granary floor,
  Thy hair soft-lifted by the winnowing wind;
Or on a self-reaped furrow sound asleep,
  Drowsed with the fume of poppies, while thy hook
    Spares the next swath and all its twinéd flowers
And sometimes like a gleaner thou dost keep
  Steady thy laden head across a brook;
  Or by a cider-press, with patient look,
    Thou watchest the last oozings, hours by hours

Where are the songs of Spring? Ay, where are they?
  Think not of them, thou hast thy music too,
    While barréd clouds bloom the soft-dying day,
  And touch the stubble-plains with rosy hue;
Then in a wailful choir, the small gnats mourn
  Among the river sallows, borne aloft
    Or sinking as the light wind lives or dies;
And full-grown lambs loud bleat from hilly bourn;
  Hedge-crickets sing; and now with.treble soft
  The red-breast whistles from a garden-croft,
    And gathering swallows twitter in the skies.

On Melancholy

No, no! go not to Lethe, neither twist
   Wolf's-bane, tight-rooted, for its poisonous wine;
Nor suffer thy pale forehead to be kissed
   By nightshade, ruby grape of Proserpine;
Make not your rosary of yew-berries,
    Nor let the beetle nor the death-moth be
      Your mournful Psyche, nor the downy owl
A partner in your sorrow's mysteries;
    For shade to shade will come too drowsily,
      And drown the wakeful anguish of the soul.

But when the melancholy fit shall fall
   Sudden from heaven like a weeping cloud,
That fosters the droop-headed flowers all,
   And hides the green hill in an April shroud;
Then glut thy sorrow on a morning rose,
    Or on the rainbow of the salt sand-wave,
      Or on the wealth of globéd peonies;
Or if thy mistress some rich anger shows,
    Emprison her soft hand, and let her rave,
      And feed deep, deep upon her peerless eyes.

She dwells with Beauty—Beauty that must die;
   And Joy, whose hand is ever at his lips
Bidding adieu; and aching Pleasure nigh,
   Turning to poison while the bee-mouth sips:
Ay, in the very temple of Delight
    Veiled Melancholy has her sovran shrine,
      Though seen of none save him whose strenuous tongue
    Can burst Joy's grape against his palate fine:
His soul shall taste the sadness of her might,
      And be among her cloudy trophies hung.

Sonnet on the Sea

It keeps eternal whispering around
   Desolate shores, and with its mighty swell
   Gluts twice ten thousand caverns, till the spell
Of Hecate leaves them their old shadowy sound.
Often 'tis in such gentle temper found,
   That scarcely will the very smallest shell
   Be moved for days from whence it sometime fell,
When last the winds of heaven were unbound.
Oh ye! who have your eye-balls vexed and tired,
   Feast them upon the wideness of the Sea;
Oh ye! whose ears are dinned with uproar rude,
   Or fed too much with cloying melody,—
Sit ye near some old cavern's mouth, and brood
Until ye start, as if the sea-nymphs quired!

Sonnet to Sleep

O soft embalmer of the still midnight!
   Shutting, with careful fingers and benign,
Our gloom-pleased eyes, embowered from the light,
   Enshaded in forgetfulness divine;
O soothest Sleep! if so it please thee, close,
   In midst of this thine hymn, my willing eyes,
Or wait the amen, ere thy poppy throws
   Around my bed its lulling charities;
   Then save me, ·or the passéd day will shine
Upon my pillow, breeding many woes;
   Save me from curious conscience, that still lord⌐
Its strength, for darkness burrowing like a mole;
   Turn the key deftly in the oiléd wards,
And seal the hushéd casket of my soul.

Ballad: La Belle Dame sans Merci

   O what can ail thee, knight-at-arms,
      Alone and palely loitering?
   The sedge has withered from the lake,
      And no birds sing.

O what can ail thee, knight-at-arms,
   So haggard and so woe-begone?
The squirrel's granary is full,
   And the harvest's done.

I see a lily on thy brow
   With anguish moist and fever dew,
And on thy cheeks a fading rose
   Fast withereth too.

I met a lady in the meads,
   Full beautiful—a faery's child,
Her hair was long, her foot was light,
   And her eyes were wild.

I made a garland for her head,
   And bracelets too, and fragrant zone,
She looked at me as she did love.
   And made sweet moan.

I set her on my pacing steed,
   And nothing else saw all day long,
For sidelong would she bend, and sing
   A faery's song.

She found me roots of relish sweet,
   And honey wild, and manna dew,
And sure in language strange she said—
   "I love thee true!"

She took me to her elfin grot,
   And there she wept and sighed full sore,
And there I shut her wild, wild eyes
   With kisses four.

And there she lulléd me asleep,
   And there I dreamed—ah, woe betide!
The latest dream I ever dreamed
   On the cold hill's side.

I saw pale kings and princes too,
   Pale warriors, death-pale were they all;
They cried—"La Belle Dame sans Merci
   Hath thee in thrall!"

I saw their starved lips in the gloam,
   With horrid warning gapéd wide,
And I awoke and found me here,
   On the cold hill's side.

And this is why I sojourn here,
   Alone and palely loitering,
Though the sedge is withered from the lake,
   And no birds sing.

FROM The Eve of St. Agnes

Out went the taper as she hurried in;
Its little smoke in pallid moonshine died:
She closed the door, she panted, all akin
To spirits of the air, and visions wide:
No uttered syllable, or, woe betide!
But to her heart, her heart was voluble,
Paining with eloquence her balmy side;
As though a tongueless nightingale should swell
Her throat in vain, and die, heart-stifled, in her dell.

A casement high and triple-arched there was,
All garlanded with carven imageries,
Of fruits and flowers, and bunches of knot-grass,
And diamonded with panes of quaint device,
Innumerable of stains and splendid dyes,
As are the tiger-moth's deep-damasked wings;
And in the midst, 'mong thousand heraldries,
And twilight saints, and dim emblazonings,
A shielded scutcheon blushed with blood of queens and kings.

Full on this casement shone the wintry moon,
And threw warm gules on Madeline's fair breast,
As down she knelt for Heaven's grace and boon;
Rose-bloom fell on her hands, together prest,

And on her silver cross soft amethyst,
And on her hair a glory, like a saint:
She seemed a splendid angel, newly drest,
Save wings, for heaven:—Porphyro grew faint:
She knelt, so pure a thing, so free from mortal taint.

Anon his heart revives: her vespers done,
Of all its wreathéd pearls her hair she frees;
Unclasps her warméd jewels one by one;
Loosens her fragrant boddice; by degrees
Her rich attire creeps rustling to her knees:
Half-hidden, like a mermaid in sea-weed,
Pensive awhile she dreams awake, and sees,
In fancy, fair St. Agnes in her bed,
But dares not look behind, or all the charm is fled.

Soon, trembling in her soft and chilly nest,
In sort of wakeful swoon, perplexed she lay,
Until the poppied warmth of sleep oppressed
Her soothéd limbs, and soul fatigued away;
Flown, like a thought, until the morrow-day;
Blissfully havened both from joy and pain;
Clasped like a missal where swart Paynims pray;
Blinded alike from sunshine and from rain,
As though a rose should shut, and be a bud again.

Stolen to this paradise, and so entranced,
Porphyro gazed upon her empty dress,
And listened to her breathing, if it chanced
To wake into a slumberous tenderness;
Which when he heard, that minute did he bless,
And breathed himself: then from the closet crept,
Noiseless as fear in a wide wilderness,
And over the hushed carpet, silent, stept,
And 'tween the curtains peeped, where lo!—how fast she slept!

Then by the bed-side, where the faded moon
Made a dim, silver twilight, soft he set
A table, and, half anguished, threw thereon
A cloth of woven crimson, gold, and jet:—
O for some drowsy Morphean amulet!

The boisterous, midnight, festive clarion,
The kettle-drum, and far-heard clarionet,
Affray his ears, though but in dying tone:—
The hall-door shuts again, and all the noise is gone.

And still she slept an azure-lidded sleep,
In blanchéd linen, smooth, and lavendered,
While he from forth the closet brought a heap
Of candied apple, quince, and plum, and gourd;
With jellies soother than the creamy curd,
And lucent syrops, tinct with cinnamon;
Manna, and dates, in argosy transferred
From Fez; and spiced dainties, every one
From silken Samarcand to cedared Lebanon.

These delicates he heaped with glowing hand
On golden dishes and in baskets bright
Of wreathéd silver: sumptuous they stand
In the retiréd quiet of the night,
Filling the chilly room with perfume light.—
"And now, my love, my seraph fair, awake!
Thou art my heaven, and I thine eremite:
Open thine eyes, for meek St. Agnes' sake,
Or I shall drowse beside thee, so my soul doth ache."

Thus whispering, his warm unnervéd arm
Sank in her pillow. Shaded was her dream
By the dusk curtains:—'twas a midnight charm
Impossible to melt as iced stream:
The lustrous salvers in the moonlight gleam;
Broad golden fringe upon the carpet lies:
It seemed he never, never could redeem
From such a steadfast spell his lady's eyes;
So mused awhile, entoiled in wooféd phantasies.

FROM *Isabella or The Pot of Basil*

1.

Fair Isabel, poor simple Isabel!
   Lorenzo, a young palmer in Love's eye!
They could not in the self-same mansion dwell
   Without some stir of heart, some malady;

They could not sit at meals but feel how well
    It soothed each to be the other by;
They could not, sure, beneath the same roof sleep,
But to each other dream, and nightly weep.

With every morn their love grew tenderer,
    With every eve deeper and tenderer still;
He might not in house, field, or garden stir,
    But her full shape would all his seeing fill;
And his continual voice was pleasanter
    To her, than noise of trees or hidden rill;
Her lute-string gave an echo of his name,
She spoilt her half-done broidery with the same.

He knew whose gentle hand was at the latch,
    Before the door had given her to his eyes;
And from her chamber-window he would catch
    Her beauty farther than the falcon spies;
And constant as her vespers would he watch,
    Because her face was turned to the same skies;
And with sick longing all the night outwear,
To hear her morning-step upon the stair.

A whole long month of May in this sad plight
    Made their cheeks paler by the break of June:
"To-morrow will I bow to my delight,
    To-morrow will I ask my lady's boon."—
"O may I never see another night,
    Lorenzo, if thy lips breathe not love's tune."—
So spake they to their pillows; but, alas,
Honeyless days and nights did he let pass;

Until sweet Isabella's untouched cheek
    Fell sick within the rose's just domain,
Fell thin as a young mother's, who doth seek
    By every lull to cool her infant's pain:
"How ill she is!" said he, "I may not speak
    And yet I will, and tell my love all plain:
If looks speak love-laws, I will drink her tears,
And at the least 'twill startle off her cares."

So said he one fair morning, and all day
   His heart beat awfully against his side;
And to his heart he inwardly did pray
   For power to speak; but still the ruddy tide
Stifled his voice, and pulsed resolve away—
   Fevered his high conceit of such a bride,
Yet brought him to the meekness of a child:
Alas! when passion is both meek and wild!

So once more he had waked and anguished
   A dreary night of love and misery,
If Isabel's quick eye had not been wed
   To every symbol on his forehead high;
She saw it waxing very pale and dead,
   And straight all flushed; so, lisped tenderly,
"Lorenzo!"—here she ceased her timid quest,
But in her tone and look he read the rest.

"O Isabella! I can half perceive
   That I may speak my grief into thine ear;
If thou didst ever anything believe,
   Believe how I love thee, believe how near
My soul is to its doom: I would not grieve
   Thy hand by unwelcome pressing, would not fear
Thine eyes by gazing; but I cannot live
Another night, and not my passion shrive.

"Love: thou art leading me from wintry cold,
   Lady! thou leadest me to summer clime,
And I must taste the blossoms that unfold
   In its ripe warmth this gracious morning time."
So said, his erewhile timid lips grew bold,
   And poesied with hers in dewy rhyme:
Great bliss was with them, and great happiness
Grew, like a lusty flower in June's caress.

Parting they seemed to tread upon the air,
   Twin roses by the zephyr blown apart
Only to meet again more close, and share
   The inward fragrance of each other's heart.

She, to her chamber gone, a ditty fair
   Sang, of delicious love and honeyed dart;
He with light steps went up a western hill,
And bade the sun farewell, and joyed his fill.

All close they met again, before the dusk
   Had taken from the stars its pleasant veil,
All close they met, all eves, before the dusk
   Had taken from the stars its pleasant veil,
Close in a bower of hyacinth and musk,
   Unknown of any, free from whispering tale.
Ah! better had it been for ever so,
Than idle ears should pleasure in their woe.

Were they unhappy then?—It cannot be—
   Too many tears for lovers have been shed,
Too many sighs give we to them in fee,
   Too much of pity after they are dead,
Too many doleful stories do we see,
   Whose matter in bright gold were best be read;
Except in such a page where Theseus' spouse
Over the pathless waves towards him bows.

But for the general award of love,
   The little sweet doth kill much bitterness;
Though Dido silent is in under-grove,
   And Isabella's was a great distress,
Though young Lorenzo in warm Indian clove
   Was not embalmed, this truth is not the less—
Even bees, the little almsmen of spring-bowers,
Know there is richest juice in poison-flowers.

2.

O Melancholy, linger here awhile!
   O Music, Music, breathe despondingly!
O Echo, Echo, from some sombre isle,
   Unknown, Lethean, sigh to us—O sigh!
Spirits in grief, lift up your heads, and smile;
   Lift up your heads, sweet Spirits, heavily,
And make a pale light in your cypress glooms,
Tinting with silver wan your marble tombs

Moan hither, all ye syllables of woe,
    From the deep throat of sad Melpomene!
Through bronzed lyre in tragic order go,
    And touch the strings into a mystery;
Sound mournfully upon the winds and low;
    For simple Isabel is soon to be
Among the dead: She withers, like a palm
Cut by an Indian for its juicy balm.

O leave the palm to wither by itself;
    Let not quick Winter chill its dying hour!—
It may not be—those Baälites of pelf,
    Her brethren, noted the continual shower
From her dead eyes; and many a curious elf,
    Among her kindred, wondered that such dower
Of youth and beauty should be thrown aside
By one marked out to be a Noble's bride.

And furthermore, her brethren wondered much
    Why she sat drooping by the Basil green,
And why it flourished, as by magic touch;
    Greatly they wondered what the thing might mean:
They could not surely give belief, that such
    A very nothing would have power to wean
Her from her own fair youth, and pleasures gay,
And even remembrance of her love's delay.

Therefore they watched a time when they might sift
    This hidden whim; and long they watched in vain;
For seldom did she go to chapel-shrift,
    And seldom felt she any hunger-pain:
And when she left, she hurried back, as swift
    As bird on wing to breast its eggs again:
And, patient as a hen-bird, sat her there
Beside her Basil, weeping through her hair.

Yet they contrived to steal the Basil-pot,
    And to examine it in secret place:
The thing was vile with green and livid spot,
    And yet they knew it was Lorenzo's face:

The guerdon of their murder they had got,
    And so left Florence in a moment's space,
Never to turn again.—Away they went,
With blood upon their heads, to banishment.

O Melancholy, turn thine eyes away!
    O Music, Music, breathe despondingly!
O Echo, Echo, on some other day,
    From isles Lethean, sigh to us—O sigh!
Spirits of grief, sing not your "Well-a-way!"
    For Isabel, sweet Isabel, will die;
Will die a death too lone and incomplete,
Now they have ta'en away her Basil sweet.

And so she pined, and so she died forlorn,
    Imploring for her Basil to the last.
No heart was there in Florence but did mourn
    In pity of her love, so overcast.
And a sad ditty of this story borne
    From mouth to mouth through all the country pass'd:
Still is the burthen sung—"O cruelty,
To steal my Basil-pot away from me!"

FROM *Endymion*

1.

A thing of beauty is a joy for ever:
Its loveliness increases; it will never
Pass into nothingness; but still will keep
A bower quiet for us, and a sleep
Full of sweet dreams, and health, and quiet breathing.
Therefore, on every morrow, are we wreathing
A flowery band to bind us to the earth,
Spite of despondence, of the inhuman dearth
Of noble natures, of the gloomy days,
Of all the unhealthy and o'er-darkened ways
Made for our searching: yes, in spite of all,
Some shape of beauty moves away the pall
From our dark spirits. Such the sun, the moon,
Trees old and young, sprouting a shady boon

For simple sheep; and such are daffodils
With the green world they live in; and clear rills
That for themselves a cooling covert make
'Gainst the hot season; the mid-forest brake,
Rich with a sprinkling of fair musk-rose blooms:
And such too is the grandeur of the dooms
We have imagined for the mighty dead;
All lovely tales that we have heard or read:
An endless fountain of immortal drink,
Pouring unto us from the heaven's brink.

Nor do we merely feel these essences
For one short hour; no, even as the trees
That whisper round a temple become soon
Dear as the temple's self, so does the moon,
The passion poesy, glories infinite,
Haunt us till they become a cheering light
Unto our souls, and bound to us so fast,
That, whether there be shine, or gloom o'ercast,
They always must be with us, or we die.

2.

And, truly, I would rather be struck dumb
Than speak against this ardent listlessness:
For I have ever thought that it might bless
The world with benefits unknowingly;
As does the nightingale, up-perchéd high,
And cloistered among cool and bunchéd leaves—
She sings but to her love, nor e'er conceives
How tiptoe Night holds back her dark-grey hood.
Just so may love, although 'tis understood
The mere commingling of passionate breath,
Produce more than our searching witnesseth:
What I know not: but who, of men, can tell
That flowers would bloom, or that green fruit would swell
To melting pulp, that fish would have bright mail,
The earth its dower of river, wood, and vale,
The meadows runnels, runnels pebble-stones,
The seed its harvest, or the lute its tones,
Tones ravishment, or ravishment its sweet,
If human souls did never kiss and greet?

3.

> O sovereign power of love! O grief! O balm!
> All records, saving thine, come cool, and calm,
> And shadowy, through the mist of passéd years:
> For others, good or bad, hatred and tears,
> Have become indolent; but touching thine,
> One sigh doth echo, one poor sob doth pine,
> One kiss brings honey-dew from buried days.
> The woes of Troy, towers smothering o'er their blaze,
> Stiff-holden shields, far-piercing spears, keen blades,
> Struggling, and blood, and shrieks—all dimly fades
> Into some backward corner of the brain;
> Yet, in our very souls, we feel amain
> The close of Troilus and Cressid sweet.
> Hence, pageant history! hence, gilded cheat!
> Swart planet in the universe of deeds!
> Wide sea, that one continuous murmur breeds
> Along the pebbled shore of memory!
> Many old rotten-timbered boats there be
> Upon thy vaporous bosom, magnified
> To goodly vessels; many a sail of pride,
> And golden-keeled, is left unlaunched and dry.
> But wherefore this? What care, though owl did fly
> About the great Athenian admiral's mast?
> What care, though striding Alexander past
> The Indus with his Macedonian numbers?
> Though old Ulysses tortured from his slumbers
> The glutted Cyclops, what care?—Juliet leaning
> Amid her window-flowers,—sighing,—weaning
> Tenderly her fancy from its maiden snow,
> Doth more avail than these: the silver flow
> Of Hero's tears, the swoon of Imogen,
> Fair Pastorella in the bandit's den,
> Are things to brood on with more ardency
> Than the death-day of empires.

4.

> Beneath my palm-trees, by the river side,
> I sat a-weeping: what enamoured bride

Cheated by shadowy wooer from the clouds,
    But hides and shrouds
Beneath dark palm-trees by a river side?

And as I sat, over the light blue hills
There came a noise of revellers: the rills
Into the wide stream came of purple hue—
    'Twas Bacchus and his crew!
The earnest trumpet spake, and silver thrills
From kissing cymbals made a merry din—
    'Twas Bacchus and his kind!
Like to a moving vintage down they came,
Crowned with green leaves, and faces all on flame;
All madly dancing through the pleasant valley,
    To scare thee, Melancholy!
O then, O then, thou wast a simple name!
And I forgot thee, as the berried holly
By shepherds is forgotten, when in June,
Tall chestnuts keep away the sun and moon:—
    I rushed into the folly!

Within his car, aloft, young Bacchus stood,
Trifling his ivy-dart, in dancing mood,
    With sidelong laughing;
And little rills of crimson wine imbrued
His plump white arms, and shoulders, enough white
    For Venus' pearly bite;
And near him rode Silenus on his ass,
Pelted with flowers as he on did pass
    Tipsily quaffing.

Whence came ye, merry Damsels, whence came ye,
So many, and so many, and such glee?
Why have ye left your forest haunts, why left
    Your nuts in oak-tree cleft?—
"For wine, for wine we left our kernel tree;
For wine we left our heath, and yellow brooms,
    And cold mushrooms;

For wine we follow Bacchus through the earth;
Great god of breathless cups and chirping mirth!
Come hither, fair lady, and joinéd be
    To our mad minstrelsy!"

Over wide streams and mountains great we went,
And, save when Bacchus kept his ivy tent,
Onward the tiger and the leopard pants,
    With Asian elephants:
Onward these myriads—with song and dance,
With zebras striped, and sleek Arabians' prance,
Web-footed alligators, crocodiles,
Bearing upon their scaly backs, in files,
Plump infant laughers mimicking the coil
Of seamen, and stout galley-rowers' toil:
With toying oars and silken sails they glide,
    Nor care for wind and tide.

Mounted on panthers' furs and lions' manes,
From rear to van they scour about the plains;
A three days' journey in a moment done;
And always, at the rising of the sun,
About the wilds they hunt with spear and horn,
    On spleenful unicorn.

I saw Osirian Egypt kneel adown
    Before the vine-wreath crown!
I saw parched Abyssinia rouse and sing
    To the silver cymbals' ring!
I saw the whelming vintage hotly pierce
    Old Tartary the fierce!

The kings of Ind their jewel-sceptres vail,
And from their treasures scatter pearléd hail;
Great Brahma from his mystic heaven groans,
    And all his priesthood moans,
Before young Bacchus' eye-wink turning pale.
Into these regions came I, following him,
Sick-hearted, weary—so I took a whim
To stray away into these forests drear,
    Alone, without a peer:
And I have told thee all thou mayest hear.

FROM *Hyperion*

1.

As when, upon a trancéd summer-night,
Those green-robed senators of mighty woods,
Tall oaks, branch-charméd by the earnest stars,
Dream, and so dream all night without a stir,
Save from one gradual solitary gust
Which comes upon the silence, and dies off,
As if the ebbing air had but one wave:
So came these words and went; the while in tears
She touched her fair large forehead to the ground,
Just where her falling hair might be outspread
A soft and silken mat for Saturn's feet.

2.

O leave them, Muse! O leave them to their woes
For thou art weak to sing such tumults dire:
A solitary sorrow best befits
Thy lips, and antheming a lonely grief.
Leave them, O Muse! for thou anon wilt find
Many a fallen old Divinity
Wandering in vain about bewildered shores.
Meantime touch piously the Delphic harp,
And not a wind of heaven but will breathe
In aid soft warble from the Dorian flute;
For lo! 'tis for the Father of all verse.
Flush everything that hath a vermeil hue,
Let the rose glow intense and warm the air,
And let the clouds of even and of morn
Float in voluptuous fleeces o'er the hills;
Let the red wine within the goblet boil,
Cold as a bubbling well; let faint-lipped shells,
On sands or in great deeps, vermilion turn
Through all their labyrinths; and let the maid
Blush keenly, as with some warm kiss surprised.
Chief isle of the embowered Cyclades,
Rejoice, O Delos, with thine olives green,
And poplars, and lawn-shading palms, and beech,
In which the Zephyr breathes the loudest song,
And hazels thick dark-stemmed beneath the shade:
Apollo is once more the golden theme!

"Bright Star! Would I Were Steadfast as Thou Art"

Bright star! would I were steadfast as thou art—
  Not in lone splendour hung aloft the night,
And watching, with eternal lids apart,
  Like Nature's patient, sleepless Eremite,
The moving waters at their priestlike task
  Of pure ablution round earth's human shores,
Or gazing on the new soft fallen mask
  Of snow upon the mountains and the moors—
No—yet still steadfast, still unchangeable,
  Pillowed upon my fair love's ripening breast,
To feel for ever its soft fall and swell,
  Awake for ever in a sweet unrest,
Still, still to hear her tender-taken breath,
And so live ever—or else swoon to death.

GEORGE DARLEY

(1795–1846)

Siren Chorus

Troop home to silent grots and caves,
  Troop home! and mimic as you go
The mournful winding of the waves
  Which to their dark abysses flow.

At this sweet hour all things beside
  In amorous pairs to covert creep,
The swans that brush the evening tide
  Homeward in snowy couples keep.

In his green den the murmuring seal
  Close by his sleek companion lies,
While singly we to bedward steal,
  And close in fruitless sleep our eyes.

In bowers of love men take their rest,
  In loveless bowers we sigh alone,
With bosom-friends are others blest,
  But we have none! but we have none!

HARTLEY COLERIDGE
(1796–1849)
Song

She is not fair to outward view
    As many maidens be,
Her loveliness I never knew
    Until she smiled on me;
Oh! then I saw her eye was bright,
A well of love, a spring of light.

But now her looks are coy and cold,
    To mine they ne'er reply,
And yet I cease not to behold
    The love-light in her eye:
Her very frowns are fairer far
Than smiles of other maidens are.

THOMAS HOOD
(1799–1845)
Autumn

I saw old Autumn in the misty morn
Stand shadowless like Silence, listening
To silence, for no lonely bird would sing
Into his hollow ear from woods forlorn,
Nor lowly hedge nor solitary thorn;
Shaking his languid locks all dewy bright
With tangled gossamer that fell by night,
    Pearling his coronet of golden corn.

Where are the songs of Summer? With the sun,
Oping the dusky eyelids of the south,
Till shade and silence waken up as one,
And Morning sings with a warm odorous mouth.
Where are the merry birds? Away, away,
On panting wings through the inclement skies,
    Lest owls should prey
    Undazzled at noonday,
And tear with horny beak their lustrous eyes.

Where are the blossoms of Summer? In the west,
Blushing their last to the last sunny hours,
When the mild Eve by sudden Night is prest
Like tearful Proserpine, snatched from her flowers
   To a most gloomy breast.
Where is the pride of Summer—the green prime—
The many, many leaves all twinkling? Three
   On the mossed elm; three on the naked lime
Trembling—and one upon the old oak tree.
   Where is the Dryads' immortality?
Gone into mournful cypress and dark yew,
Or wearing the long gloomy Winter through
   In the smooth holly's green eternity.

The squirrel gloats on his accomplished hoard,
The ants have brimmed their garners with ripe grain,
   And honey bees have stored
The sweets of Summer in their luscious cells;
The swallows all have winged across the main;
And here the Autumn melancholy dwells,
And sighs her tearful spells,
Amongst the sunless shadows of the plain.
   Alone, alone,
   Upon a mossy stone,
She sits and reckons up the dead and gone
With the last leaves for a love-rosary,
Whilst all the withered world looks drearily,
Like a dim picture of the drownéd past
In the hushed mind's mysterious far away,
Doubtful what ghostly thing will steal the last
Into that distance, grey upon the grey.

O go and sit with her, and be o'ershaded
Under the languid downfall of her hair:
She wears a coronal of flowers faded
Upon her forehead, and a face of care;
There is enough of withered everywhere
To make her bower—and enough of gloom;
There is enough of sadness to invite,
If only for the rose that died—whose doom
Is Beauty's—she that with the living bloom

Of conscious cheeks most beautifies the light;
There is enough of sorrowing, and quite
Enough of bitter fruits the earth doth bear—
Enough of chilly droppings for her bowl;
Enough of fear and shadowy despair,
To frame her cloudy prison for the soul.

The Water Lady

Alas, the moon should ever beam
To show what man should never see!
I saw a maiden on a stream,
And fair was she!

I stayed awhile, to see her throw
Her tresses back, that all beset
The fair horizon of her brow
With clouds of jet.

I stayed a little while to view
Her cheek, that wore in place of red
The bloom of water, tender blue,
Daintily spread.

I stayed to watch, a little space,
Her parted lips if she would sing;
The waters closed above her face
With many a ring.

And still I stayed a little more,
Alas! she never comes again;
I throw my flowers from the shore,
And watch in vain.

I know my life will fade away,
I know that I must vainly pine,
For I am made of mortal clay,
But she's divine.

Sonnet

It is not death, that sometime in a sigh
This eloquent breath shall take its speechless flight;
That sometime these bright stars, that now reply
In sunlight to the sun, shall set in night:
That this warm conscious flesh shall perish quite,
And all life's ruddy springs forget to flow;
That thoughts shall cease, and the immortal sprite
Be lapped in alien clay, and laid below;
It is not death to know this—but to know
That pious thoughts, which visit at new graves
In tender pilgrimage, will cease to go
So duly and so oft—and when grass waves
Over the past-away, there may be then
No resurrection in the minds of men.

Silence

There is a silence where hath been no sound,
There is a silence where no sound may be,
In the cold grave—under the deep, deep sea,
Or in wide desert where no life is found,
Which hath been mute, and still must sleep profound;
No voice is hushed—no life treads silently,
But clouds and cloudy shadows wander free,
That never spoke, over the idle ground:
But in green ruins, in the desolate walls
Of antique palaces, where Man hath been,
Though the dun fox, or wild hyena calls,
And owls, that flit continually between,
Shriek to the echo, and the low winds moan,
There the true Silence is, self-conscious and alone.

THOMAS BABINGTON MACAULAY, LORD MACAULAY
(1800–1859)

Epitaph on a Jacobite

To my true king I offered free from stain
Courage and faith; vain faith, and courage vain.
For him I threw lands, honours, wealth, away,
And one dear hope that was more prized than they.
For him I languished in a foreign clime,
Grey-haired with sorrow in my manhood's prime;
Heard on Lavernia Scargill's whispering trees,
And pined by Arno for my lovelier Tees;
Beheld each night my home in fevered sleep,
Each morning started from the dream to weep;
Till God, who saw me tried too sorely, gave
The resting place I asked, an early grave.
O thou, whom chance leads to this nameless stone,
From that proud country which was once mine own,
By those white cliffs I never more must see,
By that dear language which I spake like thee,
Forget all feuds, and shed one English tear
O'er English dust. A broken heart lies here.

WINTHROP MACKWORTH PRAED
(1802–1839)

FROM *The Belle of the Ball-Room*

Our love was like most other loves;—
    A little glow, a little shiver,
A rose-bud, and a pair of gloves,
    And "Fly not yet"—upon the river;
Some jealousy of some one's heir,
    Some hopes of dying broken-hearted,
A miniature, a lock of hair,
    The usual vows,—and then we parted.

We parted; months and years rolled by;
    We met again four summers after:
Our parting was all sob and sigh;
    Our meeting was all mirth and laughter:

For in my heart's most secret cell
There had been many other lodgers;
And she was not the ball-room's Belle,
But only—Mrs. Something Rogers!

RALPH WALDO EMERSON

(1803–1882)

"And When I Am Entombéd..."

And when I am entombéd in my place,
Be it remembered of a single man,
He never, though he dearly loved his race,
For fear of human eyes swerved from his plan.

FROM Ode Inscribed to W. H. Channing

The God who made New Hampshire
Taunted the lofty land
With little men;—
Small bat and wren
House in the oak:—
If earth-fire cleave
The upheaved land, and bury the folk,
The southern crocodile would grieve.
Virtue palters; Right is hence;
Freedom praised, but hid;
Funeral eloquence
Rattles the coffin-lid.

The horseman serves the horse,
The neatherd serves the neat,
The merchant serves the purse,
The eater serves his meat;
'Tis the day of the chattel,
Web to weave, and corn to grind;
Things are in the saddle,
And ride mankind.

There are two laws discrete,
Not reconciled,—
Law for man, and law for thing;
The last builds town and fleet,
But it runs wild,
And doth the man unking.

Let man serve law for man;
Live for friendship, live for love,
For truth's and harmony's behoof;
The state may follow how it can,
As Olympus follows Jove.

Yet do not I implore
The wrinkled shopman to my sounding woods,
Nor bid the unwilling senator
Ask votes of thrushes in the solitudes.
Every one to his chosen work;—
Foolish hands may mix and mar;
Wise and sure the issue are.
Round they roll till dark is light,
Sex to sex, and even to odd;—
The over-god
Who marries Right to Might
Who peoples, unpeoples,—
He who exterminates
Races by stronger races,
Black by white faces,—
Knows to bring honey
Out of the lion;
Grafts gentlest scion
On pirate and Turk.

Forbearance

Hast thou named all the birds without a gun?
Loved the wood-rose, and left it on its stalk?
At rich men's tables eaten bread and pulse?
Unarmed, faced danger with a heart of trust?

And loved so well a high behavior,
In man or maid, that thou from speech refrained,
Nobility more nobly to repay?
O, be my friend, and teach me to be thine!

Give All to Love

Give all to love;
Obey thy heart;
Friends, kindred, days,
Estate, good-fame,
Plans, credit and the Muse,—
Nothing refuse.

'Tis a brave master;
Let it have scope:
Follow it utterly,
Hope beyond hope:
High and more high
It dives into noon,
With wing unspent,
Untold intent;
But it is a god,
Knows its own path
And the outlets of the sky.

It was never for the mean;
It requireth courage stout.
Souls above doubt,
Valor unbending,
It will reward,—
They shall return
More than they were,
And ever ascending.

Leave all for love;
Yet, hear me, yet,
One word more thy heart behoved,
One pulse more of firm endeavor,—

Keep thee to-day,
To-morrow, forever,
Free as an Arab
Of thy beloved.

Cling with life to the maid;
But when the surprise,
First vague shadow of surmise,
Flits across her bosom young,
Of a joy apart from thee,
Free be she, fancy-free;
Nor thou detain her vesture's hem,
Nor the palest rose she flung
From her summer diadem.

Though thou loved her as thyself,
As a self of purer clay,
Though her parting dims the day,
Stealing grace from all alive;
Heartily know,
When half-gods go,
The gods arrive.

Bacchus

Bring me wine, but wine which never grew
In the belly of the grape,
Or grew on vine whose tap-roots, reaching through
Under the Andes to the Cape,
Suffer no savor of the earth to scape.

Let its grapes the morn salute
From a nocturnal root,
Which feels the acrid juice
Of Styx and Erebus;
And turns the woe of Night
By its own craft, to a more rich delight.

We buy ashes for bread;
We buy diluted wine;
Give me of the true,—
Whose ample leaves and tendrils curled
Among the silver hills of heaven
Draw everlasting dew;
Wine of wine,
Blood of the world,
Form of forms, and mould of statures,
That I intoxicated,
And by the draught assimilated,
May float at pleasure through all natures;
The bird-language rightly spell,
And that which roses say so well.

Wine that is shed
Like the torrents of the sun
Up the horizon walls,
Or like the Atlantic streams, which run
When the South Sea calls.
Water and bread,
Food which needs no transmuting,
Rainbow-flowering, wisdom-fruiting,
Wine which is already man,
Food which teach and reason can.

Wine which Music is,—
Music and wine are one,—
That I, drinking this,
Shall hear far Chaos talk with me;
Kings unborn shall walk with me;
And the poor grass shall plot and plan
What it will do when it is man.
Quickened so, will I unlock
Every crypt of every rock.

I thank the joyful juice
For all I know;—
Winds of remembering
Of the ancient being blow,
And seeming-solid walls of use
Open and flow.

Pour, Bacchus! the remembering wine;
Retrieve the loss of me and mine!
Vine for vine be antidote,
And the grape requite the lote!
Haste to cure the old despair,—
Reason in Nature's lotus drenched,
The memory of ages quenched;
Give them again to shine;
Let wine repair what this undid;
And where the infection slid,
A dazzling memory revive;
Refresh the faded tints,
Recut the aged prints,
And write my old adventures with the pen
Which on the first day drew,
Upon the tablets blue,
The dancing Pleiads and eternal men.

FROM *Concord Hymn*

By the rude bridge that arched the flood,
  Their flag to April's breeze unfurled,
Here once the embattled farmers stood
  And fired the shot heard round the world.

The foe long since in silence slept;
  Alike the conqueror silent sleeps;
And Time the ruined bridge has swept
  Down the dark stream which seaward creeps.

Days

Daughters of Time, the hypocritic Days,
Muffled and dumb like barefoot dervishes,
And marching single in an endless file,
Bring diadems and fagots in their hands.
To each they offer gifts after his will,

Bread, kingdoms, stars, and sky that holds them all.
I, in my pleached garden, watched the pomp,
Forgot my morning wishes, hastily
Took a few herbs and apples, and the Day
Turned and departed silently. I, too late,
Under her solemn fillet saw the scorn.

April

The April winds are magical
And thrill our tuneful frames;
The garden walks are passional
To bachelors and dames.
The hedge is gemmed with diamonds,
The air with Cupids full,
The cobweb clues of Rosamond
Guide lovers to the pool.
Each dimple in the water,
Each leaf that shades the rock
Can cozen, pique and flatter,
Can parley and provoke.
Goodfellow, Puck and goblins,
Know more than any book.
Down with your doleful problems,
And court the sunny brook.
The south-winds are quick-witted,
The schools are sad and slow,
The masters quite omitted
The lore we care to know.

Heroism

Ruby wine is drunk by knaves,
Sugar spends to fatten slaves,
Rose and vine-leaf deck buffoons;
Thunder-clouds are Jove's festoons,
Drooping oft in wreaths of dread,
Lightning-knotted round his head;

The hero is not fed on sweets,
Daily his own heart he eats;
Chambers of the great are jails,
And head-winds right for royal sails.

Brahma

If the red slayer think he slays,
    Or if the slain think he is slain,
They know not well the subtle ways
    I keep, and pass, and turn again.

Far or forgot to me is near;
    Shadow and sunlight are the same;
The vanished gods to me appear;
    And one to me are shame and fame.

They reckon ill who leave me out;
    When me they fly, I am the wings;
I am the doubter and the doubt,
    And I the hymn the Brahmin sings.

The strong gods pine for my abode,
    And pine in vain the sacred Seven;
But thou, meek lover of the good!
    Find me, and turn thy back on heaven.

THOMAS LOVELL BEDDOES
(1803–1849)
Song

How many times do I love thee, dear?
    Tell me how many thoughts there be
        In the atmosphere
        Of a new-fall'n year,
Whose white and sable hours appear
    The latest flake of Eternity:—
So many times do I love thee, dear.

How many times do I love again?
  Tell me how many beads there are
    In a silver chain
    Of evening rain,
Unravelled from the tumbling main,
  And threading the eye of a yellow star:—
So many times do I love again.

Torrismond

Dream-Pedlary

If there were dreams to sell
  What would you buy?
Some cost a passing bell;
  Some a light sigh,
That shakes from Life's fresh crown
Only a roseleaf down.
If there were dreams to sell,
Merry and sad to tell,
And the crier rung the bell,
  What would you buy?

A cottage lone and still,
  With bowers nigh,
Shadowy, my woes to still,
  Until I die.
Such pearl from Life's fresh crown
Fain would I shake me down.
Were dreams to have at will,
This would best heal my ill,
  This would I buy.

But there were dreams to sell,
  Ill didst thou buy;
Life is a dream, they tell,
  Waking, to die.
Dreaming a dream to prize,
Is wishing ghosts to rise;
  And, if I had the spell
  To call the buried, well,
    Which one would I?

If there are ghosts to raise,
    What shall I call,
Out of hell's murky haze,
    Heaven's blue hall?
Raise my loved longlost boy
To lead me to his joy.
        There are no ghosts to raise;
        Out of death lead no ways;
            Vain is the call.

Know'st thou not ghosts to sue?
    No love thou hast.
Else lie, as I will do,
    And breathe thy last,
So out of Life's fresh crown
Fall like a rose-leaf down.
        Thus are the ghosts to woo;
        Thus are all dreams made true,
            Ever to last!

Love-in-Idleness

He: "Shall I be your first love, lady, shall I be your first?
    Oh! then I'll fall before you down on my velvet knee
    And deeply bend my rosy head and press it upon thee,
And swear that there is nothing more for which my heart doth
        thirst,
        But a downy kiss and pink
        Between your lips' soft chink."

She: "Yes, you shall be my first love, boy, and you shall be my
        first,
    And I will raise you up again unto my bosom's fold;
    And when you kisses many a one on lip and cheek have told,
I'll let you loose upon the grass, to leave me if you durst;
        And so we'll toy away
        The night beside the day."

He: "But let me be your second love, but let me be your
        second,
    For then I'll tap so gently, dear, upon your window pane,

And creep between the curtains in, where never man has
lain,
And never leave thy gentle side till the morning star hath
beckoned,
Within the silken lace
Of thy young arms' embrace."

She: "Well thou shalt be my second love, yes, gentle boy, my
second,
And I will wait at eve for thee within my lonely bower,
And yield unto thy kisses, like a bud to April's shower,
From moonset till the tower-clock the hour of dawn hath
reckoned,
And lock thee with my arms
All silent up in charms."

He: "No, I will be thy third love, lady, aye, I will be the third,
And break upon thee, bathing, in woody place alone,
And catch thee to my saddle and ride o'er stream and stone,
And press thee well, and kiss thee well, and never speak a
word,
Till thou hast yielded up
The first taste of love's cup."

She: "Then thou shalt not be my first love, boy, nor my sec-
ond, nor my third;
If thou'rt the first, I'll laugh at thee and pierce thy flesh
with thorns;
If the second, from my chamber pelt with jeering laugh and
scorns;
And if thou darest be the third, I'll draw my dirk unheard
And cut thy heart in two,—
And then die, weeping you."

Song

Who tames the lion now?
Who smooths Jove's wrinkles now?
Who is the reckless wight
That in the horrid middle

Of the deserted night
Doth play upon man's brain,
  As on a wanton fiddle,
The mad and magic strain,
The reeling tripping sound,
To which the world goes round?
  Sing heigh! ho! diddle!
    And then say—
Love, quotha, Love? Nay, nay!
It is a spirit fine
Of ale or ancient wine,
  Lord Alcohol, the drunken fay,
    Lord Alcohol alway!

Who maketh pipe-clay man
Think all that nature can?
Who dares the gods to flout,
  Lay fate beneath the table,
And make him stammer out
  A thousand monstrous things,
  For history a fable,
  Dish-clouts for kings?
And send the world along
Singing a ribald song
  Of heighho! Babel?
    Who, I pray—
Love, quotha, Love? Nay, nay!
It is a spirit fine
Of ale or ancient wine,
  Lord Alcohol, the drunken fay,
    Lord Alcohol alway!

The Phantom-Wooer

A ghost, that loved a lady fair,
Ever in the starry air
  Of midnight at her pillow stood;
And, with a sweetness skies above
The luring words of human love,
  Her soul the phantom wooed.

Sweet and sweet is their poisoned note,
The little snakes' of silver throat,
In mossy skulls that nest and lie,
Ever singing, "Die, oh! die."

Young soul put off your flesh, and come
With me into the quiet tomb,
　　Our bed is lovely, dark, and sweet;
The earth will swing us, as she goes,
Beneath our coverlid of snows,
　　And the warm leaden sheet.
Dear and dear is their poisoned note,
The little snakes' of silver throat,
In mossy skulls that nest and lie,
Ever singing, "Die, oh! die."

Song

Strew not earth with empty stars,
　　Strew it not with roses,
Nor feathers from the crest of Mars,
　　Nor summer's idle posies.
'Tis not the primrose-sandalled moon,
　　Nor cold and silent morn,
Nor he that climbs the dusty noon,
Nor mower war with scythe that drops,
Stuck with helmed and turbanned tops
　　Of enemies new shorn.

Ye cups, ye lyres, ye trumpets know,
Pour your music, let it flow,
'Tis Bacchus' son who walks below.

JAMES CLARENCE MANGAN
(1803–1849)

Dark Rosaleen

O my dark Rosaleen,
　　Do not sigh, do not weep!
The priests are on the ocean green,
　　They march along the deep.

There's wine from the royal Pope,
  Upon the ocean green;
And Spanish ale shall give you hope,
  My dark Rosaleen!
  My own Rosaleen!
Shall glad your heart, shall give you hope,
Shall give you health and help, and hope,
  My dark Rosaleen.

Over hills and through dales,
  Have I roamed for your sake;
All yesterday I sailed with sails
  On river and on lake.
The Erne, at its highest flood,
  I dashed across unseen,
For there was lightning in my blood,
  My dark Rosaleen!
  My own Rosaleen!
Oh! there was lightning in my blood,
Red lightning lightened through my blood,
  My dark Rosaleen!

All day long in unrest,
  To and fro do I move,
The very soul within my breast
  Is wasted for you, love!
The heart in my bosom faints
  To think of you, my Queen,
My life of life, my saint of saints,
  My dark Rosaleen!
  My own Rosaleen!
To hear your sweet and sad complaints,
My life, my love, my saint of saints,
  My dark Rosaleen!

Woe and pain, pain and woe,
  Are my lot, night and noon,
To see your bright face clouded so,
  Like to the mournful moon.
But yet will I rear your throne
  Again in golden sheen;

'Tis you shall reign, shall reign alone,
  My dark Rosaleen!
  My own Rosaleen!
'Tis you shall have the golden throne,
'Tis you shall reign, shall reign alone,
  My dark Rosaleen!

Over dews, over sands,
  Will I fly for your weal:
Your holy, delicate white hands
  Shall girdle me with steel.
At home in your emerald bowers,
  From morning's dawn till e'en,
You'll pray for me, my flower of flowers,
  My dark Rosaleen!
  My fond Rosaleen!
You'll think of me through daylight's hours,
My virgin flower, my flower of flowers,
  My dark Rosaleen!

I could scale the blue air,
  I could plough the high hills,
Oh, I could kneel all night in prayer,
  To heal your many ills!
And one beamy smile from you
  Would float like light between
My toils and me, my own, my true,
  My dark Rosaleen!
  My fond Rosaleen!
Would give me life and soul anew,
A second life, a soul anew,
  My dark Rosaleen!

O! the Erne shall run red
  With redundance of blood,
The earth shall rock beneath our tread,
  And flames wrap hill and wood,
And gun-peal, and slogan cry
  Wake many a glen serene,

Ere you shall fade, ere you shall die,
   My dark Rosaleen!
   My own Rosaleen!
The Judgment Hour must first be nigh
Ere you can fade, ere you can die,
   My dark Rosaleen!

ELIZABETH BARRETT BROWNING

(1806–1861)

Sonnets from the Portuguese

I

I thought once how Theocritus had sung
Of the sweet years, the dear and wished-for years,
Who each one in a gracious hand appears
To bear a gift for mortals, old or young:
And, as I mused it in his antique tongue,
I saw, in gradual vision through my tears,
The sweet, sad years, the melancholy years,
Those of my own life, who by turns had flung
A shadow across me. Straightway I was 'ware,
So weeping, how a mystic Shape did move
Behind me, and drew me backward by the hair;
And a voice said in mastery, while I strove,—
"Guess now who holds thee?"—"Death," I said. But, there,
The silver answer rang,—"Not Death, but Love."

VI

Go from me. Yet I feel that I shall stand
Henceforward in thy shadow. Nevermore
Alone upon the threshold of my door
Of individual life, I shall command
The uses of my soul, nor lift my hand
Serenely in the sunshine as before,
Without the sense of that which I forbore—
Thy touch upon the palm. The widest land
Doom takes to part us, leaves thy heart in mine
With pulses that beat double. What I do

And what I dream include thee, as the wine
Must taste of its own grapes. And when I sue
God for myself, He hears that name of thine,
And sees within my eyes the tears of two.

XIV

If thou must love me, let it be for nought
Except for love's sake only. Do not say
"I love her for her smile—her look—her way
Of speaking gently,—for a trick of thought
That falls in well with mine, and certes brought
A sense of pleasant ease on such a day"—
For these things in themselves, Belovéd, may
Be changed, or change for thee,—and love, so wrought,
May be unwrought so. Neither love me for
Thine own dear pity's wiping my cheeks dry,—
A creature might forget to weep, who bore
Thy comfort long, and lose thy love thereby!
But love me for love's sake, that evermore
Thou mayst love on, through love's eternity.

XXII

When our two souls stand up erect and strong,
Face to face, silent, drawing nigh and nigher,
Until the lengthening wings break into fire
At either curvéd point,—what bitter wrong
Can the earth do to us, that we should not long
Be here contented? Think. In mounting higher,
The angels would press on us and aspire
To drop some golden orb of perfect song
Into our deep, dear silence. Let us stay
Rather on earth, Belovéd,—where the unfit
Contrarious moods of men recoil away
And isolate pure spirits, and permit
A place to stand and love in for a day,
With darkness and the death-hour rounding it.

XXVIII

My letters! all dead paper, mute and white!
And yet they seem alive and quivering
Against my tremulous hands which loose the string

And let them drop down on my knee to-night.
This said,—he wished to have me in his sight
Once, as a friend: this fixed a day in spring
To come and touch my hand . . . a simple thing,
Yet I wept for it!—this, . . . the paper's light . . .
Said, *Dear, I love thee;* and I sank and quailed
As if God's future thundered on my past.
This said, *I am thine*—and so its ink has paled
With lying on my heart that beat too fast.
And this . . . O Love, thy words have ill availed
If, what this said, I dared repeat at last!

XXXII

The first time that the sun rose on thine oath
To love me, I looked forward to the moon
To slacken all those bonds which seemed too soon
And quickly tied to make a lasting troth.
Quick-loving hearts, I thought, may quickly loathe;
And, looking on myself, I seemed not one
For such man's love!—more like an out-of-tune
Worn viol, a good singer would be wroth
To spoil his song with, and which, snatched in haste,
Is laid down at the first ill-sounding note.
I did not wrong myself so, but I placed
A wrong on *thee.* For perfect strains may float
'Neath master-hands, from instruments defaced,—
And great souls, at one stroke, may do and doat.

XXXV

If I leave all for thee, wilt thou exchange
And be all to me? Shall I never miss
Home-talk and blessing and the common kiss
That comes to each in turn, nor count it strange,
When I look up, to drop on a new range
Of walls and floors, another home than this?
Nay, wilt thou fill that place by me which is
Filled by dead eyes too tender to know change?
That's hardest. If to conquer love, has tried,
To conquer grief, tries more, as all things prove;
For grief indeed is love and grief beside.

Alas, I have grieved so I am hard to love.
Yet love me—wilt thou? Open thine heart wide,
And fold within the wet wings of thy dove.

XXXVIII

First time he kissed me, he but only kissed
The fingers of this hand wherewith I write;
And ever since, it grew more clean and white,
Slow to world-greetings, quick with its "Oh, list,"
When the angels speak. A ring of amethyst
I could not wear here, plainer to my sight,
Than that first kiss. The second passed in height
The first, and sought the forehead, and half missed,
Half falling on the hair. O beyond meed!
That was the chrism of love, which love's own crown,
With sanctifying sweetness, did precede.
The third upon my lips was folded down
In perfect, purple state; since when, indeed,
I have been proud and said, "My love, my own."

XLIII

How do I love thee? Let me count the ways.
I love thee to the depth and breadth and height
My soul can reach, when feeling out of sight
For the ends of Being and ideal Grace.
I love thee to the level of everyday's
Most quiet need, by sun and candle-light.
I love thee freely, as men strive for Right;
I love thee purely, as they turn from Praise.
I love thee with the passion put to use
In my old griefs, and with my childhood's faith.
I love thee with a love I seemed to lose
With my lost saints,—I love thee with the breath,
Smiles, tears, of all my life!—and, if God choose,
I shall but love thee better after death.

The Cry of the Children

φεῦ, φεῦ· τί προσδέρκεσθε μ' ὄμμασιν, τέκνα;

Medea: Do ye hear the children weeping, O my brothers,
　　Ere the sorrow comes with years?
They are leaning their young heads against their
　　　mothers,
　　And *that* cannot stop their tears.
The young lambs are bleating in the meadows,
　　The young birds are chirping in the nest,
The young fawns are playing with the shadows,
　　The young flowers are blowing toward the west—
But the young, young children, O my brothers,
　　They are weeping bitterly!
They are weeping in the playtime of the others,
　　In the country of the free.

Do you question the young children in their sorrow,
　　Why their tears are falling so?
The old man may weep for his to-morrow
　　Which is lost in Long Ago;
The old tree is leafless in the forest,
　　The old year is ending in the frost,
The old wound, if stricken, is the sorest,
　　The old hope is hardest to be lost:
But the young, young children, O my brothers,
　　Do you ask them why they stand
Weeping sore before the bosoms of their mothers,
　　In our happy Fatherland?

They look up with their pale and sunken faces,
　　And their looks are sad to see,
For the man's hoary anguish draws and presses
　　Down the cheeks of infancy;
"Your old earth," they say, "is very dreary,
　　Our young feet," they say, "are very weak;
Few paces have we taken, yet are weary—
　　Our grave-rest is very far to seek:

Ask the aged why they weep, and not the children,
    For the outside earth is cold,
And we young ones stand without, in our bewilder-
        ing,
    And the graves are for the old."

"True," say the children, "it may happen
    That we die before our time:
Little Alice died last year, her grave is shapen
    Like a snowball, in the rime.
We looked into the pit prepared to take her:
    Was no room for any work in the close clay!
From the sleep wherein she lieth none will wake her,
    Crying, 'Get up, little Alice! it is day.'
If you listen by that grave, in sun and shower,
    With your ear down, little Alice never cries;
Could we see her face, be sure we should not know
        her,
    For the smile has time for growing in her eyes:
And merry go her moments, lulled and stilled in
    The shroud by the kirk-chime.
It is good when it happens," say the children,
    "That we die before our time."

Alas, alas, the children! They are seeking
    Death in life, as best to have:
They are binding up their hearts away from breaking,
    With a cerement from the grave.
Go out, children, from the mine and from the city,
    Sing out, children, as the little thrushes do;
Pluck you handfuls of the meadow-cowslips pretty,
    Laugh aloud, to feel your fingers let them through!
But they answer, "Are your cowslips of the meadows
    Like our weeds anear the mine?
Leave us quiet in the dark of the coal-shadows,
    From your pleasures fair and fine!

"For oh," say the children, "we are weary
    And we cannot run or leap;
If we cared for any meadows, it were merely
    To drop down in them and sleep.

Our knees tremble sorely in the stooping,
    We fall upon our faces, trying to go;
And, underneath our heavy eyelids drooping
    The reddest flower would look as pale as snow.
For, all day, we drag our burden tiring
    Through the coal-dark, underground;
Or, all day, we drive the wheels of iron
    In the factories, round and round.

"For all day the wheels are droning, turning;
    Their wind comes in our faces,
Till our hearts turn, our heads with pulses burning,
    And the walls turn in their places:
Turns the sky in the high window, blank and reeling,
    Turns the long light that drops adown the wall,
Turn the black flies that crawl along the ceiling:
    All are turning, all the day, and we with all.
And all day, the iron wheels are droning,
    And sometimes we could pray,
'O ye wheels' (breaking out in a mad moaning)
    'Stop! be silent for to-day!' "

Ay! be silent! Let them hear each other breathing
    For a moment, mouth to mouth!
Let them touch each other's hands, in a fresh wreath-
        ing
    Of their tender human youth!
Let them feel that this cold metallic motion
    Is not all the life God fashions or reveals:
Let them prove their living souls against the notion
    That they live in you, or under you, O wheels!
Still, all day, the iron wheels go onward,
    Grinding life down from its mark;
And the children's souls, which God is calling sun-
        ward,
    Spin on blindly in the dark.

Now tell the poor young children, O my brothers,
    To look up to Him, and pray;
So the blessèd One who blesseth all the others,
    Will bless them another day.

They answer, "Who is God that He should hear us,
    While the rushing of the iron wheels is stirred?
When we sob aloud, the human creatures near us
    Pass by, hearing not, or answer not a word.
And *we* hear not (for the wheels in their resounding)
    Strangers speaking at the door:
Is it likely God, with angels singing round Him,
    Hears our weeping any more?

"Two words, indeed, of praying we remember,
    And at midnight's hour of harm,
'Our Father', looking upward in the chamber,
    We say softly for a charm.
We know no other words except 'Our Father',
    And we think that, in some pause of angels' song,
God may pluck them with the silence sweet to gather,
    And hold both within His right hand which is
        strong.
'Our Father!' If He heard us, He would surely
    (For they call Him good and mild)
Answer, smiling down the steep world very purely,
    'Come and rest with me, my child.'

"But, no!" say the children, weeping faster,
    "He is speechless as a stone:
And they tell us, of His image is the master
    Who commands us to work on.
Go to!" say the children,—"up in Heaven,
    Dark, wheel-like, turning clouds are all we find.
Do not mock us; grief has made us unbelieving:
    We look up for God; but tears have made us
        blind."
Do you hear the children weeping and disproving,
    O my brothers, what ye preach?
For God's possible is taught by His world's loving,
    And the children doubt of each.

And well may the children weep before you!
    They are weary ere they run;
They have never seen the sunshine, nor the glory
    Which is brighter than the sun.

They know the grief of man, without its wisdom;
　　They sink in man's despair, without its calm;
Are slaves, without the liberty in Christdom,
　　Are martyrs, by the pang without the palm:
Are worn as if with age, yet unretrievingly
　　The harvest of its memories cannot reap,—
Are orphans of the earthly love and heavenly.
　　Let them weep! let them weep!

They look up with their pale and sunken faces,
　　And their look is dread to see,
For they mind you of their angels in high places,
　　With eyes turned on Deity.
"How long," they say, "how long, O cruel nation,
　　Will you stand, to move tho world, on a child's
　　　　heart,—
Stifle down with a mailed heel its palpitation,
　　And tread onward to your throne amid the mart?
Our blood splashes upward, O gold-heaper,
　　And your purple shows your path!
But the child's sob in the silence curses deeper
　　Than the strong man in his wrath."

HENRY WADSWORTH LONGFELLOW
(1807–1882)

Hymn to the Night

I heard the trailing garments of the Night
　　Sweep through her marble halls!
I saw her sable skirts all fringed with light
　　From the celestial walls!

I felt her presence, by its spell of might,
　　Stoop o'er me from above;
The calm, majestic presence of the Night,
　　As of the one I love.

I heard the sounds of sorrow and delight,
　　The manifold soft chimes,
That fill the haunted chambers of the Night,
　　Like some old poet's rhymes.

From the cool cisterns of the midnight air
  My spirit drank repose;
The fountain of perpetual peace flows there,—
  From those deep cisterns flows.

O holy Night! from thee I learn to bear
  What man has borne before!
Thou layest thy finger on the lips of Care,
  And they complain no more.

Peace! Peace! Orestes-like I breathe this prayer!
  Descend with broad-winged flight,
The welcome, the thrice-prayed for, the most fair,
  The best-belovéd Night!

Serenade

Stars of the summer night!
    Far in yon azure deeps,
Hide, hide your golden light!
    She sleeps!
My lady sleeps!
    Sleeps!

Moon of the summer night!
    Far down yon western steeps,
Sink, sink in silver light!
    She sleeps!
My lady sleeps!
    Sleeps!

Wind of the summer night!
    Where yonder woodbine creeps,
Fold, fold thy pinions light!
    She sleeps!
My lady sleeps!
    Sleeps!

Dreams of the summer night!
　　Tell her, her lover keeps
Watch! while in slumbers light
　　She sleeps!
My lady sleeps!
　　Sleeps!

The Spanish Student

Suspiria

Take them, O Death! and bear away
　　Whatever thou canst call thine own!
Thine image, stamped upon this clay,
　　Doth give thee that, but that alone!

Take them, O Grave! and let them lie
　　Folded upon thy narrow shelves,
As garments by the soul laid by,
　　And precious only to ourselves!

Take them, O great Eternity!
　　Our little life is but a gust
That bends the branches of thy tree,
　　And trails its blossoms in the dust!

My Lost Youth

Often I think of the beautiful town
　　That is seated by the sea;
Often in thought go up and down
The pleasant streets of that dear old town,
　　And my youth comes back to me.
　　　　And a verse of a Lapland song
　　　　Is haunting my memory still:
　　　　"A boy's will is the wind's will,
And the thoughts of youth are long, long thoughts."

I can see the shadowy lines of its trees,
 And catch, in sudden gleams,
The sheen of the far-surrounding seas,
And islands that were the Hesperides
 Of all my boyish dreams.
  And the burden of that old song,
  It murmurs and whispers still:
  "A boy's will is the wind's will,
And the thoughts of youth are long, long thoughts."

I remember the black wharves and the slips,
 And the sea-tides tossing free;
And Spanish sailors with bearded lips,
And the beauty and mystery of the ships,
 And the magic of the sea.
  And the voice of the wayward song
  Is singing and saying still:
  "A boy's will is the wind's will,
And the thoughts of youth are long, long thoughts."

I remember the bulwarks by the shore,
 And the fort upon the hill;
The sunrise gun, with its hollow roar,
The drum-beat repeated o'er and o'er,
 And the bugle wild and shrill.
  And the music of that old song
  Throbs in my memory still:
  "A boy's will is the wind's will,
And the thoughts of youth are long, long thoughts."

I remember the sea-fight far away,
 How it thundered o'er the tide!
And the dead captains, as they lay
In their graves, o'erlooking the tranquil bay,
 Where they in battle died.
  And the sound of that mournful song
  Goes through me with a thrill:
  "A boy's will is the wind's will,
And the thoughts of youth are long, long thoughts."

I can see the breezy dome of groves,
  The shadows of Deering's Woods;
And the friendships old and the early loves
Come back with a Sabbath sound, as of doves
  In quiet neighborhoods.
    And the verse of that sweet old song,
    It flutters and murmurs still:
    "A boy's will is the wind's will,
And the thoughts of youth are long, long thoughts."

I remember the gleams and glooms that dart
  Across the school-boy's brain;
The song and the silence in the heart,
That in part are prophecies, and in part
  Are longings wild and vain.
    And the voice of that fitful song
    Sings on, and is never still:
    "A boy's will is the wind's will,
And the thoughts of youth are long, long thoughts."

There are things of which I may not speak;
  There are dreams that cannot die;
There are thoughts that make the strong heart weak,
And bring a pallor into the cheek,
  And a mist before the eye.
    And the words of that fatal song
    Come over me like a chill:
    "A boy's will is the wind's will,
And the thoughts of youth are long, long thoughts."

Strange to me now are the forms I meet
  When I visit the dear old town;
But the native air is pure and sweet,
And the trees that o'ershadow each well-known street,
  As they balance up and down,
    Are singing the beautiful song,
    Are sighing and whispering still:
    "A boy's will is the wind's will,
And the thoughts of youth are long, long thoughts."

And Deering's Woods are fresh and fair,
    And with joy that is almost pain
My heart goes back to wander there,
And among the dreams of the days that were,
    I find my lost youth again.
        And the strange and beautiful song,
        The groves are repeating it still:
        "A boy's will is the wind's will,
And the thoughts of youth are long, long thoughts."

"Some Day, Some Day"

Some day, some day,
O troubled breast,
Shalt thou find rest.

If Love in thee
To grief give birth,
Six feet of earth
Can more than he;
There calm and free
And unoppressed
Shalt thou find rest.

The unattained
In life at last,
When life is passed,
Shall all be gained;
And no more pained,
No more distressed,
Shalt thou find rest.

Divina Commedia

Oft have I seen at some cathedral door
    A laborer, pausing in the dust and heat,
    Lay down his burden, and with reverent feet
Enter, and cross himself, and on the floor
Kneel to repeat his paternoster o'er;
    Far off the noises of the world retreat;
    The loud vociferations of the street

Become an undistinguishable roar.
So, as I enter here from day to day,
    And leave my burden at this minster gate,
Kneeling in prayer, and not ashamed to pray,
    The tumult of the time disconsolate
To inarticulate murmurs dies away,
    While the eternal ages watch and wait.

Ultima Thule
(DEDICATION)

With favoring winds o'er sunlit seas,
We sailed for the Hesperides,
The land where the golden apples grow;
But that, ah! that was long ago.

How far, since then, the ocean streams
Have swept us from that land of dreams,
That land of fiction and of truth,
The lost Atlantis of our youth!

Whither, ah, whither? Are not these
The tempest-haunted Hebrides,
Where sea-gulls scream, and breakers roar,
And wreck and sea-weed line the shore?

Ultima Thule! Utmost Isle!
Here in thy harbors for a while
We lower our sails; a while we rest
From the unending, endless quest.

JOHN GREENLEAF WHITTIER
(1807–1892)
"I Call the Old Time Back..."

I call the old time back: I bring these lays
To thee, in memory of the summer days
When, by our native streams and forest ways,

We dreamed them over; while the rivulets made
Songs of their own, and the great pine-trees laid
On warm noon-lights the masses of their shade.

And *she* was with us, living o'er again
Her life in ours, despite of years and pain,—
The autumn's brightness after latter rain.

Beautiful in her holy peace as one
Who stands, at evening, when the work is done,
Glorified in the setting of the sun!

Her memory makes our common landscape seem
Fairer than any of which painters dream,
Lights the brown hills and sings in every stream;

For she whose speech was always truth's pure gold
Heard, not unpleased, its simple legends told,
And loved with us the beautiful and old.

OLIVER WENDELL HOLMES

(1809–1894)

The Voiceless

We count the broken lyres that rest
    Where the sweet wailing singers slumber,
But o'er their silent sister's breast
    The wild-flowers who will stoop to number?
A few can touch the magic string,
    And noisy Fame is proud to win them:—
Alas for those that never sing,
    But die with all their music in them!

Nay, grieve not for the dead alone
    Whose song has told their hearts' sad story,—
Weep for the voiceless, who have known
    The cross without the crown of glory!
Not where Leucadian breezes sweep
    O'er Sappho's memory-haunted billow,
But where the glistening night-dews weep
    On nameless sorrow's churchyard pillow.

O hearts that break and give no sign
  Save whitening lip and fading tresses,
Till Death pours out his longed-for wine
  Slow-dropped from Misery's crushing presses,—
If singing breath or echoing chord
  To every hidden pang were given,
What endless melodies were poured,
  As sad as earth, as sweet as heaven!

After a Lecture on Keats

The wreath that star-crowned Shelley gave
Is lying on thy Roman grave,
Yet on its turf young April sets
Her store of slender violets;
Though all the Gods their garlands shower,
I too may bring one purple flower.
Alas! what blossom shall I bring,
That opens in my Northern spring?
The garden beds have all run wild,
So trim when I was yet a child;
Flat plantains and unseemly stalks
Have crept across the gravel walks;
The vines are dead, long, long ago,
The almond buds no longer blow.
No more upon its mound I see
The azure, plume-bound fleur-de-lis;
Where once the tulips used to show,
In straggling tufts the pansies grow;
The grass has quenched my white-rayed gem,
The flowering "Star of Bethlehem",
Though its long blade of glossy green
And pallid stripe may still be seen.
Nature, who treads her nobles down,
And gives their birthright to the clown,
Has sown her base-born weedy things
About the garden's queens and kings.
Yet one sweet flower of ancient race
Springs in the old familiar place.
When snows were melting down the vale,

And Earth unlaced her icy mail,
And March his stormy trumpet blew,
And tender green came peeping through,
I loved the earliest one to seek
That broke the soil with emerald beak,
And watch the trembling bells so blue
Spread on the column as it grew.
Meek child of earth! thou wilt not shame
The sweet, dead poet's holy name;
The God of music gave thee birth,
Called from the crimson-spotted earth,
Where, sobbing his young life away,
His own fair Hyacinthus lay.
The hyacinth my garden gave
Shall lie upon that Roman grave!

EDWARD FITZGERALD

(1809–1883)

Rubáiyát of Omar Khayyám of Naishápúr

Wake! For the Sun, who scattered into flight
The Stars before him from the Field of Night,
    Drives Night along with them from Heav'n, and strikes
The Sultán's Turret with a Shaft of Light.

Before the phantom of False morning died,
Methought a Voice within the Tavern cried,
    "When all the Temple is prepared within,
Why nods the drowsy Worshipper outside?"

And, as the Cock crew, those who stood before
The Tavern shouted—"Open then the door!
    You know how little while we have to stay,
And, once departed, may return no more."

Now the New Year reviving old Desires,
The thoughtful Soul to Solitude retires,
    Where the White Hand of Moses on the Bough
Puts out, and Jesus from the Ground suspires.

Iram indeed is gone with all his Rose,
And Jamshyd's Sev'n-ring'd Cup where no one knows;
   But still a Ruby gushes from the Vine,
And many a Garden by the Water blows.

And David's lips are lockt; but in divine
High-piping Péhleví, with "Wine! Wine! Wine!
   Red Wine!"—the Nightingale cries to the Rose
That sallow cheek of hers t' incarnadine.

Come, fill the Cup, and in the fire of Spring
Your Winter-garment of Repentance fling;
   The Bird of Time has but a little way
To flutter—and the Bird is on the Wing.

Whether at Naishápúr or Babylon,
Whether the Cup with sweet or bitter run,
   The Wine of Life keeps oozing drop by drop,
The Leaves of Life keep falling one by one.

Each Morn a thousand Roses brings, you say;
Yes, but where leaves the Rose of Yesterday?
   And this first Summer month that brings the Rose
Shall take Jamshyd and Kaikobád away.

Well, let it take them! What have we to do
With Kaikobád the Great, or Kaikhosrú?
   Let Zál and Rustum thunder as they will,
Or Hátim call to Supper—heed not you.

With me along the strip of Herbage strown
That just divides the desert from the sown,
   Where name of Slave and Sultán is forgot—
And Peace to Máhmúd on his golden Throne!

A Book of Verses underneath the Bough,
A Jug of Wine, a Loaf of Bread—and Thou
   Beside me singing in the Wilderness—
Oh, Wilderness were Paradise enow!

Some for the Glories of This World; and some
Sigh for the Prophet's Paradise to come;
    Ah, take the Cash, and let the Credit go,
Nor heed the rumble of a distant Drum!

Look to the blowing Rose about us—Lo,
"Laughing," she says, "into the world I blow,
    At once the silken tassel of my Purse
Tear, and its Treasure on the Garden throw."

And those who husbanded the Golden grain,
And those who flung it to the winds like Rain,
    Alike to no such aureate Earth are turn'd
As, buried once, Men want dug up again.

The Worldly Hope men set their Hearts upon
Turns Ashes—or it prospers; and anon,
    Like Snow upon the Desert's dusty Face
Lighting a little hour or two—was gone.

Think, in this batter d Caravanserai
Whose portals are alternate Night and Day,
    How Sultán after Sultán with his Pomp
Abode his destin'd Hour, and went his way.

They say the Lion and the Lizard keep
The Courts where Jamshyd gloried and drank deep;
    And Bahrám, that great Hunter—the Wild Ass
Stamps o'er his Head, but cannot break his Sleep.

I sometimes think that never blows so red
The Rose as where some buried Caesar bled;
    That every Hyacinth the Garden wears
Dropt in her Lap from some once lovely Head.

And this reviving Herb whose tender Green
Fledges the River-Lip on which we lean—
    Ah, lean upon it lightly! for who knows
From what once lovely lip it springs unseen!

Ah, my Belovéd, fill the Cup that clears
To-Day of past Regret and future Fears:
   To-morrow!—Why, To-morrow I may be
Myself with Yesterday's Sev'n thousand Years.

For some we loved, the loveliest and the best
That from his Vintage rolling Time has prest,
   Have drunk their Cup a Round or two before,
And one by one crept silently to rest.

And we, that now make merry in the Room
They left, and Summer dresses in new bloom,
   Ourselves must we beneath the Couch of Earth
Descend—ourselves to make a Couch—for whom!

Ah, make the most of what we yet may spend,
Before we too into the Dust descend;
   Dust into Dust, and under Dust, to lie,
Sans Wine, sans Song, sans Singer, and—sans End!

Alike for those who for To-Day prepare,
And those that after some To-Morrow stare,
   A Muezzín from the Tower of Darkness cries,
"Fools! your reward is neither Here nor There."

Why, all the Saints and Sages who discuss'd
Of the Two Worlds so learnedly are thrust
   Like foolish Prophets forth; their Words to Scorn
Are scatter'd, and their Mouths are stopt with Dust.

Myself when young did eagerly frequent
Doctor and Saint, and heard great argument
   About it and about: but evermore
Came out by that same door where in I went.

With them the seed of Wisdom did I sow,
And with my own hand wrought to make it grow;
   And this was all the Harvest that I reap'd—
"I came like Water, and like Wind I go."

Into this Universe, and *Why* not knowing,
Nor *Whence*, like Water willy-nilly flowing;
   And out of it, as Wind along the Waste,
I know not *Whither*, willy-nilly blowing.

What, without asking, hither hurried *Whence?*
And, without asking, *Whither* hurried hence!
   Oh, many a Cup of this forbidden Wine
Must drown the memory of that insolence!

Up from Earth's Centre through the Seventh Gate
I rose, and on the Throne of Saturn sate,
   And many a Knot unravel'd by the Road;
But not the Master-knot of Human Fate.

There was the Door to which I found no Key;
There was the Veil through which I could not see:
   Some little talk awhile of Me and Thee
There was—and then no more of Thee and Me.

Earth could not answer; nor the Seas that mourn
In flowing Purple, of their Lord forlorn;
   Nor rolling Heaven, with all his Signs reveal'd
And hidden by the sleeve of Night and Morn.

Then of the Thee in Me who works behind
The Veil, I lifted up my hands to find
   A Lamp amid the Darkness; and I heard,
As from Without—"The Me Within Thee Blind!"

Then, to the Lip of this poor earthen Urn
I lean'd, the Secret of my Life to learn:
   And Lip to Lip it murmur'd—"While you live,
Drink!—for, once dead, you never shall return."

I think the Vessel, that with fugitive
Articulation answer'd, once did live
   And drink: and Ah! the passive Lip I kiss'd
How many Kisses might it take—and give!

For I remember stopping by the way
To watch a Potter thumping his wet Clay,
　　And with its all-obliterated Tongue
It murmur'd—"Gently, Brother, gently, pray!"

And has not such a Story from of Old
Down Man's successive generations roll'd
　　Of such a clod of saturated Earth
Cast by the Maker into Human Mould?

And not a drop that from our Cups we throw
For Earth to drink of, but may steal below
　　To quench the fire of Anguish in some Eye
There hidden—far beneath, and long ago.

As then the Tulip for her morning sup
Of Heav'nly Vintage from the soil looks up,
　　Do you devoutly do the like, till Heav'n
To Earth invert you—like an empty Cup.

Perplext no more with Human or Divine,
To-morrow's tangle to the winds resign,
　　And lose your fingers in the tresses of
The Cypress-slender Minister of Wine.

And if the Wine you drink, the Lip you press,
End in what All begins and ends in—Yes:
　　Think then you are To-Day what Yesterday
You were—To-Morrow you shall not be less.

So when that Angel of the darker Drink
At last shall find you by the river-brink,
　　And, offering his Cup, invite your Soul
Forth to your Lips to quaff—you shall not shrink.

Why, if the Soul can fling the Dust aside,
And naked on the Air of Heaven ride,
　　Were't not a Shame—were't not a Shame for him
In this clay carcase crippled to abide?

'Tis but a Tent where takes his one day's rest
A Sultán to the realm of Death addrest;
    The Sultán rises, and the dark Ferrásh
Strikes, and prepares it for another Guest.

And fear not lest Existence closing your
Account, and mine, should know the like no more;
    The Eternal Sáki from that Bowl has pour'd
Millions of Bubbles like us, and will pour.

When You and I behind the Veil are past,
Oh, but the long, long while the World shall last,
    Which of our Coming and Departure heeds
As the Sea's self should heed a pebble-cast.

A Moment's Halt—a momentary taste
Of Being from the Well amid the Waste—
    And Lo!—the phantom Caravan has reach'd
The Nothing it set out from—Oh, make haste!

Would you that spangle of Existence spend
About The Secret—quick about it, Friend!
    A Hair perhaps divides the False and True—
And upon what, prithee, may life depend?

A Hair perhaps divides the False and True-
Yes; and a single Alif were the clue—
    Could you but find it—to the Treasure-house,
And peradventure to The Master too;

Whose secret Presence, through Creation's veins
Running Quicksilver-like eludes your pains;
    Taking all shapes from Máh to Máhi; and
They change and perish all—but He remains;

A moment guess'd—then back behind the Fold
Immerst of Darkness round the Drama roll'd
    Which, for the Pastime of Eternity,
He doth Himself contrive, enact, behold.

But if in vain, down on the stubborn floor
Of Earth, and up to Heav'n's unopening Door,
   You gaze To-Day, while You are You—how then
To-Morrow, You when shall be You no more?

Waste not your hour, nor in the vain pursuit
Of This and That endeavour and dispute;
   Better be jocund with the fruitful Grape
Than sadden after none, or bitter, Fruit.

You know, my Friends, with what a brave Carouse
I made a Second Marriage in my house;
   Divorced old barren Reason from my Bed,
And took the Daughter of the Vine to Spouse.

For "Is" and "Is-Not" though with Rule and Line
And "Up-And-Down" by Logic I define,
   Of all that one should care to fathom, I
Was never deep in anything but—Wine.

Ah, but my Computations, People say,
Reduced the Year to better Reckoning? Nay,
   'Twas only striking from the Calendar
Unborn To-morrow and dead Yesterday.

And lately, by the Tavern Door agape,
Came shining through the Dusk an Angel Shape
   Bearing a Vessel on his Shoulder; and
He bid me taste of it; and 'twas—the Grape!

The Grape that can with Logic absolute
The Two-and-Seventy jarring Sects confute:
   The Sovereign Alchemist that in a trice
Life's leaden metal into Gold transmute:

The mighty Mahmúd, Allah-breathing Lord,
That all the misbelieving and black Horde
   Of Fears and Sorrows that infest the Soul
Scatters before him with his whirlwind Sword.

Why, be this Juice the Growth of God, who dare
Blaspheme the twisted tendril as a Snare?
    A Blessing, we should use it, should we not?
And if a Curse—why, then, Who set it there?

I must abjure the Balm of Life, I must,
Scared by some After-reckoning ta'en on trust,
    Or lured with Hope of some Diviner Drink,
To fill the Cup—when crumbled into Dust!

Oh threats of Hell and Hopes of Paradise!
One thing at least is certain—*This* Life flies;
    One thing is certain and the rest is Lies;
The Flower that once has blown for ever dies.

Strange, is it not? that of the myriads who
Before us pass'd the door of Darkness through,
    Not one returns to tell us of the Road,
Which to discover we must travel too.

The Revelations of Devout and Learn'd
Who rose before us, and as Prophets burn'd,
    Are all but Stories, which, awoke from Sleep
They told their comrades, and to Sleep return'd.

I sent my Soul through the Invisible.
Some letter of the After-life to spell:
    And by and by my Soul return'd to me,
And answer'd "I Myself am Heav'n and Hell:"

Heav'n but the Vision of fulfill'd Desire,
And Hell the Shadow from a Soul on fire,
    Cast on the Darkness into which Ourselves,
So late emerged from, shall so soon expire.

We are no other than a moving row
Of Magic Shadow-shapes that come and go
    Round with the Sun-illumined Lantern held
In Midnight by the Master of the Show;

But helpless Pieces of the Game He plays
Upon this Chequer-board of Nights and Days;
   Hither and thither moves, and checks, and slays,
And one by one back in the Closet lays.

The Ball no question makes of Ayes and Noes,
But Here or There as strikes the Player goes;
   And He that toss'd you down into the Field,
He knows about it all—HE knows—HE knows!

The Moving Finger writes; and, having writ,
Moves on: nor all your Piety nor Wit
   Shall lure it back to cancel half a Line,
Nor all your Tears wash out a Word of it.

And that inverted Bowl they call the Sky,
Whereunder crawling coop'd we live and die,
   Lift not your hands to *It* for help—for It
As impotently moves as you or I.

With Earth's first Clay They did the Last Man knead,
And there of the Last Harvest sow'd the Seed:
   And the first Morning of Creation wrote
What the Last Dawn of Reckoning shall read.

Yesterday *This* Day's Madness did prepare;
To-Morrow's Silence, Triumph, or Despair:
   Drink! for you know not whence you came, nor why:
Drink! for you know not why you go, nor where.

I tell you this—When, started from the Goal,
Over the flaming shoulders of the Foal
   Of Heav'n Parwín and Mushtarí they flung,
In my predestined Plot of Dust and Soul

The Vine had struck a fibre: which about
If clings my being—let the Dervish flout;
   Of my Base metal may be filed a Key
That shall unlock the Door he howls without.

And this I know: whether the one True Light
Kindle to Love, or Wrath-consume me quite,
    One Flash of It within the Tavern caught
Better than in the Temple lost outright.

What! out of Senseless Nothing to provoke
A conscious Something to resent the yoke
    Of unpermitted Pleasure, under pain
Of Everlasting Penalties, if broke!

What! from his helpless Creature be repaid
Pure Gold for what he lent him dross-allay'd—
    Sue for a Debt he never did contract,
And cannot answer—Oh the sorry trade!

Oh Thou, who didst with pitfall and with gin
Beset the Road I was to wander in,
    Thou wilt not with Predestined Evil round
Enmesh, and then impute my Fall to Sin!

Oh Thou, who Man of baser Earth didst make,
And ev'n with Paradise devise the Snake:
    For all the Sin wherewith the Face of Man
Is blacken'd—Man's forgiveness give—and take!

*   *   *   *   *   *

As under cover of departing Day
Slunk hunger-stricken Ramazán away,
    Once more within the Potter's house alone
I stood, surrounded by the Shapes of Clay.

Shapes of all Sorts and Sizes, great and small,
That stood along the floor and by the wall;
    And some loquacious Vessels were; and some
Listen'd perhaps, but never talk'd at all.

Said one among them—"Surely not in vain
My substance of the common Earth was ta'en
    And to this Figure moulded, to be broke,
Or trampled back to shapeless Earth again."

Then said a Second—"Ne'er a peevish Boy
Would break the Bowl from which he drank in joy;
    And He that with his hand the Vessel made
Will surely not in after Wrath destroy."

After a momentary silence spake
Some Vessel of a more ungainly Make;
    "They sneer at me for leaning all awry;
What! did the Hand then of the Potter shake?"

Whereat some one of the loquacious Lot—
I think a Súfi pipkin—waxing hot—
    "All this of Pot and Potter—Tell me then,
Who is the Potter, pray, and who the Pot?"

"Why," said another, "Some there are who tell
Of one who threatens he will toss to Hell
    The luckless Pots he marr'd in making—Pish!
He's a Good Fellow, and 'twill all be well."

"Well," murmur'd one, "Let whoso make or buy,
My Clay with long Oblivion is gone dry:
    But fill me with the old familiar Juice,
Methinks I might recover by and by."

So while the Vessels one by one were speaking,
The little Moon look'd in that all were seeking:
    And then they jogg'd each other, "Brother, Brother!
Now for the Porter's shoulder-knot a-creaking!"

        *   *   *   *   *   *

Ah, with the Grape my fading Life provide,
And wash the Body whence the Life has died,
    And lay me, shrouded in the living Leaf,
By some not unfrequented Garden-side.

That ev'n my buried Ashes such a snare
Of Vintage shall fling up into the Air
    As not a True-believer passing by
But shall be overtaken unaware.

Indeed the Idols I have loved so long
Have done my credit in this World much wrong:
    Have drown'd my Glory in a shallow Cup,
And sold my Reputation for a Song.

Indeed, indeed, Repentance oft before
I swore—but was I sober when I swore?
    And then and then came Spring, and Rose-in-hand
My thread-bare Penitence apieces tore.

And much as Wine has played the Infidel,
And robb'd me of my Robe of Honour—Well,
    I wonder often what the Vintners buy
One half so precious as the stuff they sell.

Yet Ah, that Spring should vanish with the Rose!
That Youth's sweet-scented manuscript should close!
    The Nightingale that in the branches sang,
Ah whence, and whither flown again, who knows!

Would but the Desert of the Fountain yield
One glimpse—if dimly, yet indeed, reveal'd,
    To which the fainting Traveller might spring,
As springs the trampled herbage of the field!

Would but some wingéd Angel ere too late
Arrest the yet unfolded Roll of Fate,
    And make the stern Recorder otherwise
Enregister, or quite obliterate!

Ah Love! could you and I with Him conspire
To grasp this sorry Scheme of Things entire,
    Would not we shatter it to bits—and then
Re-mould it nearer to the Heart's Desire!

    ✿   ✿   ✿   ✿   ✿   ✿

Yon rising Moon that looks for us again—
How oft hereafter will she wax and wane;
    How oft hereafter rising look for us
Through this same Garden—and for *one* in vain!

And when like her, oh Sáki, you shall pass
Among the Guests Star-scatter'd on the Grass,
    And in your joyous errand reach the spot
Where I made One—turn down an empty Glass!

Tamám

ALFRED TENNYSON, LORD TENNYSON

(1809–1892)

Mariana

Mariana in the moated grange.
Measure for Measure

With blackest moss the flower-plots
    Were thickly crusted, one and all:
The rusted nails fell from the knots
    That held the pear to the gable-wall.
The broken sheds looked sad and strange:
    Unlifted was the clinking latch;
    Weeded and worn the ancient thatch
Upon the lonely moated grange.
    She only said, "My life is dreary,
        He cometh not," she said;
    She said, "I am aweary, aweary,
        I would that I were dead!"

Her tears fell with the dews at even;
    Her tears fell ere the dews were dried;
She could not look on the sweet heaven,
    Either at morn or eventide.
After the flitting of the bats,
    When thickest dark did trance the sky,
    She drew her casement-curtain by,
And glanced athwart the glooming flats.
    She only said, "The night is dreary,
        He cometh not," she said;
    She said, "I am aweary, aweary,
        I would that I were dead!"

Upon the middle of the night,
  Waking she heard the night-fowl crow;
The cock sung out an hour ere light:
  From the dark fen the oxen's low
Came to her: without hope of change,
  In sleep she seemed to walk forlorn,
  Till cold winds woke the gray-eyed morn
About the lonely moated grange.
  She only said, "The day is dreary,
    He cometh not," she said;
  She said, "I am aweary, aweary,
    I would that I were dead!"

About a stone-cast from the wall
  A sluice with blackened waters slept,
And o'er it many, round and small,
  The clustered marish-mosses crept.
Hard by a poplar shook alway,
  All silver-green with gnarléd bark:
  For leagues no other tree did mark
The level waste, the rounding gray.
  She only said, "My life is dreary,
    He cometh not," she said;
  She said, "I am aweary, aweary,
    I would that I were dead!"

And ever when the moon was low,
  And the shrill winds were up and away,
In the white curtain, to and fro,
  She saw the gusty shadow sway.
But when the moon was very low,
  And wild winds bound within their cell,
  The shadow of the poplar fell
Upon her bed, across her brow.
  She only said, "The night is dreary,
    He cometh not," she said;
  She said, "I am aweary, aweary,
    I would that I were dead!"

All day within the dreamy house,
  The doors upon their hinges creaked;

The blue fly sung in the pane; the mouse
   Behind the mouldering wainscot shrieked,
Or from the crevice peered about.
   Old faces glimmered thro' the doors,
   Old footsteps trod the upper floors,
Old voices called her from without.
   She only said, "My life is dreary,
     He cometh not," she said;
   She said, "I am aweary, aweary,
     I would that I were dead!"

The sparrow's chirrup on the roof,
   The slow clock ticking, and the sound
Which to the wooing wind aloof
   The poplar made, did all confound
Her sense; but most she loathed the hour
   When the thick-moted sunbeam lay
   Athwart the chamber, and the day
Was sloping toward his western bower.
   Then, said she, "I am very dreary,
     He will not come," she said;
   She wept, "I am aweary, aweary,
     Oh God, that I were dead!"

Choric Song of the Lotos-Eaters

There is sweet music here that softer falls
Than petals from blown roses on the grass,
Or night-dews on still waters between walls
Of shadowy granite, in a gleaming pass;
Music that gentlier on the spirit lies
Than tired eyelids upon tired eyes;
Music that brings sweet sleep down from the blissful skies.
Here are cool mosses deep,
And through the moss the ivies creep,
And in the stream the long-leaved flowers weep,
And from the craggy ledge the poppy hangs in sleep.

Why are we weighed upon with heaviness,
And utterly consumed with sharp distress,
While all things else have rest from weariness?
All things have rest: why should we toil alone,
We only toil, who are the first of things,
And make perpetual moan,
Still from one sorrow to another thrown;
Nor ever fold our wings,
And cease from wanderings,
Nor steep our brows in slumber's holy balm;
Nor hearken what the inner spirit sings,
"There is no joy but calm!"—
Why should we only toil, the roof and crown of things?

Lo! in the middle of the wood,
The folded leaf is wooed from out the bud
With winds upon the branch, and there
Grows green and broad, and takes no care,
Sun-steeped at noon, and in the moon
Nightly dew-fed; and turning yellow
Falls, and floats adown the air.
Lo! sweetened with the summer light,
The full-juiced apple, waxing over-mellow,
Drops in a silent autumn night.
All its allotted length of days
The flower ripens in its place,
Ripens and fades, and falls, and hath no toil,
Fast-rooted in the fruitful soil.

Hateful is the dark-blue sky,
Vaulted o'er the dark-blue sea.
Death is the end of life; ah, why
Should life all labour be?
Let us alone. Time driveth onward fast,
And in a little while our lips are dumb.
Let us alone. What is it that will last?
All things are taken from us, and become
Portions and parcels of the dreadful past.
Let us alone. What pleasure can we have
To war with evil? Is there any peace
In ever climbing up the climbing wave?

All things have rest, and ripen toward the grave
In silence—ripen, fall, and cease:
Give us long rest or death, dark death, or dreamful ease.

How sweet it were, hearing the downward stream,
With half-shut eyes ever to seem
Falling asleep in a half-dream!
To dream and dream, like yonder amber light,
Which will not leave the myrrh-bush on the height;
To hear each other's whispered speech;
Eating the Lotos day by day,
To watch the crisping ripples on the beach,
And tender curving lines of creamy spray;
To lend our hearts and spirits wholly
To the influence of mild-minded melancholy;
To muse and brood and live again in memory,
With those old faces of our infancy
Heaped over with a mound of grass,
Two handfuls of white dust, shut in an urn of brass!

Dear is the memory of our wedded lives,
And dear the last embraces of our wives
And their warm tears; but all hath suffered change;
For surely now our household hearths are cold,
Our sons inherit us, our looks are strange,
And we should come like ghosts to trouble joy.
Or else the island princes over-bold
Have eat our substance, and the minstrel sings
Before them of the ten years' war in Troy,
And our great deeds, as half-forgotten things.
Is there confusion in the little isle?
Let what is broken so remain.
The Gods are hard to reconcile;
'Tis hard to settle order once again.
There *is* confusion worse than death,
Trouble on trouble, pain on pain,
Long labour unto aged breath,
Sore task to hearts worn out by many wars
And eyes grown dim with gazing on the pilot-stars.

But, propt on beds of amaranth and moly,
How sweet—while warm airs lull us, blowing lowly—
With half-dropt eyelid still,
Beneath a heaven dark and holy,
To watch the long bright river drawing slowly
His waters from the purple hill—
To hear the dewy echoes calling
From cave to cave through the thick-twined vine—
To watch the emerald-coloured water falling
Through many a woven acanthus-wreath divine!
Only to hear and see the far-off sparkling brine,
Only to hear were sweet, stretched out beneath the pine.

The Lotos blooms below the barren peak,
The Lotos blows by every winding creek;
All day the wind breathes low with mellower tone;
Through every hollow cave and alley lone
Round and round the spicy downs the yellow Lotos-dust is
        blown.
We have had enough of action, and of motion we,
Rolled to starboard, rolled to larboard, when the surge was
        seething free,
Where the wallowing monster spouted his foam-fountains
        in the sea.

Let us swear an oath, and keep it with an equal mind,
In the hollow Lotos-land to live and lie reclined
On the hills like Gods together, careless of mankind.
For they lie beside their nectar, and the bolts are hurled
Far below them in the valleys, and the clouds are lightly
        curled
Round their golden houses, girdled with the gleaming world;
Where they smile in secret, looking over wasted lands,
Blight and famine, plague and earthquake, roaring deeps and
        fiery sands,
Clanging fights, and flaming towns, and sinking ships and
        praying hands.
But they smile, they find a music centred in a doleful song
Steaming up, a lamentation and an ancient tale of wrong,
Like a tale of little meaning though the words are strong;
Chanted from an ill-used race of men that cleave the soil,

Sow the seed, and reap the harvest with enduring toil,
Storing yearly little dues of wheat, and wine and oil;
Till they perish and they suffer—some, 'tis whispered—down
    in hell
Suffer endless anguish, others in Elysian valleys dwell,
Resting weary limbs at last on beds of asphodel.
Surely, surely, slumber is more sweet than toil, the shore
Than labour in the deep mid-ocean, wind and wave and oar;
O, rest, brother mariners, we will not wander more.

Œnone

There lies a vale in Ida, lovelier
Than all the valleys of Ionian hills.
The swimming vapour slopes athwart the glen,
Puts forth an arm, and creeps from pine to pine,
And loiters, slowly drawn. On either hand
The lawns and meadow-ledges midway down
Hang rich in flowers, and far below them roars
The long brook falling thro' the clov'n ravine
In cataract after cataract to the sea.
Behind the valley topmost Gargarus
Stands up and takes the morning: but in front
The gorges, opening wide apart, reveal
Troas and Ilion's column'd citadel,
The crown of Troas.
                Hither came at noon
Mournful Œnone, wandering forlorn
Of Paris, once her playmate on the hills.
Her cheek had lost the rose, and round her neck
Floated her hair or seemed to float in rest.
She, leaning on a fragment twined with vine,
Sang to the stillness, till the mountain-shade
Sloped downward to her seat from the upper cliff.

"O mother Ida, many-fountained Ida,
Dear mother Ida, harken ere I die.
For now the noonday quiet holds the hill:
The grasshopper is silent in the grass:
The lizard, with his shadow on the stone,

Rests like a shadow, and the winds are dead.
The purple flower droops: the golden bee
Is lily-cradled: I alone awake.
My eyes are full of tears, my heart of love,
My heart is breaking, and my eyes are dim,
And I am all aweary of my life.

"O mother Ida, many-fountained Ida,
Dear mother Ida, harken ere I die.
Hear me, O Earth, hear me, O Hills, O Caves
That house the cold crowned snake! O mountain brooks,
I am the daughter of a River-God,
Hear me, for I will speak, and build up all
My sorrow with my song, as yonder walls
Rose slowly to a music slowly breathed,
A cloud that gathered shape: for it may be
That, while I speak of it, a little while
My heart may wander from its deeper woe.

"O mother Ida, many-fountained Ida,
Dear mother Ida, harken ere I die.
I waited underneath the dawning hills,
Aloft the mountain lawn was dewy-dark,
And dewy-dark aloft the mountain-pine:
Beautiful Paris, evil-hearted Paris,
Leading a jet-black goat white-horned, white-hooved,
Came up from reedy Simois all alone.

"O mother Ida, harken ere I die.
Far off the torrent called me from the cleft:
Far up the solitary morning smote
The streaks of virgin snow. With down-dropt eyes
I sat alone: white-breasted like a star
Fronting the dawn he moved; a leopard skin
Drooped from his shoulder but his sunny hair
Clustered about his temples like a God's:
And his cheeks brightened as the foam-bow brightens
When the wind blows the foam, and all my heart
Went forth to embrace him coming ere he came.

"Dear mother Ida, harken ere I die.
He smiled, and opening out his milk-white palm
Disclosed a fruit of pure Hesperian gold,
That smelt ambrosially, and while I looked
And listened, the full-flowing river of speech
Came down upon my heart.
          " 'My own Œnone,
Beautiful-browed Œnone, my own soul,
Behold this fruit, whose gleaming rind ingrav'n
"For the most fair," would seem to award it thine,
As lovelier than whatever Oread haunt
The knolls of Ida, loveliest in all grace
Of movement, and the charm of married brows.'

"Dear mother Ida, harken ere I die.
He prest the blossom of his lips to mine,
And added 'This was cast upon the board,
When all the full-faced presence of the Gods
Ranged in the halls of Peleus; whereupon
Rose feud, with question unto whom 'twere due:
But light-foot Iris brought it yester-eve,
Delivering, that to me, by common voice
Elected umpire, Heré comes to-day,
Pallas and Aphrodité, claiming each
This meed of fairest. Thou, within the cave
Behind yon whispering tuft of oldest pine,
Mayst well behold them unbeheld, unheard
Hear all, and see thy Paris judge of Gods.'

"Dear mother Ida, harken ere I die.
It was the deep midnoon: one silvery cloud
Had lost his way between the piney sides
Of this long glen. Then to the bower they came,
Naked they came to that smooth-swarded bower,
And at their feet the crocus brake like fire,
Violet, amaracus, and asphodel,
Lotos and lilies: and a wind arose,
And overhead the wandering ivy and vine,
This way and that, in many a wild festoon
Ran riot, garlanding the gnarléd boughs
With bunch and berry and flower thro' and thro'.

"O mother Ida, harken ere I die.
On the tree-tops a crested peacock lit,
And o'er him flowed a golden cloud, and leaned
Upon him, slowly dropping fragrant dew.
Then first I heard the voice of her, to whom
Coming thro' Heaven, like a light that grows
Larger and clearer, with one mind the Gods
Rise up for reverence. She to Paris made
Proffer of royal power, ample rule
Unquestioned, overflowing revenue
Wherewith to embellish state, 'from many a vale
And river-sundered champaign clothed with corn,
Or laboured mine undrainable of ore.
Honour,' she said, 'and homage, tax and toll,
From many an inland town and haven large,
Mast-thronged beneath her shadowing citadel
In glassy bays among her tallest towers.'

"O mother Ida, harken ere I die.
Still she spake on and still she spake of power,
'Which in all action is the end of all;
Power fitted to the season; wisdom-bred
And throned of wisdom—from all neighbour crowns
Alliance and allegiance, till thy hand
Fail from the sceptre-staff. Such boon from me,
From me, Heaven's Queen, Paris, to thee king-born,
A shepherd all thy life but yet king-born,
Should come most welcome, seeing men, in power
Only, are likest gods, who have attained
Rest in a happy place and quiet seats
Above the thunder, with undying bliss
In knowledge of their own supremacy.'

"Dear mother Ida, harken ere I die.
She ceased, and Paris held the costly fruit
Out at arm's-length, so much the thought of power
Flattered his spirit; but Pallas where she stood
Somewhat apart, her clear and bared limbs
O'erthwarted with the brazen-headed spear
Upon her pearly shoulder leaning cold,

The while, above, her full and earnest eye
Over her snow-cold breast and angry cheek
Kept watch, waiting decision, made reply.

" 'Self-reverence, self-knowledge, self-control,
These three alone lead life to sovereign power.
Yet not for power (power of herself
Would come uncalled for) but to live by law,
Acting the law we live by without fear;
And, because right is right, to follow right
Were wisdom in the scorn of consequence.'

"Dear mother Ida, harken ere I die.
Again she said: 'I woo thee not with gifts.
Sequel of guerdon could not alter me
To fairer. Judge thou me by what I am
So shalt thou find me fairest.
                              Yet, indeed,
If gazing on divinity disrobed
Thy mortal eyes are frail to judge of fair,
Unbias'd by self-profit, oh! rest thee sure
That I shall love thee well and cleave to thee,
So that my vigour, wedded to thy blood,
Shall strike within thy pulses, like a God's,
To push thee forward thro' a life of shocks,
Dangers, and deeds, until endurance grow
Sinewed with action, and the full-grown will,
Circled thro' all experiences, pure law,
Commeasure perfect freedom.'
                              "Here she ceased,
And Paris pondered, and I cried, 'O Paris,
Give it to Pallas!' but he heard me not,
Or hearing would not hear me, woe is me!

"Oh mother Ida, many-fountained Ida,
Dear mother Ida, harken ere I die.
Idalian Aphrodité beautiful,
Fresh as the foam, new-bathed in Paphian wells,
With rosy slender fingers backward drew
From her warm brows and bosom her deep hair
Ambrosial, golden round her lucid throat

And shoulder: from the violets her light foot
Shone rosy-white, and o'er her rounded form
Between the shadows of the vine-bunches
Floated the glowing sunlights, as she moved.

"Dear mother Ida, harken ere I die.
She with a subtle smile in her mild eyes,
The herald of her triumph, drawing nigh
Half-whispered in his ear, 'I promise thee
The fairest and most loving wife in Greece.'
She spoke and laughed: I shut my sight for fear:
But when I looked, Paris had raised his arm,
And I beheld great Heré's angry eyes,
As she withdrew into the golden cloud,
And I was left alone within the bower;
And from that time to this I am alone,
And I shall be alone until I die.

"Yet, mother Ida, harken ere I die.
Fairest—why fairest wife? am I not fair?
My love hath told me so a thousand times.
Methinks I must be fair, for yesterday,
When I past by, a wild and wanton pard,
Eyed like the evening star, with playful tail
Crouched fawning in the weed. Most loving is she?
Ah me, my mountain shepherd, that my arms
Were wound about thee, and my hot lips prest
Close, close to thine in that quick-fallen dew
Of fruitful kisses, thick as Autumn rains
Flash in the pools of whirling Simois.

"O mother, hear me yet before I die.
They came, they cut away my tallest pines,
My tall dark pines, that plumed the craggy ledge
High over the blue gorge, and all between
The snowy peak and snow-white cataract
Fostered the callow eaglet—from beneath
Whose thick mysterious boughs in the dark morn
The panther's roar came muffled, while I sat
Low in the valley. Never, never more
Shall lone Œnone see the morning mist

Sweep thro' them; never see them overlaid
With narrow moon-lit slips of silver cloud,
Between the loud stream and the trembling stars.

"O mother, hear me yet before I die.
I wish that somewhere in the ruined folds,
Among the fragments tumbled from the glens,
Or the dry thickets, I could meet with her
The Abominable, that uninvited came
Into the fair Peleïan banquet-hall,
And cast the golden fruit upon the board,
And bred this change; that I might speak my mind,
And tell her to her face how much I hate
Her presence, hated both of Gods and men.

"O mother, hear me yet before I die.
Hath he not sworn his love a thousand times,
In this green valley, under this green hill,
Ev'n on this hand, and sitting on this stone?
Sealed it with kisses? watered it with tears?
O happy tears, and how unlike to these!
O happy Heaven, how canst thou see my face?
O happy earth, how canst thou bear my weight?
O death, death, death, thou ever-floating cloud,
There are enough unhappy on this earth,
Pass by the happy souls, that love to live:
I pray thee, pass before my light of life,
And shadow all my soul, that I may die.
Thou weighest heavy on the heart within,
Weigh heavy on my eyelids: let me die.

"O mother, hear me yet before I die.
I will not die alone, for fiery thoughts
Do shape themselves within me, more and more,
Whereof I catch the issue, as I hear
Dead sounds at night come from the inmost hills,
Like footsteps upon wool. I dimly see
My far-off doubtful purpose, as a mother
Conjectures of the features of her child
Ere it is born: her child!—a shudder comes
Across me: never child be born of me,
Unblest, to vex me with his father's eyes!

"O mother, hear me yet before I die.
Hear me, O earth. I will not die alone,
Lest their shrill happy laughter come to me
Walking the cold and starless road of death
Uncomforted, leaving my ancient love
With the Greek woman. I will rise and go
Down into Troy, and ere the stars come forth
Talk with the wild Cassandra, for she says
A fire dances before her, and a sound
Rings ever in her ears of armed men.
What this may be I know not, but I know
That, whatsoe'er I am by night and day,
All earth and air seem only burning fire."

FROM *The Princess*

1.

The splendour falls on castle walls
    And snowy summits old in story;
The long light shakes across the lakes,
    And the wild cataract leaps in glory,
Blow, bugle, blow, set the wild echoes flying,
Blow, bugle; answer, echoes, dying, dying, dying.

O hark, O hear! how thin and clear,
    And thinner, clearer, farther going!
O, sweet and far from cliff and scar
    The horns of Elfland faintly blowing!
Blow, let us hear the purple glens replying,
Blow, bugle; answer, echoes, dying, dying, dying.

O love, they die in yon rich sky,
    They faint on hill or field or river;
Our echoes roll from soul to soul,
    And grow for ever and for ever.
Blow, bugle, blow, set the wild echoes flying,
And answer, echoes, answer, dying, dying, dying.

2.

Tears, idle tears, I know not what they mean,
Tears from the depth of some divine despair
Rise in the heart, and gather to the eyes,
In looking on the happy autumn-fields,
And thinking of the days that are no more.

Fresh as the first beam glittering on a sail,
That brings our friends up from the under-world,
Sad as the last which reddens over one
That sinks with all we love below the verge;
So sad, so fresh, the days that are no more.

Ah, sad and strange as in dark summer dawns
The earliest pipe of half-awakened birds
To dying ears, when unto dying eyes
The casement slowly grows a glimmering square;
So sad, so strange, the days that are no more.

Dear as remembered kisses after death,
And sweet as those by hopeless fancy feigned
On lips that are for others; deep as love,
Deep as first love, and wild with all regret;
O Death in Life, the days that are no more!

3.

Now sleeps the crimson petal, now the white;
Nor waves the cypress in the palace walk;
Nor winks the gold fin in the porphyry font.
The fire-fly wakens; waken thou with me.

Now droops the milk-white peacock like a ghost,
And like a ghost she glimmers on to me.

Now lies the Earth all Danaë to the stars,
And all thy heart lies open unto me.

Now slides the silent meteor on, and leaves
A shining furrow, as thy thoughts in me.

Now folds the lily all her sweetness up,
And slips into the bosom of the lake.
So fold thyself, my dearest, thou, and slip
Into my bosom and be lost in me.

4.

    Come down, O maid, from yonder mountain height.
What pleasure lives in height (the shepherd sang)
In height and cold, the splendour of the hills?
But cease to move so near the heavens, and cease
To glide a sunbeam by the blasted pine,
To sit a star upon the sparkling spire;
And come, for Love is of the valley, come,
For Love is of the valley, come thou down
And find him; by the happy threshold, he,
Or hand in hand with Plenty in the maize,
Or red with spirted purple of the vats,
Or foxlike in the vine; nor cares to walk
With Death and Morning on the Silver Horns,
Nor wilt thou snare him in the white ravine,
Nor find him dropt upon the firths of ice,
That huddling slant in furrow-cloven falls
To roll the torrent out of dusky doors.
But follow; let the torrent dance thee down
To find him in the valley; let the wild
Lean-headed eagles yelp alone, and leave
The monstrous ledges there to slope, and spill
Their thousand wreaths of dangling water-smoke,
That like a broken purpose waste in air.
So waste not thou, but come; for all the vales
Await thee; azure pillars of the hearth
Arise to thee; the children call, and I
Thy shepherd pipe, and sweet is every sound,
Sweeter thy voice, but every sound is sweet;
Myriads of rivulets hurrying through the lawn,
The moan of doves in immemorial elms,
And murmuring of innumerable bees.

FROM *In Memoriam*

XXXV

Yet if some voice that man could trust
  Should murmur from the narrow house,
  "The cheeks drop in, the body bows;
Man dies, nor is there hope in dust;"

Might I not say? "Yet even here
  But for one hour, O Love, I strive
  To keep so sweet a thing alive."
But I should turn mine ears and hear

The moanings of the homeless sea,
  The sound of streams that swift or slow
  Draw down Æonian hills, and sow
The dust of continents to be;

And Love would answer with a sigh,
  "The sound of that forgetful shore
  Will change my sweetness more and more,
Half-dead to know that I shall die."

LXXXII

Dip down upon the northern shore,
  O sweet new-year delaying long;
  Thou doest expectant Nature wrong;
Delaying long, delay no more.

What stays thee from the clouded noons,
  Thy sweetness from its proper place?
  Can trouble live with April days,
Or sadness in the summer moons?

Bring orchis, bring the foxglove spire,
  The little speedwell's darling blue,
  Deep tulips dashed with fiery dew,
Laburnums, dropping-wells of fire.

O thou, new-year, delaying long,
  Delayest the sorrow in my blood,
  That longs to burst a frozen bud
And flood a fresher throat with song.

XC

When rosy plumelets tuft the larch,
  And rarely pipes the mounted thrush,
  Or underneath the barren bush
Flits by the sea-blue bird of March;

Come, wear the form by which I knew
  Thy spirit in time among thy peers;
  The hope of unaccomplished years
Be large and lucid round thy brow.

When summer's hourly-mellowing change
  May breathe, with many roses sweet,
  Upon the thousand waves of wheat
That rippled round the lowly grange.

Come; not in watches of the night,
  But where the sunbeam broodeth warm,
  Come, beauteous in thine after form,
And like a finer light in light.

CXIV

Now fades the last long streak of snow,
  Now burgeons every maze of quick
  About the flowering squares, and thick
By ashen roots the violets blow.

Now rings the woodland loud and long,
  The distance takes a lovelier hue,
  And drowned in yonder living blue
The lark becomes a sightless song.

Now dance the lights on lawn and lea,
  The flocks are whiter down the vale,
  And milkier every milky sail
On winding stream or distant sea;

Where now the seamew pipes, or dives
   In yonder greening gleam, and fly
   The happy birds, that change their sky
To build and brood, that live their lives

From land to land; and in my breast
   Spring wakens too, and my regret
   Becomes an April violet,
And buds and blossoms like the rest.

Ulysses

It little profits that an idle king,
By this still hearth, among these barren crags,
Matched with an aged wife, I mete and dole
Unequal laws unto a savage race,
That hoard, and sleep, and feed, and know not me.
I cannot rest from travel; I will drink
Life to the lees. All times I have enjoyed
Greatly, have suffered greatly, both with those
That loved me, and alone; on shore, and when
Through scudding drifts the rainy Hyades
Vext the dim sea. I am become a name;
For always roaming with a hungry heart
Much have I seen and known,—cities of men
And manners, climates, councils, governments,
Myself not least, but honoured of them all,—
And drunk delight of battle with my peers,
Far on the ringing plains of windy Troy.
I am a part of all that I have met;
Yet all experience is an arch wherethrough
Gleams that untravelled world whose margin fades
For ever and for ever when I move.
How dull it is to pause, to make an end,
To rust unburnished, not to shine in use!
As though to breathe were life! Life piled on life
Were all too little, and of one to me
Little remains; but every hour is saved
From that eternal silence, something more,

A bringer of new things; and vile it were
For some three suns to store and hoard myself,
And this gray spirit yearning in desire
To follow knowledge like a sinking star,
Beyond the utmost bound of human thought.

This is my son, mine own Telemachus,
To whom I leave the sceptre and the isle,—
Well-loved of me, discerning to fulfill
This labour, by slow prudence to make mild
A rugged people, and through soft degrees
Subdue them to the useful and the good.
Most blameless is he, centred in the sphere
Of common duties, decent not to fail
In offices of tenderness, and pay
Meet adoration to my household gods,
When I am gone. He works his work, I mine.
There lies the port; the vessel puffs her sail;
There gloom the dark, broad seas. My mariners,
Souls that have toiled and wrought, and thought with me,—
That ever with a frolic welcome took
The thunder and the sunshine, and opposed
Free hearts, free foreheads,—you and I are old;
Old age hath yet his honour and his toil.
Death closes all; but something ere the end,
Some work of noble note, may yet be done,
Not unbecoming men that strove with Gods.
The lights begin to twinkle from the rocks;
The long day wanes; the slow moon climbs; the deep
Moans round with many voices. Come, my friends,
'Tis not too late to seek a newer world.
Push off, and sitting well in order smite
The sounding furrows; for my purpose holds
To sail beyond the sunset, and the baths
Of all the western stars, until I die.
It may be that the gulfs will wash us down;
It may be we shall touch the Happy Isles,
And see the great Achilles, whom we knew.
Though much is taken, much abides; and though
We are not now that strength which in old days
Moved earth and heaven, that which we are, we are,—

One equal temper of heroic hearts,
 Made weak by time and fate, but strong in will
To strive, to seek, to find, and not to yield.

Crossing the Bar

Sunset and evening star,
 And one clear call for me!
And may there be no moaning of the bar,
 When I put out to sea,

But such a tide as moving seems asleep,
 Too full for sound and foam,
When that which drew from out the boundless deep
 Turns again home.

Twilight and evening bell,
 And after that the dark!
And may there be no sadness of farewell,
 When I embark;

For though from out our bourne of Time and Place
 The flood may bear me far,
I hope to see my Pilot face to face
 When I have crost the bar.

EDGAR ALLAN POE

(1809–1849)

The Raven

Once upon a midnight dreary, while I pondered weak and
 weary,
Over many a quaint and curious volume of forgotten lore,
While I nodded, nearly napping, suddenly there came a
 tapping,
As of someone gently rapping, rapping at my chamber door.
" 'Tis some visitor," I muttered, "tapping at my chamber door—
 Only this, and nothing more."

Ah, distinctly I remember it was in the bleak December,
And each separate dying ember wrought its ghost upon the
      floor.
Eagerly I wished the morrow;—vainly I had sought to borrow
From my books surcease of sorrow—sorrow for the lost
      Lenore—
For the rare and radiant maiden whom the angels name
      Lenore—
          Nameless here for evermore.

And the silken sad uncertain rustling of each purple curtain
Thrilled me—filled me with fantastic terrors never felt before;
So that now, to still the beating of my heart, I stood repeating,
" 'Tis some visitor entreating entrance at my chamber door—
Some late visitor entreating entrance at my chamber door;—
          This it is, and nothing more."

Presently my soul grew stronger; hesitating then no longer,
"Sir," said I, "or Madam, truly your forgiveness I implore;
But the fact is I was napping, and so gently you came rapping,
And so faintly you came tapping, tapping at my chamber door,
That I scarce was sure I heard you"—here I opened wide the
      door;—
          Darkness there, and nothing more.

Deep into the darkness peering, long I stood there, wonder-
      ing, fearing,
Doubting, dreaming dreams no mortals ever dared to dream
      before;
But the silence was unbroken, and the stillness gave no token,
And the only word there spoken was the whispered word,
      "Lenore!"
This I whispered, and an echo murmured back the word,
      "Lenore!"—
          Merely this, and nothing more.

Back into the chamber turning, all my soul within me burning,
Soon again I heard a tapping somewhat louder than before.
"Surely," said I, "surely that is something at my window
      lattice:

Let me see, then, what thereat is, and this mystery explore—
Let my heart be still a moment and this mystery explore;—
     'Tis the wind and nothing more."

Open here I flung the shutter, when, with many a flirt and
    flutter,
In there stepped a stately raven of the saintly days of yore;
Not the least obeisance made he; not a minute stopped or
    stayed he;
But, with mien of lord or lady, perched above my chamber
    door—
Perched upon a bust of Pallas just above my chamber door—
     Perched and sat, and nothing more.

Then this ebony bird beguiling my sad fancy into smiling,
By the grave and stern decorum of the countenance it wore.
"Though thy crest be shorn and shaven, thou," I said, "art
    sure no craven,
Ghastly grim and ancient raven wandering from the Nightly
    shore—
Tell me what thy lordly name is on the Night's Plutonian
    shore!"
     Quoth the Raven, "Nevermore."

Much I marvelled this ungainly fowl to hear discourse so
    plainly,
Though its answer little meaning—little relevancy bore;
For we cannot help agreeing that no living human being
Ever yet was blest with seeing bird above his chamber door—
Bird or beast upon the sculptured bust above his chamber
    door,
     With such name as "Nevermore."

But the raven, sitting lonely on the placid bust, spoke only
That one word, as if his soul in that one word he did outpour.
Nothing further then he uttered—not a feather then he
    fluttered—
Till I scarcely more than muttered, "Other friends have flown
    before,
On the morrow *he* will leave me, as my hopes have flown
    before."
     Then the bird said, "Nevermore."

Startled at the stillness broken by reply so aptly spoken,
"Doubtless," said I, "what it utters is its only stock and store,
Caught from some unhappy master whom unmerciful Disaster
Followed fast and followed faster till his songs one burden
      bore—
Till the dirges of his Hope that melancholy burden bore
          Of 'Never—nevermore'."

But the Raven still beguiling all my fancy into smiling,
Straight I wheeled a cushioned seat in front of bird, and bust
      and door;
Then upon the velvet sinking, I betook myself to linking
Fancy unto fancy, thinking what this ominous bird of yore—
What this grim, ungainly, ghastly, gaunt and ominous bird
      of yore
          Meant in croaking, "Nevermore."

This I sat engaged in guessing, but no syllable expressing
To the fowl whose fiery eyes now burned into my bosom's
      core;
This and more I sat divining, with my head at ease reclining
On the cushion's velvet lining that the lamplight gloated o'er,
But whose velvet violet lining with the lamplight gloating o'er,
          She shall press, ah, nevermore!

Then methought the air grew denser, perfumed from an
      unseen censer
Swung by Seraphim whose footfalls tinkled on the tufted
      floor.
"Wretch," I cried, "thy God hath lent thee—by these angels he
      hath sent thee
Respite—respite and nepenthe, from the memories of Lenore!
Quaff, oh quaff this kind nepenthe and forget this lost Lenore!"
          Quoth the Raven, "Nevermore."

"Prophet!" said I, "thing of evil!—prophet still, if bird or
      devil!—
Whether Tempter sent, or whether tempest tossed thee here
      ashore,
Desolate yet all undaunted, on this desert land enchanted—
On this home by horror haunted—tell me truly, I implore—

Is there—*is* there balm in Gilead?—tell me—tell me, I implore!"
       Quoth the Raven, "Nevermore."

"Prophet!" said I, "thing of evil!—prophet still, if bird or devil!
By that Heaven that bends above us—by that God we both
    adore—
Tell this soul with sorrow laden if, within the distant Aidenn,
It shall clasp a sainted maiden whom the angels name Lenore—
Clasp a rare and radiant maiden whom the angels name
    Lenore."
       Quoth the Raven, "Nevermore."

"Be that word our sign in parting, bird or fiend," I shrieked,
    upstarting-
"Get thee back into the tempest and the Night's Plutonian
    shore!
Leave no black plume as a token of that lie thy soul hath
    spoken!
Leave my loneliness unbroken! quit the bust above my door!
Take thy beak from out my heart, and thy form from off my
    door!"
       Quoth the Raven, "Nevermore."

And the Raven, never flitting, still is sitting, still is sitting
On the pallid bust of Pallas just above my chamber door;
And his eyes have all the seeming of a demon's that is
    dreaming,
And the lamplight o'er him streaming throws his shadow on
    the floor;
And my soul from out that shadow that lies floating on the
    floor
       Shall be lifted—nevermore!

Ulalume

    The skies they were ashen and sober;
      The leaves they were crispéd and sere—
      The leaves they were withering and sere;
    It was night in the lonesome October
      Of my most immemorial year;

It was hard by the dim lake of Auber,
    In the misty mid region of Weir—
It was down by the dark tarn of Auber,
    In the ghoul-haunted woodland of Weir.

Here once, through an alley Titanic,
    Of cypress, I roamed with my Soul—
    Of cypress, with Psyche, my Soul.
These were days when my heart was volcanic
    As the scoriac rivers that roll—
    As the lavas that restlessly roll
Their sulphurous currents down Yaanek
    In the ultimate climes of the pole—
That groan as they roll down Mount Yaanek
    In the realms of the boreal pole.

Our talk had been serious and sober,
    But our thoughts they were palsied and sere—
    Our memories were treacherous and sere—
For we knew not the month was October,
    And we marked not the night of the year—
    (Ah, night of all nights in the year!)
We noted not the dim lake of Auber—
    (Though once we had journeyed down here),
Remembered not the dark tarn of Auber,
    Nor the ghoul-haunted woodland of Weir.

And now, as the night was senescent,
    And star-dials pointed to morn—
    As the star-dials hinted of morn—
At the end of our path a liquescent
    And nebulous lustre was born,
Out of which a miraculous crescent
    Arose with a duplicate horn—
Astarte's bediamonded crescent
    Distinct with its duplicate horn.

And I said—"She is warmer than Dian:
    She rolls through an ether of sighs—
    She revels in a region of sighs:

She has seen that the tears are not dry on
   These cheeks, where the worm never dies,
And has come past the stars of the Lion
   To point out the path to the skies—
   To the Lethean peace of the skies—
Come up, in despite of the Lion,
   To shine on us with her bright eyes—
Come up through the lair of the Lion,
   With love in her luminous eyes."

But Psyche, uplifting her finger,
   Said—"Sadly this star I mistrust—
   Her pallor I strangely mistrust:—
Oh hasten!—oh, let us not linger!
   Oh, fly!—let us fly!—for we must."
In terror she spoke, letting sink her
   Wings until they trailed in the dust—
In agony sobbed, letting sink her
   Plumes till they trailed in the dust—
   Till they sorrowfully trailed in the dust.

I replied—"This is nothing but dreaming:
   Let us on by this tremulous light!
   Let us bathe in this crystalline light!
Its Sibyllic splendour is beaming
   With Hope and in Beauty to-night:—
   See!—it flickers up the sky through the night!
Ah, we safely may trust to its gleaming,
   And be sure it will lead us aright—
We safely may trust to a gleaming
   That cannot but guide us aright,
   Since it flickers up to Heaven through the night."

Thus I pacified Psyche and kissed her,
   And tempted her out of her gloom—
   And conquered her scruples and gloom;
And we passed to the end of the vista,
   But were stopped by the door of a tomb—
   By the door of a legended tomb;

And I said—"What is written, sweet sister,
  On the door of this legended tomb?"
She replied—"Ulalume—Ulalume—
  'Tis the vault of thy lost Ulalume!"

Then my heart it grew ashen and sober
  As the leaves that were crispéd and sere—
  As the leaves that were withering and sere,
And I cried—"It was surely October
  On *this* very night of last year
  That I journeyed—I journeyed down here—
  That I brought a dread burden down here—
  On this night of all nights in the year,
  Ah, what demon has tempted me here?
Well I know, now, this dim lake of Auber—
  This misty mid region of Weir—
Well I know, now, this dank tarn of Auber,
  This ghoul-haunted woodland of Weir."

The Valley of Unrest

Once it smiled a silent dell
Where the people did not dwell;
They had gone unto the wars,
Trusting to the mild-eyed stars,
Nightly, from their azure towers,
To keep watch above the flowers,
In the midst of which all day
The red sunlight lazily lay.
Now each visitor shall confess
The sad valley's restlessness.
Nothing there is motionless—
Nothing save the airs that brood
Over the magic solitude.
Ah, by no wind are stirred those trees
That palpitate like the chill seas
Around the misty Hebrides!
Ah, by no wind those clouds are driven
That rustle through the unquiet Heaven
Uneasily, from morn till even,

Over the violets there that lie
In myriad types of the human eye—
Over the lilies there that wave
And weep above a nameless grave!
They wave:—from out their fragrant tops
Eternal dews come down in drops.
They weep:—from off their delicate stems
Perennial tears descend in gems.

The City in the Sea

Lo! Death has reared himself a throne
In a strange city lying alone
Far down within the dim West,
Where the good and the bad and the worst and the best
Have gone to their eternal rest.
There shrines and palaces and towers
(Time-eaten towers that tremble not!)
Resemble nothing that is ours.
Around, by lifting winds forgot,
Resignedly beneath the sky
The melancholy waters lie.

No rays from the holy heaven come down
On the long night-time of that town:
But light from out the lurid sea
Streams up the turrets silently—
Gleams up the pinnacles far and free—
Up domes—up spires—up kingly halls—
Up fanes—up Babylon-like walls—
Up shadowy long-forgotten bowers
Of sculptured ivy and stone flowers—
Up many and many a marvellous shrine
Whose wreathéd friezes intertwine
The viol, the violet, and the vine.
Resignedly beneath the sky
The melancholy waters lie.
So blend the turrets and shadows there
That all seem pendulous in air,
While from a proud tower in the town
Death looks gigantically down.

There open fanes and gaping graves
Yawn level with the luminous waves;
But not the riches there that lie
In each idol's diamond eye—
Not the gaily-jewelled dead
Tempt the waters from their bed;
For no ripples curl, alas!
Along that wilderness of glass—
No swellings tell that winds may be
Upon some far-off happier sea—
No heavings hint that winds have been
On seas less hideously serene.

But lo, a stir is in the air!
The wave—there is a movement there!
As if the towers had thrust aside,
In slightly sinking, the dull tide—
As if their tops had feebly given
A void within the filmy Heaven.
The waves have now a redder glow—
The hours are breathing faint and low—
And when, amid no earthly moans,
Down, down that town shall settle hence,
Hell, rising from a thousand thrones,
Shall do it reverence.

To One in Paradise

Thou wast all that to me, love,
    For which my soul did pine—
A green isle in the sea, love,
    A fountain and a shrine,
All wreathed with fairy fruits and flowers,
    And all the flowers were mine.

Ah, dream too bright to last!
    Ah, starry Hope! that didst arise
But to be overcast!

A voice from out the Future cries,
"On! on!"—but o'er the Past
  (Dim gulf!) my spirit hovering lies
Mute, motionless, aghast!

For, alas! alas! with me
  The light of Life is o'er!
  "No more—no more—no more—"
(Such language holds the solemn sea
  To the sands upon the shore)
Shall bloom the thunder-blasted tree
  Or the stricken eagle soar!

And all my days are trances,
  And all my nightly dreams
Are where thy grey eye glances,
  And where thy footstep gleams—
In what ethereal dances,
  By what eternal streams.

The Haunted Palace

In the greenest of our valleys
  By good angels tenanted,
Once a fair and stately palace—
  Radiant palace—reared its head.
In the monarch Thought's dominion—
  It stood there!
Never seraph spread a pinion
  Over fabric half so fair!

Banners yellow, glorious, golden,
  On its roof did float and flow,
(This—all this—was in the olden
  Time long ago,)

And every gentle air that dallied,
    In that sweet day,
Along the ramparts plumed and pallid,
    A wingéd odour went away.

Wanderers in that happy valley,
    Through two luminous windows, saw
Spirits moving musically,
    To a lute's well-tunéd law,
Round about a throne where, sitting
    (Porphyrogene!)
In state his glory well-befitting,
    The ruler of the realm was seen.

And all with pearl and ruby glowing
    Was the fair palace door,
Through which came flowing, flowing, flowing,
    And sparkling evermore,
A troop of Echoes, whose sweet duty
    Was but to sing,
In voices of surpassing beauty,
    The wit and wisdom of their king.

But evil things, in robes of sorrow,
    Assailed the monarch's high estate.
(Ah, let us mourn!—for never morrow
    Shall dawn upon him desolate!)
And round about his home the glory
    That blushed and bloomed,
Is but a dim-remembered story
    Of the old time entombed.

And travellers, now, within that valley,
    Through the red-litten windows see
Vast forms, that move fantastically
    To a discordant melody,
While, like a ghastly rapid river,
    Through the pale door
A hideous throng rush out forever
    And laugh—but smile no more.

Annabel Lee

It was many and many a year ago,
    In a kingdom by the sea,
That a maiden there lived whom you may know
    By the name of ANNABEL LEE;
And this maiden she lived with no other thought
    Than to love and be loved by me.

I was a child and *she* was a child,
    In this kingdom by the sea;
But we loved with a love which was more than love—
    I and my Annabel Lee;
With a love that the wingéd seraphs of heaven
    Coveted her and me.

And this was the reason that, long ago,
    In this kingdom by the sea,
A wind blew out of a cloud, chilling
    My beautiful Annabel Lee;
So that her highborn kinsmen came
    And bore her away from me,
To shut her up in a sepulchre
    In this kingdom by the sea.

The angels, not half so happy in heaven,
    Went envying her and me—
Yes!—that was the reason (as all men know,
    In this kingdom by the sea)
That the wind came out of the cloud by night,
    Chilling and killing my Annabel Lee.

But our love it was stronger by far than the love
    Of those who were older than we—
    Of many far wiser than we—
And neither the angels in heaven above,
    Nor the demons down under the sea,
Can ever dissever my soul from the soul
    Of the beautiful Annabel Lee.

For the moon never beams without bringing me dreams
  Of the beautiful Annabel Lee;
And the stars never rise but I feel the bright eyes
  Of the beautiful Annabel Lee;
And so, all the night-tide, I lie down by the side
Of my darling—my darling—my life and my bride,
  In the sepulchre there by the sea,
  In her tomb by the sounding sea.

To Helen

Helen, thy beauty is to me
  Like those Nicaean barks of yore,
That gently o'er a perfumed sea,
  The weary, wayworn wanderer bore
  To his own native shore.

On desperate seas long wont to roam,
  Thy hyacinth hair, thy classic face,
Thy Naiad airs have brought me home
  To the glory that was Greece
  And the grandeur that was Rome.

Lo! in yon brilliant window-niche
  How statue-like I see thee stand,
The agate lamp within thy hand!
  Ah, Psyche, from the regions which
  Are Holy Land!

WILLIAM MAKEPEACE THACKERAY

(1811–1863)

FROM *The Chronicle of the Drum*

Ah, gentle, tender lady mine!
  The winter wind blows cold and shrill;
Come, fill me one more glass of wine,
  And give the silly fools their will.

And what care we for war and wrack,
 And kings and heroes rise and fall?
Look yonder, in his coffin black,
 There lies the greatest of them all.

To pluck him down, and keep him up,
 Died many million human souls.—
'Tis twelve o'clock and time to sup:
 Bid Mary heap the fire with coals.

He captured many thousand guns;
 He wrote "The Great" before his name;
And dying, only left his sons
 The recollection of his shame.

Though more than half the world was his,
 He died without a rood his own;
And borrowed from his enemies
 Six foot of ground to lie upon.

He fought a thousand glorious wars,
 And more than half the world was his,
And somewhere now, in yonder stars,
 Can tell, mayhap, what greatness is.

The Ballad of Bouillabaisse

A street there is in Paris famous,
 For which no rhyme our language yields,
Rue Neuve des Petits Champs its name is—
 The New Street of the Little Fields.
And here's an inn, not rich and splendid,
 But still in comfortable case;
The which in youth I oft attended,
 To eat a bowl of Bouillabaisse.

This Bouillabaisse a noble dish is—
 A sort of soup or broth, or brew,
Or hotchpotch of all sorts of fishes,
 That Greenwich never could outdo;

Green herbs, red peppers, mussels, saffron,
 Soles, onions, garlic, roach, and dace:
All these you eat at Terré's tavern,
 In that one dish of Bouillabaisse.

Indeed, a rich and savoury stew 'tis;
 And true philosophers, methinks,
Who love all sorts of natural beauties,
 Should love good victuals and good drinks.
And Cordelier or Benedictine
 Might gladly, sure, his lot embrace,
Nor find a fast-day too afflicting,
 Which served him up a Bouillabaisse.

I wonder if the house still there is?
 Yes, here the lamp is, as before;
The smiling red-cheeked *écaillère* is
 Still opening oysters at the door.
Is Terré still alive and able?
 I recollect his droll grimace:
He'd come and sit before your table,
 And hope you liked your Bouillabaisse.

We enter—nothing's changed or older.
 "How's Monsieur Terré, waiter, pray?"
The waiter stares and shrugs his shoulder—
 "Monsieur is dead this many a day."
"It is the lot of saint and sinner,
 So honest Terré's run his race."
"What will Monsieur require for dinner?"
 "Say, do you still cook Bouillabaisse?"

"Oh, oui, Monsieur," 's the waiter's answer;
 "Quel vin Monsieur désire-t-il?"
"Tell me a good one."—"That I can, Sir;
 The Chambertin with yellow seal."
"So Terré's gone," I say, and sink in
 My old accustomed corner-place;
"He's done with feasting and with drinking,
 With Burgundy and Bouillabaisse."

My old accustomed corner here is,
   The table still is in the nook;
Ah! vanished many a busy year is
   This well-known chair since last I took.
When first I saw ye, *cari luoghi,*
   I'd scarce a beard upon my face,
And now a grizzled, grim old fogy,
   I sit and wait for Bouillabaisse.

Where are you, old companions trusty
   Of early days here met to dine?
Come, waiter! quick, a flagon crusty—
   I'll pledge them in the good old wine.
The kind old voices and old faces
   My memory can quick retrace;
Around the board they take their places,
   And share the wine and Bouillabaisse.

There's Jack has made a wondrous marriage;
   There's laughing Tom is laughing yet;
There's brave Augustus drives his carriage;
   There's poor old Fred in the *Gazette;*
On James's head the grass is growing:
   Good Lord! the world has wagged apace
Since here we set the claret flowing,
   And drank, and ate the Bouillabaisse.

Ah me! how quick the days are flitting!
   I mind me of a time that's gone,
When here I'd sit, as now I'm sitting,
   In this same place—but not alone.
A fair young form was nestled near me,
   A dear, dear face looked fondly up,
And sweetly spoke and smiled to cheer me
   —There's no one now to share my cup.

I drink it as the Fates ordain it.
   Come, fill it, and have done with rhymes:
Fill up the lonely glass, and drain it
   In memory of dear old times.

Welcome the wine, whate'er the seal is;
　And sit you down, and say your grace
With thankful heart, whate'er the meal is.
　Here comes the smoking Bouillabaisse!

ROBERT HINCKLEY MESSINGER

(1811–1874)

A Winter Wish

Old wine to drink!
　Ay, give the slippery juice
That drippeth from the grape thrown loose
　Within the tun;
Plucked from beneath the cliff
Of sunny-sided Teneriffe,
　And ripened 'neath the blink
　　Of India's sun!
Tempered with well-boiled water!
　Peat whiskey hot,
These make the long night shorter—
　Forgetting not
Good stout old English porter.

Old wood to burn!
Ay, bring the hill-side beech
From where the owlets meet and screech,
　And ravens croak;
The crackling pine, and cedar sweet;
Bring too a clump of fragrant peat,
　Dug 'neath the fern;
　　The knotted oak,
　　A fagot too, perhaps,
Whose bright flame, dancing, winking,
Shall light us at our drinking;
　While the oozing sap
Shall make sweet music to our thinking.

Old books to read!
Ay, bring those nodes of wit,
The brazen-clasped, the vellum writ,
　Time-honored tomes!

The same my sire scanned before,
The same my grandsire thumbéd o'er,
The same his sire from college bore,
    The well-earned meed
        Of Oxford's domes:
        Old Homer blind,
Old Horace, rake Anacreon, by
Old Tully, Plautus, Terence lie;
Mort Arthur's olden minstrelsie,
Quaint Burton, quainter Spenser, ay!
And Gervase Markham's venerie—
    Nor leave behind
The holye Book by which we live and die.

Old friends to talk!
Ay, bring those chosen few,
The wise, the courtly, and the true,
    So rarely found;
Him for my wine, him for my stud,
Him for my easel, distich, bud
    In mountain walk!
        Bring Walter good,
With soulful Fred, and learned Will,
And thee, my alter ego (dearer still
    For every mood).

These add a bouquet to my wine!
These add a sparkle to my pine!
    If these I tine,
Can books, or fire, or wine be good?

ROBERT BROWNING

(1812–1889)

Song

Give her but a least excuse to love me!
When—where—
How—can this arm establish her above me,
If fortune fixed her as my lady there,

There already, to eternally reprove me?
  ("Hist!"—said Kate the Queen;
  But "Oh!"—cried the maiden, binding her tresses,
  " 'Tis only a page that carols unseen,
  Crumbling your hounds their messes!")

Is she wronged?—To the rescue of her honour,
My heart!
Is she poor?—What costs it to be styled a donor?
Merely an earth to cleave, a sea to part.
But that fortune should have thrust all this upon her!
  ("Nay, list!"—bade Kate the Queen;
  And still cried the maiden, binding her tresses,
  " 'Tis only a page that carols unseen,
  Fitting your hawks their jesses!")

Pippa Passes

The Lost Leader

Just for a handful of silver he left us,
  Just for a riband to stick in his coat—
Found the one gift of which fortune bereft us,
  Lost all the others she lets us devote;
They, with the gold to give, doled him out silver,
  So much was theirs who so little allowed:
How all our copper had gone for his service!
  Rags—were they purple, his heart had been proud!
We that had loved him so, followed him, honoured him,
  Lived in his mild and magnificent eye,
Learned his great language, caught his clear accents,
  Made him our pattern to live and to die!
Shakespeare was of us, Milton was for us,
  Burns, Shelley, were with us,—they watch from their graves!
He alone breaks from the van and the freemen,
  —He alone sinks to the rear and the slaves!

We shall march prospering,—not through his presence;
  Songs may inspirit us,—not from his lyre;
Deeds will be done,—while he boasts his quiescence,
  Still bidding crouch whom the rest bade aspire:

Blot out his name, then, record one lost soul more,
   One task more declined, one more foot-path untrod,
One more devils'-triumph and sorrow for angels,
   One wrong more to man, one more insult to God!
Life's night begins: let him never come back to us!
   There would be doubt, hesitation, and pain,
Forced praise on our part—the glimmer of twilight,
   Never glad confident morning again!
Best fight on well, for we taught him—strike gallantly,
   Menace our heart ere we master his own;
Then let him receive the new knowledge and wait us
   Pardoned in heaven, the first by the throne!

The Confessional
(SPAIN)

It is a lie—their Priests, their Pope,
   Their Saints, their . . . all they fear or hope
Are lies, and lies— there! through my door
   And ceiling, there! and walls and floor,
There, lies, they lie—shall still be hurled
   Till spite of them I reach the world!

You think Priests just and holy men!
   Before they put me in this den
I was a human creature too,
   With flesh and blood like one of you,
A girl that laughed in beauty's pride
   Like lilies in your world outside.

I had a lover—shame avaunt!
   This poor wrenched body, grim and gaunt,
Was kissed all over till it burned,
   By lips the truest, love e'er turned
His heart's own tint: one night they kissed
   My soul out in a burning mist.

So, next day when the accustomed train
   Of things grew round my sense again,
"That is a sin," I said: and slow

With downcast eyes to church I go,
And pass to the confession-chair,
And tell the old mild father there.

But when I falter Beltran's name,
"Ha?" quoth the father; "much I blame
The sin; yet wherefore idly grieve?
Despair not—strenuously retrieve!
Nay I will turn this love of thine
To lawful love, almost divine;

"For he is young, and led astray,
This Beltran, and he schemes, men say,
To change the laws of church and state;
So, thine shall be an angel's fate,
Who, ere the thunder breaks, should roll
Its cloud away and save his soul.

"For, when he lies upon thy breast,
Thou mayst demand and be possessed
Of all his plans, and next day steal
To me, and all those plans reveal,
That I and every priest, to purge
His soul, may fast and use the scourge."

That father's beard was long and white,
With love and truth his brow seemed bright;
I went back, all on fire with joy,
And, that same evening, bade the boy
Tell me, as lovers should, heart-free,
Something to prove his love of me.

He told me what he would not tell
For hope of heaven or fear of hell;
And I lay listening in such pride!
And, soon as he had left my side,
Tripped to the church by morning-light
To save his soul in his despite.

I told the father all his schemes,
Who were his comrades, what their dreams;
"And now make haste," I said, "to pray
The one spot from his soul away;
To-night he comes, but not the same
Will look!" At night he never came.

Nor next night; and the after-morn,
I went forth with a strength new-born.
The church was empty; something drew
My steps into the street; I knew
It led me to the market-place:
Where, lo, on high, the father's face!

That horrible black scaffold dressed,
That stapled block . . . God sink the rest!
That head strapped back, that blinding vest,
Those knotted hands and naked breast,
Till near one busy hangman pressed,
And, on the neck these arms caressed . . .

No part in aught they hope or fear!
No heaven with them, no hell!—and here,
No earth, not so much space as pens
My body in their worst of dens
But shall bear God and man my cry,
Lies—lies, again—and still, they lie!

Meeting at Night

The grey sea and the long black land;
And the yellow half-moon large and low;
And the startled little waves that leap
In fiery ringlets from their sleep,
As I gain the cove with pushing prow,
And quench its speed i' the slushy sand.

Then a mile of warm sea-scented beach;
Three fields to cross till a farm appears;
A tap at the pane, the quick sharp scratch

And blue spurt of a lighted match,
And a voice less loud, through its joys and fears,
Than the two hearts beating each to each!

A Woman's Last Word

Let's contend no more, Love,
    Strive nor weep:
All be as before, Love,
    —Only sleep!

What so wild as words are?
    I and thou
In debate, as birds are,
    Hawk on bough!

See the creature stalking
    While we speak!
Hush and hide the talking,
    Cheek on cheek!

What so false as truth is,
    False to thee?
Where the serpent's tooth is
    Shun the tree—

Where the apple reddens
    Never pry—
Lest we lose our Edens,
    Eve and I.

Be a god and hold me
    With a charm!
Be a man and fold me
    With thine arm!

Teach me, only teach, Love!
    As I ought
I will speak thy speech, Love,
    Think thy thought—

Meet, if thou require it,
    Both demands,
Laying flesh and spirit
    In thy hands.

That shall be to-morrow
    Not to-night:
I must bury sorrow
    Out of sight:

—Must a little weep, Love,
    (Foolish me!)
And so fall asleep, Love,
    Loved by thee.

Respectability

Dear, had the world in its caprice
    Deigned to proclaim "I know you both,
    Have recognised your plighted troth,
Am sponsor for you: live in peace."
How many precious months and years
    Of youth had passed, that sped so fast,
    Before we found it out at last,
The world, and what it fears?

How much of priceless life were spent
    With men that every virtue decks,
    And women models of their sex,
Society's true ornament,—
Ere we dared wander, nights like this,
    Through wind and rain, and watch the Seine,
    And feel the Boulevart break again
To warmth and light and bliss?

I know! the world proscribes not love;
    Allows my finger to caress
    Your lips' contour and downiness,
Provided it supply a glove.

The world's good word!—the Institute!
  Guizot receives Montalembert!
  Eh? Down the court three lampions flare:
Put forward your best foot!

Women and Roses

I dream of a rose-red tree.
And which of its roses three
Is the dearest rose to me?

Round and round, like a dance of snow
In a dazzling drift, as its guardians, go
Floating the women faded for ages,
Sculptured in stone, on the poet's pages.
Then follow women fresh and gay,
Living and loving and loved to-day.
Last, in the rear, flee the multitude of maidens,
Beauties yet unborn. And all, to one cadence,
They circle their rose on my rose tree.

Dear rose, thy term is reached,
Thy leaf hangs loose and bleached:
Bees pass it unimpeached.

Stay then, stoop, since I cannot climb,
You, great shapes of the antique time!
How shall I fix you, fire you, freeze you,
Break my heart at your feet to please you?
Oh, to possess and be possessed!
Hearts that beat 'neath each pallid breast!
Once but of love, the poesy, the passion,
Drink but once and die!—In vain, the same fashion,
They circle their rose on my rose tree.

Dear rose, thy joy's undimmed,
Thy cup is ruby-rimmed,
Thy cup's heart nectar-brimmed.

Deep, as drops from a statue's plinth
The bee sucked in by the hyacinth,
So will I bury me while burning,
Quench like him at a plunge my yearning,
Eyes in your eyes, lips on your lips!
Fold me fast where the cincture slips,
Prison all my soul in eternities of pleasure,
Girdle me for once! But no—the old measure,
They circle their rose on my rose tree.

Dear rose without a thorn,
Thy bud's the babe unborn:
First streak of a new morn.

Wings, lend wings for the cold, the clear!
What is far conquers what is near.
Roses will bloom nor want beholders,
Sprung from the dust where our flesh moulders.
What shall arrive with the cycle's change?
A novel grace and a beauty strange.
I will make an Eve, be the artist that began her,
Shaped her to his mind!—Alas! in like manner
They circle their rose on my rose tree.

FROM *In a Gondola*

He sings
I send my heart up to thee, all my heart
    In this my singing.
For the stars help me, and the sea bears part;
    The very night is clinging
Closer to Venice' streets to leave one space
    Above me, whence thy face
May light my joyous heart to thee its dwelling-place.

She speaks
Say after me, and try to say
My very words, as if each word
Came from you of your own accord,

In your own voice, in your own way:
"This woman's heart and soul and brain
Are mine as much as this gold chain
She bids me wear; which" (say again)
"I choose to make by cherishing
A precious thing, or choose to fling
Over the boat-side, ring by ring."
And yet once more say . . . no word more!
Since words are only words. Give o'er!

Unless you call me, all the same,
Familiarly by my pet name,
Which if the Three should hear you call,
And me reply to, would proclaim
At once our secret to them all.
Ask of me, too, command me, blame—
Do, break down the partition-wall
'Twixt us, the daylight world beholds
Curtained in dusk and splendid folds!
What's left but—all of me to take?
I am the Three's: prevent them, slake
Your thirst! 'Tis said, the Arab sage,
In practising with gems, can loose
Their subtle spirit in his cruce
And leave but ashes: so, sweet mage,
Leave them my ashes when thy use
Sucks out my soul, thy heritage!

He sings

Past we glide, and past and past!
    What's that poor Agnese doing
Where they make the shutters fast?
    Grey Zanobi's just a-wooing
To his couch the purchased bride:
    Past we glide!

Past we glide, and past, and past!
    Why's the Pucci Palace flaring
Like a beacon to the blast?
    Guests by hundreds, not one caring
If the dear host's neck were wried:
    Past we glide!

She sings
The moth's kiss, first!
Kiss me as if you made believe
You were not sure, this eve,
How my face, your flower, had pursed
Its petals up; so, here and there
You brush it, till I grow aware
Who wants me, and wide ope I burst.

The bee's kiss, now!
Kiss me as if you entered gay
My heart at some noonday,
A bud that dares not disallow
The claim, so all is rendered up,
And passively its shattered cup
Over your head to sleep I bow.

He muses
Oh, which were best, to roam or rest?
The land's lap or the water's breast?
To sleep on yellow millet-sheaves,
Or swim in lucid shallows just
Eluding water-lily leaves,
An inch from Death's black fingers, thrust
To lock you, whom release he must;
Which life were best on Summer eves?

Still he muses
What if the Three should catch at last
Thy serenader? While there's cast
Paul's cloak about my head, and fast
Gian pinions me, Himself has past
His stylet through my back; I reel;
And . . . is it thou I feel?

They trail me, these three godless knaves,
Past every church that sains and saves,
Nor stop till, where the cold sea raves
By Lido's wet accursed graves,
They scoop mine, roll me to its brink,
And . . . on thy breast I sink!

She speaks

To-morrow, if a harp-string, say,
Is used to tie the jasmine back
That overfloods my room with sweets,
Contrive your Zorzi somehow meets
My Zanze! If the ribbon's black,
The Three are watching: keep away!

Your gondola—let Zorzi wreathe
A mesh of water-weeds about
Its prow, as if he unaware
Had struck some quay or bridge-foot stair!
That I may throw a paper out
As you and he go underneath.

There's Zanze's vigilant taper; safe are we.
Only one minute more to-night with me?
Resume your past self of a month ago!
Be you the bashful gallant, I will be
The lady with the colder breast than snow.
Now bow you, as becomes, nor touch my hand
More than I touch yours when I step to land,
And say, "All thanks, Siora!"—
                              Heart to heart
And lips to lips! Yet once more, ere we part,
Clasp me and make me thine, as mine thou art!

He is surprised, and stabbed

It was ordained to be so, sweet!—and best
Comes now, beneath thine eyes, upon thy breast.
Still kiss me! Care not for the cowards! Care
Only to put aside thy beauteous hair
My blood will hurt! The Three, I do not scorn
To death, because they never lived: but I
Have lived indeed, and so—(yet one more kiss)—can die!

The Bishop Orders His Tomb
at Saint Praxed's Church

(ROME, 15—)

Vanity, saith the preacher, vanity!
Draw round my bed: is Anselm keeping back?
Nephews—sons mine . . . ah God, I know not! Well—
She, men would have to be your mother once,
Old Gandolf envied me, so fair she was!
What's done is done, and she is dead beside,
Dead long ago, and I am Bishop since,
And as she died so must we die ourselves,
And thence ye may perceive the world's a dream.
Life, how and what is it? As here I lie
In this state-chamber, dying by degrees,
Hours and long hours in the dead night, I ask
"Do I live, am I dead?" Peace, peace seems all.
Saint Praxed's ever was the church for peace;
And so, about this tomb of mine. I fought
With tooth and nail to save my niche, ye know:
—Old Gandolf cozened me, despite my care;
Shrewd was the snatch from out the corner South
He graced his carrion with, God curse the same!
Yet still my niche is not so cramped but thence
One sees the pulpit o' the epistle-side,
And somewhat of the choir, those silent seats,
And up into the aery dome where live
The angels, and a sunbeam's sure to lurk:
And I shall fill my slab of basalt there,
And 'neath my tabernacle take my rest,
With those nine columns round me, two and two,
The odd one at my feet where Anselm stands:
Peach-blossom marble all, the rare, the ripe
As fresh-poured red wine of a mighty pulse.
—Old Gandolf with his paltry onion-stone,
Put me where I may look at him! True peach,
Rosy and flawless: how I earned the prize!
Draw close: that conflagration of my church
—What then? So much was saved if aught were missed!
My sons, ye would not be my death? Go dig

The white-grape vineyard where the oil-press stood,
Drop water gently till the surface sink,
And if ye find . . . Ah God, I know not, I! . . .
Bedded in store of rotten fig-leaves soft,
And corded up in a tight olive-frail,
Some lump, ah God, of *lapis lazuli,*
Big as a Jew's head cut off at the nape,
Blue as a vein o'er the Madonna's breast . . .
Sons, all have I bequeathed you, villas, all,
That brave Frascati villa with its bath,
So, let the blue lump poise between my knees,
Like God the Father's globe on both his hands
Ye worship in the Jesu Church so gay,
For Gandolf shall not choose but see and burst!
Swift as a weaver's shuttle fleet our years:
Man goeth to the grave, and where is he?
Did I say basalt for my slab, sons? Black—
'Twas ever antique-black I meant! How else
Shall ye contrast my frieze to come beneath?
The bas-relief in bronze ye promised me,
Those Pans and Nymphs ye wot of, and perchance
Some tripod, thyrsus, with a vase or so,
The Saviour at his sermon on the mount,
Saint Praxed in a glory, and one Pan
Ready to twitch the Nymph's last garment off,
And Moses with the tables . . . but I know
Ye mark me not! What do they whisper thee,
Child of my bowels, Anselm? Ah, ye hope
To revel down my villas while I gasp
Bricked o'er with beggar's mouldy travertine
Which Gandolf from his tomb-top chuckles at!
Nay, boys, ye love me—all of jasper, then!
'Tis jasper ye stand pledged to, lest I grieve.
My bath must needs be left behind, alas!
One block, pure green as a pistachio-nut,
There's plenty jasper somewhere in the world—
And have I not Saint Praxed's ear to pray
Horses for ye, and brown Greek manuscripts,
And mistresses with great smooth marbly limbs?
—That's if ye carve my epitaph aright,
Choice Latin, picked phrase, Tully's every word,

No gaudy ware like Gandolf's second line—
Tully, my masters? Ulpian serves his need!
And then how I shall lie through centuries,
And hear the blessed mutter of the mass,
And see God made and eaten all day long,
And feel the steady candle-flame, and taste
Good strong thick stupefying incense-smoke!
For as I lie here, hours of the dead night,
Dying in state and by such slow degrees,
I fold my arms as if they clasped a crook,
And stretch my feet forth straight as stone can point,
And let the bedclothes, for a mortcloth, drop
Into great laps and folds of sculptor's-work:
And as you tapers dwindle, and strange thoughts
Grow, with a certain humming in my ears,
About the life before I lived this life,
And this life too, popes, cardinals, and priests,
Saint Praxed at his sermon on the mount,
Your tall pale mother with her talking eyes,
And new-found agate urns as fresh as day,
And marble's language, Latin pure, discreet,
—Aha, ELUCESCEBAT quoth our friend?
No Tully, said I, Ulpian at the best!
Evil and brief hath been my pilgrimage.
All *lapis*, all, sons! Else I give the Pope
My villas! Will ye ever eat my heart?
Ever your eyes were as a lizard's quick,
They glitter like your mother's for my soul,
Or ye would heighten my impoverished frieze,
Piece out its starved design, and fill my vase
With grapes, and add a vizor and a Term,
And to the tripod ye would tie a lynx
That in his struggle throws the thyrsus down,
Whereon I am to lie till I must ask
"Do I live, am I dead?" There, leave me, there!
For ye have stabbed me with ingratitude
To death—ye wish it—God, ye wish it! Stone—
Gritstone, a-crumble! Clammy squares which sweat
As if the corpse they keep were oozing through—
And no more *lapis* to delight the world!
Well, go! I bless ye. Fewer tapers there,

But in a row: and, going, turn your backs
—Ay, like departing altar-ministrants,
And leave me in my church, the church for peace,
That I may watch at leisure if he leers—
Old Gandolf, at me, from his onion-stone,
As still he envied me, so fair she was!

Fra Lippo Lippi

I am poor brother Lippo, by your leave!
You need not clap your torches to my face.
Zooks, what's to blame? you think you see a monk!
What, 'tis past midnight, and you go the rounds,
And here you catch me at an alley's end
Where sportive ladies leave their doors ajar?
The Carmine's my cloister: hunt it up,
Do,—harry out, if you must show your zeal,
Whatever rat, there, haps on his wrong hole,
And nip each softling of a wee white mouse,
Weke, weke, that's crept to keep him company!
Aha, you know your betters? Then, you'll take
Your hand away that's fiddling on my throat,
And please to know me likewise. Who am I?
Why, one, sir, who is lodging with a friend
Three streets off—he's a certain . . . how d'ye call?
Master—a . . . Cosimo of the Medici,
In the house that caps the corner. Boh! you were best!
Remember and tell me, the day you're hanged,
How you affected such a gullet's-gripe!
But you, sir, it concerns you that your knaves
Pick up a manner nor discredit you:
Zooks, are we pilchards, that they sweep the streets
And count fair prize what comes into their net?
He's Judas to a tittle, that man is!
Just such a face! Why, sir, you make amends.
Lord, I'm not angry! Bid your hangdogs go
Drink out this quarter-florin to the health
Of the munificent House that harbours me
(And many more beside, lads! more beside!)

And all's come square again. I'd like his face—
His, elbowing on his comrade in the door
With the pike and lantern,—for the slave that holds
John Baptist's head a-dangle by the hair
With one hand ("look you, now," as who should say)
And his weapon in the other, yet unwiped!
It's not your chance to have a bit of chalk,
A wood-coal or the like? or you should see!
Yes, I'm the painter, since you style me so.
What, brother Lippo's doings, up and down,
You know them and they take you? like enough!
I saw the proper twinkle in your eye—
'Tell you, I liked your looks at very first.
Let's sit and set things straight now, hip to haunch.
Here's spring come, and the nights one makes up bands
To roam the town and sing out carnival,
And I've been three weeks shut within my mew,
A-painting for the great man, saints and saints
And saints again. I could not paint all night—
Ouf! I leaned out of window for fresh air.
There came a hurry of feet and little feet,
A sweep of lute-strings, laughs, and whifts of song,—
Flower o' the broom,
Take away love, and our earth is a tomb!
Flower o' the quince,
I let Lisa go, and what good's in life since?
Flower o' the thyme—and so on. Round they went.
Scarce had they turned the corner when a titter
Like the skipping of rabbits by moonlight,—three slim shapes—
And a face that looked up . . . zooks, sir, flesh and blood,
That's all I'm made of! Into shreds it went,
Curtain and counterpane and coverlet,
All the bed-furniture—a dozen knots,
There was a ladder! down I let myself,
Hands and feet, scrambling somehow, and so dropped,
And after them. I came up with the fun
Hard by Saint Laurence, hail fellow, well met,—
Flower o' the rose,
If I've been merry, what matter who knows?
And so as I was stealing back again
To get to bed and have a bit of sleep

Ere I rise up to-morrow and go work
On Jerome knocking at his poor old breast
With his great round stone to subdue the flesh,
You snap me of the sudden. Ah, I see!
Though your eye twinkles still, you shake your head—
Mine's shaved,—a monk, you say—the sting's in that!
If Master Cosimo announced himself,
Mum's the word naturally; but a monk!
Come, what am I a beast for? tell us, now!
I was a baby when my mother died
And father died and left me in the street.
I starved there, God knows how, a year or two
On fig skins, melon-parings, rinds and shucks,
Refuse and rubbish. One fine frosty day,
My stomach being empty as your hat,
The wind doubled me up and down I went.
Old Aunt Lapaccia trussed me with one hand,
(Its fellow was a stinger as I knew)
And so along the wall, over the bridge,
By the straight cut to the convent. Six words, there,
While I stood munching my first bread that month:
"So, boy, you're minded," quoth the good fat father
Wiping his own mouth, 'twas refection-time,—
"To quit this very miserable world?
Will you renounce" . . . The mouthful of bread? thought I;
By no means! Brief, they made a monk of me;
I did renounce the world, its pride and greed,
Palace, farm, villa, shop, and banking-house,
Trash, such as these poor devils of Medici
Have given their hearts to—all at eight years old.
Well, sir, I found in time, you may be sure,
'Twas not for nothing—the good bellyful,
The warm serge and the rope that goes all round,
And day-long blessed idleness beside!
"Let's see what the urchin's fit for"—that came next.
Not overmuch their way, I must confess.
Such a to-do! They tried me with their books.
Lord, they'd have taught me Latin in pure waste!
Flower o' the clove,
All the Latin I construe is, "amo" I love!

But, mind you, when a boy starves in the streets
Eight years together, as my fortune was,
Watching folk's faces to know who will fling
The bit of half-stripped grape-bunch he desires,
And who will curse or kick him for his pains—
Which gentleman processional and fine,
Holding a candle to the Sacrament,
Will wink and let him lift a plate and catch
The droppings of the wax to sell again,
Or holla for the Eight and have him whipped,—
How say I?—nay, which dog bites, which lets drop
His bone from the heap of offal in the street,—
Why, soul and sense of him grow sharp alike,
He learns the look of things, and none the less
For admonition from the hunger-pinch.
I had a store of such remarks, be sure,
Which, after I found leisure, turned to use.
I drew men's faces on my copy-books,
Scrawled them within the antiphonary's marge,
Joined legs and arms to the long music-notes,
Found nose and eyes and chin for A's and B's,
And made a string of pictures of the world
Betwixt the ins and outs of verb and noun,
On the wall, the bench, the door. The monks looked black.
"Nay," quoth the Prior, "turn him out, d'ye say?
In no wise. Lose a crow and catch a lark.
What if at last we get our man of parts,
We Carmelites, like those Camaldolese
And Preaching Friars, to do our church up fine
And put the front on it that ought to be!"
And hereupon he bade me daub away.
Thank you! my head being crammed, their walls a blank,
Never was such prompt disemburdening.
First, every sort of monk, the black and white,
I drew them, fat and lean: then, folks at church,
From good old gossips waiting to confess
Their cribs of barrel-droppings, candle-ends,—
To the breathless fellow at the altar-foot,
Fresh from his murder, safe and sitting there
With the little children round him in a row

Of admiration, half for his beard and half
For that white anger of his victim's son
Shaking a fist at him with one fierce arm,
Signing himself with the other because of Christ
(Whose sad face on the cross sees only this
After the passion of a thousand years)
Till some poor girl, her apron o'er her head
Which the intense eyes looked through, came at eve
On tip-toe, said a word, dropped in a loaf,
Her pair of earrings and a bunch of flowers
The brute took growling, prayed, and then was gone.
I painted all, then cried " 'tis ask and have—
Choose, for more's ready!"—laid the ladder flat,
And showed my covered bit of cloister-wall.
The monks closed in a circle and praised loud
Till checked,—taught what to see and not to see,
Being simple bodies,—"that's the very man!
Look at the boy who stoops to pat the dog!
That woman's like the Prior's niece who comes
To care about his asthma: it's the life!"
But there my triumph's straw-fire flared and funked—
Their betters took their turn to see and say:
The Prior and the learned pulled a face
And stopped all that in no time. "How? what's here?
Quite from the mark of painting, bless us all!
Faces, arms, legs and bodies like the true
As much as pea and pea! it's devil's-game!
Your business is not to catch men with show,
With homage to the perishable clay,
But lift them over it, ignore it all,
Make them forget there's such a thing as flesh.
Your business is to paint the souls of men—
Man's soul, and it's a fire, smoke . . . no it's not . .
It's vapour done up like a new-born babe—
(In that shape when you die it leaves your mouth)
It's . . . well, what matters talking, it's the soul!
Give us no more of body than shows soul!
Here's Giotto, with his Saint a-praising God,
That sets us praising,—why not stop with him?
Why put all thoughts of praise out of our heads
With wonder at lines, colours, and what not?

Paint the soul, never mind the legs and arms!
Rub all out, try at it a second time.
Oh, that white smallish female with the breasts,
She's just my niece . . . Herodias, I would say,—
Who went and danced and got men's heads cut off—
Have it all out!" Now, is this sense, I ask?
A fine way to paint soul, by painting body
So ill, the eye can't stop there, must go further
And can't fare worse! Thus, yellow does for white
When what you put for yellow's simply black,
And any sort of meaning looks intense
When all beside itself means and looks nought.
Why can't a painter lift each foot in turn,
Left foot and right foot, go a double step,
Make his flesh liker and his soul more like,
Both in their order? Take the prettiest face,
The Prior's niece . . . patron-saint—is it so pretty
You can't discover if it means hope, fear,
Sorrow or joy? won't beauty go with these?
Suppose I've made her eyes all right and blue,
Can't I take breath and try to add life's flash,
And then add soul and heighten them threefold?
Or say there's beauty with no soul at all—
(I never saw it—put the case the same—)
If you get simple beauty and nought else,
You get about the best thing God invents,—
That's somewhat. And you'll find the soul you have missed,
Within yourself, when you return Him thanks.
"Rub all out!" Well, well, there's my life, in short,
And so the thing has gone on ever since.
I've grown a man no doubt, I've broken bounds—
You should not take a fellow eight years old
And make him swear to never kiss the girls.
I'm my own master, paint now as I please—
Having a friend, you see, in the Corner-house!
Lord, it's fast holding by the rings in front—
Those great rings serve more purposes than just
To plant a flag in, or tie up a horse!
And yet the old schooling sticks, the old grave eyes
Are peeping o'er my shoulder as I work,
The heads shake still—"It's Art's decline, my son!

You're not of the true painters, great and old;
Brother Angelico's the man, you'll find;
Brother Lorenzo stands his single peer:
Fag on at flesh, you'll never make the third!"
Flower o' the pine,
You keep your mistr . . . manners, and I'll stick to mine!
I'm not the third, then: bless us, they must know!
Don't you think they're the likeliest to know,
They with their Latin? so, I swallow my rage,
Clench my teeth, suck my lips in tight, and paint
To please them—sometimes do and sometimes don't,
For, doing most, there's pretty sure to come
A turn, some warm eve finds me at my saints—
A laugh, a cry, the business of the world—
(*Flower o' the peach,*
Death for us all, and his own life for each!)
And my whole soul revolves, the cup runs over,
The world and life's too big to pass for a dream,
And I do these wild things in sheer despite,
And play the fooleries you catch me at,
In pure rage! The old mill-horse, out at grass
After hard years, throws up his stiff heels so,
Although the miller does not preach to him
The only good of grass is to make chaff.
What would men have? Do they like grass or no—
May they or mayn't they? all I want's the thing
Settled for ever one way: as it is,
You tell too many lies and hurt yourself.
You don't like what you only like too much,
You do like what, if given you at your word,
You find abundantly detestable.
For me, I think I speak as I was taught—
I always see the Garden and God there
A-making man's wife—and, my lesson learned,
The value and significance of flesh,
I can't unlearn ten minutes afterwards.

You understand me: I'm a beast, I know.
But see, now—why, I see as certainly
As that the morning-star's about to shine,
What will hap some day. We've a youngster here

Comes to our convent, studies what I do,
Slouches and stares and lets no atom drop—
His name is Guidi—he'll not mind the monks—
They call him Hulking Tom, he lets them talk—
He picks my practice up –he'll paint apace,
I hope so—though I never live so long,
I know what's sure to follow. You be judge!
You speak no Latin more than I, belike—
However, you're my man, you've seen the world
—The beauty and the wonder and the power,
The shapes of things, their colours, lights and shades,
Changes, surprises,—and God made it all!
—For what? Do you feel thankful, ay or no,
For this fair town's face, yonder river's line,
The mountain round it and the sky above,
Much more the figures of man, woman, child,
These are the frame to? What's it all about?
To be passed over, despised? or dwelt upon,
Wondered at? oh, this last of course!—you say.
But why not do as well as say,—paint these
Just as they are, careless what comes of it?
God's works—paint anyone, and count it crime
To let a truth slip. Don't object, "His works
Are here already—nature is complete:
Suppose you reproduce her—(which you can't)
There's no advantage! you must beat her, then."
For, don't you mark? we're made so that we love
First when we see them painted, things we have passed
Perhaps a hundred times nor cared to see;
And so they are better, painted—better to us,
Which is the same thing. Art was given for that—
God uses us to help each other so,
Lending our minds out. Have you noticed, now,
Yon cullion's hanging face? A bit of chalk,
And trust me but you should, though! How much more,
If I drew higher things with the same truth!
That were to take the Prior's pulpit-place,
Interpret God to all of you! oh, oh,
It makes me mad to see what men shall do
And we in our graves! This world's no blot for us,
Nor blank—it means intensely, and means good:

To find its meaning is my meat and drink.
"Ay, but you don't so instigate to prayer!"
Strikes in the Prior: "when your meaning's plain
It does not say to folk—remember matins,
Or, mind you fast next Friday!" Why, for this
What need of art at all? A skull and bones,
Two bits of stick nailed cross-wise, or, what's best
A bell to chime the hour with, does as well.
I painted a Saint Laurence six months since
At Prato, splashed the fresco in fine style:
"How looks my painting, now the scaffold's down?"
I ask a brother: "Hugely," he returns—
"Already not one phiz of your three slaves
Who turn the Deacon off his toasted side,
But's scratched and prodded to our heart's content,
The pious people have so eased their own
When coming to say prayers there in a rage:
We get on fast to see the bricks beneath.
Expect another job this time next year,
For pity and religion grow i' the crowd—
Your painting serves its purpose!" Hang the fools!

—That is—you'll not mistake an idle word
Spoke in a huff by a poor monk, God wot,
Tasting the air in this spicy night which turns
The unaccustomed head like Chianti wine!
Oh, the church knows! don't misreport me, now!
It's natural a poor monk out of bounds
Should have his apt word to excuse himself:
And hearken how I plot to make amends.
I have bethought me: I shall paint a piece
. . . There's for you! Give me six months, then go, see
Something in Sant' Ambrogio's! Bless the nuns!
They want a cast of my office. I shall paint
God in the midst, Madonna and her babe,
Ringed by a bowery, flowery angel-brood,
Lilies and vestments and white faces, sweet
As puff on puff of grated orris-root
When ladies crowd to church at midsummer.

And then in the front, of course a saint or two—
Saint John, because he saves the Florentines,
Saint Ambrose, who puts down in black and white
The convent's friends and gives them a long day,
And Job, I must have him there past mistake,
The man of Uz, (and Us without the z,
Painters who need his patience.) Well, all these
Secured at their devotions, up shall come
Out of a corner when you least expect,
As one by a dark stair into a great light,
Music and talking, who but Lippo! I!—
Mazed, motionless and moonstruck—I'm the man!
Back I shrink—what is this I see and hear?
I, caught up with my monk's things by mistake,
My old serge gown and rope that goes all round,
I, in this presence, this pure company!
Where's a hole, where's a corner for escape?
Then steps a sweet angelic slip of a thing
Forward, puts out a soft palm—"Not so fast!"
—Addresses the celestial presence, "nay—
He made you and devised you, after all,
Though he's none of you! Could Saint John there, draw—
His camel-hair make up a painting-brush?
We come to brother Lippo for all that,
Iste perfecit opus!" So, all smile—
I shuttle sideways with my blushing face
Under the cover of a hundred wings
Thrown like a spread of kirtles when you're gay
And play hot cockles, all the doors being shut,
Till, wholly unexpected, in there pops
The hothead husband! Thus I scuttle off
To some safe bench behind, not letting go
The palm of her, the little lily thing
That spoke the good word for me in the nick,
Like the Prior's niece . . . Saint Lucy, I would say.
And so all's saved for me, and for the church
A pretty picture gained. Go, six months hence!
Your hand, sir, and good-bye: no lights, no lights!
The street's hushed, and I know my own way back,
Don't fear me! There's the grey beginning. Zooks!

Song

Nay but you, who do not love her,
  Is she not pure gold, my mistress?
Holds earth aught—speak truth—above her?
  Aught like this tress, see, and this tress,
And this last fairest tress of all,
So fair, see, ere I let it fall?

Because, you spend your lives in praising;
  To praise, you search the wide world over:
Then why not witness, calmly gazing,
  If earth holds aught—speak truth—above her?
Above this tress, and this, I touch
But cannot praise, I love so much!

Confessions

What is he buzzing in my ears?
  "Now that I come to die,
Do I view the world as a vale of tears?"
  Ah, reverend sir, not I!

What I viewed there once, what I view again
  Where the physic bottles stand
On the table's edge,—is a suburb lane,
  With a wall to my bedside hand.

That lane sloped, much as the bottles do,
  From a house you could descry
O'er the garden-wall: is the curtain blue
  Or green to a healthy eye?

To mine, it serves for the old June weather
  Blue above lane and wall;
And that farthest bottle labelled "Ether"
  Is the house o'ertopping all.

At a terrace, somewhere near the stopper,
　　There watched for me, one June,
A girl; I know, sir, it's improper,
　　My poor mind's out of tune.

Only, there was a way . . . you crept
　　Close by the side, to dodge
Eyes in the house, two eyes except:
　　They styled their house "The Lodge".

What right had a lounger up their lane?
　　But, by creeping very close,
With the good wall's help—their eyes might strain
　　And stretch themselves to Oes,

Yet never catch her and me together,
　　As she left the attic, there,
By the rim of the bottle labelled "Ether",
　　And stole from stair to stair,

And stood by the rose-wreathed gate. Alas,
　　We loved, sir—used to meet:
How sad and bad and mad it was—
　　But then, how it was sweet!

Youth and Art

It once might have been, once only:
　　We lodged in a street together,
You, a sparrow on the housetop lonely,
　　I, a lone she-bird of his feather.

Your trade was with sticks and clay,
　　You thumbed, thrust, patted and polished,
Then laughed "They will see some day
　　"Smith made, and Gibson demolished."

My business was song, song, song;
　　I chirped, cheeped, trilled and twittered,
"Kate Brown's on the boards ere long,
　　And Grisi's existence embittered!"

I earned no more by a warble
   That you by a sketch in plaster;
You wanted a piece of marble,
   I needed a music-master.

We studied hard in our styles,
   Chipped each at a crust like Hindoos,
For air looked out on the tiles,
   For fun watched each other's windows.

You lounged, like a boy of the South,
   Cap and blouse—nay, a bit of a beard too;
Or you got it, rubbing your mouth
   With fingers the clay adhered to.

And I—soon managed to find
   Weak points in the flower-fence facing,
Was forced to put up a blind
   And be safe in my corset-lacing.

No harm! It was not my fault
   If you never turned your eye's tail up
As I shook upon E *in alt,*
   Or ran the chromatic scale up:

For spring bade the sparrows pair,
   And the boys and girls gave guesses,
And stalls in our street looked rare
   With bulrush and watercresses.

Why did not you pinch a flower
   In a pellet of clay and fling it?
Why did not I put a power
   Of thanks in a look, or sing it?

I did look, sharp as a lynx,
   (And yet the memory rankles)
When models arrived, some minx
   Tripped up-stairs, she and her ankles.

But I think I gave you as good!
   "That foreign fellow—who can know
How she pays, in a playful mood,
   For his tuning her that piano?"

Could you say so, and never say
   "Suppose we join hands and fortunes,
And I fetch her from over the way,
   Her, piano, and long tunes and short tunes?"

No, no: you would not be rash,
   Nor I rasher and something over:
You've to settle yet Gibson's hash,
   And Grisi yet lives in clover.

But you meet the Prince at the Board,
   I'm queen myself at *bals-paré*,
I've married a rich old lord,
   And you're dubbed knight and an R.A.

Each life's unfulfilled, you see;
   It hangs still, patchy and scrappy:
We have not sighed deep, laughed free,
   Starved, feasted, despaired—been happy.

And nobody calls you a dunce,
   And people suppose me clever:
This could have happened but once,
   And we missed it, lost it for ever.

FROM One Word More
(TO E.B.B.)

There they are, my fifty men and women
Naming me the fifty poems finished!
Take them, Love, the book and me together:
Where the heart lies, let the brain lie also.

Rafael made a century of sonnets,
Made and wrote them in a certain volume
Dinted with the silver-pointed pencil
Else he only used to draw Madonnas:
These, the world might view—but one, the volume.

Who that one, you ask? Your heart instructs you.
Did she live and love it all her life-time?
Did she drop, his lady of the sonnets,
Die, and let it drop beside her pillow
Where it lay in place of Rafael's glory,
Rafael's cheek so duteous and so loving—
Cheek, the world was wont to hail a painter's,
Rafael's cheek, her love had turned a poet's?

You and I would rather read that volume,
(Taken to his beating bosom by it)
Lean and list the bosom-beats of Rafael,
Would we not? than wonder at Madonnas—
Her, San Sisto names, and Her, Foligno,
Her, that visits Florence in a vision,
Her, that's left with lilies in the Louvre—
Seen by us and all the world in circle.

You and I will never read that volume.
Guido Reni, like his own eye's apple
Guarded long the treasure-book and loved it.
Guido Reni dying, all Bologna
Cried, and the world cried too, "Ours, the treasure!"
Suddenly, as rare things will, it vanished.

Dante once prepared to paint an angel:
Whom to please? You whisper "Beatrice."
While he mused and traced it and retraced it,
(Peradventure with a pen corroded
Still by drops of that hot ink he dipped for,
When, his left-hand i' the hair o' the wicked,
Back he held the brow and pricked its stigma,
Bit into the live man's flesh for parchment,
Loosed him, laughed to see the writing rankle,
Let the wretch go festering through Florence)—
Dante, who loved well because he hated,
Hated wickedness that hinders loving,
Dante standing, studying his angel—
In there broke the folk of his Inferno.
Says he—"Certain people of importance"

(Such he gave his daily dreadful line to)
"Entered and would seize, forsooth, the poet."
Says the poet—"Then I stopped my painting."

You and I would rather see that angel,
Painted by the tenderness of Dante,
Would we not?—than read a fresh Inferno.

You and I will never see that picture.
While he mused on love and Beatrice,
While he softened o'er his outlined angel,
In they broke, those "people of importance":
We and Bice bear the loss for ever.

What of Rafael's sonnets, Dante's picture?
This: no artist lives and loves, that longs not
Once, and only once, and for one only,
(Ah, the prize!) to find his love a language
Fit and fair and simple and sufficient—
Using nature that's an art to others,
Not, this one time, art that's turned his nature.
Ay, of all the artists living, loving,
None but would forego his proper dowry,—
Does he paint? he fain would write a poem,—
Does he write? he fain would paint a picture,
Put to proof art alien to the artist's,
Once, and only once, and for one only,
So to be the man and leave the artist,
Gain the man's joy, miss the artist's sorrow.

I shall never, in the years remaining,
Paint you pictures, no, nor carve you statues,
Make you music that should all-express me;
So it seems: I stand on my attainment.
This of verse alone, one life allows me;
Verse and nothing else have I to give you.
Other heights in other lives, God willing:
All the gifts from all the heights, your own, Love!

Yet a semblance of resource avails us—
Shade so finely touched, love's sense must seize it.
Take these lines, look lovingly and nearly,
Lines I write the first time and the last time.
He who works in fresco, steals a hair-brush,
Curbs the liberal hand, subservient proudly,
Cramps his spirit, crowds its all in little,
Makes a strange art of an art familiar,
Fills his lady's missal-marge with flowerets.
He who blows through bronze, may breathe through silver,
Fitly serenade a slumbrous princess.
He who writes, may write for once as I do.

Love, you saw me gather men and women,
Live or dead or fashioned by my fancy,
Enter each and all, and use their service,
Speak from every mouth,—the speech, a poem.
Hardly shall I tell my joys and sorrows,
Hopes and fears, belief and disbelieving:
I am mine and yours—the rest be all men's,
Karshish, Cleon, Norbert and the fifty.
Let me speak this once in my true person,
Not as Lippo, Roland or Andrea,
Though the fruit of speech be just this sentence:
Pray you, look on these my men and women,
Take and keep my fifty poems finished;
Where my heart lies, let my brain lie also!
Poor the speech; be how I speak, for all things.

Not but that you know me! Lo, the moon's self!
Here in London, yonder late in Florence,
Still we find her face, the thrice-transfigured.
Curving on a sky imbrued with colour,
Drifted over Fiesole by twilight,
Came she, our new crescent of a hair's-breadth.
Full she flared it, lamping Samminiato,
Rounder 'twixt the cypresses and rounder,
Perfect till the nightingales applauded.
Now, a piece of her old self, impoverished,
Hard to greet, she traverses the houseroofs,
Hurries with unhandsome thrift of silver,
Goes dispiritedly, glad to finish.

What, there's nothing in the moon noteworthy?
Nay: for if that moon could love a mortal,
Use, to charm him (so to fit a fancy),
All her magic ('tis the old sweet mythos),
She would turn a new side to her mortal,
Side unseen of herdsman, huntsman, steersman—
Blank to Zoroaster on his terrace,
Blind to Galileo on his turret,
Dumb to Homer, dumb to Keats—him, even!
Think, the wonder of the moonstruck mortal—
When she turns round, comes again in heaven,
Opens out anew for worse or better!
Proves she like some portent of an iceberg
Swimming full upon the ship it founders,
Hungry with huge teeth of splintered crystals?
Proves she as the paved work of a sapphire
Seen by Moses when he climbed the mountain?

What were seen? None knows, none ever shall know.
Only this is sure—the sight were other,
Not the moon's same side, born late in Florence,
Dying now impoverished here in London.
God be thanked, the meanest of his creatures
Boasts two soul-sides, one to face the world with,
One to show a woman when he loves her!

This I say of me, but think of you, Love!
This to you—yourself my moon of poets!
Ah, but that's the world's side, there's the wonder,
Thus they see you, praise you, think they know you!
There, in turn I stand with them and praise you—
Out of my own self, I dare to phrase it.
But the best is when I glide from out them,
Cross a step or two of dubious twilight,
Come out on the other side, the novel
Silent silver lights and darks undreamed of,
Where I hush and bless myself with silence.

Oh, their Rafael of the dear Madonnas,
Oh, their Dante of the dread Inferno,
Wrote one song—and in my brain I sing it,
Drew one angel—borne, see, on my bosom!

Epilogue

At the midnight in the silence of the sleep-time,
    When you set your fancies free,
Will they pass to where—by death, fools think, imprisoned
    Low he lies who once so loved you, whom you loved so,
            —Pity me?

Oh to love so, be so loved, yet so mistaken!
    What had I on earth to do
With the slothful, with the mawkish, the unmanly?
    Like the aimless, helpless, hopeless, did I drivel
            —Being—who?

One who never turned his back but marched breast forward,
    Never doubted clouds would break,
Never dreamed, though right were worsted, wrong would
        triumph,
    Held we fall to rise, are baffled to fight better,
            Sleep to wake.

No, at noonday in the bustle of man's work-time,
    Greet the unseen with a cheer!
Bid him forward, breast and back as either should be,
    "Strive and thrive!" cry "Speed,—fight on, fare ever
            There as here!"

CHARLOTTE BRONTË

(1816–1855)

On the Death of Anne Brontë

        There's little joy in life for me,
            And little terror in the grave;
        I've lived the parting hour to see
            Of one I would have died to save.

        Calmly to watch the failing breath,
            Wishing each sigh might be the last;
        Longing to see the shade of death
            O'er those belovéd features cast;

The cloud, the stillness that must part
　The darling of my life from me;
And then to thank God from my heart,
　To thank him well and fervently;

Although I knew that we had lost
　The hope and glory of our life;
And now, benighted, tempest-tossed,
　Must bear alone the weary strife.

HENRY DAVID THOREAU

(1817–1862)

"Low-Anchored Cloud"

Low-anchored cloud,
Newfoundland air,
Fountain-head and source of rivers,
Dew-cloth, dream drapery,
And napkin spread by fays;
Drifting meadow of the air,
Where bloom the daisied banks and violets,
And in whose fenny labyrinth
The bittern booms and heron wades;
Spirit of lakes and seas and rivers,
Bear only perfumes and the scent
Of healing herbs to just men's fields!

A Week on the Concord and Merrimack Rivers

"Woof of the Sun..."

Woof of the sun, ethereal gauze,
Woven of Nature's richest stuffs,
Visible heat, air-water, and dry sea,
Last conquest of the eye;
Toil of the day displayed, sun-dust,
Aerial surf upon the shores of earth,
Ethereal estuary, frith of light,

Breakers of air, billows of heat,
Fine summer spray on inland seas;
Bird of the sun, transparent-winged
Owlet of noon, soft-pinioned,
From heat or stubble rising without song;
Establish thy serenity o'er the fields.

A Week on the Concord and Merrimack Rivers

The Atlantides

The smothered streams of love, which flow
More bright than Phlegethon, more low,
Island us ever, like the sea,
In an Atlantic mystery.
Our fabled shores none ever reach,
No mariner has found our beach,
Surely our mirage now is seen,
And neighbouring waves with floating green,
Yet still the oldest charts contain
Some dotted outline of our main;
In ancient times midsummer days
Unto the western islands' gaze,
To Teneriffe and the Azores,
Have shown our faint and cloud-like shores.

But sink not yet, ye desolate isles,
Anon your coast with commerce smiles,
And richer freights ye'll furnish far
Than Africa or Malabar.
Be fair, be fertile evermore,
Ye rumored but untrodden shore,
Princes and monarchs will contend
Who first unto your land shall send,
And pawn the jewels of their crown
To call your distant soil their own.

A Week on the Concord and Merrimack Rivers

"All Things Are Current Found"

All things are current found
On earthly ground,
Spirits, and elements
Have their descents.

Night and day, year on year,
High and low, far and near,
These are our own aspects,
These are our own regrets.

Ye gods of the shore,
Who abide evermore,
I see your far headland,
Stretching on either hand;

I hear the sweet evening sounds
From your undecaying grounds;
Cheat me no more with time,
Take me to your clime.

A Week on the Concord and Merrimack Rivers

"Light-Winged Smoke..."

Light-winged Smoke, Icarian bird,
Melting thy pinions in thy upward flight,
Lark without song, and messenger of dawn,
Circling above the hamlets as thy nest;
Or else, departing dream, and shadowy form
Of midnight vision, gathering up thy skirts;
By night star-veiling, and by day
Darkening the light and blotting out the sun;
Go thou my incense upward from this hearth,
And ask the gods to pardon this clear flame.

Walden

EMILY JANE BRONTË

(1818–1848)

The Old Stoic

Riches I hold in light esteem,
  And love I laugh to scorn;
And lust of fame was but a dream,
  That vanished with the morn:

And if I pray, the only prayer
  That moves my lips for me
Is, "Leave the heart that now I bear,
  And give me liberty!"

Yes, as my swift days near their goal,
  'Tis all that I implore;—
In life and death a chainless soul,
  With courage to endure.

"Tell Me, Tell Me..."

Tell me, tell me, smiling child,
  What the past is like to thee?
"An autumn evening, soft and mild,
  With a wind that sighs mournfully."

Tell me, what is the present hour?
  "A green and flowery spray,
Where a young bird sits gathering its power
  To mount and fly away."

And what is the future, happy one?
  "A sea beneath a cloudless sun—
A mighty, glorious, dazzling sea,
  Stretching into infinity."

"The Sun Has Set..."

The sun has set, and the long grass now
  Waves dreamily in the evening wind;
And the wild bird has flown from that old grey stone
  In some warm nook a couch to find.

In all the lonely landscape round
I see no light and hear no sound,
Except the wind that far away
Comes sighing o'er the heathy sea.

"Sleep Brings No Joy..."

Sleep brings no joy to me,
  Remembrance never dies;
My soul is given to misery,
  And lives in sighs.

Sleep brings no rest to me;
  The shadows of the dead,
My wakening eyes may never see,
  Surround my bed.

Sleep brings no hope to me;
  In soundest sleep they come,
And with their doleful imagery
  Deepen the gloom.

Sleep brings no strength to me,
  No power renewed to brave:
I only sail a wilder sea,
  A darker wave.

Sleep brings no friend to me
  To soothe and aid to bear;
They all gaze on—how scornfully!
  And I despair.

Sleep brings no wish to fret
My harassed heart beneath:
My only wish is to forget
In endless sleep of death.

"A Little While, a Little While"

A little while, a little while,
The noisy crowd are barred away;
And I can sing and smile—
A little while I've holiday!

Where wilt thou go, my harassed heart?
Full many a land invites thee now;
And places near, and far apart
Have rest for thee, my weary brow—

There is a spot mid barren hills,
Where winter howls and driving rain,
But if the dreary tempest chills,
There is a light that warms again.

The house is old, the trees are bare,
And moonless bends the misty dome,
But what on earth is half so dear—
So longed for as the hearth of home?

The mute bird sitting on the stone,
The dank moss dripping from the wall,
The garden-walk with weeds o'er grown,
I love them—how I love them all!

Shall I go there? or shall I seek
Another clime, another sky,
Where tongues familiar music speak
In accents dear t' memory?

Yes, as I mused, the naked room,
The flickering firelight died away,
And from the midst of cheerless gloom
I passed to bright, unclouded day.

A little and a lone green lane,
    That opened on a common wide;
A distant, dreamy, dim blue chain
    Of mountains circling every side;

A heaven so clear, an earth so calm,
    So sweet, so soft, so hushed an air;
And, deepening still the dream-like charm,
    Wild moor-sheep feeding everywhere.

That was the scene—I knew it well;
    I knew the path-ways far and near,
That, winding o'er each billowy swell,
    Marked out the tracks of wandering deer.

Could I have lingered but an hour,
    It had well paid a week of toil;
But truth has banished fancy's power,
    I hear my dungeon bars recoil.

Even as I stood with raptured eye,
    Absorbed in bliss so deep and dear,
My hour of rest had fleeted by,
    And given me back to weary care.

FROM *"I Am the Only Being..."*

I am the only being whose doom
    No tongue would ask, no eye would mourn;
I've never caused a thought of gloom,
    A smile of joy, since I was born.

In secret pleasure, secret tears,
    This changeful life has slipped away,
As friendless after eighteen years,
    As lone as on my natal day.

"I Gazed Within…"

I gazed within thy earnest eyes,
  And read the sorrow brooding there;
I heard thy young breast torn with sighs,
  And envied such despair.

Go to the grave in youth's bare woe!
That dream was written long ago.

At Castle Wood

The day is done, the winter sun
  Is setting in its sullen sky;
And drear the course that has been run,
  And dim the hearts that slowly die.

No star will light my coming night;
  No morn of hope for me will shine;
I mourn not heaven would blast my sight,
  And I ne'er longed for joys divine.

Through life's hard task I did not ask
  Celestial aid, celestial cheer:
I saw my fate without its mask,
  And met it too without a tear.

The grief that pressed my aching breast
  Was heavier far than earth can be;
And who would dread eternal rest
  When labour's hour was agony?

Dark falls the fear of this despair
  On spirits born of happiness;
But I was bred the mate of care,
  The foster-child of sore distress.

No sighs for me, no sympathy,
  No wish to keep my soul below;
The heart is dead in infancy,
  Unwept for let the body go.

"No Coward Soul..."

No coward soul is mine,
No trembler in the world's storm-troubled sphere:
  I see Heaven's glories shine,
And Faith shines equal, arming me from Fear.

  O God within my breast,
Almighty, ever-present Deity!
  Life, that in me hast rest
As I, undying Life, have power in Thee!

  Vain are the thousand creeds
That move men's hearts: unutterably vain;
  Worthless as withered weeds,
Or idlest froth amid the boundless main,

  To waken doubt in one
Holding so fast by Thy infinity,
  So surely anchored on
The steadfast rock of Immortality.

  With wide-embracing love
Thy Spirit animates eternal years,
  Pervades and broods above,
Changes, sustains, dissolves, creates, and rears.

  Though earth and moon were gone,
And suns and universes ceased to be,
  And Thou wert left alone,
Every existence would exist in Thee.

  There is not room for Death,
Nor atom that his might could render void:
  Since Thou art Being and Breath
And what Thou art may never be destroyed.

ARTHUR HUGH CLOUGH

(1819–1861)

The Latest Decalogue

Thou shalt have one God only; who
Would be at the expense of two?
No graven images may be
Worshipped, except the currency:
Swear not at all; for, for thy curse
Thine enemy is none the worse:
At church on Sunday to attend
Will serve to keep the world thy friend:
Honour thy parents; that is, all
From whom advancement may befall:
Thou shalt not kill; but needst not strive
Officiously to keep alive:
Do not adultery commit;
Advantage rarely comes of it:
Thou shalt not steal; an empty feat,
When it's so lucrative to cheat:
Bear not false witness; let the lie
Have time on its own wings to fly:
Thou shalt not covet; but tradition
Approves all forms of competition.
The sum of all is, thou shalt love,
If any body, God above:
At any rate shall never labour
More than thyself to love thy neighbour.

"Say Not the Struggle..."

Say not the struggle nought availeth,
    The labour and the wounds are vain,
The enemy faints not, nor faileth,
    And as things have been, things remain.

If hopes were dupes, fears may be liars;
    It may be, in yon smoke concealed,

Your comrades chase e'en now the fliers,
   And, but for you, possess the field.

For while the tired waves, vainly breaking,
   Seem here no painful inch to gain,
Far back, through creeks and inlets making,
   Comes silent, flooding in, the main.

And not by eastern windows only,
   When daylight comes, comes in the light,
In front, the sun climbs slow, how slowly,
   But westward, look, the land is bright.

WALT WHITMAN

(1819–1892)

FROM *Starting from Paumanok*

Starting from fish-shape Paumanok where I was born,
Well-begotten, and rais'd by a perfect mother,
After roaming many lands, lover of populous pavements,
Dweller in Mannahatta my city, or on southern savannas,
Or a soldier camp'd or carrying my knapsack and gun, or a
   miner in California,
Or rude in my home in Dakota's woods, my diet meat, my
   drink from the spring,
Or withdrawn to muse and meditate in some deep recess,
Far from the clank of crowds intervals passing rapt and happy,
Aware of the fresh free giver the flowing Missouri, aware of
   mighty Niagara,
Aware of the buffalo herds grazing the plains, the hirsute
   and strong-breasted bull,
Of earth, rocks, Fifth-month flowers experienced, stars, rain,
   snow, my amaze,
Having studied the mocking-bird's tones and the flight of the
   mountain-hawk,
And heard at dawn the unrivall'd one, the hermit thrush from
   the swamp-cedars,
Solitary, singing in the West, I strike up for a New World . . .

FROM Song of Myself

I celebrate myself, and sing myself,
And what I assume you shall assume,
For every atom belonging to me as good belongs to you.

I loafe and invite my soul,
I lean and loafe at my ease observing a spear of summer grass.

My tongue, every atom of my blood, form'd from this soil,
   this air,
Born here of parents born here from parents the same, and
   their parents the same,
I, now thirty-seven years old in perfect health begin,
Hoping to cease not till death.

Creeds and schools in abeyance,
Retiring back a while sufficed at what they are, but never
   forgotten,
I harbor for good or bad, I permit to speak at every hazard,
Nature without check with original energy.

.   .   .   .   .

A child said What is the grass? fetching it to me with full
   hands;
How could I answer the child? I do not know what it is any
   more than he.
I guess it must be the flag of my disposition, out of hopeful
   green stuff woven.

Or I guess it is the handkerchief of the Lord,
A scented gift and remembrancer designedly dropt,
Bearing the owner's name someway in the corners, that we
   may see and remark, and say Whose?

Or I guess it is a uniform hieroglyphic,
And it means, Sprouting alike in broad zones and narrow
   zones,
Growing among black folks as among white,
Kanuck, Tuckahoe, Congressman, Cuff, I give them the same,
   I receive them the same.

And now it seems to me the beautiful uncut hair of graves.

Tenderly will I use you curling grass,
It may be you transpire from the breasts of young men,
It may be if I had known them I would have loved them,
It may be you are from old people, or from offspring taken
    soon out of their mothers' laps,
And here you are the mothers' laps.

This grass is very dark to be from the white heads of old
    mothers,
Darker than the colorless beards of old men,
Dark to come from under the faint red roofs of mouths.

O I perceive after all so many uttering tongues,
And I perceive they do not come from the roofs of mouths
    for nothing.

I wish I could translate the hints about the dead young men
    and women,
And the hints about old men and mothers, and the offspring
    taken soon out of their laps.

What do you think has become of the young and old men?
And what do you think has become of the women and chil-
    dren?

They are alive and well somewhere,
The smallest sprout shows there is really no death,
And if ever there was it led forward life, and does not wait
    at the end to arrest it,
And ceas'd the moment life appear'd.

All goes onward and outward, nothing collapses,
And to die is different from what any one supposed, and
    luckier.

    .   .   .   .   .

Walt Whitman, a kosmos, of Manhattan the son,
Turbulent, fleshy, sensual, eating, drinking and breeding,
No sentimentalist, no stander above men and women or apart
    from them,
No more modest than immodest.

Unscrew the locks from the doors!
Unscrew the doors themselves from their jambs!

Whoever degrades another degrades me,
And whatever is done or said returns at last to me.

Through me the afflatus surging and surging, through me the
    current and index.

I speak the pass-word primeval, I give the sign of democracy,
By God! I will accept nothing which all cannot have their
    counterpart of on the same terms.

Through me many long dumb voices,
Voices of the interminable generations of prisoners and slaves,
Voices of the diseas'd and despairing and of thieves and
    dwarfs,
Voices of cycles of preparation and accretion,
And of the threads that connect the stars, and of wombs and
    of the father-stuff,
And of the rights of them the others are down upon,
And of the deform'd, trivial, flat, foolish, despised,
Fog in the air, beetles rolling balls of dung.

Through me forbidden voices,
Voices of sexes and lusts, voices veil'd and I remove the veil,
Voices indecent by me clarified and transfigur'd.

       .   .   .   .   .

I think I could turn and live with animals, they are so placid
    and self-contain'd,
I stand and look at them long and long.

They do not sweat and whine about their condition,
They do not lie awake in the dark and weep for their sins,
They do not make me sick discussing their duty to God,
Not one is dissatisfied, not one is demented with the mania of
    owning things,
Not one kneels to another, nor to his kind that lived thou·
    sands of years ago,
Not one is respectable or unhappy over the whole earth.

.   .   .   .   .

I have said that the soul is not more than the body,
And I have said that the body is not more than the soul,
And nothing, not God, is greater to one than one's self is,
And whoever walks a furlong without sympathy walks to his
    own funeral dressed in his own shroud,
And I or you pocketless of a dime may purchase the pick of
    the earth,
And to glance with an eye or show a bean in its pod confounds
    the learning of all times,
And there is no trade or employment but the young man fol-
    lowing it may become a hero,
And there is no object so soft but it makes a hub for the
    wheel'd universe,
And I say to any man or woman, Let your soul stand cool
    and composed before a million universes.

And I say to mankind, Be not curious about God,
For I who am curious about each am not curious about God,
(No array of terms can say how much I am at peace about
    God and about death.)

I hear and behold God in every object, yet understand God
    not in the least,
Nor do I understand who there can be more wonderful than
    myself.

From Pent-Up Aching Rivers

From pent-up aching rivers,
From that of myself without which I were nothing,
From what I am determin'd to make illustrious, even if I stand
    sole among men,
From my own voice resonant, singing the phallus,
Singing the song of procreation,
Singing the need of superb children and therein superb
    grown people,
Singing the muscular urge and the blending,
Singing the bedfellow's song, (O resistless yearning!
O for any and each the body correlative attracting!

O for you whoever you are your correlative body! O it, more
    than all else, you delighting!)
From the hungry gnaw that eats me night and day,
From native moments, from bashful pains, singing them,
Seeking something yet unfound though I have diligently
    sought it many a long year,
Singing the true song of the soul fitful at random,
Renascent with grossest Nature or among animals,
Of that, of them and what goes with them my poems inform-
    ing,
Of the smell of apples and lemons, of the pairing of birds,
Of the wet of woods, of the lapping of waves,
Of the mad pushes of waves upon the land, I them chanting.
The overture lightly sounding, the strain anticipating,
The welcome nearness, the sight of the perfect body,
The swimmer swimming naked in the bath, or motionless on
    his back lying and floating,
The female form approaching, I pensive, love-flesh tremulous
    aching,
The divine list for myself or you or for any one making,
The face, the limbs, the index from head to foot, and what
    it arouses,
The mystic deliria, the madness amorous, the utter abandon-
    ment,
(Hark close and still what I now whisper to you,
I love you, O you entirely possess me,
O that you and I could escape from the rest and go utterly off,
    free and lawless,
Two hawks in the air, two fishes swimming in the sea not
    more lawless than we;)
The furious storm through me careering, I passionately trem-
    bling,
The oath of the inseparableness of two together, of the
    woman that loves me and whom I love more than my
    life, that oath swearing,
(O I willingly stake all for you,
O let me be lost if it must be so!
O you and I! what is it to us what the rest do or think?
What is all else to us? only that we enjoy each other and
    exhaust each other if it must be so;)
From the master, the pilot I yield the vessel to,

The general commanding me, commanding all, from him per-
    mission taking,
From time the programme hastening (I have loiter'd too long
    as it is)
From sex, from the warp and from the woof,
From privacy, from frequent repinings alone,
From plenty of persons near and yet the right person not near,
From the soft sliding of hands over me and thrusting of fin-
    gers through my hair and beard,
From the long sustain'd kiss upon the mouth or bosom,
From the close pressure that makes me or any man drunk,
    fainting with excess,
From what the divine husband knows, from the work of
    fatherhood,
From exultation, victory and relief, from the bedfellow's em-
    brace in the night,
From the act-poems of eyes, hands, hips and bosoms,
From the cling of the trembling arm,
From the bending curve and the clinch,
From side by side the pliant coverlet off-throwing,
From the one so unwilling to have me leave, and me just as
    unwilling to leave,
(Yet a moment O tender waiter, and I return,)
From the hour of shining stars and dropping dews,
From the night a moment I emerging flitting out,
Celebrate you act divine and you children prepared for,
And you stalwart loins.

Out of the Rolling Ocean the Crowd

Out of the rolling ocean the crowd came a drop gently to me,
Whispering *I love you, before long I die,*
I have travel'd a long way merely to look on you to touch you,
For I could not die till I once look'd on you,
For I fear'd I might afterwards lose you.

Now we have met, we have look'd, we are safe,
Return in peace to the ocean my love,
I too am part of that ocean my love, we are not so much
    separated,

Behold the great rondure, the cohesion of all, how perfect!
But as for me, for you, the irresistible sea is to separate us,
As for an hour carrying us diverse, yet cannot carry us diverse
    forever;
Be not impatient—a little space—know you I salute the air,
    the ocean and the land,
Every day at sundown for your dear sake my love.

FROM *Song of the Open Road*

Afoot and light-hearted I take to the open road,
Healthy, free, the world before me,
The long brown path before me leading wherever I choose.
Henceforth I ask not good-fortune, I myself am good-fortune,
Henceforth I whimper no more, postpone no more, need noth-
    ing,
Done with indoor complaints, libraries, querulous criticisms,
Strong and content I travel the open road.

The earth, that is sufficient,
I do not want the constellations any nearer,
I know they are very well where they are,
I know they suffice for those who belong to them.

.   .   .   .   .

I think heroic deeds were all conceiv'd in the open air, and
    all free poems also,
I think I could stop here myself and do miracles,
I think whatever I shall meet on the road I shall like, and
    whoever beholds me shall like me,
I think whoever I see must be happy.

From this hour I ordain myself loos'd of limits and imaginary
    lines,
Going where I list, my own master total and absolute,
Listening to others, considering well what they say,
Pausing, searching, receiving, contemplating,
Gently, but with undeniable will, divesting myself of the holds
    that would hold me.

I inhale great draughts of space,
The east and the west are mine, and the north and the south
    are mine.

I am larger, better than I thought,
I did not know I held so much goodness.

    •   •   •   •   •

Now if a thousand perfect men were to appear it would not
    amaze me,
Now if a thousand beautiful forms of women appear'd it
    would not astonish me.

Now I see the secret of the making of the best persons,
It is to grow in the open air and to eat and sleep with the
    earth.

    •   •   •   •   •

Listen! I will be honest with you,
I do not offer the old smooth prizes, but offer rough new
    prizes,
These are the days that must happen to you:
You shall not heap up what is call'd riches,
You shall scatter with lavish hand all that you earn or achieve,
You but arrive at the city to which you were destined, you
        hardly settle yourself to satisfaction before you are
        call'd by an irresistible call to depart,
You shall be treated to the ironical smiles and mockings of
        those who remain behind you,
What beckonings of love you receive you shall only answer
        with passionate kisses of parting,
You shall not allow the hold of those who spread their reach'd
        hands toward you.

    •   •   •   •   •

Allons! the road is before us!
It is safe—I have tried it—my own feet have tried it well—be
    not detain'd!
Let the paper remain on the desk unwritten, and the book
    on the shelf unopen'd!

Let the tools remain in the workshop! let the money remain
      unearn'd!
Let the school stand! mind not the cry of the teacher!
Let the preacher preach in his pulpit! let the lawyer plead
      in the court, and the judge expound the law.

Camerado, I give you my hand!
I give you my love more precious than money,
I give you myself before preaching or law;
Will you give me yourself? will you come travel with me?
Shall we stick by each other as long as we live?

FROM *Out of the Cradle Endlessly Rocking*

Out of the cradle endlessly rocking,
Out of the mocking-bird's throat, the musical shuttle,
Out of the Ninth-month midnight,
Over the sterile sands and the fields beyond, where the child
      leaving his bed wander'd alone, bareheaded, barefoot,
Down from the shower'd halo,
Up from the mystic play of shadows, twining and twisting as
      if they were alive,
Out from the patches of briers and blackberries,
From the memories of the bird that chanted to me,
From your memories sad brother, from the fitful risings and
      fallings I heard,
From under that yellow half-moon late-risen and swollen as if
      with tears,
From those beginning notes of yearning and love there in the
      mist.
From the thousand responses of my heart never to cease,
From the myriad thence-arous'd words,
From the word stronger and more delicious than any,
From such as now they start the scene revisiting,
As a flock, twittering, rising, or overhead passing,
Borne hither, ere all eludes me, hurriedly,
A man, yet by these tears a little boy again,
Throwing myself on the sand, confronting the waves,
I, chanter of pains and joys, uniter of here and hereafter,
Taking all hints to use them, but swiftly leaping beyond them,
A reminiscence sing.

As Toilsome I Wander'd Virginia's Woods

As toilsome I wander'd Virginia's woods,
To the music of rustling leaves kick'd by my feet (for 'twas
     autumn)
I mark'd at the foot of a tree the grave of a soldier;
Mortally wounded he and buried on the retreat, (easily all
     could I understand,)
The halt of a mid-day hour, when up! no time to lose—yet this
     sign left,
On a tablet scrawl'd and nail'd on the tree by the grave,
Bold, cautious, true, and my loving comrade.

Long, long I muse, then on my way go wandering,
Many a changeful season to follow, and many a scene of life,
Yet at times through changeful season and scene, abrupt,
     alone, or in the crowded street,
Comes before me the unknown soldier's grave, comes the
     inscription rude in Virginia's woods,
Bold, cautious, true, and my loving comrade.

The Wound-Dresser

An old man bending I come among new faces,
Years looking backward resuming in answer to children,
Come tell us old man, as from young men and maidens that
     love me,
(Arous'd and angry, I'd thought to beat the alarum, and urge
     relentless war,
But soon my fingers fail'd me, my face droop'd and I resign'd
     myself
To sit by the wounded and soothe them, or silently watch the
     dead;)
Years hence of these scenes, of these furious passions, these
     chances,
Of unsurpass'd heroes, (was one side so brave? the other was
     equally brave;)
Now be witness again, paint the mightiest armies of earth,
Of those armies so rapid so wondrous what saw you to tell
     us?

What stays with you latest and deepest? of curious panics,
Of hard-fought engagements or sieges tremendous what deep-
　　est remains?

O maidens and young men I love and that love me,
What you ask of my days those the strangest and sudden your
　　talking recalls,
Soldier alert I arrive after a long march cover'd with sweat
　　and dust,
In the nick of time I come, plunge in the fight, loudly shout in
　　the rush of successful charge,
Enter the captur'd works—yet lo, like a swift-running river
　　they fade,
Pass and are gone they fade—I dwell not on soldiers' perils or
　　soldiers' joys,
(Both I remember well—many the hardships, few the joys,
　　yet I was content.)

But in silence, in dreams' projections,
While the world of gain and appearance and mirth goes on,
So soon what is over forgotten, and waves wash the imprints
　　off the sand,
With hinged knees returning I enter the doors (while for you
　　up there,
Whoever you are, follow without noise and be of strong
　　heart.)

Bearing the bandages, water and sponge,
Straight and swift to my wounded I go,
Where they lie on the ground after the battle brought in,
Where their priceless blood reddens the grass the ground,
Or to the rows of the hospital tent, or under the roof'd hospi-
　　tal,
To the long row of cots up and down each side I return,
To each and all one after another I draw near, not one do I
　　miss,
An attendant follows holding a tray, he carries a refuse pail,
Soon to be filled with clotted rags and blood, emptied, and
　　fill'd again.

I onward go, I stop,
With hinged knees and steady hand to dress wounds,
I am firm with each, the pangs are sharp but unavoidable,

One turns to me his appealing eyes—poor boy! I never knew
you,
Yet I think I could not refuse this moment to die for you, if
that would save you.

On, on I go, (open doors of time! open hospital doors!)
The crush'd head I dress, (poor crazed hand tear not the
bandage away)
The neck of the cavalry-man with the bullet through and
through I examine,
Hard the breathing rattles, quite glazed already the eye, yet
life struggles hard,
(Come sweet death! be persuaded O beautiful death! In
mercy come quickly)

From the stump of the arm, the amputated hand,
I undo the clotted lint, remove the slough, wash off the mat-
ter and blood,
Back on the pillow the soldier bends with curv'd neck and
side-falling head,
His eyes are closed, his face is pale, he dares not look on the
bloody stump,
And has not yet look'd on it.

I dress a wound in the side, deep, deep,
But a day or two more, for see the frame all wasted and sink-
ing,
And the yellow-blue countenance see.

I dress the perforated shoulder, the foot with the bullet-
wound,
Cleanse the one with a gnawing and putrid gangrene, so sick-
ening, so offensive,
While the attendant stands behind aside me holding the tray
and pail.
I am faithful, I do not give out,
The fractur'd thigh, the knee, the wound in the abdomen,
These and more I dress with impassive hand, (yet deep in
my breast a fire, a burning flame.)

Thus in silence in dreams' projections,
Returning, resuming, I thread my way through the hospitals,
The hurt and wounded I pacify with soothing hand,

I sit by the restless all the dark night, some are so young,
Some suffer so much, I recall the experience sweet and sad,
(Many a soldier's loving arms about this neck have cross'd
          and rested,
Many a soldier's kiss dwells on these bearded lips.)

When Lilacs Last in the Dooryard Bloom'd

When lilacs last in the dooryard bloom'd,
And the great star early droop'd in the western sky in the
          night,
I mourn'd, and yet shall mourn with ever-returning spring.

Ever-returning spring, trinity sure to me you bring,
Lilac blooming perennial and drooping star in the west,
And thought of him I love.

O powerful western fallen star!
O shades of night—O moody, tearful night!
O great star disappear'd—O the black murk that hides the
          star!
O cruel hands that hold me powerless—O helpless soul of me!
O harsh surrounding cloud that will not free my soul.

In the dooryard fronting an old farm-house near the white-
          wash'd palings,
Stands the lilac-bush tall-growing with heart-shaped leaves
          of rich green,
With many a pointed blossom rising delicate, with the per-
          fume strong I love,
With every leaf a miracle—and from this bush in the door-
          yard,
With delicate-color'd blossoms and heart-shaped leaves of
          rich green,
A sprig with its flowers I break.

In the swamp in secluded recesses,
A shy and hidden bird is warbling a song.

Solitary the thrush,
The hermit withdrawn to himself, avoiding the settlements,
Sings by himself a song.

Song of the bleeding throat,
Death's outlet song of life, (for well dear brother I know,
If thou wast not granted to sing thou would'st surely die.)

Over the breast of the spring, the land, amid cities,
Amid lanes and through old woods, where lately the violets
          peep'd from the ground, spotting the gray debris,
Amid the grass in the fields each side of the lanes, passing the
          endless grass,
Passing the yellow-speared wheat, every grain from its shroud
          in the dark-brown fields uprisen,
Passing the apple-tree blows of white and pink in the orchards,
Carrying a corpse to where it shall rest in the grave,
Night and day journeys a coffin.

Coffin that passes through lanes and streets,
Through day and night with the great cloud darkening the
          land,
With the pomp of the inloop'd flags with the cities draped
          in black,
With the show of the States themselves as of crape-veil'd
          women standing,
With processions long and winding and the flambeaus of the
          night,
With the countless torches lit, with the silent sea of faces
          and the unbared heads,
With the waiting depot, the arriving coffin, and the sombre
          faces,
With dirges through the night, with the thousand voices ris-
          ing strong and solemn,
With all the mournful voices of the dirges pour'd around the
          coffin,
The dim-lit churches and the shuddering organs—where amid
          these you journey,
With the tolling tolling bells' perpetual clang,
Here, coffin that slowly passes,
I give you my sprig of lilac.

(Nor for you, for one alone,
Blossoms and branches green to coffins all I bring,
For fresh as the morning, thus would I chant a song for you
            O sane and sacred death.

All over bouquets of roses,
O death, I cover you over with roses and early lilies,
But mostly and now the lilac that blooms the first,
Copious I break, I break the sprigs from the bushes,
With loaded arms I come, pouring for you,
For you and the coffins of all of you O death.)

O western orb sailing the heaven,
Now I know what you must have meant as a month since I
            walk'd,
As I walk'd in silence the transparent shadowy night,
As I saw you had something to tell as you bent to me night
            after night,
As you droop'd from the sky low down as if to my side,
            (while the other stars all look'd on,)
As we wander'd together the solemn night, (for something I
            know not what kept me from sleep,)
As the night advanced, and I saw on the rim of the west how
            full you were of woe,
As I stood on the rising ground in the breeze in the cool
            transparent night,
As I watch'd where you pass'd and was lost in the netherward
            black of the night,
As my soul in its trouble dissatisfied sank, as where you, sad
            orb,
Concluded, dropt in the night, and was gone.

Sing on there in the swamp,
O singer bashful and tender, I hear your notes, I hear your
            call,
I hear, I come presently, I understand you,
But a moment I linger, for the lustrous star has detain'd me,
The star my departing comrade holds and detains me.

O how shall I warble myself for the dead one there I
            loved?

And how shall I deck my song for the large sweet soul that
     has gone?
And what shall my perfume be for the grave of him I love?

Sea-winds blown from east and west,
Blown from the Eastern sea and blown from the Western
     sea, till there on the prairies meeting,
These and with these and the breath of my chant,
I'll perfume the grave of him I love.

O what shall I hang on the chamber walls?
And what shall the pictures be that I hang on the walls,
To adorn the burial-house of him I love?

Pictures of growing spring and farms and homes,
With the Fourth-month eve at sundown, and the gray smoke
     lucid and bright,
With floods of the yellow gold of the gorgeous, indolent,
     sinking sun, burning, expanding the air,
With the fresh sweet herbage under foot, and the pale
     green leaves of the trees prolific,
In the distance the flowing glaze, the breast of the river, with
     a wind-dapple here and there,
With ranging hills on the banks, with many a line against the
     sky, and shadows,
And the city at hand with dwellings so dense, and stacks of
     chimneys,
And all the scenes of life and the workshops, and the workmen
     homeward returning.

Lo, body and soul—this land,
My own Manhattan with spires, and the sparkling and hurry-
     ing tides, and the ships,
The varied and ample land, the South and the North in the
     light, Ohio's shores and flashing Missouri,
And ever the far-spreading prairies cover'd with grass and
     corn.

Lo, the most excellent sun so calm and haughty,
The violet and purple morn with just-felt breezes,
The gentle soft-born measureless light,

The miracles spreading bathing all, the fulfill'd noon,
The coming eve delicious, the welcome night and the stars,
Over my cities shining all, enveloping man and land.

Sing on, sing on, you gray-brown bird,
Sing from the swamps, the recesses, pour your chant from
      the bushes,
Limitless out of the dusk, out of the cedars and pines.

Sing on dearest brother, warble your reedy song,
Loud human song, with voice of uttermost woe.

O liquid and free and tender!
O wild and loose to my soul—O wondrous singer!
You only I hear—yet the star holds me, (but will soon depart)
Yet the lilac with mastering odor holds me.

Now while I sat in the day and look'd forth,
In the close of the day with its light and the fields of spring,
      and the farmers preparing their crops,
In the large unconscious scenery of my land with its lakes
      and forests,
In the heavenly aerial beauty, (after the perturb'd winds
      and the storms,)
Under the arching heavens of the afternoon swift passing,
      and the voices of children and women,
The many-moving sea-tides, and I saw the ships how they
      sail'd,
And the summer approaching with richness, and the fields all
      busy with labor,
And the infinite separate houses, how they all went on, each
      with its meals and minutia of daily usages,
And the streets how their throbbings throbb'd, and the
      cities pent—lo, then and there,
Falling upon them all and among them all, enveloping me
      with the rest,
Appear'd the cloud, appear'd the long black trail,
And I knew death, its thought, and the sacred knowledge of
      death.

Then with the knowledge of death as walking one side of me,
And the thought of death close-walking the other side of
        me,
And I in the middle as with companions, and as holding the
        hands of companions,
I fled forth to the hiding receiving night that talks not,
Down to the shores of the water, the path by the swamp in
        the dimness,
To the solemn shadowy cedars and ghostly pines so still.

And the singer so shy to the rest receiv'd me,
The gray-brown bird I know receiv'd us comrades three,
And he sang the carol of death, and a verse for him I love.

From deep secluded recesses,
From the fragrant cedars and the ghostly pines so still,
Came the carol of the bird.

And the charm of the carol rapt me,
As I held as if by their hands my comrades in the night,
And the voice of my spirit tallied the song of the bird.

Come lovely and soothing death,
Undulate round the world, serenely arriving, arriving,
In the day, in the night, to all, to each,
Sooner or later delicate death.

Prais'd be the fathomless universe,
For life and joy, and for objects and knowledge curious,
And for love, sweet love—but praise! praise! praise!
For the sure-enwinding arms of cool-enfolding death!

Dark mother always gliding near with soft feet,
Have none chanted for thee a chant of fullest welcome?
Then I chant it for thee, I glorify thee above all,
I bring thee a song that when thou must indeed come, come
        unfalteringly.

Approach strong deliveress,
When it is so, when thou hast taken them I joyously sing the
        dead,

Lost in the loving floating ocean of thee,
Laved in the flood of thy bliss O death.

From me to thee glad serenades,
Dances for thee I propose saluting thee, adornments and
    feastings for thee,
And the sights of the open landscape and the high-spread sky
    are fitting,
And life and the fields, and the huge and thoughtful night.

The night in silence under many a star,
The ocean shore and the husky whispering wave whose voice
    I know,
And the soul turning to thee O vast and well-veil'd death,
And the body gratefully nestling close to thee.

Over the tree-tops I float thee a song,
Over the rising and sinking waves, over the myriad fields and
    the prairies wide,
Over the dense-pack'd cities all and the teeming wharves and
    ways,
I float this carol with joy, with joy to thee O death.

To the tally of my soul,
Loud and strong kept up the gray-brown bird,
With pure deliberate notes spreading filling the night.

Loud in the pines and cedars dim,
Clear in the freshness moist and the swamp-perfume,
And I with my comrades there in the night.

While my sight that was bound in my eyes unclosed,
As to long panoramas of visions.

And I saw askant the armies,
I saw as in noiseless dreams hundreds of battle-flags,
Borne through the smoke of the battles and pierc'd with
    missiles I saw them,
And carried hither and yon through the smoke, and torn
    and bloody,

And at last but a few shreds left on the staffs, (and all in
    silence,)
And the staffs all splinter'd and broken.

I saw battle-corpses, myriads of them,
And the white skeletons of young men, I saw them,
I saw the debris and debris of all the slain soldiers of the
    war,
But I saw they were not as was thought,
They themselves were fully at rest, they suffer'd not,
The living remain'd and suffer'd, the mother suffer'd,
And the wife and the child and the musing comrade suffer'd,
And the armies that remain'd suffer'd.

Passing the visions, passing the night,
Passing unloosing the hold of my comrades' hands,
Passing the song of the hermit bird and the tallying song of
    my soul,
Victorious song, death's outlet song, yet varying ever-altering
    song,
As low and wailing, yet clear the notes, rising and falling,
    flooding the night,
Sadly sinking and fainting, as warning and warning, and yet
    again bursting with joy,
Covering the earth and filling the spread of the heaven,
As that powerful psalm in the night I heard from recesses,
Passing, I leave thee lilac with heart-shaped leaves,
I leave thee there in the door-yard, blooming, returning with
    spring.

I cease from my song for thee,
From my gaze on thee in the west, fronting the west, com-
    muning with thee,
O comrade lustrous with silver face in the night.

Yet each to keep and all, retrievements out of the night,
The song, the wondrous chant of the gray-brown bird,
And the tallying chant, the echo arous'd in my soul,
With the lustrous and drooping star with the countenance
    full of woe,

With the holders holding my hand nearing the call of the
    bird,
Comrades mine and I in the midst, and their memory ever to
    keep, for the dead I loved so well,
For the sweetest, wisest soul of all my days and lands—and
    this for his dear sake,
Lilac and star and bird twined with the chant of my soul,
There in the fragrant pines and cedars dusk and dim.

To a Common Prostitute

Be composed—be at ease with me—I am Walt Whitman,
    liberal and lusty as Nature,
Not till the sun excludes you do I exclude you,
Not till the waters refuse to glisten for you and the leaves to
    rustle for you, do my words refuse to glisten and
    rustle for you.
My girl I appoint with you an appointment, and I charge
    you that you make preparation to be worthy to meet
    me,
And I charge you that you be patient and perfect till I come.

Till then I salute you with a significant look that you do not
    forget me.

Darest Thou Now O Soul

Darest thou now O soul,
Walk out with me toward the unknown region,
Where neither ground is for the feet nor any path to follow?

No map there, nor guide,
Nor voice sounding, nor touch of human hand,
Nor face with blooming flesh, nor lips, nor eyes, are in that
    land.

1 know it not O soul,
Nor dost thou, all is a blank before us,
All waits undream'd of in that region, that inaccessible land.

Till when the ties loosen,
All but the ties eternal, Time and Space,
Nor darkness, gravitation, sense, nor any bounds bounding us.

Then we burst forth, we float,
In Time and Space O soul, prepared for them,
Equal, equipt at last, (O joy, O fruit of all) them to fulfil
     O soul.

CHARLES KINGSLEY

(1819–1875)

"When All the World..."

When all the world is young, lad,
    And all the trees are green;
And every goose a swan, lad,
    And every lass a queen;
Then hey for boot and horse, lad,
    And round the world away:
Young blood must have its course, lad,
    And every dog his day.

When all the world is old, lad,
    And all the trees are brown;
And all the sport is stale, lad,
    And all the wheels run down;
Creep home, and take your place there,
    The spent and maimed among:
God grant you find one face there,
    You loved when all was young.

The Water Babies

JAMES RUSSELL LOWELL

(1819–1891)

She Came and Went

As a twig trembles, which a bird
    Lights on to sing, then leaves unbent,
So is my memory thrilled and stirred;—
    I only know she came and went.

As clasps some lake, by gusts unriven,
  The blue dome's measureless content,
So my soul held that moment's heaven;—
  I only know she came and went.

As, at one bound, our swift spring heaps
  The orchard full of bloom and scent,
So clove her May my wintry sleeps;—
  I only know she came and went.

An angel stood and met my gaze,
  Through the low doorway of my tent;
The tent is struck, the vision stays;—
  I only know she came and went.

Oh, when the room grows slowly dim,
  And life's last oil is nearly spent,
One gush of light these eyes will brim,
  Only to think she came and went.

HERMAN MELVILLE

(1819–1891)

"The Ribs and Terrors..."

The ribs and terrors in the whale,
  Arched over me a dismal gloom,
While all God's sun-lit waves rolled by,
  And lift* me deepening down to doom.

I saw the opening maw of hell,
  With endless pains and sorrows there;
Which none but they that feel can tell—
  Oh, I was plunging to despair.

In black distress, I called my God,
  When I could scarce believe Him mine,
He bowed His ear to my complaints—
  No more the whale did me confine.

With speed He flew to my relief,
  As on a radiant dolphin borne;
Awful, yet bright, as lightning shone
  The face of my Deliverer God.

* Left (?)

My song for ever shall record
   That terrible, that joyful hour;
I give the glory to my God,
   His all the mercy and the power.

Moby-Dick

The March into Virginia
(JULY 1861)

Did all the lets and bars appear
   To every just or larger end,
Whence should come the trust and cheer?
   Youth must its ignorant impulse lend—
Age finds place in the rear.
   All wars are boyish, and are fought by boys,
The champions and enthusiasts of the state:
   Turbid ardours and vain joys
     Not barrenly abate—
   Stimulants to the power mature,
     Preparatives of fate.

Who here forecasteth the event?
What heart but spurns at precedent
And warnings of the wise,
Contemned foreclosures of surprise?
The banners play, the bugles call,
The air is blue and prodigal.
   No berrying party, pleasure-wooed,
No picnic party in the May,
Ever went less loth than they
   Into that leafy neighborhood.
In Bacchic glee they file toward Fate,
Moloch's uninitiate;
Expectancy, and glad surmise
Of battle's unknown mysteries.
All they feel is this: 'tis glory,
A rapture sharp, though transitory,
Yet lasting in belaurelled story.
So they gaily go to fight,
Chatting left and laughing right.

But some who this blithe mood present,
　　As on in lightsome files they fare,
Shall die experienced ere three days are spent—
　　Perish, enlightened by the volleyed glare;
Or shame survive, and like to adamant,
　　The throe of Second Manassas share.

Shiloh, a Requiem
(APRIL 1862)

Skimming lightly, wheeling still,
　　The swallows fly low
Over the field in clouded days,
　　The forest-field of Shiloh—
Over the field where April rain
Solaced the parched one stretched in pain
Through the pause of night
That followed the Sunday fight
　　Around the church of Shiloh—
The church so lone, the log-built one,
That echoed to many a parting groan
　　　And natural prayer
　　Of dying foemen mingled there—
Foemen at morn, but friends at eve—
　　Fame or country least their care:
(What like a bullet can undeceive!)
　　But now they lie low,
While over them the swallows skim
　　And all is hushed at Shiloh.

FROM John Marr

Since as in night's deck-watch ye show,
Why, lads, so silent here to me,
Your watchmate of times long ago?

Once, for all the darkling sea,
You your voices raised how clearly,
Striking in when tempest sung;

Hoisting up the storm-sail cheerly,
Life is storm—let storm! you rung.
Taking things as fated merely,
Childlike though the world ye spanned;
Nor holding unto life too dearly,
Ye who held your lives in hand—
Skimmers, who on oceans four
Petrels were, and larks ashore.

O, not from memory lightly flung,
Forgot, like strains no more availing,
The heart to music haughtier strung;
Nay, frequent near me, never staling,
Whose good feeling kept ye young,
Like tides that enter creek or stream,
Ye come, ye visit me, or scem
Swimming out from seas of faces,
Alien myriads memory traces,
To enfold me in a dream!

I yearn as ye. But rafts that strain,
Parted, shall they lock again?
Twined we were, entwined, then riven,
Ever to new embracements driven,
Shifting gulf-weed of the main!
And how if one here shift no more,
Lodged by the flinging surge ashore?
Nor less, as now, in eve's decline,
Your shadowy fellowship is mine.
Ye float around me, form and feature:—
Tattooings, ear-rings, love-locks curled;
Barbarians of man's simpler nature,
Unworldly servers of the world.
Yea, present all, and dear to me,
Though shades, or scouring China's sea.

Whither, whither, merchant-sailors,
Witherward now in roaring gales?
Competing still, ye huntsman-whalers,
In leviathan's wake what boat prevails?
And man-of-war's men, whereaway?

If now no dinned drum beat to quarters
On the wilds of midnight waters—
Foemen looming through the spray;
Do yet your gangway lanterns, streaming,
Vainly strive to pierce below,
When tilted from the slant plank gleaming,
A brother you see to darkness go?

But, gunmates lashed in shotted canvas,
If where long watch-below ye keep,
Never the shrill *"All hands up hammocks!"*
Breaks the spell that charms your sleep,
And summoning trumps might vainly call,
And booming guns implore—
A beat, a heart-beat musters all,
One heart-beat at heart-core.
It musters. But to clasp, retain;
To see you at the halyards main—
To hear your chorus once again!

To Ned

Where is the world we roved, Ned Bunn?
    Hollows thereof lay rich in shade
By voyagers old inviolate thrown
    Ere Paul Pry cruised with Pelf and Trade.
To us old lads some thoughts come home
Who roamed a world young lads no more shall roam.

Nor less the satiate year impends
    When, wearying of routine-resorts,
The pleasure-hunter shall break loose,
    Ned, for our Pantheistic ports:—
Marquesas and glenned isles that be
Authentic Edens in a Pagan sea.

The charm of scenes untried shall lure,
    And, Ned, a legend urge the flight—
The Typee-truants under stars
    Unknown to Shakespeare's *Midsummer-Night;*

And man, if lost to Saturn's Age,
Yet feeling life no Syrian pilgrimage.

But, tell, shall he, the tourist, find
  Our isles the same in violet-glow
Enamouring us what years and years—
  Ah, Ned, what years and years ago!
Well, Adam advances, smart in pace,
But scarce by violets that advance you trace.

But we, in anchor-watches calm,
  The Indian Psyche's languor won,
And, musing, breathed primeval balm
  From Edens ere yet overrun,
Marvelling mild if mortal twice,
Here and hereafter, touch a Paradise.

Lone Founts

Though fast youth's glorious fable flies,
View not the world with worldling's eyes;
Nor turn with weather of the time.
Foreclose the coming of surprise:
Stand where Posterity shall stand;
Stand where the Ancients stood before,
And, dipping in lone founts thy hand,
Drink of the never-varying lore:
Wise once, and wise thence evermore.

Art

In placid hours well pleased we dream
Of many a brave unbodied scheme.
But form to lend, pulsed life create,
What unlike things must meet and mate:
A flame to melt—a wind to freeze;
Sad patience—joyous energies;

Humility—yet pride and scorn;
Instinct and study; love and hate;
Audacity—reverence. These must mate
And fuse with Jacob's mystic heart,
To wrestle with the angel—Art.

Fragments of a Lost Gnostic Poem
of the Twelfth Century

Found a family, build a state,
The pledged event is still the same:
Matter in end will never abate
His ancient brutal claim.

Indolence is heaven's ally here,
And energy the child of hell:
The Good Man pouring from his pitcher clear
But brims the poisoned well.

L'Envoi: The Return of the Sire de Nesle
(A.D. 16—)

My towers at last! These rovings end,
Their thirst is slaked in larger dearth:
The yearning infinite recoils,
    For terrible is earth.

Kaf thrusts his snouted crags through fog:
Araxes swells beyond his span,
And knowledge poured by pilgrimage
    Overflows the banks of man.

But thou, my stay, thy lasting love
One lonely good, let this but be!
Weary to view the wide world's swarm,
    But blest to fold but thee.

Immolated

Children of my happier prime,
When One yet lived with me, and threw
Her rainbow over life and time,
Even Hope, my bride, and mother to you!
O, nurtured in sweet pastoral air,
And fed on flowers and light and dew
Of morning meadows—spare, ah, spare
Reproach; spare, and upbraid me not
That, yielding scarce to reckless mood,
But jealous of your future lot,
I sealed you in a fate subdued.
Have I not saved you from the dread
Theft, and ignoring which need be
The triumph of the insincere
Unanimous Mediocrity?
Rest therefore, free from all despite,
Snugged in the arms of comfortable night.

Camoens

(BEFORE)

And ever must I fan this fire?
Thus ever in flame on flame aspire?
Ever restless, restless, craving rest—
The Imperfect toward Perfection pressed!
Yea, for the God demands thy best.
The world with endless beauty teems,
And thought evokes new worlds of dreams:
Hunt then the flying herds of themes!
And fan, still fan, thy fervid fire,
Until thy crucibled gold shall show
That fire can purge as well as glow.
In ordered ardour, nobly strong,
Flame to the height of epic song.

(AFTER)
Camoens in the Hospital

What now avails the pageant verse,
Trophies and arms with music borne?
Base is the world; and some rehearse
Now noblest meet ignoble scorn,
Vain now thy ardour, vain thy fire,
Delirium mere, unsound desire;
Fate's knife hath ripped thy corded lyre.
Exhausted by the exacting lay,
Thou dost but fall a surer prey
To wile and guile ill understood;
While they who work them, fair in face,
Still keep their strength in prudent place,
And claim they worthier run life's race,
Serving high God with useful good.

Falstaff's Lament over Prince Hal Become Henry V

One that I cherished,
Yea, loved as a son—
Up early, up late with,
My promising one:
No use in good nurture,
None, lads, none!

Here on this settle
He wore the true crown,
King of good fellows,
And Fat Jack was one—
Now, Beadle of England
In formal array—
Best fellow alive
On a throne flung away!

Companions and cronies
Keep fast and lament;—
Come drawer, more sack here
To drown discontent;

For now intuitions
Shall wither to codes,
Pragmatised morals
Shall libel the gods.

One I instructed,
Yea, talked to—alone:
Precept—example
Clean away thrown!

Sorrow makes thirsty:
Sack, drawer, more sack!—
One that I prayed for,
I, Honest Jack!

To bring down these gray hairs—
To cut his old pal!
But, I'll be magnanimous—
Here's to thee, Hal!

MATTHEW ARNOLD

(1822–1888)

Shakespeare

Others abide our question. Thou art free.
We ask and ask: Thou smilest and art still,
Out-topping knowledge. For the loftiest hill
That to the stars uncrowns his majesty,
Planting his steadfast footsteps in the sea,
Making the Heaven of Heavens his dwelling-place,
Spares but the cloudy border of his base
To the foil'd searching of mortality:
And thou, who didst the stars and sunbeams know,
Self-school'd, self-scann'd, self-honour'd, self-secure,
Didst walk on earth unguess'd at. Better so!
All pains the immortal spirit must endure,
All weakness that impairs, all griefs that bow,
Find their sole voice in that victorious brow.

The Forsaken Merman

Come, dear children, let us away;
Down and away below.
Now my brothers call from the bay;
Now the great winds shoreward blow;
Now the salt tides seaward flow;
Now the wild white horses play,
Champ and chafe and toss in the spray.
Children dear, let us away.
This way, this way.

Call her once before you go.
Call once yet.
In a voice that she will know:
"Margaret! Margaret!"
Children's voices should be dear
(Call once more) to a mother's ear:
Children's voices, wild with pain.
Surely she will come again.
Call her once and come away.
This way, this way.
"Mother dear, we cannot stay."
The wild white horses foam and fret.
Margaret! Margaret!

Come, dear children, come away down.
Call no more.
One last look at the white-wall'd town,
And the little grey church on the windy shore.
Then come down.
She will not come though you call all day.
Come away, come away.

Children dear, was it yesterday
We heard the sweet bells over the bay?
In the caverns where we lay,
Through the surf and through the swell,
The far-off sound of a silver bell?
Sand-strewn caverns, cool and deep,

Where the winds are all asleep;
Where the spent lights quiver and gleam;
Where the salt weed sways in the stream;
Where the sea-beasts rang'd all round
Feed in the ooze of their pasture-ground;
Where the sea-snakes coil and twine,
Dry their mail and bask in the brine;
Where great whales come sailing by,
Sail and sail, with unshut eye,
Round the world for ever and aye?
When did music come this way?
Children dear, was it yesterday?

Children dear, was it yesterday
(Call yet once) that she went away?
Once she sate with you and me,
On a red gold throne in the heart of the sea,
And the youngest sate on her knee.
She comb'd its bright hair, and she tended it well,
When down swung the sound of the far-off bell.
She sigh'd, she look'd up through the clear green sea.
She said: "I must go, for my kinsfolk pray
In the little grey church on the shore to-day.
'Twill be Easter-time in the world—ah me!
And I lose my poor soul, Merman, here with thee."
I said: "Go up, dear heart, through the waves;
Say thy prayer, and come back to the kind sea-caves."
She smil'd, she went up through the surf in the bay.
Children dear, was it yesterday?

Children dear, were we long alone?
"The sea grows stormy, the little ones moan.
Long prayers," I said, "in the world they say.
Come," I said, and we rose through the surf in the bay.
We went up the beach, by the sandy down
Where the sea-stocks bloom, to the white-wall'd town.
Through the narrow pav'd streets, where all was still,
To the little grey church on the windy hill.
From the church came a murmur of folk at their prayers,
For we stood without in the cold blowing airs.
We climb'd on the graves, on the stones, worn with rains,

And we gaz'd up the aisle through the small leaded panes.
She sate by the pillar; we saw her clear:
"Margaret, hist! come quick, we are here.
Dear heart," I said, "we are long alone.
The sea grows stormy, the little ones moan."
But, ah, she gave me never a look,
For her eyes were seal'd to the holy book.
Loud prays the priest; shut stands the door.
Come away, children, call no more.
Come away, come down, call no more.

Down, down, down.
Down to the depths of the sea.
She sits at her wheel in the humming town,
Singing most joyfully.
Hark, what she sings: "O joy, O joy,
For the humming street, and the child with its toy.
For the priest, and the bell, and the holy well.
For the wheel where I spun,
And the blessed light of the sun."
And so she sings her fill,
Singing most joyfully,
Till the shuttle falls from her hand,
And the whizzing wheel stands still.
She steals to the window, and looks at the sand;
And over the sand at the sea;
And her eyes are set in a stare;
And anon there breaks a sigh,
And anon there drops a tear,
From a sorrow-clouded eye,
And a heart sorrow-laden,
A long, long sigh,
For the cold strange eyes of a little Mermaiden,
And the gleam of her golden hair.

Come away, away children.
Come children, come down.
The hoarse wind blows colder;
Lights shine in the town.
She will start from her slumber
When gusts shake the door;

She will hear the winds howling,
Will hear the waves roar.
We shall see, while above us
The waves roar and whirl.
A ceiling of amber,
A pavement of pearl.
Singing, "Here came a mortal,
But faithless was she.
And alone dwell for ever
The kings of the sea."

But, children, at midnight,
When soft the winds blow;
When clear falls the moonlight;
When spring-tides are low:
When sweet airs come seaward
From heaths starr'd with broom;
And high rocks throw mildly
On the blanch'd sands a gloom:
Up the still, glistening beaches,
Up the creeks we will hie;
Over banks of bright seaweed
The ebb-tide leaves dry.
We will gaze, from the sand-hills,
At the white sleeping town;
At the church on the hill-side—
    And then come back down.
Singing, "There dwells a lov'd one,
But cruel is she.
She left lonely for ever
The kings of the sea."

Requiescat

Strew on her roses, roses,
    And never a spray of yew.
In quiet she reposes:
    Ah! would that I did too.

Her mirth the world required:
　　She bathed it in smiles of glee.
But her heart was tired, tired,
　　And now they let her be.

Her life was turning, turning,
　　In mazes of heat and sound.
But for peace her soul was yearning,
　　And now peace laps her round.

Her cabin'd, ample Spirit,
　　It flutter'd, and fail'd for breath.
To-night it doth inherit
　　The vasty Hall of Death.

The Scholar Gipsy

Go, for they call you, Shepherd, from the hill;
　　Go, Shepherd, and untie the wattled cotes:
　　　No longer leave thy wistful flock unfed,
　　Nor let thy bawling fellows rack their throats,
　　　Nor the cropp'd grasses shoot another head.
　　　　But when the fields are still,
　　And the tired men and dogs all gone to rest,
　　　And only the white sheep are sometimes seen
　　　Cross and recross the strips of moon-blanch'd green;
　　　　Come, Shepherd, and again renew the quest.

Here, where the reaper was at work of late,
　　In this high field's dark corner, where he leaves
　　　His coat, his basket, and his earthen cruse,
　　And in the sun all morning binds the sheaves,
　　　Then here, at noon, comes back his stores to use;
　　　　Here will I sit and wait,
　　While to my ear from uplands far away
　　　The bleating of the folded flocks is borne,
　　　With distant cries of reapers in the corn—
　　　　All the live murmur of a summer's day.

Screen'd in this nook o'er the high, half-reap'd field,
  And here till sun-down, Shepherd, will I be.
    Through the thick corn the scarlet poppies peep,
  And round green roots and yellowing stalks I see
    Pale blue convolvulus in tendrils creep:
      And air-swept lindens yield
  Their scent, and rustle down their perfum'd showers
    Of bloom on the bent grass where I am laid,
    And bower me from the August sun with shade;
      And the eye travels down to Oxford's towers:

And near me on the grass lies Glanvil's book—
  Come, let me read the oft-read tale again,
    The story of the Oxford scholar poor
  Of pregnant parts and quick inventive brain,
    Who, tir'd of knocking at Preferment's door,
      One summer morn forsook
  His friends, and went to learn the Gipsy lore,
    And roamed the world with that wild brotherhood,
    And came, as most men deem'd, to little good,
      But came to Oxford and his friends no more.

But once, years after, in the country lanes,
  Two scholars whom at college erst he knew
    Met him, and of his way of life inquir'd.
  Whereat he answered that the Gipsy crew,
    His mates, had arts to rule as they desir'd
      The workings of men's brains;
  And they can bind them to what thoughts they will:
    "And I," he said, "the secret of their art,
    When fully learned, will to the world impart:
      But it needs heaven-sent moments for this skill."

This said, he left them, and return'd no more,
  But rumours hung about the country side
    That the lost Scholar long was seen to stray,
  Seen by rare glimpses, pensive and tongue-tied,
    In hat of antique shape, and cloak of grey,
      The same the Gipsies wore.

Shepherds had met him on the Hurst in spring;
    At some lone alehouse in the Berkshire moors,
      On the warm ingle bench, the smock-frock'd boors
        Had found him seated at their entering.

But, mid their drink and clatter, he would fly:
    And I myself seem half to know thy looks,
      And put the shepherds, Wanderer, on thy trace;
    And boys who in lone wheatfields scare the rooks
      I ask if thou hast passed their quiet place;
        Or in my boat I lie
Moor'd to the cool bank in the summer heats,
    Mid wide grass meadows which the sunshine fills,
    And watch the warm green-muffled Cumner hills,
      And wonder if thou haunt'st their shy retreats.

For most, I know, thou lov'st retired ground.
    Thee, at the ferry, Oxford riders blithe,
      Returning home on summer nights, have met
    Crossing the stripling Thames at Bab-lock-hithe,
      Trailing in the cool stream thy fingers wet,
        As the slow punt swings round:
    And leaning backwards in a pensive dream,
      And fostering in thy lap a heap of flowers
      Pluck'd in shy fields and distant Wychwood bowers,
        And thine eyes resting on the moonlit stream:

And then they land, and thou art seen no more.
    Maidens who from the distant hamlet come
      To dance around the Fyfield elm in May,
    Oft through the darkening fields have seen thee roam,
      Or cross a stile into the public way.
        Oft thou hast given them store
    Of flowers—the frail-leaf'd, white anemone—
      Dark bluebells drench'd with dews of summer eves—
      And purple orchises with spotted leaves—
        But none has words she can report of thee.

And, above Godstow Bridge, when hay-time's here
    In June, and many a scythe in sunshine flames,
      Men who through those wild fields of breezy grass

Where black-wing'd swallows haunt the glittering Thames,
　To bathe in the abandon'd lasher pass,
　　Have often pass'd thee near
Sitting upon the river bank o'ergrown:
　Mark'd thy outlandish garb, thy figure spare,
　Thy dark vague eyes, and soft abstracted air;
　　But, when they came from bathing, thou wert gone.

At some lone homestead in the Cumner hills,
　Where at her open door the housewife darns,
　　Thou hast been seen, or hanging on a gate
To watch the threshers in the mossy barns.
　Children, who early range these slopes and late
　　For cresses from the rills,
Have known thee watching, all an April day,
　The springing pastures and the feeding kine;
　And mark'd thee, when the stars come out and shine,
　　Through the long dewy grass move slow away.

In autumn, on the skirts of Bagley wood,
　Where most the Gipsies by the turf-edg'd way
　　Pitch their smok'd tents, and every bush you see
With scarlet patches tagged and shreds of grey,
　Above the forest ground call'd Thessaly—
　　The blackbird picking food
Sees thee, nor stops his meal, nor fears at all;
　So often has he known thee past him stray
　Rapt, twirling in thy hand a wither'd spray,
　　And waiting for the spark from Heaven to fall.

And once, in winter, on the causeway chill
　Where home through flooded fields foot-travellers go,
　　Have I not pass'd thee on the wooden bridge
Wrapt in thy cloak and battling with the snow,
　Thy face towards Hinksey and its wintry ridge?
　　And thou hast climb'd the hill
And gain'd the white brow of the Cumner range,
　Turn'd once to watch, while thick the snowflakes fall,
　The line of festal light in Christ-Church hall—
　　Then sought thy straw in some sequester'd grange.

But what—I dream! Two hundred years are flown
  Since first thy story ran through Oxford halls,
    And the grave Glanvil did the tale inscribe
  That thou wert wander'd from the studious walls
    To learn strange arts, and join a Gipsy tribe:
      And thou from earth art gone
    Long since, and in some quiet churchyard laid;
      Some country nook, where o'er thy unknown grave
      Tall grasses and white flowering nettles wave—
        Under a dark red-fruited yew-tree's shade.

No, no, thou hast not felt the lapse of hours.
  For what wears out the life of mortal men?
    'Tis that from change to change their being rolls:
  'Tis that repeated shocks, again, again,
    Exhaust the energy of strongest souls,
      And numb the elastic powers.
    Till having us'd our nerves with bliss and teen,
      And tir'd upon a thousand schemes our wit,
      To the just-pausing Genius we remit
        Our worn-out life, and are—what we have been.

Thou hast not liv'd, why should'st thou perish, so?
  Thou hadst *one* aim, *one* business, *one* desire:
    Else wert thou long since number'd with the dead—
  Else hadst thou spent like other men thy fire.
    The generations of thy peers are fled,
      And we ourselves shall go;
    But thou possessest an immortal lot,
      And we imagine thee exempt from age
      And living as thou liv'st on Glanvil's page,
        Because thou hadst—what we, alas, have not!

For early didst thou leave the world, with powers
  Fresh, undiverted to the world without,
    Firm to their mark, not spent on other things;
  Free from the sick fatigue, the languid doubt,
      Which much to have tried, in much been baffled, brings.
        O Life unlike to ours!

Who fluctuate idly without term or scope,
　Of whom each strives, nor knows for what he strives,
　　And each half lives a hundred different lives;
　　　Who wait like thee, but not, like thee, in hope.

Thou waitest for the spark from Heaven: and we,
　Vague half-believers of our casual creeds,
　　Who never deeply felt, nor clearly will'd,
　Whose insight never has borne fruit in deeds,
　　Whose weak resolves never have been fulfill'd;
　　　For whom each year we see
　Breeds new beginnings, disappointments new;
　　Who hesitate and falter life away,
　　And lose to-morrow the ground won to-day—
　　　Ah, do not we, Wanderer, await it too?

Yes, we await it, but it still delays,
　And then we suffer; and amongst us One,
　　Who most has suffer'd, takes dejectedly
　His seat upon the intellectual throne;
　　And all his store of sad experience he
　　　Lays bare of wretched days;
　Tells us his misery's birth and growth and signs,
　　And how the dying spark of hope was fed,
　　And how the breast was sooth'd, and how the head,
　　　And all his hourly varied anodynes.

This for our wisest: and we others pine,
　And wish the long unhappy dream would end,
　　And waive all claim to bliss, and try to bear,
　With close-lipp'd Patience for our only friend,
　　Sad Patience, too near neighbour to Despair:
　　　But none has hope like thine.
　Thou through the fields and through the woods dost stray,
　　Roaming the country side, a truant boy,
　　Nursing thy project in unclouded joy,
　　　And every doubt long blown by time away.

O born in days when wits were fresh and clear,
　And life ran gaily as the sparkling Thames;
　　Before this strange disease of modern life,

With its sick hurry, its divided aims,
   Its heads o'ertax'd, its palsied hearts, was rife—
     Fly hence, our contact fear!
Still fly, plunge deeper in the bowering wood!
   Averse, as Dido did with gesture stern
   From her false friend's approach in Hades turn,
     Wave us away, and keep thy solitude.

Still nursing the unconquerable hope,
   Still clutching the inviolable shade,
     With a free onward impulse brushing through,
   By night, the silver'd branches of the glade—
     Far on the forest skirts, where none pursue,
       On some mild pastoral slope
   Emerge, and resting on the moonlit pales,
     Freshen thy flowers, as in former years,
     With dew, or listen with enchanted ears,
       From the dark dingles, to the nightingales.

But fly our paths, our feverish contact fly!
   For strong the infection of our mental strife,
     Which, though it gives no bliss, yet spoils for rest;
   And we should win thee from thy own fair life,
     Like us distracted, and like us unblest.
       Soon, soon thy cheer would die,
   Thy hopes grow timorous, and unfix'd thy powers,
     And thy clear aims be cross and shifting made:
     And then thy glad perennial youth would fade,
       Fade, and grow old at last, and die like ours.

They fly our greetings, fly our speech and smiles!
   As some grave Tyrian trader, from the sea,
     Descried at sunrise an emerging prow
   Lifting the cool-hair'd creepers stealthily,
     The fringes of a southward-facing brow
       Among the Aegean isles;
   And saw the merry Grecian coaster come,
     Freighted with amber grapes, and Chian wine,
     Green bursting figs, and tunnies steeped in brine;
       And knew the intruders on his ancient home,

The young light-hearted Masters of the waves;
   And snatch'd his rudder, and shook out more sail,
      And day and night held on indignantly
O'er the blue Midland waters with the gale,
      Betwixt the Syrtes and soft Sicily,
         To where the Atlantic raves
Outside the Western Straits, and unbent sails
      There, where down cloudy cliffs, through sheets of foam,
      Shy traffickers, the dark Iberians come;
         And on the beach undid his corded bales.

FROM *Stanzas from the Grande Chartreuse*

For rigorous teachers seized my youth,
And purged its faith, and trimm'd its fire,
Show'd me the high white star of Truth,
There bade me gaze, and there aspire;
Even now their whispers pierce the gloom:
What dost thou in this living tomb?

Forgive me, masters of the mind!
At whose behest I long ago
So much unlearnt, so much resign'd!
I come not here to be your foe.
I seek these anchorites, not in ruth,
To curse and to deny your truth;

Not as their friend or child I speak!
But as on some far northern strand,
Thinking of his own gods, a Greek
In pity and mournful awe might stand
Before some fallen Runic stone—
For both were faiths, and both are gone.

Wandering between two worlds, one dead,
The other powerless to be born,
With nowhere yet to rest my head,
Like these, on earth I wait forlorn.
Their faith, my tears, the world deride;
I come to shed them at their side.

Dover Beach

The sea is calm to-night.
The tide is full, the moon lies fair
Upon the straits;—on the French coast the light
Gleams and is gone; the cliffs of England stand
Glimmering and vast, out in the tranquil bay.
Come to the window, sweet is the night-air!
Only, from the long line of spray
Where the sea meets the moon-blanch'd land,
Listen! you hear the grating roar
Of pebbles which the waves draw back, and fling,
At their return, up the high strand,
Begin, and cease, and then again begin,
With tremulous cadence slow, and bring
The eternal note of sadness in.

Sophocles long ago
Heard it on the Ægean, and it brought
Into his mind the turbid ebb and flow
Of human misery; we
Find also in the sound a thought,
Hearing it by this distant northern sea.

The Sea of Faith
Was once, too, at the full, and round earth's shore
Lay like the folds of a bright girdle furl'd.
But now I only hear
Its melancholy, long, withdrawing roar,
Retreating, to the breath
Of the night-wind, down the vast edges drear
And naked shingles of the world.

Ah, love, let us be true
To one another! for the world, which seems
To lie before us like a land of dreams,
So various, so beautiful, so new,
Hath really neither joy, nor love, nor light,
Nor certitude, nor peace, nor help for pain;
And we are here as on a darkling plain
Swept with confused alarms of struggle and flight,
Where ignorant armies clash by night.

WILLIAM JOHNSON CORY
(1823–1892)

Heraclitus

They told me, Heraclitus, they told me you were dead,
They brought me bitter news to hear and bitter tears to shed.
I wept as I remembered how often you and I
Had tired the sun with talking and sent him down the sky.

And now that thou art lying, my dear old Carian guest,
A handful of grey ashes, long, long ago at rest,
Still are thy pleasant voices, thy nightingales, awake;
For Death, he taketh all away, but them he cannot take.

From the Greek

COVENTRY KERSEY DIGHTON PATMORE
(1823–1896)

FROM *The Angel in the House*

An idle poet, here and there,
Looks round him; but, for all the rest
The world, unfathomably fair,
Is duller than a witling's jest.

Love wakes men, once a lifetime each;
They lift their heavy lids and look;
And, lo, what one sweet page can teach
They read with joy, then shut the book:

And some give thanks, and some blaspheme,
And most forget; but, either way,
That and the child's unheeded dream
Is all the light of all their day.

The Toys

My little Son, who looked from thoughtful eyes,
And moved and spoke in quiet grown-up wise,
Having my law the seventh time disobeyed,

I struck him, and dismissed
With hard words and unkissed,
—His Mother, who was patient, being dead.
Then, fearing lest his grief should hinder sleep,
I visited his bed,
But found him slumbering deep,
With darkened eyelids, and their lashes yet
From his late sobbing wet.
And I, with moan,
Kissing away his tears, left others of my own;
For, on a table drawn beside his head,
He had put, within his reach,
A box of counters and a red-veined stone,
A piece of glass abraded by the beach,
And six or seven shells,
A bottle with bluebells,
And two French copper coins, ranged there with careful art,
To comfort his sad heart.
So when that night I prayed
To God, I wept, and said:
Ah, when at last we lie with trancéd breath,
Not vexing Thee in death,
And Thou rememberest of what toys
We made our joys,
How weakly understood
Thy great commanded good,
Then fatherly not less
Than I whom Thou hast moulded from the clay,
Thou'lt leave Thy wrath, and say,
"I will be sorry for their childishness."

WILLIAM ALLINGHAM

(1824--1889)

The Fairies

Up the airy mountain,
  Down the rushy glen,
We daren't go a-hunting
  For fear of little men.

Wee folk, good folk,
  Trooping all together;
Green jacket, red cap,
  And white owl's feather!

Down along the rocky shore
  Some make their home—
They live on crispy pancakes
  Of yellow tide-foam;
Some in the reeds
  Of the black mountain-lake,
With frogs for their watch-dogs,
  All night awake.

High on the hill-top
  The old King sits;
He is now so old and grey,
  He's nigh lost his wits.
With a bridge of white mist
  Columbkill he crosses,
On his stately journeys
  From Slieveleague to Rosses;
Or going up with music
  On cold starry nights,
To sup with the Queen
  Of the gay Northern Lights.

They stole little Bridget
  For seven years long;
When she came down again,
  Her friends were all gone.
They took her lightly back,
  Between the night and morrow;
They thought that she was fast asleep,
  But she was dead with sorrow.
They have kept her ever since
  Deep within the lake,
On a bed of flag-leaves,
  Watching till she wake.

By the craggy hill-side,
    Through the mosses bare,
They have planted thorn-trees,
    For pleasure here and there.
Is any man so daring
    As dig them up in spite,
He shall find their sharpest thorns
    ·In his bed at night.

Up the airy mountain,
    Down the rushy glen,
We daren't go a-hunting
    For fear of little men.
Wee folk, good folk,
    Trooping all together;
Green jacket, red cap,
    And white owl's feather!

GEORGE MEREDITH

(1828–1909)

Love in the Valley

Under yonder beech-tree single on the green-sward,
    Couched with her arms behind her golden head,
Knees and tresses folded to slip and ripple idly,
    Lies my young love sleeping in the shade.
Had I the heart to slide an arm beneath her,
    Press her parting lips as her waist I gather slow,
Waking in amazement she could not but embrace me:
    Then would she hold me and never let me go?

Shy as the squirrel and wayward as the swallow,
    Swift as the swallow along the river's light
Circleting the surface to meet his mirrored winglets,
    Fleeter she seems in her stay than in her flight.
Shy as the squirrel that leaps among the pine-tops,
    Wayward as the swallow overhead at set of sun,
She whom I love is hard to catch and conquer,
    Hard, but O the glory of the winning were she won!

When her mother tends her before the laughing mirror,
  Tying up her laces, looping up her hair,
Often she thinks, were this wild thing wedded,
  More love should I have, and much less care.
When her mother tends her before the lighted mirror,
  Loosening her laces, combing down her curls,
Often she thinks, were this wild thing wedded,
  I should miss but one for many boys and girls.

Heartless she is as the shadow in the meadows
  Flying to the hills on a blue and breezy noon.
No, she is athirst and drinking up her wonder:
  Earth to her is young as the slip of the new moon.
Deals she an unkindness, 'tis but her rapid measure,
  Even as in a dance; and her smile can heal no less:
Like the swinging May-cloud that pelts the flowers with
    hailstones
  Off a sunny border, she was made to bruise and bless.

Lovely are the curves of the white owl sweeping
  Wavy in the dusk lit by one large star.
Lone on the fir-branch, his rattle-note unvaried,
  Brooding o'er the gloom, spins the brown eve-jar.
Darker grows the valley, more and more forgetting:
  So were it with me if forgetting could be willed.
Tell the grassy hollow that holds the bubbling well-spring,
  Tell it to forget the source that keeps it filled.

Stepping down the hill with her fair companions,
  Arm in arm, all against the raying West,
Boldly she sings, to the merry tune she marches,
  Brave is her shape, and sweeter unpossessed.
Sweeter, for she is what my heart first awaking
  Whispered the world was; morning light is she.
Love that so desires would fain keep her changeless;
  Fain would fling the net, and fain have her free.

Happy, happy time, when the white star hovers
  Low over dim fields fresh with bloomy dew,
Near the face of dawn, that draws athwart the darkness,
  Threading it with colour, like yewberries the yew.

Thicker crowd the shades as the grave East deepens
  Glowing, and with crimson a long cloud swells.
Maiden still the morn is; and strange she is, and secret;
  Strange her eyes; her cheeks are cold as cold sea-shells.

Sunrays, leaning on our southern hills and lighting
  Wild cloud-mountains that drag the hills along,
Oft ends the day of your shifting brilliant laughter
  Chill as a dull face frowning on a song.
Ay, but shows the South-West a ripple-feathered bosom
  Blown to silver while the clouds are shaken and ascend,
Scaling the mid-heavens as they stream, there comes a sunset
  Rich, deep like love in beauty without end.

When at dawn she sighs, and like an infant to the window
  Turns grave eyes craving light, released from dreams,
Beautiful she looks, like a white water-lily
  Bursting out of bud in havens of the streams.
When from bed she rises clothed from neck to ankle
  In her long nightgown sweet as boughs of May,
Beautiful she looks, like a tall garden lily
  Pure from the night, and splendid for the day.

Mother of the dews, dark eye-lashed twilight,
  Low-lidded twilight, o'er the valley's brim,
Rounding on thy breast sings the dew-delighted sky-lark,
  Clear as though the dewdrops had their voice in him.
Hidden where the rose-flush drinks the rayless planet,
  Fountain-full he pours the spraying fountain-showers.
Let me hear her laughter, I would have her ever
  Cool as dew in twilight, the lark above the flowers.

All the girls are out with their baskets for the primrose;
  Up lanes, woods through, they troop in joyful bands.
My sweet leads: she knows not why, but now she loiters,
  Eyes the bent anemones, and hangs her hands.
Such a look will tell that the violets are peeping,
  Coming the rose: and unaware a cry
Springs in her bosom for odours and for colour,
  Covert and the nightingale; she knows not why.

Kerchiefed head and chin she darts between her tulips,
  Streaming like a willow grey in arrowy rain:
Some bend beaten cheek to gravel, and their angel
  She will be; she lifts them, and on she speeds again.
Black the driving raincloud breasts the iron gateway:
  She is forth to cheer a neighbour lacking mirth.
So when sky and grass met rolling dumb for thunder
  Saw I once a white dove, sole light of earth.

Prim little scholars are the flowers of her garden,
  Trained to stand in rows, and asking if they please.
I might love them well but for loving more the wild ones:
  O my wild ones! they tell me more than these.
You, my wild one, you tell of honied field-rose,
  Violet, blushing eglantine in life; and even as they,
They by the wayside are earnest of your goodness,
  You are of life's, on the banks that line the way.

Peering at her chamber the white crowns the red rose,
  Jasmine winds the porch with stars two and three.
Parted is the window; she sleeps; the starry jasmine
  Breathes a falling breath that carries thoughts of me.
Sweeter unpossessed, have I said of her my sweetest?
  Not while she sleeps: while she sleeps the jasmine breathes,
Luring her to love; she sleeps; the starry jasmine
  Bears me to her pillow under white rose-wreaths.

Yellow with birdfoot-trefoil are the grass-glades;
  Yellow with cinquefoil of the dew-grey leaf;
Yellow with stone-crop; the moss-mounds are yellow;
  Blue-necked the wheat sways, yellowing to the sheaf.
Green-yellow bursts from the copse the laughing yaffle;
  Sharp as a sickle is the edge of shade and shine:
Earth in her heart laughs looking at the heavens,
  Thinking of the harvest: I look and think of mine.

This I may know: her dressing and undressing
  Such a change of light shows as when the skies in sport
Shift from cloud to moonlight; or edging over thunder
  Slips a ray of sun; or sweeping into port

White sails furl; or on the ocean borders
   White sails lean along the waves leaping green.
Visions of her shower before me, but from eyesight
   Guarded she would be like the sun were she seen.

Front door and back of the mossed old farmhouse
   Open with the morn, and in a breezy link
Freshly sparkles garden to stripe-shadowed orchard,
   Green across a rill where on sand the minnows wink.
Busy in the grass the early sun of summer
   Swarms, and the blackbird's mellow fluting notes
Call my darling up with round and roguish challenge:
   Quaintest, richest carol of all the singing throats!

Cool was the woodside; cool as her white dairy
   Keeping sweet the cream-pan; and there the boys from
      school,
Cricketing below, rushed brown and red with sunshine;
   O the dark translucence of the deep-eyed cool!
Spying from the farm, herself she fetched a pitcher
   Full of milk, and tilted for each in turn the beak.
Then a little fellow, mouth up and on tiptoe,
   Said "I will kiss you": she laughed and leaned her cheek.

Doves of the fir-wood walling high our red roof
   Through the long noon coo, crooning through the coo.
Loose droop the leaves, and down the sleepy roadway
   Sometimes pipes a chaffinch; loose droops the blue.
Cows flap a slow tail knee-deep in the river,
   Breathless, given up to sun and gnat and fly.
Nowhere is she seen; and if I see her nowhere,
   Lightning may come, straight rains and tiger sky.

O the golden sheaf, the rustling treasure-armful!
   O the nutbrown tresses nodding interlaced!
O the treasure-tresses one another over
   Nodding! O the girdle slack about the waist!
Slain are the poppies that shot their random scarlet
   Quick amid the wheatears: wound about the waist,
Gathered, see these brides of Earth one blush of ripeness!
   O the nutbrown tresses nodding interlaced!

Large and smoky red the sun's cold disk drops,
  Clipped by naked hills, on violet shaded snow:
Eastward large and still lights up a bower of moonrise,
  Whence at her leisure steps the moon aglow.
Nightlong on black print-branches our beech-tree
  Gazes in this whiteness: nightlong could I.
Here may life on death or death on life be painted.
  Let me clasp her soul to know she cannot die!

Gossips count her faults; they scour a narrow chamber
  Where there is no window, read not heaven or her.
"When she was a tiny," one aged woman quavers,
  Plucks at my heart and leads me by the ear.
Faults she had once as she learnt to run and tumbled:
  Faults of feature some see, beauty not complete.
Yet, good gossips, beauty that makes holy
  Earth and air, may have faults from head to feet.

Hither she comes; she comes to me; she lingers,
  Deepens her brown eyebrows, while in new surprise
High rise the lashes in wonder of a stranger;
  Yet am I the light and living of her eyes.
Something friends have told her fills her heart to brimming,
  Nets her in her blushes, and wounds her, and tames.—
Sure of her haven, O like a dove alighting,
  Arms up, she dropped: our souls were in our names.

Soon will she lie like a white-frost sunrise.
  Yellow oats and brown wheat, barley pale as rye,
Long since your sheaves have yielded to the thresher,
  Felt the girdle loosened, seen the tresses fly.
Soon will she lie like a blood-red sunset.
  Swift with the to-morrow, green-winged Spring!
Sing from the South-West, bring her back the truants,
  Nightingale and swallow, song and dipping wing.

Soft new beech-leaves, up to beamy April
  Spreading bough on bough a primrose mountain, you
Lucid in the moon, raise lilies to the skyfields,
  Youngest green transfused in silver shining through:

Fairer than the lily, than the wild white cherry:
　　Fair as in image my seraph love appears
Borne to me by dreams when dawn is at my eyelids:
　　Fair as in the flesh she swims to me on tears.

Could I find a place to be alone with heaven,
　　I would speak my heart out: heaven is my need.
Every woodland tree is flushing like the dogwood,
　　Flashing like the whitebeam, swaying like the reed.
Flushing like the dogwood crimson in October;
　　Streaming like the flag-reed South-West blown;
Flashing as in gusts the sudden-lighted whitebeam:
　　All seem to know what is for heaven alone.

FROM *Modern Love*

VI

It chanced his lips did meet her forehead cool.
She had no blush, but slanted down her eye.
Shamed nature, then, confesses love can die:
And most she punishes the tender fool
Who will believe what honours her the most!
Dead! Is it dead? She has a pulse, and flow
Of tears, the price of blood-drops, as I know,
For whom the midnight sobs around Love's ghost,
Since then I heard her, and so will sob on.
The love is here; it has but changed its aim.
O bitter barren woman! what's the name?
The name, the name, the new name thou hast won?
Behold me striking the world's coward stroke!
That will I not do, though the sting is dire.
—Beneath the surface this, while by the fire
They sat, she laughing at a quiet joke.

XII

Not solely that the Future she destroys,
And the fair life which in the distance lies
For all men, beckoning out from dim rich skies:
Nor that the passing hour's supporting joys

Have lost the keen-edged flavour, which begat
Distinction in old times, and still should breed
Sweet Memory, and Hope,—earth's modest seed,
And heaven's high-prompting: not that the world is flat
Since that soft-luring creature I embraced,
Among the children of Illusion went:
Methinks with all this loss I were content,
If the mad Past, on which my foot is based,
Were firm, or might be blotted: but the whole
Of life is mixed: the mocking Past will stay:
And if I drink oblivion of a day,
So shorten I the stature of my soul.

ΛΛΛ

What are we first? First, animals; and next
Intelligences at a leap; on whom
Pale lies the distant shadow of the tomb,
And all that draweth on the tomb for text.
Into which state comes Love, the crowning sun:
Beneath whose light the shadow loses form.
We are the lords of life, and life is warm.
Intelligence and instinct now are one.
But nature says: "My children most they seem
When they least know me: therefore I decree
That they shall suffer." Swift doth young Love flee,
And we stand wakened, shivering from our dream.
Then if we study Nature we are wise,
Thus do the few who live but with the day:
The scientific animals are they.—
Lady, this is my sonnet to your eyes.

XLII

I am to follow her. There is much grace
In women when thus bent on martyrdom.
They think that dignity of soul may come,
Perchance, with dignity of body. Base!
But I was taken by that air of cold
And statuesque sedateness, when she said
"I'm going"; lit a taper, bowed her head,
And went, as with the stride of Pallas bold.
Fleshly indifference horrible! The hands

Of Time now signal: O, she's safe from me!
Within those secret walls what do I see?
Where first she set the taper down she stands:
Not Pallas: Hebe shamed! Thoughts black as death,
Like a stirred pool in sunshine break. Her wrists
I catch: she faltering, as she half resists,
"You love . . . ? love . . . ? love . . . ?" all on
        an indrawn breath.

XLVII

We saw the swallows gathering in the sky,
And in the osier-isle we heard them noise.
We had not to look back on summer joys,
Or forward to a summer of bright dye:
But in the largeness of the evening earth
Our spirits grew as we went side by side.
The hour became her husband and my bride.
Love that had robbed us so, thus blessed our dearth!
The pilgrims of the year waxed very loud
In multitudinous chatterings, as the flood
Full brown came from the West, and like pale blood
Expanded to the upper crimson cloud.
Love that had robbed us of immortal things,
This little moment mercifully gave,
Where I have seen across the twilight wave
The swan sail with her young beneath her wings.

L

Thus piteously Love closed what he begat:
The union of this ever-diverse pair!
These two were rapid falcons in a snare,
Condemned to do the flitting of the bat.
Lovers beneath the singing sky of May,
They wandered once; clear as the dew on flowers:
But they fed not on the advancing hours:
Their hearts held cravings for the buried day.
Then each applied to each that fatal knife,
Deep questioning, which probes to endless dole.
Ah, what a dusty answer gets the soul
When hot for certainties in this our life!—
In tragic hints here see what evermore

Moves dark as yonder midnight ocean's force,
Thundering like ramping hosts of warrior horse,
To throw that faint thin line upon the shore!

Appreciation

Earth was not Earth before her sons appeared,
Nor Beauty Beauty ere young Love was born:
And thou when I lay hidden wast as morn
At city-windows, touching eyelids bleared;
To none by her fresh wingedness endeared;
Unwelcome unto revellers outworn.
I the last echoes of Diana's horn
In woodland heard, and saw thee come, and cheered.
No longer wast thou then mere light, fair soul!
And more than simple duty moved thy feet.
New colours rose in thee, from fear, from shame,
From hope, effused: though not less pure a scroll
May men read on the heart I taught to beat:
That change in thee, if not thyself, I claim.

Lucifer in Starlight

On a starred night Prince Lucifer uprose.
Tired of his dark dominion swung the fiend
Above the rolling ball in cloud part screened,
Where sinners hugged their spectre of repose.
Poor prey to his hot fit of pride were those.
And now upon his western wing he leaned,
Now his huge bulk o'er Afric's sands careened,
Now the black planet shadowed Arctic snows.
Soaring through wider zones that pricked his scars
With memory of the old revolt from Awe,
He reached a middle height, and at the stars,
Which are the brain of heaven, he looked, and sank.
Around the ancient track marched, rank on rank,
The army of unalterable law.

DANTE GABRIEL ROSSETTI

(1828–1882)

A Little While

A little while a little love
   The hour yet bears for thee and me
   Who have not drawn the veil to see
If still our heaven be lit above.
Thou merely, at the day's last sigh,
   Hast felt thy soul prolong the tone;
And I have heard the night-wind cry
   And deemed its speech mine own.

A little while a little love
   The scattering autumn hoards for us
   Whose bower is not yet ruinous
Nor quite unleaved our songless grove.
Only across the shaken boughs
   We hear the flood-tides seek the sea,
And deep in both our hearts they rouse
   One wail for thee and me.

A little while a little love
   May yet be ours who have not said
   The word it makes our eyes afraid
To know that each is thinking of.
Not yet the end: be our lips dumb
   In smiles a little season yet:
I'll tell thee, when the end is come,
   How we may best forget.

Three Shadows

I looked and saw your eyes
   In the shadow of your hair,
As a traveller sees the stream
   In the shadow of the wood;

And I said, "My faint heart sighs,
   Ah me! to linger there,
To drink deep and to dream
   In that sweet solitude."

I looked and saw your heart
   In the shadow of your eyes,
As a seeker sees the gold
   In the shadow of the stream;
And I said, "Ah me! what art
   Should win the immortal prize,
Whose want must make life cold
   And Heaven a hollow dream?"

I looked and saw your love
   In the shadow of your heart,
As a diver sees the pearl
   In the shadow of the sea;
And I murmured, not above
   My breath, but all apart,—
"Ah! you can love, true girl,
   And is your love for me?"

Autumn Song

Know'st thou not at the fall of the leaf
How the heart feels a languid grief
   Laid on it for a covering,
   And how sleep seems a goodly thing
In Autumn at the fall of the leaf?

And how the swift beat of the brain
Falters because it is in vain,
   In Autumn at the fall of the leaf
   Knowest thou not? and how the chief
Of joys seems—not to suffer pain?

Know'st thou not at the fall of the leaf
How the soul feels like a dried sheaf
   Bound up at length for harvesting,
   And how death seems a comely thing
In Autumn at the fall of the leaf?

For a Venetian Pastoral by Giorgione

Water, for anguish of the solstice:—nay,
But dip the vessel slowly,—nay, but lean
And hark how at its verge the wave sighs in
Reluctant. Hush! beyond all depth away
The heat lies silent at the brink of day:
Now the hand trails upon the viol-string
That sobs, and the brown faces cease to sing,
Sad with the whole of pleasure. Whither stray
Her eyes now, from whose mouth the slim pipes creep
And leave it pouting, while the shadowed grass
Is cool against her naked side? Let be:—
Say nothing now unto her lest she weep,
Nor name this ever. Be it as it was,—
Life touching lips with immortality.

FROM *The House of Life*

1.

A Sonnet is a moment's monument,—
Memorial from the Soul's eternity
To one dead deathless hour. Look that it be,
Whether for lustral rite or dire portent,
Of its own arduous fullness reverent:
Carve it in ivory or in ebony,
As Night or Day may rule; and let Time see
Its flowering crest impearled and orient.

A Sonnet is a coin: its face reveals
The soul,—its converse, to what Power 'tis due:—
Whether for tribute to the august appeals
Of Life, or dower in Love's high retinue,
It serve; or, mid the dark wharf's cavernous breath,
In Charon's palm it pay the toll to Death.

2. LOVESIGHT

When do I see thee most, beloved one?
When in the light the spirits of mine eyes
Before thy face, their altar, solemnize

The worship of that Love through thee made known?
Or when in the dusk hours (we two alone),
 Close-kissed and eloquent of still replies
 Thy twilight-hidden glimmering visage lies,
And my soul only sees thy soul its own?

O love, my love! if I no more should see
Thyself, nor on the earth the shadow of thee,
 Nor image of thine eyes in any spring,—
How then should sound upon Life's darkening slope
The ground-whirl of the perished leaves of Hope,
 The wind of Death's imperishable wing?

3.   WITHOUT HER

What of her glass without her? The blank grey
 There where the pool is blind of the moon's face.
 Her dress without her? The tossed empty space
Of cloud-rack whence the moon has passed away.
Her paths without her? Day's appointed sway
 Usurped by desolate night. Her pillowed place
 Without her? Tears, ah me! for love's good grace,
And cold forgetfulness of night or day.

What of the heart without her? Nay, poor heart,
 Of thee what word remains ere speech be still?
 A wayfarer by barren ways and chill,
Steep ways and weary, without her thou art,
Where the long cloud, the long wood's counterpart,
 Sheds doubled darkness up the labouring hill.

4.   THE CHOICE

I

Eat thou and drink; to-morrow thou shalt die.
 Surely the earth, that's wise being very old,
 Needs not our help. Then loose me, love, and hold
Thy sultry hair up from my face; that I

May pour for thee this golden wine, brim-high,
   Till round the glass thy fingers glow like gold.
   We'll drown all hours: thy song, while hours are toll'd,
Shall leap, as fountains veil the changing sky.

Now kiss, and think that there are really those,
   My own high-bosomed beauty, who increase
     Vain gold, vain lore, and yet might choose our way!
     Through many years they toil; then on a day
   They die not,—for their life was death,—but cease;
And round their narrow lips the mould falls close.

II

Watch thou and fear; to-morrow thou shalt die.
   Or art thou sure thou shalt have time for death?
   Is not the day which God's word promiseth
To come man knows not when? In yonder sky
Now while we speak, the sun speeds forth: can I
   Or thou assure him of his goal? God's breath
   Even at this moment haply quickeneth
The air to a flame; till spirits, always nigh
Though screened and hid, shall walk the daylight here.
   And dost thou prate of all that men shall do?
     Canst thou, who hast but plagues, presume to be
     Glad in his gladness that comes after thee?
   Will *his* strength slay *thy* worm in Hell? Go to:
Cover thy countenance, and watch, and fear.

III

Think thou and act; to-morrow thou shalt die.
   Outstretched in the sun's warmth upon the shore,
   Thou say'st: "Man's measured path is all gone o'er:
Up all his years, steeply, with strain and sigh,
Man clomb until he touched the truth; and I,
   Even I, am he whom it was destined for."
   How should this be? Art thou then so much more
Than they who sowed, that thou shouldst reap thereby?

Nay, come up hither. From this wave-washed mound
   Unto the furthest flood-brim look with me;

Then reach on with thy thought till it be drowned.
 Miles and miles distant though the last line be,
And though thy soul sail leagues and leagues beyond,—
 Still, leagues beyond those leagues, there is more sea.

The Ballad of Dead Ladies

Tell me now in what hidden way is
 Lady Flora the hidden Roman?
Where's Hipparchia, and where is Thais,
 Neither of them the fairer woman?
 Where is Echo, beheld of no man,
Only heard in river and mere,—
 She whose beauty was more than human? . . .
But where are the snows of yester-year?

Where's Héloïse, the learned nun,
 For whose sake Abeillard, I ween,
Lost manhood and put priesthood on?
 (From Love he won such dule and teen!)
 And where, I pray you, is the Queen
Who willed that Buridan should steer
 Sewed in a sack's mouth down the Seine? . . .
But where are the snows of yester-year?

White Queen Blanche, like a queen of lilies,
 With a voice like any mermaiden,—
Bertha Broadfoot, Beatrice, Alice,
 And Ermengarde the lady of Maine,—
 And that good Joan whom Englishmen
At Rouen doomed and burned her there,—
 Mother of God, where are they then? . . .
But where are the snows of yester-year?

Nay, never ask this week, fair lord,
 Where they are gone, nor yet this year,
Save with thus much for an overword,—
 But where are the snows of yester-year?

From the French of FRANÇOIS VILLON, 1450

Beauty
(A COMBINATION FROM SAPPHO)

Like the sweet apple which reddens upon the topmost bough,
A-top on the topmost twig,—which the pluckers forgot some-
    how,—
Forgot it not, nay, but got it not, for none could get it till now.

Like the wild hyacinth which on the hills is found,
Which the passing feet of the shepherds for ever tear and
    wound,
Until the purple blossom is trodden into the ground.

SILAS WEIR MITCHELL

(1829–1914)

A Decanter of Madeira, Aged 86,
to George Bancroft, Aged 86

Good master, you and I were born
    In "Teacup days" of hoop and hood,
And when the silver cue hung down,
    And toasts were drunk, and wine was good;

When kin of mine (a jolly brood)
    From sideboards looked, and knew full well
What courage they had given the beau,
    How generous made the blushing belle.

Ah me! what gossip could I prate
    Of days when doors were locked at dinners!
Believe me, I have kissed the lips
    Of many pretty saints—or sinners.

Lip service have I done, alack!
    I don't repent, but come what may,
What ready lips, sir, I have kissed,
    Be sure at least I shall not say.

Two honest gentlemen are we,—
   I Demi John, whole George are you;
When Nature grew us one in years
   She meant to make a generous brew.

She bade me store for festal hours
   The sun our south-side vineyard knew;
To sterner tasks she set your life,
   As statesman, writer, scholar, grew.

Years eighty-six have come and gone;
   At last we meet. Your health to-night.
Take from this board of friendly hearts
   The memory of a proud delight.

The days that went have made you wise.
   There's wisdom in my rare bouquet.
I'm rather paler than I was;
   And on my soul, you're growing gray.

I like to think, when Toper Time
   Has drained the last of me and you,
Some here shall say, They both were good,—
   The wine we drank, the man we knew.

CHRISTINA GEORGINA ROSSETTI

(1830–1894)

FROM *Monna Innominata*

XI

Many in after times will say of you
"He loved her"—while of me what will they say?
Not that I loved you more than just in play,
For fashion's sake as idle women do.
Even let them prate; who know not what we knew
Of love and parting in exceeding pain,
Of parting hopeless here to meet again,
Hopeless on earth, and heaven is out of view.
But by my heart of love laid bare to you,

My love that you can make not void nor vain,
Love that foregoes you but to claim anew
Beyond this passage of the gate of death,
I charge you at the Judgment make it plain
My love of you was life and not a breath.

XIV

Youth gone, and beauty gone if ever there
Dwelt beauty in so poor a face as this;
Youth gone and beauty, what remains of bliss?
I will not bind fresh roses in my hair,
To shame a cheek at best but little fair,—
Leave youth his roses, who can bear a thorn,—
I will not seek for blossoms anywhere,
Except such common flowers as blow with corn.
Youth gone and beauty gone, what doth remain?
The longing of a heart pent up forlorn,
A silent heart whose silence loves and longs;
The silence of a heart which sang its songs
While youth and beauty made a summer morn,
Silence of love that cannot sing again.

Song

When I am dead, my dearest,
    Sing no sad songs for me;
Plant thou no roses at my head,
    Nor shady cypress tree:
Be the green grass above me
    With showers and dewdrops wet:
And if thou wilt, remember,
    And if thou wilt, forget.

I shall not see the shadows,
    I shall not feel the rain;
I shall not hear the nightingale
    Sing on as if in pain:
And dreaming through the twilight
    That doth not rise nor set,
Haply I may remember,
    And haply may forget.

Song

Oh roses for the flush of youth,
　　And laurel for the perfect prime;
But pluck an ivy branch for me
　　Grown old before my time.

Oh violets for the grave of youth,
　　And bay for those dead in their prime;
Give me the withered leaves I chose
　　Before in the old time.

Remember

Remember me when I am gone away,
Gone far away into the silent land;
When you can no more hold me by the hand,
Nor I half turn to go yet turning stay.
Remember me when no more day by day
You tell me of our future that you plann'd:
Only remember me; you understand
It will be late to counsel then or pray.
Yet if you should forget me for a while
And afterwards remember, do not grieve:
For if the darkness and corruption leave
A vestige of the thoughts that once I had,
Better by far you should forget and smile
Than that you should remember and be sad.

FROM The Prince's Progress

Too late for love, too late for joy,
　　Too late, too late!
You loitered on the road too long,
　　You trifled at the gate:
The enchanted dove upon her branch
　　Died without a mate;
The enchanted princess in her tower
　　Slept, died, behind the grate;
Her heart was starving all this while
　　You made it wait.

Ten years ago, five years ago,
　One year ago,
Even then you had arrived in time,
　Though somewhat slow;
Then you had known her living face
　Which now you cannot know:
The frozen fountain would have leaped,
　The buds gone on to blow,
The warm south wind would have awaked
　To melt the snow.

Is she fair now as she lies?
　Once she was fair;
Meet queen for any kindly king,
　With gold-dust on her hair.
Now these are poppies in her locks,
　White poppies she must wear;
Must wear a veil to shroud her face
　And the want graven there:
Or is the hunger fed at length,
　Cast off the care?

We never saw her with a smile
　Or with a frown;
Her bed seemed never soft to her,
　Though tossed of down;
She little heeded what she wore,
　Kirtle, or wreath, or gown;
We think her white brows often ached
　Beneath her crown,
Till silvery hairs showed in her locks
　That used to be so brown.

We never heard her speak in haste;
　Her tones were sweet,
And modulated just so much
　As it was meet:
Her heart sat silent through the noise
　And concourse of the street.

There was no hurry in her hands,
  No hurry in her feet;
There was no bliss drew nigh to her,
  That she might run to greet.

You should have wept her yesterday,
  Wasting upon her bed:
But wherefore should you weep to-day
  That she is dead?
Lo, we who love weep not to-day,
  But crown her royal head.
Let be these poppies that we strew,
  Your roses are too red:
Let these be poppies, not for you
  Cut down and spread.

A Birthday

My heart is like a singing bird
  Whose nest is in a watered shoot:
My heart is like an apple-tree
  Whose boughs are bent with thickset fruit;
My heart is like a rainbow shell
  That paddles in a halcyon sea;
My heart is gladder than all these
  Because my love is come to me.

Raise me a dais of silk and down;
  Hang it with vair and purple dyes;
Carve it in doves and pomegranates,
  And peacocks with a hundred eyes;
Work it in gold and silver grapes,
  In leaves and silver fleurs-de-lys;
Because the birthday of my life
  Is come, my love is come to me.

Echo

Come to me in the silence of the night;
　Come in the speaking silence of a dream;
Come with soft rounded cheeks and eyes as bright
　As sunlight on a stream;
　　Come back in tears,
O memory, hope, love of finished years.

O dream how sweet, too sweet, too bitter sweet,
　Whose wakening should have been in Paradise,
Where souls brimfull of love abide and meet;
　Where thirsty longing eyes
　　Watch the slow door
That opening, letting in, lets out no more.

Yet come to me in dreams, that I may live
　My very life again though cold in death:
Come back to me in dreams, that I may give
　Pulse for pulse, breath for breath:
　　Speak low, lean low,
As long ago, my love, how long ago.

Up-Hill

Does the road wind up-hill all the way?
　Yes, to the very end.
Will the day's journey take the whole long day?
　From morn to night, my friend.

But is there for the night a resting-place?
　A roof for when the slow dark hours begin.
May not the darkness hide it from my face?
　You cannot miss that inn.

Shall I meet other wayfarers at night?
　Those who have gone before.
Then must I knock, or call when just in sight?
　They will not keep you standing at that door.

Shall I find comfort, travel-sore and weak?
Of labour you shall find the sum.
Will there be beds for me and all who seek?
Yea, beds for all who come.

Twice

I took my heart in my hand,
    (O my love, O my love),
I said: Let me fall or stand,
    Let me live or die,
But this once hear me speak—
    (O my love, O my love)—
Yet a woman's words are weak;
    You should speak, not I.

You took my heart in your hand
    With a friendly smile,
With a critical eye you scanned,
    Then set it down,
And said: It is still unripe
    Better wait awhile;
Wait while the skylarks pipe,
    Till the corn grows brown.

As you set it down it broke—
    Broke, but did not wince;
I smiled at the speech you spoke,
    At your judgment that I heard:
But I have not often smiled
    Since then, nor questioned since,
Nor cared for corn-flowers wild,
    Nor sung with the singing bird.

I take my heart in my hand,
    O my God, O my God,
My broken heart in my hand:
    Thou hast seen, judge Thou.

My hope was written on sand,
   O my God, O my God:
Now let Thy judgment stand—
   Yea, judge me now.

This contemned of a man,
   This marred one heedless day,
This heart take Thou to scan
   Both within and without:
Refine with fire its gold,
   Purge Thou its dross away—
Yea hold it in Thy hold,
   Whence none can pluck it out.

I take my heart in my hand—
   I shall not die, but live—
Before Thy face I stand;
   I, for Thou callest such:
All that I have I bring,
   All that I am I give;
Smile Thou and I shall sing,
   But shall not question much.

EMILY DICKINSON

(1830–1886)

"My Life Closed Twice..."

My life closed twice before its close;
   It yet remains to see
If Immortality unveil
   A third event to me,

So huge, so hopeless to conceive,
   As these that twice befell.
Parting is all we know of heaven,
   And all we need of hell.

"Doubt Me ..."

Doubt me, my dim companion!
Why, God would be content
With but a fraction of the love
Poured thee without a stint.
The whole of me, forever,
What more the woman can,—
Say quick, that I may dower thee
With last delight I own!

It cannot be my spirit,
For that was thine before,
I ceded all of dust I knew,—
What opulence the more
Had I, a humble maiden,
Whose farthest of degree
Was that she might
Some distant heaven,
Dwell timidly with thee!

"I'm Ceded ..."

I'm ceded, I've stopped being theirs;
The name they dropped upon my face
With water, in the country church,
Is finished using now,
And they can put it with my dolls,
My childhood, and the string of spools
I've finished threading too.

Baptized before without the choice,
But this time consciously, of grace
Unto supremest name,
Called to my full, the crescent dropped,
Existence's whole arc filled up
With one small diadem.

My second rank, too small the first,
Crowned, crowing on my father's breast,
A half unconscious queen;
But this time, adequate, erect,
With will to choose or to reject,
And I choose—just a throne.

"I'm Wife..."

I'm wife; I've finished that,
That other state;
I'm Czar, I'm woman now:
It's safer so.

How odd the girl's life looks
Behind this soft eclipse!
I think that earth seems so
To those in heaven now.

This being comfort, then
That other kind was pain;
But why compare?
I'm wife! stop there!

"Proud of My Broken Heart..."

Proud of my broken heart since thou didst break it,
    Proud of the pain I did not feel till thee.
Proud of my night since thou with moons dost slake it,
    Not to partake thy passion, my humility.

"Heart, We Will Forget Him!"

Heart, we will forget him!
    You and I, to-night!
You may forget the warmth he gave,
    I will forget the light.

When you have done, pray tell me,
    That I my thoughts may dim;
Haste! lest while you're lagging,
    I may remember him!

"Title Divine Is Mine"

Title divine is mine
The Wife without
The Sign.
Acute degree
Conferred on me—
Empress of Calvary,
Royal all but the
Crown
Betrothed, without the swoon
God gives us women
When two hold
Garnet to garnet,
Gold to gold—
Born—Bridalled—
Shrouded—
In a day
Tri-Victory—
"My Husband"
Women say
Stroking the melody,
Is this the way?

"This Quiet Dust..."

This quiet dust was Gentlemen and Ladies,
    And Lads and Girls;
Was laughter and ability and sighing,
    And frocks and curls.
This passive place a Summer's nimble mansion,
    Where Bloom and Bees
Fulfilled their Oriental Circuit,
    Then ceased like these.

JAMES THOMSON

(1834–1882)

FROM *The City of Dreadful Night*

PROEM

Lo, thus, as prostrate, "In the dust I write
　My heart's deep languor and my soul's sad tears."
Yet why evoke the spectres of black night
　To blot the sunshine of exultant years?
Why disinter dead faith from mouldering hidden?
Why break the seals of mute despair unbidden,
　And wail life's discords into careless ears?

Because a cold rage seizes one at whiles
　To show their bitter old and wrinkled truth
Stripped naked of all vesture that beguiles,
　False dreams, false hopes, false masks and modes of youth;
Because it gives some sense of power and passion
In helpless impotence to try to fashion
　Our woe in living words howe'er uncouth.

Surely I write not for the hopeful young,
　Or those who deem their happiness of worth,
Or such as pasture and grow fat among
　The shows of life and feel not doubt nor dearth,
Or pious spirits with a God above them
To sanctify and glorify and love them,
　Or sages who foresee a heaven on earth.

For none of these I write, and none of these
　Could read the writing if they deigned to try:
So may they flourish in their due degrees,
　On our sweet earth and in their unplaced sky.
If any cares for the weak words here written,
It must be some one desolate, Fate-smitten,
　Whose faith and hope are dead, and who would die.

Yes, here and there some weary wanderer
　In that same city of tremendous night
Will understand the speech, and feel a stir
　Of fellowship in all-disastrous fight;

"I suffer mute and lonely, yet another
Uplifts his voice to let me know a brother
   Travels the same wild paths though out of sight."

O sad Fraternity, do I unfold
   Your dolorous mysteries shrouded from of yore?
Nay, be assured; no secret can be told
   To any who divined it not before:
None uninitiate by many a presage
Will comprehend the language of the message,
   Although proclaimed aloud for evermore.

I

The City is of Night; perchance of Death,
   But certainly of Night; for never there
Can come the lucid morning's fragrant breath
   After the dewy dawning's cold grey air;
The moon and stars may shine with scorn or pity;
The sun has never visited that city,
   For it dissolveth in the daylight fair.

Dissolveth like a dream of night away;
   Though present in distempered gloom of thought
And deadly weariness of heart all day.
   But when a dream night after night is brought
Throughout a week, and such weeks few or many
Recur each year for several years, can any
   Discern that dream from real life in aught?

For life is but a dream whose shapes return,
   Some frequently, some seldom, some by night
And some by day, some night and day: we learn,
   The while all change and many vanish quite,
In their recurrence with recurrent changes
A certain seeming order; where this ranges
   We count things real; such is memory's might.

A river girds the city west and south,
   The main north channel of a broad lagoon,
Regurging with the salt tides from the mouth;
   Waste marshes shine and glister to the moon

For leagues, then moorland black, then stony ridges;
Great piers and causeways, many noble bridges,
   Connect the town and islet suburbs strewn.

Upon an easy slope it lies at large,
   And scarcely overlaps the long curved crest
Which swells out two leagues from the river marge.
   A trackless wilderness rolls north and west,
Savannahs, savage woods, enormous mountains,
Bleak uplands, black ravines with torrent fountains;
   And eastward rolls the shipless sea's unrest.

The city is not ruinous, although
   Great ruins of an unremembered past,
With others of a few short years ago
   More sad, are found within its precincts vast.
The street-lamps always burn; but scarce a casement
In house or palace front from roof to basement
   Doth glow or gleam athwart the mirk air cast.

The street-lamps burn amidst the baleful glooms,
   Amidst the soundless solitudes immense
Of rangéd mansions dark and still as tombs.
   The silence which benumbs or strains the sense
Fulfils with awe the soul's despair unweeping:
Myriads of habitants are ever sleeping,
   Or dead, or fled from nameless pestilence!

Yet as in some necropolis you find
   Perchance one mourner to a thousand dead,
So there; worn faces that look deaf and blind
   Like tragic masks of stone. With weary tread,
Each wrapt in his own doom, they wander, wander,
Or sit foredone and desolately ponder
   Through sleepless hours with heavy drooping head.

Mature men chiefly, few in age or youth,
   A woman rarely, now and then a child:
A child! If here the heart turns sick with ruth
   To see a little one from birth defiled,

Or lame or blind, as preordained to languish
Through youthless life, think how it bleeds with anguish
    To meet one erring in that homeless wild.

They often murmur to themselves, they speak
    To one another seldom, for their woe
Broods maddening inwardly, and scorns to wreak
    Itself abroad; and if at whiles it grow
To frenzy which must rave, none heeds the clamour,
Unless there waits some victim of like glamour,
    To rave in turn, who lends attentive show.

The City is of Night, but not of Sleep;
    There sweet sleep is not for the weary brain;
The pitiless hours like years and ages creep,
    A night seems termless hell. This dreadful strain
Of thought and consciousness which never ceases,
Or which some moments' stupor but increases,
    This, worse than woe, makes wretches there insane.

They leave all hope behind who enter there:
    One certitude while sane they cannot leave,
One anodyne for torture and despair;
    The certitude of Death, which no reprieve
Can put off long; and which, divinely tender,
But waits the outstretched hand to promptly render
    That draught whose slumber nothing can bereave.

XIII

Of all things human which are strange and wild
    This is perchance the wildest and most strange,
And showeth man most utterly beguiled,
    To those who haunt that sunless City's range;
That he bemoans himself for aye, repeating
How time is deadly swift, how life is fleeting,
    How naught is constant on the earth but change.

The hours are heavy on him and the days;
    The burden of the months he scarce can bear;
And often in his secret soul he prays
    To sleep through barren periods unaware,

Arousing at some longed-for date of pleasure;
Which having passed and yielded him small treasure,
  He would outsleep another term of care.

Yet in his marvellous fancy he must make
  Quick wings for Time, and see it fly from us;
This Time that crawleth like a monstrous snake,
  Wounded and slow and very venomous;
Which creeps blindwormlike round the earth and ocean,
Distilling poison at each painful motion,
  And seems condemned to circle ever thus.

And since he cannot spend and use aright
  The little time here given him in trust,
But wasteth it in weary undelight
  Of foolish toil and trouble, strife and lust,
He naturally claimeth to inherit
The everlasting Future, that his merit
  May have full scope; as surely is most just.

O length of the intolerable hours,
  O nights that are as aeons of slow pain,
O Time, too ample for our vital powers,
  O Life, whose woeful vanities remain
Immutable for all of all our legions
Through all the centuries and in all the regions,
  Not of your speed and variance *we* complain.

We do not ask a longer term of strife,
  Weakness and weariness and nameless woes;
We do not claim renewed and endless life
  When this which is our torment here shall close,
An everlasting conscious inanition!
We yearn for speedy death in full fruition,
  Dateless oblivion and divine repose.

FROM *Sunday up the River*

I

I looked out into the morning,
  I looked out into the west:
The soft blue eye of the quiet sky
  Still drooped in dreamy rest;

The trees were still like clouds there,
  The clouds like mountains dim;
The broad mist lay, a silver bay
  Whose tide was at the brim.

I looked out into the morning,
  I looked out into the east:
The flood of light upon the night
  Had silently increased;

The sky was pale with fervour,
  The distant trees were grey,
The hill-lines drawn like waves of dawn
  Dissolving in the day.

I looked out into the morning;
  Looked east, looked west, with glee:
O richest day of happy May,
  My love will spend with me!

XVIII

The wine of Love is music,
  And the feast of Love is song:
And when Love sits down to the banquet,
    Love sits long;

Sits long and ariseth drunken,
  But not with the feast and the wine;
He reeleth with his own heart,
    That great rich Vine.

FROM *Sunday at Hampstead*

X

As we rush, as we rush in the Train,
    The trees and the houses go wheeling back,
But the starry heavens above the plain
    Come flying on our track.

All the beautiful stars of the sky,
    The silver doves of the forest of Night,
Over the dull earth swarm and fly,
    Companions of our flight.

We will rush ever on without fear;
    Let the goal be far, the flight be fleet!
For we carry the Heavens with us, Dear,
    While the Earth slips from our feet!

WILLIAM MORRIS

(1834–1896)

Summer Dawn

Pray but one prayer for me 'twixt thy closed lips,
    Think but one thought of me up in the stars.
    The summer night waneth, the morning light slips,
Faint and grey 'twixt the leaves of the aspen, betwixt the
        cloud-bars,
That are patiently waiting there for the dawn:
    Patient and colourless, though Heaven's gold
Waits to float through them along with the sun.
Far out in the meadows, above the young corn,
    The heavy elms wait, and restless and cold
The uneasy wind rises; the roses are dun;
Through the long twilight they pray for the dawn.
Round the lone house in the midst of the corn.
    Speak but one word to me over the corn,
    Over the tender, bowed locks of the corn.

FROM *The Life and Death of Jason*

1.

I know a little garden-close,
Set thick with lily and red rose,
Where I would wander if I might
From dewy dawn to dewy night,
And have one with me wandering.

And though within it no birds sing,
And though no pillared house is there,
And though the apple boughs are bare
Of fruit and blossom, would to God,
Her feet upon the green grass trod,
And I beheld them as before.

There comes a murmur from the shore,
And in the place two fair streams are,
Drawn from the purple hills afar,
Drawn down unto the restless sea;
The hills whose flowers ne'er fed the bee,
The shore no ship has ever seen,
Still beaten by the billows green,
Whose murmur comes unceasingly
Unto the place for which I cry.

For which I cry both day and night,
For which I let slip all delight,
That maketh me both deaf and blind,
Careless to win, unskilled to find,
And quick to lose what all men seek.

Yet tottering as I am and weak,
Still have I left a little breath
To seek within the jaws of death
An entrance to that happy place,
To seek the unforgotten face
Once seen, once kissed, once reft from me
Anigh the murmuring of the sea.

2.

The Sirens: O happy seafarers are ye,
And surely all your ills are past,

And toil upon the land and sea,
    Since ye are brought to us at last.

To you the fashion of the world,
    Wide lands laid waste, fair cities burned,
And plagues, and kings from kingdoms hurled,
    Are nought, since hither ye have turned.

For as upon this beach we stand,
    And o'er our heads the sea-fowl flit,
Our eyes behold a glorious land,
    And soon shall ye be kings of it.

Orpheus: A little more, a little more,
    O carriers of the Golden Fleece,
A little labour with the oar,
    Before we reach the land of Greece.

E'en now perchance faint rumours reach
    Men's ears of this our victory,
And draw them down unto the beach
    To gaze across the empty sea.

But since the longed-for day is nigh,
    And scarce a God could stay us now,
Why do ye hang your heads and sigh,
    Hindering for nought our eager prow?

The Sirens: Ah, had ye chanced to reach the home
    On which your fond desires were set,
Into what troubles had ye come?
    Short love and joy and long regret.

But now, but now, when ye have lain
    Asleep with us a little while
Beneath the washing of the main,
    How calm shall be your waking smile!

For ye shall smile to think of life
    That knows no troublous change or fear,

No unavailing bitter strife,
　That ere its time brings trouble near.

Orpheus: Is there some murmur in your ears,
　　That all that we have done is nought,
　And nothing ends our cares and fears,
　　Till the last fear on us is brought?

The Sirens: Alas! and will ye stop your ears,
　　In vain desire to do aught,
　And wish to live 'mid cares and fears,
　　Until the last fear makes you nought?

Orpheus: Is not the May-time now on earth,
　　When close against the city wall
　The folks are singing in their mirth,
　　While on their heads the May-flowers fall?

The Sirens: Yes, May is come, and its sweet breath
　　Shall well-nigh make you weep to-day,
　And pensive with swift-coming death,
　　Shall ye be satiate of the May.

Orpheus: Shall not July bring fresh delight,
　　As underneath green trees ye sit,
　And o'er some damsel's body white
　　The noontide shadows change and flit?

The Sirens: No new delight July shall bring
　　But ancient fear and fresh desire,
　And, spite of every lovely thing,
　　Of July surely shall ye tire.

Orpheus: And now, when August comes on thee,
　　And 'mid the golden sea of corn
　The merry reapers thou mayst see,
　　Wilt thou still think the earth forlorn?

The Sirens: Set flowers upon thy short-lived head,
   And in thine heart forgetfulness
  Of man's hard toil, and scanty bread,
   And weary of those days no less.

Orpheus: Or wilt thou climb the sunny hill,
   In the October afternoon,
  To watch the purple earth's blood fill
   The grey vat to the maiden's tune?

The Sirens: When thou beginnest to grow old,
   Bring back remembrance of thy bliss
  With that the shining cup doth hold,
   And weary helplessly of this.

Orpheus: Or pleasureless shall we pass by
   The long cold night and leaden day,
  That song and tale and minstrelsy
   Shall make as merry as the May?

The Sirens: List then, to-night, to some old tale
   Until the tears o'erflow thine eyes;
  But what shall all these things avail
   When sad to-morrow comes and dies?

Orpheus: And when the world is born again,
   And with some fair love, side by side,
  Thou wanderest 'twixt the sun and rain,
   In that fresh love-begetting tide;

  Then, when the world is born again,
   And the sweet year before thee lies,
  Shall thy heart think of coming pain,
   Or vex itself with memories?

The Sirens: Ah! then the world is born again
   With burning love unsatisfied,
  And new desires fond and vain,
   And weary days from tide to tide.

Ah! when the world is born again,
  A little day is soon gone by,
When thou, unmoved by sun or rain,
  Within a cold straight house shall lie.

FROM *The Earthly Paradise*

1.

Of Heaven or Hell I have no power to sing,
I cannot ease the burden of your fears,
Or make quick-coming death a little thing,
Or bring again the pleasure of past years,
Nor for my words shall ye forget your tears,
Or hope again for aught that I can say,
The idle singer of an empty day.

But rather, when aweary of your mirth,
From full hearts still unsatisfied ye sigh,
And, feeling kindly unto all the earth,
Grudge every minute as it passes by,
Made the more mindful that the sweet days die—
Remember me a little then I pray,
The idle singer of an empty day.

The heavy trouble, the bewildering care
That weighs us down who live and earn our bread,
These idle verses have no power to bear;
So let me sing of names remembéréd,
Because they, living not, can ne'er be dead,
Or long time take their memory quite away
From us poor singers of an empty day.

Dreamer of dreams, born out of my due time,
Why should I strive to set the crooked straight?
Let it suffice me that my murmuring rhyme
Beats with light wing against the ivory gate,
Telling a tale not too importunate
To those who in the sleepy region stay,
Lulled by the singer of an empty day.

2.

O June, O June, that we desired so,
Wilt thou not make us happy on this day?
Across the river thy soft breezes blow
Sweet with the scent of beanfields far away,
Above our heads rustle the aspens grey,
Calm is the sky with harmless clouds beset,
No thought of storm the morning vexes yet.

See, we have left our hopes and fears behind
To give our very hearts up unto thee;
What better place than this then could we find
By this sweet stream that knows not of the sea,
That guesses not the city's misery,
This little stream whose hamlets scarce have names
This far-off, lonely mother of the Thames?

Here then, O June, thy kindness will we take;
And if indeed but pensive men we seem,
What should we do? thou wouldst not have us wake
From out the arms of this rare happy dream
And wish to leave the murmur of the stream,
The rustling boughs, the twitter of the birds,
And all thy thousand peaceful happy words.

FROM *Ogier the Dane*

Haec: In the white-flowered hawthorn brake,
Love, be merry for my sake;
Twine the blossoms in my hair,
Kiss me where I am most fair—
Kiss me, love! for who knoweth
What thing cometh after death?

Ille: Nay, the garlanded gold hair
Hides thee where thou art most fair;
Hides the rose-tinged hills of snow—
Ay, sweet love, I have thee now!
Kiss me, love! for who knoweth
What thing cometh after death?

Haec: Shall we weep for a dead day,
        Or set Sorrow in our way?
        Hidden by my golden hair,
        Wilt thou weep that sweet days wear?
        Kiss me, love! for who knoweth
        What thing cometh after death?

Ille: Weep, O Love, the days that flit,
          Now, while I can feel thy breath;
        Then may I remember it
          Sad and old, and near my death.
        Kiss me, love! for who knoweth
        What thing cometh after death?

FROM Love Is Enough

Love is Enough: though the World be a-waning
And the woods have no voice but the voice of complaining,
    Though the sky be too dark for dim eyes to discover
The gold-cups and daisies fair blooming thereunder,
Though the hills be held shadows, and the sea a dark wonder,
    And this day draw a veil over all deeds passed over,
Yet their hands shall not tremble, their feet shall not falter;
The void shall not weary, the fear shall not alter
    These lips and these eyes of the loved and the lover.

ALGERNON CHARLES SWINBURNE
(1837–1909)
FROM The Triumph of Time

I have put my days and dreams out of mind
    Days that are over, dreams that are done.
Though we seek life through, we shall surely find
    There is none of them clear to us now, not one.
But clear are these things; the grass and the sand,
Where, sure as the eyes reach, ever at hand,
With lips wide open and face burnt blind,
    The strong sea-daisies feast on the sun.

The low downs lean to the sea; the stream,
  One loose thin pulseless tremulous vein,
Rapid and vivid and dumb as a dream,
  Works downward, sick of the sun and the rain;
No wind is rough with the rank rare flowers;
The sweet sea, mother of loves and hours,
Shudders and shines as the grey winds gleam,
  Turning her smile to a fugitive pain.

Mother of loves that are swift to fade,
  Mother of mutable winds and hours.
A barren mother, a mother-maid,
  Cold and clean as her faint salt flowers.
I would we twain were even as she,
Lost in the night and the light of the sea,
Where faint sounds falter and wan beams wade,
  Break, and are broken, and shed into showers.

The loves and hours of the life of a man,
  They are swift and sad, being born of the sea.
Hours that rejoice and regret for a span,
  Born with a man's breath, mortal as he;
Loves that are lost ere they come to birth,
Weeds of the wave, without fruit upon earth.
I lose what I long for, save what I can,
  My love, my love, and no love for me!

It is not much that a man can save
  On the sands of life, in the straits of time,
Who swims in sight of the great third wave
  That never a swimmer shall cross or climb.
Some waif washed up with the strays and spars
That ebb-tide shows to the shore and the stars;
Weed from the water, grass from a grave,
  A broken blossom, a ruined rhyme.

There will no man do for your sake, I think,
  What I would have done for the least word said.
I had wrung life dry for your lips to drink,
  Broken it up for your daily bread:

Body for body and blood for blood,
As the flow of the full sea risen to flood
That yearns and trembles before it sink,
    I had given, and lain down for you, glad and dead

Yea, hope at highest and all her fruit,
    And time at fullest and all his dower,
I had given you surely, and life to boot,
    Were we once made one for a single hour.
But now, you are twain, you are cloven apart,
Flesh of his flesh, but heart of my heart;
And deep in one is the bitter root,
    And sweet for one is the lifelong flower.

I will go back to the great sweet mother,
    Mother and lover of men, the sea.
I will go down to her, I and none other,
    Close with her, kiss her and mix her with me;
Cling to her, strive with her, hold her fast:
O fair white mother, in days long past
Born without sister, born without brother,
    Set free my soul as thy soul is free.

O fair green-girdled mother of mine,
    Sea, that art clothed with the sun and the rain,
Thy sweet hard kisses are strong like wine,
    Thy large embraces are keen like pain.
Save me and hide me with all thy waves,
Find me one grave of thy thousand graves,
Those pure cold populous graves of thine
    Wrought without hand in a world without stain

I shall sleep, and move with the moving ships,
    Change as the winds change, veer in the tide;
My lips will feast on the foam of thy lips,
    I shall rise with thy rising, with thee subside;
Sleep, and not know if she be, if she were,
Filled full with life to the eyes and hair,
As a rose is fulfilled to the roseleaf tips
    With splendid summer and perfume and pride.

This woven raiment of nights and days,
　　Were it once cast off and unwound from me,
Naked and glad would I walk in thy ways,
　　Alive and aware of thy ways and thee;
Clear of the whole world, hidden at home,
Clothed with the green and crowned with the foam
A pulse of the life of thy straits and bays,
　　A vein in the heart of the streams of the sea.

There lived a singer in France of old
　　By the tideless dolorous midland sea.
In a land of sand and ruin and gold
　　There shone one woman, and none but she.
And finding life for her love's sake fail,
Being fain to see her, he bade set sail,
Touched land, and saw her as life grew cold,
　　And praised God, seeing; and so died he.

Died, praising God for his gift and grace:
　　For she bowed down to him weeping, and said
"Live"; and her tears were shed on his face
　　Or ever the life in his face was shed.
The sharp tears fell through her hair, and stung
Once, and her close lips touched him and clung
Once, and grew one with his lips for a space;
　　And so drew back, and the man was dead.

O brother, the gods were good to you.
　　Sleep, and be glad while the world endures.
Be well content as the years wear through;
　　Give thanks for life, and the loves and lures;
Give thanks for life, O brother, and death,
For the sweet last sound of her feet, her breath,
For gifts she gave you, gracious and few,
　　Tears and kisses, that lady of yours.

Rest, and be glad of the gods; but I,
　　How shall I praise them, or how take rest?
There is not room under all the sky
　　For me that know not of worst or best,

Dream or desire of the days before,
Sweet things or bitterness, any more.
Love will not come to me now though I die,
    As love came close to you, breast to breast.

I shall never be friends again with roses;
    I shall loathe sweet tunes, where a note grown strong
Relents and recoils, and climbs and closes,
    As a wave of the sea turned back by song.
There are sounds where the soul's delight takes fire,
Face to face with its own desire;
A delight that rebels, a desire that reposes;
I shall hate sweet music my whole life long.

A Leave-Taking

Let us go hence, my songs; she will not hear.
Let us go hence together without fear;
Keep silence now, for singing time is over,
And over all old things and all things dear.
She loves not you nor me as all we love her.
Yea, though we sang as angels in her ear,
        She would not hear.

Let us rise up and part; she will not know.
Let us go seaward as the great winds go,
Full of blown sand and foam; what help is here?
There is no help, for all these things are so,
And all the world is bitter as a tear.
And how these things are, though ye strove to show,
        She would not know.

Let us go home and hence; she will not weep.
We gave love many dreams and days to keep,
Flowers without scent, and fruits that would not grow,
Saying "If thou wilt, thrust in thy sickle and reap".
All is reaped now; no grass is left to mow;
And we that sowed, though all we fell on sleep,
        She would not weep.

Let us go hence and rest; she will not love.
She shall not hear us if we sing hereof,
Nor see love's ways, how sore they are and steep.
Come hence, let be, lie still; it is enough.
Love is a barren sea, bitter and deep;
And though she saw all heaven in flower above,
      She would not love.

Let us give up, go down; she will not care.
Though all the stars made gold of all the air,
And the sea moving saw before it move
One moon-flower making all the foam-flowers fair;
Though all those waves went over us, and drove
Deep down the stifling lips and drowning hair,
      She would not care.

Let us go hence, go hence; she will not see.
Sing all once more together; surely she,
She too, remembering days and words that were,
Will turn a little toward us, sighing; but we,
We are hence, we are gone, as though we had not been there.
Nay, and though all men seeing had pity on me,
      She would not see.

FROM *Anactoria*

Thee too the years shall cover; thou shalt be
As the rose born of one same blood with thee,
As a song sung, as a word said, and fall
Flower-wise, and be not any more at all,
Nor any memory of thee anywhere;
For never Muse has bound above thine hair
The high Pierian flower whose graft outgrows
All summer kinship of the mortal rose
And colour of deciduous days, nor shed
Reflux and flush of heaven about thine head,
Nor reddened brows made pale by floral grief
With splendid shadow from that lordlier leaf.
Yea, thou shalt be forgotten like spilt wine,
Except these kisses of my lips on thine

Brand them with immortality; but me—
Men shall not see bright fire nor hear the sea,
Nor mix their hearts with music, nor behold
Cast forth of heaven, with feet of awful gold
And plumeless wings, that make the bright air blind,
Lightning, with thunder for a hound behind
Hunting through fields unfurrowed and unsown,
But in the light and laughter, in the moan
And music, and in grasp of lip and hand
And shudder of water that makes felt on land
The immeasurable tremor of all the sea,
Memories shall mix and metaphors of me.
Like me shall be the shuddering calm of night,
When all the winds of the world for pure delight
Close lips that quiver and fold up wings that ache
When nightingales are louder for love's sake,
And leaves tremble like lute-strings or like fire;
Like me the one star swooning with desire
Even at the cold lips of the sleepless moon,
As I at thine; like me the waste white noon,
Burnt through with barren sunlight; and like me
The land-stream and the tide-stream in the sea.
I am sick with time as these with ebb and flow,
And by the yearning in my veins I know
The yearning sound of waters; and mine eyes
Burn as that beamless fire which fills the skies
With troubled stars and travailing things of flame;
And in my heart the grief consuming them
Labours, and in my veins the thirst of these,
And all the summer travail of the trees
And all the winter sickness; and the earth,
Filled full with deadly works of death and birth,
Sore spent with hungry lusts of birth and death,
Has pain like mine in her divided breath;
Her spring of leaves is barren, and her fruit
Ashes; her boughs are burdened, and her root
Fibrous and gnarled with poison; underneath
Serpents have gnawn it through with tortuous teeth
Made sharp upon the bones of all the dead,
And wild birds rend her branches overhead.
These, woven as raiment for his word and thought,

These hath God made, and me as these, and wrought
Song, and hath lit it at my lips; and me
Earth shall not gather though she feed on thee.
As a tear shed shalt thou be shed; but I—
Lo, earth may labour, men live long and die,
Years change and stars, and the high God devise
New things, and old things wane before his eyes
Who wields and wrecks them, being more strong than they—
But, having made me, me he shall not slay.
Nor slay nor satiate, like those herds of his
Who laugh and live a little, and their kiss
Contents them, and their loves are swift and sweet,
And sure death grasps and gains them with slow feet,
Love they or hate they, strive or bow the knees—
And all these end; he hath his will of these.
Yea, but albeit he slay me, hating me—
Albeit he hide me in the deep dear sea
And cover me with cool wan foam, and ease
This soul of mine as any soul of these,
And give me water and great sweet waves, and make
The very sea's name lordlier for my sake,
The whole sea sweeter—albeit I die indeed
And hide myself and sleep and no man heed,
Of me the high God hath not all his will.
Blossom of branches, and on each high hill
Clear air and wind, and under in clamorous vales
Fierce noises of the fiery nightingales,
Buds burning in the sudden spring like fire,
The wan washed sand and the waves' vain desire,
Sails seen like blown white flowers at sea, and words
That bring tears swiftest, and long notes of birds
Violently singing till the whole world sings—
I Sappho shall be one with all these things,
With all high things for ever; and my face
Seen once, my songs once heard in a strange place,
Cleave to men's lives, and waste the days thereof
With gladness and much sadness and long love.
Yea, they shall say, earth's womb has borne in vain
New things, and never this best thing again;
Borne days and men, borne fruits and wars and wine,
Seasons and songs, but no song more like mine.

And they shall know me as ye who have known me here,
Last year when I loved Atthis, and this year
When I love thee; and they shall praise me and say:
"She hath all time as all we have our day,
Shall she not live and have her will"—even I?
For these shall give me of their souls, shall give
Life, and the days and loves wherewith I live,
Shall quicken me with loving, fill with breath,
Save me and serve me, strive for me with death.
Alas, that neither moon nor snow nor dew
Nor all cold things can purge me wholly through,
Assuage me nor allay me nor appease,
Till supreme sleep shall bring me bloodless ease;
Till time wax faint in all his periods;
Till fate undo the bondage of the gods,
And lay, to slake and satiate me all through,
Lotus and Lethe on my lips like dew,
And shed around and over and under me
Thick darkness and the insuperable sea.

Rococo

Take hands and part with laughter;
   Touch lips and part with tears;
Once more and no more after,
   Whatever comes with years.
We twain shall not remeasure
   The ways that left us twain;
Nor crush the lees of pleasure
   From sanguine grapes of pain.

We twain once well in sunder,
   What will the mad gods do
For hate with me, I wonder,
   Or what for love with you?
Forget them till November,
   And dream there's April yet;
Forget that I remember,
   And dream that I forget.

Time found our tired love sleeping,
  And kissed away his breath;
But what should we do weeping,
  Though light love sleep to death?
We have drained his lips at leisure,
  Till there's not left to drain
A single sob of pleasure,
  A single pulse of pain.

Dream that the lips once breathless
  Might quicken if they would;
Say that the soul is deathless;
  Dream that the gods are good;
Say March may wed September,
  And time divorce regret;
But not that you remember,
  And not that I forget.

We have heard from hidden places
  What love scarce lives and hears:
We have seen on fervent faces
  The pallor of strange tears:
We have trod the wine-vat's treasure,
  Whence, ripe to steam and stain,
Foams round the feet of pleasure
  The blood-red must of pain.

Remembrance may recover
  And time bring back to time
The name of your first lover,
  The ring of my first rhyme;
But rose-leaves of December
  The frosts of June shall fret,
The day that you remember,
  The day that I forget.

The snake that hides and hisses
  In heaven we twain have known;
The grief of cruel kisses,
  The joy whose mouth makes moan;

The pulse's pause and measure,
   Where in one furtive vein
Throbs through the heart of pleasure
   The purpler blood of pain.

We have done with tears and treasons
   And love for treason's sake;
Room for the swift new seasons,
   The years that burn and break,
Dismantle and dismember
   Men's days and dreams, Juliette;
For love may not remember,
   But time will not forget.

Life treads down love in flying,
   Time withers him at root,
Bring all dead things and dying,
   Reaped sheaf and ruined fruit,
Where, crushed by three days' pressure,
   Our three days' love lies slain;
And earlier leaf of pleasure,
   And latter flower of pain.

Breathe close upon the ashes,
   It may be flame will leap;
Unclose the soft close lashes,
   Lift up the lids, and weep.
Light love's extinguished ember,
   Let one tear leave it wet
For one that you remember
   And ten that you forget.

Rondel

Kissing her hair I sat against her feet,
Wove and unwove it, wound and found it sweet;
Made fast therewith her hands, drew down her eyes,
Deep as deep flowers and dreamy like dim skies;
With her own tresses bound and found her fair,
   Kissing her hair.

Sleep were no sweeter than her face to me,
Sleep of cold sea-bloom under the cold sea;
What pain could get between my face and hers?
What new sweet thing would love not relish worse?
Unless, perhaps, white death had kissed me there,
        Kissing her hair?

The Garden of Proserpine

Here, where the world is quiet;
    Here, where all trouble seems
Dead winds' and spent waves' riot
    In doubtful dreams of dreams;
I watch the green field growing
For reaping folk and sowing,
For harvest-time and mowing,
    A sleepy world of streams.

I am tired of tears and laughter,
    And men that laugh and weep;
Of what may come hereafter
    For men that sow to reap:
I am weary of days and hours,
Blown buds of barren flowers,
Desires and dreams and powers
    And everything but sleep.

Here night has death for neighbour,
    And far from eye or ear
Wan waves and wet winds labour,
    Weak ships and spirits steer;
They drive adrift, and whither
They wot not who make thither;
But no such winds blow hither,
    And no such things grow here.

No growth of moor or coppice,
    No heather-flower or vine,
But bloomless buds of poppies,
    Green grapes of Proserpine,

Pale beds of blowing rushes
Where no leaf blooms or blushes
Save this whereout she crushes
    For dead men deadly wine.

Pale, without name or number,
    In fruitless fields of corn,
They bow themselves and slumber
    All night till light is born;
And like a soul belated,
In hell and heaven unmated,
By cloud and mist abated,
    Comes out of darkness morn.

Though one were strong as seven,
    He too with death shall dwell,
Nor wake with wings in heaven,
    Nor weep for pains in hell;
Though one were fair as roses,
His beauty clouds and closes;
And well though love reposes,
    In the end it is not well.

Pale, beyond porch and portal,
    Crowned with calm leaves, she stands,
Who gathers all things mortal
    With cold immortal hands;
Her languid lips are sweeter
Than love's who fears to greet her
To men that mix and meet her
    From many times and lands.

She waits for each and other,
    She waits for all men born;
Forgets the earth her mother,
    The life of fruits and corn;
And spring and seed and swallow
Take wing for her and follow
Where summer song rings hollow,
    And flowers are put to scorn.

There go the old loves that wither,
    The old loves with wearier wings;
And all dead years draw thither,
    And all disastrous things;
Dead dreams of days forsaken,
Blind buds that snows have shaken,
Wild leaves that winds have taken,
    Red strays of ruined springs.

We are not sure of sorrow,
    And joy was never sure;
To-day will die to-morrow;
    Time stoops to no man's lure;
And love, grown faint and fretful,
With lips but half regretful
Sighs, and with eyes forgetful
    Weeps that no loves endure.

From too much love of living,
    From hope and fear set free,
We thank with brief thanksgiving
    Whatever gods may be
That no life lives for ever;
That dead men rise up never;
That even the weariest river
    Winds somewhere safe to sea.

An Interlude

In the greenest growth of the Maytime,
    I rode where the woods were wet,
Between the dawn and the daytime;
    The spring was glad that we met.

There was something the season wanted,
    Though the ways and the woods smelt sweet;
The breath of your lips that panted,
    The pulse of the grass at your feet.

You came, and the sun came after,
    And the green grew golden above;
And the flag-flowers lightened with laughter,
    And the meadow-sweet shook with love.

Your feet in the full-grown grasses,
    Moved soft as a weak wind blows;
You passed me as April passes,
    With face made out of a rose.

By the stream where the stems were slender,
    Your bright foot paused at the sedge;
It might be to watch the tender
    Light leaves in the springtime hedge,

On boughs that the sweet month blanches
    With flowery frost of May:
It might be a bird in the branches,
    It might be a thorn in the way.

I waited to watch you linger
    With foot drawn back from the dew,
Till a sunbeam straight like a finger
    Struck sharp through the leaves at you.

And a bird overhead sang *Follow*,
    And a bird to the right sang *Here;*
And the arch of the leaves was hollow,
    And the meaning of May was clear.

I saw where the sun's hand pointed,
    I knew what the bird's note said;
By the dawn and the dewfall anointed,
    You were queen by the gold on your head.

As the glimpse of a burnt-out ember
    Recalls a regret of the sun,
I remember, forget, and remember
    What Love saw done and undone.

I remember the way we parted,
  The day and the way we met;
You hoped we were both broken-hearted,
  And knew we should both forget.

And May with her world in flower
  Seemed still to murmur and smile
As you murmured and smiled for an hour;
  I saw you turn at the stile.

A hand like a white wood-blossom
  You lifted, and waved, and passed,
With head hung down to the bosom,
  And pale, as it seemed, at last.

And the best and the worst of this is
  That neither is most to blame
If you've forgotten my kisses
  And I've forgotten your name.

At Parting

For a day and a night Love sang to us, played with us,
  Folded us round from the dark and the light;
And our hearts were fulfilled of the music he made with us,
Made with our hearts and our lips while he stayed with us,
  Stayed in mid passage his pinions from flight
    For a day and a night.

From his foes that kept watch with his wings had he hidden
    us,
  Covered us close from the eyes that would smite,
From the feet that had tracked and the tongues that had chid-
    den us
Sheltering in shade of the myrtles forbidden us
  Spirit and flesh growing one with delight
    For a day and a night.

But his wings will not rest and his feet will not stay for us:
   Morning is here in the joy of its might;
With his breath has he sweetened a night and a day for us;
Now let him pass, and the myrtles make way for us;
   Love can but last in us here at his height
       For a day and a night.

Ave atque Vale
(IN MEMORY OF CHARLES BAUDELAIRE)

> Nous devrions pourtant lui porter quelques fleurs;
> Les morts, les pauvres morts, ont de grandes douleurs,
> Et quand Octobre souffle, émondeur des vieux arbres,
> Son vent mélancolique à l'entour de leurs marbres,
> Certe, ils doivent trouver les vivants bien ingrats.
>   —Les Fleurs du Mal

Shall I strew on thee rose or rue or laurel,
   Brother, on this that was the veil of thee?
   Or quiet sea-flower moulded by the sea,
Or simplest growth of meadow-sweet or sorrel,
   Such as the summer-sleepy Dryads weave,
   Waked up by snow-soft sudden rains at eve?
Or wilt thou rather, as on earth before,
   Half-faded fiery blossoms, pale with heat
   And full of bitter summer, but more sweet
To thee than gleanings of a northern shore
   Trod by no tropic feet?

For always thee the fervid languid glories
   Allured of heavier suns in mightier skies;
   Thine ears knew all the wandering watery sighs
Where the sea sobs round Lesbian promontories,
   The barren kiss of piteous wave to wave
   That knows not where is that Leucadian grave
Which hides too deep the supreme head of song.
   Ah, salt and sterile as her kisses were,
   The wild sea winds her and the green gulfs bear
Hither and thither, and vex and work her wrong,
   Blind gods that cannot spare.

Thou sawest, in thine old singing season, brother,
    Secrets and sorrows unbeheld of us:
Fierce loves, and lovely leaf-buds poisonous,
Bare to thy subtler eye, but for none other
       Blowing by night in some unbreathed-in clime;
       The hidden harvest of luxurious time,
Sin without shape, and pleasure without speech;
       And where strange dreams in a tumultuous sleep
       Make the shut eyes of stricken spirits weep;
And with each face thou sawest the shadow of each,
    Seeing as men sow men reap.

O sleepless heart and sombre soul unsleeping,
       That were athirst for sleep and no more life
       And no more love, for peace and no more strife!
Now the dim gods of death have in their keeping
       Spirit and body and all the springs of song,
       Is it well now where love can do no wrong,
Where stingless pleasure has no foam or fang
       Behind the unopening closure of her lips?
       Is it well now where soul from body slips
And flesh from bone divides without a pang
    As dew from flower-bell drips?

It is enough; the end and the beginning
       Are one thing to thee, who art past the end.
       O hand unclasped of unbeholden friend,
For thee no fruits to pluck, no palms for winning,
       No triumph and no labour and no lust,
       Only dead yew-leaves and a little dust.
O quiet eyes wherein the light saith nought,
       Whereto the day is dumb, nor any night
       With obscure finger silences your sight,
Nor in your speech the sudden soul speaks thought,
    Sleep, and have sleep for light.

Now all strange hours and all strange loves are over,
       Dreams and desires and sombre songs and sweet,
       Hast thou found place at the great knees and feet
Of some pale Titan-woman like a lover,
       Such as thy vision here solicited,
       Under the shadow of her fair vast head,

The deep division of prodigious breasts,
        The solemn slope of mighty limbs asleep,
        The weight of awful tresses that still keep
The savour and shade of old-world pine-forests
        Where the wet hill-winds weep?

Hast thou found any likeness for thy vision?
        O gardener of strange flowers, what bud, what bloom,
        Hast thou found sown, what gathered in the gloom?
What of despair, of rapture, of derision,
        What of life is there, what of ill or good?
        Are the fruits grey like dust or bright like blood?
Does the dim ground grow any seed of ours,
        The faint fields quicken any terrene root,
        In low lands where the sun and moon are mute
And all the stars keep silence? Are there flowers
        At all, or any fruit?

Alas, but though my flying song flies after,
        O sweet strange elder singer, thy more fleet
        Singing, and footprints of thy fleeter feet,
Some dim derision of mysterious laughter
        From the blind tongue-less warders of the dead,
        Some gainless glimpse of Proserpine's veiled head,
Some little sound of unregarded tears
        Wept by effaced unprofitable eyes,
        And from pale mouths some cadence of dead sighs—
These only, these the hearkening spirit hears,
        Sees only such things rise.

Thou art far too far for wings of words to follow,
        Far too far off for thought or any prayer.
        What ails us with thee, who art wind and air?
What ails us gazing where all seen is hollow?
        Yet with some fancy, yet with some desire,
        Dreams pursue death as winds a flying fire,
Our dreams pursue our dead and do not find.
        Still, and more swift than they, the thin flame flies,
        The low light fails us in elusive skies,
Still the foiled earnest ear is deaf, and blind
        Are still the eluded eyes.

Not thee, O never thee, in all time's changes,
    Not thee, but this the sound of thy sad soul,
    The shadow of thy swift spirit, this shut scroll
I lay my hand on, and not death estranges
    My spirit from communion of thy song—
    These memories and these melodies that throng
Veiled porches of a Muse funereal—
    These I salute, these touch, these clasp and fold
    As though a hand were in my hand to hold,
Or through mine ears a mourning musical
    Of many mourners rolled.

I among these, I also, in such station
    As when the pyre was charred, and piled the sods,
    And offering to the dead made, and their gods,
The old mourners had, standing to make libation,
    I stand, and to the gods and to the dead
    Do reverence without prayer or praise, and shed
Offering to these unknown, the gods of gloom,
    And what of honey and spice my seedlands bear,
    And what I may of fruits in this chilled air,
And lay, Orestes-like, across the tomb
    A curl of severed hair.

But by no hand nor any treason stricken,
    Not like the low-lying head of Him, the King,
    The flame that made of Troy a ruinous thing,
Thou liest, and on this dust no tears could quicken
    There fall no tears like theirs that all men hear
    Fall tear by sweet imperishable tear
Down the opening leaves of holy poets' pages.
    Thee not Orestes, not Electra mourns;
    But bending us-ward with memorial urns
The most high Muses that fufil all ages
    Weep, and our God's heart yearns.

For, sparing of his sacred strength, not often
    Among us darkling here the lord of light
    Makes manifest his music and his might
In hearts that open and in lips that soften
    With the soft flame and heat of songs that shine.
    Thy lips indeed he touched with bitter wine,

And nourished them indeed with bitter bread;
    Yet surely from his hand thy soul's food came,
    The fire that scarred thy spirit at his flame
Was lighted, and thine hungering heart he fed
    Who feeds our hearts with fame.

Therefore he too now at thy soul's sunsetting,
    God of all suns and songs, he too bends down
    To mix his laurel with thy cypress crown,
And save thy dust from blame and from forgetting.
    Therefore he too, seeing all thou wert and art,
    Compassionate, with sad and sacred heart,
Mourns thee of many his children the last dead,
    And hallows with strange tears and alien sighs
    Thine unmelodious mouth and sunless eyes,
And over thine irrevocable head
    Sheds light from the under skies.

And one weeps with him in the ways Lethean,
    And stains with tears her changing bosom chill:
    That obscure Venus of the hollow hill,
That thing transformed which was the Cytherean,
    With lips that lost their Grecian laugh divine
    Long since, and face no more called Erycine;
A ghost, a bitter and luxurious god.
    Thee also with fair flesh and singing spell
    Did she, a sad and second prey, compel
Into the footless places once more trod,
    And shadows hot from hell.

And now no sacred staff shall break in blossom,
    No choral salutation lure to light
    A spirit sick with perfume and sweet night
And love's tired eyes and hands and barren bosom.
    There is no help for these things; none to mend
    And none to mar; not all our songs, O friend,
Will make death clear or make life durable.
    Howbeit with rose and ivy and wild vine
    And with wild notes about this dust of thine
At least I fill the place where white dreams dwell
    And wreathe an unseen shrine.

Sleep; and if life was bitter to thee, pardon,
    If sweet, give thanks; thou hast no more to live;
    And to give thanks is good, and to forgive.
Out of the mystic and the mournful garden
    Where all day through thine hands in barren braid
    Wove the sick flowers of secrecy and shade,
Green buds of sorrow and sin, and remnants grey,
    Sweet-smelling, pale with poison, sanguine-hearted,
    Passions that sprang from sleep and thoughts that
        started,
Shall death not bring us all as thee one day
    Among the days departed?

For thee, O now a silent soul, my brother,
    Take at my hands this garland, and farewell.
    Thin is the leaf, and chill the wintry smell,
And chill the solemn earth, a fatal mother,
    With sadder than the Niobean womb,
    And in the hollow of her breasts a tomb.
Content thee, howsoe'er, whose days are done;
    There lies not any troublous thing before,
    Nor sight nor sound to war against thee more,
For whom all winds are quiet as the sun,
    All waters as the shore.

Choruses from Atalanta in Calydon

1.

    When the hounds of spring are on winter's traces,
        The mother of months in meadow or plain
    Fills the shadows and windy places
        With lisp of leaves and ripple of rain;
    And the brown bright nightingale amorous
    Is half assuaged for Itylus,
    For the Thracian ships and the foreign faces,
        The tongueless vigil, and all the pain.

    Come with bows bent and with emptying of quivers,
        Maiden most perfect, lady of light,
    With a noise of winds and many rivers,
        With a clamour of waters, and with might;

Bind on thy sandals, O thou most fleet,
Over the splendour and speed of thy feet;
For the faint east quickens, the wan west shivers,
   Round the feet of the day and the feet of the night.

Where shall we find her, how shall we sing to her,
   Fold our hands round her knees, and cling?
O that man's heart were as fire and could spring to her,
   Fire, or the strength of the streams that spring!
For the stars and the winds are unto her
As raiment, as songs of the harp-player;
For the risen stars and the fallen cling to her,
   And the southwest-wind and the west-wind sing.

For winter's rains and ruins are over,
   And all the season of snows and sins;
The days dividing lover and lover,
   The light that loses, the night that wins;
And time remembered is grief forgotten,
And frosts are slain and flowers begotten,
And in green underwood and cover
   Blossom by blossom the spring begins.

The full streams feed on flowers of rushes,
   Ripe grasses trammel a travelling foot,
The faint fresh flame of the young year flushes
   From leaf to flower and flower to fruit;
And fruit and leaf are as gold and fire,
And the oat is heard above the lyre,
And the hooféd heel of a satyr crushes
   The chestnut-husk at the chestnut-root.

And Pan by noon and Bacchus by night,
   Fleeter of foot than the fleet-foot kid,
Follows with dancing and fills with delight
   The Maenad and the Bassarid;
And soft as lips that laugh and hide
The laughing leaves of the trees divide,
And screen from seeing and leave in sight
   The god pursuing, the maiden hid.

The ivy falls with the Bacchanal's hair
   Over her eyebrows hiding her eyes;
The wild vine slipping down leaves bare
   Her bright breast shortening into sighs,
The wild vine slips with the weight of its leaves,
But the berried ivy catches and cleaves
To the limbs that glitter, the feet that scare
   The wolf that follows, the fawn that flies.

2.

   Before the beginning of years
     There came to the making of man
   Time, with a gift of tears;
     Grief with a glass that ran;
   Pleasure, with pain for leaven;
     Summer, with flowers that fell;
   Remembrance fallen from heaven,
     And madness risen from hell;
   Strength without hands to smite;
     Love that endures for a breath;
   Night, the shadow of light,
     And life, the shadow of death.

And the high gods took in hand
   Fire, and the falling of tears,
And a measure of sliding sand
   From under the feet of the years;
And froth and drift of the sea;
   And dust of the labouring earth;
And bodies of things to be
   In the houses of death and of birth;
And wrought with weeping and laughter,
   And fashioned with loathing and love
With life before and after
   And death beneath and above,
For a day and a night and a morrow,
   That his strength might endure for a span
With travail and heavy sorrow,
   The holy spirit of man.

From the winds of the north and the south
  They gathered as unto strife;
They breathed upon his mouth,
  They filled his body with life;
Eyesight and speech they wrought
  For the veils of the soul therein,
A time for labour and thought,
  A time to serve and to sin;
They gave him light in his ways,
  And love, and a space for delight,
And beauty and length of days,
  And night, and sleep in the night.
His speech is a burning fire;
  With his lips he travaileth;
In his heart is a blind desire,
  In his eyes foreknowledge of death;
He weaves, and is clothed with derision;
  Sows, and he shall not reap;
His life is a watch or a vision
  Between a sleep and a sleep.

8.

Who hath given man speech? or who hath set therein
A thorn for peril and a snare for sin?
For in the word his life is and his breath,
  And in the word his death,
That madness and the infatuate heart may breed
  From the word's womb the deed
And life bring one thing forth ere all pass by,
Even one thing which is ours yet cannot die—
Death. Hast thou seen him ever anywhere,
Time's twin-born brother, imperishable as he
Is perishable and plaintive, clothed with care
  And mutable as sand,
But death is strong and full of blood and fair
And perdurable and like a lord of land?
Nay, time thou seest not, death thou wilt not see
Till life's right hand be loosened from thine hand
  And thy life-days from thee.

For the gods very subtly fashion
   Madness with sadness upon earth:
Not knowing in any wise compassion,
   Nor holding pity of any worth;
And many things they have given and taken,
   And wrought and ruined many things;
The firm land they have loosed and shaken,
   And sealed the sea with all her springs;
They have wearied time with heavy burdens
   And vexed the lips of life with breath:
Set men to labour and given them guerdons,
   Death, and great darkness after death:
Put moans into the bridal measure
   And on the bridal wools a stain;
And circled pain about with pleasure,
   And girdled pleasure about with pain;
And strewed one marriage-bed with tears and fire
For extreme loathing and supreme desire.

What shall be done with all these tears of ours?
   Shall they make watersprings in the fair heaven
To bathe the brows of morning? or like flowers
   Be shed and shine before the starriest hours,
   Or made the raiment of the weeping Seven?
Or rather, O our masters, shall they be
Food for the famine of the grievous sea,
   A great well-head of lamentation
Satiating the sad gods? or fall and flow
Among the years and seasons to and fro,
   And wash their feet with tribulation
And fill them full with grieving ere they go?
   Alas, our lords, and yet alas again,
Seeing all your iron heaven is gilt as gold
   But all we smite thereat in vain;
Smite the gates barred with groanings manifold,
   And all the floors are paven with our pain.
Yea, and with weariness of lips and eyes,
With breaking of the bosom, and with sighs,
   We labour, and are clad and fed with grief
And filled with days we would not fain behold

And nights we would not hear of; we wax old,
  All we wax old and wither like a leaf.
We are outcast, strayed between bright sun and moon;
  Our light and darkness are as leaves of flowers,
Black flowers and white, that perish; and the noon
  As midnight, and the night as daylight hours.
  A little fruit a little while is ours,
    And the worm finds it soon.

But up in heaven the high gods one by one
  Lay hands upon the draught that quickeneth,
Fulfilled with all tears shed and all things done,
  And stir with soft imperishable breath
  The bubbling bitterness of life and death,
And hold it to our lips and laugh; but they
Preserve their lips from tasting night or day,
  Lest they too change and sleep, the fates that spun,
The lips that made us and the hands that slay;
  Lest all these change, and heaven bow down to none.
Change and be subject to the secular sway
  And terrene revolution of the sun.
Therefore they thrust it from them, putting time away.

I would the wine of time, made sharp and sweet
  With multitudinous days and nights and tears
  And many mixing savours of strange years,
Were no more trodden of them under feet,
  Cast out and spilt about their holy places:
That life were given them as a fruit to eat
And death to drink as water; that the light
Might ebb, drawn backward from their eyes, and night
  Hide for one hour the imperishable faces.
That they might rise up sad in heaven, and know
Sorrow and sleep, one paler than young snow,
  One cold as blight of dew and ruinous rain;
Rise up and rest and suffer a little, and be
Awhile as all things born with us and we,
  And grieve as men, and like slain men be slain.

For now we know not of them; but one saith
  The gods are gracious, praising God; and one,

When hast thou seen? or hast thou felt his breath
  Touch, nor consume thine eyelids as the sun,
Nor fill thee to the lips with fiery death?
  None hath beheld him, none
Seen above other gods and shapes of things,
Swift without feet and flying without wings,
Intolerable, not clad with death or life,
  Insatiable, not known of night or day,
The lord of love and loathing and of strife
  Who gives a star and takes a sun away;
Who shapes the soul, and makes her a barren wife
  To the earthly body and grievous growth of clay;
Who turns the large limbs to a little flame
  And binds the great sea with a little sand;
Who makes desire, and slays desire with shame;
  Who shakes the heaven as ashes in his hand;
Who, seeing the light and shadow for the same,
  Bids day waste night as fire devours a brand,
Smites without sword, and scourges without rod;
  The supreme evil, God.

Yea, with thine hate, O God, thou hast covered us,
  One saith, and hidden our eyes away from sight,
And made us transitory and hazardous,
  Light things and slight;
Yet have men praised thee, saying, He hath made man thus,
  And he doeth right.
Thou hast kissed us, and hast smitten; thou hast laid
Upon us with thy left hand life, and said,
Live: and again thou hast said, Yield up your breath,
And with thy right hand laid upon us death.
Thou hast sent us sleep, and stricken sleep with dreams,
  Saying, Joy is not, but love of joy shall be;
Thou hast made sweet springs for all the pleasant streams,
  In the end thou hast made them bitter with the sea.
Thou hast fed one rose with dust of many men;
  Thou hast marred one face with fire of many tears;
Thou hast taken love, and given us sorrow again;
  With pain thou hast filled us full to the eyes and ears.
Therefore because thou art strong, our father, and we
  Feeble; and thou art against us, and thine hand

Constrains us in the shallows of the sea
   And breaks us at the limits of the land;
Because thou hast bent thy lightnings as a bow,
   And loosed the hours like arrows; and let fall
Sins and wild words and many a wingéd woe
   And wars among us, and one end of all;
Because thou hast made the thunder, and thy feet
   Are as a rushing water when the skies
Break, but thy face as an exceeding heat
   And flames of fire the eyelids of thine eyes;
Because thou art over all who are over us;
   Because thy name is life and our name death;
Because thou art cruel and men are piteous,
   And our hands labour and thine hand scattereth;
Lo, with hearts rent and knees made tremulous,
   Lo, with ephemeral lips and casual breath,
     At least we witness of thee ere we die
That these things are not otherwise, but thus;
   That each man in his heart sigheth, and saith,
     That all men even as I,
All we are against thee, against thee, O God most high.

THOMAS HARDY

(1840–1928)

The Impercipient
(AT A CATHEDRAL SERVICE)

That with this bright believing band
   I have no claim to be,
That faiths by which my comrades stand
   Seem fantasies to me,
And mirage-mists their Shining Land,
   Is a strange destiny.

Why thus my soul should be consigned
   To infelicity,
Why always I must feel as blind
   To sights my brethren see,
Why joys they've found I cannot find,
   Abides a mystery.

Since heart of mine knows not that ease
   Which they know; since it be
That He who breathes All's Well to these
   Breathes no All's Well to me,
My lack might move their sympathies
   And Christian charity!

I am like a gazer who should mark
   An inland company
Standing upfingered, with, "Hark! hark!
   The glorious distant sea!"
And feel, "Alas, 'tis but yon dark
   And wind-swept pine to me!"

Yet I would bear my shortcomings
   With meet tranquillity,
But for the charge that blessed things
   I'd liefer not have be.
O, doth a bird deprived of wings
   Go earth-bound wilfully!

.   .   .

Enough. As yet disquiet clings
   About us. Rest shall we.

To an Unborn Pauper Child

Breathe not, hid Heart: cease silently,
And though thy birth-hour beckons thee,
   Sleep the long sleep:
   The Doomsters heap
Travails and teens around us here
And Time-wraiths turn our songsingings to fear.

Hark, how the people surge and sigh,
And laughters fail, and greetings die:
   Hopes dwindle; yea,
   Faiths waste away,
Affections and enthusiasms numb;
Thou canst not mend these things if thou dost come.

Had I the ear of wombéd souls
Ere their terrestrial chart unrolls,
  And thou wert free
  To cease, or be,
Then would I tell thee all I know,
And put it to thee: Wilt thou take Life so?

Vain vow! No hint of mine may hence
To theeward fly: to thy locked sense
  Explain none can
  Life's pending plan:
Thou wilt thy ignorant entry make
Though skies spout fire and blood and nations quake.

Fain would I, dear, find some shut plot
Of earth's wide wold for thee, where not
  One tear, one qualm,
  Should break the calm.
But I am weak as thou and bare;
No man can change the common lot to rare.

Must come and bide. And such are we—
Unreasoning, sanguine, visionary—
  That I can hope
  Health, love, friends, scope
In full for thee; can dream thou wilt find
Joys seldom yet attained by humankind!

Shut Out That Moon

Close up the casement, draw the blind,
 Shut out that stealing moon,
She wears too much the guise she wore
 Before our lutes were strewn
With years-deep dust, and names we read
 On a white stone were hewn.

Step not out on the dew-dashed lawn
 To view the Lady's Chair,
Immense Orion's glittering form,
 The Less and Greater Bear:
Stay in; to such sights we were drawn
 When faded ones were fair.

Brush not the bough for midnight scents
    That come forth lingeringly,
And wake the same sweet sentiments
    They breathed to you and me
When living seemed a laugh, and love
    All it was said to be.

Within the common lamp-lit room
    Prison my eyes and thought;
Let dingy details crudely loom,
    Mechanic speech be wrought:
Too fragrant was Life's early bloom,
    Too tart the fruit it brought!

The Conformers

Yes; we'll wed, my little fay,
    And you shall write you mine,
And in a villa chastely gray
    We'll house, and sleep, and dine.
    But those night-screened, divine,
    Stolen trysts of heretofore,
We of choice ecstasies and fine
            Shall know no more.

The formal faced cohue
    Will then no more upbraid
With smiting smiles and whisperings two
    Who have thrown less loves in shade.
    We shall no more evade
    The searching light of the sun,
Our game of passion will be played,
            Our dreaming done.

We shall not go in stealth
    To rendezvous unknown,
But friends will ask me of your health,
    And you about my own.

When we abide alone,
No leapings each to each,
But syllables in frigid tone
Of household speech.

When down to dust we glide
Men will not say askance,
As now: "How all the country side
Rings with their mad romance!"
But as they graveward glance
Remark: "In them we lose
A worthy pair, who helped advance
Sound parish views."

Let Me Enjoy

Let me enjoy the earth no less
Because the all-enacting Might
That fashioned forth its loveliness
Had other aims than my delight.

About my path there flits a Fair,
Who throws me not a word or sign;
I'll charm me with her ignoring air,
And laud the lips not meant for mine.

From manuscripts of moving song
Inspired by scenes and souls unknown,
I'll pour out raptures that belong
To others, as they were my own.

And some day hence, toward Paradise
And all its blest—if such should be—
I will lift glad, afar-off eyes,
Though it contain no place for me.

Afterwards

When the Present has latched its postern behind my tremu-
  lous stay,
  And the May month flaps its glad green leaves like wings,
Delicate-filmed as a new-spun silk, will the neighbours say,
  "He was a man who used to notice such things?"

If it be in the dusk when, like an eyelid's soundless blink,
  The dewfall-hawk comes crossing the shades to alight
Upon the wind-warped upland thorn, a gazer may think,
  "To him this must have been a familiar sight."

If I pass during some nocturnal blackness, mothy and warm,
  When the hedgehog travels furtively over the lawn,
One may say, "He strove that such innocent creatures should
  come to no harm,
  But he could do little for them; and now he is gone."

If, when hearing that I have been stilled at last, they stand
  at the door,
  Watching the full-starred heavens that winter sees,
Will this thought rise on those who will meet my face no
  more,
  "He was one who had an eye for such mysteries?"

And will any say when my bell of quittance is heard in the
  gloom,
  And a crossing breeze cuts a pause in its outrollings,
Till they rise again, as they were a new bell's boom,
  "He hears it not now, but used to notice such things?"

HENRY AUSTIN DOBSON

(1840–1921)

On a Fan That Belonged
to the Marquise de Pompadour

  Chicken-skin, delicate, white,
    Painted by Carlo Vanloo,
  Loves in a riot of light,
    Roses and vaporous blue;
    Hark to the dainty *frou-frou!*

Picture above if you can,
  Eyes that would melt as the dew,—
This was the Pompadour's fan!

See how they rise at the sight,
  Thronging the *Œil de Bœuf* through,
Courtiers as butterflies bright,
  Beauties that Fragonard drew,
Talon-rouge, falbala, queue,
  Cardinal, Duke,—to a man,
  Eager to sigh or to sue,—
This was the Pompadour's fan!

Ah! but things more than polite
  Hung on this toy, *voyez-vous!*
Matters of state and of might,
  Things that great ministers do,
  Things that, maybe, overthrew
Those in whose brains they began;
  Here was the sign and the cue,—
This was the Pompadour's fan!

ENVOY

Where are the secrets it knew?
  Weavings of plot and of plan?
But where is the Pompadour, too?
  This was the Pompadour's *Fan!*

WILFRID SCAWEN BLUNT

(1840–1922)

FROM *Esther*

L

He who has once been happy is for aye
  Out of destruction's reach. His fortune then
Holds nothing secret, and Eternity,
  Which is a mystery to other men,
Has like a woman given him its joy.
  Time is his conquest. Life, if it should fret,
Has paid him tribute. He can bear to die.
  He who has once been happy! When I set

The world before me and survey its range,
　　Its mean ambitions, its scant fantasies,
The shreds of pleasure which for lack of change
　　Men wrap around them and call happiness,
The poor delights which are the tale and sum
Of the world's courage in its martyrdom;

LI

When I hear laughter from a tavern door,
　　When I see crowds agape and in the rain
Watching on tiptoe and with stifled roar
　　To see a rocket fired or a bull slain,
When misers handle gold, when orators
　　Touch strong men's hearts with glory till they weep,
When cities deck their streets for barren wars
　　Which have laid waste their youth, and when I keep
Calmly the count of my own life and see
　　On what poor stuff my manhood's dreams were fed
Till I too learned what dole of vanity
　　Will serve a human soul for daily bread,
—Then I remember that I once was young
And lived with Esther the world's gods among.

FROM *The Love Sonnets of Proteus*

AS TO HIS CHOICE OF HER

If I had chosen thee, thou shouldst have been
A virgin proud, untamed, immaculate,
Chaste as the morning star, a saint, a queen,
Scarred by no wars, no violence of hate.
Thou shouldst have been of soul commensurate
With thy fair body, brave and virtuous
And kind and just; and, if of poor estate,
At least an honest woman for my house.
I would have had thee come of honoured blood
And honourable nurture. Thou shouldst bear
Sons to my pride and daughters to my heart,
And men should hold thee happy, wise, and good.
Lo, thou art none of this, but only fair.
Yet must I love thee, dear, and as thou art.

HE HAS FALLEN FROM THE HEIGHT OF HIS LOVE

Love, how ignobly hast thou met thy doom!
Ill-seasoned scaffolding by which, full-fraught
With passionate youth and mighty hopes, we clomb
To our heart's heaven, fearing, doubting, naught!
Oh love, thou wert too frail for such mad sport,
Too rotten at thy core, designed too high:
And we who trusted thee our death have bought,
And bleeding on the ground must surely die.
—I will not see her. What she now may be
I care not. For the dream within my brain
Is fairer, nobler, and more kind than she;
And with that vision I can mock at pain.
God! Was there ever woman half so sweet,
Or death so bitter, or at such dear feet?

ON THE NATURE OF LOVE

You ask my love. What shall my love then be?
A hope, an aspiration, a desire?
The soul's eternal charter writ in fire
Upon the earth, the heavens, and the sea?
You ask my love. The carnal mystery
Of a soft hand, of finger-tips that press,
Of eyes that kindle and of lips that kiss,
Of sweet things known to thee and only thee?
You ask my love. What love can be more sweet
Than hope or pleasure? Yet we love in vain.
The soul is more than joy, the life than meat.
The sweetest love of all were love in pain,
And that I will not give. So let it be.
—Nay, give me any love, so it be love of thee.

IN ANSWER TO A QUESTION

Why should I hate you, love, or why despise
For that last proof of tenderness you gave?
The battle is not always to the brave,

Nor life's sublimest wisdom to the wise.
True courage often is in frightened eyes,
And reason in sweet lips that only rave.
There is a weakness stronger than the grave,
And blood poured out has overcome the skies.
—Nay, love, I honour you the more for this,
That you have rent the veil, and ushered in
A fellow soul to your soul's holy place.
And why should either blush that we have been
One day in Eden, in our nakedness?
—'Tis conscience makes us sinners, not our sin.

FAREWELL TO JULIET

Lame, impotent conclusion to youth's dreams
Vast as all heaven! See, what glory lies
Entangled here in these base stratagems,
What virtue done to death! O glorious sighs,
Sublime beseechings, high cajoleries,
Fond wraths, brave ruptures, all that sometime was
Our daily bread of gods beneath the skies,
How are ye ended, in what utter loss!
Time was, time is, and time is yet to come,
Till even time itself shall have its end.
These were eternal. And behold, a tomb!
Come, let us laugh and eat and drink. God send
What all the world must need one day as we,
Speedy oblivion, rest for memory.

ST. VALENTINE'S DAY

To-day, all day, I rode upon the Down,
With hounds and horsemen, a brave company.
On this side in its glory lay the sea,
On that the Sussex Weald, a sea of brown.
The wind was light, and brightly the sun shone,
And still we galloped on from gorse to gorse.
And once, when checked, a thrush sang, and my horse
Pricked his quick ears as to a sound unknown.

I knew the Spring was come. I knew it even
Better than all by this, that through my chase
In bush and stone and hill and sea and heaven
I seemed to see and follow still your face.
Your face my quarry was. For it I rode,
My horse a thing of wings, myself a god.

TO ONE ON HER WASTE OF TIME

Why practise, love, this small economy
Of your heart's favours? Can you keep a kiss
To be enjoyed in age? And would the free
Expense of pleasure leave you penniless?
Nay, nay. Be wise. Believe me, pleasure is
A gambler's token, only gold to-day.
The day of love is short, and every bliss
Untasted now is a bliss thrown away.
'Twere pitiful, in truth, such treasures should
Lie by like miser's crusts till mouldy grown.
Think you the hand of age will be less rude
In touching your sweet bosom than my own?
Alas, what matter, when our heads are grey,
Whether you loved or did not love to-day?

TO ONE WHO WOULD MAKE CONFESSION

Oh! leave the Past to bury its own dead.
The Past is naught to us, the Present all.
What need of last year's leaves to strew Love's bed?
What need of ghosts to grace a festival?
I would not, if I could, those days recall,
Those days not ours. For us the feast is spread,
The lamps are lit, and music plays withal.
Then let us love and leave the rest unsaid.
This island is our home. Around it roar
Great gulfs and oceans, channels, straits, and seas.
What matter in what wreck we reached the shore,
So we both reached it? We can mock at these.
Oh! leave the Past, if Past indeed there be.
I would not know it. I would know but thee.

Song

Oh fly not, Pleasure, pleasant-hearted Pleasure,
    Fold me thy wings, I prithee, yet and stay.
For my heart no measure
Knows nor other treasure
    To buy a garland for my love to-day.

And thou too, Sorrow, tender-hearted Sorrow,
    Thou grey-eyed mourner, fly not yet away.
For I fain would borrow
Thy sad weeds to-morrow
    To make a mourning for love's yesterday.

The voice of Pity, Time's divine dear Pity,
    Moved me to tears. I dared not say them nay,
But went forth from the city
Making thus my ditty
    Of fair love lost for ever and a day.

FROM *The Wisdom of Merlyn*

What then is Merlyn's message, his word to thee weary of
    pain,
Man, on thy desolate march, thy search for an adequate
    cause, for a thread, for a guiding rein,
Still in the maze of thy doubts and fears, to bring thee thy joy
    again?

Thou hast tried to climb to the sky; thou hast called it a
    firmament;
Thou hast found it a thing infirm, a heaven which is no haven,
    a bladder punctured and rent,
A mansion frail as the rainbow mist, as thy own soul impotent.

Thou hast clung to a dream in thy tears; thou hast stayed thy
    rage with a hope;
Thou hast anchored thy wreck to a reed, a cobweb spread for
    thy sail, with sand for thy salvage rope;
Thou hast made thy course with a compass marred, a toy for
    thy telescope.

What hast thou done with thy days? Bethink thee, Man, that
    alone
Thou of all sentient things, hast learned to grieve in thy joy,
    hast earned thee the malison
Of going sad without cause of pain, a weeper and woe-begone.

Why? For the dream of a dream of another than this fair life
Joyous to all but thee, by every creature beloved in its spring-
    time of passion rife,
By every creature but only thee, sad husband with sadder
    wife,

Scared at thought of the end, at the simple logic of death,
Scared at the old Earth's arms outstretched to hold thee again,
    thou child of an hour, of a breath,
Seeking refuge with all but her, the mother that comforteth.

Merlyn's message is this: he would bid thee have done with
    pride.
What has it brought thee but grief, thy parentage with the
    Gods, thy kinship with beasts denied?
What thy lore of a life to come in a cloud-world deified?

O thou child which art Man, distraught with a shadow of ill!
O thou fool of thy dreams, thou gatherer rarely of flowers but
    of fungi of evil smell,
Poison growths of the autumn woods, rank mandrake and
    mort-morell!

Take thy joy with the rest, the bird, the beast of the field,
Each one wiser than thou, which frolic in no dismay, which
    seize what the seasons yield,
And lay thee down when thy day is done content with the
    unrevealed.

Take the thing which thou hast. Forget thy kingdom unseen.
Lean thy lips on the Earth; she shall bring new peace to thy
    eyes with her healing vesture green.
Drink once more at her fount of love, the one true hippocrene.

O thou child of thy fears! Nay, shame on thy childish part,
Weeping when called to thy bed. Take cheer. When the shad-
　　ows come, when the crowd is leaving the mart,
Then shalt thou learn that thou needest sleep, Death's kindly
　　arms for thy heart.

SIDNEY LANIER

(1842–1881)

FROM *The Symphony*

I speak for each no-tonguéd tree
That, spring by spring, doth nobler be,
And dumbly and most wistfully
His mighty prayerful arms outspreads
Above men's oft-unheeding heads,
And his big blessing downward sheds.
I speak for all-shaped blooms and leaves,
Lichens on stones and moss on eaves,
Grasses and grains in ranks and sheaves;
Broad-fronded ferns and keen-leafed canes,
And briery mazes bounding lanes,
And marsh-plants, thirsty-cupped for rains,
And milky stems and sugary veins;
For every long-armed woman-vine
That round a piteous tree doth twine;
For passionate odors, and divine
Pistils, and petals crystalline;
All purities of shady springs,
All shynesses of film-winged things
That fly from tree-trunks and bark-rings;
All modesties of mountain-fawns
That leap to covert from wild lawns,
And tremble if the day but dawns;
All sparklings of small beady eyes
Of birds, and sidelong glances wise
Wherewith the jay hints tragedies;
All piquancies of prickly burs,
And smoothnesses of downs and furs
Of eiders and of minivers;
All limpid honeys that do lie

At stamen-bases, nor deny
The humming-birds' fine roguery,
Bee-thighs, nor any butterfly;
All gracious curves of slender wings,
Bark-mottlings, fibre-spiralings,
Fern-wavings and leaf-flickerings;
Each dial-marked leaf and flower-bell
Wherewith in every lonesome dell
Time to himself his hours doth tell;
All tree-sounds, rustlings of pine-cones,
Wind-sighings, doves' melodious moans,
And night's unearthly under-tones;
All placid lakes and waveless deeps,
All cool reposing mountain-steeps,
Vale-calms and tranquil lotos-sleeps;—
Yea, all fair forms, and sounds, and lights,
And warmths, and mysteries, and mights,
Of Nature's utmost depths and heights,
—These doth my timid tongue present,
Their mouthpiece and leal instrument
And servant, all love-eloquent.

GERARD MANLEY HOPKINS

(1844–1889)

Heaven—Haven

(A NUN TAKES THE VEIL)

I have desired to go
   Where springs not fail,
To fields where flies no sharp and sided hail
   And a few lilies blow.

And I have asked to be
   Where no storms come,
Where the green swell is in the havens dumb,
   And out of the swing of the sea.

The Habit of Perfection

Elected Silence, sing to me
And beat upon my whorlèd ear,
Pipe me to pastures still and be
The music that I care to hear.

Shape nothing, lips; be lovely-dumb:
It is the shut, the curfew sent
From there where all surrenders come
Which only makes you eloquent.

Be shellèd, eyes, with double dark
And find the uncreated light:
This ruck and reel which you remark
Coils, keeps, and teases simple sight.

Palate, the hutch of tasty lust,
Desire not to be rinsed with wine:
The can must be so sweet, the crust
So fresh that comes in fasts divine!

Nostrils, your careless breath that spend
Upon the stir and keep of pride,
What relish shall the censers send
Along the sanctuary side!

O feel-of-primrose hands, O feet
That want the yield of plushy sward,
But you shall walk the golden street
And you unhouse and house the Lord.

And, Poverty, be thou the bride
And now the marriage feast begun,
And lily-coloured clothes provide
Your spouse not laboured-at nor spun.

In the Valley of the Elwy

I remember a house where all were good
  To me, God knows, deserving no such thing:
  Comforting smell breathed at very entering,
Fetched fresh, as I suppose, off some sweet wood.
That cordial air made those kind people a hood
  All over, as a bevy of eggs the mothering wing
  Will, or mild nights the new morsels of spring:
Why, it seemed of course; seemed of right it should.

Lovely the woods, waters, meadows, combes, vales,
All the air things wear that build this world of Wales;
  Only the inmate does not correspond:
God, lover of souls, swaying considerate scales,
Complete thy creature dear O where it fails,
  Being mighty a master, being a father and fond.

The Starlight Night

Look at the stars! look, look up at the skies!
  O look at all the fire-folk sitting in the air!
  The bright boroughs, the circle-citadels there!
Down in dim woods the diamond delves! the elves'-eyes!
The grey lawns cold where gold, where quickgold lies!
  Wind-beat whitebeam! airy abeles set on a flare!
  Flake-doves sent floating forth at a farmyard scare!—
Ah well! it is all a purchase, all is a prize.

Buy then! bid then!—What?—Prayer, patience, alms, vows.
Look, look: a May-mess, like on orchard boughs!
  Look! March-bloom, like on mealed-with-yellow sallows!
These are indeed the barn; withindoors house
The shocks. This piece-bright paling shuts the spouse
  Christ home, Christ and his mother and all his hallows.

Pied Beauty

Glory be to God for dappled things—
    For skies of couple-colour as a brinded cow;
      For rose-moles all in stipple upon trout that swim;
Fresh-firecoal chestnut-falls; finches' wings;
    Landscape plotted and pieced—fold, fallow, and plough;
      And áll Trádes, their gear and tackle and trim.
All things counter, original, spare, strange;
    Whatever is fickle, freckled (who knows how?)
      With swift, slow; sweet, sour; adazzle, dim;
He fathers-forth whose beauty is past change:
        Praise him.

ANDREW LANG

(1844–1912)

The Odyssey

As one that for a weary space has lain
    Lulled by the song of Circe and her wine,
    In gardens near the pale of Proserpine,
Where that Aeaean isle forgets the main,
And only the low lutes of love complain,
    And only shadows of wan lovers pine;
    As such an one were glad to know the brine
Salt on his lips, and the large air again—

So gladly, from the songs of modern speech
    Men turn, and see the stars, and feel the free
    Shrill wind beyond the close of heavy flowers;
    And, through the music of the languid hours,
They hear like ocean on a western beach
    The surge and thunder of the Odyssey.

ARTHUR WILLIAM EDGAR O'SHAUGHNESSY
(1844–1881)

FROM *Ode*

We are the music-makers,
    And we are the dreamers of dreams,
Wandering by lone sea-breakers,
    And sitting by desolate streams;
World-losers and world-forsakers,
    On whom the pale moon gleams:
Yet we are the movers and shakers
    Of the world for ever, it seems.

With wonderful deathless ditties
We build up the world's great cities,
    And out of a fabulous story
    We fashion an empire's glory:
One man with a dream, at pleasure,
    Shall go forth and conquer a crown;
And three with a new song's measure
    Can trample an empire down.

We, in the ages lying
    In the buried past of the earth,
Built Nineveh with our sighing,
    And Babel itself with our mirth;
And o'erthrew them with prophesying
    To the old of the new world's worth;
For each age is a dream that is dying,
    Or one that is coming to birth.

ROBERT BRIDGES
(1844–1930)

Pater Filio

Sense with keenest edge unuséd,
    Yet unsteel'd by scathing fire;
Lovely feet as yet unbruiséd
    On the ways of dark desire;
Sweetest hope that lookest smiling
O'er the wilderness defiling!

Why such beauty, to be blighted
  By the swarm of foul destruction?
Why such innocence delighted,
  When sin stalks to thy seduction?
All the litanies e'er chaunted
Shall not keep thy faith undaunted.

I have pray'd the sainted Morning
  To unclasp her hands to hold thee;
From resignful Eve's adorning
  Stol'n a robe of peace to enfold thee;
With all charms of man's contriving
Arm'd thee for thy lonely striving.

Me too once unthinking Nature
  —Whence Love's timeless mockery took me,—
Fashion'd so divine a creature,
  Yea, and like a beast forsook me.
I forgave, but tell the measure
Of her crime in thee, my treasure.

To L.B.C.L.M.

I love all beauteous things,
  I seek and adore them;
God hath no better praise,
And man in his hasty days
  Is honoured for them.

I too will something make
  And joy in the making;
Altho' to-morrow it seem
Like the empty words of a dream
  Remembered on waking.

On a Dead Child

Perfect little body, without fault or stain on thee,
  With promise of strength and manhood full and fair!
    Though cold and stark and bare,
The bloom and the charm of life doth awhile remain on thee.

Thy mother's treasure wert thou;—alas! no longer
  To visit her heart with wondrous joy; to be
    Thy father's pride;—ah, he
Must gather his faith together, and his strength make stronger.

To me, as I move thee now in the last duty,
  Dost thou with a turn or gesture anon respond;
    Startling my fancy fond
With a chance attitude of the head, a freak of beauty.

Thy hand clasps, as 'twas wont, my finger, and holds it:
  But the grasp is the clasp of Death, heart-breaking and stiff;
    Yet feels to my hand as if
'Twas still thy will, thy pleasure and trust that enfolds it.

So I lay thee there, thy sunken eyelids closing,—
  Go lie thou there in thy coffin, thy last little bed!—
    Propping thy wise, sad head,
Thy firm pale hands across thy chest disposing.

So quiet! doth the change content thee?
  Death, whither hath he taken thee?
  To a world, do I think, that rights the disaster of this?
    The vision of which I miss,
Who weep for the body, and wish but to warm thee and
    awaken thee?

Ah! little at best can all our hopes avail us
  To lift this sorrow, or cheer us, when in the dark,
    Unwilling, alone we embark,
And the things we have seen and have known and have heard
    of, fail us.

ALICE MEYNELL
(1849–1922)
A Letter from a Girl to Her Own Old Age

    Listen, and when thy hand this paper presses,
    O time-worn woman, think of her who blesses
    What thy thin fingers touch, with her caresses.

O mother, for the weight of years that break thee!
O daughter, for slow time must yet awake thee,
And from the changes of my heart must make thee.

O fainting traveller, morn is grey in heaven.
Dost thou remember how the clouds were driven?
And are they calm about the fall of even?

Pause near the ending of thy long migration,
For this one sudden hour of desolation
Appeals to one hour of thy meditation.

Suffer, O silent one, that I remind thee
Of the great hills that stormed the sky behind thee,
Of the wild winds of power that have resigned thee.

Know that the mournful plain where thou must wander
Is but a grey and silent world, but ponder
The misty mountains of the morning yonder.

Listen:—the mountain winds with rain were fretting,
And sudden gleams the mountain-tops besetting.
I cannot let thee fade to death, forgetting.

What part of this wild heart of mine I know not
Will follow with thee where the great winds blow not,
And where young flowers of the mountain grow not.

         *   *   *   *

I have not writ this letter of divining
To make a glory of thy silent pining,
A triumph of thy mute and strange declining.

Only one youth, and the bright life was shrouded.
Only one morning, and the day was clouded.
And one old age with all regrets is crowded.

O hush, O hush! thy tears my words are steeping.
O hush, hush, hush! So full, the fount of weeping?
Poor eyes, so quickly moved, so near to sleeping?

Pardon the girl; such strange desires beset her.
Poor woman, lay aside the mournful letter
That breaks thy heart; the one who wrote, forget her.

The one who now thy faded features guesses,
With filial fingers thy grey hair caresses,
With mournful tears thy mournful twilight blesses.

Renouncement

I must not think of thee; and, tired yet strong,
   I shun the love that lurks in all delight—
   The love of thee—and in the blue heaven's height,
And in the dearest passage of a song.
Oh, just beyond the sweetest thoughts that throng
   This breast, the thought of thee waits hidden yet bright;
   But it must never, never come in sight;
I must stop short of thee the whole day long.
But when sleep comes to close each difficult day,
   When night gives pause to the long watch I keep,
And all my bonds I needs must loose apart,
Must doff my will as raiment laid away,—
   With the first dream that comes with the first sleep
I run, I run, I am gather'd to thy heart.

WILLIAM ERNEST HENLEY

(1849–1903)

I.M.
R. T. Hamilton Bruce

Out of the night that covers me,
   Black as the Pit from pole to pole,
I thank whatever gods may be
   For my unconquerable soul.

In the fell clutch of circumstance
   I have not winced nor cried aloud.
Under the bludgeonings of chance
   My head is bloody, but unbowed.

Beyond this place of wrath and tears
   Looms but the horror of the shade,
And yet the menace of the years
   Finds, and shall find, me unafraid.

It matters not how strait the gate,
    How charged with punishments the scroll,
I am the master of my fate:
    I am the captain of my soul.

"Fill a Glass with Golden Wine"

Fill a glass with golden wine,
    And the while your lips are wet
Set their perfume unto mine,
    And forget,
Every kiss we take and give
Leaves us less of life to live.

Yet again! your whim and mine
    In a happy while have met.
All your sweets to me resign,
    Nor regret
That we press with every breath,
Sighed or singing, nearer death.

To A.D.

The nightingale has a lyre of gold,
    The lark's is a clarion call,
And the blackbird plays but a boxwood flute,
    But I love him best of all.

For his song is all of the joy of life,
    And we in the mad, spring weather,
We two have listened till he sang
    Our hearts and lips together.

"On the Way to Kew"

On the way to Kew
By the river old and gray,
Where in the Long Ago
We laughed and loitered so,
I met a ghost to-day,

A ghost that told of you—
A ghost of low replies
And sweet, inscrutable eyes
Coming up from Richmond
As you used to do.

By the river old and gray,
The enchanted Long Ago
Murmured and smiled anew.
On the way to Kew,
March had the laugh of May,
The bare boughs looked aglow,
And old immortal words
Sang in my breast like birds,
Coming up from Richmond
As I used with you.

With the life of Long Ago
Lived my thoughts of you.
By the river old and gray
Flowing his appointed way
As I watched I knew
What is so good to know—
Not in vain, not in vain,
Shall I look for you again
Coming up from Richmond
On the way to Kew.

Epilogue to Rhymes and Rhythms

These, to you now, O, more than ever now—
Now that the Ancient Enemy
Has passed, and we, we two that are one, have seen
A piece of perfect Life
Turn to so ravishing a shape of Death
The Arch-Discomforter might well have smiled
In pity and pride,
Even as he bore his lovely and innocent spoil
From those home-kingdoms he left desolate.

Poor windlestraws
On the great, sullen, roaring pool of Time
And Chance and Change, I know!
But they are yours, as I am, till we attain
That end for which we make, we two that are one:
A little, exquisite Ghost
Between us, smiling with the serenest eyes
Seen in this world, and calling, calling still
In that clear voice whose infinite subtleties
Of sweetness, thrilling back across the grave,
Break the poor heart to hear:—
                    "Come, Dadsie, come!
Mama, how long—how long!"

ROBERT LOUIS STEVENSON

(1850–1894)

The Celestial Surgeon

If I have faltered more or less
In my great task of happiness;
If I have moved among my race
And shown no glorious morning face;
If beams from happy human eyes
Have moved me not; if morning skies,
Books, and my food, and summer rain
Knocked on my sullen heart in vain:—
Lord, thy most pointed pleasure take
And stab my spirit broad awake;
Or, Lord, if too obdurate I,
Choose thou, before that spirit die,
A piercing pain, a killing sin,
And to my dead heart run them in!

The Vagabond

Give to me the life I love,
    Let the lave go by me,
Give the jolly heaven above
    And the byway nigh me.

Bed in the bush with stars to see,
    Bread I dip in the river—
There's the life for a man like me,
    There's the life for ever.

Let the blow fall soon or late,
    Let what will be o'er me;
Give the face of earth around
    And the road before me.
Wealth I seek not, hope nor love,
    Nor a friend to know me;
All I seek the heaven above
    And the road below me.

Or let autumn fall on me
    Where afield I linger,
Silencing the bird on tree,
    Biting the blue finger:
White as meal the frosty field—
    Warm the fireside haven—
Not to autumn will I yield,
    Not to winter even!

Let the blow fall soon or late,
    Let what will be o'er me;
Give the face of earth around,
    And the road before me.
Wealth I ask not, hope nor love,
    Nor a friend to know me;
All I ask the heaven above,
    And the road below me.

Requiem

Under the wide and starry sky
Dig the grave and let me lie.
Glad did I live and gladly die,
    And I laid me down with a will.

This be the verse you grave for me:
Here he lies where he longed to be;
Home is the sailor, home from sea,
    And the hunter home from the hill.

OSCAR WILDE

(1856–1900)

FROM *The Ballad of Reading Gaol*

In Debtor's Yard the stones are hard,
    And the dripping wall is high,
So it was there he took the air
    Beneath the leaden sky,
And by each side a Warder walked,
    For fear the man might die.

Or else he sat with those who watched
    His anguish night and day;
Who watched him when he rose to weep,
    And when he crouched to pray;
Who watched him lest himself should rob
    Their scaffold of its prey.

The Governor was strong upon
    The Regulations Act:
The Doctor said that Death was but
    A scientific fact:
And twice a day the Chaplain called,
    And left a little tract.

And twice a day he smoked his pipe,
    And drank his quart of beer:
His soul was resolute, and held
    No hiding-place for fear;
He often said that he was glad
    The hangman's hands were near.

But why he said so strange a thing
    No Warder dared to ask:

For he to whom a watcher's doom
   Is given as his task,
Must set a lock upon his lips,
   And make his face a mask.

Or else he might be moved, and try
   To comfort or console:
And what should Human Pity do
   Pent up in Murderers' Hole?
What word of grace in such a place
   Could help a brother's soul?

With slouch and swing around the ring
   We trod the Fools' Parade!
We did not care: we knew we were
   The Devil's Own Brigade:
And shaven head and feet of lead
   Make a merry masquerade.

We tore the tarry rope to shreds
   With blunt and bleeding nails;
We rubbed the doors, and scrubbed the floors,
   And cleaned the shining rails:
And, rank by rank, we soaped the plank,
   And clattered with the pails.

We sewed the sacks, we broke the stones,
   We turned the dusty drill:
We banged the tins, and bawled the hymns,
   And sweated on the mill:
But in the heart of every man
   Terror was lying still.

So still it lay that every day
   Crawled like a weed-clogged wave:
And we forgot the bitter lot
   That waits for fool and knave,
Till once, as we tramped in from work,
   We passed an open grave.

With yawning mouth the yellow hole
   Gaped for a living thing;
The very mud cried out for blood
   To the thirsty asphalt ring:
And we knew that ere one dawn grew fair
   Some prisoner had to swing.

Right in we went, with soul intent
   On Death and Dread and Doom:
The hangman, with his little bag,
   Went shuffling through the gloom:
And each man trembled as he crept
   Into his numbered tomb.

That night the empty corridors
   Were full of forms of Fear,
And up and down the iron town
   Stole feet we could not hear,
And through the bars that hide the stars
   White faces seemed to peer.

He lay as one who lies and dreams
   In a pleasant meadow-land,
The watchers watched him as he slept,
   And could not understand
How one could sleep so sweet a sleep
   With a hangman close at hand.

But there is no sleep when men must weep
   Who never yet have wept:
So we—the fool, the fraud, the knave—
   That endless vigil kept,
And through each brain on hands of pain
   Another's terror crept.

Alas! it is a fearful thing
   To feel another's guilt!
For, right within, the sword of Sin
   Pierced to its poisoned hilt,
And as molten lead were the tears we shed
   For the blood we had not spilt.

The Warders with their shoes of felt
  Crept by each padlocked door,
And peeped and saw, with eyes of awe,
  Gray figures on the floor,
And wondered why men knelt to pray
  Who never prayed before.

All through the night we knelt and prayed,
  Mad mourners of a corse!
The troubled plumes of midnight were
  The plumes upon a hearse:
And bitter wine upon a sponge
  Was the savour of Remorse.

The grey cock crew, the red cock crew,
  But never came the day;
And crooked shapes of terror crouched
  In the corners where we lay:
And each evil sprite that walks by night
  Before us seemed to play.

      *   *   *   *   *

The morning wind began to moan,
  But still the night went on;
Through its giant loom the web of gloom
  Crept till each thread was spun:
And, as we prayed, we grew afraid
  Of the Justice of the Sun.

The moaning wind went wandering round
  The weeping prison-wall:
Till like a wheel of turning steel
  We felt the minutes crawl:
O moaning wind! what had we done
  To have such a seneschal?

At last I saw the shadowed bars,
  Like a lattice wrought in lead,
Move right across the whitewashed wall
  That faced my three-planked bed,
And I knew that somewhere in the world
  God's dreadful dawn was red.

At six o'clock we cleaned our cells,
  At seven all was still,
But the sough and swing of a mighty wing
  The prison seemed to fill,
For the Lord of Death, with icy breath,
  Had entered in to kill.

He did not pass in purple pomp,
  Nor ride a moon-white steed,
Three yards of cord and a sliding board
  Are all the gallows' need:
So with rope of shame the Herald came
  To do the secret deed.

We were as men who through a fen
  Of filthy darkness grope:
We did not dare to breathe a prayer,
  Or to give our anguish scope:
Something was dead in each of us,
  And what was dead was Hope.

For Man's grim Justice goes its way,
  And will not swerve aside:
It slays the weak, it slays the strong,
  It has a deadly stride:
With iron heel it slays the strong,
  The monstrous parricide!

We waited for the stroke of eight:
  Each tongue was thick with thirst:
For the stroke of eight is the stroke of Fate
  That makes a man accursed,
And Fate will use a running noose
  For the best man and the worst.

We had no other thing to do,
  Save to wait for the sign to come:
So, like things of stone in a valley lone,
  Quiet we sat and dumb:
But each man's heart beat thick and quick,
  Like a madman on a drum!

With sudden shock, the prison-clock
   Smote on the shivering air,
And from all the jail rose up a wail
   Of impotent despair,
Like the sound that frightened marshes hear
   From some leper in his lair.

And as one sees most dreadful things
   In the crystal of a dream,
We saw the greasy hempen rope
   Hooked to the blackened beam,
And heard the prayer the hangman's snare
   Strangled into a scream.

And all the woe that moved him so
   That he gave that bitter cry,
And the wild regrets, and the bloody sweats,
   None knew so well as I:
For he who lives more lives than one
   More deaths than one must die.

JOHN DAVIDSON

(1857–1909)

In Romney Marsh

As I went down to Dymchurch Wall,
   I heard the South sing o'er the land;
I saw the yellow sunlight fall
   On knolls where Norman churches stand.

And ringing shrilly, taut and lithe,
   Within the wind a core of sound,
The wire from Romney town to Hythe
   Alone its airy journey wound.

A veil of purple vapour flowed
   And trailed its fringe along the Straits;
The upper air like sapphire glowed;
   And roses filled Heaven's central gates.

Masts in the offing wagged their tops;
    The swinging waves pealed on the shore;
The saffron beach, all diamond drops
    And beads of surge, prolonged the roar.

As I came up from Dymchurch Wall,
    I saw above the Downs' low crest
The crimson brands of sunset fall,
    Flicker and fade from out the west.

Night sank: like flakes of silver fire
    The stars in one great shower came down;
Shrill blew the wind; and shrill the wire
    Rang out from Hythe to Romney town.

The darkly shining salt sea drops
    Streamed as the waves clashed on the shore;
The beach, with all its organ stops
    Pealing again, prolonged the roar.

Waiting

Within unfriendly walls
    We starve—or starve by stealth.
Oxen fatten in their stalls;
    You guard the harrier's health:
They never can be criminals,
    And can't compete for wealth.
        From the mansion and the palace
            Is there any help or hail
        For the tenants of the alleys,
            Of the workhouse and the jail?

Though lands await our toil,
    And earth half-empty rolls,
Cumberers of English soil,
    We cringe for orts and doles—
Prosperity's accustomed foil,
    Millions of useless souls.
        In the gutters and the ditches
            Human vermin festering lurk—
        We, the rust upon your riches;
            We, the flaw in all your work.

Come down from where you sit;
  We look to you for aid.
Take us from the miry pit,
  And lead us undismayed:
Say: "Even you, outcast, unfit,
  Forward with sword and spade!"
    And myriads of us idle
      Would thank you through our tears,
    Though you drove us with a bridle,
      And a whip about our ears.

From cloudy cape to cape
  The teeming waters seethe;
Golden grain and purple grape
  The regions overwreathe.
Will no one help us to escape?
  We scarce have room to breathe.
    You might try to understand us:
      We are waiting night and day
    For a captain to command us,
      And the word we must obey.

ALFRED EDWARD HOUSMAN

(1859–1936)

"Loveliest of Trees..."

Loveliest of trees, the cherry now
Is hung with bloom along the bough,
And stands about the woodland ride
Wearing white for Eastertide.

Now, of my threescore years and ten,
Twenty will not come again,
And take from seventy springs a score,
It only leaves me fifty more.

And since to look at things in bloom
Fifty springs are little room,
About the woodlands I will go
To see the cherry hung with snow.

"When I Was One-and-Twenty"

When I was one-and-twenty
    I heard a wise man say,
"Give crowns and pounds and guineas
    But not your heart away;
Give pearls away and rubies
    But keep your fancy free."
But I was one-and-twenty,
    No use to talk to me.

When I was one-and-twenty
    I heard him say again,
"The heart out of the bosom
    Was never given in vain;
'Tis paid with sighs a-plenty
    And sold for endless rue."
And I am two-and-twenty,
    And oh, 'tis true, 'tis true.

"Into My Heart an Air . . ."

Into my heart an air that kills
    From yon far country blows:
What are those blue remembered hills,
    What spires, what farms are those?

That is the land of lost content,
    I see it shining plain,
The happy highways where I went
    And cannot come again.

Epitaph on an Army of Mercenaries

These, in the day when heaven was falling,
    The hour when earth's foundations fled,
Followed their mercenary calling
    And took their wages and are dead.

Their shoulders held the sky suspended;
 They stood, and earth's foundations stay;
What God abandoned, these defended,
 And saved the sum of things for pay.

"I to My Perils"

I to my perils
  Of cheat and charmer
  Came clad in armour
    By stars benign;
Hope lies to mortals
  And most believe her,
  But man's deceiver
    Was never mine.

The thoughts of others
  Were light and fleeting,
  Of lovers' meeting
    Or luck or fame;
Mine were of trouble
  And mine were steady,
  So I was ready
    When trouble came.

For My Funeral

O thou that from thy mansion
  Through time and place to roam,
Dost sent abroad thy children,
  And then dost call them home,

That men and tribes and nations
  And all thy hand hath made
May shelter them from sunshine
  In thine eternal shade:

We now to peace and darkness
And earth and thee restore
Thy creature that thou madest
And wilt cast forth no more.

FRANCIS THOMPSON

(1859–1907)

The Hound of Heaven

I fled Him, down the nights and down the days;
  I fled Him, down the arches of the years;
I fled Him, down the labyrinthine ways
  Of my own mind; and in the midst of tears
I hid from Him, and under running laughter.
      Up vistaed hopes I sped;
      And shot, precipitated,
Adown Titanic glooms of chasméd fears,
  From those strong Feet that followed, followed after.
      But with unhurrying chase,
      And unperturbéd pace,
    Deliberate speed, majestic instancy,
      They beat—and a Voice beat
      More instant than the Feet—
    "All things betray thee, who betrayest Me."

      I pleaded, outlaw-wise,
By many a hearted casement, curtained red,
  Trellised with intertwining charities
(For, though I knew His love Who followéd,
      Yet was I sore adread
Lest, having Him, I must have naught beside);
But, if one little casement parted wide,
  The gust of His approach would clash it to.
Fear wist not to evade, as Love wist to pursue.
Across the margent of the world I fled,
  And troubled the gold gateways of the stars,
  Smiting for shelter on their clangéd bars;
      Fretted to dulcet jars
And silvern chatter the pale ports o' the moon.

I said to dawn, Be sudden; to eve, Be soon;
  With thy young skiey blossoms heap me over
     From this tremendous Lover!
Float thy vague veil about me, lest He see!
    I tempted all His servitors, but to find
My own betrayal in their constancy,
In faith to Him their fickleness to me,
  Their traitorous trueness, and their loyal deceit.
To all swift things for swiftness did I sue;
  Clung to the whistling mane of every wind,
     But whether they swept, smoothly fleet,
    The long savannahs of the blue;
     Or whether thunder-driven
    They clanged his chariot 'thwart a heaven
Flashy with flying lightnings round the spurn o' their feet:—
  Fear wist not to evade as Love wist to pursue
     Still with unhurrying chase,
     And unperturbéd pace,
    Deliberate speed, majestic instancy,
     Came on the following Feet,
     And a Voice above their beat—
    "Naught shelters thee, who wilt not shelter Me."

I sought no more that after which I strayed
    In face of man or maid;
But still within the little children's eyes
    Seems something, something that replies;
They at least are for me, surely for me!
I turned me to them very wistfully;
But, just as their young eyes grew sudden fair
    With dawning answers there,
Their angel plucked them from me by the hair.
"Come then, ye other children, Nature's—share
With me" (said I) "your delicate fellowship;
    Let me greet you lip to lip,
    Let me twine with you caresses,
     Wantoning
    With our Lady-Mother's vagrant tresses,
     Banqueting
    With her in her wind-walled palace,
    Underneath her azured daïs,

Quaffing as your taintless way is,
From a chalice
Lucent-weeping out of the dayspring.
So it was done:
I in their delicate fellowship was one—
Drew the bolts of Nature's secrecies.
I knew all the swift importings
On the wilful face of skies;
I knew how the clouds arise
Spuméd of the wild sea-snortings;
All that's born or dies
Rose and drooped with—made them shapers
Of mine own moods, or wailful or divine—
With them joyed and was bereaven.
I was heavy with the even,
When she lit her glimmering tapers
Round the day's dead sanctities.
I laughed in the morning's eyes.
I triumphed and I saddened with all weather,
Heaven and I wept together,
And its sweet tears were salt with mortal mine;
Against the red throb of its sunset-heart
I laid my own to beat,
And share commingling heat;
But not by that, by that, was eased my human smart.
In vain my tears were wet on Heaven's grey cheek.
For ah! we know not what each other says,
These things and I; in sound *I* speak—
Their sound is but their stir, they speak by silences.
Nature, poor stepdame, cannot slake my drouth;
Let her, if she would owe me,
Drop yon blue bosom-veil of sky, and show me
The breasts o' her tenderness:
Never did any milk of hers once bless
My thirsting mouth.
Nigh and nigh draws the chase,
With unperturbéd pace,
Deliberate speed, majestic instancy;
And past those noiséd Feet
A voice comes yet more fleet—
"Lo! naught contents thee, who content'st not Me."

Naked I wait Thy love's uplifted stroke!
My harness piece by piece Thou hast hewn from me,
　　　And smitten me to my knee;
　　　I am defenceless utterly.
　　　I slept, methinks, and woke,
And, slowly gazing, find me stripped in sleep.
In the rash lustihead of my young powers,
　　　I shook the pillaring hours
And pulled my life upon me; grimed with smears,
I stand amid the dust o' the mounded years—
My mangled youth lies dead beneath the heap.
My days have crackled and gone up in smoke,
Have puffed and burst as sun-starts on a stream.
　　　Yea, faileth now even dream
The dreamer, and the lute the lutanist;
Even the linkéd fantasies, in whose blossomy twist
I swung the earth a trinket at my wrist,
Are yielding; cords of all too weak account
For earth with heavy griefs so overplussed.
　　　Ah! is Thy love indeed
A weed, albeit an amaranthine weed,
Suffering no flowers except its own to mount?
　　　Ah! must—
　　　Designer infinite!—
Ah! must Thou char the wood ere Thou canst limn with it?
My freshness spent its wavering shower i' the dust;
And now my heart is as a broken fount,
Wherein tear-droppings stagnate, spilt down ever
　　　From the dank thoughts that shiver
Upon the sighful branches of my mind.
　　　Such is; what is to be?
The pulp so bitter, how shall taste the rind?
I dimly guess what Time in mists confounds;
Yet ever and anon a trumpet sounds
From the hid battlements of Eternity;
Those shaken mists a space unsettle, then
Round the half-glimpséd turrets slowly wash again.
　　　But not ere him who summoneth
　　　I first have seen, enwound
With glooming robes purpureal, cypress-crowned;
His name I know, and what his trumpet saith.

Whether man's heart or life it be which yields
   Thee harvest, must Thy harvest fields
   Be dunged with rotten death?

    Now of that long pursuit
    Comes on at hand the bruit;
  That Voice is round me like a bursting sea:
    "And is thy earth so marred,
    Shattered in shard on shard?
  Lo, all things fly thee, for thou fliest Me!
  Strange, piteous, futile thing!
Wherefore should any set thee love apart?
Seeing none but I makes much of naught"
    (He said)
"And human love needs human meriting:
    How hast thou merited—
Of all man's clotted clay the dingiest clot?
    Alack, thou knowest not
How little worthy of any love thou art!
Whom wilt thou find to love ignoble thee
    Save Me, save only Me?
All which I took from thee I did but take,
    Not for thy harms,
But just that thou might'st seek it in My arms.
    All which thy child's mistake
Fancies as lost, I have stored for thee at home;
    Rise, clasp My hand, and come!"
    Halts by me that footfall:
    Is my gloom, after all,
  Shade of His hand, outstretched caressingly?
    "Ah, fondest, blindest, weakest,
    I am He whom thou seekest!
Thou dravest love from thee, who dravest Me."

VICTOR PLARR
(1863–1929)

Epitaphium Citharistriae

Stand not uttering sedately
   Trite oblivious praise above her!
Rather say you saw her lately
   Lightly kissing her last lover.

Whisper not "There is a reason
  Why we bring her no white blossom:"
Since the snowy bloom's in season,
  Strow it on her sleeping bosom:

Oh, for it would be a pity
  To o'erpraise her or to flout her:
She was wild, and sweet, and witty—
  Let's not say dull things about her.

GEORGE SANTAYANA

(1863–1952)

Ode

My heart rebels against my generation,
That talks of freedom and is slave to riches,
And, toiling 'neath each day's ignoble burden,
    Boasts of the morrow.

No space for noonday rest or midnight watches,
No purest joy of breathing under heaven!
Wretched themselves, they heap, to make them happy,
    Many possessions.

But thou, O silent Mother, wise, immortal,
To whom our toil is laughter,—take, divine one,
This vanity away, and to thy lover
    Give what is needful:—

A staunch heart, nobly calm, averse to evil,
The windy sky for breath, the sea, the mountain,
A well-born, gentle friend, his spirit's brother,
    Ever beside him.

What would you gain, ye seekers, with your striving,
Or what vast Babel raise you on your shoulders?
You multiply distresses, and your children
    Surely will curse you.

O leave them rather friendlier gods, and fairer
Orchards and temples, and a freer bosom!
What better comforter have we, or what other
　　　Profit in living,

Than to feed, sobered by the truth of Nature,
Awhile upon her bounty and her beauty,
And hand her torch of gladness to the ages
　　　Following after?

She hath not made us, like her other children,
Merely for peopling of her spacious kingdoms,
Beasts of the wild, or insects of the summer,
　　　Breeding and dying.

But also that we might, half knowing, worship
The deathless beauty of her guiding vision,
And learn to love, in all things mortal, only
　　　What is eternal.

On the Death of a Metaphysician

Unhappy dreamer, who outwinged in flight
The pleasant region of the things I love,
And soared beyond the sunshine, and above
The golden cornfields and the dear and bright
Warmth of the hearth,—blasphemer of delight,
Was your proud bosom not at peace with Jove,
That you sought, thankless for his guarded grove,
The empty horror of abysmal night?
Ah, the thin air is cold above the moon!
I stood and saw you fall, befooled in death,
As, in your numbéd spirit's fatal swoon,
You cried you were a god, or were to be;
I heard with feeble moan your boastful breath
Bubble from depths of the Icarian sea.

"We Needs Must Be Divided..."

We needs must be divided in the tomb,
For I would die among the hills of Spain,
And o'er the treeless melancholy plain
Await the coming of the final gloom.
But thou—O pitiful!—wilt find scant room
Among thy kindred by the northern main,
And fade into the drifting mist again,
The hemlocks' shadow, or the pines' perfume.
Let gallants lie beside their ladies' dust,
In one cold grave, with mortal love inurned;
Let the sea part our ashes, if it must.
The souls fled thence which love immortal burned,
For they were wedded without bond of lust,
And nothing of our heart to earth returned.

WILLIAM BUTLER YEATS

(1865–1939)

A Faery Song

*(SUNG BY THE PEOPLE OF FAERY OVER DIARMUID AND
GRANIA, IN THEIR BRIDAL SLEEP UNDER A CROMLECH)*

We who are old, old and gay,
O so old!
Thousands of years, thousands of years,
If all were told:

Give to these children, new from the world,
Silence and love;
And the long dew-dripping hours of the night,
And the stars above:

Give to these children, new from the world,
Rest far from men.
Is anything better, anything better?
Tell us it then:

Us who are old, old and gay,
O so old!
Thousands of years, thousands of years,
If all were told.

The Lover Tells of the Rose in His Heart

All things uncomely and broken, all things worn out and old,
The cry of a child by the roadway, the creak of a lumbering
cart,
The heavy steps of the ploughman, splashing the wintry
mould,
Are wronging your image that blossoms a rose in the deeps
of my heart.

The wrong of unshapely things is a wrong too great to be told;
I hunger to build them anew and sit on a green knoll apart,
With the earth and the sky and the water, re-made, like a
casket of gold
For my dreams of your image that blossoms a rose in the
deeps of my heart.

FROM *The Land of Heart's Desire*

The wind blows out of the gates of the day,
The wind blows over the lonely of heart,
And the lonely of heart is withered away;
While the fairies dance in a place apart,
Shaking their milk-white feet in a ring,
Tossing their milk-white arms in the air;
For they hear the wind laugh and murmur and sing
Of a land where even the old are fair,
And even the wise are merry of tongue;
But I heard a reed of Coolaney say—
"When the wind has laughed and murmured and sung,
The lonely of heart is withered away."

FROM *Deirdre*

"Why is it," Queen Edain said,
"If I do but climb the stair
To the tower overhead,
When the winds are calling there,

Or the gannets calling out,
    In waste places of the sky,
There's so much to think about,
    That I cry, that I cry?"

But her goodman answered her:
    "Love would be a thing of nought
Had not all his limbs a stir
    Born out of immoderate thought;
Were he anything by half,
    Were his measure running dry,
Lovers, if they may not laugh,
    Have to cry, have to cry."

But is Edain worth a song?
    Now the hunt begins anew?
Praise the beautiful and strong;
    Praise the redness of the yew;
Praise the blossoming apple-stem.
    But our silence had been wise.
What is all our praise to them,
    That have one another's eyes?

When Helen Lived

We have cried in our despair
That men desert,
For some trivial affair
Or noisy, insolent sport,
Beauty that we have won
From bitterest hours;
Yet we, had we walked within
Those topless towers
Where Helen walked with her boy,
Had given but as the rest
Of the men and women of Troy,
A word and a jest.

FROM A Prayer for My Daughter

I have walked and prayed for this young child an hour
And heard the sea-wind scream upon the tower,
And under the arches of the bridge, and scream
In the elms above the flooded stream;
Imagining in excited reverie
That the future years had come,
Dancing to a frenzied drum
Out of the murderous innocence of the sea.

May she be granted beauty and yet not
Beauty to make a stranger's eye distraught,
Or hers before a looking-glass, for such,
Being made beautiful overmuch,
Consider beauty a sufficient end,
Lose natural kindness and maybe
The heart-revealing intimacy
That chooses right, and never find a friend.

In courtesy I'd have her chiefly learned;
Hearts are not had as a gift but hearts are earned
By those that are not entirely beautiful;
Yet many, that have played the fool
For beauty's very self, has charm made wise,
And many a poor man that has roved,
Loved and thought himself beloved,
From a glad kindness cannot take his eyes.

My mind, because the minds that I have loved,
The sort of beauty that I have approved,
Prosper but little, has dried up of late,
Yet knows that to be choked with hate
May well be of all evil chances chief.
If there's no hatred in a mind
Assault and battery of the wind
Can never tear the linnet from the leaf.

An Intellectual hatred is the worst,
So let her think opinions are accursed.
Have I not seen the loveliest woman born
Out of the mouth of Plenty's horn,
Because of her opinionated mind
Barter that horn and every good
By quiet natures understood
For an old bellows full of angry wind?

And may her bridegroom bring her to a house
Where all's accustomed, ceremonious;
For arrogance and hatred are the wares
Peddled in the thoroughfares.
How but in custom and in ceremony
Are innocence and beauty born?
Ceremony's a name for the rich horn,
And custom for the spreading laurel tree.

Sailing to Byzantium

That is no country for old men. The young
In one another's arms, birds in the trees,
—Those dying generations—at their song,
The salmon-falls, the mackerel-crowded seas,
Fish, flesh, or fowl, commend all summer long
Whatever is begotten, born and dies.
Caught in that sensual music all neglect
Monuments of unageing intellect.

An aged man is but a paltry thing,
A tattered coat upon a stick, unless
Soul clap its hands and sing, and louder sing
For every tatter in its mortal dress,
Nor is there singing school but studying
Monuments of its own magnificence;
And therefore I have sailed the seas and come
To the holy city of Byzantium.

O sages standing in God's holy fire
As in the gold mosaic of a wall,
Come from the holy fire, perne in a gyre,
And be the singing-masters of my soul.
Consume my heart away; sick with desire
And fastened to a dying animal
It knows not what it is; and gather me
Into the artifice of eternity.

Once out of nature I shall never take
My bodily form from any natural thing,
But such a form as Grecian goldsmiths make
Of hammered gold and gold enamelling
To keep a drowsy Emperor awake;
Or set upon a golden bough to sing
To lords and ladies of Byzantium
Of what is past, or passing, or to come.

ARTHUR SYMONS

(1865–1945)

Declaration

Child, I will give you rings to wear,
And, if you love them, dainty dresses,
Flowers for your bosom and your hair,
And, if you love them, fond caresses;

And I will give you of my days,
And I will leave, when you require it,
My dreams, my books, my wonted ways,
Content if only you desire it.

Take for your own my life, my heart,
And for your love's sake I forgive you;
I only ask you for your heart,
Because I have no heart to give you.

Wanderer's Song

I have had enough of women, and enough of love,
But the land waits, and the sea waits, and day and night is
    enough;
Give me a long white road, and grey wide path of the sea,
And the wind's will and the bird's will, and the heart-ache
    still in me.

Why should I seek out sorrow, and give gold for strife?
I have loved much and wept much, but tears and love are
    not life;
The grass calls to my heart, and the foam to my blood cries
    up,
And the sun shines and the road shines, and the wine's in the
    cup.

I have had enough of wisdom, and enough of mirth,
For the way's one and the end's one, and it's soon to the
    ends of the earth;
And it's then good-night and to bed, and if heels or heart ache,
Well, it's sound sleep and long sleep, and sleep too deep to
    wake.

RUDYARD KIPLING

(1865–1936)

The Long Trail

There's a whisper down the field where the year has shot her
    yield,
  And the ricks stand grey to the sun,
Singing: "Over then, come over, for the bee has quit the
    clover,
  And your English summer's done."

    You have heard the beat of the off-shore wind,
    And the thresh of the deep-sea rain;
    You have heard the song—how long? how long?
    Pull out on the trail again!

Ha' done with the tents of Shem, dear lass,
We've seen the seasons through,
And it's time to turn on the old trail, our own trail, the
    out trail,
Pull out, pull out, on the Long Trail—the trail that is al-
    ways new!

It's North you may run to the rime-ringed sun
    Or South to the blind Horn's hate;
Or East all the way into Mississippi Bay,
    Or West to the Golden Gate—
        Where the blindest bluffs hold good, dear lass,
        And the wildest tales are true,
        And the men bulk big on the old trail, our own trail, the
            out trail,
        And life runs large on the Long Trail—the trail that is
            always new.

The days are sick and cold, and the skies are grey and old,
    And the twice-breathed airs blow damp;
And I'd sell my tired soul for the bucking beam-sea roll
    Of a black Bilbao tramp,
        With her load-line over her hatch, dear lass,
        And a drunken Dago crew,
        And her nose held down on the old trail, our own trail,
            the out trail
        From Cadiz south on the Long Trail—the trail that is
            always new.

There be triple ways to take, of the eagle or the snake,
    Or the way of a man with a maid;
But the sweetest way to me is a ship's upon the sea
    In the heel of the North-East Trade.
        Can you hear the crash on her bows, dear lass,
        And the drum of the racing screw,
        As she ships it green on the old trail, our own trail, the
            out trail,
        As she lifts and 'scends on the Long Trail—the trail that
            is always new?

See the shaking funnels roar, with the Peter at the fore,
  And the fenders grind and heave,
And the derricks clack and grate, as the tackle hooks the
    crate,
  And the fall-rope whines through the sheave;
    It's "Gang-plank up and in," dear lass,
    It's "Hawsers warp her through!"
    And it's "All clear aft" on the old trail, our own trail, the
    out trail,
    We're backing down on the Long Trail—the trail that is
    always new.

O the mutter overside, when the port-fog holds us tied,
  And the sirens hoot their dread,
When foot by foot we creep o'er the hueless viewless deep
  To the sob of the questing lead!
    It's down by the Lower Hope, dear lass,
    With the Gunfleet Sands in view,
    Till the Mouse swings green on the old trail, our own
    trail, the out trail,
    And the Gull Light lifts on the Long Trail—the trail that
    is always new.

O the blazing tropic night, when the wake's a welt of light
  That holds the hot sky tame,
And the steady fore-foot snores through the planet-powdered
    floors
  Where the scared whale flukes in flame!
    Her plates are flaked by the sun, dear lass,
    And her ropes are taut with dew,
    For we're booming down on the old trail, our own trail,
    the out trail,
    We're sagging south on the Long Trail—the trail that
    is always new.

Then home, get her home, where the drunken rollers comb,
  And the shouting seas drive by,
And the engines stamp and ring, and wet bows reel and
    swing,
  And the Southern Cross rides high!
    Yes, the old lost stars wheel back, dear lass,

That blaze in the velvet blue.
They're all old friends on the old trail, our own trail, the
out trail,
They're God's own guides on the Long Trail—the trail
that is always new.

Fly forward, O my heart, from the Foreland to the Start—
We're steaming all too slow,
And its twenty thousand mile to our little lazy isle
Where the trumpet-orchids blow!
You have heard the call of the off-shore wind
And the voice of the deep-sea rain:
You have heard the song. How long—how long?
Pull out on the trail again!

The Lord knows what we may find, dear lass,
And the Deuce knows what we may do—
But we're back once more on the old trail, our own trail, the
out trail,
We're down, hull-down, on the Long Trail—the trail that is
always new!

Screw-Guns

Smokin' my pipe on the mountings, sniffin' the mornin' cool,
I walks in my old brown gaiters along o' my old brown mule,
With seventy gunners be'ind me, and never a beggar forgets
It's only the pick of the Army that handles the dear little pets
—'Tss! 'Tss!
For you all love the screw-guns—the screw-guns they all
love you!
So when we call round with a few guns, o' course you
will know what to do—hoo! hoo!
Jest send in your Chief and surrender—it's worse if you
fights or you runs:
You can go where you please, you can skid up the trees,
but you don't get away from the guns!

They sends us along where the roads are, but mostly we goes
where they ain't.

We'd climb up the side of a sign-board an' trust to the stick
    o' the paint:
We've chivvied the Naga an' Looshai; we've given the Afree-
    deeman fits;
For we fancies ourselves at two thousand, we guns that are
    built in two bits—'Tss! 'Tss!
      For you all love the screw-guns . . .

If a man doesn't work, why, we drills 'im an' teaches 'im 'ow
    to behave.
If a beggar can't march, why, we kills 'im an' rattles 'im into
    'is grave.
You've got to stand up to our business an' spring without
    snatchin' or fuss.
D'you say that you sweat with the field-guns? By God, you
    must lather with us—'Tss! 'Tss!
      For you all love the screw-guns . . .

The eagles is screamin' around us, the river's a-moanin' below,
We're clear o' the pine an' the oak-scrub, we're out on the
    rocks an' the snow,
An' the wind is as thin as a whip-!ash what carries away to
    the plains
The rattle an' stamp o' the lead-mules—the jinglety-jink o'
    the chains—'Tss! 'Tss!
      For you all love the screw-guns . . .

There's a wheel on the Horns o' the Mornin', an' a wheel on
    the edge o' the Pit,
An' a drop into nothin' beneath you as straight as a beggar
    can spit:
With the sweat runnin' out o' your shirt-sleeves, an' the sun
    off the snow in your face,
An' 'arf o' the men on the drag-ropes to hold the old gun in
    'er place—'Tss! 'Tss!
      For you all love the screw-guns . . .

Smokin' my pipe on the mountings, sniffin' the mornin' cool,
I climbs in my old brown gaiters along o' my old brown mule.
The monkey can say what our road was—the wild-goat 'e
    knows where we passed.

Stand easy, you long-eared old darlin's! Out drag-ropes! With
　　shrapnel! Hold fast—'Tss! 'Tss!
　　For you all love the screw-guns—the screw-guns they all
　　　　love you!
　　So when we take tea with a few guns, o' course you will
　　　　know what to do—hoo! hoo!
　　Jest send in your Chief an' surrender—it's worse if you
　　　　fights or you runs:
　　You may hide in the caves, they'll be only your graves,
　　　　but you can't get away from the guns!

Shillin' a Day

My name is O'Kelly, I've heard the Revelly
From Birr to Bareilly, from Leeds to Lahore,
Hong-Kong and Peshawur,
Lucknow and Etawah,
And fifty-five more all endin' in "pore."
Black Death and his quickness, the depth and the thickness
Of sorrow and sickness I've known on my way,
But I'm old and I'm nervis,
I'm cast from the Service,
And all I deserve is a shillin' a day.

Chorus:　　Shillin' a day,
　　　　Bloomin' good pay—
　　　　Lucky to touch it, a shillin' a day!

Oh, it drives me half crazy to think of the days I
Went slap for the Ghazi, my sword at my side,
When we rode Hell-for-leather
Both squadrons together,
That didn't care whether we lived or we died.
But it's no use despairin', my wife must go charin'
An' me commissairin', the pay-bills to better,
So if me you be'old
In the wet and the cold,
By the Grand Metropold, won't you give me a letter?

Full Chorus: Give 'im a letter—
'Can't do no better,
Late Troop-Sergeant-Major an'—runs with a
letter!
Think what 'e's been,
Think what 'e's seen,
Think of his pension an'—
GAWD SAVE THE QUEEN!

Recessional

(1897)

God of our fathers, known of old,
Lord of our far-flung battle-line,
Beneath whose awful Hand we hold
Dominion over palm and pine—
Lord God of Hosts, be with us yet,
Lest we forget—lest we forget!

The tumult and the shouting dies;
The Captains and the Kings depart:
Still stands Thine ancient sacrifice,
An humble and a contrite heart.
Lord God of Hosts, be with us yet,
Lest we forget—lest we forget!

Far-called, our navies melt away;
On dune and headland sinks the fire:
Lo, all our pomp of yesterday
Is one with Nineveh and Tyre!
Judge of the Nations, spare us yet,
Lest we forget—lest we forget!

If, drunk with sight of power, we loose
Wild tongues that have not Thee in awe,
Such boastings as the Gentiles use,
Or lesser breeds without the Law—
Lord God of Hosts, be with us yet,
Lest we forget—lest we forget!

For heathen heart that puts her trust
   In reeking tube and iron shard,
All valiant dust that builds on dust,
   And guarding, calls not Thee to guard,
For frantic boast and foolish word—
Thy mercy on Thy people, Lord!

ERNEST DOWSON

(1867–1900)

Vitae Summa Brevis Spem Nos Vetat Incohare Longam

They are not long, the weeping and the laughter,
   Love and desire and hate:
I think they have no portion in us after
      We pass the gate.

They are not long, the days of wine and roses:
   Out of a misty dream
Our path emerges for a while, then closes
      Within a dream.

Non Sum Qualis Eram Bonae sub Regno Cynarae

Last night, ah, yesternight, betwixt her lips and mine
There fell thy shadow, Cynara! thy breath was shed
Upon my soul between the kisses and the wine;
And I was desolate and sick of an old passion,
   Yea, I was desolate and bow'd my head:
I have been faithful to thee, Cynara! in my fashion.

All night upon mine heart I felt her warm heart beat,
Night-long within mine arms in love and sleep she lay;
Surely the kisses of her bought red mouth were sweet;
But I was desolate and sick of an old passion,
   When I awoke and found the dawn was gray:
I have been faithful to thee, Cynara! in my fashion.

I have forgot much, Cynara! gone with the wind,
Flung roses, roses, riotously with the throng,
Dancing, to put thy pale lost lilies out of mind;
But I was desolate and sick of an old passion,
   Yea, all the time, because the dance was long:
I have been faithful to thee, Cynara! in my fashion.

I cried for madder music and for stronger wine,
But when the feast is finish'd and the lamps expire,
Then falls thy shadow, Cynara! the night is thine;
And I am desolate and sick of an old passion,
   Yea, hungry for the lips of my desire:
I have been faithful to thee, Cynara! in my fashion.

A.E.—GEORGE WILLIAM RUSSELL

(1867–1935)

Chivalry

I dreamed I saw that ancient Irish queen,
Who from her dun, as dawn had opened wide,
Saw the tall foemen rise on every side,
And gazed with kindling eye upon the scene,
And in delight cried, "Noble is their mien."
"Most kingly are they," her own host replied,
Praising the beauty, bravery, and pride
As if the foe their very kin had been.
And then I heard the innumerable hiss
Of human adders, nation with poisonous breath
Spitting at nation, as if the dragon's rage
Would claw the spirit, and I woke at this,
Knowing the soul of man was sick to death
And I was weeping in the Iron Age.

LIONEL JOHNSON

(1867–1902)

The Precept of Silence

I know you: solitary griefs,
Desolate passions, aching hours!
I know you: tremulous beliefs,
Agonized hopes, and ashen flowers!

The winds are sometimes sad to me;
The starry spaces, full of fear:
Mine is the sorrow on the sea,
And mine the sigh of places drear.

Some players upon plaintive strings
Publish their wistfulness abroad:
I have not spoken of these things
Save to one man, and unto God.

EDGAR LEE MASTERS

(1869–1950)

The Hill

Where are Elmer, Herman, Bert, Tom and Charley,
The weak of will, the strong of arm, the clown, the boozer,
     the fighter?
All, all, are sleeping on the hill.

One passed in a fever,
One was burned in a mine,
One was killed in a brawl,
One died in a jail,
One fell from a bridge toiling for children and wife—
All, all are sleeping, sleeping, sleeping on the hill.

Where are Ella, Kate, Mag, Lizzie and Edith,
The tender heart, the simple soul, the loud, the proud, the
     happy one?—
All, all, are sleeping on the hill.

One died in shameful child-birth,
One of a thwarted love,
One at the hands of a brute in a brothel,
One of a broken pride, in the search for heart's desire,
One after life in far-away London and Paris
Was brought home to her little space by Ella and Kate and
     Mag—
All, all are sleeping, sleeping, sleeping on the hill.

Where are Uncle Isaac and Aunt Emily,
And old Towny Kincaid and Sevigne Houghton,
And Major Walker who had talked
With venerable men of the revolution?—
All, all, are sleeping on the hill.

They brought them dead sons from the war,
And daughters whom life had crushed,
And their children, fatherless, crying—
All, all are sleeping, sleeping, sleeping on the hill.

Where is old Fiddler Jones
Who played with life all his ninety years,
Braving the sleet with bared breast,
Drinking, rioting, thinking neither of wife nor kin,
Nor gold, nor love, nor heaven?
Lo! he babbles of the fish-frys of long ago,
Of the horse-races of long ago at Clary's Grove,
Of what Abe Lincoln said
One time at Springfield.

Howard Lamson

Ice cannot shiver in the cold,
Nor stones shrink from the lapping flame.
Eyes that are sealed no more have tears;
Ears that are stopped hear nothing ill;
Hearts turned to silt are strange to pain;
Tongues that are dumb report no loss;
Hands stiffened, well may idle be;
No sigh is from a breathless breast.
Beauty may fade, but closed eyes see not;
Sorrow may wail, but stopped ears hear not;
Nothing to say is for dumb tongues.
The rolling earth rolls on and on
With trees and stones and winding streams—
My dream is what the hillside dreams!

EDWIN ARLINGTON ROBINSON

(1869–1935)

For a Dead Lady

No more with overflowing light
Shall fill the eyes that now are faded,
Nor shall another's fringe with night
Their woman-hidden world as they did.
No more shall quiver down the days
The flowing wonder of her ways,
Whereof no language may requite
The shifting and the many-shaded.

The grace, divine, definitive,
Clings only as a faint forestalling;
The laugh that love could not forgive
Is hushed, and answers to no calling;
The forehead and the little ears
Have gone where Saturn keeps the years;
The breast where roses could not live
Has done with rising and with falling.

The beauty, shattered by the laws
That have creation in their keeping,
No longer trembles at applause,
Or over children that are sleeping;
And we who delve in beauty's lore
Know all that we have known before
Of what inexorable cause
Makes Time so vicious in his reaping.

Momus

"Where's the need of singing now?"—
Smooth your brow,
Momus, and be reconciled,
For King Kronos is a child—
Child and father,
Or god rather,
And all gods are wild.

"Who reads Byron any more?"
Shut the door,
Momus, for I feel a draught;
Shut it quick, for some one laughed.—
"What's become of
Browning? Some of
Wordsworth lumbers like a raft?

"What are poets to find here?"—
Have no fear:
When the stars are shining blue
There will yet be left a few
Themes availing—
And these failing,
Momus, there'll be you.

Mr. Flood's Party

Old Eben Flood, climbing alone one night
Over the hill between the town below
And the forsaken upland hermitage
That held as much as he should ever know
On earth again of home, paused warily.
The road was his with not a native near;
And Eben, having leisure, said aloud,
For no man else in Tilbury Town to hear:

"Well, Mr. Flood, we have the harvest moon
Again, and we may not have many more;
The bird is on the wing, the poet says,
And you and I have said it here before.
Drink to the bird." He raised up to the light
The jug that he had gone so far to fill,
And answered huskily: "Well, Mr. Flood,
Since you propose it, I believe I will."

Alone, as if enduring to the end
A valiant armor of scarred hopes outworn,
He stood there in the middle of the road
Like Roland's ghost winding a silent horn.

Below him, in the town among the trees,
Where friends of other days had honored him,
A phantom salutation of the dead
Rang thinly till old Eben's eyes were dim.

Then, as a mother lays her sleeping child
Down tenderly, fearing it may awake,
He set the jug down slowly at his feet
With trembling care, knowing that most things break;
And only when assured that on firm earth
It stood, as the uncertain lives of men
Assuredly did not, he paced away,
And with his hand extended paused again:

"Well, Mr. Flood, we have not met like this
In a long time; and many a change has come
To both of us, I fear, since last it was
We had a drop together. Welcome home!"
Convivially returning with himself,
Again he raised the jug up to the light;
And with an acquiescent quaver said:
"Well, Mr. Flood, if you insist, I might.

"Only a very little, Mr. Flood—
For auld lang syne. No more, sir; that will do."
So, for the time, apparently it did,
And Eben evidently thought so too;
For soon amid the silver loneliness
Of night he lifted up his voice and sang,
Secure, with only two moons listening,
Until the whole harmonious landscape rang—

"For auld lang syne." The weary throat gave out,
The last word wavered, and the song was done.
He raised again the jug regretfully
And shook his head, and was again alone.
There was not much that was ahead of him,
And there was nothing in the town below—
Where strangers would have shut the many doors
That many friends had opened long ago.

None of my fairy kinsmen
    Make music with me now;
Alone the raths I wander
    Or ride the whitethorn bough;
But the wild swans they know me,
    And the horse that draws the plough.

STEPHEN CRANE

(1871–1900)

War Is Kind

Do not weep, maiden, for war is kind.
Because your lover threw wild hands toward the sky
And the affrighted steed ran on alone,
Do not weep.
War is kind.

    Hoarse, booming drums of the regiment,
    Little souls who thirst for fight,
    These men were born to drill and die.
    The unexplained glory flies above them,
    Great is the battle-god, great, and his kingdom—
    A field where a thousand corpses lie.

Do not weep, babe, for war is kind.
Because your father tumbled in the yellow trenches,
Raged at his breast, gulped and died,
Do not weep.
War is kind.

    Swift blazing flag of the regiment,
    Eagle with crest of red and gold,
    These men were born to drill and die.
    Point for them the virtue of slaughter,
    Make plain to them the excellence of killing
    And a field where a thousand corpses lie.

Mother whose heart hung humble as a button
On the bright splendid shroud of your son,
Do not weep.
War is kind.

"A Newspaper Is..."

A newspaper is a collection of half-injustices
Which, bawled by boys from mile to mile,
Spreads its curious opinion
To a million merciful and sneering men,
While families cuddle the joys of the fireside
When spurred by tale of dire lone agony.
A newspaper is a court
Where every one is kindly and unfairly tried
By a squalor of honest men.
A newspaper is a market
Where wisdom sells its freedom
And melons are crowned by the crowd.
A newspaper is a game
Where his error scores the player victory
While another's skill wins death.
A newspaper is a symbol;
It is feckless life's chronicle,
A collection of loud tales,
Concentrating eternal stupidities,
That in remote ages lived unhaltered,
Roaming through a fenceless world.

RALPH HODGSON

(1871-   )

Time, You Old Gipsy Man

Time, you old gipsy man,
    Will you not stay,
Put up your caravan
    Just for one day?

All things I'll give you
Will you be my guest,
Bells for your jennet
Of silver the best,
Goldsmiths shall beat you
A great golden ring,

Peacocks shall bow to you,
Little boys sing.
Oh, and sweet girls will
Festoon you with may,
Time, you old gipsy,
Why hasten away?

Last week in Babylon,
Last night in Rome,
Morning, and in the crush
Under Paul's dome;
Under Paul's dial
You tighten your rein—
Only a moment, and off once again;
Off to some city
Now blind in the womb,
Off to another
Ere that's in the tomb.

Time, you old gipsy man,
    Will you not stay,
Put up your caravan
    Just for one day?

JOHN McCRAE

(1872–1918)

In Flanders Fields

In Flanders fields the poppies blow
Between the crosses, row on row,
    That mark our place; and in the sky
    The larks, still bravely singing, fly
Scarce heard amid the guns below.

We are the Dead. Short days ago
We lived, felt dawn, saw sunset glow,
    Loved and were loved, and now we lie
    In Flanders fields.

Take up our quarrel with the foe:
To you from failing hands we throw
The torch; be yours to hold it high.
If ye break faith with us who die
We shall not sleep, though poppies grow
In Flanders fields.

FORD MADOX FORD

(1873–1939)

FROM *On Heaven*

. . . And my dear one sat in the shadows; very softly she
      wept:—
Such joy is in Heaven,
In the cool of the even,
After the burden and toil of the days,
After the heat and haze
In the vine-hills; or in the shady
Whispering groves in high passes up in the Alpilles
Guarding the castle of God.

And I went on talking towards her unseen face:
"So it is, so it goes, in this beloved place,
There shall be never a grief but passes; no, not any;
There shall be such bright light and no blindness;
There shall be so little awe and so much loving-kindness;
There shall be a little longing and enough care,
There shall be a little labour and enough of toil
To bring back the lost flavour of our human coil;
Not enough to taint it;
And all that we desire shall prove as fair as we can paint it."
For, though that may be the very hardest trick of all
God set Himself, who fashioned this goodly hall,
Thus He has made Heaven;
Even Heaven.

For God is a good man; God is a kind man;
In the darkness He came walking to our table beneath the
      planes,

And spoke
So kindly to my dear,
With a little joke,
Giving Himself some pains
To take away her fear
Of His Stature,
So as not to abash her,
In no way at all to dash her new pleasure beneath the planes,
In the cool of the even
In Heaven.

That, that is God's nature,
For God's a good brother, and God is no blind man,
And God's a good mother and loves sons who're rovers,
And God is our father and loves all good lovers,
He has a kindly smile for many a poor sinner;
He takes note to make it up to poor wayfarers on sodden
        roads;
Such as bear heavy loads
He takes note of, and of all that toil on bitter seas and frosty
        lands,
He takes care that they shall all have good at His hands;
Well He takes note of a poor old cook,
Cooking your dinner;
And much He loves sweet joys in such as ever took
Sweet joy on earth. He has a kindly smile for a kiss
Given in a shady nook.
And in the golden book
Where the accounts of His estate are kept,
All the round, golden sovereigns of bliss,
Known by poor lovers, married or never yet married,
Whilst the green world waked, or the black world quietly
        slept;
All joy, all sweetness, each sweet sigh that's sighed—
Their accounts are kept,
And carried
By the love of God to His own credit's side.
So that is why He came to our table to welcome my dear,
        dear bride,
In the cool of the even
In front of a café in Heaven.

A Solis Ortus Cardine...

Oh, quiet peoples sleeping bed by bed
Beneath grey roof-trees in the glimmering West,
We who can see the silver grey and red
Rise over No Man's Land—salute your rest.

Oh, quiet comrades, sleeping in the clay
Beneath a turmoil you need no more mark,
We who have lived through yet another day
Salute your graves at setting in of dark.

And rising from your beds or from the clay
You, dead, or far from lines of slain and slayers,
Thro' your eternal or your finite day
Give us your prayers!

WALTER DE LA MARE

(1873–1956)

An Epitaph

Here lies a most beautiful lady,
Light of step and heart was she;
I think she was the most beautiful lady
That ever was in the West Country.
But beauty vanishes; beauty passes;
However rare—rare it be;
And when I crumble, who will remember
This lady of the West Country?

The Listeners

"Is there anybody there?" said the Traveller,
Knocking on the moonlit door;
And his horse in the silence champed the grasses
Of the forest's ferny floor:
And a bird flew up out of the turret,
Above the Traveller's head:

And he smote upon the door again a second time;
   "Is there anybody there?" he said.
But no one descended to the Traveller;
   No head from the leaf-fringed sill
Leaned over and looked into his grey eyes,
   Where he stood perplexed and still.
But only a host of phantom listeners
   That dwelt in the lone house then
Stood listening in the quiet of the moonlight
   To that voice from the world of men:
Stood thronging the faint moonbeams on the dark stair,
   That goes down to the empty hall,
Hearkening in an air stirred and shaken
   By the lonely Traveller's call.
And he felt in his heart their strangeness,
   Their stillness answering his cry,
While his horse moved, cropping the dark turf,
   'Neath the starred and leafy sky;
For he suddenly smote on the door, even
   Louder, and lifted his head:—
"Tell them I came, and no one answered,
   That I kept my word," he said.
Never the least stir made the listeners,
   Though every word he spake
Fell echoing through the shadowiness of the still house
   From the one man left awake:
Ay, they heard his foot upon the stirrup,
   And the sound of iron on stone,
And how the silence surged softly backward,
   When the plunging hoofs were gone.

All That's Past

Very old are the woods;
   And the buds that break
Out of the brier's boughs,
   When March winds wake.
So old with their beauty are—
   Oh, no man knows
Through what wild centuries
   Roves back the rose.

Very old are the brooks;
   And the rills that rise
Where snow sleeps cold beneath
   The azure skies
Sing such a history
   Of come and gone
Their every drop is as wise
   As Solomon.

Very old are we men;
   Our dreams are tales
Told in dim Eden
   By Eve's nightingales;
We wake and whisper awhile,
   But, the day gone by,
Silence and sleep like fields
   Of amaranth lie.

Clear Eyes

Clear eyes do dim at last,
   And cheeks outlive their rose.
Time, heedless of the past,
   No loving-kindness knows;
Chill unto mortal lip
   Still Lethe flows.

Griefs, too, but brief while stay,
   And sorrow, bring o'er,
Its salt tears shed away,
   Woundeth the heart no more.
Stealthily lave those waters
   That solemn shore.

Ah, then, sweet face burn on,
   While yet quick memory lives!
And Sorrow, ere thou art gone,
   Know that my heart forgives—
Ere yet, grown cold in peace,
   It loves not, nor grieves.

GILBERT KEITH CHESTERTON
(1874–1936)

Wine and Water

Old Noah he had an ostrich farm and fowls on the largest
scale,
He ate his egg with a ladle in an egg-cup big as a pail,
And the soup he took was Elephant Soup, and the fish he
took was Whale,
But they all were small to the cellar he took when he set out
to sail,
And Noah he often said to his wife when he sat down to dine,
"I don't care where the water goes if it doesn't get into the
wine."

The cataract of the cliff of heaven fell blinding off the brink
As if it would wash the stars away as suds go down a sink,
The seven heavens came roaring down for the throats of hell
to drink,
And Noah he cocked his eye and said, "It looks like rain, I
think,
The water has drowned the Matterhorn as deep as a Mendip
mine,
But I don't care where the water goes if it doesn't get into
the wine."

But Noah he sinned, and we have sinned; on tipsy feet we
trod,
Till a great big black teetotaller was sent to us for a rod,
And you can't get wine at a P. S. A., or chapel, or Eisteddfod,
For the Curse of Water has come again because of the wrath
of God,
And water is on the Bishop's board and the Higher Thinker's
shrine,
But I don't care where the water goes if it doesn't get into
the wine.

On a Prohibitionist Poem

Though Shakespeare's Mermaid, ocean's mightiest daughter,
With vintage could the seas incarnadine:
And Keats's name that was not writ in water
    Was often writ in wine;

Though wine that seeks the loftiest habitation
Went to the heads of Villon and Verlaine,
Yet Hiram Hopper needs no inspiration
    But water on the brain.

Elegy in a Country Churchyard

The men that worked for England
They have their graves at home:
And bees and birds of England
About the cross can roam.

But they that fought for England,
Following a falling star,
Alas, alas for England
They have their graves afar.

And they that rule in England,
In stately conclave met,
Alas, alas for England
They have no graves as yet.

ANONYMOUS

(19TH CENTURY)

"I Know Where I'm Going"

I know where I'm going,
I know who's going with me,
I know who I love,
But the dear knows who I'll marry.

I'll have stockings of silk,
Shoes of fine green leather,
Combs to buckle my hair
And a ring for every finger.

Feather beds are soft,
Painted rooms are bonny;
But I'd leave them all
To go with my love Johnny.

Some say he's dark,
I say he's bonny,
He's the flower of them all
My handsome, coaxing Johnny.

I know where I'm going,
I know who's going with me,
I know who I love,
But the dear knows who I'll marry.

TRUMBULL STICKNEY
(1874–1904)

Mnemosyne

It's autumn in the country I remember.

How warm a wind blew here about the ways!
And shadows on the hillside lay to slumber
During the long sun-sweetened summer-days.

It's cold abroad the country I remember.

The swallows veering skimmed the golden grain
At midday with a wing aslant and limber;
And yellow cattle browsed upon the plain.

It's empty down the country I remember.

I had a sister lovely in my sight:
Her hair was dark, her eyes were very sombre;
We sang together in the woods at night.

It's lonely in the country I remember.

The babble of our children fills my ears,
And on our hearth I stare the perished ember
To flames that show all starry thro' my tears.

It's dark about the country I remember.

There are the mountains where I lived. The path
Is slushed with cattle-tracks and fallen timber,
The stumps are twisted by the tempests' wrath.

But that I knew these places are my own,
I'd ask how came such wretchedness to cumber
The earth, and I to people it alone.

It rains across the country I remember.

AMY LOWELL

(1874–1925)

Little Ivory Figures Pulled with String

Is it the tinkling of mandolins which disturbs you?
Or the dropping of bitter-orange petals among the coffee-
cups?
Or the slow creeping of the moonlight between the olive-
trees?
Drop! Drop! the rain
Upon the thin plates of my heart.

String your blood to chord with this music,
Stir your heels upon the cobbles to the rhythm of a dance-
tune.
They have slim thighs and arms of silver;
The moon washes away their garments;
They make a pattern of fleeing feet in the branch shadows,

And the green grapes knotted about them
Burst as they press against one another.
  The rain knocks upon the plates of my heart,
  They are crumpled with its beating.

Would you drink only from your brains, Old Man?
See, the moonlight has reached your knees,
It falls upon your head in an accolade of silver.
Rise up on the music,
Fling against the moon-drifts in a whorl of young light
    bodies:
Leaping grape clusters,
Vine leaves tearing from a grey wall.
You shall run, laughing, in a braid of women,
And weave flowers with the frosty spines of thorns.
Why do you gaze into your glass,
And jar the spoons with your finger-tapping?
  The rain is rigid on the plates of my heart.
  The murmur of it is loud—loud.

ROBERT FROST

(1875-   )

The Pasture

I'm going out to clean the pasture spring;
I'll only stop to rake the leaves away
(And wait to watch the water clear, I may):
I shan't be gone long.—You come too.

I'm going out to fetch the little calf
That's standing by the mother. It's so young
It totters when she licks it with her tongue.
I shan't be gone long.—You come too.

My November Guest

My sorrow, when she's here with me,
   Thinks these dark days of autumn rain
Are beautiful as days can be;

She loves the bare, the withered tree;
　　She walks the sodden pasture lane.

Her pleasure will not let me stay.
　　She talks and I am fain to list:
She's glad the birds are gone away,
She's glad her simple worsted grey
　　Is silver now with clinging mist.

The desolate, deserted trees,
　　The faded earth, the heavy sky,
The beauties she so truly sees,
She thinks I have no eye for these,
　　And vexes me for reason why.

Not yesterday I learned to know
　　The love of bare November days
Before the coming of the snow;
But it were vain to tell her so,
　　And they are better for her praise.

After Apple-Picking

My long two-pointed ladder's sticking through a tree
Toward heaven still,
And there's a barrel that I didn't fill
Beside it, and there may be two or three
Apples I didn't pick upon some bough.
But I am done with apple-picking now.
Essence of winter sleep is on the night,
The scent of apples: I am drowsing off.
I cannot rub the strangeness from my sight
I got from looking through a pane of glass
I skimmed this morning from the drinking trough
And held against the world of hoary grass.
It melted, and I let it fall and break.
But I was well
Upon my way to sleep before it fell,
And I could tell
What form my dreaming was about to take.

Magnified apples appear and disappear.
Stem end and blossom end,
And every fleck of russet showing clear.
My instep arch not only keeps the ache,
It keeps the pressure of a ladder-round.
I feel the ladder sway as the boughs bend.
And I keep hearing from the cellar bin
The rumbling sound
Of load on load of apples coming in.
For I have had too much
Of apple-picking: I am overtired
Of the great harvest I myself desired.
There were ten thousand thousand fruit to touch,
Cherish in hand, lift down, and not let fall.
For all
That struck the earth,
No matter if not bruised or spiked with stubble,
Went surely to the cider-apple heap
As of no worth.
One can see what will trouble
This sleep of mine, whatever sleep it is.
Were he not gone,
The woodchuck could say whether it's like his
Long sleep, as I describe its coming on,
Or just some human sleep.

Storm Fear

When the wind works against us in the dark,
And pelts with snow
The lowly chamber window on the east,
And whispers with a sort of stifled bark,
The beast,
"Come out! Come out!"—
It costs no inward struggle not to go,
Ah, no!
I count our strength,
Two and a child,
Those of us not asleep subdued to mark
How the cold creeps as the fire dies at length,—

How drifts are piled
Dooryard and road ungraded,
Till even the comforting barn grows far away
And my heart owns a doubt
Whether 'tis in us to arise with day
And save ourselves unaided.

Mending Wall

Something there is that doesn't love a wall,
That sends the frozen-ground-swell under it,
And spills the upper boulders in the sun;
And makes gaps even two can pass abreast.
The work of hunters is another thing:
I have come after them and made repair
Where they have left not one stone on a stone,
But they would have the rabbit out of hiding,
To please the yelping dogs. The gaps I mean,
No one has seen them made or heard them made,
But at spring mending-time we find them there.
I let my neighbor know beyond the hill;
And on a day we meet to walk the line
And set the wall between us once again.
We keep the wall between us as we go.
To each the boulders that have fallen to each.
And some are loaves and some so nearly balls
We have to use a spell to make them balance:
"Stay where you are until our backs are turned!"
We wear our fingers rough with handling them.
Oh, just another kind of out-door game,
One on a side. It comes to little more:
There where it is we do not need the wall:
He is all pine and I am apple orchard.
My apple trees will never get across
And eat the cones under his pines, I tell him.
He only says, "Good fences make good neighbors."
Spring is the mischief in me, and I wonder
If I could put a notion in his head:
"*Why* do they make good neighbors? Isn't it
Where there are cows? But here there are no cows.

Before I built a wall I'd ask to know
What I was walling in or walling out,
And to whom I was like to give offence.
Something there is that doesn't love a wall,
That wants it down." I could say "Elves" to him,
But it's not elves exactly, and I'd rather
He said it for himself. I see him there
Bringing a stone grasped firmly by the top
In each hand, like an old-stone savage armed.
He moves in darkness as it seems to me,
Not of woods only and the shade of trees.
He will not go behind his father's saying.
And he likes having thought of it so well
He says again, "Good fences make good neighbors."

FROM *Two Witches*

THE WITCH OF COÖS

I stayed the night for shelter at a farm
Behind the mountain, with a mother and son,
Two old-believers. They did all the talking.

MOTHER. Folks think a witch who has familiar spirits
She could call up to pass a winter evening,
But won't, should be burned at the stake or something.
Summoning spirits isn't "Button, button,
Who's got the button," I would have them know.

SON. Mother can make a common table rear
And kick with two legs like an army mule.

MOTHER. And when I've done it, what good have I done?
Rather than tip a table for you, let me
Tell you what Ralle the Sioux Control once told me.
He said the dead had souls, but when I asked him
How could that be—I thought the dead were souls,
He broke my trance. Don't that make you suspicious
That there's something the dead are keeping back?
Yes, there's something the dead are keeping back.

SON. You wouldn't want to tell him what we have
Up attic, mother?

MOTHER. Bones—a skeleton.

SON. But the headboard of mother's bed is pushed
Against the attic door: the door is nailed.
It's harmless. Mother hears it in the night
Halting perplexed behind the barrier
Of door and headboard. Where it wants to get
Is back into the cellar where it came from.

MOTHER. We'll never let them, will we, son! We'll never!

SON. It left the cellar forty years ago
And carried itself like a pile of dishes
Up one flight from the cellar to the kitchen,
Another from the kitchen to the bedroom,
Another from the bedroom to the attic,
Right past both father and mother, and neither stopped it.
Father had gone upstairs; mother was downstairs.
I was a baby: I don't know where I was.

MOTHER. The only fault my husband found with me—
I went to sleep before I went to bed,
Especially in winter when the bed
Might just as well be ice and the clothes snow.
The night the bones came up the cellar-stairs
Toffile had gone to bed alone and left me,
But left an open door to cool the room off
So as to sort of turn me out of it.
I was just coming to myself enough
To wonder where the cold was coming from,
When I heard Toffile upstairs in the bedroom
And thought I heard him downstairs in the cellar.
The board we had laid down to walk dry-shod on
When there was water in the cellar in spring
Struck the hard cellar bottom. And then someone
Began the stairs, two footsteps for each step,
The way a man with one leg and a crutch,

Or a little child, comes up. It wasn't Toffile:
It wasn't anyone who could be there.
The bulkhead double-doors were double-locked
And swollen tight and buried under snow.
The cellar windows were banked up with sawdust
And swollen tight and buried under snow.
It was the bones. I knew them—and good reason.
My first impulse was to get to the knob
And hold the door. But the bones didn't try
The door; they halted helpless on the landing,
Waiting for things to happen in their favor.
The faintest restless rustling ran all through them.
I never could have done the thing I did
If the wish hadn't been too strong in me
To see how they were mounted for this walk.
I had a vision of them put together
Not like a man, but like a chandelier.
So suddenly I flung the door wide on him.
A moment he stood balancing with emotion,
And all but lost himself. (A tongue of fire
Flashed out and licked along his upper teeth.
Smoke rolled inside the sockets of his eyes.)
Then he came at me with one hand outstretched,
The way he did in life once; but this time
I struck the hand off brittle on the floor,
And fell back from him on the floor myself.
The finger-pieces slid in all directions.
(Where did I see one of those pieces lately?
Hand me my button-box—it must be there.)
I sat up on the floor and shouted, "Toffile,
It's coming up to you." It had its choice
Of the door to the cellar or the hall.
It took the hall door for the novelty,
And set off briskly for so slow a thing,
Still going every which way in the joints, though,
So that it looked like lightning or a scribble,
From the slap I had just now given its hand.
I listened till it almost climbed the stairs
From the hall to the only finished bedroom,
Before I got up to do anything;
Then ran and shouted, "Shut the bedroom door,

Toffile, for my sake!" "Company?" he said,
"Don't make me get up; I'm too warm in bed."
So lying forward weakly on the handrail
I pushed myself upstairs, and in the light
(The kitchen had been dark) I had to own
I could see nothing. "Toffile, I don't see it.
It's with us in the room though. It's the bones."
"What bones?" "The cellar bones—out of the grave."
That made him throw his bare legs out of bed
And sit up by me and take hold of me.
I wanted to put out the light and see
If I could see it, or else mow the room,
With our arms at the level of our knees,
And bring the chalk-pile down. "I'll tell you what—
It's looking for another door to try.
The uncommonly deep snow has made him think
Of his old song, *The Wild Colonial Boy,*
He always used to sing along the tote road.
He's after an open door to get outdoors.
Let's trap him with an open door up attic."
Toffile agreed to that, and sure enough,
Almost the moment he was given an opening,
The steps began to climb the attic stairs.
I heard them. Toffile didn't seem to hear them.
"Quick!" I slammed to the door and held the knob.
"Toffile, get nails." I made him nail the door shut
And push the headboard of the bed against it.
Then we asked was there anything
Up attic that we'd ever want again.
The attic was less to us than the cellar.
If the bones liked the attic, let them have it.
Let them stay in the attic. When they sometimes
Come down the stairs at night and stand perplexed
Behind the door and headboard of the bed,
Brushing their chalky skull with chalky fingers,
With sounds like the dry rattling of a shutter,
That's what I sit up in the dark to say—
To no one any more since Toffile died.
Let them stay in the attic since they went there.
I promised Toffile to be cruel to them
For helping them be cruel once to him.

SON. We think they had a grave down in the cellar.

MOTHER. We know they had a grave down in the cellar.

SON. We never could find out whose bones they were.

MOTHER. Yes, we could too, son. Tell the truth for once.
They were a man's his father killed for me.
I mean a man he killed instead of me.
The least I could do was to help dig their grave.
We were about it one night in the cellar.
Son knows the story: but 'twas not for him
To tell the truth, suppose the time had come.
Son looks surprised to see me end a lie
We'd kept all these years between ourselves
So as to have it ready for outsiders.
But tonight I don't care enough to lie—
I don't remember why I ever cared.
Toffile, if he were here, I don't believe
Could tell you why he ever cared himself. . . .

She hadn't found the finger-bone she wanted
Among the buttons poured out in her lap.
I verified the name next morning: Toffile.
The rural letter box said Toffile Lajway.

Fire and Ice

Some say the world will end in fire,
Some say in ice.
From what I've tasted of desire
I hold with those who favor fire.
But if it had to perish twice,
I think I know enough of hate
To say that for destruction ice
Is also great
And would suffice.

Stopping by Woods on a Snowy Evening

Whose woods these are I think I know.
His house is in the village though;
He will not see me stopping here
To watch his woods fill up with snow.

My little horse must think it queer
To stop without a farmhouse near
Between the woods and frozen lake
The darkest evening of the year.

He gives his harness bells a shake
To ask if there is some mistake.
The only other sound's the sweep
Of easy wind and downy flake.

The woods are lovely, dark and deep,
But I have promises to keep,
And miles to go before I sleep,
And miles to go before I sleep.

JOHN MASEFIELD

(1878–   )

FROM Reynard the Fox

The cobbler bent at his wooden foot,
Beating sprigs in a broken boot;
He wore old glasses with thick horn rim,
He scowled at his work, for his sight was dim.
His face was dingy, his lips were grey,
From trimming sparrowbills day by day.
As he turned his boot he heard a noise
At his garden-end, and he thought, "It's boys."
Like a rocket shot to a ship ashore
The lean red bolt of his body tore,
Like a ripple of wind running swift on grass;
Like a shadow on wheat when a cloud blows past,
Like a turn at the buoy in a cutter sailing

When the bright green gleam lips white at the railing,
Like the April snake whipping back to sheath,
Like the gannets' hurtle on fish beneath,
Like a kestrel chasing, like a sickle reaping,
Like all things swooping, like all things sweeping,
Like a hound for stay, like a stag for swift,
With his shadow beside like spinning drift

❊   ❊   ❊   ❊   ❊

Past the gibbet-stock all stuck with nails,
Where they hanged in chains what had hung at jails,
Past Ashmundshowe where Ashmund sleeps,
And none but the tumbling peewit weeps,
Past Curlew Calling, the gaunt grey corner
Where the curlew comes as a summer mourner,
Past Blowbury Beacon, shaking his fleece,
Where all winds hurry and none brings peace;
Then down on the mile-long green decline,
Where the turf's like spring and the air's like wine
Where the sweeping spurs of the downland spill
Into Wan Brook Valley and Wan Dyke Hill.

❊   ❊   ❊   ❊   ❊

On he went with a galloping rally
Past Maesbury Camp for Wan Brook Valley.
The blood in his veins went romping high,
"Get on, on, on, to the earth or die."
The air of the downs went purely past
Till he felt the glory of going fast,
Till the terror of death, though there indeed,
Was lulled for a while by his pride of speed.
He was romping away from the hounds and hunt,
He had Wan Dyke Hill and his earth in front,
In one mile more when his point was made
He would rest in safety from dog or spade;
Nose between paws he would hear the shout
Of the "Gone to earth!" to the hounds without,
The whine of the hounds, and their cat-feet gadding,
Scratching the earth, and their breath pad-padding;
He would hear the horn call hounds away,
And rest in peace till another day.

On Growing Old

Be with me, Beauty, for the fire is dying;
My dog and I are old, too old for roving.
Man, whose young passion sets the spindrift flying,
Is soon too lame to march, too cold for loving.
I take the book and gather to the fire,
Turning old yellow leaves; minute by minute
The clock ticks to my heart. A withered wire,
Moves a thin ghost of music in the spinet.
I cannot sail your seas, I cannot wander
Your cornland, nor your hill-land, nor your valleys
Ever again, nor share the battle yonder
Where the young knight the broken squadron rallies.
Only stay quiet while my mind remembers
The beauty of fire from the beauty of embers.

Beauty, have pity! for the strong have power,
The rich their wealth, the beautiful their grace,
Summer of man its sunlight and its flower,
Spring-time of man all April in a face.
Only, as in the jostling in the Strand,
Where the mob thrusts or loiters or is loud,
The beggar with the saucer in his hand
Asks only a penny from the passing crowd,
So, from this glittering world with all its fashion,
Its fire, and play of men, its stir, its march,
Let me have wisdom, Beauty, wisdom and passion,
Bread to the soul, rain when the summers parch.
Give me but these, and though the darkness close
Even the night will blossom as the rose.

EDWARD THOMAS

(1878–1917)

The Sign-Post

The dim sea glints chill. The white sun is shy,
And the skeleton weeds and the never-dry,
Rough, long grasses keep white with frost
At the hill-top by the finger-post;

The smoke of the traveller's-joy is puffed
Over hawthorn berry and hazel tuft.
I read the sign. Which way shall I go?
A voice says: You would not have doubted so
At twenty. Another voice gentle with scorn
Says: At twenty you wished you had never been born.
One hazel lost a leaf of gold
From a tuft at the tip, when the first voice told
The other he wished to know what 'twould be
To be sixty by this same post. "You shall see,"
He laughed—and I had to join his laughter—
"You shall see; but either before or after,
Whatever happens, it must befall.
A mouthful of earth to remedy all
Regrets and wishes shall be freely given;
And if there be a flaw in that heaven
'Twill be freedom to wish, and your wish may be
To be here or anywhere talking to me,
No matter what the weather, on earth,
At any age between death and birth,—
To see what day or night can be,
The sun and the frost, the land and the sea,
Summer, Autumn, Winter, Spring,—
With a poor man of any sort, down to a king,
Standing upright out in the air
Wondering where he shall journey, O where?"

CARL SANDBURG

(1878–   )

Chicago

Hog Butcher for the World,
Tool Maker, Stacker of Wheat,
Player with Railroads and the Nation's Freight Handler;
Stormy, husky, brawling,
City of the Big Shoulders:
They tell me you are wicked and I believe them, for I have
    seen your painted women under the gas lamps luring
    the farm boys.

And they tell me you are crooked and I answer: Yes, it is
true I have seen the gunman kill and go free to kill
again.
And they tell me you are brutal and my reply is: On the
faces of women and children I have seen the marks
of wanton hunger.
And having answered so I turn once more to those who
sneer at this my city, and I give them back the sneer
and say to them:
Come and show me another city with lifted head singing so
proud to be alive and coarse and strong and cunning.
Flinging magnetic curses amid the toil of piling job on job,
here is a tall bold slugger set vivid against the little
soft cities;
Fierce as a dog with tongue lapping for action, cunning as a
savage pitted against the wilderness,
Bareheaded,
Shoveling,
Wrecking,
Planning,
Building, breaking, rebuilding.
Under the smoke, dust all over his mouth, laughing with
white teeth,
Under the terrible burden of destiny laughing as a young
man laughs,
Laughing even as an ignorant fighter laughs who has never
lost a battle,
Bragging and laughing that under his wrist is the pulse, and
under his ribs the heart of the people,
Laughing!
Laughing the stormy, husky, brawling laughter of Youth,
half-naked, sweating, proud to be Hog Butcher, Tool
Maker, Stacker of Wheat, Player with Railroads and
Freight Handler to the Nation.

Cool Tombs

When Abraham Lincoln was shoveled into the tombs he
forgot the copperheads and the assassin . . . in the dust, in
the cool tombs.

And Ulysses Grant lost all thought of con men and Wall Street, cash and collateral turned ashes . . . in the dust, in the cool tombs.

Pocahontas' body, lovely as a poplar, sweet as a red haw in November or a paw-paw in May, did she wonder, does she remember? . . . in the dust, in the cool tombs?

Take any streetful of people buying clothes and groceries, cheering a hero or throwing confetti and blowing tin horns . . . tell me if the lovers are losers . . . tell me if any get more than the lovers . . . in the dust . . . in the cool tombs.

VACHEL LINDSAY

(1879–1931)

The Eagle That Is Forgotten

(JOHN P. ALTGELD. BORN DECEMBER 30, 1847;
DIED MARCH 12, 1902)

Sleep softly . . . eagle forgotten . . . under the stone.
Time has its way with you there, and the clay has its own.

"We have buried him now," thought your foes, and in secret
    rejoiced.
They made a brave show of their mourning, their hatred
    unvoiced,
They had snarled at you, barked at you, foamed at you, day
    after day,
Now you were ended. They praised you, . . . and laid you
    away.

The others that mourned you in silence and terror and truth,
The widow bereft of her crust, the boy without youth,
The mocked and the scorned and the wounded, the lame and
    the poor
That should have remembered forever, . . . remember no
    more.

Where are those lovers of yours, on what name do they call,
The lost, that in armies wept over your funeral pall?

They call on the names of a hundred high-valiant ones
A hundred white eagles have risen, the sons of your sons,
The zeal in their wings is a zeal that your dreaming began,
The valor that wore out your soul in the service of man.

Sleep softly, . . . eagle forgotten, . . . under the stone.
Time has its way with you there, and the clay has its own.
Sleep on, O brave-hearted, O wise man, that kindled the
    flame—
To live in mankind is far more than to live in a name,
To live in mankind, far, far more . . . than to live in a
    name.

HAROLD MONRO

(1879–1932)

Midnight Lamentation

When you and I go down
Breathless and cold,
Our faces both worn back
To earthly mould,
How lonely we shall be!
What shall we do,
You without me,
I without you?

I cannot bear the thought
You, first, may die,
Nor of how you will weep,
Should I.
We are too much alone;
What can we do
To make our bodies one:
You, me; I, you?

We are most nearly born
Of one same kind;
We have the same delight,
The same true mind.

Must we then part, we part;
Is there no way
To keep a beating heart
And light of day?

I could now rise and run
Through street on street
To where you are breathing—you,
That we might meet,
And that your living voice
Might sound above
Fear, and we two rejoice
Within our love.

How frail the body is,
And we are made
As only in decay
To lean and fade.
I think too much of death;
There is a gloom
When I can't hear your breath
Calm in some room.

O, but how suddenly
Either may droop;
Countenance be so white,
Body stoop.
Then there may be a place
Where fading flowers
Drop on a lifeless face
Through weeping hours.

Is then nothing safe?
Can we not find
Some everlasting life
In our one mind?
I feel it like disgrace
Only to understand
Your spirit through your word,
Or by your hand.

I cannot find a way
Through love and through;
I cannot reach beyond
Body, to you.
When you or I must go
Down evermore,
There'll be no more to say
—But a locked door.

WALLACE STEVENS

(1879–1955)

The Emperor of Ice-Cream

Call the roller of big cigars,
The muscular one, and bid him whip
In kitchen cups concupiscent curds.
Let the wenches dawdle in such dress
As they are used to wear, and let the boys
Bring flowers in last month's newspapers.
Let be be the finale of seem.
The only emperor is the emperor of ice-cream.

Take from the dresser of deal,
Lacking the three glass knobs, that sheet
On which she embroidered fantails once
And spread it so as to cover her face.
If her horny feet protrude, they come
To show how cold she is, and dumb.
Let the lamp affix its beam.
The only emperor is the emperor of ice-cream.

Peter Quince at the Clavier

I

Just as my fingers on these keys
Make music, so the self-same sounds
On my spirit make a music too.

Music is feeling then, not sound;
And thus it is that what I feel,
Here in this room, desiring you,
Thinking of your blue-shadowed silk,
Is music. It is like the strain
Waked in the elders by Susanna:

Of a green evening, clear and warm,
She bathed in her still garden, while
The red-eyed elders, watching, felt

The basses of their being throb
In witching chords, and their thin blood
Pulse pizzicati of Hosanna.

II

In the green evening, clear and warm,
Susanna lay.
She searched
The touch of springs,
And found
Concealed imaginings.
She sighed
For so much melody.

Upon the bank she stood
In the cool
Of spent emotions.
She felt, among the leaves,
The dew
Of old devotions.

She walked upon the grass,
Still quavering.
The winds were like her maids,
On timid feet,
Fetching her woven scarves,
Yet wavering.

A breath upon her hand
Muted the night.

She turned—
A cymbal clashed,
And roaring horns.

III

Soon, with a noise like tambourines,
Came her attendant Byzantines.

They wondered why Susanna cried
Against the elders by her side:

And as they whispered, the refrain
Was like a willow swept by rain.

Anon their lamps' uplifted flame
Revealed Susanna and her shame.

And then the simpering Byzantines
Fled, with a noise like tambourines.

IV

Beauty is momentary in the mind—
The fitful tracing of a portal;
But in the flesh it is immortal.

The body dies; the body's beauty lives.
So evenings die, in their green going,
A wave, interminably flowing.

So gardens die, their meek breath scenting
The cowl of Winter, done repenting.
So maidens die, to the auroral
Celebration of a maiden's choral.

Susanna's music touched the bawdy strings
Of those white elders; but, escaping,
Left only Death's ironic scraping.
Now in its immortality, it plays
On the clear viol of her memory,
And makes a constant sacrament of praise.

Not Ideas about the Thing
but the Thing Itself

At the earliest ending of winter,
In March, a scrawny cry from outside
Seemed like a sound in his mind.

He knew that he heard it,
A bird's cry, at daylight or before,
In the early March wind.

The sun was rising at six,
No longer a battered panache above snow . . .
It would have been outside.

It was not from the vast ventriloquism
Of sleep's faded papier-mâché . . .
The sun was coming from outside.

That scrawny cry—it was
A chorister whose c preceded the choir.
It was part of the colossal sun,

Surrounded by its choral rings,
Still far away. It was like
A new knowledge of reality.

WILSON PUGSLEY MacDONALD
(1880–

Exit

Easily to the old
Opens the hard ground:
But when youth grows cold,
And red lips have no sound,
Bitterly does the earth
Open to receive
And bitterly do the grasses
In the churchyard grieve.

Cold clay knows how to hold
An agéd hand;
But how to comfort youth
It does not understand.
Even the gravel rasps
In a dumb way
When youth comes homing
Before its day.

Elizabeth's hair was made
To warm a man's breast,
And her lips called like roses
To be caressed;
But grim the Jester
Who gave her hair to lie
On the coldest lover
Under the cold sky.

But Elizabeth never knew
Nor will learn now,
How the long wrinkle comes
On the white brow;
Nor will she ever know,
In her robes of gloom,
How chill is a dead child
From a warm womb.

O clay, so tender
When a flower is born!
Press gently as she dreams
In her bed forlorn.
They who come early
Must weary of their rest—
Lie softly, then, as light
On her dear breast.

Unflowered is her floor,
Her roof is unstarred.
Is this then the ending—
Here, shuttered and barred?
Nay, not the ending;

She will awake
Or the heart of the earth
That enfolds her will break.

Easily to the old
Opens the hard ground:
But when youth grows cold,
And red lips have no sound,
Bitterly does the earth
Open to receive
And bitterly do the grasses
In the churchyard grieve.

RALPH CHAPLIN

(1880–   )

"Mourn Not the Dead . . ."

Mourn not the dead that in the cool earth lie—
Dust unto dust—
The calm sweet earth that mothers all who die
As all men must;

Mourn not your captured comrades who must dwell—
Too strong to strive—
Each in his steel-bound coffin of a cell, buried alive;

But rather mourn the apathetic throng—
The coward and the meek—
Who see the world's great anguish and its wrong
And dare not speak.

LASCELLES ABERCROMBIE

(1881–1938)

Epitaph

Sir, you shall notice me: I am the Man;
I am Good Fortune: I am satisfied.
All I desired, more than I could desire,
I have: everything has gone right with me.

Life was a hiding-place that played me false;
I croucht ashamed, and still was seen and scorned:
But now I am not seen. I was a fool,
And now I know what wisdom dare not know:
For I know Nothing. I was a slave, and now
I have ungoverned freedom and the wealth
That cannot be conceived: for I have Nothing.
I lookt for beauty and I longed for rest,
And now I have perfection: nay, I am
Perfection: I am nothing, I am dead.

JOSEPH CAMPBELL

(1881–   )

The Old Woman

As a white candle
In a holy place,
So is the beauty
Of an agéd face.

As the spent radiance
Of the winter sun,
So is a woman
With her travail done.

Her brood gone from her,
And her thoughts as still
As the waters
Under a ruined mill.

PADRAIC COLUM

(1881–   )

A Drover

To Meath of the pastures,
From wet hills by the sea,
Through Leitrim and Longford,
Go my cattle and me.

I hear in the darkness
Their slipping and breathing—
I name them the by-ways
They're to pass without heeding.

Then the wet, winding roads,
Brown bogs with black water,
And my thoughts on white ships
And the King o' Spain's daughter.

O farmer, strong farmer!
You can spend at the fair,
But your face you must turn
To your crops and your care;

And soldiers, red soldiers!
You've seen many lands,
But you walk two by two,
And by captain's commands!

O the smell of the beasts,
The wet wind in the morn,
And the proud and hard earth
Never broken for corn!

And the crowds at the fair,
The herds loosened and blind,
Loud words and dark faces,
And the wild blood behind!

(O strong men with your best
I would strive breast to breast,
I could quiet your herds
With my words, with my words!)

I will bring you, my kine,
Where there's grass to the knee,
But you'll think of scant croppings
Harsh with salt of the sea.

JAMES JOYCE

(1882–1941)

"I Hear an Army Charging . . ."

I hear an army charging upon the land,
 And the thunder of horses plunging, foam about their
  knees:
Arrogant, in black armour, behind them stand,
 Disdaining the reins, with fluttering whips, the charioteers.

They cry unto the night their battle-name:
 I moan in sleep when I hear afar their whirling laughter.
They cleave the gloom of dreams, a blinding flame,
 Clanging, clanging upon the heart as upon an anvil.

They come shaking in triumph their long, green hair:
 They come out of the sea and run shouting by the shore.
My heart, have you no wisdom thus to despair?
 My love, my love, my love, why have you left me alone?

She Weeps over Rahoon

Rain on Rahoon falls softly, softly falling,
Where my dark lover lies.
Sad is his voice that calls me, sadly calling,
At grey moonrise.

Love, hear thou
How soft, how sad his voice is ever calling.
Ever unanswered and the dark rain falling,
Then as now.

Dark too our hearts, O love, shall lie and cold
As his sad heart has lain
Under the moongrey nettles, the black mould
And muttering rain.

A Memory of the Players in a Mirror
at Midnight

They mouth love's language. Gnash
The thirteen teeth
Your lean jaws grin with. Lash
Your itch and quailing, nude greed of the flesh.
Love's breath in you is stale, worded or sung,
As sour as cat's breath,
Harsh of tongue.

This grey that stares
Lies not, stark skin and bone.
Leave greasy lips their kissing. None
Will choose her what you see to mouth upon.
Dire hunger holds his hour.
Pluck forth your heart, saltblood, a fruit of tears.
Pluck and devour!

JAMES STEPHENS

(1882–1950)

Deirdre

Do not let any woman read this verse!
It is for men, and after them their sons,
And their son's sons!

The time comes when our hearts sink utterly;
When we remember Deirdre, and her tale,
And that her lips are dust.

Once she did tread the earth: men took her hand;
They looked into her eyes and said their say,
And she replied to them.

More than two thousand years it is since she
Was beautiful: she trod the waving grass;
She saw the clouds.

Two thousand years! The grass is still the same;
The clouds as lovely as they were that time
When Deirdre was alive.

But there has been again no woman born
Who was so beautiful; not one so beautiful
Of all the women born.

Let all men go apart and mourn together!
No man can ever love her! Not a man
Can dream to be her lover!

No man can bend before her! No man say—
What could one say to her? There are no words
That one could say to her!

Now she is but a story that is told
Beside the fire! No man can ever be
The friend of that poor queen!

THOMAS ERNEST HULME

(1883–1917)

Autumn

A touch of cold in the Autumn night—
I walked abroad,
And saw the ruddy moon lean over a hedge
Like a red-faced farmer.
I did not stop to speak, but nodded,
And round about were the wistful stars
With white faces like town children.

Conversion

Light-hearted I walked into the valley wood
In the time of hyacinths,
Till beauty like a scented cloth

Cast over, stifled me. I was bound
Motionless and faint of breath
By loveliness that is her own eunuch.

Now pass I to the final river
Ignominiously, in a sack, without sound,
As any peeping Turk to the Bosphorus.

WILLIAM CARLOS WILLIAMS

(1883–   )

Peace on Earth

The Archer is wake!
The Swan is flying!
Gold against blue
An Arrow is lying.
There is hunting in heaven—
Sleep safe till tomorrow.

The Bears are abroad!
The Eagle is screaming!
Gold against blue
Their eyes are gleaming!
Sleep!
Sleep safe till tomorrow.

The Sisters lie
With their arms intertwining;
Gold against blue
Their hair is shining!
The Serpent writhes!
Orion is listening!
Gold against blue
His sword is glistening!
Sleep!
There is hunting in heaven—
Sleep safe till tomorrow.

The Yachts

contend in a sea which the land partly encloses
shielding them from the too heavy blows
of an ungoverned ocean which when it chooses

tortures the biggest hulls, the best man knows
to pit against its beating, and sinks them pitilessly.
Mothlike in mists, scintillant in the minute

brilliance of cloudless days, with broad bellying sails
they glide to the wind tossing green water
from their sharp prows while over them the crew crawls

ant like, solicitously grooming them, releasing,
making fast as they turn, lean far over and having
caught the wind again, side by side, head for the mark.

In a well guarded arena of open water surrounded by
lesser and greater craft which, sycophant, lumbering
and flittering follow them, they appear youthful, rare

as the light of a happy eye, live with the grace
of all that in the mind is feckless, free and
naturally to be desired. Now the sea which holds them

is moody, lapping their glossy sides, as if feeling
for some slightest flaw but fails completely.
Today no race. Then the wind comes again. The yachts

move, jockeying for a start, the signal is set and they
are off. Now the waves strike at them but they are too
well made, they slip through, though they take in canvas.

Arms with hands grasping seek to clutch at the prows.
Bodies thrown recklessly in the way are cut aside.
It is a sea of faces about them in agony, in despair

until the horror of the race dawns staggering the mind,
the whole sea become an entanglement of watery bodies
lost to the world bearing what they cannot hold. Broken,

beaten, desolate, reaching from the dead to be taken up
they cry out, failing, failing! their cries rising
in waves still as the skillful yachts pass over.

ANNA WICKHAM

(1884–   )

The Fresh Start

O give me back my rigorous English Sunday
And my well-ordered house, with stockings washed on Mon-
    day.
Let the House-Lord, that kindly decorous fellow,
Leave happy for his Law at ten, with a well-furled umbrella.
Let my young sons observe my strict house rules,
Imbibing Tory principles, at Tory schools.

Two years now I have sat beneath a curse
And in a fury poured out frenzied verse.
Such verse as held no beauty and no good
And was at best new curious vermin-food.

My dog is rabid, and my cat is lean,
And not a pot in all this place is clean.
The locks have fallen from my hingeless doors,
And holes are in my credit and my floors.

There is no solace for me, but in sooth
To have said baldly certain ugly truth.
Such scavenger's work was never yet a woman's,
My wardrobe's more a scarecrow's than a human's.

I'm off to the House-goddess for her gift.
"O give me Circumspection, Temperance, Thrift;
Take thou this lust of words, this fevered itching,
And give me faith in darning, joy of stitching!"

When this hot blood is cooled by kindly Time
Controlled and schooled, I'll come again to Rhyme.
Sure of my methods, morals and my gloves,
I'll write chaste sonnets of imagined Loves.

JAMES ELROY FLECKER

(1884–1915)

The Dying Patriot

Day breaks on England down the Kentish hills,
Singing in the silence of the meadow-footing rills,
Day of my dreams, O day!
I saw them march from Dover, long ago,
With a silver cross before them, singing low,
Monks of Rome from their home where the blue seas break
in foam,
Augustine with his feet of snow.

Noon strikes on England, noon on Oxford town,
—Beauty she was statue cold—there's blood upon her
gown:
Noon of my dreams, O noon!
Proud and godly kings had built her, long ago,
With her towers and tombs and statues all arow,
With her fair and floral air and the love that lingers there,
And the streets where the great men go!

Evening on the olden, the golden sea of Wales,
When the first star shivers and the last wave pales:
O evening dreams!
There's a house that Britons walked in, long ago,
Where now the springs of ocean fall and flow,
And the dead robed in red and sea-lilies overhead
Sway when the long winds blow.

Sleep not, my country: though night is here, afar
Your children of the morning are clamorous for war:
Fire in the night, O dreams!
Though she send you as she sent you, long ago,
South to desert, east to ocean, west to snow,
West of these out to seas colder than the Hebrides I must go
Where the fleet of stars is anchored and the young Star-
captains glow.

DAVID HERBERT LAWRENCE

(1885–1930)

FROM *The Virgin Mother*

I kiss you good-bye, my darling,
Our ways are different now;
You are a seed in the night-time,
I am a man, to plough
The difficult glebe of the future
For seed to endow.

I kiss you good-bye, my dearest,
It is finished between us here.
Oh, if I were calm as you are,
Sweet and still on your bier!
Oh God, if I had not to leave you
Alone, my dear.

Is the last word now uttered?
Is the farewell said?
Spare me the strength to leave you
Now you are dead.
I must go, but my soul lies helpless
Beside your bed.

River Roses

By the Isar, in the twilight
We were wandering and singing,
By the Isar, in the evening
We climbed the huntsman's ladder and sat swinging
In the fir-tree overlooking the marshes,
While river met with river, and the ringing
Of their pale-green glacier water filled the evening.

By the Isar, in the twilight
We found the dark wild roses
Hanging red at the river; and simmering
Frogs were singing, and over the river closes
Was savour of ice and roses; and glimmering

Fear was abroad. We whispered: "No one knows us.
Let it be as the snake disposes
Here in this simmering marsh."

Song of a Man Who Has Come Through

Not I, not I, but the wind that blows through me!
A fine wind is blowing the new direction of Time.
If only I let it bear me, carry me, if only it carry me!
If only I am sensitive, subtle, oh, delicate, a winged gift!
If only, most lovely of all, I yield myself and am borrowed
By the fine, fine wind that takes its course through the chaos
    of the world
Like a fine, an exquisite chisel, a wedge-blade inserted;
If only I am keen and hard like the sheer tip of a wedge
Driven by invisible blows,
The rock will split, we shall come at the wonder, we shall
    find the Hesperides.

    Oh, for the wonder that bubbles into my soul,
    I would be a good fountain, a good well-head,
    Would blur no whisper, spoil no expression.

    What is the knocking?
    What is the knocking at the door in the night?
    It is somebody wants to do us harm.

    No, no, it is the three strange angels.
    Admit them, admit them.

Sinners

    The big mountains sit still in the afternoon light,
        Shadows in their lap;
    The bees roll round in the wild-thyme with delight.

    We sitting here among the cranberries
        So still in the gap
    Of rock, distilling our memories,

Are sinners! Strange! The bee that blunders
  Against me goes off with a laugh.
A squirrel cocks his head on the fence, and wonders

What about sin?—For, it seems
  The mountains have
No shadow of us on their snowy forehead of dreams

As they ought to have. They rise above us
  Dreaming
For ever. One even might think that they love us.

Little red cranberries cheek to cheek,
Two great dragon-flies wrestling;
You, with your forehead nestling
Against me, and bright peak shining to peak—

There's a love-song for you!—Ah, if only
  There were no teeming
Swarms of mankind in the world, and we were less lonely!

Bavarian Gentians

Not every man has gentians in his house
in soft September, at slow, sad Michaelmas.

Bavarian gentians, big and dark, only dark
darkening the day-time torch-like with the smoking blueness
    of Pluto's gloom,
ribbed and torch-like, with their blaze of darkness spread
    blue
down flattening into points, flattened under the sweep of
    white day
torch-flower of the blue-smoking darkness, Pluto's dark-blue
    daze,
black lamps from the halls of Dis, burning dark blue,
giving off darkness, blue darkness, as Demeter's pale lamps
    give off light,
lead me then, lead me the way.

Reach me a gentian, give me a torch
let me guide myself with the blue, forked torch of this flower
down the darker and darker stairs, where blue is darkened
    on blueness,
even where Persephone goes, just now, from the frosted
    September
to the sightless realm where darkness is awake upon the dark
and Persephone herself is but a voice
or a darkness invisible enfolded in the deeper dark
of the arms Plutonic, and pierced with the passion of dense
    gloom,
among the splendour of torches of darkness, shedding dark-
    ness on the lost bride and her groom.

Ship of Death

I sing of autumn and the falling fruit
and the long journey towards oblivion.

The apples falling like great drops of dew
to bruise themselves an exit from themselves.

Have you built your ship of death, oh, have you?
Build then your ship of death, for you will need it!

Can man his own quietus make
with a bare bodkin?

With daggers, bodkins, bullets man can make
a bruise or break of exit for his life
but is that a quietus, oh tell me, is it quietus?

Quietus is the goal of the long journey,
the longest journey towards oblivion.

Slips out the soul, invisible one, wrapped still
in the white shirt of the mind's experiences
and folded in the dark-red, unseen
mantle of the body's still mortal memories.

Frightened and alone, the soul slips out of the house
or is pushed out
to find himself on the crowded, arid margins of existence.

Oh, it is not so easy, I tell you it is not so easy
to set softly forth on the longest journey, the longest journey.

It is easy to be pushed out of the silvery city of the body
through any breach in the wall,
thrust out on to the grey grey beaches of shadow,
the long marginal stretches of existence, crowded with lost
    souls
that intervene between our tower and the shaking sea of the
    beyond.

Oh build your ship of death, oh build it in time
and build it lovingly, and put it between the hands of your
    soul.

Once outside the gate of the walled silvery life of days,
once outside upon the grey marsh beaches, where lost souls
    moan
in millions, unable to depart,
having no boat to launch upon the shaken, soundless
deepest and longest of seas,
once outside the gate,
what will you do, if you have no ship of the soul?

Oh pity the dead that are dead but cannot take
the journey, still they moan and beat
against the silvery adamant walls of this our exclusive exist-
    ence.
They moan and beat, they gnash, they rage,
they fall upon the new outcoming souls with rage,
and they send arrows of anger, bullets and bombs of frustra-
    tion
over the adamant walls of this, our by-no-means impregnable
    existence.

Pity, oh pity the poor dead that are only ousted from life,
and crowd there on the grey mud beaches of the margins,

gaunt and horrible,
waiting, waiting till at last the ancient boatman with the
     common barge
shall take them abroad, towards the great goal of oblivion.

Pity the poor gaunt dead that cannot die
into the distance with receding oars,
but must roam like outcast dogs on the margins of life,
and think of them, and with the soul's deep sigh
waft nearer to them the bark of delivery.

But, for myself, but for my soul, dear soul,
let me build a little ship with oars and food
and little dishes, and all accoutrements
dainty and ready for the departing soul.
And put it between the hands of the trembling soul.

So that when the hour comes, and the last door closes behind
     him,
he shall slip down the shores invisible
between the half-visible hordes
to where the furthest and longest sea
touches the margins of our life's existence
with wincing unwilling waves.

And launching there his little ship,
wrapped in the dark-red mantle of the body's memories,
the little, slender soul sits swiftly down, and takes the oars,
and draws away, away, away towards the dark depths,
fathomless deep ahead, far, far from the grey shores
that fringe with shadow all this world's existence.

Over the sea, over the furthest sea
on the longest journey,
past the jutting rocks of shadow,
past the lurking octopus arms of agonised memory,
past the strange whirlpools of remembered greed,
through the dead weed of a life-time's falsity,
slow, slow, my soul in his little ship,
on the most soundless of all seas,
taking the longest journey.

Pulling the long oars of a life-time's courage,
drinking the confident water from the little jug,
and eating the brave bread of a wholesome knowledge,
row, little soul, row on,
on the longest journey, towards the greatest goal;

Neither straight nor crooked, neither here nor there,
but shadows folded on deeper shadows,
and deeper, to a core of sheer oblivion,
like the convolutions of shadow-shell,
or deeper, like the foldings and involvings of a womb.

Drift on, drift on, my soul, towards the most pure,
most dark oblivion.
And at the penultimate porches, the dark-red mantle
of the body's memories slips and is absorbed
into the shell-like, womb-like convoluted shadow.

And round the great final bend of unbroken dark,
the skirt of the spirit's experience has melted away,
the oars have gone from the boat, and the little dishes
gone, gone, and the boat dissolves like pearl,
as the soul at last slips perfect into the goal, the core
of sheer oblivion and of utter peace,
the womb of silence in the living night.

Ah peace, ah lovely peace, most lovely lapsing
of this my soul into the plasm of peace.

Oh lovely last, last lapse of death, into pure oblivion,
at the end of the longest journey
peace, complete peace!
But can it be that also it is procreation?

Oh build your ship of death,
oh build it!
Oh, nothing matters but the longest journey.

EZRA POUND

(1885–   )

Δώρια

Be in me as the eternal moods
    of the bleak wind, and not
As transient things are—
    gaiety of flowers.
Have me in the strong loneliness
    of sunless cliffs
And of grey waters.
    Let the gods speak softly of us
In days hereafter,
    The shadowy flowers of Orcus
Remember thee.

The Return

See, they return; ah, see the tentative
Movements, and the slow feet,
The trouble in the pace and the uncertain
Wavering!

See, they return, one, and by one,
With fear, as half-awakened;
As if the snow should hesitate
And murmur in the wind,
        and half turn back;
These were the "Wing'd-with-Awe,"
    Inviolable.

Gods of the wingéd shoe!
With them the silver hounds
        sniffing the trace of air!

Haie! Haie!
        These were the swift to harry;
These the keen-scented;
These were the souls of blood.

Slow on the leash,
        pallid the leash-men!

FROM *Canto LXXXI*

What thou lovest well remains,
   the rest is dross
What thou lov'st well shall not be reft from thee
What thou lov'st well is thy true heritage
Whose world, or mine or theirs
    or is it of none?
First came the seen, then thus the palpable
  Elysium, though it were in the halls of hell,
What thou lovest well is thy true heritage

The ant's a centaur in his dragon world.
Pull down thy vanity, it is not man
Made courage, or made order, or made grace,
  Pull down thy vanity, I say pull down.
Learn of the green world what can be thy place
In scaled invention or true artistry,
Pull down thy vanity,
    Paquin pull down!
The green casque has outdone your elegance.

"Master thyself, then others shall thee beare"
  Pull down thy vanity
Thou art a beaten dog beneath the hail,
A swollen magpie in a fitful sun,
Half black half white
Nor knowst'ou wing from tail
Pull down thy vanity
    How mean thy hates
Fostered in falsity,
    Pull down thy vanity,
Rathe to destroy, niggard in charity,
Pull down thy vanity,
    I say pull down.

But to have done instead of not doing
    this is not vanity
To have, with decency, knocked
That a Blunt should open
    To have gathered from the air a live tradition

or from a fine old eye the unconquered flame
This is not vanity.
    Here error is all in the not done,
all in the diffidence that faltered.

ELINOR WYLIE

(1885–1928)

The Eagle and the Mole

Avoid the reeking herd,
Shun the polluted flock,
Live like that stoic bird,
The eagle of the rock.

The huddled warmth of crowds
Begets and fosters hate;
He keeps, above the clouds,
His cliff inviolate.

When flocks are folded warm,
And herds to shelter run,
He sails above the storm,
He stares into the sun.

If in the eagle's track
Your sinews cannot leap,
Avoid the lathered pack,
Turn from the steaming sheep.

If you would keep your soul
From spotted sight or sound,
Live like the velvet mole;
Go burrow underground

And there hold intercourse
With roots of trees and stones,
With rivers at their source,
And disembodied bones.

SIEGFRIED SASSOON

(1886–   )

Aftermath

Have you forgotten yet? . . .
For the world's events have rumbled on since those gagged
    days,
Like traffic checked awhile at the crossing of city ways:
And the haunted gap in your mind has filled with thoughts
    that flow
Like clouds in the lit heaven of life; and you're a man re-
    prieved to go,
Taking your peaceful share of Time, with joy to spare.
But the past is just the same,—and War's a bloody game . . .
Have you forgotten yet? . . .
*Look down, and swear by the slain of the War that you'll
    never forget?*

Do you remember the dark months you held the sector at
    Mametz,—
The nights you watched and wired and dug and piled sand-
    bags on parapets?
Do you remember the rats; and the stench
Of corpses rotting in front of the front-line trench,—
And dawn coming, dirty-white, and chill with a hopeless
    rain?
Do you ever stop and ask, "Is it all going to happen again?"

Do you remember that hour of din before the attack,—
And the anger, the blind compassion that seized and shook
    you then
As you peered at the doomed and haggard faces of your
    men?
Do you remember the stretcher-cases lurching back
With dying eyes and lolling heads,—those ashen-grey
Masks of the lads who once were keen and kind and gay?

Have you forgotten yet? . . .
*Look up, and swear by the green of the Spring that you'll
    never forget.*

H.D.
(HILDA DOOLITTLE)

(1886–   )

Sitalkas

Thou art come at length
more beautiful
than any cool god
in a chamber under
Lycia's far coast,
than any high god
who touches us not
here in the seeded grass,
aye, than Argestes
scattering the broken leaves.

Lethe

Nor skin nor hide nor fleece
   Shall cover you,
Nor curtain of crimson nor fine
Shelter of cedar-wood be over you,
   Nor the fir-tree
   Nor the pine.

Nor sight of whin nor gorse
   Nor river-yew,
Nor fragrance of flowering bush,
Nor wailing of reed-bird to waken you,
   Nor of linnet,
   Nor of thrush.

Nor word nor touch nor sight
   Of lover, you
Shall long through the night but for this:
The roll of the full tide to cover you
   Without question,
   Without kiss.

FROM *Hymen*

Never more will the wind
Cherish you again,
Never more will the rain.

Never more
Shall we find you bright
In the snow and wind.

The snow is melted,
The snow is gone,
And you are flown:

Like a bird out of our hand,
Like a light out of our heart,
You are gone.

ROBINSON JEFFERS

(1887–   )

Signpost

Civilized, crying how to be human again: this will tell you
    how.
Turn outward, love things, not men, turn right away from
    humanity,
Let that doll lie. Consider if you like how the lilies grow,
Lean on the silent rock until you feel its divinity
Make your veins cold, look at the silent stars, let your eyes
Climb the great ladder out of the pit of yourself and man.
Things are so beautiful, your love will follow your eyes;
Things are the God, you will love God, and not in vain,
For what we love, we grow to it, we share its nature. At
    length
You will look back along the stars' rays and see that even
The poor doll humanity has a place under heaven.
Its qualities repair their mosaic around you, the chips of
    strength
And sickness; but now you are free, even to become human,
But born of the rock and the air, not of a woman.

Shine, Perishing Republic

While this America settles in the mould of its vulgarity, heav-
      ily thickening to empire,
And protest, only a bubble in the molten mass, pops and
      sighs out, and the mass hardens,

I sadly smiling remember that the flower fades to make fruit,
      the fruit rots to make earth
Out of the mother; and through the spring exultances, ripe-
      ness and decadence; and home to the mother.

You making haste haste on decay: not blameworthy; life is
      good, be it stubbornly long or suddenly
A mortal splendor: meteors are not needed less than moun-
      tains: shine, perishing republic.

But for my children, I would have them keep their distance
      from the thickening center; corruption
Never has been compulsory, when the cities lie at the mon-
      ster's feet there are left the mountains.

And boys, be in nothing so moderate as in love of man, a
      clever servant, insufferable master.
There is the trap that catches noblest spirits, that caught—
      they say—God, when he walked on earth.

EDITH SITWELL
(1887–   )

An Old Woman Laments in Spring-Time

I walk on grass as soft as wool,
Or fluff that our old fingers pull
From beaver or from miniver,—
Sweet-sounding as a dulcimer,—

A poor old woman creeping where
The young can never pry and stare.
I am so old, I should be gone,—
Too old to warm in the kind sun

My wrinkled face; my hat that flaps
Will hide it, and my cloak has laps
That trail upon the grass as I
Like some warm shade of spring creep by.

And all the laden fruit-boughs spread
Into a silver sound, but dead
Is the wild dew I used to know,
Nor will the morning music grow.

I sit beneath these coral boughs
Where the air's silver plumage grows
And flows like water with a sigh.
Fed with sweet milk of lilies, I

Still feel the dew like amber gums,
That from the richest spice-tree comes,
Drip down upon my turbanned head,
Trembling and ancient as the Dead,

Beneath these floating branches' shade.
Yet long ago, a lovely maid,
On grass, a fading silver tune
Played on an ancient dulcimer,
(And soft as wool of miniver)

I walked like a young antelope,
And Day was but an Ethiop,
Beside my fairness shining there—
Like black shade seemed the brightest air

When I was lovely as the snows,—
A fading starriness that flows . . .
Then, far-off Death seemed but the shade
That those heavenly branches made.

EDWIN MUIR

(1887–   )

The Road

There is a road that turning always
    Cuts off the country of Again.
Archers stand there on every side
    And as it runs time's deer is slain,
    And lies where it has lain.

The busy clock shows never an hour.
    All flies and all in flight must tarry.
The hunter shoots the empty air
    Far on before the quarry,
    Which falls though nothing's there to parry.

The lion couching in the centre
    With mountain head and sunset brow
Rolls down the everlasting slope
    Bones picked an age ago,
    And the bones rise up and go.

There the beginning finds the end
    Before beginning ever can be,
And the great runner never leaves
    The starting and the finishing tree,
    The budding and the fading tree.

There the ship sailing safe in harbour
    Long since in many a sea was drowned.
The treasure burning in her hold
    So near will never be found,
    Sunk past all sound.

There a man on a summer evening
    Reclines at ease upon his tomb
And is his mortal effigy.
    And there within the womb,
    The cell of doom,

The ancestral deed is thought and done,
　　And in a million Edens fall
A million Adams drowned in darkness,
　　For small is great and great is small,
　　And a blind seed all.

LEONARD BACON

(1887–1954)

Chorus from a Tragedy

The world is no longer good.
Men's hearts no more are kind.
There is coldness in the mind,
Bitterness in the blood.
And I am not resigned.

When they talk of burning things
That touch me to the heart,
They trammel music and art,
They wither Ariel's wings
Or tear his pinions apart,

Anatomizing, digesting,
Drying the sap that ran
Once in the brain of man
Riotous and unresting,
Guiltless of plot or plan.

There is no pulse in the vein.
And the staunch muscle has slacked.
A blight has devoured the bract.
Color dies to a stain.
Wisdom dwindles to fact.

And I feel as dead as the ash
Of an unregarded fire.
The elements of desire,
Lovely and wild and rash,
Separate and retire.

We shall not have things as they were,
Not as they were before.
If I had the heart to restore,
Would the chestnut thicken its burr?
Would the olive leaf once more?

MARIANNE MOORE

(1887–   )

Silence

My father used to say,
"Superior people never make long visits,
have to be shown Longfellow's grave
or the glass flowers at Harvard.
Self-reliant like the cat—
that takes its prey to privacy,
the mouse's limp tail hanging like a shoelace from its mouth—
they sometimes enjoy solitude,
and can be robbed of speech
by speech which has delighted them.
The deepest feeling always shows itself in silence;
not in silence, but restraint."
Nor was he insincere in saying, "Make my house your inn."
Inns are not residences.

A Talisman

Under a splintered mast,
Torn from the ship and cast
    Near her hull,

A stumbling shepherd found
Embedded in the ground,
    A seagull

Of lapis lazuli,
A scarab of the sea,
    With wings spread—

Curling its coral feet,
Parting its beak to greet
Men long dead.

Poetry

I, too, dislike it: there are things that are important beyond
    all this fiddle.
Reading it, however, with a perfect contempt for it, one
    discovers in
it, after all, a place for the genuine.
    Hands that can grasp, eyes
    that can dilate, hair that can rise
      if it must, these things are important not because a

high-sounding interpretation can be put upon them but be-
    cause they are
useful. When they become so derivative as to become un-
    intelligible
the same thing may be said for all of us, that we
    do not admire what
    we cannot understand: the bat
      holding on upside down or in quest of something to

eat, elephants pushing, a wild horse taking a roll, a tireless
    wolf under
a tree, the immovable critic twitching his skin like a horse
    that feels a flea, the base-
ball fan, the statistician—
    nor is it valid
      to discriminate against "business documents and

school-books"; all these phenomena are important. One must
    make a distinction
however: when dragged into prominence by half poets, the
    result is not poetry,
nor till the poets among us can be
    "literalists of
    the imagination"—above
      insolence and triviality and can present

for inspection, "imaginary gardens with real toads in them,"
        shall we have
    it. In the meantime, if you demand on the one hand,
    the raw material of poetry in
        all its rawness and
        that which is on the other hand
        genuine, you are interested in poetry.

In Distrust of Merits

Strengthened to live, strengthened to die for
        medals and positioned victories?
They're fighting, fighting, fighting the blind
        man who thinks he sees,—
who cannot see that the enslaver is
enslaved; the hater, harmed. O shining O
        firm star, O tumultuous
                ocean lashed till small things go
        as they will, the mountainous
                wave makes us who look, know

depth. Lost at sea before they fought! O
        star of David, star of Bethlehem,
O black imperial lion
        of the Lord—emblem
of a risen world—be joined at last, be
joined. There is hate's crown beneath which all is
                death; there's love's without which none
                        is king; the blessed deeds bless
                the halo. As contagion
                        of sickness makes sickness,

contagion of trust can make trust. They're
        fighting in deserts and caves, one by
one, in battalions and squadrons;
        they're fighting that I
may yet recover from the disease, My
Self; some have it lightly; some will die. "Man

wolf to man?" And we devour
        ourselves. The enemy could not
have made a greater breach in our
        defenses. One pilot-

ing a blind man can escape him, but
        Job disheartened by false comfort knew
that nothing is so defeating
        as a blind man who
can see. O alive who are dead, who are
proud not to see, O small dust of the earth
        that walks so arrogantly,
                trust begets power and faith is
        an affectionate thing. We
                vow, we make this promise

to the fighting—it's a promise—"We'll
        never hate black, white, red, yellow, Jew,
Gentile, Untouchable." We are
        not competent to
make our vows. With set jaw they are fighting,
fighting, fighting, —some we love whom we know,
        some we love but know not—that
                hearts may feel and not be numb.
        It cures me; or am I what
                I can't believe in? Some

in snow, some on crags, some in quicksands,
        little by little, much by much, they
are fighting fighting fighting that where
        there was death there may
be life. "When a man is prey to anger,
he is moved by outside things; when he holds
        his ground in patience patience
                patience, that is action or
        beauty," the soldier's defense
                and hardest armor for

the fight. The world's an orphans' home. Shall
        we never have peace without sorrow?

without pleas of the dying for
    help that won't come? O
quiet form upon the dust, I cannot
look and yet I must. If these great patient
    dyings—all these agonies
        and woundbearings and bloodshed—
    can teach us how to live, these
    dyings were not wasted.

Hate-hardened heart, O heart of iron,
    iron is iron till it is rust.
There never was a war that was
    not inward; I must
fight till I have conquered in myself what
causes war, but I would not believe it.
    I inwardly did nothing.
        O Iscariotlike crime!
    Beauty is everlasting
        and dust is for a time.

RUPERT BROOKE

(1887–1915)

The Hill

Breathless, we flung us on the windy hill,
    Laughed in the sun, and kissed the lovely grass.
    You said, "Through glory and ecstasy we pass;
Wind, sun, and earth remain, the birds sing still,
When we are old, are old . . ." "And when we die
    All's over that is ours; and life burns on
Through other lovers, other lips," said I,
    "Heart of my heart, our heaven is now, is won!"

"We are earth's best, that learnt her lesson here.
    Life is our cry. We have kept the faith!" we said;
    "We shall go down with unreluctant tread
Rose-crowned into the darkness!" . . . Proud we were,
And laughed, that had such brave true things to say,
    —And then you suddenly cried, and turned away.

The Soldier

If I should die, think only this of me:
  That there's some corner of a foreign field
That is for ever England. There shall be
  In that rich earth a richer dust concealed;
A dust whom England bore, shaped, made aware;
  Gave, once, her flowers to love, her ways to roam,
A body of England's breathing English air,
  Washed by the rivers, blest by suns of home.

And think, this heart, all evil shed away,
  A pulse in the eternal mind, no less
    Gives somewhere back the thoughts by England given;
Her sights and sounds; dreams happy as her day;
  And laughter, learnt of friends; and gentleness,
    In hearts at peace, under an English heaven.

ALAN SEEGER

(1888–1916)

"I Have a Rendezvous with Death"

I have a rendezvous with Death
  At some disputed barricade,
When Spring comes back with rustling shade
  And apple-blossoms fill the air—
I have a rendezvous with Death
  When Spring brings back blue days and fair.

It may be he shall take my hand
  And lead me into his dark land
And close my eyes and quench my breath—
  It may be I shall pass him still.
I have a rendezvous with Death
  On some scarred slope of battered hill,
When Spring comes round again this year
  And the first meadow-flowers appear.

God knows 'twere better to be deep
  Pillowed in silk and scented down,

Where Love throbs out in blissful sleep,
Pulse nigh to pulse, and breath to breath,
Where hushed awakenings are dear . . .
But I've a rendezvous with Death
At midnight in some flaming town,
When Spring trips north again this year,
And I to my pledged word am true,
I shall not fail that rendezvous.

THOMAS STEARNS ELIOT

(1888–   )

The Love Song of J. Alfred Prufrock

> S'io credessi che mia risposta fosse
> A persona che mai tornasse al mondo,
> Questa fiamma staria senza più scosse.
> Ma perciocché giammai di questo fondo
> Non tornò vivo alcun, s'i'odo il vero
> Senza tema d'infamia ti rispondo.

Let us go then, you and I,
When the evening is spread out against the sky
Like a patient etherised upon a table;
Let us go, through certain half-deserted streets,
The muttering retreats
Of restless nights in one-night cheap hotels
And sawdust restaurants with oyster-shells:
Streets that follow like a tedious argument
Of insidious intent
To lead you to an overwhelming question . . .
Oh, do not ask, "What is it?"
Let us go and make our visit.

In the room the women come and go
Talking of Michelangelo.

The yellow fog that rubs its back upon the window-panes,
The yellow smoke that rubs its muzzle on the window-panes
Licked its tongue into the corners of the evening,
Lingered upon the pools that stand in drains,
Let fall upon its back the soot that falls from chimneys,

Slipped by the terrace, made a sudden leap,
And seeing that it was a soft October night,
Curled once about the house, and fell asleep.

And indeed there will be time
For the yellow smoke that slides along the street,
Rubbing its back upon the window-panes;
There will be time, there will be time
To prepare a face to meet the faces that you meet;
There will be time to murder and create,
And time for all the works and days of hands
That lift and drop a question on your plate;
Time for you and time for me,
And time yet for a hundred indecisions,
And for a hundred visions and revisions,
Before the taking of a toast and tea.

In the room the women come and go
Talking of Michelangelo.

And indeed there will be time
To wonder, "Do I dare?" and, "Do I dare?"
Time to turn back and descend the stair,
With a bald spot in the middle of my hair—
(They will say: "How his hair is growing thin!")
My morning coat, my collar mounting firmly to the chin,
My necktie rich and modest, but asserted by a simple pin—
(They will say: "But how his arms and legs are thin!")
Do I dare
Disturb the universe?
In a minute there is time
For decisions and revisions which a minute will reverse.

For I have known them all already, known them all:—
Have known the evenings, mornings, afternoons,
I have measured out my life with coffee spoons;
I know the voices dying with a dying fall
Beneath the music from a farther room.
    So how should I presume?

And I have known the eyes already, known them all—
The eyes that fix you in a formulated phrase,
And when I am formulated, sprawling on a pin,
When I am pinned and wriggling on the wall,
Then how should I begin
To spit out all the butt-ends of my days and ways?
　　And how should I presume?

And I have known the arms already, known them all—
Arms that are braceleted and white and bare
(But in the lamplight, downed with light brown hair!)
Is it perfume from a dress
That makes me so digress?
Arms that lie along a table, or wrap about a shawl.
　　And should I then presume?
　　And how should I begin?

.　　.　　.　　.　　.

Shall I say, I have gone at dusk through narrow streets
And watched the smoke that rises from the pipes
Of lonely men in shirt-sleeves, leaning out of windows? . . .

I should have been a pair of ragged claws
Scuttling across the floors of silent seas.

.　　.　　.　　.　　.

And the afternoon, the evening, sleeps so peacefully!
Smoothed by long fingers,
Asleep . . . tired . . . or it malingers,
Stretched on the floor, here beside you and me.
Should I, after tea and cakes and ices,
Have the strength to force the moment to its crisis?
But though I have wept and fasted, wept and prayed,
Though I have seen my head (grown slightly bald) brought
　　　　in upon a platter,
I am no prophet—and here's no great matter;
I have seen the moment of my greatness flicker,
And I have seen the eternal Footman hold my coat, and
　　　　snicker,
And in short, I was afraid.

And would it have been worth it, after all,
After the cups, the marmalade, the tea,
Among the porcelain, among some talk of you and me,
Would it have been worth while,
To have bitten off the matter with a smile,
To have squeezed the universe into a ball
To roll it toward some overwhelming question,
To say: "I am Lazarus, come from the dead,
Come back to tell you all, I shall tell you all"—
If one, settling a pillow by her head,
    Should say: "That is not what I meant at all.
    That is not it, at all."

And would it have been worth it, after all,
Would it have been worth while,
After the sunsets and the dooryards and the sprinkled streets,
After the novels, after the teacups, after the skirts that trail
        along the floor—
And this, and so much more?—
It is impossible to say just what I mean!
But as if a magic lantern threw the nerves in patterns on a
        screen:
Would it have been worth while
If one, settling a pillow or throwing off a shawl,
And turning toward the window, should say:
    "That is not it at all,
    That is not what I meant, at all."

.   .   .   .   .

No! I am not Prince Hamlet, nor was meant to be;
Am an attendant lord, one that will do
To swell a progress, start a scene or two,
Advise the prince; no doubt, an easy tool,
Deferential, glad to be of use,
Politic, cautious, and meticulous;
Full of high sentence, but a bit obtuse;
At times, indeed, almost ridiculous—
Almost, at times, the Fool.

I grow old . . . I grow old . . .
I shall wear the bottoms of my trousers rolled.

Shall I part my hair behind? Do I dare to eat a peach?
I shall wear white flannel trousers, and walk upon the beach.
I have heard the mermaids singing, each to each.

I do not think that they will sing to me.

I have seen them riding seaward on the waves
Combing the white hair of the waves blown back
When the wind blows the water white and black.

We have lingered in the chambers of the sea
By sea-girls wreathed with seaweed red and brown
Till human voices wake us, and we drown.

La Figlia Che Piange

O quam te memorem virgo . . .

Stand on the highest pavement of the stair—
Lean on a garden urn—
Weave, weave the sunlight in your hair—
Clasp your flowers to you with a pained surprise—
Fling them to the ground and turn
With a fugitive resentment in your eyes:
But weave, weave the sunlight in your hair.

So I would have had him leave,
So I would have had her stand and grieve,
So he would have left
As the soul leaves the body torn and bruised,
As the mind deserts the body it has used.
I should find
Some way incomparably light and deft,
Some way we both should understand,
Simple and faithless as a smile and shake of the hand.

She turned away, but with the autumn weather
Compelled my imagination many days,
Many days and many hours:
Her hair over her arms and her arms full of flowers.

And I wonder how they should have been together!
I should have lost a gesture and a pose.
Sometimes these cogitations still amaze
The troubled midnight and the noon's repose.

"Eyes That Last I Saw in Tears"

Eyes that last I saw in tears
Through division
Here in death's dream kingdom
The golden vision reappears
I see the eyes but not the tears
This is my affliction

This is my affliction
Eyes I shall not see again
Eyes of decision
Eyes I shall not see unless
At the door of death's other kingdom
Where, as in this,
The eyes outlast a little while
A little while outlast the tears
And hold us in derision.

FROM Four Quartets

(FROM Burnt Norton)

v

Words move, music moves
Only in time; but that which is only living
Can only die. Words, after speech, reach
Into the silence. Only by the form, the pattern,
Can words or music reach
The stillness, as a Chinese jar still
Moves perpetually in its stillness.
Not the stillness of the violin, while the note lasts,
Not that only, but the co-existence,
Or say that the end precedes the beginning,

And the end and the beginning were always there
Before the beginning and after the end.
And all is always now. Words strain,
Crack and sometimes break, under the burden,
Under the tension, slip, slide, perish,
Decay with imprecision, will not stay in place,
Will not stay still. Shrieking voices
Scolding, mocking, or merely chattering,
Always assail them. The Word in the desert
Is most attacked by voices of temptation,
The crying shadow in the funeral dance,
The loud lament of the disconsolate chimera.

The detail of the pattern is movement,
As in the figure of the ten stairs.
Desire itself is movement
Not in itself desirable;
Love is itself unmoving,
Only the cause and end of movement,
Timeless, and undesiring
Except in the aspect of time
Caught in the form of limitation
Between un-being and being.
Sudden in a shaft of sunlight
Even while the dust moves
There rises the hidden laughter
Of children in the foliage
Quick now, here, now, always—
Ridiculous the waste sad time
Stretching before and after.

JOHN CROWE RANSOM

(1888-   )

Tom, Tom, the Piper's Son

Grim in my little black coat as the sleazy beetle,
And gone of hue,
Lonely, a man reputed for softening little,
Loving few—

Mournfully going where men assemble, unfriended, pushing
With laborious wares,
And glaring with little grey eyes at whom I am brushing,
Who would with theirs—

Full of my thoughts as I trudge here and trundle yonder,
Eyes on the ground,
Tricked by white birds or tall women into no wonder,
And no sound—

Yet privy to great dreams, and secret in vainglory,
And hot and proud,
And poor and bewildered, and longing to hear my own story
Rehearsed aloud—

How I have passed, involved in these chances and choices,
By certain trees
Whose tiny attent auricles receive the true voices
Of the wordless breeze—

And against me the councils of spirits were not then dark-
        ened
Who thereby house,
As I set my boots to the path beneath them, and hearkened
To the talking boughs—

How one said, "This ambulant worm, he is strangely other
Than they suppose"—
But one, "He was sired by his father and damned by his
        mother,
And acknowledges those"—

And then: "Nay, nay—this man is a changeling, and knows
        not—
This was a Prince
From a far great kingdom—and should return, but goes
        not—
Long years since"—

But like a King I was subject to a King's condition,
And I marched on,
Not testing at eavesdrop the glory of my suspicion,
And the talkers were gone—

And duly appeared I on the very clock-throb appointed
In the litten room,
Nor was hailed with that love that leaps to the Heir anointed:
"Hush, hush, he is come!"

CONRAD AIKEN

(1889–   )

FROM *Time in the Rock*

XX

And you who love, you who attach yourselves
to another mouth, who in the depth of night
speak without speech act without conscious action
in all that lamentable struggle to be another
to make that other yourself, to find that other,
to make two one

                    who would be tree and earth
cloud and ocean, movement and stillness,
object and shadow

                    what can we learn from you
pathetic ones, poor victims of the will,
wingless angels who beat with violent arms,
what can we learn from your tragic effort

is there a secret here, an unambiguous
message, a leaf blown from another star,
that thus all stand and watch you, thus all envy,
all emulate? must we be violent too?

O patience, let us be patient and discern
in this lost leaf all that can be discerned;
and let us learn, from this sad violence learn,
all that in midst of violence can be learned.

Blind Date

No more the swanboat on the artificial lake
its paddled path through neon lights shall take;
the stars are turned out on the immortal Ferris wheel,
dark and still are the cars of the Virginia Reel.
Baby, it is the last of all blind dates,
and this we keep with the keeper of the golden gates.

For the last time, my darling, the chute-the-chutes,
the Tunnel of Love, the cry "all men are brutes,"
the sweaty dance-hall with the juke-box playing,
pretzels and beer, and our young love a-Maying:
baby, it is the last of all blind dates,
and this we keep with the keeper of the golden gates.

The radios in a thousand taxis die;
at last man's music fades from the inhuman sky;
as, short or long, fades out the impermanent wave
to find in the ether or the earth its grave.
Baby, it is the last of all blind dates,
and this we keep with the keeper of the golden gates.

Hold hands and kiss, it will never come again,
look in your own eyes and remember the deep pain,
how hollow the world is, like a bubble burst,
yes, and all beauty by some wretchedness accursed!
Baby, it is the last of all blind dates,
and this we keep with the keeper of the golden gates.

Love now the footworn grass, the trampled flowers,
and the divided man of crowds, for he is ours—
love him, yes, love him now, this sundered being,
who most himself seeks when himself most fleeing—
baby, it is the last of all blind dates,
and this we keep with the keeper of the golden gates.

But look—the scenic railway is flashed from red to green—
and swiftly beneath our feet as this machine
our old star plunges down the precipitous sky,
down the hurrahs of space! So soon to die!—
But baby, it is the last of all blind dates;
and we shall keep it with the keeper of the golden gates.

ISAAC ROSENBERG

(1890–1918)

Break of Day in the Trenches

The darkness crumbles away—
It is the same old druid Time as ever.
Only a live thing leaps my hand—
A queer sardonic rat—
As I pull the parapet's poppy
To stick behind my ear.
Droll rat, they would shoot you if they knew
Your cosmopolitan sympathies
(And God knows what antipathies).
Now you have touched this English hand
You will do the same to a German—
Soon, no doubt, if it be your pleasure
To cross the sleeping green between.
It seems you inwardly grin as you pass
Strong eyes, fine limbs, haughty athletes
Less chanced than you for life,
Bonds to the whims of murder,
Sprawled in the bowels of the earth,
The torn fields of France.
What do you see in our eyes
As the shrieking iron and flame
Hurled through still heavens?
What quaver—what heart aghast?
Poppies whose roots are in man's veins
Drop, and are ever dropping;
But mine in my ear is safe,
Just a little white with the dust.

OSBERT SITWELL

(1892–   )

Mrs. Southern's Enemy

Even as the shadows of the statues lengthen,
While, when the glowing glass below is broken,
The plunging images are shaken,
For the young, blue-wingéd god is woken,

Sighs, stretches, shivers, till his muscles strengthen
So he can trample down the flowers, forsaken
By their droning, golden-liveried lovers, tumble
Among them till their red mouths tremble,
Already in the ancient house, whose shadow dies
With the slow opening of its hundred eyes,
Already, even then, Night the Black Panther
Is slinking, creeping down the corridors,
Lithe-swinging on her velvet paws,
Sharpening her treacherous claws
To frighten children.

And then it is
                I seem to see again
That grey typhoon we knew as Mrs. Southern,
Spinning along the darkened passages,
Watching things, tugging things,
Seeing to things,
                And putting things to rights.
Oh, would that the cruel daylight too,
Could give us back again
Dear Mrs. Southern,
Dear selfless, blue-lipped Mrs. Southern,
Cross, mumbling and transparent Mrs. Southern,
With her grey hair,
                Grey face,
                        And thinly-bitter smile,
In wide blue skirt, white-spotted, and white apron;
On the very top of her head she carried a cap,
An emblem of respect and respectability, while
As though she were a Hindu charmer of snakes,
Her hair lay coiled and tame at the back of her head.
But her actual majesty was really the golden glory,
Through which she moved, a hurrying fly
Enshrined in rolling amber,
As she spun along in a twisting column of golden atoms,
A halo of gold motes above and about her,
A column of visible, virtuous activity.
Her life was a span of hopeless conflict,
For she battled against Time,
That never-vanquished and invisible foe.

She did not recognise her enemy,
She thought him Dust:
But what is Dust,
Save Time's most lethal weapon,
His faithful ally and our sneaking foe,
Through whom Time steals and covers all we know,
The very instrument through whom he overcame
Great Nineveh and Rome and Carthage,
Ophir and Trebizond and Ephesus,
Now deep, all deep, so deep in dust?
Even the lean and arid archaeologist,
Who bends above the stones, and peers and ponders,
Will be his, too, one day.
Dust loads the dice,
Then challenges to play,
Each layer of dust upon a chair or table
A tablet to his future victory.
And Dust is cruel, no victory despising,
However slight,
And Dust is greedy, eats the very bones;
So that, in the end, still not content
With trophies such as Helen of Troy,
Or with the conquering golden flesh of Cleopatra
(She, perhaps, understood the age-long battle,
For did she not prefer to watch her pearl
Dissolve in amber wine,
Thus herself enjoying
Its ultimate disintegration,
Than let Dust conquer such a thing of beauty?
Was not the asp, fruit-hidden,
The symbol of such understanding?),
He needs must seize upon Mrs. Southern,
Poor mumbling, struggling, blue-lipped Mrs. Southern,
For Dust is insatiate and invincible.

FROM *England Reclaimed*

Sound out, proud trumpets,
And you, bugles, blow
Over the English Dead,

Not slain in battle, in no sense sublime,
These rustic figures caught at last by Time,
And yet their blood was warm and red
As any roses that in England grow
To these anonymous armies of the Dead.
    Blow, bugles, blow;
Sound out, proud trumpets, let your brazen thunder
    Wake them, to make them pass
    Before us under the wide sky.
    Thunder, drums and trumpets, thunder,
    Wake them, to rise from where they lie
Under,
    Under
        Under
            The green grass
        Under the wide grey sky.

ARCHIBALD MacLEISH

(1892–   )

You, Andrew Marvel

And here face down beneath the sun
And here upon earth's noonward height
To feel the always coming on
The always rising of the night:

To feel creep up the curving east
The earthy chill of dusk and slow
Upon those under lands the vast
And ever climbing shadow grow

And strange at Ecbatan the trees
Take leaf by leaf the evening strange
The flooding dark about their knees
The mountains over Persia change

And now at Kermanshah the gate
Dark empty and the withered grass
And through the twilight now the late
Few travelers in the westward pass

And Baghdad darken and the bridge
Across the silent river gone
And through Arabia the edge
Of evening widen and steal on

And deepen on Palmyra's street
The wheel rut in the ruined stone
And Lebanon fade out and Crete
High through the clouds and overblown

And over Sicily the air
Still flashing with the landward gulls
And loom and slowly disappear
The sails above the shadowy hulls

And Spain go under and the shore
Of Africa the gilded sand
And evening vanish and no more
The low pale light across that land

Nor now the long light on the sea:

And here face downward in the sun
To feel how swift how secretly
The shadow of the night comes on . . .

"Not Marble nor the Gilded Monuments"

The praisers of women in their proud and beautiful poems,
Naming the grave mouth and the hair and the eyes,
Boasted those they loved should be forever remembered:
These were lies.

The words sound but the face in the Istrian sun is forgotten.
The poet speaks but to her dead ears no more.
The sleek throat is gone—and the breast that was troubled to
    listen:
Shadow from door.

Therefore I will not praise your knees nor your fine walking
Telling you men shall remember your name as long

As lips move or breath is spent or the iron of English
Rings from a tongue.

I shall say you were young and your arms straight, and your
    mouth scarlet:
I shall say you will die and none will remember you:
Your arms change, and none remember the swish of your
    garments,
Nor the click of your shoe.

Not with my hand's strength, not with difficult labor
Springing the obstinate words to the bones of your breast
And the stubborn line to your young stride and the breath to
    your breathing
And the beat to your haste
Shall I prevail on the hearts of unborn men to remember.

(What is a dead girl but a shadowy ghost
Or a dead man's voice but a distant and vain affirmation
Like dream words most)

Therefore I will not speak of the undying glory of women.
I will say you were young and straight and your skin fair
And you stood in the door and the sun was a shadow of
    leaves on your shoulders
And a leaf on your hair—

I will not speak of the famous beauty of dead women:
I will say the shape of a leaf lay once on your hair.
Till the world ends and the eyes are out and the mouths broken
Look! It is there!

EDNA ST. VINCENT MILLAY

(1892–1950)

"Oh, Sleep Forever in the Latmian Cave"

Oh, sleep forever in the Latmian cave,
Mortal Endymion, darling of the Moon!
Her silver garments by the senseless wave
Shouldered and dropped and on the shingle strewn,

Her fluttering hand against her forehead pressed,
Her scattered looks that trouble all the sky,
Her rapid footsteps running down the west—
Of all her altered state, oblivious lie!
Whom earthen you, by deathless lips adored,
Wild-eyed and stammering to the grasses thrust,
And deep into her crystal body poured
The hot and sorrowful sweetness of the dust:
Whereof she wanders mad, being all unfit
For mortal love, that might not die of it.

FROM *Sonnets*

XIX

What lips my lips have kissed, and where, and why,
I have forgotten, and what arms have lain
Under my head till morning; but the rain
Is full of ghosts to-night, that tap and sigh
Upon the glass and listen for reply,
And in my heart there stirs a quiet pain
For unremembered lads that not again
Will turn to me at midnight with a cry.
Thus in the winter stands the lonely tree,
Nor knows what birds have vanished one by one,
Yet knows its boughs more silent than before:
I cannot say what loves have come and gone,
I only know that summer sang in me
A little while, that in me sings no more.

WILFRED OWEN

(1893–1918)

Greater Love

Red lips are not so red
 As the stained stones kissed by the English dead.
Kindness of wooed and wooer
Seems shame to their love pure.
O Love, your eyes lose lure
 When I behold eyes blinded in my stead!

Your slender attitude
  Trembles not exquisite like limbs knife-skewed,
Rolling and rolling there
Where God seems not to care;
Till the fierce Love they bear
  Cramps them in death's extreme decrepitude.

Your voice sings not so soft,—
  Though even as wind murmuring through raftered loft,—
Your dear voice is not dear,
Gentle, and evening clear,
As theirs whom none now hear,
  Now earth has stopped the piteous mouths that coughed.

Heart, you were never hot,
  Nor large, nor full like hearts made great with shot,
And though your hand be pale,
Paler are all which trail
Your cross through flame and hail:
  Weep, you may weep, for you may touch them not.

The Show

  My soul looked down from a vague height with Death,
  As unremembering how I rose or why,
  And saw a sad land, weak with sweats of dearth,
  Gray, cratered like the moon with hollow woe,
  And fitted with great pocks and scabs of plagues.

  Across its beard, that horror of harsh wire,
  There moved thin caterpillars, slowly uncoiled.
  It seemed they pushed themselves to be as plugs
  Of ditches, where they writhed and shrivelled, killed.

  By them had slimy paths been trailed and scraped
  Round myriad warts that might be little hills.

  From gloom's last dregs these long-strung creatures crept
  And vanished out of dawn down hidden holes.

(And smell came up from those foul openings
As out of mouths, or deep wounds deepening.)

On dithering feet upgathered, more and more,
Brown strings, towards strings of gray, with bristling spines,
All migrants from green fields, intent on mire.

Those that were gray, of more abundant spawns,
Ramped on the rest and ate them and were eaten.

I saw their bitten backs curve, loop, and straighten,
I watched those agonies curl, lift, and flatten.

Whereat, in terror what that sight might mean
I reeled and shivered earthward like a feather.

And Death fell with me, like a deepening moan.
And He, picking a manner of worm, which half had hid
Its bruises in the earth, but crawled no further,
Showed me its feet, the feet of many men,
And the fresh-severed head of it, my head.

Anthem for Doomed Youth

What passing-bells for these who die as cattle?
Only the monstrous anger of the guns.
Only the stuttering rifles' rapid rattle
Can patter out their hasty orisons.
No mockeries for them from prayers or bells,
Nor any voice of mourning save the choirs,—
The shrill, demented choirs of wailing shells;
And bugles calling for them from sad shires.

What candles may be held to speed them all?
Not in the hands of boys, but in their eyes
Shall shine the holy glimmers of good-byes.
The pallor of girls' brows shall be their pall;
Their flowers the tenderness of silent minds,
And each slow dusk a drawing-down of blinds.

ALDOUS HUXLEY

(1894–   )

Ninth Philosopher's Song

God's in His Heaven: He never issues
    (Wise man!) to visit this world of ours.
Unchecked the cancer gnaws our tissues,
    Stops to lick chops and then again devours.

Those find, who most delight to roam
    'Mid castles of remotest Spain,
That there's, thank Heaven, no place like home;
    So they set out upon their travels again.

Beauty for some provides escape,
    Who gains a happiness in eyeing
The gorgeous buttocks of the ape
    Or Autumn sunsets exquisitely dying.

And some to better worlds than this
    Mount up on wings as frail and misty
As passion's all-too-transient kiss
    (Though afterwards—oh, *omne animal triste!*)

But I, too rational by half
    To live but where I bodily am,
Can only do my best to laugh,
    Can only sip my misery dram by dram.

While happier mortals take to drink,
    A dolorous dipsomaniac,
Fuddled with grief I sit and think,
    Looking upon the bile when it is black.

Then brim the bowl with atrabilious liquor!
    We'll pledge our Empire vast across the flood:
For Blood, as all men know, than Water's thicker,
    But Water's wider, thank the Lord, than Blood.

Frascati's

Bubble-breasted swells the dome
Of this my spiritual home,
From whose nave the chandelier,
Schaffhausen frozen, tumbles sheer.
We in the round balcony sit,
Lean o'er and look into the pit
Where feed the human bears beneath,
Champing with their gilded teeth.
What negroid holiday makes free
With such priapic revelry?
What songs? What gongs? What nameless rites?
What gods like wooden stalagmites?
What steams of blood or kidney pie?
What blasts of Bantu melody?
Ragtime . . . But when the wearied Band
Swoons to a waltz, I take her hand,
And there we sit in blissful calm,
Quietly sweating palm to palm.

MARK VAN DOREN

(1894–   )

Epitaphs: For a Fickle Man

Two women had these words engraved:
The first and last of whom he tired.
One told the other, while they lived,
The thing between them he desired.
What now it is they do not know,
Or where he seeks it round the sun.
They only ask the wind to blow,
And that his will be ever done.

The End

I sing of ghosts and people under ground,
Or if they live, absented from green sound.
Not that I dote on death or being still;

But what men would is seldom what they will,
And there is farthest meaning in an end
Past the wild power of any word to mend.
The telltale stalk, and silence at the close,
Is most that may be read of man or rose.
Death is our outline, and a stillness seals
Even the living heart that loudest feels.
I am in love with joy, but find it wrapped
In a queer earth, at languages unapt;
With shadows sprinkled over, and no mind
To speak for them and prove they are designed.
I sing of men and shadows, and the light
That none the less shines under them by night.
Then lest I be dog enemy of day,
I add old women talking by the way;
And, not to grow insensible to noise,
Add gossip girls and western-throated boys.

EDWARD ESTLIN CUMMINGS

(1894–   )

Song

All in green went my love riding
on a great horse of gold
into the silver dawn.

four lean hounds crouched low and smiling
the merry deer ran before.

Fleeter be they than dappled dreams
the swift sweet deer
the red rare deer.

four red roebuck at a white water
the cruel bugle sang before.

Horn at hip went my love riding
riding the echo down
into the silver dawn.

four lean hounds crouched low and smiling
the level meadows ran before.

Softer be they than slippered sheep
the lean' lithe deer
the fleet flown deer.

Four fleet does at a gold valley
the famished arrow sang before.

Bow at belt went my love riding
riding the mountain down
into the silver dawn.

four lean hounds crouched low and smiling
the sheer peaks ran before.

Paler be they than daunting death
the sleek slim deer
the tall tense deer.

Four tall stags at a green mountain
the lucky hunter sang before.

All in green went my love riding
on a great horse of gold
into the silver dawn.

four lean hounds crouched low and smiling
my heart fell dead before.

"the Cambridge ladies who live in furnished souls"

the Cambridge ladies who live in furnished souls
are unbeautiful and have comfortable minds
(also, with the church's protestant blessings
daughters, unscented shapeless spirited)
they believe in Christ and Longfellow, both dead,

are invariably interested in so many things—
at the present writing one still finds
delighted fingers knitting for the is it Poles?
perhaps. While permanent faces coyly bandy
scandal of Mrs. N and Professor D
. . . the Cambridge ladies do not care, above
Cambridge if sometimes in its box of
sky lavender and cornerless, the
moon rattles like a fragment of angry candy

"what if a much of a which of a wind"

what if a much of a which of a wind
gives the truth to summer's lie;
bloodies with dizzying leaves the sun
and yanks immortal stars awry?
Blow king to beggar and queen to seem
(blow friend to fiend:blow space to time)
—when skies are hanged and oceans drowned,
the single secret will still be man

what if a keen of a lean wind flays
screaming hills with sleet and snow:
strangles valleys by ropes of thing
and stifles forests in white ago?
Blow hope to terror;blow seeing to blind
(blow pity to envy and soul to mind)
—whose hearts are mountains,roots are trees,
it's they shall cry hello to the spring

what if a dawn of a doom of a dream
bites this universe in two,
peels forever out of his grave
and sprinkles nowhere with me and you?
Blow soon to never and never to twice
(blow life to isn't:blow death to was)
—all nothing's only our hugest home;
the most who die,the more we live

HOWARD PHELPS PUTNAM

(1894–1948)

Hasbrouck and the Rose

Hasbrouck was there and so were Bill
And Smollet Smith the poet, and Ames was there.
After his thirteenth drink, the burning Smith,
Raising his fourteenth trembling in the air,
Said, "Drink with me, Bill, drink up to the Rose."
But Hasbrouck laughed like old men in a myth,
Inquiring, "Smollet, are you drunk? What rose?"
And Smollet said, "I drunk? It may be so;
Which comes from brooding on the flower, the flower
I mean toward which mad hour by hour
I travel brokenly; and I shall know,
With Hermes and the alchemists—but, hell,
What use is it talking that way to you?
Hard-boiled, unbroken egg, what can you care
For the enfolded passion of the Rose?"
Then Hasbrouck's voice rang like an icy bell:
"Arcane romantic flower, meaning what?
Do you know what it meant? Do I?
We do not know.
Unfolded pungent rose, the glowing bath
Of ecstasy and clear forgetfulness;
Closing and secret bud one might achieve
By long debauchery—
Except that I have eaten it, and so
There is no call for further lunacy.
In Springfield, Massachusetts, I devoured
The mystic, the improbable, the Rose.
For two nights and a day, rose and rosette,
And petal after petal and the heart,
I had my banquet by the beams
Of four electric stars which shone
Weakly into my room, for there,
Drowning their light and gleaming at my side,
Was the incarnate star
Whose body bore the stigma of the Rose.
And that is all I know about the flower;

I have eaten it—It has disappeared.
There is no Rose."

Young Smollet Smith let fall his glass; he said
"Oh Jesus, Hasbrouck, am I drunk or dead?"

ROBERT GRAVES

(1895–   )

The Bards

The bards falter in shame, their running verse
Stumbles, with marrow-bones the drunken diners
Pelt them for their delay.
It is a something fearful in the song,
Plagues them—an unknown grief that like a churl
Goes common-place in cowskin
And bursts unheralded, crowing and coughing,
An unpilled holly-club twirled in his hand,
Into their many-shielded, samite-curtained,
Jewel-bright hall where twelve kings sit at chess
Over the white-bronze pieces and the gold;
And by a gross enchantment
Flails down the rafters and leads off the queens—
The wild-swan-breasted, the rose-ruddy-cheeked,
Raven-haired daughters of their admiration—
To stir his black pots and to bed on straw.

The Climate of Thought

The climate of thought has seldom been described.
It is no terror of Caucasian frost,
Nor yet that brooding Hindu heat
For which a loin-rag and a dish of rice
Suffice until the pestilent monsoon.
But, without winter, blood would run too thin;
Or, without summer, fires would burn too long.
In thought the seasons run concurrently.

Thought has a sea to gaze, not voyage on;
And hills, to rough the edge of the bland sky,
Not to be climbed in search of blander prospect;
Few birds, sufficient for such caterpillars
As are not fated to turn butterflies;
Few butterflies, sufficient for the flowers
That are the luxury of a full orchard;
Wind, sometimes, in the evening chimneys; rain
On the early morning roof, on sleepy sight;
Snow streaked upon the hilltop, feeding
The fond brook at the valley-head
That greens the valley and that parts the lips;
The sun, simple, like a country neighbour;
The moon, grand, not fanciful with clouds.

Counting the Beats

You, love, and I,
(He whispers) you and I,
And if no more than only you and I
What care you or I?

Counting the beats,
Counting the slow heart beats,
The bleeding to death of time in slow heart beats,
Wakeful they lie.

Cloudless day,
Night, and a cloudless day;
Yet the huge storm will burst upon their heads one day
From a bitter sky.

Where shall we be,
(She whispers) where shall we be,
When death strikes home, O where then shall we be
Who were you and I?

Not there but here,
(He whispers) only here,

As we are, here, together, now and here,
Always you and I.

Counting the beats,
Counting the slow heart beats,
The bleeding to death of time in slow heart beats,
Wakeful they lie.

EDMUND BLUNDEN

(1896–   )

Into the Salient

Sallows like heads in Polynesia,
With few and blood-stuck hairs,
Mud-layered cobble-stones,
Soldiers in smoky sheds, blackening uniforms and walls with
    their cookery;
Shell-holes in roofs, in roads,
Even in advertisements
Of bicycles and beer;
The Middle Ages gone to sleep, and woken up to this—
A salvo, four flat slamming explosions.
When you come out the wrong side of the ruin, you are
    facing Hill Sixty,
Hill Sixty is facing you.
You have been planted on the rim of a volcano,
Which will bring forth its fruit, at any second.
Better to be shielded from these facts;
There is a cellar, or was just now.
If the wreck isn't knocked in on us all,
We may emerge past the two Belgian policemen,
The owners' representatives,
Standing in their capes on the steps of the hollow estaminet
Open at all hours to all the winds
At the Poperinghe end of Ypres.
O if we do, if time will pass in time,
We will march
With rifles butt-upwards, in our teeth, any way you like,
Into seven days of country where you come out any door.

An Infantryman

Painfully writhed the few last weeds upon those houseless
    uplands,
    Cleft pods had dropt their blackened seeds into the tram-
      pled clay,
Wind and rain were running loose, and icy flew the whiplash;
    Masked guns like autumn thunder drummed the outcast
    year away.

Hidden a hundred yards ahead with winter's blinding pas-
    sion,
    The mule-track appeared half dead, even war's hot blood
    congealed;
The half-dug trenches brimmed like troughs, the camps lay
    slushed and empty,
    Unless those bitter whistlings proved Death's army in the
    field.

Over the captured ridge above the hurt battalion waited,
    And hardly had sense left to prove if ghost or living passed
From hole to hole with sunken eyes and slow ironic orders,
    While fiery fountains burst and clanged—and there your
    lot was cast.

Yet I saw your health and youth go brightening the vortex,
    The ghosts on guard, the storm uncouth were then no
    match for you;
You smiled, you sang, your courage rang, and to this day I
    hear it,
    Sunny as a May-day dance, along that spectral avenue.

STEPHEN VINCENT BENÉT
(1898-1943)

FROM *John Brown's Body*

This is the hidden place that hiders know.
This is where hiders go.
Step softly, the snow that falls here is different snow,

The rain has a different sting.
Step softly, step like a cloud, step softly as the least
Whisper of air against the beating wing,
And let your eyes be sealed
With two blue muscadines
Stolen from secret vines
Or you will never find, in the lost field,
The table spread, the signs of the hidden feast.

This is where hiders live.
This is the tentative
And outcast corner where hiders steal away
To bake their hedgehogs in a lump of clay,
To raise their crops and children wild and shy
And let the world go by
In accidental marches of armed wrath
That stumble blindly past the buried path.
Step softly, step like a whisper, but do not speak
Or you will never see
The furriness curled within the hollow tree,
The shadow-dance upon the wilderness creek.

This is the hiders' house.
This is the ark of pine-and-willow-boughs.
This is the quiet place.
You may call now, but let your call be sweet
As clover-honey strained through silver sieves
And delicate as the dust upon the moth
Or you will never find your fugitives.
Call once, and call again,
Then, if the lifted strain
Has the true color and substance of the wild,
You may perceive, if you have lucky eyes,
Something that ran away from being wise
And changed silk ribbons for a greener cloth,
Some budding-horned and deer-milk-suckled child,
Some lightness, moving toward you on light feet,
Some girl with indolent passion in her face.

HART CRANE

(1899–1932)

Voyages: II

—And yet this great wink of eternity,
Of rimless floods, unfettered leewardings,
Samite sheeted and processioned where
Her undinal vast belly moonward bends,
Laughing the wrapt inflections of our love;

Take this Sea, whose diapason knells
On scrolls of silver snowy sentences,
The sceptered terror of whose sessions rends
As her demeanors motion well or ill,
All but the pieties of lovers' hands.

And onward, as bells off San Salvador
Salute the crocus lusters of the stars,
In these poinsettia meadows of her tides,—
Adagios of islands, O my Prodigal,
Complete the dark confessions her veins spell.

Mark how her turning shoulders wind the hours,
And hasten while her penniless rich palms
Pass superscription of bent foam and wave,—
Hasten, while they are true,—sleep, death, desire,
Close round one instant in one floating flower.

Bind us in time, O seasons clear, and awe.
O minstrel galleons of Carib fire,
Bequeath us to no earthly shore until
Is answered in the vortex of our grave
The seal's wide spindrift gaze toward paradise.

FROM *The Bridge*

THE RIVER

Stick your patent name on a signboard
brother—all over—going west—young man
Tintex—Japalac—Certain-teed Overalls ads

and land sakes! under the new playbill ripped
in the guaranteed corner—see Bert Williams what?
Minstrels when you steal a chicken just
save me the wing for if it isn't
Erie it ain't for miles around a
Mazda—and the telegraphic night coming on Thomas
a Ediford—and whistling down the tracks
a headlight rushing with the sound—can you
imagine—while an express makes time like
SCIENCE—COMMERCE and the HOLYGHOST
RADIO ROARS IN EVERY HOME WE HAVE THE NORTHPOLE
WALLSTREET AND VIRGINBIRTH WITHOUT STONES OR
WIRES OR EVEN RUNNing brooks connecting ears
and no more sermons windows flashing roar
Breathtaking—as you like it . . . eh?

                          So the 20th Century —so
whizzed the Limited—roared by and left
three men, still hungry on the tracks, ploddingly
watching the tail lights wizen and converge, slipping gimleted and neatly out of sight.

The last bear, shot drinking in the Dakotas,
Loped under wires that span the mountain stream.
Keen instruments, strung to a vast precision
Bind town to town and dream to ticking dream.
But some men take their liquor slow—and count
—Though they'll confess no rosary nor clue—
The river's minute by the far brook's year.
Under a world of whistles, wires and steam
Caboose-like they go ruminating through
Ohio, Indiana—blind baggage—
To Cheyenne tagging . . . Maybe Kalamazoo.

Time's renderings, time's blendings they construe
As final reckonings of fire and snow;
Strange bird-wit, like the elemental gist
Of unwalled winds they offer, singing low
My Old Kentucky Home and Casey Jones,
Some Sunny Day. I heard a road-gang chanting so.
And afterwards, who had a colt's eyes—one said,

"Jesus! O I remember watermelon days!" And sped
High in a cloud of merriment, recalled
"—And when my Aunt Sally Simpson smiled," he drawled—
"It was almost Louisiana, long ago."

"There's no place like Booneville though, Buddy,"
One said, excising a last burr from his vest,
"—For early trouting." Then peering in the can,
"—But I kept on the tracks." Possessed, resigned,
He trod the fire down pensively and grinned,
Spreading dry shingles of a beard. . . .

                                        Behind
My father's cannery works I used to see
Rail-squatters ranged in nomad raillery,
The ancient men—wifeless or runaway
Hobo-trekkers that forever search
An empire wilderness of freight and rails.
Each seemed a child, like me, on a loose perch,
Holding to childhood like some termless play.
John, Jake, or Charley, hopping the slow freight
—Memphis to Tallahassee—riding the rods,
Blind fists of nothing, humpty-dumpty clods.

Yet they touch something like a key perhaps.
From pole to pole across the hills, the states
—They know a body under the wide rain;
Youngsters with eyes like fjords, old reprobates
With racetrack jargon,—dotting immensity
They lurk across her, knowing her yonder breast
Snow-silvered, sumac-stained or smoky blue—
Is past the valley-sleepers, south or west.
—As I have trod the rumorous midnights, too,

And past the circuit of the lamp's thin flame
(O Nights that brought me to her body bare!)
Have dreamed beyond the print that bound her name.
Trains sounding the long blizzards out—I heard
Wail into distances I knew were hers.

Papooses crying on the wind's long mane
Screamed redskin dynasties that fled the brain,
—Dead echoes! But I knew her body there,
Time like a serpent down her shoulder, dark,
And space, an eaglet's wing, laid on her hair.

Under the Ozarks, domed by Iron Mountain,
The old gods of the rain lie wrapped in pools
Where eyeless fish curvet a sunken fountain
And re-descend with corn from querulous crows.
Such pilferings make up their timeless eatage,
Propitiate them for their timber torn
By iron, iron—always the iron dealt cleavage!
They doze now, below axe and powder horn.

And Pullman breakfasters glide glistening steel
From tunnel into field—iron strides the dew—
Straddles the hill, a dance of wheel on wheel.
You have a half-hour's wait at Siskiyou,
Or stay the night and take the next train through.
Southward, near Cairo passing, you can see
The Ohio merging,—borne down Tennessee;
And if it's summer and the sun's in dusk
Maybe the breeze will lift the River's musk
—As though the waters breathed that you might know
Memphis Johnny, Steamboat Bill, Missouri Joe.
Oh, lean from the window, if the train slows down,
As though you touched hands with some ancient clown,
—A little while gaze absently below
And hum Deep River with them while they go.

Yes, turn again and sniff once more—look see,
O Sheriff, Brakeman and Authority—
Hitch up your pants and crunch another quid,
For you, too, feed the River timelessly.
And few evade full measure of their fate;
Always they smile out eerily what they seem.
I could believe he joked at heaven's gate—
Dan Midland—jolted from the cold brake-beam.

Down, down—born pioneers in time's despite,
Grimed tributaries to an ancient flow—
They win no frontier by their wayward plight,
But drift in stillness, as from Jordan's brow.

You will not hear it as the sea; even stone
Is not more hushed by gravity . . . But slow,
As loth to take more tribute—sliding prone
Like one whose eyes were buried long ago

The River, spreading, flows—and spends your dream.
What are you, lost within this tideless spell?
You are your father's father, and the stream—
A liquid theme that floating niggers swell.

Damp tonnage and alluvial march of days—
Nights turbid, vascular with silted shale
And roots surrendered down of moraine clays:
The Mississippi drinks the farthest dale.

O quarrying passion, undertowed sunlight!
The basalt surface drags a jungle grace
Ocherous and lynx-barred in lengthening might;
Patience! and you shall reach the biding place!

Over De Soto's bones the freighted floors
Throb past the City storied of three thrones.
Down two more turns the Mississippi pours
(Anon tall ironsides up from salt lagoons)

And flows within itself, heaps itself free.
All fades but one thin skyline 'round . . . Ahead
No embrace opens but the stinging sea;
The River lifts itself from its long bed,

Poised wholly on its dream, a mustard glow
Tortured with history, its one will—flow!
—The passion spreads in wide tongues, choked and slow,
Meeting the Gulf, hosannas silently below.

ALLEN TATE

(1899–   )

Shadow and Shade

The shadow streamed into the wall—
The wall, break-shadow in the blast;
We lingered wordless while a tall
Shade enclouded the shadow's cast.

The torrent of the reaching shade
Broke shadow into all its parts,
What then had been of shadow made
Found exigence in fits and starts

Where nothing properly had name
Save that still element the air,
Burnt the sea of universal frame
In which impounded now we were:

I took her hand, I shut her eyes
And all her shadow clove with shade,
Shadow was crushed beyond disguise
But, being fear, was unafraid.

I asked fair shadow at my side:
What more shall fiery shade require?
We lay there in the immense tide
Of shade and shadowy desire

And saw the dusk assail the wall,
The black surge, mounting, crash the stone!
Companion of this lust, we fall,
I said, lest we should die alone.

Ode to the Confederate Dead

Row after row with strict impunity
The headstones yield their names to the element,
The wind whirrs without recollection;
In the riven troughs the splayed leaves

Pile up, of nature the casual sacrament
To the seasonal eternity of death,
Then driven by the fierce scrutiny
Of heaven to their business in the vast breath,
They sough the rumor of mortality.

Autumn is desolation in the plot
Of a thousand acres where these memories grow
From the inexhaustible bodies that are not
Dead, but feed the grass row after rich row.
Think of the autumns that have come and gone—
Ambitious November with the humors of the year,
With a particular zeal for every slab,
Staining the uncomfortable angels that rot
On the slabs, a wing chipped here, an arm there:
The brute curiosity of an angel's stare
Turns you, like them, to stone,
Transforms the heaving air,
Till plunged to a heavier world below
You shift your sea-space blindly
Heaving, turning like the blind crab.

Dazed by the wind, only the wind
The leaves flying, plunge

You know who have waited by the wall
The twilit certainty of an animal;
Those midnight restitutions of the blood
You know—the immitigable pines, the smoky frieze
Of the sky, the sudden call; you know the rage—
The cold pool left by the mounting flood—
The rage of Zeno and Parmenides.
You who have waited for the angry resolution
Of those desires that should be yours tomorrow,
You know the unimportant shrift of death
And praise the vision
And praise the arrogant circumstance
Of those who fall
Rank upon rank, hurried beyond decision—
Here by the sagging gate, stopped by the wall.

Seeing, seeing only the leaves
Flying, plunge and expire

Turn your eyes to the immoderate past
Turn to the inscrutable infantry rising
Demons out of the earth—they will not last.
Stonewall, Stonewall—and the sunken fields of hemp,
Shiloh, Antietam, Malvern Hill, Bull Run.
Lost in that orient of the thick and fast
You will curse the setting sun.

Cursing only the leaves crying
Like an old man in a storm

You hear the shout—the crazy hemlocks point
With troubled fingers to the silence which
Smothers you, a mummy, in time.
                              The hound bitch
Toothless and dying, in a musty cellar
Hears the wind only.

                    Now that the salt of their blood
Stiffens the saltier oblivion of the sea,
Seals the malignant purity of the flood,
What shall we who count our days and bow
Our heads with a commercial woe
In the ribboned coats of grim felicity,
What shall we say of the bones, unclean,
Whose verdurous anonymity will grow?
The ragged arms, the ragged heads and eyes
Lost in these acres of the insane green?
The gray lean spiders come, they come and go;
In a tangle of willows without light
The singular screech-owl's bright
Invisible lyric seeds the mind
With the furious murmur of their chivalry.

We shall say only, the leaves
Flying, plunge and expire

We shall say only, the leaves whispering
In the improbable mist of nightfall
That flies on multiple wing:
Night is the beginning and the end
And in between the ends of distraction
Waits mute speculation, the patient curse
That stones the eyes, or like the jaguar leaps
For his own image in a jungle pool, his victim.

What shall we say who have knowledge
Carried to the heart? Shall we take the act
To the grave? Shall we, more hopeful, set up the grave
In the house? The ravenous grave?

　　　　　　　　　　Leave now
The shut gate and the decomposing wall:
The gentle serpent, green in the mulberry bush,
Riots with his tongue through the hush—
Sentinel of the grave who counts us all!

LÉONIE ADAMS

(1899–　　)

Country Summer

Now the rich cherry, whose sleek wood,
And top with silver petals traced
Like a strict box its gems encased,
Has spilt from out that cunning lid,
All in an innocent green round,
Those melting rubies which it hid;
With moss ripe-strawberry-encrusted,
So birds get half, and minds lapse merry
To taste the deep-red lark's-bite berry,
And blackcap-bloom is yellow-dusted.

The wren that thieved it in the eaves
A trailer of the rose could catch
To her poor droopy sloven thatch,
And side by side with the wren's brood—
O lovely time of beggars' luck—

Opens the quaint and hairy bud;
And full and golden is the yield
Of cows that never have to house,
But all night nibble under boughs,
Or cool their sides in the moist field.

Into the rooms flow meadow airs,
The warm farm baking smell's blown round.
Inside and out, and sky and ground
Are much the same; the wishing star,
Hesperus, kind and early born,
Is risen only finger-far;
All stars stand close in summer air,
And tremble, and look mild as amber;
When wicks are lighted in the chamber,
They are like stars which settled there.

Now straightening from the flowery hay,
Down the still light the mowers look,
Or turn, because their dreaming shook,
And they waked half to other days,
When left alone in yellow stubble,
The rusty-coated mare would graze.
Yet thick the lazy dreams are born,
Another thought can come to mind,
But like the shivering of the wind,
Morning and evening in the corn.

SACHEVERELL SITWELL

(1900–   )

Variation on a Theme by John Lyly

What mournful metamorphosis
Changed my days: mocked time that flies:
My life, a beating clock that is,
Turning to endless song that dies:
So while I sigh here as a reed,
I, dying, live, that lived, indeed?

The hills' green tumbling fields I climbed
For hollow music from the shore,
That with the cooling wind's voice rhymed,
Both mingling through the wood's green core;
Till leaves and branches both do sing
With wind and water echoing.

One day I trod the river bank
And sang into the gentle wind,
The wood god tangled, wet and dank,
Leaped through the leaves and came behind;
He ran with goat's feet, chasing me,
Until I fell back wearily.

My heart, that beating clock, stopped dead,
And I was changed into a brake;
My limbs that cheated him, my head,
All turned to reed that wind can shake;
So do I mock time, blowing here;
One winter's sighs make not a year.

He comes and cuts himself a quill,
To make my image with his breath;
He tries at mine, his lips, to fill,
But music mocks him like my death;
No sooner a shrill note he blows,
Than it has fled, as water flows.

And so this ghost of me escapes,
It flies from him each time he plays;
And I shall never feel his rapes,
Till music in a reed pipe stays;
Till then, he'll find me still a reed,
Though sighing at his breath, indeed.

KENNETH SLESSOR

(1901–   )

Metempsychosis

Suddenly to become John Benbow, walking down William
    Street
With a tin trunk and a five-pound note, looking for a place
    to eat,
And a peajacket the colour of a shark's behind
That a Jew might buy in the morning . . .

To fry potatoes (God save us!) if you feel inclined,
Or to kiss the landlady's daughter, and no one mind,
In a peel-paper bedroom with a whistling jet
And a picture of the Holy Virgin . . .

Wake in a shaggy bale of blankets with a fished-up cigarette,
Picking over "Turfbird's Tattle" for a Sunday morning bet,
With a bottle in the wardrobe easy to reach
And a blast of onions from the landing . . .

Tattooed with foreign ladies' tokens, a heart and dagger
    each,
In places that make the delicate female inquirer screech,
And over a chest smoky with gunpowder-blue—
Behold!—a mermaid piping through a coach-horn!

Banjo-playing, firing off guns, and other momentous things
    to do,
Such as blowing through peashooters at hawkers to improve
    the view—

Suddenly paid-off and forgotten in Woolloomooloo . . .

Suddenly to become John Benbow. . . .

ROY CAMPBELL

(1902–1957)

The Zebras

From the dark woods that breathe of fallen showers,
Harnessed with level rays in golden reins,
The zebras draw the dawn across the plains
Wading knee-deep among the scarlet flowers.
The sunlight, zithering their flanks with fire,
Flashes between the shadows as they pass
Barred with electric tremors through the grass
Like wind along the gold strings of a lyre.
Into the flushed air snorting rosy plumes
That smoulder round their feet in drifting fumes,
With dove-like voices call the distant fillies,
While round the herds the stallion wheels his flight,
Engine of beauty volted with delight,
To roll his mare among the trampled lilies.

from *Talking Bronco*

THE VOLUNTEER'S REPLY TO THE POET
("WILL IT BE SO AGAIN?")

. . . So the soldier replied to the Poet,
Oh yes! it will all be the same,
But a bloody sight worse, and you know it
Since you have a hand in the game:
And you'll be the first in the racket
To sell us a similar dope,
Wrapped up in a rosier packet,
But noosed with as cunning a rope.
You coin us the catchwords and phrases
For which to be slaughtered; and then,
While thousands are blasted to blazes,
Sit picking your nose with your pen.
We know what you're bursting to tell us,
By heart. It is all very fine.
We must swallow the bait that you sell us
And pay for your Hook and your Line.
But his pride for a soldier suffices

Since someone must carry the can;
In war, or depression, or crisis,
It's what you expect of a man.
But when we have come to the Isthmus
That bridges the Slump to the War,
We shall contact a new Father Christmas
Like the one we contacted before,
Deploring the one he replaces
Like you do (it's part of the show!)
But with those same mincing grimaces
And that mealy old kisser we know!
And he'll patent a cheap cornucopia
For all that our purse can afford,
And rent us a flat in Utopia
With dreams for our lodging and board.
And we'll hand in our Ammo and Guns
As we handed them in once before,
And we'll lock them up safe; till our sons
Are conscripted for Freedom once more.
We can die for our faith by the million
And laugh at our bruises and scars,
But hush! for the Poet-Civilian
Is weeping, between the cigars.
Mellifluous, sweeter than Cadbury's,
The M.O.I. Nightingale (Hush!)
Is lining his pockets with Bradburies
So his feelings come out with a rush,
For our woes are the cash in his kitty
When his voice he so kindly devotes
In sentiment, pathos, and pity,
To bringing huge lumps to our throats
Of our widows, and sweethearts, and trollops,
Since it sells like hot cakes to the town
As he doles out the Goitre in dollops
And the public is gulping it down.
Oh well may he weep for the soldier,
Who weeps at a guinea a tear,
For although his invention gets mouldier,
It keeps him his job in the rear.
When my Mrs. the organ is wheeling
And my adenoids wheeze to the sky,

He will publish the hunger I'm feeling
And rake in his cheque with a sigh:
And when with a trayful of matches
And laces, you hawk in the street,
O comrades, in tatters and patches,
Rejoice! since we're in for a treat:
For when we have died in the gutter
To safeguard his income and state,
Be sure that the Poet will utter
Some beautiful thoughts on our Fate!

CECIL DAY LEWIS

(1904–   )

FROM *From Feathers to Iron*

XIV

Now the full-throated daffodils,
Our trumpeters in gold,
Call resurrection from the ground
And bid the year be bold.

To-day the almond tree turns pink,
The first flush of the spring;
Winds loll and gossip through the town
Her secret whispering.

Now too the bird must try his voice
Upon the morning air;
Down drowsy avenues he cries
A novel great affair.

He tells of royalty to be;
How with her train of rose
Summer to coronation comes
Through waving wild hedgerows.

To-day crowds quicken in a street,
The fish leaps in the flood:
Look there, gasometer rises,
And here bough swells to bud.

For our love's luck, our stowaway,
Stretches in his cabin;
Our youngster joy barely conceived
Shows up beneath the skin.

Our joy was but a gusty thing
Without sinew or wit,
An infant flyaway; but now
We make a man of it.

PHYLLIS McGINLEY

(1905–   )

Midcentury Love Letter

Stay near me. Speak my name. Oh, do not wander
By a thought's span, heart's impulse, from the light
We kindle here. You are my sole defender
(As I am yours) in this precipitous night,
Which over earth, till common landmarks alter,
Is falling, without stars, and bitter cold.
We two have but our burning selves for shelter.
Huddle against me. Give me your hand to hold.

So might two climbers lost in mountain weather
On a high slope and taken by the storm,
Desperate in the darkness, cling together
Under one cloak and breathe each other warm.
Stay near me. Spirit, perishable as bone,
In no such winter can survive alone.

WILLIAM EMPSON

(1906–   )

Missing Dates

Slowly the poison the whole blood stream fills.
It is not the effort nor the failure tires.
The waste remains, the waste remains and kills.

It is not your system or clear sight that mills
Down small to the consequence a life requires;
Slowly the poison the whole blood stream fills.

They bled an old dog dry yet the exchange rills
Of young dog blood gave but a month's desires;
The waste remains, the waste remains and kills.

It is the Chinese tombs and the slag hills
Usurp the soil, and not the soil retires.
Slowly the poison the whole blood stream fills.

Not to have fire is to be a skin that shrills.
The complete fire is death. From partial fires
The waste remains, the waste remains and kills.

It is the poems you have lost, the ills
From missing dates, at which the heart expires.
Slowly the poison the whole blood stream fills.
The waste remains, the waste remains and kills.

WYSTAN HUGH AUDEN

(1907–   )

"O for Doors to Be Open"

O for doors to be open and an invite with gilded edges
To dine with Lord Lobcock and Count Asthma on the plat-
    inum benches,
With the somersaults and fireworks, the roast and the smack-
    ing kisses—
                Cried the cripples to the silent statue,
                The six beggared cripples.

And Garbo's and Cleopatra's wits to go astraying,
In a feather ocean with me to go fishing and playing
Still jolly when the cock has burst himself with crowing—
                Cried the six cripples to the silent statue,
                The six beggared cripples.

And to stand on green turf among the craning yelling faces,
Dependent on the chestnut, the sable, the Arabian horses,
And me with a magic crystal to foresee their places—
    Cried the six cripples to the silent statue,
    The six beggared cripples.

And this square to be a deck, and these pigeons sails to rig
And to follow the delicious breeze like a tantony pig
To the shaded feverless islands where the melons are big—
    Cried the six cripples to the silent statue,
    The six beggared cripples.

And these shops to be turned to tulips in a garden bed,
And me with my stick to thrash each merchant dead
As he pokes from a flower his bald and wicked head—
    Cried the six cripples to the silent statue,
    The six beggared cripples.

And a hole in the bottom of heaven, and Peter and Paul
And each smug surprised saint like parachutes to fall,
And every one-legged beggar to have no legs at all—
    Cried the six cripples to the silent statue,
    The six beggared cripples.

Ballad: "O What Is That Sound . . ."

O what is that sound which so thrills the ear
    Down in the valley drumming, drumming?
Only the scarlet soldiers, dear,
    The soldiers coming.

O what is that light I see flashing so clear
    Over the distance brightly, brightly?
Only the sun on their weapons, dear,
    As they step lightly.

O what are they doing with all that gear;
    What are they doing this morning, this morning?
Only the usual maneuvers, dear,
    Or perhaps a warning.

O why have they left the road down there,
  Why are they suddenly wheeling, wheeling?
Perhaps a change in the orders, dear;
  Why are you kneeling?

O haven't they stopped for the doctor's care,
  Haven't they reined their horses, their horses?
Why, they are none of them wounded, dear,
  None of these forces.

O is it the parson they want, with white hair;
  Is it the parson, is it, is it?
No, they are passing his gateway, dear,
  Without a visit.

O it must be the farmer who lives so near,
  It must be the farmer, so cunning, so cunning?
They have passed the farm already, dear,
  And now they are running.

O where are you going? Stay with me here!
  Were the vows you swore me deceiving, deceiving?
No, I promised to love you, dear,
  But I must be leaving.

O it's broken the lock and splintered the door,
  O it's the gate where they're turning, turning;
Their feet are heavy on the floor
  And their eyes are burning.

In Memory of W. B. Yeats

I

He disappeared in the dead of winter:
The brooks were frozen, the airports almost deserted,
And snow disfigured the public statues;
The mercury sank in the mouth of the dying day.
O all the instruments agree
The day of his death was a dark cold day.

Far from his illness
The wolves ran on through the evergreen forests,
The peasant river was untempted by the fashionable quays;
By mourning tongues
The death of the poet was kept from his poems.

But for him it was his last afternoon as himself,
An afternoon of nurses and rumors;
The provinces of his body revolted,
The squares of his mind were empty,
Silence invaded the suburbs,
The current of his feeling failed: he became his admirers.

Now he is scattered among a hundred cities
And wholly given over to unfamiliar affections;
To find his happiness in another kind of wood
And be punished under a foreign code of conscience.
The words of a dead man
Are modified in the guts of the living.

But in the importance and noise of tomorrow
When the brokers are roaring like beasts on the floor of the
    Bourse,
And the poor have the sufferings to which they are fairly
    accustomed,
And each in the cell of himself is almost convinced of his
    freedom;
A few thousand will think of this day
As one thinks of a day when one did something slightly
    unusual.
O all the instruments agree
The day of his death was a dark cold day.

II

You were silly like us: your gift survived it all;
The parish of rich women, physical decay,
Yourself; mad Ireland hurt you into poetry.
Now Ireland has her madness and her weather still,
For poetry makes nothing happen: it survives
In the valley of its saying where executives
Would never want to tamper; it flows south

From ranches of isolation and the busy griefs,
Raw towns that we believe and die in; it survives,
A way of happening, a mouth.

III

Earth, receive an honored guest;
William Yeats is laid to rest:
Let the Irish vessel lie
Emptied of its poetry.

Time that is intolerant
Of the brave and innocent,
And indifferent in a week
To a beautiful physique,

Worships language and forgives
Everyone by whom it lives;
Pardons cowardice, conceit,
Lays its honours at their feet.

Time that with this strange excuse
Pardoned Kipling and his views,
And will pardon Paul Claudel,
Pardons him for writing well.

In the nightmare of the dark
All the dogs of Europe bark,
And the living nations wait,
Each sequestered in its hate;

Intellectual disgrace
Stares from every human face,
And the seas of pity lie
Locked and frozen in each eye.

Follow, poet, follow right
To the bottom of the night,
With your unconstraining voice
Still persuade us to rejoice;

With the farming of a verse
Make a vineyard of the curse,
Sing of human unsuccess
In a rapture of distress;

In the deserts of the heart
Let the healing fountain start,
In the prison of his days
Teach the free man how to praise.

LOUIS MacNEICE

(1907–   )

Aubade

Having bitten on life like a sharp apple
Or, playing it like a fish, been happy,

Having felt with fingers that the sky is blue,
What have we after that to look forward to?

Not the twilight of the gods but a precise dawn
Of sallow and grey bricks, and newsboys crying war.

Bagpipe Music

It's no go the merry-go-round, it's no go the rickshaw,
All we want is a limousine and a ticket for the peepshow.
Their knickers are made of crêpe-de-chine, their shoes are
       made of python,
Their halls are lined with tiger rugs and their walls with
       heads of bison.

John MacDonald found a corpse, put it under the sofa,
Waited till it came to life and hit it with a poker,
Sold its eyes for souvenirs, sold its blood for whiskey,
Kept its bones for dumb-bells to use when he was fifty.

It's no go the Yogi-Man, it's no go Blavatsky,
All we want is a bank balance and a bit of skirt in a taxi.

Annie MacDougall went to milk, caught her foot in the
    heather,
Woke to hear a dance record playing of Old Vienna.
It's no go your maidenheads, it's no go your culture,
All we want is a Dunlop tyre and the devil mend the punc-
    ture.

The Laird o'Phelps spent Hogmannay declaring he was
    sober;
Counted his feet to prove the fact and found he had one foot
    over.
Mrs. Carmichael had her fifth, looked at the job with re-
    pulsion,
Said to the midwife "Take it away; I'm through with over-
    production."

It's no go the gossip column, it's no go the Ceilidh,
All we want is a mother's help and a sugar-stick for the baby.

Willie Murray cut his thumb, couldn't count the damage,
Took the hide of an Ayrshire cow and used it for a bandage.
His brother caught three hundred cran when the seas were
    lavish,
Threw the bleeders back in the sea and went upon the
    parish.

It's no go the Herring Board, it's no go the Bible,
All we want is a packet of fags when our hands are idle.

It's no go the picture palace, it's no go the stadium,
It's no go the country cot with a pot of pink geraniums.
It's no go the Government grants, it's no go the elections,
Sit on your arse for fifty years and hang your hat on a
    pension.

It's no go my honey love, it's no go my poppet;
Work your hands from day to day, the winds will blow the
    profit.
The glass is falling hour by hour, the glass will fall for ever,
But if you break the bloody glass you won't hold up the
    weather.

KATHLEEN RAINE

(1908–   )

The Pythoness

I am that serpent-haunted cave
Whose navel breeds the fates of men.
All wisdom issues from a hole in the earth:
The gods form in my darkness, and dissolve again.

From my blind womb all kingdoms come,
And from my grave seven sleepers prophesy.
No babe unborn but wakens to my dream,
No lover but at last entombed in me shall lie.

I am that feared and longed-for burning place
Where man and phoenix are consumed away,
And from my low polluted bed arise
New sons, new suns, new skies.

THEODORE ROETHKE

(1908–   )

Big Wind

Where were the greenhouses going,
Lunging into the lashing
Wind driving water
So far down the river
All the faucets stopped?—
So we drained the manure-machine
For the steam plant,
Pumping the stale mixture
Into the rusty boilers,
Watching the pressure gauge
Waver over to red,
As the seams hissed
And the live steam
Drove to the far
End of the rose-house,
Where the worst wind was,
Creaking the cypress window-frames,

Cracking so much thin glass
We stayed all night,
Stuffing the holes with burlap;
But she rode it out,
That old rose-house,
She hove into the teeth of it,
The core and pith of that ugly storm,
Ploughing with her stiff prow,
Bucking into the wind-waves
That broke over the whole of her,
Flailing her sides with spray,
Flinging long strings of wet across the roof-top,
Finally veering, wearing themselves out, merely
Whistling thinly under the wind-vents;
She sailed into the calm morning,
Carrying her full cargo of roses.

STEPHEN SPENDER

(1909-   )

Thoughts during an Air Raid

Of course, the entire effort is to put myself
Outside the ordinary range
Of what are called statistics. A hundred are killed
In the outer suburbs. Well, well, I carry on.
So long as the great "I" is propped upon
This girdered bed which seems more like a hearse,
In the hotel bedroom with flowering wallpaper
Which rings in wreathes above, I can ignore
The pressure of those names under my fingers
Heavy and black as I rustle the paper,
The wireless wail in the lounge margin.
Yet supposing that a bomb should dive
Its nose right through this bed, with me upon it?
The thought is obscene. Still, there are many
To whom my death would be only a name,
One figure in a column. The essential is
That all the "I"s should remain separate
Propped up under flowers, and no one suffer
For his neighbour. Then horror is postponed

For everyone until it settles on him
And drags him to that incommunicable grief
Which is all mystery or nothing.

"I Think Continually of Those . . ."

I think continually of those who were truly great.
Who, from the womb, remembered the soul's history
Through corridors of light where the hours are suns,
Endless and singing. Whose lovely ambition
Was that their lips, still touched with fire,
Should tell of the Spirit, clothed from head to foot in song.
And who hoarded from the Spring branches
The desires falling across their bodies like blossoms.

What is precious is never to forget
The delight of the blood drawn from ageless springs
Breaking through rocks in worlds before our earth.
Never to deny its pleasure in the morning simple light
Nor its grave evening demand for love.
Never to allow gradually the traffic to smother
With noise and fog, the flowering of the Spirit.

Near the snow, near the sun, in the highest fields,
See how these names are fêted by the waving grass,
And by the streamers of white cloud
And whispers of wind in the listening sky.
The names of those who in their lives fought for life,
Who wore at their hearts the fire's centre.
Born of the sun, they travelled a short while toward the sun,
And left the vivid air signed with their honour.

FREDERIC PROKOSCH

(1909-   )

Eclogue

No one dies cleanly now,
All, all of us rot away:
No longer down the wood

Angelic shapes delight
The innocent and gay.
Poisonous things are spared,
The gifted are the sad
And solitude breeds hate.
Yellow is every bough,
No one dies cleanly now.

All, all of us rot away.
In broken barges drift
The warm and cinnamon-skinned
And in black Europe's wind
The ice-edged lanterns sway.
The carousels are silent,
The towns are torn by sea
And in their coiling streets
The dragon snares his prey
Till all of us rot away!

No longer down the wood
May the tall victor lead
The shy swan-breasted maid
Or generous pageants move.
The loved are sick of love,
Love is strangled with words:
Beauty sighs in her bed:
The faithful, calm and good
Follow the songs of birds
No longer down the wood.

Angelic shapes delight
Only the perpetual child.
The murderer plans his night
And the green hunter's horn
Drives the unwanted wild.
O mourn, willows, weep!
Till the clear spring return
And to the warming heart
The curious wonders creep;
A cry; a living sleep.

WILLIAM ROBERT RODGERS

(1909–   )

Neither Here nor There

In that land all is and nothing's ought;
No owners or notices, only birds;
No walls anywhere, only lean wire of words
Worming brokenly out from eaten thought;
No oats growing, only ankle-lace grass
Easing and not resenting the feet that pass;
No enormous beasts, only names of them;
No bones made, bans laid, or boons expected,
No contracts, entails, hereditaments,
Anything at all that might tie or lien.

In that land all's lackadaisical;
No lakes of coddled spawn, and no locked ponds
Of settled purpose, no netted fishes;
But only inkling streams and running fronds
Fritillaried with dreams, weedy with wishes;
No arrogant talk is heard, haggling phrase,
But undertones, and hesitance, and haze;
On clear days mountains of meaning are seen
Humped high on the horizon; no one goes
To con their meaning, no one cares or knows.

In that land all's flat, indifferent; there
Is neither springing house nor hanging tent,
No aims are entertained, and nothing is meant,
For there are no ends and no trends, no roads,
Only follow your nose to anywhere.
No one is born there, no one stays or dies,
For it is a timeless land, it lies
Between the act and the attrition, it
Marks off bound from rebound, make from break, tit
From tat, also today from tomorrow.
No Cause there comes to term, but each departs
Elsewhere to whelp its deeds, expel its darts;
There are no homecomings, of course, no good-byes
In that land, neither yearning nor scorning,
Though at night there is the smell of morning.

ELIZABETH BISHOP

(1911–   )

The Fish

I caught a tremendous fish
and held him beside the boat
half out of water, with my hook
fast in a corner of his mouth.
He didn't fight.
He hadn't fought at all.
He hung a grunting weight,
battered and venerable
and homely. Here and there
his brown skin hung in strips
like ancient wall-paper,
and its pattern of darker brown
was like wall-paper:
shapes like full-blown roses
stained and lost through age.
He was speckled with barnacles,
fine rosettes of lime,
and infested
with tiny white sea-lice,
and underneath two or three
rags of green weed hung down.
While his gills were breathing in
the terrible oxygen
—the frightening gills
fresh and crisp with blood,
that can cut so badly—
I thought of the coarse white flesh
packed in like feathers,
the big bones and the little bones,
the dramatic reds and blacks
of his shiny entrails,
and the pink swim-bladder
like a big peony.
I looked into his eyes
which were far larger than mine
but shallower, and yellowed,

the irises backed and packed
with tarnished tinfoil
seen through the lenses
of old scratched isinglass.
They shifted a little, but not
to return my stare.
—It was more like the tipping
of an object toward the light.
I admired his sullen face,
the mechanism of his jaw,
and then I saw
that from his lower lip
—if you could call it a lip—
grim, wet, and weapon-like,
hung five old pieces of fish-line,
or four and a wire leader
with the swivel still attached,
with all their five hooks
grown firmly in his mouth.
A green line, frayed at the end
where he broke it, two heavier lines,
and a fine black thread
still crimped from the strain and snap
when it broke and he got away.
Like medals with their ribbons
frayed and wavering,
a five-haired beard of wisdom
trailing from his aching jaw.
I stared and stared
and victory filled up
the little rented boat,
from the pool of bilge
where oil had spread a rainbow
around the rusted engine
to the bailer rusted orange,
the sun-cracked thwarts,
the oarlocks on their strings,
the gunnels—until everything
was rainbow, rainbow, rainbow!
And I let the fish go.

GEORGE BARKER

(1913–   )

Sonnet to My Mother

Most near, most dear, most loved and most far,
Under the window where I often found her
Sitting as huge as Asia, seismic with laughter,
Gin and chicken helpless in her Irish hand,
Irresistible as Rabelais but most tender for
The lame dogs and hurt birds that surround her,—
She is a procession no one can follow after
But be like a little dog following a brass band.

She will not glance up at the bomber or condescend
To drop her gin and scuttle to a cellar,
But lean on the mahogany table like a mountain
Whom only faith can move, and so I send
O all my faith and all my love to tell her
That she will move from mourning into morning.

To Any Member of My Generation

What was it you remember?—the summer mornings
Down by the river at Richmond with a girl,
And as you kissed, clumsy in bathing costumes,
History guffawed in a rosebush. O what a warning—
If only we had known, if only we had known!
And when you looked in mirrors was this meaning
Plain as the pain in the centre of a pearl?
Horrible tomorrow in goddamning postures
Making absurd the past we cannot disown?

Whenever we kissed we cocked the future's rifles
And from our wildoat words, like dragons' teeth,
Death underfoot now arises. When we were gay
Dancing together in what we hoped was life,
Who was it in our arms but the whores of death
Whom we have found in our beds today, today?

DELMORE SCHWARTZ

(1913–   )

FROM *The Repetitive Heart*

III

All clowns are masked and all *personae*
Flow from choices; sad and gay, wise,
Moody and humorous are chosen faces,
And yet not so! For all are circumstances,
Given, like a tendency
To colds or like blond hair and wealth,
Or war and peace or gifts for mathematics,
Fall from the sky, rise from the ground, stick to us
In time, surround us: Socrates is mortal.

Gifts and choices! All men are masked,
And we are clowns who think to choose our faces
And we are taught in time of circumstances
And we have colds, blond hair and mathematics,
For we have gifts which interrupt our choices,
And all our choices grasp in Blind Man's Buff:
"My wife was very different, after marriage,"
"I practise law, but botany's my pleasure,"
Save postage stamps or photographs,
But save your soul! Only the past is immortal.

Decide to take a trip, read books of travel,
Go quickly! Even Socrates is mortal,
Mention the name of happiness: it is
Atlantis, Ultima Thule, or the limelight,
Cathay or Heaven. But go quickly
And remember: there are circumstances,
And he who chooses chooses what is given,
And he who chooses is ignorant of Choice,
—Choose love, for love is full of children,
Full of choices, children choosing
Botany, mathematics, law and love,
So full of choices! So full of children!
And the past is immortal, the future is inexhaustible!

KARL SHAPIRO

(1913–   )

Buick

As a sloop with a sweep of immaculate wing on her delicate
spine
And a keel as steel as a root that holds in the sea as she
leans,
Leaning and laughing, my warm-hearted beauty, you ride,
you ride,
You tack on the curves with parabola speed and a kiss of
good-bye,
Like a thoroughbred sloop, my new high-spirited spirit, my
kiss.

As my foot suggests that you leap in the air with your hips
of a girl,
My finger that praises your wheel and announces your voices
of song,
Flouncing your skirts, you blueness of joy, you flirt of polite-
ness,
You leap, you intelligence, essence of wheelness with silvery
nose,
And your platinum clocks of excitement stir like the hairs of
a fern.

But how alien you are from the booming belts of your birth
and the smoke
Where you turned on the stinging lathes of Detroit and
Lansing at night
And shrieked at the torch in your secret parts and the amo-
rous tests,
But now with your eyes that enter the future of roads you
forget;
You are all instinct with your phosphorous glow and your
streaking hair.

And now when we stop it is not as the bird from the shell
that I leave
Or the leathery pilot who steps from his bird with a sneer
of delight,

And not as the ignorant beast do you squat and watch me
    depart,
But with exquisite breathing you smile, with satisfaction of
    love,
And I touch you again as you tick in the silence and settle
    in sleep.

HENRY REED

(1914–   )

Lessons of the War: Naming of Parts

Today we have naming of parts. Yesterday,
We had daily cleaning. And tomorrow morning,
We shall have what to do after firing. But today,
Today we have naming of parts. Japonica
Glistens like coral in all of the neighbouring gardens,
    And today we have naming of parts.

This is the lower sling swivel. And this
Is the upper sling swivel, whose use you will see,
When you are given your slings. And this is the piling swivel,
Which in your case you have not got. The branches
Hold in the gardens their silent, eloquent gestures,
    Which in our case we have not got.

This is the safety-catch, which is always released
With an easy flick of the thumb. And please do not let me
See anyone using his finger. You can do it quite easy
If you have any strength in your thumb. The blossoms
Are fragile and motionless, never letting anyone see
    Any of them using their finger.

And this you can see is the bolt. The purpose of this
Is to open the breech, as you see. We can slide it
Rapidly backwards and forwards: we call this
Easing the spring. And rapidly backwards and forwards
The early bees are assaulting and fumbling the flowers:
    They call it easing the Spring.

They call it easing the Spring: it is perfectly easy
If you have any strength in your thumb: like the bolt,
And the breech, and the cocking-piece, and the point of
     balance,
Which in our case we have not got; and the almond-blossom
Silent in all of the gardens and the bees going backwards
     and forwards,
     For today we have naming of parts.

DYLAN THOMAS

(1914–1953)

"The Force That through the Green Fuse . . ."

The force that through the green fuse drives the flower
Drives my green age; that blasts the roots of trees
Is my destroyer.
And I am dumb to tell the crooked rose
My youth is bent by the same wintry fever.

The force that drives the water through the rocks
Drives my red blood; that dries the mouthing streams
Turns mine to wax.
And I am dumb to mouth unto my veins
How at the mountain spring the same mouth sucks.

The hand that whirls the water in the pool
Stirs the quicksand; that ropes the blowing wind
Hauls my shroud sail.
And I am dumb to tell the hanging man
How of my clay is made the hangman's lime.

The lips of time leech to the fountain head;
Love drips and gathers, but the fallen blood
Shall calm her sores.
And I am dumb to tell a weather's wind
How time has ticked a heaven round the stars.

And I am dumb to tell the lover's tomb
How at my sheet goes the same crooked worm.

"Light Breaks Where No Sun Shines"

Light breaks where no sun shines;
Where no sea runs, the waters of the heart
Push in their tides;
And, broken ghosts with glowworms in their heads,
The things of light
File through the flesh where no flesh decks the bones.

A candle in the thighs
Warms youth and seed and burns the seeds of age;
Where no seed stirs,
The fruit of man unwrinkles in the stars,
Bright as a fig;
Where no wax is, the candle shows its hairs.

Dawn breaks behind the eyes;
From poles of skull and toe the windy blood
Slides like a sea;
Nor fenced, nor staked, the gushers of the sky
Spout to the rod
Divining in a smile the oil of tears.

Night in the sockets rounds,
Like some pitch moon, the limit of the globes;
Day lights the bone;
Where no cold is, the skinning gales unpin
The winter's robes;
The film of spring is hanging from the lids.

Light breaks on secret lots,
On tips of thought where thoughts smell in the rain;
When logics die,
The secret of the soil grows through the eye,
And blood jumps in the sun;
Above the waste allotments the dawn halts.

Fern Hill

Now as I was young and easy under the apple boughs
About the lilting house and happy as the grass was green,
    The night above the dingle starry,
        Time let me hail and climb
    Golden in the heydays of his eyes,
And honored among wagons I was prince of the apple towns
And once below a time I lordly had the trees and leaves
        Trail with daisies and barley
    Down the rivers of the windfall light.

And as I was green and carefree, famous among the barns
About the happy yard and singing as the farm was home,
    In the sun that is young once only,
        Time let me play and be
    Golden in the mercy of his means,
And green and golden I was huntsman and herdsman, the
        calves
Sang to my horn, the foxes on the hills barked clear and cold,
        And the sabbath rang slowly
    In the pebbles of the holy streams.

All the sun long it was running, it was lovely, the hay
Fields high as the house, the tunes from the chimneys, it was
        air
    And playing, lovely and watery
        And fire green as grass.
    And nightly under the simple stars
As I rode to sleep the owls were bearing the farm away,
All the moon long I heard, blessed among stables, the night-
        jars
    Flying with the ricks, and horses
        Flashing into the dark.

And then to awake, and the farm, like a wanderer white
With the dew, come back, the cock on his shoulder: it was
        all
    Shining, it was Adam and maiden,
        The sky gathered again
    And the sun grew round that very day.
So it must have been after the birth of the simple light

In the first, spinning place, the spellbound horses walking
　　warm
　　Out of the whinnying green stable
　　On to the fields of praise.

And honored among foxes and pheasants by the gay house
Under the new made clouds and happy as the heart was long,
　　In the sun born over and over,
　　I ran my heedless ways,
　　My wishes raced through the house high hay
And nothing I cared, at my sky blue trades, that time allows
In all his tuneful turning so few and such morning songs
　　Before the children green and golden
　　Follow him out of grace,

Nothing I cared, in the lamb white days, that time would
　　take me
Up to the swallow thronged loft by the shadow of my hand,
　　In the moon that is always rising,
　　Nor that riding to sleep
　　I should hear him fly with the high fields
And wake to the farm forever fled from the childless land.
Oh as I was young and easy in the mercy of his means,
　　Time held me green and dying
　　Though I sang in my chains like the sea.

Do Not Go Gentle into That Good Night

　　Do not go gentle into that good night,
　　Old age should burn and rave at close of day;
　　Rage, rage against the dying of the light.

　　Though wise men at their end know dark is right,
　　Because their words had forked no lightning they
　　Do not go gentle into that good night.

　　Good men, the last wave by, crying how bright
　　Their frail deeds might have danced in a green bay,
　　Rage, rage against the dying of the light.

Wild men who caught and sang the sun in flight,
And learn, too late, they grieved it on its way,
Do not go gentle into that good night.

Grave men, near death, who see with blinding sight
Blind eyes could blaze like meteors and be gay,
Rage, rage against the dying of the light.

And you, my father, there on the sad height,
Curse, bless, me now with your fierce tears, I pray.
Do not go gentle into that good night.
Rage, rage against the dying of the light.

ROBERT LOWELL

(1917–   )

The Quaker Graveyard in Nantucket

(FOR WARREN WINSLOW, DEAD AT SEA)

> Let man have dominion over the fishes of the sea
> and the fowls of the air and the beasts and the whole
> earth, and every creeping creature that moveth upon
> the earth.

I

A brackish reach of shoal off Madaket,—
The sea was still breaking violently and night
Had steamed into our North Atlantic Fleet,
When the drowned sailor clutched the drag-net. Light
Flashed from his matted head and marble feet,
He grappled at the net
With the coiled, hurdling muscles of his thighs:
The corpse was bloodless, a botch of reds and whites,
Its open, staring eyes
Were lustreless dead-lights
Or cabin-windows on a stranded hulk
Heavy with sand. We weight the body, close
Its eyes and heave it seaward whence it came,
Where the heel-headed dogfish barks its nose
On Ahab's void and forehead; and the name
Is blocked in yellow chalk.

Sailors, who pitch this portent at the sea
Where dreadnoughts shall confess
Its hell-bent deity,
When you are powerless
To sand-bag this Atlantic bulwark, faced
By the earth-shaker, green, unwearied, chaste
In his steel scales: ask for no Orphean lute
To pluck life back. The guns of the steeled fleet
Recoil and then repeat
The hoarse salute.

II

Whenever winds are moving and their breath
Heaves at the roped-in bulwarks of this pier,
The terns and sea-gulls tremble at your death
In these home waters. Sailor, can you hear
The Pequod's sea wings, beating landward, fall
Headlong and break on our Atlantic wall
Off 'Sconset, where the yawing S-boats splash
The bellbuoy, with ballooning spinnakers,
As the entangled, screeching mainsheet clears
The blocks: off Madaket, where lubbers lash
The heavy surf and throw their long lead squids
For blue-fish? Sea-gulls blink their heavy lids
Seaward. The winds' wings beat upon the stones,
Cousin, and scream for you and the claws rush
At the sea's throat and wring it in the slush
Of this old Quaker graveyard where the bones
Cry out in the long night for the hurt beast
Bobbing by Ahab's whaleboats in the East.

III

All you recovered from Poseidon died
With you, my cousin, and the harrowed brine
Is fruitless on the blue beard of the god,
Stretching beyond us to the castles in Spain,
Nantucket's westward haven. To Cape Cod
Guns, cradled on the tide,
Blast the eelgrass about a waterclock

Of bilge and backwash, roil the salt and sand
Lashing earth's scaffold, rock
Our warships in the hand
Of the great God, where time's contrition blues
Whatever it was these Quaker sailors lost
In the mad scramble of their lives. They died
When time was open-eyed,
Wooden and childish; only bones abide
There, in the nowhere, where their boats were tossed
Sky-high, where mariners had fabled news
Of Is, the whited monster. What it cost
Them is their secret. In the sperm-whale's slick
I see the Quakers drown and hear their cry:
"If God himself had not been on our side,
If God himself had not been on our side,
When the Atlantic rose against us, why,
Then it had swallowed us up quick."

IV

This is the end of the whaleroad and the whale
Who spewed Nantucket bones on the thrashed swell
And stirred the troubled waters to whirlpools
To send the Pequod packing off to hell:
This is the end of them, three-quarters fools,
Snatching at straws to sail
Seaward and seaward on the turntail whale,
Spouting out blood and water as it rolls,
Sick as a dog to these Atlantic shoals:
Clamavimus, O depths. Let the sea-gulls wail

For water, for the deep where the high tide
Mutters to its hurt self, mutters and ebbs.
Waves wallow in their wash, go out and out,
Leave only the death-rattle of the crabs,
The beach increasing, its enormous snout
Sucking the ocean's side.
This is the end of running on the waves;
We are poured out like water. Who will dance
The mast-lashed master of Leviathans
Up from this field of Quakers in their unstoned graves?

V

When the whale's viscera go and the roll
Of its corruption overruns this world
Beyond tree-swept Nantucket and Wood's Hole
And Martha's Vineyard, Sailor, will your sword
Whistle and fall and sink into the fat?
In the great ash-pit of Jehoshaphat
The bones cry for the blood of the white whale,
The fat flukes arch and whack about its ears,
The death-lance churns into the sanctuary, tears
The gun-blue swingle, heaving like a flail,
And hacks the coiling life out: it works and drags
And rips the sperm-whale's midriff into rags,
Gobbets of blubber spill to wind and weather,
Sailor, and gulls go round the stoven timbers
Where the morning stars sing out together
And thunder shakes the white surf and dismembers
The red flag hammered in the mast-head. Hide
Our steel, Jonas Messias, in Thy side.

VI

OUR LADY OF WALSINGHAM

There once the penitents took off their shoes
And then walked barefoot the remaining mile;
And the small trees, a stream and hedgerows file
Slowly along the munching English lane,
Like cows at the old shrine, until you lose
Track of your dragging pain.
The stream flows down under the druid tree,
Shiloah's whirlpools gurgle and make glad
The castle of God. Sailor, you were glad
And whistled Sion by that stream. But see:

Our Lady, too small for her canopy,
Sits near the altar. There's no comeliness
At all or charm in that expressionless
Face with its heavy eyelids. As before,
This face, for centuries a memory,
Non est species, neque decor,

Expressionless, expresses God: it goes
Past castled Sion. She knows what God knows,
Not Calvary's Cross nor crib at Bethlehem
Now, and the world shall come to Walsingham.

VII

The empty winds are creaking and the oak
Splatters and splatters on the cenotaph,
The boughs are trembling and a gaff
Bobs on the untimely stroke
Of the greased wash exploding on a shoal-bell
In the old mouth of the Atlantic. It's well;
Atlantic, you are fouled with the blue sailors,
Sea-monsters, upward angel, downward fish:
Unmarried and corroding, spare of flesh,
Mart once of supercilious, wing'd clippers;
Atlantic, where your bell-trap guts its spoil
You could cut the brackish winds with a knife
Here in Nantucket, and cast up the time
When the Lord God formed man from the sea's slime
And breathed into his face the breath of life,
And blue-lung'd combers lumbered to the kill.
The Lord survives the rainbow of his will.

RICHARD WILBUR

(1921–   )

After the Last Bulletins

After the last bulletins the windows darken
And the whole city founders easily and deep,
Sliding on all its pillows
To the thronged Atlantis of personal sleep,

And the wind rises. The wind rises and bowls
The day's litter of news in the alleys. Trash
Tears itself on the railings,
Soars and falls with a soft crash,

Tumbles and soars again. Unruly flights
Scamper the park, and taking a statue for dead
Strike at positive eyes,
Batter and flap the stolid head

And scratch the noble name. In empty lots
Our journals spiral in a fierce noyade
Of all we thought to think,
Or caught in corners cramp and wad

And twist our words. And some from gutters flail
Their tatters at the tired patrolman's feet,
Like all that fisted snow
That cried beside his long retreat

Damn you! damn you! to the emperor's horse's heels.
Oh none too soon through the air white and dry
Will the clear announcer's voice
Beat like a dove, and you and I

From the heart's anarch and responsible town
Rise by the subway-mouth to life again,
Bearing the morning papers,
And cross the park where saintlike men,

White and absorbed, with stick and bag remove
The litter of the night, and footsteps rouse
With confident morning sound
The songbirds in the public boughs.

INDEX OF POETS

INDEX OF FIRST LINES
AND TITLES

ACKNOWLEDGMENTS

INDEX OF POETS

INDEX OF FIRST LINES AND TITLES

ACKNOWLEDGMENTS

The editor wishes to express his gratitude for permission to reprint selections from the works of those authors listed below. The listing shows the volume or volumes from which the selections from each poet's work were taken, and the individuals or firms from whom permission was obtained. When dates are given, they refer to United States copyright registration, not necessarily the dates of the volumes mentioned. Permissions for poems that have been added to the Revised, Mid-Century Edition are acknowledged on pages 1296–1297.

ORIGINAL EDITION

ABERCROMBIE, LASCELLES: *Poems.* Oxford University Press, Oxford.

A.E. (GEORGE WILLIAM RUSSELL): *Collected Poems.* 1926. The Macmillan Company, N.Y.

AIKEN, CONRAD: *Time In the Rock.* Copr. 1932, 1933, 1934, 1935, 1936 by Conrad Aiken. Charles Scribner's Sons, N.Y.

AUDEN, W. H.: "Look, Stranger!" from *On This Island,* 1937. Random House, Inc., N.Y. Also from *Look, Stranger!* Faber & Faber Ltd, London.

BACON, LEONARD: *Bullinger Bound and Other Poems.* Copr. 1938 by Leonard Bacon. Harper & Brothers, N.Y.

BELLOC, HILAIRE: *Sonnets and Verse.* Sheed & Ward, Inc., N.Y.

BENÉT, STEPHEN VINCENT: *John Brown's Body.* Copr. 1927, 1928 by Stephen Vincent Benét. Published by Farrar & Rinehart, N.Y.

BINYON, LAURENCE: *Collected Poems.* 1922. The Macmillan Company, N.Y.

BLUNDEN, EDMUND: *Poems, 1914–1930.* A. D. Peters, agent, London.

BRIDGES, ROBERT: *Poems.* Oxford University Press, Oxford.

BROOKE, RUPERT: *The Collected Poems of Rupert Brooke.* Copr. 1915 by Dodd, Mead & Company, Inc., N.Y. *Complete Poems.* McClelland & Stewart Ltd., Toronto. The author's representative and Sidgwick & Jackson Ltd., London.

CAMPBELL, ROY: *Adamastor.* Faber & Faber Ltd, London.

CHAPLIN, RALPH: *Bars and Shadows.* 1921. Nellie Seeds Nearing, Ridgewood, N.J., and the author.

CHESTERTON, G. K.: *The Collected Poems of G. K. Chesterton.* Copr. 1911, 1932 by Dodd, Mead & Company, Inc., N.Y. The executrix and Methuen & Co., Ltd., London.

CLOUGH, ARTHUR HUGH: Last four lines of "The Latest Decalogue" from *Oxford Anthology of English Poetry.* 1935. Oxford University Press, N.Y.

COLUM, PADRAIC: *Wild Earth.* 1916. The Macmillan Company, N.Y.

CUMMINGS, E. E.: *Collected Poems.* Copr. 1923, 1925, 1931, 1935, 1938 by E. E. Cummings. Published by Harcourt, Brace and Company, Inc., N.Y.

DAVIDSON, JOHN: "In Romney Marsh" from *Ballads and Songs;* "Waiting" from *Fleet Street Eclogues.* John Lane The Bodley Head Ltd, London. Both in *Fleet Street and Other Poems.* Modern Library, N.Y.

DAVIES, WILLIAM HENRY: *The Poems of W. H. Davies.* Oxford University Press, N.Y. Jonathan Cape Ltd, London.

DE LA MARE, WALTER: *Collected Poems.* 1941. Henry Holt and Company, N.Y. Faber & Faber Ltd, London.

DICKINSON, EMILY: *The Poems of Emily Dickinson,* edited by Martha Dickinson Bianchi and Alfred Leete Hampson. Reprinted

1293

by permission of Little, Brown &
Company, Boston.

DOUGLAS, LORD ALFRED: *Sonnets
and Lyrics.* The author.

ELIOT, T. S.: *Collected Poems of
T. S. Eliot.* Copr. 1934, 1936 by
Harcourt, Brace and Company,
Inc., N.Y. Faber & Faber Ltd,
London.

FORD, FORD MADOX: *Collected
Poems of Ford Madox Ford.*
1936. Oxford University Press,
N.Y.

FROST, ROBERT: *Collected Poems.*
1939, 1941. Henry Holt & Company, N.Y.

HARDY, THOMAS: *Collected Poems.*
1925. The Macmillan Company,
N.Y.

H.D. (HILDA DOOLITTLE): *Collected Poems of H.D.* 1925. Liveright Publishing Corp., N.Y.

HODGSON, RALPH: *Poems.* 1917.
The Macmillan Company, N.Y.

HOUSMAN, A. E.: "I to my perils"
and "For my funeral" from *More
Poems.* 1936. Leland Hayward,
Inc., N.Y. "Epitaph on an Army
of Mercenaries" from *Last Poems.*
1922. All others from *A Shrop-
shire Lad,* Authorized Edition,
1924. Henry Holt and Company,
N.Y.

HUXLEY, ALDOUS: *Leda.* Copr. 1929
by Aldous Huxley. Harper &
Brothers, N.Y. The Macmillan
Company Ltd., Toronto. The
author and Chatto & Windus,
London.

JEFFERS, ROBINSON: "Shine, Perishing Republic" from *Roan Stallion, Tamar.* 1925. "Signpost"
from *Solstice and Other Poems.*
1935. Random House, Inc., N.Y.

JOYCE, JAMES: *Collected Poems.*
1918, 1927. The Viking Press,
Inc., N.Y.

KIPLING, RUDYARD: All from *Rudyard Kipling's Verse, Inclusive
Edition, 1885–1932.* Copr. 1891–
1932. Reprinted by permission
from Doubleday, Doran and
Company, Inc., N.Y. "Reces-
sional" from *The Five Nations;*
all others from *Barrack Room*

Ballads. The Macmillan Company Ltd., London and Toronto.

LAWRENCE, D. H.: "The Ship of
Death" and "Bavarian Gentians"
from *Last Poems.* Copr. 1933 by
Frieda Lawrence. All others from
Collected Poems. 1929. The Vi-
king Press, Inc., N.Y. Mrs.
Frieda Lawrence and William
Heinemann, Ltd., London.

LEWIS, C. DAY: *Collected Poems.*
1935. Random House, Inc., N.Y.
From Feathers to Iron. Hogarth
Press, London, and the author.

LOWELL, AMY: "Little Ivory Figures
Pulled with String" from *Pictures
of the Floating World.* 1919.
Houghton Mifflin Company, Boston.

MACDONALD, WILSON: *Out of the
Wilderness.* 1926. The author.

MACLEISH, ARCHIBALD: *Poems,
1924–1933.* 1935. Houghton Mifflin Company, Boston.

MACNEICE, LOUIS: *Poems.* 1937.
Random House, Inc., N.Y. Faber & Faber Ltd, London.

MASEFIELD, JOHN: *Poems.* 1935.
The Macmillan Company, N.Y.

MASTERS, EDGAR LEE: *Spoon River
Anthology.* 1916. The author.

MCCRAE, JOHN: *In Flanders Fields
and Other Poems.* 1919. G. P.
Putnam's Sons, N.Y.

MEREDITH, GEORGE: *Poems.* Revised edition Copr. 1897, 1898 by
George Meredith. Charles Scribner's Sons, N.Y. Constable & Co.
Ltd., London.

MEW, CHARLOTTE: "Sea Love"
from *The Farmer's Bride.* "Moorland Night" from *The Rambling
Sailor.* The Poetry Bookshop,
London.

MEYNELL, ALICE: *Poems.* Copr.
1923 by Wilfrid Meynell. Charles
Scribner's Sons, N.Y.

MILLAY, EDNA ST. VINCENT: "Oh,
Sleep Forever" from *Fatal Inter-
view.* Copr. 1931 by Edna St.
Vincent Millay. "What Lips My
Lips" from *The Harp Weaver
and Other Poems.* Copr. 1920,
1921, 1922, 1923 by Edna St.
Vincent Millay. Published by
Harper & Brothers, N.Y.

MITCHELL, SILAS WEIR: *Collected Poems*. 1914. The Pennsylvania Company, Philadelphia.

MONRO, HAROLD: *The Earth for Sale*. The Poetry Bookshop, London, and Mrs. Harold Monro.

MOORE, MARIANNE: "Silence" from *Selected Poems*. 1935. The Macmillan Company, N.Y. "A Talisman" from *Observations*. 1924. The author.

OWEN, WILFRED: *Poems*. Mrs. Owen and Chatto & Windus, London.

PLARR, VICTOR: *In the Dorian Mood*. John Lane The Bodley Head Ltd, London.

POUND, EZRA: *Personae: The Collected Poems of Ezra Pound*. 1926. Liveright Publishing Corp., N.Y., and Virginia Rice, agent.

PROKOSCH, FREDERIC: *Carnival*. Copr. 1938 by Harper & Brothers, N.Y. The author and Chatto & Windus, London.

PUTNAM, HOWARD PHELPS: *Five Seasons*. 1931. Charles Scribner's Sons, N.Y.

RANSOM, JOHN CROWE: *Chills and Fever*. 1924. Alfred A. Knopf, Inc., N.Y.

ROBINSON, EDWIN ARLINGTON: "Mr. Flood's Party" from *Collected Poems*. 1937. The Macmillan Company, N.Y. "For a Dead Lady" and "Momus" from *The Town down the River*. Copr. 1910 by Charles Scribner's Sons, N.Y.

ROSENBERG, ISAAC: *Poems*. William Heinemann, Ltd., London.

SANDBURG, CARL: *Cornhuskers*, 1918. Henry Holt and Company, N.Y.

SANTAYANA, GEORGE: *Poems*. Copr. 1901, 1923 by Charles Scribner's Sons, N.Y. Constable & Co. Ltd., London.

SASSOON, SIEGFRIED: *Picture Show*. Published by E. P. Dutton & Co., N.Y.

SCHWARTZ, DELMORE. *In Dreams Begin Responsibilities*. 1939. New Directions, Norfolk, Conn.

SEEGER, ALAN: *Poems*. 1916 Charles Scribner's Sons, N.Y.

SPENDER, STEPHEN: *The Still Centre*. Faber & Faber Ltd, London.

STEPHENS, JAMES: *Collected Poems*. 1926. The Macmillan Company, N.Y.

STEVENS, WALLACE: *Harmonium*, 1923. Alfred A. Knopf, Inc., N.Y.

SWINBURNE, ALGERNON CHARLES: *Collected Poetical Works*. Harper & Brothers, N.Y. *Complete Works*. William Heinemann, Ltd., London.

SIMONS, ARTHUR: *Poems*. Dodd, Mead & Company, Inc., N.Y. William Heinemann, Ltd., London.

TATE, ALLEN: *Selected Poems*. 1937. Charles Scribner's Sons, N.Y.

THOMAS, DYLAN: *The World I Breathe*. 1939. New Directions, Norfolk, Conn. *The Map of Love*. J. M. Dent & Sons, Ltd., London.

VAN DOREN, MARK: *The Collected Poems of Mark Van Doren*. 1939. Henry Holt and Company, N.Y., and the author.

WICKHAM, ANNA: *The Contemplative Quarry* and *The Man with a Hammer*. 1921. Harcourt, Brace and Company, Inc., N.Y.

WILLIAMS, WILLIAM CARLOS: *Complete Collected Poems of William Carlos Williams*. 1938. New Directions, Norfolk, Conn.

WYLIE, ELINOR: *Nets to Catch the Wind* in *Collected Poems of Elinor Wylie*. 1921. Alfred A. Knopf, Inc., N.Y.

YEATS, WILLIAM BUTLER: "The Land of Heart's Desire" and "Deirdre" from *Collected Plays*. 1934. All others from *Collected Poems*. 1933. The Macmillan Company, N.Y.

REVISED, MID-CENTURY EDITION

ADAMS, LÉONIE: *Poems: A Selection.* Copr. 1954 by Léonie Adams. Funk & Wagnalls Company, N.Y.

AIKEN, CONRAD: "Blind Date" from *Collected Poems.* Copr. 1953 by Conrad Aiken. Oxford University Press, Inc., N.Y.

AUDEN, W. H.: "Ballad," Copr. 1937 by Random House, Inc., and "In Memory of W. B. Yeats," Copr. 1940 by W. H. Auden, both from *The Collected Poetry of W. H. Auden.* By permission of Random House, Inc., N.Y.

BARKER, GEORGE: *Selected Poems.* Copr. 1941 by the Macmillan Company, N.Y. By permission of the author.

BISHOP, ELIZABETH: *Poems: North and South—A Cold Spring.* Copr. 1946 by Elizabeth Bishop. Houghton Mifflin Company, Boston.

CAMPBELL, ROY: "The Volunteer's Reply to the Poet" from *Talking Bronco.* Henry Regnery Company, Chicago.

CRANE, HART: *The Collected Poems of Hart Crane.* Copr. 1933 by Liveright, Inc. By permission of Liveright Publishing Corporation, N.Y.

CUMMINGS, E. E.: "the Cambridge ladies who live in furnished souls" and "what if a much of a which of a wind" from *Poems, 1923–1954.* Copr. © 1923, 1944, 1951 by E. E. Cummings. Harcourt, Brace and Company, Inc., N.Y. By permission of Brandt & Brandt, N.Y.

ELIOT, T. S.: Part V of "Burnt Norton" from *Four Quartets.* Copr. 1943 by T. S. Eliot. Harcourt, Brace and Company, Inc., N.Y.

EMPSON, WILLIAM: *Collected Poems of William Empson.* Copr. 1935, 1940, 1949 by William Empson. Harcourt, Brace and Company, Inc., N.Y.

FROST, ROBERT: "The Witch of Coös" from "Two Witches," "Fire and Ice," and "Stopping by Woods on a Snowy Evening" from *Complete Poems of Robert Frost.* Copr. 1930, 1949 by Henry Holt and Company, Inc., N.Y. By permission of the publisher.

GRAVES, ROBERT: *Collected Poems 1955.* Copr. 1955 by Robert Graves. Doubleday & Company, Inc., N.Y. By permission of the author.

LINDSAY, VACHEL: *Collected Poems.* Copr. 1913 by The Macmillan Company, N.Y. By permission of the publisher.

LOWELL, ROBERT: *Lord Weary's Castle.* Copr. 1944, 1946 by Robert Lowell. Harcourt, Brace and Company, Inc., N.Y.

MacNEICE, LOUIS: "Bagpipe Music" from *Poems, 1925–1940.* Copr. 1937, 1939 by Louis MacNeice. Random House, Inc., N.Y.

McGINLEY, PHYLLIS: *The Love Letters of Phyllis McGinley.* Copr. 1953, 1954 by Phyllis McGinley. The Viking Press, Inc., N.Y. "Midcentury Love Letter" originally appeared in *The New Yorker.*

MOORE, MARIANNE: "Poetry" and "In Distrust of Merits" from *Collected Poems.* Copr. 1951 by Marianne Moore. The Macmillan Company, N.Y.

MUIR, EDWIN: *Collected Poems, 1921–1951.* Grove Press, Inc., N.Y.

OWEN, WILFRED: "The Show" from *Poems of Wilfred Owen.* All rights reserved. New Directions, publishers, Norfolk, Connecticut.

POUND, EZRA: "From 'Canto LXXXI'" from *The Cantos.* Copr. 1934, 1937, 1940, 1948 by Ezra Pound. New Directions, publishers, Norfolk, Connecticut.

RAINE, KATHLEEN: *The Pythoness and Other Poems.* Farrar, Straus and Cudahy, Inc., N.Y.